Conte

Germany: the "Lander"

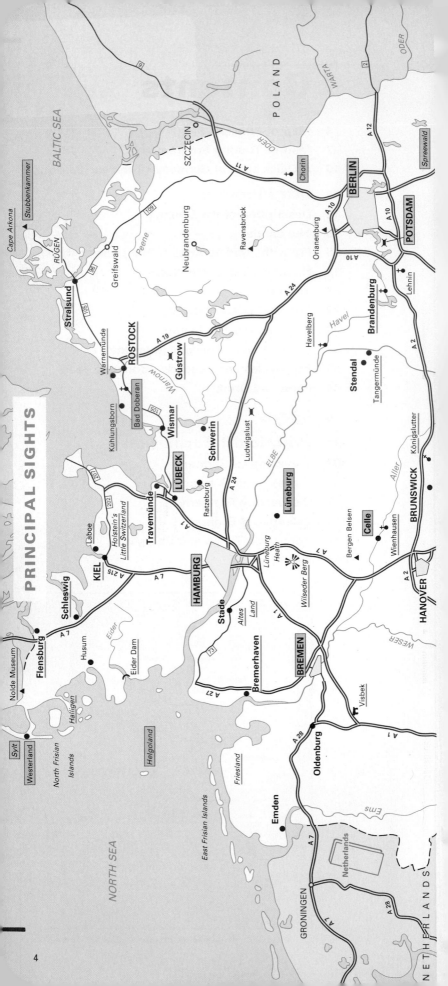

A QUICK LOOK AT GERMANY

A Federal State – Subdivided throughout history into different regions that were largely autonomous, owing allegiance to no single capital (Berlin was only capital of the Reich for 70 years), Germany has naturally gravitated towards a governmental structure that is federal in origin.

The **Fundamental Law** established in 1949 guarantees the liberty of the individual and defines the principles underlying the institutions of the Republic. The Federal Parliament is composed of two chambers: the **Bundestag**, a national assembly of 500 members elected by universal suffrage, is invested with legislative power, chooses the Chancellor, and controls the government; the **Bundesrat**, a federal council comprising 41 members drawn from the local governments administering the Länder, or provinces, is concerned with certain aspects of legislative power, particularly when they affect the Länder.

At the head of the Federal government, the Chancellor, who is invested with wide-ranging powers, defines the broad lines of policy. The Federal President (Bundespräsident) is elected by a Federal Assembly composed of the members of the Bundestag and an equal number of representatives from the parliaments of the Länder. It is he who concludes treaties with foreign states, decides upon or revokes the appointment of judges and Federal functionaries as well as Federal ministers suggested by the Chancellor, and verifies that the laws of the Constitution are respected.

The Federal Republic comprises 16 **Länder** (eleven of which formed the old West Germany plus the five added in 1990 which were re-constituted from the 15 districts of the former East German Democratic Republic - *see p 15*). Each Land organizes its constitution within the terms of the Fundamental Law. Apart from questions concerning the Federal authority – foreign affairs, defence matters, financial policy – each enjoys wide powers, notably in the spheres of education, culture and professional training. They are responsible, in addition, for the application of Federal laws and numerous administrative functions.

Industrial Dynamism – Despite the devastation inflicted during the final years of the Second World War and the dismantling of industrial potential demanded by the Allies after the capitulation of Hitler's Reich, the Federal Republic has raised itself to the position of the world's fourth industrial power and the second biggest exporter. This success is the result of a **social market economy**, linking private enterprise to social progress, in which unions and management work together as partners.

The decline of Germany's traditional iron and steel industry has been compensated by dynamic advances in the fields of mechanics (machine-tools, electro-technology) and automobile construction (the world's third largest producer). Numerous smaller businesses maintain the reputation of the country's optical industry and its talent for the manufacture of precision machinery. Craftwork too occupies an important place in the economy, as exemplified in the annual Munich International Fair, the largest in the world.

Progressive Towns – The political disintegration of the old Germany raised many provincial cities to the status of local capital. The absence, for almost a half-century, of a national capital at once political and economic, added to the federal character of institutions in West Germany, has permitted a certain number of towns to develop an unexpected industrial and cultural influence. Such centres as Cologne, Düsseldorf, Hanover, Frankfurt and Munich, but also Dresden and Leipzig, each with its university, its theatre and its symphony orchestra, organize every year a series of festivals, congresses and commercial fairs which confirm their position as cradles of modern culture and win them international acclaim.

THE FOUR SEASONS

Continuous interaction between oceanic and continental air masses determines the atmospheric conditions over Germany, producing a climate notable for its instability – even turbulence – especially in the north of the country. The months which are the least cloudy, although not necessarily the warmest, are normally April and May in coastal regions, June and September in the interior.

Throughout the year, the climate is bracing and breezy on the North Sea coast, a little milder on the Baltic. But life tends to be active in each case because of the prevailing west winds.

From April onwards, the Rhine Valley and southern Germany as a whole enjoy calm, mild weather brightened with the blossom of fruit trees and orchards. On the shores of Lake Constance, in the valleys of the Inn and the Salzach, the arrival of the Föhn – a cool, dry south wind blowing violently down from the Alps – hastens the approach of springtime.

Summer in the centre of the country is marked by a rapid rise in temperature, particularly in the sheltered depressions of the Hercynian massifs (the plains of the Upper Rhine for instance), where the heat can become heavy and thundery. At such times holidaymakers are especially glad of the bathing facilities and the various opportunities for forest walks. In the Alps, the climate at this time of the year is very variable, depending on the orientation of valleys, the direction of local winds, which way the slopes face, etc.

Often enough in late October and mid-November the sun reappears in a kind of Indian summer, known locally as the "Altweibersommer" (old women's summer), which enhances autumn tints marvellously, particularly in southern Germany. But night falls fast. From the first chill days of winter, the Bavarian Alps, the Allgäu, the Black Forest, the Sauerland and the Harz begin to be hidden beneath a carpet of snow.

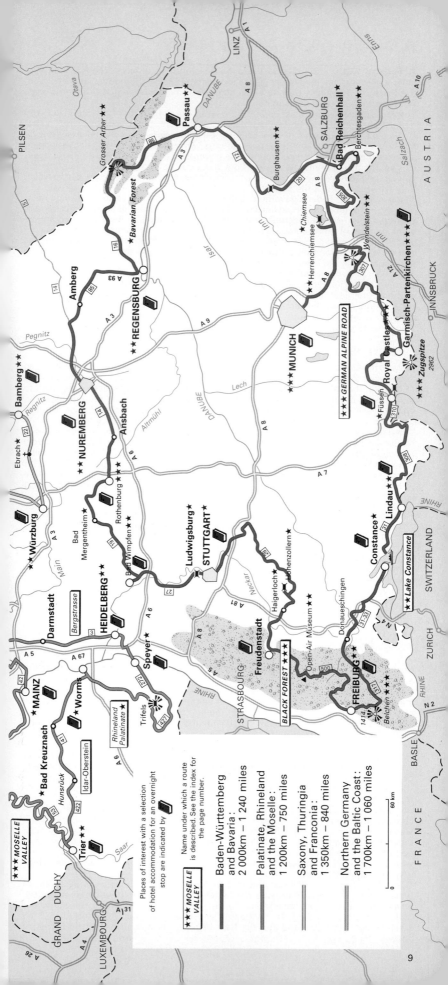

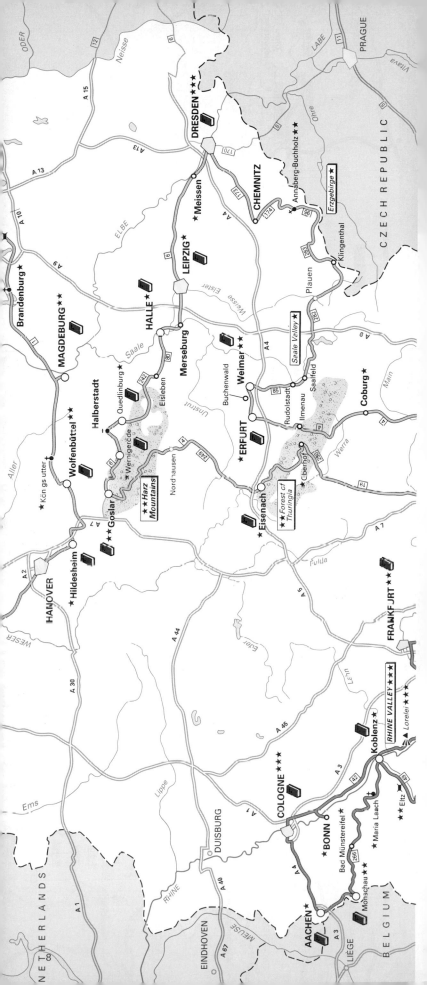

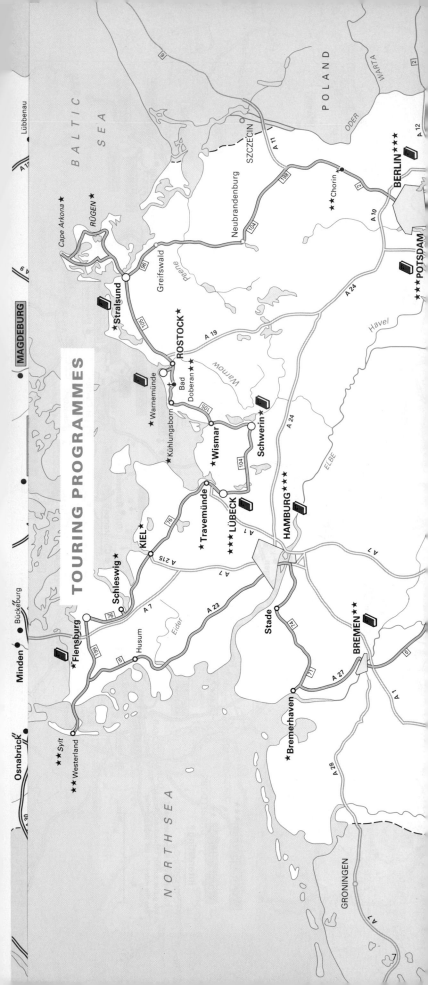

TOURING PROGRAMMES

Introduction

DESCRIPTION OF THE COUNTRY

In the heart of Europe, bordered by the Alps to the south and by the Baltic Sea to the north, Germany is virtually without natural frontiers to the east and the west. Such a lack of barriers, and the subsequent accessibility to outside influences has had a profound effect on the country's history and civilization.

THREE HUGE NATURAL REGIONS

Modern Germany covers an area of 356 000km^2 - 139 000sq miles. Geologically and geographically, this vast area is divided into three separate regions. In the **north**, the immense **Germano-Polish Plain**, formed by the glaciation of the Quaternary era, owes the fact that it was scarcely touched by the Hercynian and Alpine mountain-building movements to the resistance of its crystalline base.

In the **centre**, during the Primary era, the formidable **Hercynian folding** created a complex of minor massifs – today degraded and for the most part wooded – separated by geographic depressions. The most important of these Hercynian massifs are the Black Forest, the Rhenish schist massif, and – encircling Bohemia – the Böhmerwald, the Bavarian Forest, the Erzgebirge (or metal-bearing mountains) and the Riesengebirge. On the edges of this Hercynian zone accumulated the coal-bearing deposits of the Ruhr and Silesia which led to the industrial expansion of the 19C.

The sedimentary basin of Swabia-Franconia, its vast area drained by the Main and the Neckar, offers a less dramatic landscape: abutting the Black Forest on the west and the Swabian Jura to the south, the limestone plateau is patterned with lines of hills sculpted according to the resistance of the varied strata.

In the **south**, the Alpine portion of Germany confines itself to the **Pre-Alps**, where the debris torn up and crushed during the final exertions of Quaternary glaciation formed the Bavarian plateau – a huge area stretching in a gentle slope as far as the Danube.

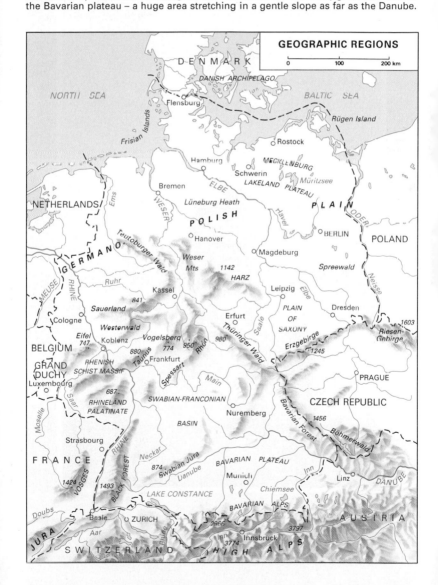

The letter ß (eszett) which is to be found only in the German alphabet, appears in the text transcribed as "ss".

THE SCENERY

Northern Germany

Lower Rhine Valley and Westphalia – Lush, green and flat, protected from flooding, the plain of the Lower Rhine, with its cosy houses, brings to mind the landscape of the neighbouring Netherlands. There is similar scenery around Münster, on the Westphalian plain, where the farmlands patterned by hedges and trees offer the additional attraction of many moated castles (Wasserburgen).

Great Northern Plain – Despite its apparent monotony, this enormous area (which extends eastwards into Poland but is confined, so far as Germany is concerned, between the Ems and the Oder) does offer a certain variety of landscapes.

In the south, below the Weser and Harz foothills, the Börde country lies between the Weser and the Elbe – a region covered by an alluvial topsoil whose fertility is legendary. Farms and market gardens flourish in this densely populated zone, which is favoured also with mineral deposits rich in iron and potassium.

Further north, on either side of the Elbe, is the Geest – a region with little to recommend it geographically, since it was covered by the Scandinavian glaciers right up to Palaeolithic times. This has resulted in poor drainage and soils that are too sandy: between Berlin and the Baltic, the Mecklenburg plateau is scattered with shallow lakes interspersed with morainic deposits that bear witness to the prolonged glacial presence. The Baltic coast has been little affected by erosion, thanks to the relatively shallow depth of the sea, and local currents have been strong enough to link up the rocky islets at Rügen with the mainland to form the Darss peninsula.

The Spree and the Havel, meandering through the flatlands, supply the lakeland regions of the Spreewald and Potsdam.

West of the Lower Weser, and in the Worpswede neighbourhood north of Bremen, peat bogs (Moore) alternate with very wet pastureland. Most of the peat moors are now under cultivation, after drainage using Dutch methods.

The nature reserve south of Lüneburg, however, has preserved for all time a typical stretch of the original moorland.

Loop of the Saar at Cloef

North Sea Coast – Huge areas of cultivation have been reclaimed from the vast mudflats once uncovered here at low tide. Germany's two largest seaports, Hamburg and Bremen, lie at the inner ends of the Elbe and Weser estuaries.

Schleswig-Holstein – There is a striking contrast between Germany's North Sea coast, scoured by the ocean winds and constantly threatened by storms, and the Baltic shoreline, where the flat, wooded countryside is deeply penetrated by arms of the sea (Förde), and calm waters lap peacefully against picturesque fishing villages and sandy beaches. Naturally the principal towns are built on this eastern side of the peninsula – with the exception of Husum. Inland, the many lakes and woods make up Holstein's enticing "Little Switzerland", while further west – towards the harsh Atlantic weather – there is an alternation of dunes, marshes and moorland.

Central Germany

The Rhenish Schist Massif – This ancient geologic mass, cut through by the Rhine – the only real channel of communication between the north and south of the country – the Lahn and the Moselle, comprises the highlands known as the Eifel, the Westerwald, the Taunus and the Hunsrück. They share the same inhospitable climate and the same evidence of volcanic activity, witness the crater lakes or Maare *(qv)* of the Eifel plateau. The Eifel will be familiar to motoring enthusiasts as the home of the Nurburgring Grand Prix race circuit. The Upper Sauerland, a thickly wooded, mountainous region (841m - 2 760ft), acts as a water reserve for the Ruhr industrial area, thanks to its many dams.

Mountains of Upper Hessen and the Weser – Between the Rhenish schist massif and the forest of Thuringia (Thüringer Wald) lies a confused amalgam of heights, some of them volcanic (Vogelsberg, Rhön), and depressions which have been used as a highway linking north and south by German invaders throughout the ages. Between Westphalia and the north, the Weser Mountains – extended westwards by the Teutoburger Wald – form a barrier that is breached at the Porta Westfalica, near Minden. Further to the east, the Erzgebirge (metal-bearing mountains) form a natural frontier with Czechoslovakia.

Harz Mountains – This relatively high range (1 142m - 3 747ft at the Brocken) enjoys a real mountain climate, characterized by heavy snowfalls in winter.

Southern Germany

Plain of the Upper Rhine – Between Basle and the Bingen Gap, a soil of exceptionally fertile loess, added to a climate which combines little rain, an advanced spring and a very hot summer, has produced a rich agricultural yield (hops, corn and tobacco) and a terrain highly suitable for the cultivation of vines. The whole of this low-lying, productive tract has become a crossroads for the rest of Europe, which is why certain towns – Frankfurt, for instance – have profited internationally from their development.

Black Forest – This crystalline massif (1 493m - 4 899ft at the Feldberg), which overlooks the Rhine gap, is relatively well populated.
A beneficial climate and important thermal resources guarantee it a high proportion of tourists.

Swabian-Franconian Basin – Franconia, formed by vast plateaux only gently folded, is bordered on the southeast by the small limestone massif of the Franconian Jura which produces Germany's finest building stone, and to the north and northeast by the heavily wooded crystalline ranges flanking Bohemia and Thuringia.
Swabia, once ruled by the kings of Württemberg, offers a great variety of landscapes – barred to the south by the blue line of the Swabian Jura, which rises to 874m - 2 867ft. Small valleys, enlivened by orchards and vineyards, alternate here with the gentle slopes of wooded hillsides.

The Alps and the Bavarian Plateau – The Bavarian Alps and the Alps of Allgäu offer impressive contrasts between the sombre green of their forests and the shades of grey colouring their rocks and escarpments, especially when the sky behind them is a brilliant blue. The Zugspitze, the highest point in Germany, reaches 2 962m - 9 720ft.
Torrents such as the Isar, the Lech and the Iller, rushing down from the mountains throughout the ages, have carved out wide corridors suitable for the cultivation of the land and the development of towns (Ulm, Augsburg and Munich).

NATURE AND CONSERVATION

The preservation of natural assets, particularly of trees, is of prime concern to Germans today.

The Forest – The colossal forests of the old Germania are of course no more than a memory, but the long survival of feudal customs and the difficulties of adapting undergrowth to the establishment of pastureland have resulted over the centuries in a remarkable preservation of wooded country. Such regions, gravely menaced today by pollution, are now the subject of protective measures greatly supported in their application by the ecological conscience of the great majority of the German people. Forests of deciduous trees flourish above all in the centre of the country, in the zone of the Hercynian massifs. In the Westerwald, the Thüringer Wald, the Weser Mountains and the land around Kassel, there are still magnificent beechwoods. Clumps of beech and spruce predominate in the Swabian Jura, the Harz and the heights of the Black Forest. Superb oaks cover the Spessart and the Reinhardswald, while the homogeneous carpet of conifers is found mainly in the Alps.

The Parks – Whether it be a municipal park or the grounds of a spa, an English garden at Munich or one in the formal French style at Brühl, a Romantic fantasy like Linderhof or a contemporary design such as can be found in the Ruhr, all German parks have one thing in common: the impeccable standard of their upkeep.
Every other year, one of these great parks hosts the National Horticultural Exhibition or Bundesgartenschau (Stuttgart is the chosen place for 1993).
In Germany there are many **natural parks** (Naturpark), the details and extent of which can be found in Michelin maps ▨▨, ▨▨ and ▨▨. These must not be confused with the great number of **nature reserves** (Naturschutzgebiet), which are less extensive and frequently play a scientific role justifying certain restrictions of access. The natural parks are kept, especially in forest regions, specifically for the pleasure of walkers. The biggest are in the Altmühl Valley, in Swiss Franconia and the Bergstrasse-Odenwald. The Palatinate nature park (Pfälzer Wald) is limited in the south by France's North Vosges Regional Park; that of the southern Eifel (Südeifel), which also straddles a frontier, includes Luxemburg's "Little Switzerland". Between Berlin and the Oder lies the Märkische Schweiz.
There are also National Parks in Germany. Among them are the Watten-Meer on the North Sea coast, the Bavarian Forest in the southeast, Swiss Saxony (Niedersächisisches) in the east and the Hochharz in the north centre.
Apart from these official parks, all mountain ranges of any importance and most woods near holiday resorts are crisscrossed with public footpaths, well sign-posted and – if they qualify as a "Waldlehrpfad" – posted with information on local flora and fauna.

THE LÄNDER

LAND	AREA	POPULATION	CAPITAL
Baden-Württemberg (Baden-Württemberg)	35 751 km² 13 530sq miles	9 400 000	Stuttgart
Bavaria (Bayern)	70 555 km² 27 213sq miles	11 000 000	Munich
Berlin (Berlin)	833 km² 310sq miles	3 400 000	Berlin
Brandenburg (Brandenburg)	26 000 km² 10 036sq miles	2 700 000	Potsdam
Bremen (Bremen)	404 km² 156sq miles	682 000	Bremen
Hamburg (Hamburg)	755 km² 292sq miles	1 600 000	Hamburg
Hessen (Hessen)	21 114 km² 8 106sq miles	5 600 000	Wiesbaden
Lower Saxony (Niedersachsen)	47 344 km² 18 258sq miles	7 200 000	Hanover
Mecklenburg-West Pomerania (Mechlenburg-Vorpommern)	22 500 km² 8 685sq miles	2 100 000	Schwerin
Rhineland-Palatinate (Rheinland-Pfalz)	19 849 km² 7 662sq miles	3 700 000	Mainz
Rhineland-Westphalia (Nordrhein-Westfalen)	34 070 km² 13 124sq miles	16 900 000	Düsseldorf
Saar (Saarland)	2 570 km² 965sq miles	1 100 000	Saarbrücken
Saxony (Sachsen)	17 000 km² 6 562sq miles	4 900 000	Dresden
Saxony-Anhalt (Sachsen-Anhalt)	25 000 km² 9 650sq miles	3 000 000	Magdeburg
Schleswig-Holstein (Schleswig-Holstein)	15 729 km² 6 060sq miles	2 600 000	Kiel
Thuringia (Thüringen)	15 209 km² 5 867sq miles	2 500 000	Erfurt

Traditional Costumes – There has been a tendency since the Second World War for these to be phased out. Nevertheless, men in Upper Bavaria, still wear leather shorts, a Loden cloth jacket with horn buttons, and the famous "Tyrolean hat" adorned with a tuft of chamois beard or badger's tail. The impression this outfit makes on tourists is of course one of the main reasons it remains in favour.

Authentic regional costumes are worn in the Schwalm country (the region of Alsfeld, Ziegenhain and Marburg), where women working in the fields are still dressed at times in the old-style short, flared skirt and white stockings. At such popular festivals as the Schwalm Salad Fair, the young girls are charming in their heavy, tight-fitting ceremonial costumes embroidered in brilliant colours and crowned with a tiny red hood – the living illustration, for the Brothers Grimm, of their celebrated fairy tale.

To see other regional costumes – for example, those of the Black Forest, the Kleinwalsertal or the region of Forchheim – it is usually necessary to attend a carnival, pageant or local fête.

The **Dirndl**, so often worn by women in Bavaria, is not in fact attached to any specific folklore or tradition. But the charm of the gathered skirt, the puff-sleeved bodice, and the pinafore trimmed with gaily coloured designs ensures a continual demand for the costume as a souvenir.

Young girl from the Schwalm region

FROM THE MIDDLE AGES

After the Treaty of Verdun in AD 843, Germany united from the Baltic Sea to the Alps all those peoples sharing a common language and culture. Faced with constant incursrions from the barbarians, a number of powerful princes asserted their authority, and it was from among these that eventual kings of Germany were elected. It was Otto I, who was finally created "Emperor" by the Pope.

	ARCHITECTURE	SCULPTURE / PAINTING	MUSIC
1000	St Michael's, HILDESHEIM SPEYER Cathedral TRIER Cathedral (west front)	• Wall paintings (OBERZELL, Reichenau Island)	
1100	Abbey Church, MARIA LAACH	• Wall paintings, ALPIRSBACH	
		• Lectern, FREUDENSTADT	
1200	BAMBERG and NAUMBURG Cathedrals St Gereon's, Cologne WORMS Cathedral (west chancel) COLOGNE Cathedral	• Shrine of the Magi Kings, (COLOGNE Cathedral) • Knight of BAMBERG • Statues of the Margrave Ekkehardt and his wife Uta, (NAUMBURG Cathedral)	HARTMANN von AUE REINMAR WALTHER von der VOGELWEIDE MINNESÄNGER
1300	St Mary's, LÜBECK FREIBURG Cathedral (west tower: belfry and spire)		
1400	ULM Cathedral (west front)		
1500	HEIDELBERG Castle St Anne's, ANNABERG	V. STOSS T. RIEMENSCHNEIDER HOLBEIN the YOUNGER H.B. GRIEN M. GRÜNEWALD S. LOCHNER M. SCHONGAUER P. VISCHER A. DÜRER A. ALTDORFER CRANACH the ELDER	J. WALTHER H. SACHS H. FINCK MASTERSINGERS LUTHRAN CHORALE
1600	• Town Hall, Augsburg	A. ELSHEIMER MERIAN E. HOLL	H. SCHÜTZ
1700	• The Zwinger, DRESDEN • Sans-Souci Palace, POTSDAM • OTTOBEUREN Abbey • WIES Church	M.D. POPPELMANN G. KNOBELSDORFF C. D. ASAM B. NEUMANN D. ZIMMERMANN A. SCHLÜTER E. Q. ASAM B. PERMOSER	C.P.E. BACH W.A. MOZART G. F. HANDEL J. HAYDN C. W. GLUCK D. BUXTEHUDE J. S. BACH G. P. TELEMANN J. PACHELBEL
1800	• NEUSCHWANSTEIN Castle	C. F. SCHINKEL A. von HILDEBRAND C.D. FRIEDRICH BIEDERMEIER	F. MENDELSSOHN L. van BEETHOVEN C. M. von WEBER R. SCHUMANN R. WAGNER
1900	D. BÖHM W. GROPIUS P. BEHRENS	E. L. KIRCHNER E. BARLACH J. BEUYS M. BECKMANN M. LIEBERMANN O. DIX F. MARC M. ERNST JUGENDSTIL	P. HINDEMITH G. MAHLER J. BRAHMS H. WOLF R. STRAUSS K. WEILL
2000	BAUHAUS		K.-H. STOCKHAUSEN

Otto I became the founder of the Holy Roman Empire. For a long time after that, the control of the Papacy itself was the Empire's principal objective, but when this policy failed and the organization was reduced just to Germany, the different territorial principalities grew stronger and the "Empire" shrank in fact to what in time developed into an elective monarchy.

LITERATURE	RELIGION AND PHILOSOPHY	HISTORY	ECONOMY, SCIENCE AND TECHNOLOGY	
		SAXON DYNASTY **Ottonian Emperors** **SALIAN DYNASTY**	Growth of trade Founding of the monasteries	1000
SONG OF THE NIBELUNGEN	POPE GREGORY VII. • CANOSSA 1077	Henry IV		
				1100
HEINRICH von VELDEKE	Concordat of Worms (1122)		• Demographic growth	
GOTTFRIED von STRASSBURG / WOLFRAM von ESCHENBACH	ALEXANDER III	**House of HOHENSTAUFEN** Conrad III Emperor Frederick I Barbarossa	• Expansion towards the East	
	TEUTONIC ORDER 1190 Third Crusade		• Working of the mineral deposits in Silesia and Thuringia	1200
Master ECKHART / ALBERTUS MAGNUS	Sixth Crusade	Frederick II (King of Sicily) Rudolph I of Habsburg	• HANSEATIC LEAGUE: growth of Baltic trade • Growth of towns	
H. SUSO / J. TAULER		**House of LUXEMBOURG**		1300
		Charles IV The Golden Bull	• Famines • BLACK DEATH 1349 • Demographic decline	
	Council of Constance The Hussite Controversy	Sigismund		1400
		House of HABSBURG	• GUTENBERG	
M. LUTHER / PARACELSUS / H. SACHS	1517: Luther exhibits his 95 "theses" on the door of the church at Wittenberg 1521: Luther is excommunicated 1530. Confession of Augsburg 1546: death of Luther	Maximilian I (1493-1519) acquires the duchy of Burgundy and the rich Netherlands by marriage Maximilian I Emperor Charles V • Peace of AUGSBURG 1555 Rudolf II	Powerful Merchant Families (The FUGGERS and the WELSERS) • Rapid urban Expansion	1500
J. J. GRIMMELSHAUSEN / F. FISCHAR / A. GRYPHIUS / M. OPITZ / D. C. LOHENSTEIN		Matthias II • THIRTY YEARS WAR	• KEPLER: astronomical telescope	1600
W. G. LEIBNIZ		• Peace of WESTPHALIA 1648 Revocation of the Edict of Nantes French Huguenots arrive	• LEIBNIZ: differential and integral calculus	
		Rise of BRANDENBURG and PRUSSIAN Rulers THE HOHENZOLLERN	• BÖTTGER: Saxon porcelain • FAHRENHEIT: mercury thermometer	1700
J. C. GOTTSCHED / F. von SCHILLER / G. E. LESSING / NOVALIS / F. G. KLOPSTOCK / H. von KLEIST / C. WIELAND / E. T. A. HOFFMANN / J. von EICHENDORFF / J. W. von GOETHE / AUFKLÄRUNG / J. G. von HERDER / E. KANT / J. G. FICHTE		• Seven Years War		
H. HEINE / J. and W. GRIMM / K. MARX / F. ENGELS / G. W. F. HEGEL / A. SCHOPENHAUER		• Confederation of the Rhine • Chancellor Otto von Bismarck • North German Confederation	• DRAIS: draisienne (prototype of the bicycle) • HAHNEMANN: homeopathy	1800
G. HAUPTMANN / T. MANN / H. HESSE / E. BRECHT / E. HUSSERL / F. NIETZSCHE		• SECOND REICH	• G. DAIMLER and K. BENZ: internal combustion engine • DIESEL engine • RÖNTGEN: X-rays • PLANCK: quantum theory • EINSTEIN: theory of relativity • O. HAHN: nuclear fission	1900
H. BÖLL / G. GRASS / M. HEIDEGGER / K. JASPERS		FIRST WORLD WAR • Weimar Republic • THIRD REICH SECOND WORLD WAR		
		• TREATY OF GERMAN REUNIFICATION		2000

(vertical label: Investiture Controversy)
(vertical label: Counter-Reformation)
(vertical label: HANSEATIC LEAGUE)

HISTORICAL TABLE AND NOTES

The Origins

The first human occupation of the territories which lie between the Rhine and the Elbe is thought to have been at the time of Neanderthal Man *(qv)*, during the final stages of the Ice Age about 60 000 years ago. From the 10C to the 6C BC, Germans arrived from the north and east. Looking to expand their territory and themselves under pressure from both Slav and Asiatic invaders, they crossed the Rhine to invade Celtic countries before being contained and then forced to retreat by the Romans.

Romans and Germans

1C AD	In the year 9, annihilation of 3 Roman legions under the command of Varus by Arminius, the leader of the Germans *(qv)*. Demarcation of the limit of Roman colonization by a fortified wall linking the Rhine and the Danube, known as the Limes.
314	Foundation of the first Christian bishopric in Germania at Trier.
c375	Pursued by the Huns, the Goths cross the Elbe.

The Frankish Empire

Early 6C	Conversion of Clovis, king of the Franks (a tribe originally based on the Rhine estuary), to Christianity. Overcoming the Alemanni in the east, he colonizes the territory later to become Franconia.
785	Charlemagne conquers the Saxons (west of the Elbe) and the Bavarians.
800	Crowning of Charlemagne by the Pope in Rome. The Emperor thus legally assumes sovereignty, on behalf of the Roman Empire, in ancient Gaul and Germania.
911	The Franks in the east choose one of their own men as King of Germania and start to quarrel with the western Franks, the nation later to become France. Colonization and conversion to Christianity of theSlav peoples east of the Elbe.

The Battle between the Priesthood and the Holy Roman Empire

962	In Rome, Otto I revives the imperial title as ruler of the Holy Roman Empire in the West, comprising the kingdoms of Germania, Italy and – after 1032 – the kingdom of Burgundy.
1073	Beginning of the reign of Pope Gregory VII, the Church's great reformer, who disputes the imperial supervision of the Papacy. A period of strife between the rival powers (Investiture Controversy) weakens the empire and threatens the unity of Christendom.
1152-1190	Frederick I ("Barbarossa") strives to reinforce the imperial power (deposition of Henry the Lion *(qv)* and dismemberment of the states of the Guelph) and to limit pontifical influence to spiritual matters. The title Holy Roman Empire derives from the reign of Frederick Barbarossa and signifies, constitutionally, that the Emperor is heir to the Caesars; that the imperial power is based on legal ties of a feudal nature.
1356	The Golden Bull, fundamental law of the Empire, inaugurates the election of the King of Germania by a college of three ecclesiastics (the archbishops of Mainz, Cologne and Trier) and four lay electors (the Duke of Saxony, the Margrave of Brandenburg, the Count of the Palatinate and the King of Bohemia).

Trade and Humanism

1358	Organization of the maritime and commercial Hanseatic League, linking more than 200 towns to guarantee the prosperity of northern Germany, and establishing Lübeck as the capital *(qv)*.
1386	Foundation of Heidelberg University, the oldest in Germany.
c1450	The invention of movable type by the printer Gutenberg in Mainz. The flowering of Humanism.

The Reformation and the Thirty Years War

Luther (1483-1546) – In 1503, Martin Luther enters the Augustinian monastery of Erfurt. A dedicated cleric, he is tormented by the problem of salvation. Appointed Professor of Theology, he finds in the Holy Scriptures (c1512-13) his answer: "Man justifies himself by his Faith, not through the workings of the Law."

Man's salvation, therefore – Luther argues – lies entirely within the gift, or Grace, of God. And to this, since he plays no part in that salvation himself, Man responds with Faith.

This concept leads him to attack the Roman traffic in indulgences and, on 31 October 1517, he exhibits on the doors of Wittenberg church 95 "theses" condemning such practices and reminding the Faithful of the primordial importance of the sacrifice on the Cross and the Grace of God. Luther is denounced in the court of Rome, refuses to retract, and in 1521 burns the Papal Bull threatening him with excommunication. Subsequently he criticizes the institutions and hierarchy of the Church and opposes to the primacy of the clergy in spiritual matters the universal priesthood of Christians conferred by baptism.

Refusing to retract once more before the Diet of Worms (1521), he is summoned before the young Charles V and banished to the outer confines of the Empire. His works are condemned to be burned.

The patronage of Frederick the Wise, Duke of Saxony, enables him to work on a translation of the Bible considered to be the first literary work in modern German.

The Edict of Worms having been confirmed in 1529 – and the controversy aggravated by an official ruling forbidding all and any religious innovations – six Princes and the representatives of 14 free towns meet in Speyer to "protest" against these decisions. From this support of the Lutheran cause, the term Protestant derives.

Martin Luther - a 16C coloured picture

| 1530 | Invited by Charles V to meet in Augsburg, theologians of the opposing faiths fail to agree, and Melanchthon draws up in the name of the Lutherans the "Confession of Augsburg" which becomes the charter of the new Protestantism. |
| 1555 | The Peace of Augsburg (*Cujus regio ejus religio* – to each state the religious faith of its people) establishes a compromise, and Protestantism is officially recognized in the states of northern Germany. |

Thirty Years War – The revival of Catholicism brought about by the Council of Trent (1545-1563), the Counter-Reformation supported by the Emperor and certain internal differences among the Protestants, added to a quarrel between Rudolf II and his brother Matthias, serve to disrupt this balance of power. The "Protestant Union", under the Elector Palatinate, gathers its forces to oppose the "Catholic League" supported by Bavaria.

The war, sparked off by a revolt in Bohemia in May 1618, is at first limited to the states ruled by the House of Austria; it spreads to become a generalized German conflict, localized physically to the west and north of the country; then finally degenerates into a European war devoid more and more of religious justification.

After the intervention of Sweden and Denmark, Protestant countries concerned at the threat menacing their national religion, Richelieu's France joins in with the intention of expelling the Habsburgs from the Franche-Comté and the Low Countries, at that time possessions of Spain. Fought almost entirely on German soil, the campaigns lay waste to the countryside, sack most of the major towns and ruin the economy. The Peace of Westphalia *(qv)* in 1648 re-establishes the rights in Germany of both faiths.

| 1689 | Provoked by the designs of Louis XIV on the west bank of the Rhine, the "War of the House of Orleans" breaks out. French troops commanded by the Marquis of Louvois devastate the Palatinate. |

The Rise of Prussia

In the 17C the Empire is weakened by internal squabbling and the sovereign pretensions of its princes. One state alone stands out through the efficiency of its organization: Prussia, fief of the Hohenzollerns. Friedrich-Wilhelm of Brandenburg, "The Great Elector" (1640-1688), and to a greater extent his son's successor, the second King of Prussia, Friedrich-Wilhelm I – known as "The King Sergeant" – were the true founders of this Prussian strength, based on a permanent army, centralized administration and national pride.

Frederick the Great (1740-1786) – Inheriting on his accession this model state with its standing army, Frederick II soon raises Prussia to the status of second power within the Empire. He challenges Austria first of all. His success during the War of Austrian Succession wins him the alliance of Silesia – and Silesia's participation in the dismemberment of Poland enables him to reinforce his eastern provinces.

Correspondant and friend of Voltaire, amateur of literature and music (he was an accomplished flautist), Frederick the Great is revered as a model of "the enlightened despot", enjoying the respect of intellectuals all over Europe. The greatness of Prussia is strengthened by his reign, marked by a meticulous administration and the renewed links forged between royalty and the nobility.

1792	Beginning of the Revolutionary Wars. Prussians defeated at Valmy.
1806	Napoleon enters Berlin. The Emperor Francis I of Austria renounces the crown of the German Holy Roman Empire, which is thereby dissolved. Creation of the Confederation of the Rhine, under the protection of France.
1813	Prussia is the bulwark of resistance to the French invader and leading force in the "War of Liberation", which ends, after "The Battle of Nations", in victory at Leipzig.

19

Map legend:

**FORMATION OF GERMAN UNITY
(1866-1871)**

0   300 km

Kingdom of Prussia in 1865
Prussian annexations in 1866
Limits of German Empire in 1871   ▬▬▬
K = Kingdom   GD = Grand Duchy
D = Duchy   ● = Free City

Towards German Unity

The dissolution of the Holy Roman Empire and the Napoleonic onslaught simplify the political map of Germany, breaking up the princeling states and secularizing the domains of the Church.
The status of most of the so-called Free Imperial Cities is abolished and a number of principalities, most of them very small, are amalgamated to form medium-sized states.

German Confederation – The Congress of Vienna establishes, in place of the Holy Roman Empire, a German Confederation of 35 autonomous states and free cities, represented by a Diet of 11 members appointed by the state and town governments, sitting at Frankfurt-on-Main and presided over by Austria. Metternich, a Rhinelander now Austrian Chancellor, becomes effective ruler of the federation, whose antiquated constitution clashes with the ideas of those liberal Germans dreaming of an independent nationhood.
The creation of a customs union (Zollverein), suggested by Prussia in 1834, goes some way towards unification through a common economic policy, but the meeting of a National German parliament at Frankfurt in 1848-49, following a revolutionary flare-up, produces no result.

Bismarck Era (1862-1890) – Bismarck, appointed Minister-President of Prussia in 1862, takes no more than eight years to impose "by fire and the sword" the unification of a "Lesser Germany" under his own rule. He thus dismisses Austrian attempts to create a "Greater Germany" extending from the North Sea to the Adriatic. Confident in the loyalty of an elite bourgeoisie born through the advance of industrialisation – and also in the neutrality of Napoleon III – he manipulates events so as to make war inevitable. He defeats the Austrians at Sadowa in the lightning campaign of 1866, thus leaving himself free to organize Germany's Northern Federation. This attaches Hanover, Hessen and Schleswig-Holstein to Prussia and unites the group with all other states north of the Main.
Then, profiting from the mistrust arising in southern Germany from the crude demands of Napoleon III – who sought the Palatinate and Luxembourg as the price of his neutrality – Bismarck works up throughout the whole of Germany a violent anti-French reaction. Finally, after the Hohenzollern candidature affair *(see Bad Ems)* has unwisely been exaggerated by the French government, he succeeds in inflaming national pride on both sides of the frontier and France declares war. The southern states unite in defence, and the whole of Germany stands shoulder-to-shoulder with Prussia.

Second Reich (1871-1918)

1870	After the victory of Sedan (September 2), the southern states open negotiations with Prussia to strengthen federal ties.
1871	On 18 January, the German Empire is proclaimed at Versailles with Wilhelm I at its head. Imperial Germany, enlarged by the acquisition of Alsace-Lorraine, remains in theory a federation – but it is in fact under Prussian domination.
1888	Wilhelm II succeeds his father.
1890	The Emperor, disliking the "Iron Chancellor's" authoritarian approach, forces Bismark's resignation. The Kaiser finds himself in the middle of a growth crisis: the demographic explosion, added to an over-rapid industrial development, has created a need for expansion that the "pan-Germanists" elevate to a creed. The Kaiser's dubious foreign policy provokes the enmity of England, Russia and France.

First World War – Erupting into an international atmosphere crackling with tension, the assassination of the Austrian Archduke Ferdinand at Sarajevo on 28 June 1914 unleashes the cataclysm. Austria's declaration of war against Serbia mobilises the armies of Europe.

1914	On 3 August, Germany declares war on France and Russia. German invasion of Belgium. Great Britain declares war on Germany 4 August. German offensive halted on the Marne; the "war of positions" begins.
1917	Russia, shaken by the Bolshevik revolution, asks for an armistice. In the West the United States, whose merchant marine has been attacked by German U-boats, declares war on the Reich.
1918	In October, an all-out counterattack by the Allies throws back the German armies, while behind their lines revolution breaks out. It is therefore a Socialist Council of People's Representatives which signs on 11 November the armistice at Réthondes.

Weimar Republic

Spartacists who formed and led the military and workingmen's Soviets behind the revolution fail to gain the support of the popular masses. Ebert, the head of the provisional government, summons the army and suppresses the revolution before the activists can consolidate their power.

On 11 August 1919, Germany adopts a Republican Constitution, virtually imposed by the victors. The Kaiser goes into exile. This "Republic without republicans" shoulders the heavy task of assuming the obligations of the Treaty of Versailles (28 June 1919): territorial concessions, loss of colonies, limitation of army and armaments, and crippling reparations.

Very quickly, the economic crisis provoked by the impossibility of re-establishing an efficient industry, plus the country's general indebtedness, results in an insane cycle of inflation; the middle classes are ruined. In 1923 the French, angry at the delay in the payment of reparations, occupy the Ruhr. The passive resistance of the German people aggravates the economic situation, and extremists come to the fore once more. On the Right, they unite around the "German National Socialist Worker's Party", which Adolf Hitler joins in 1919. Once leader of the party, he attempts to seize power in a putsch at Munich (8-9 November 1923). It fails and he is imprisoned. Freed in 1924, he waits for ten years before his next, successful, attempt.

From 1923 to 1929, Germany enjoys six years of relative calm. There is a spectacular re-establishment of the economy, encouraged by the spreading out of reparations, the French evacuation of the Ruhr and massive injections of American capital. On the international scene, Foreign Minister Gustav Stresemann recognizes the western frontiers imposed at Versailles and makes Germany a member of the League of Nations. But the worldwide financial crash of 1929 hits the German recovery hard: there is a recurrence of inflation and unemployment increases dramatically. Profiting from the general discontent, and with the cynical use of paramilitary organizations (SA and SS) prepared to resort to political violence, the National-Socialists win more than 38% of the suffrage in 1932. Management and the governing classes, seeing in Hitler a rampart against the spreading flood of Communism, allow him to accede to the post of Chancellor on 30 January 1933.

Hitler and the Third Reich

The Dictatorship – Very quickly, Hitler organizes a totalitarian state. After the Reichstag fire, in fact secretly set up by the SA on 27 February 1933, he orders the arrest of 4 000 Communist leaders and assumes total power. On 1 December, the Nazis (the word is an abbreviation of the German for National Socialist German Workers' Party) become the sole political party in the country, and this coup receives "popular approval" in a plebiscite (December 12) organized in a climate of terror. The death of President Hindenburg in August 1934 leaves Hitler absolute master of Germany – the Führer (Guide or Leader). He is now free to put into operation his blueprint for "a thousand-year Reich".

Reabsorption of the workless is obtained through a programme of public works (motorways, drainage schemes), a policy of rearmament, and the regimentation of the young. The population is subjected to a barrage of propaganda, and all forms of resistance are ruthlessly suppressed: opponents, tracked down by the Gestapo, are interned in so-called concentration camps from 1933 onwards. Persecution of the Jews becomes, with the racial laws of Nuremberg (September 1935), a radical and systematic official policy: pogroms, bans and mass arrests are the instruments of this antisemitic ideology. The arts and literature are subject to control and all works judged "decadent" forbidden. A majority of Germany's most creative artists choose exile.

To familiarize the German public with the "rights" and "wrongs" encompassed by Hitler's artistic credo an exhibition of *Entartete Kunste* – degenerate art – is held in Munich in 1937. Among the "outcasts" whose work is pilloried are Max Ernst, Oskar Kokoschka, Marc Chagall, Ernst Ludwig Kirchner and Otto Dix – artists considered today as major influences on the modern art scene. The show is contrasted with an exhibition of paintings approved by the Nazis – mainly over-life size Aryan warriors and their buxom, blonde Brünnhildes.

Hitler's foreign policy encounters little resistance on the part of the democracies. Without raising more than offended protests, he violates the Locarno Treaty by the military occupation of the Rhineland (1936), annexes Austria in the Auschluss of 1938, and browbeats Britain and France at the Munich Conference that year into accepting the return of the Sudetenland from Czechoslovakia to Germany. The progress towards war accelerates: Czechoslovakia itself is demolished in March 1939, and the unprovoked aggression against Poland on the following 1 September obliges the Allies at last to honour their undertakings.

Second World War – Germany, Mussolini's Italy and Japan are on one side, Britain, France, the United States and the Soviet Union (after an initial period of alliance with the Reich) on the other.

1940	A lightning offensive allows the Germans to invade the greater part of Western Europe. Only Britain, retreating to her island base, holds out thanks to the heroic resistance of her air force.
1941	The 22 June, Hitler attacks Russia while the Balkans are overrun and Rommel expands his offensive in North Africa. In 1942, the Third Reich is at the height of its power.
1943	Soviet counter-offensive, initiated by the victory of Stalingrad. The Americans, involved in the conflict since the Japanese attack on Pearl Harbour (December 1941), land in Sicily in July.
1944	Allied landings in Normandy (June). The 20 July, Hitler narrowly escapes a bomb attack planned by his opponents.
1945	After the suicide of the Führer (20 April), the Reich capitulates on 8 May. Germany is nothing but a wasteland of ruins. The liberation of the death camps reveals to a horrified world the reality of the Nazis' "final solution" policy of exterminating Jews and other "impure" races on a European scale (6 million dead).

Germany Today

1945	The "Big Three" (Britain, USA and USSR) meet in Potsdam to decide on the division of Germany into four zones of Occupation (France administering the fourth zone).
1946/7	Beginning of the Cold War with the confrontation of the USA and the USSR over occupation policies.
1948	Soviet blockade of the western sectors of Berlin. The Berlin Airlift.
1949	Creation (23 May) of the **Federal Republic**, comprising the three western zones. The Soviet zone becomes (7 October) the **German Democratic Republic**. Under the leadership of Konrad Adenauer, Chancellor until 1963, the Federal Republic enjoys a spectacular economic rebirth and re-establishes normal international relations.
1961	At the crisis point of the Cold War, construction (13 August) of the "Berlin Wall".
1972	Signature of a treaty between the two Germanys confirms Chancellor Willy Brandt's policy of openness towards the East (Ostpolitik).
1989	Under pressure from its citizens, the government of East Germany decides (10 November) to open the frontier between the two states. Berlin wall comes tumbling down.
1990	Free elections (May) in East Germany; ratification of the Treaty of Reunification on 3 October by Parliament sitting in the Reichstag, Berlin; eventual re-establishment of Berlin as capital of united Germany.

Konrad Adenauer

THE ARTS

Germany's geographical situation and eventful history have favoured the intrusion of artistic currents from the rest of Europe – mainly French in the Gothic period and Italian in the Renaissance. The originality of German art manifests itself above all in the sumptuous decoration of the Baroque abbeys in Bavaria.

ROMANESQUE ART (9-12C)

Pre-Romanesque Architecture – In Germany, as elsewhere in the Christian West, religious architecture developed from the adaptation of Roman lay basilicas, the long halls of worship now oriented towards the east and terminated by an apse. The central portion is raised above two or four side aisles and the whole covered with a plain wooden ceiling.

The Carolingian period is marked by the building of churches with two chancels. The western chancel sometimes forms part of another characteristic feature the **Westwerk**, a tall square tower of military appearance onto which the nave is securely anchored. The Westwerk – at Corvey for instance – frequently constitutes almost a church in itself. Such large, tall chapels, opening on the nave via galleries sometimes several storeys high, were traditionally reserved for the Emperor.

Ottonian Architecture (10C and early 11C) – The restoration of imperial dignity by Otto I in 962 was accompanied by a revival of religious architecture in Saxony and in the regions of the Meuse and Lower Rhine. The huge churches erected at this period were characterized by deeply projecting transepts and wide aisles. As yet, they had no stone vaulting. An alternation of piers and columns broke up the uniformity of the aisles, which were not yet divided by bays. The churches of St Michael at Hildesheim and St Cyriacus at Gernrode are the best examples of buildings of this period.

Rhineland Romanesque Style – At Cologne and in the surrounding countryside, several churches share in their plan a triple apse designed in the form of a clover-leaf. These tri-lobed extensions are adorned on the outside with blind arcades and a "dwarf gallery" (Zwerggalerie) – a motif of Lombard origin.

In the Middle Rhine region, the style achieves its full splendour in the majestic "imperial" cathedrals of Speyer, Mainz and Worms. These are characterized in their floor plans by a double chancel with neither ambulatory nor apsidal chapels, and sometimes by a double transept; in their elevation by a multiplicity of towers; in their exterior decoration by the use of galleries of blind arcades and Lombard bands (vertical motifs in low relief with small blind arcades linking them at the top). Typically, the roofs of these Rhineland towers are in the form of a bishop's mitre, the base decorated with a lozenge pattern.

Towards the end of the 11C, the architects of the cathedral at Speyer boldly projected groined stone vaulting over the nave. Marking the transition from Romanesque to Gothic are the churches of Limburg and Andernach and the cathedral at Naumburg, which were built with pointed vaulting early in the 13C.

GOTHIC ARCHITECTURE (13-16C)

For its great interior width, the slenderness of the two tall towers built on either side of the façade in the French style, and the height of its pointed vaulting, Cologne Cathedral is famous throughout the world. Equally inspired by the French Gothic style are the cathedrals of Regensburg, Freiburg-im-Breisgau, Magdeburg and Halberstadt.

French influence, too, may be seen in the Cistercian monasteries built in such profusion between 1150 and 1250. Their churches, usually without towers or belfries, often modified subsequently in the Baroque manner, were habitually designed with squared-off chancels flanked by rectangular chapels. Maulbronn Abbey, one of the most complete monastic ensembles remaining in Europe, is an example.

East of the Elbe, the most imposing edifices were brick-built, complete with buttresses and flying buttresses. Typical of the style (known in German as Backsteingotik) are the Church of St Nicholas at Stralsund, St Mary's in Lübeck, the town halls of those two cities, Schwerin Cathedral and the abbey church at Bad Doberan.

The Abbey Church at Bad Doberan

Late Gothic Architecture (Spätgotik) – This long period (14, 15 and 16C) is marked in Germany by the widespread building of hall-churches, usually with vaulting divided by purely decorative ribs that form stars or groining in contrast to the bareness of the walls.

St Anne's Church at Annaberg-Buchholz is exemplary of a style that allows the artists involved to express their virtuosity freed from all architectural constraint.

These **hall-churches** are completely different from those constructed on the basilical plan at the end of the Romanesque period. The aisles are now the same height as the nave, separated from it only by tall columns. The most famous examples – extra-tall buildings erected at the end of the Gothic period – are the Church of Our Lady in Munich and St George's Church, Dinkelsbühl.

Civil Architecture in the Late Middle Ages – Commercial prosperity among merchants and skilled craftsmen in the 14C and 15C led to the development in town centres of impressive town halls and half-timbered private houses, frequently adorned with painting and sculpture. Examples of such civil projects may be seen today in Regensburg, Goslar, Rothenburg and Tübingen.

A hall-church
St George's at Dinkelsbühl
1) Central nave – 2) Side aisle
3) Network vaulting

THE RENAISSANCE (1520-c1620)

The Renaissance, eclipsed by the troubles of the Reformation, is no more than an episode in the history of German architecture. Italian influence in this period is restricted to southern Germany: elegant Florentine arcading, for instance, was used by Fugger the Rich as decoration for his funerary chapel at Augsburg (1518); the Jesuits, building St Michael's Church in Munich (1589), were clearly inspired by their own Sanctuary of Jesus in Rome.

Northern Germany was influenced by Flemish and Dutch design. In the rich merchants' quarters, many-storeyed gables such as those of the Gewandhaus in Brunswick were loaded with ornamentation in the form of obelisks, scrollwork, statues, pilasters, etc. Güstrow Castle and the old town of Görlitz are important examples of Renaissance influence, while Celle, Wolfenbüttel, Bückeburg and Hamelin are saturated with the particular charm of the so-called "Weser Renaissance" *(qv)*.

BAROQUE ARCHITECTURE (17C and 18C)

Characterized by an irregularity of contour and a multiplicity of form, the Baroque seeks above all the effect of movement and contrast. Taken to its extreme, the style degenerates into Rococo, where the fantasy element is employed mainly as decoration. From the middle of the 17C, Baroque influence was most marked in Catholic southern Germany, encouraged by the Counter-Reformation's exaltation of dogmatic belief in the Real Presence, the cult of the Virgin and the saints, and in general all manifestations of popular piety.

Enterprising abbots set about rebuilding their abbeys to plans so ambitious that, today, they would seem stupefying. Masons, painters, sculptors and stuccoworkers were thus offered extraordinary opportunities. Stucco designs – worked with an amalgam of lime, plaster and wet sand that could be modelled to give a three-dimensional effect – covered every available surface.

The Masters of German and Danubian Baroque – The blossoming of the Baroque style owes much to the **Vorarlberg School** (1680-1750), of which the masters remain largely anonymous, so great was the group's corporative spirit. These architects, working chiefly in Swabia but also in Bavaria, Switzerland and even Alsace, lavished a great deal of care on the lines and perspectives of their single naves.

But, in Bavaria especially, there were also brilliant individuals, rarely specializing in a single technique, who produced designs of great subtlety – in ground plans, for example, using as a focal point a round or oval bay. Johann Michael Fischer (Diessen, Zwiefalten and Ottobeuren), the Asam brothers (Weltenburg and St John Nepomuk in Munich) and Dominikus Zimmermann (Steinhausen and Wies) were the virtuosi of this Bavarian school.

The Baroque movement in Franconia, patronized by the prince-bishops of the Schönborn family, who owned residences in Mainz, Würzburg, Speyer and Bamberg, was closely linked with the spread of similar ideas in Bohemia. The Dientzenhofer brothers decorated the palaces in Prague as well as the one in Bamberg.

Balthazar Neumann, who worked for the same prelates, dominated his contemporaries by the breadth of a culture enriched by contact with the French, Viennese and Italian masters he encountered.

The west front at Ottobeuren
Abbey Church

In Saxony, the Zwinger Palace in Dresden, joint masterpiece of the architect Pöppelmann and the sculptor Permoser, brilliantly illustrates this German Baroque with Italian roots; the refinement of the Rococo décor in the Sans-Souci Palace at Potsdam is even more astonishing, given the Prussian reputation for austerity – but is explained by the studies in France and Italy followed by the architect Knobelsdorff.

Churches – A sinuous movement, generally convex in line, animates the façades, while the superimposition of two pediments, different in design, adds vitality to the whole. The façades are additionally adorned with twin domed towers (a single tower in the case of pilgrimage churches). The later the church, the more detached are the towers.

Huge galleries stand above the lateral chapels, at the height of pilaster capitals with jutting abaci. Chapels and galleries stop at the level of the transept, giving

Vaulting at Vierzehnheiligen

it a much greater depth. Clerestory windows, pierced at gallery height, allow plenty of light to enter.

Bohemian and Franconian Baroque is typified by **complex vaulting**, round or oval bays being covered by complicated structures in which the transverse arches bow out in horse-shoe shape, only to meet in their keystones.

The **altarpiece** or reredos, focal point of the church furnishing, is treated monumentally, its design architecturally that of a triumphal arch. The arch, in carved wood or stucco, frames either a large painting or a group of statuary. Columns twisted into spiral form accentuate the concept of movement distinguishing Baroque art, and back lighting from a hidden source, with its contrasts of brightness and shadow, is equally typical.

An ornamentation that is both exaggerated and asymmetric characterizes the **Rococo** style.

Castles – The one-storey construction of these country residences was often lent additional importance when built on a raised foundation. The focal point was a circular central bloc whose convexity was evident only from the garden front.

Monumental stairways with several flights and considerable theatrical effect are often the centrepieces of the larger German castles and palaces built in the 18C. The staircase, embellished with arcaded galleries and a painted ceiling, leads to the lst floor state room whose elevation rises majestically to the roof level of the second storey. Such pompous – almost pretentious – arrangements characterize many of the great abbeys of this period, often complemented by that other ceremonial room, the library.

State staircase at
Pommersfelden Castle

THE ARRIVAL OF NEO-CLASSICISM

The example of Versailles inspired in Germany a new style of court life, particularly in the Rhineland and the Berlin of Frederick II. Many French architects were employed by the Electors of the Palatinate, of Mainz, of Trier and of Cologne; mainly, they produced plans for country mansions with names such as Monrepos (my rest) or Solitude.

Unadorned pediments, balustrades at the base of the roofs, columned porticoes at the main entrance, all indicate a desire for unobtrusive elegance outside, while the interior decoration, carried out with a lighter touch, confined itself to cornucopiae of flowers mingled with Rococo motifs that were now a little more discreet.

From 1750 on, Winckelmann's work on the art of antiquity, and the excavations taking place at Pompeii, threw a new light on Greco-Roman architecture.

A new fashion arose, in which architects favoured the Doric style, the coldest of all, and a preference for the colossal – pilasters and columns of a single "order" no longer stood one storey high but always two.

Symmetrical balance and a purely static line became the ideal to such an extent that, in some churches, a false pulpit was added to balance the genuine preacher's eyrie. As well as churches, abbeys and castles, skilled craftsmen turned their attention to commemorative monuments and museums – a new sign of their interest in the past – especially in Berlin where Schinkel, the master of the colonnade, was working. Interior decoration showed a preference for sculptured motifs such as garlands, urns, vases and friezes of pearls.

By 1830, the Neo-Classical movement had become sterile; it was superseded, except in Munich, by a renewed interest in the Gothic which became, for the Romantics, emblematic of "the old Germany".

The **Biedermeier** taste – light-weight, cushioned furniture with flowing lines, glass-fronted cabinets for the display of knick-knacks – corresponded perhaps with the later Edwardian style in England.

The year 1850 marks the beginning of the **Founders' Period** (Gründerzeit), when wealthy industrialists fell for pretentious reproductions of medieval or Renaissance furniture. Similiar pieces were to be found also in public buildings such as the Reichstag in Berlin.

CONTEMPORARY MOVEMENTS

At the beginning of the 20C, **Jugendstil** ("Style 1900") or Art Nouveau became the vogue in Germany, largely due to mass-production of well-made furniture. Of far greater importance to Germany was the growth of the idea that there could be an aesthetic for industrial design, promoted by such pioneers as Peter Behrens, Mies van der Rohe and Walter Gropius. After the First World War, Gropius was appointed head of the **Bauhaus** *(see table opposite)*.

Urban growth and the reparation of war damage called for the building or rebuilding of many churches, and architects such as Dominikus Böhm and Rudolf Schwartz were among the craftsmen who brought to light by this renewal of interest in sacred work, many of their designs being markedly austere. New concepts, too, characterized the construction of municipal and cultural enterprises such as Hans Scharoun's Philharmonia in Berlin and the Staatsgalerie of Stuttgart by the Englishman James Stirling – buildings of an architectural audacity only made possible by the development of materials and construction techniques that were entirely new.

GERMANY'S GREAT ARTISTS

Architects and Sculptors *(blue lettering)* – **Painters and Engravers** *(1)*

15th Century

Stefan LOCHNER (d 1451) – At the head of the School of Cologne: golden backgrounds, sweetness of expression, freshness of colours (**Adoration of the Magi**, Cathedral Cologne; **Virgin and Rose Bush**, Wallraf-Richartz Museum and Ludwig Museum, Cologne).

Veit STOSS (c1445-1533) – Artist and tormented genius, admirable when working in wood (**Angel's Greeting**, Church of St Laurence, Nuremberg).

Tilman RIEMENSCHNEIDER (1460-1531) – Sculptor whose works, delicately modelled, are rich in expression, intensely felt (**Tomb of Henry II the Saint**, Bamberg Cathedral; **Adam and Eve**, Franconia-Mainz Land Museum, Würzburg; **Altarpiece to the Virgin**, Creglingen Chapel).

The Master of St Severinus (late 15C) – His sense of intimacy and his iridescent colours display Dutch influence (**Christ before Pilate**, Wallraf-Richartz Museum and Ludwig Museum, Cologne).

The Master of THE LIFE OF THE VIRGIN (late 15C) – Delightful, anecdotal artist much influenced by Van der Weyden (**Vision of St Bernard**, Wallraf-Richartz Museum and Ludwig Museum, Cologne).

Friedrich HERLIN (d 1500) – Picturesque and precise realist (**Almswomen at Prayer**, Nördlingen Museum).

16th Century

Matthias GRÜNEWALD (c1460-1528) – A powerful genius, producing works of a tragic intensity (**Crucifixion**, Fine Arts Museum, Karlsruhe; **Virgin and Child**, Stuppach Church).

Albrecht DÜRER (1471-1528) – A humanist, the most famous artist of the German Renaissance school; religious scenes and portraits of extraordinary intensity; a profusion of wonderful drawings and engravings (**The Four Apostles**, **Self-Portrait with Cloak**, Old Pinakothek, Munich; **Charlemagne**, German National Museum, Nuremberg).

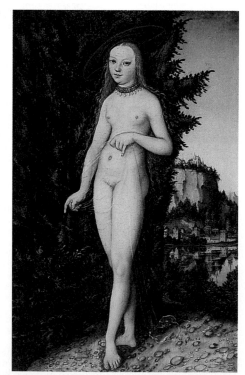

Lucas CRANACH THE ELDER (1472-1553) – Master of an important studio; portraitist of the most eminent men of the Reformation.
His sense of the wonders of nature allied him to the painters of the Danube school (**Portrait of Martin Luther**, German National Museum, Nuremberg).

Albrecht ALTDORFER (1480-1538) – Member of the Danube school *(qv)* and one of the earliest landscape painters. His use of chiaroscuro has a moving effect (**Battle of Alexander at Issus**, Old Pinakothek, Munich).

(1) Artists in the 16C were, as a rule, both painters and engravers.

Venus in a Landscape, by Lucas Cranach

Hans BALDUNG GRIEN (c1485-1545) – Artist achieving his effects by the use of unusual colours and dramatic lighting (**Altarpiece: The Coronation of the Virgin**, Freiburg Cathedral).

Hans HOLBEIN THE YOUNGER (1497-1543) – Author of religious compositions and portraits of a striking realism (**The Nativity and the Adoration of the Magi**, Freiburg Cathedral).

17th Century

Adam ELSHEIMER (1578-1610) – Elsheimer's mythological and Biblical paintings were often small scale but exquisitely worked and his influence is apparent in the work of numerous French and Italian artists (**The Flight into Egypt**, Old Pinakothek, Munich).

Elias HOLL (1573-1646) – Architect responsible for the most important buildings of the Renaissance in Germany (Town Hall, Augsburg).

Andreas SCHLÜTER (c1660-1714) – Master of Baroque sculpture in northern Germany. A most vigorous talent (**Statue of the Great Elector**, Charlottenburg, Berlin; **Masks of Dying Warriors**, Berlin Arsenal).

The MERIANS (17C) – A family of engravers specializing in plates illustrating German towns.

18th Century

Balthazar PERMOSER (1651-1732) – Sculptor to the Court of Dresden. After studying in Rome, Florence and Venice, he transplanted with great virtuosity the exuberance of Italian Baroque (**The Ramparts Pavilion**; **Nymphs Bathing**, Zwinger, Dresden).

Matthäus Daniel PÖPPELMANN (1662-1736) – Architect-in-Chief to Augustus the Strong, he worked in Prague, in Vienna and in Italy before designing his masterpiece, the **Zwinger**, in Dresden, an epitome of the Late Baroque style.

Antoine PESNE (1683-1757) – A French painter who emigrated to the Court of Friedrich II, much favoured for his use of brilliant colours (**Portraits of Friedrich II and his Sister Wilhelmina**, Private Apartments, Charlottenburg, Berlin).

Dominikus ZIMMERMANN (1685-1766) – Architect of the most successful churches in the Bavarian Rococo style (**Churches of Wies and of Steinhausen**).

Balthazar NEUMANN (1687-1753) – An architect and engineer. Technical virtuosity and the inbuilt harmony of his compositions made him master of the Baroque style (**Vierzehnheiligen Church**).

The BROTHERS ASAM – The sculptor Egid Quirin (1692-1750) and his brother, the painter and architect Cosmas Damian Asam (1686-1739) provide a splendid example of the collaboration existing between artists in the Baroque period (**Churches of the Asam Brothers**, Munich).

Georg Wenzeslaus von KNOBELSDORFF (1699-1753) – Official architect – and friend – of Frederick the Great, master of the Rococo (**Berlin Opera House; Sans-Souci**, Potsdam).

19th Century

Caspar David FRIEDRICH (1774-1840) – Artist of the Romantic school; he developed the tragic in landscape painting (**The Monk by the Sea, The Cross on the Mountain**, private apartments, Charlottenburg, Berlin; **Rambler Above a Sea of Clouds**, Fine Arts Museum, Hamburg).

Carl-Friedrich SCHINKEL (1781-1841) – Architect whose long colonnades typify the cityscape of central Berlin (**Neue Wache**, Old Museum and Schauspielhaus).

Wilhelm LEIBL (1844-1900) – Master of the Realist school (**Three Women in Church**, Fine Arts Museum, Hamburg; **Portrait of Frau Gedon**, New Pinakothek, Munich).

Adolf von HILDEBRAND (1847-1921) – As a monumental sculptor, his sureness of taste is in contrast to the excesses of most 19C artists (**Wittelsbach Fountain**, Munich).

Max LIEBERMANN (1847-1935) – Leading German Impressionist painter (**Jewish Street in Amsterdam**, Wallraf-Richartz Museum, Cologne).

20th Century

Ernst BARLACH (1870-1938) – His massive, tormented sculptures in wood and bronze are characteristic examples of the Expressionist school (**The Angel**, Antonines' Church, Cologne; **Frieze of the Listeners**, Ernst Barlach House; **The Singer**, Ratzeburg).

Dominikus BÖHM (1880-1955) – Pioneer of a new type of religious architecture (**Church of St Mary the Queen**, Cologne; **St Wolfgang's Church**, Regensburg).

The BAUHAUS – Architectural school founded in Weimar then transferred to Dessau where it was directed from 1925 to 1928 by Walter Gropius (1883-1969). The marriage of art with technique was the fundamental theme uniting the members of this school, which soon attracted a galaxy of brilliant avant-garde painters and sculptors (Bauhaus Museum, Berlin).

The EXPRESSIONISTS – German Expressionism introduced a distorted, violent and tragic vision of the world to modern painting. The movement owed much to Van Gogh and the Norwegian painter Edvard Munch (1863-1944), whose work had a marked influence in Germany. See the works of **Emil Nolde** (1867-1956) at Seebüll; and of Expressionism in general at the Brücke Museum, Berlin. The **Brücke** (Bridge) Group united from 1905 to 1913 such painters as Erich Heckel, Ernst Ludwig Kirchner, Karl Schmidt-Rottluff – whose work, with its passion for pure colour, recalls that of the Fauvists in France.

DER BLAUE REITER (The BLUE RIDER MOVEMENT) – An artistic group founded in Munich in 1911 by Kandinsky and Marc, later to be joined by Macke and Klee. Their aim was to free art from the constraint of reality, thus opening the way to abstraction (**Deer in the Forest**, by **Franz Marc**, Orangery of the Fine Arts Museum, Karlsruhe; **The Dress Shop**, by **August Macke**, Folkwang Museum, Essen)

The NEW OBJECTIVITY (NEUE SACHLICHKEIT) – An artistic current affecting all the arts around 1923, based on a realistic illustration of social facts and phenomena (**War**, by **Otto Dix**, 1932, Albertinium in Dresden).

Second half of the 20C – After the Second World War, **Group Zebra**, inheriting the New Objectivity credo, opposed the abstractions of Expressionism, and **Group Zero** (Heinz Mack, Otto Piene, Günther Vecker) inverted the treatment of the abstract by transforming thoughts into visible objects.

Josef Beuys and the artists belonging to the school of **Constructivist Sculpture** in Düsseldorf, by insisting on a direct relationship between the artist and the public (**Happenings**), hope to redefine the relative positions of art and the artist in contemporary society (**National Gallery**, Potsdamerstrasse, Berlin; **Hessen Museum**, Darmstadt; **State Gallery**, Stuttgart).

Georg Baselitz, **Anselm Kiefer** and **Sigmar Polke** belong to the new generation of German artists with growing reputations on the international scene.

Deer in the Forest, by Franz Marc

PRINCIPAL LITERARY EVENTS

Great philosophers' names appear in bold type

Middle Ages

9C	The Lay of Hildebrand.
Late 12C	National folk saga of Niebelungen.
13C	Wolfram von Eschenbach writes the epic poem *Parsifal* – the knight in quest of the Holy Grail (chalice said to have contained the blood of Christ).
1170-1228	Walther van der Vogelweide, the troubadour knight, raises medieval lyric poetry to its greatest heights.
Early 16C	Chronicle of the picaresque adventures of the buffoon Till Eulenspiegel.

The Reformation and the Thirty Years War

Only at the end of the Reformation and after the disastrous Thirty Years War was German literature in a position to develop freely.

1534	Luther finishes his translation of the Bible, the first literary work written in modern German.
1669	Grimmelshausen publishes his cautionary account of the fortunes and misfortunes of picaresque Simplicissimus.

"Aufklärung" (Age of Enlightenment)

1646-1716	**Leibniz** writes his *Theodicy* in French and in Latin; he invents differential calculus.
1729-1781	Lessing establishes the principles of the new German theatre *(Hamburg Theory of Drama)*; he writes bourgeois plays with rationalist leanings *(Kabale und Liebe)*.
1724-1804	**Kant** defines the balance between liberty and morality: man finds liberty in submission to "the categorical imperative".

"Sturm und Drang" and Classicism

In reaction against the stark rationalism of the Aufklärung, the "Sturm und Drang" movement exalts emotion, sentimentality, nature and a titanic liberty. Goethe (1749-1832), an all-round genius (science, poetry, philosophy, the drama) tempers this fashionable enthusiasm with a proposal for a classical ideal of a triumphant and harmonious humanity.

Johann Wolfgang von Goethe

1759-1805	Schiller, poet and dramatist, writes historical dramas (*Don Carlos, Wallenstein* and *William Tell*) which are in fact hymns to liberty.
1774	Werther, the novel in the form of correspondence, makes the young Goethe's reputation.
1788	Returning from Italy, Goethe publishes his great classical dramas: *Iphigenia in Tauris*, *Egmont* and *Torquato Tasso*.
1796 and 1821	*Wilhelm Meister* – a Bildungsroman (novel of educational development) in two parts.
1808 and 1832	*Faust*, the quintessence of Goethe's message to mankind.

The Romantic Movement (1790-1850)

This movement, reflecting an essential element in the German character, charts the individual soul's quest for the infinite in all its forms. It is the movement of Me. Aside from literature, it influences also the fine arts, philosophy and even politics and religion. Heidelberg, Jena and Berlin are centres from which the movement blossoms. The Romantic can create his own world from reality or from fancy and he is able to turn whatever he likes into poetry. The subconscious becomes a subject for serious study and the supernatural comes into vogue, while in religion Romantic subjectivism leads to mysticism.

1770-1831	Hegel defines the historical conscience and dialectic.
1772-1801	Novalis, poet and mystic, exalts the art and the religion of the Middle Ages; he defines the Absolute by means of "the Blue Flower symbol" (Heinrich von Ofterdingen).
1805	Publication of *The Child with the Magic Horn (Das Knaber Winderhern)*, a collecton of popular folk poems.
1810	Heinrich von Kleist writes *The Prince of Homburg*, a play about a man of action led away by his dreams. Von Kleist also publishes (1804) *The Marquise of O...*, one of a collection of 8 powerful novellae.
1812	First publication of *Grimms' Fairy Tales*.
1776-1822	E T A Hoffmann explores the supernatural in his *Tales*.

The disillusioned idealism of the Romantic Movement is succeeded by a search for realism and, after 1848, by philosophic materialism and social-critical literature.

1797-1856	Heinrich Heine, the "defrocked Romantic", poet of the *Loreley*, mingles a bitter irony with the heated emotions of a liberal "Young Germany".
1788-1860	**Arthur Schopenhauer**, pessimistic theorist of the will to live and the move towards pity.
1813-1863	Hebbel composes forceful tragedies (*Agnes Bernauer*).
1848	**Karl Marx** and **Friedrich Engels** publish their Communist *Manifesto*.
1862-1946	Gerhart Hauptmann develpos Naturalist social-critical drama (*The Weavers*).

The current period

1844-1900	**Friedrich Nietzsche** denounces, in lyrical language, the decadence of humanity, praising a future "super-man" freed from the "morality of the feeble" (*Thus Spoke Zarathustra*).
1868-1933	Stefan George publishes poems which, in their formal perfection, ally him with the French Symbolists.
1900-1930	The Austrians Rainer Maria Rilke and Hugo von Hoffmannsthal attain the peak of poetic impressionism.
1875-1955	Thomas Mann, novelist (*Buddenbrooks, Dr Faustus, The Magic Mountain* and *Death in Venice*).
1883-1924	Franz Kafka, symbolic novelist of the absurd (*The Trial, Metamorphosis, The Castle* and *America*).
1898-1956	Bertolt Brecht, social-critical dramatist (*The Threepenny Opera, Mother Courage, Galileo* and *Caucasian Chalk Circle*).
1920-1950	The Existentialist movement (**Husserl, Heidegger, Jaspers**).
Since 1945	The literary Group 47 emphasise the social role of the writer. The Nobel Prize for Literature is awarded to the novelists Hermann Hesse (1946) and Heinrich Böll (1972). Günther Grass, born in 1927, defends the role of the intellectual in society.
1900-1983	Anna Seghers, exiled since 1933, returns to East Germany after the war and questions the relationship between art and reality.

PRINCIPAL MUSICAL EVENTS

Middle Ages

12C and 13C	The Minnesänger (musical narrative poets), minstrels and troubadours who included in their number noble knights such as **Wolfram von Eschenbach** and **Walther von der Vogelweide**, draw inspiration from French lyric poetry for their songs (Minnesang = love song).
14C and 15C	The Mastersingers (Meistersinger) organize themselves into guilds. They introduce polyphony to German music (**Heinrich von Meissen** and **Hans Sachs**).

Luther (1483-1546) and the precursors of Bach

The Lutheran Reformation brings independence to German music. The new liturgy requires a new musical form: the chorale. Sung in the common tongue, this leads, later, to the German cantata and oratorio.

1529	Chorale *Ein Feste Burg* (words by Luther, music by **Johann Walther**).
1645	*The Seven Words of Christ*, by **Heinrich Schütz**, shows Italian influence (**Monteverdi**).
1637-1707	**Dietrich Buxtehude** organizes the first concerts of sacred music.

Johann Sebastian Bach (1685-1750)

His compositional expertise, his genius for invention and his total mastery of counterpoint enable Bach to excel in every branch of music he writes.

1717-1723	Position at Court of Goethen. *The Brandenburg Concertos*.
1723	Appointment as "Cantor" at St Thomas's, Leipzig. Bach's duties include the composition of a cantata every week, to be sung at the Sunday service. He has, in addition, to supervise the services at four other churches, teach Latin and singing, and find the time to compose innumerable instrumental and vocal works.
1722 and 1744	*The Well-tempered Keyboard*.

Johann Sebastian Bach

Music of the Baroque period

1665-1759	Georg Friedrich Handel, inspired and prolific Composer to the Courts of Hanover and St James, excels in both opera and oratorio (*The Messiah*, 1742).
1681-1767	**Georg Philipp Telemann**, influenced by French and Italian composers, forsakes counterpoint for melody. He originates public concerts.
Middle of 18C	Musicians of the **School of Mannheim** help establish the form of the modern symphony. **Carl Philipp Emmanuel Bach** (1714-1788) popularizes the sonata in its classic form. Appearance in Germany of the **Singspiel**, a type of popular operetta in which dialogue is interspersed with songs in the form of Lieder.
1743	Berlin's first Opera House is built.
1714-1787	**Christoph Willibald Gluck** provokes the enthusiasm of the innovators – and the horror of fans of traditional, Italian-inspired opera – by staging, in Paris, his *Iphigenia in Aulis* and *Orpheus*.

The Viennese School – Haydn and Mozart

At the height of the classic period, **Haydn** (1732-1809) establishes the definitive form of the symphony and the string quartet. **Mozart** (1756-1791) perfects both forms and creates operas that become immortal.

Beethoven (1770-1827)

Transforming the existing forms of music, Beethoven introduces new harmonies presaging the Romantic movement. The profundity of his reflection, varying from pure introspection to a wider belief in the force and universality of his art, shines out with extraordinary power. This is particularly true of the symphonies, moving and majestic, considered to be the major expression of his genius – and certainly the most popular.

1824	First performance of the *Ninth Symphony*.

The Romantics

1797-1826	**Franz Schubert** helps revive the lied blending folk and classical music in his unique style.
1786-1826	**Carl Maria von Weber** creates Germany's first Romantic opera, *Freischütz* (1821), paving the way for the characters of Wagnerian drama.
1810-1856	**Robert Schumann**, passionate and lyrical in turn, but brought up in the Germanic tradition, strives to reconcile a classical heritage with personal expression.
1833 1807	**Johannes Brahms** develops a more introverted style of German romanticism to the point of introversion.

Richard Wagner (1813-1883)

Wagner revolutionizes German opera. Music, he insists, should serve the dramatic action; it must therefore create "atmosphere", the décor of sound without which the opera's message could not be conveyed. Orchestration thus becomes of paramount importance. The singing, like the plot, is continuous, to correspond with dramatic truth. Wagnerian "Leitmotivs" – musical phrases used recurrently to denote specific characters, moods or situations – are essential to the continuity of the action.

Richard Wagner

1848	*Lohengrin*.
1876	Inauguration of the Bayreuth Festival Theatre with *The Ring*.
1882	*Parsifal*.

At the end of the 19C, **Gustav Mahler** (1860-1911), creator of the symphonic Lied, and **Hugo Wolf** (1850-1903) develop a new musical language which forms a bridge between Romanticism and Dodecaphony. **Richard Strauss** (1864-1949) unites at the same time a certain harmonic audacity with the sumptuous talent of a colourist.

Contemporary Music

Contemporary musical experimentation is derived principally from the Dodecaphonic Austrian school (**Schönberg, Berg, Webern**), with **Paul Hindemith** (1893-1963) remaining faithful to a national, traditional style.

1921	Alban Berg's *Wozzeck*.
1900-1950	**Kurt Weill**, influenced at the beginning of his career by the atonal composers, returns under the impact of jazz to tonal music, and composes *The Threepenny Opera* (1928).

From 1950 on, following the example of **Karlheinz Stockhausen**, the young generation of composers experiment progressively with electronic music.

CULTURAL LIFE

Few countries can boast a cultural life so intense, so decentralized and involving so great a proportion of the population as modern Germany.

Music and the Theatre – Amateur orchestras as well as highly-regarded professional organizations proliferate all over the country: the Berlin Philharmonic, the Gewandhaus Orchestra of Leipzig, the Bamberg Symphony Orchestra and resident radio station orchestras (Südwestfunk, Norddeutsche Rundfunk 3, Westdeutsche Rundfunk 3), and thus perpetuate a strong musical tradition.

This decentralization is equally characteristic of drama and the lyric arts. It is due to the founding of theatres by the sovereigns of the 17C and 18C and, subsequently, by the wealthier classes living in the big towns in the 19C.

Among the most important centres concentrating on music and the lyric arts, Bayreuth is celebrated for performances of the works of Wagner; Berlin, Hamburg, Dresden, Leipzig and Stuttgart for opera and ballet; and Nuremberg for organ music. Stuttgart again is renowned for choral singing, and Munich for the music of Bach and Richard Strauss. Donaueschingen, Darmstadt and Kassel are noted for performances of works by contemporary composers.

The German Cinema – The creation in 1917 of UFA (Universum Film Aktiengesellschaft) a production company of considerable means, plus the emergence of an expressionist movement linked with the troubled post-war political and social scene, produced the golden age of German cinema. Aside from the more lavish productions, the period is marked by the work of directors Robert Wiene (*The Cabinet of Dr Caligari*, 1919), Fritz Lang (*Dr Mabuse*, 1922; **Metropolis**, 1925) and Friedrich Wilhelm Murnau (*Nosferatu the Vampire*, 1922; *Faust*, 1926). Georg Wilhelm Pabst's *Lulu* (1929) and *The Blue Angel* of Josef von Sternberg (1930), with Marlene Dietrich, marked a change of direction towards realism.

This adventurous spirit was quenched with the arrival of the Third Reich, in which the cinema became no more than a tool in the service of an ideology. *The Gods of the Stadium* (Leni Riefensthal, 1938) – a glorification of the 1936 Berlin Olympics – and *Jud Süss* (Veit Harlan, 1940) remain the most striking examples.

The period immediately after the Second World War was a cultural desert for the German cinema. It was not until the 1960s that a new school of cineasts emerged to win international acclaim with such films as *The Lost Honour of Katharina Blum* (Volker Schlöndorff, 1975, in collaboration with Margarethe von Trotta), *The Tin Drum* (Schlöndorff, 1979), *The Marriage of Maria Braun* (Rainer-Werner Fassbinder, 1978), *Wozzeck* (Werner Herzog, 1979), and Wim Wenders' *American Friend* (1977) and *Wings of Desire* (1987).

PRINCIPAL MUSEUMS

Antiquities

Berlin: Pergamon Museum★★★ (Museum Island)

Cologne: Germano-Roman Museum★★★
Trier: Rhineland Museum★★

Painting and Sculpture: 13C to 18C

Cologne: Wallraf-Richartz Museum★★★
Dresden: Old Masters Gallery★★★ (Semper Gallery, Zwinger)
Kassel: Old Masters Gallery★★★ (Castle)
Munich: Old Pinakothek★★★
Nuremberg: German National Museum★★★
Berlin: Paintings Gallery★★ (Dahlem)

Frankfurt: Städel Museum★★
Hamburg: Fine Arts Museum★★
Karlsruhe: Collection of German Primitives★★ (Fine Arts Museum)
Leipzig: Fine Arts Museum★★
Stuttgart: Old Masters Section★★ (State Gallery)
Würzburg: Franconian Museum of the Main★★

Painting and Sculpture: 19C and 20C

Cologne: Ludwig Museum★★★
Dresden: Gallery of 19C and 20C Painters★★★ (Albertinum)
Berlin: Gallery of Romanticism★★ (Nationalgalerie, Charlottenburg)
Berlin: National Gallery★★ (Museum Island)

Essen: Folkwang Museum★★
Frankfurt: Städel Museum★★
Halle: Moritzburg National Gallery★★
Hamburg: Fine Arts Museum★★
Leipzig: Fine Arts Museum★★
Mannheim: Fine Arts Museum★★

Decorative Arts and Applied Arts

Dresden: Green Vault Collections★★★ (Albertinum)
Nuremberg: German National Museum★★★

Dresden: Porcelain Collection★★ (Zwinger)
Munich: Bavarian National Museum★★

Science

Bremerhaven: National Maritime Museum★★★
Munich: German Museum★★★

Dresden: Salon of Mathematics and Physics★★ (Zwinger)
Idar-Oberstein: German Museum of Precious Stones★★

Open-Air Museums

Gutach: Black Forest Open-Air Museum★★

Kiel: Schleswig-Holstein Open-Air Museum★★

FAIRY TALES AND LEGENDS

Snow White and the Seven Dwarfs – In the original story, written by the Brothers Grimm, the traditional costume worn by the dwarfs is in fact that used by miners in the Middle Ages.

Rübezahl – A giant with a red beard, a righter of wrongs. Sometimes he appears in the form of a rich merchant, sometimes as a collier in rags.

The Witches of Brocken – On the first night of May (Walpurgisnacht), they assemble for a Sabbath on the summit of the Brocken, in the Harz – a legend immortalized by a scene in Faust.

Pöppele of Hohenkrähen – From his castle perched high on a rock he surveys the highway and plots the downfall of travellers - preferably nobles or important officials.

The Heinzelmännchen – Elves who helped the craftsmen of Cologne with their secret night work – but fled forever when discovered through the curiosity of a woman.

The Seven Swabians – An unfair caricature of the people of Swabia: they aimed to conquer the world, but scattered and ran when confronted by a hare.

Baron Münchhausen – Perhaps the most famous of the extravagant literary fantasists. His fanciful adventures and exploits include a journey to the centre of the earth, a moon safari, and absurdly exaggerated deeds of heroism on the high seas. There was a real Baron Münchhausen (1720-1797) who fought with the Russian army against the Turks and is said to have wildly overstated his military prowess. It was the Hanoverian Raspe (in England at the end of the 18C) and De Crac (in France in the 19C) who grossly inflated these stories into the realms of the unreal.

Till Eulenspiegel *(see under Brunswick)*, the **Pied Piper of Hamelin** *(see under Hamelin)*, the **Nibelungen** and the **Loreley** *(see under the Rhine Valley)* are the principal characters of other, no less celebrated, legends.

BOOKS TO READ

HISTORY AND BIOGRAPHY

Exploring the Roman World: Roman Gaul and Germany. A King (British Museum Press)
A History of Germany 1815-1985. W Carr (Edward Arnold)
The Concise German History: A survey of the development of German history since 1815. AJP Taylor (Routledge)
Frederick the Great: Absolutism and Administration. W Hubatsch (Thames & Hudson)

THE ARTS

An Outline of European Architecture. N Pevsner (Penguin)
Early Medieval Art – Carolingian, Ottonian and Romanesque. J Beckwith (Thames & Hudson)
German Cathedrals. J Baum (Thames & Hudson)
Baroque Art and Architecture in Central Europe. E Hempel (Pelican)
German Architecture and the Classical Ideal 1740-1840. D Watkin and T Mellinghoff (Thames & Hudson)
Art in Germany: 1990-1939 From Expressionism to Resistance. R Heller (Prestel Art Books)
The Weimar Years: A Culture Cut Short. J Willett (Thames & Hudson)
Bauhaus. F Whitford (Thames & Hudson)
The Expressionists. W-D Dube (Thames & Hudson)
Caspar David Friedrich. H Börsch-Supan (Prestel Art Books)

TRAVEL AND MODERN GERMAN SOCIETY

Germany and the Germans. J Ardagh (Penguin)
The New Germany. D Marsch (Random Century Group)
The Origins of Modern Germany. G Barraclough (Blackwell Publishers)
Berlin: the Dispossessed City. M Simmons (Hamish Hamilton)
The Rhine. J Bentley (George Philip)
Atlas of German Wines. H Johnson (M Beazley)
Guide to the Wines of Germany. I Jamieson (Reed International)
Goodbye to Berlin. C Isherwood (Penguin)
Winter - A Berlin Family 1899-1945. L Deighton (Random Century Group)

LITERATURE

Heinrich Böll *The Lost Honour of Katharina Blum*
Bertolt Brecht *The Caucasian Chalk Circle; Threepenny Novel; Mother Courage*
Gunter Grass *The Tin Drum; The Flounder; From the Diary of a Snail*
Hermann Hesse *The Glass Bead Game; Narziss and Goldmund; Steppenwolf*
Thomas Mann *Buddenbrooks; The Magic Mountain*

FOOD AND DRINK

German food is more varied and better balanced than is generally supposed, and the composition and presentation of meals are in themselves original.

Breakfast **(Frühstück)** – there is plenty of it – includes cold meats and cheese, and there is invariably a soft-boiled egg. Lunch **(Mittagessen)** generally begins with soup, followed by a fish or meat main course always accompanied by a portion of salad (lettuce, cucumber, shredded cabbage). For the evening meal **(Abendessen)**, there will be a choice of cold meats **(Aufschnitt)**, delicatessen and cheeses, usually with a selection of different types of bread and/or rolls.

Certain dishes are served all over the country: **Wiener Schnitzel** (veal escalope fried in breadcrumbs), **Eisbein** (salted knuckle or shin of pork), **Sauerbraten** (beef in a brown sauce) and **Gulasch** (either in the form of soup or as a stew) are the most popular.

Beer and Wine – Germans are justifiably proud of their national beverage, produced by nearly 1 200 breweries throughout the country. Brewing techniques respect a purity law (Reinheitsgebot) decreed in 1516, whereby nothing but barley, hops and plain water may be used in the fabrication of **beer** (with the addition, today, of yeast).

German vineyards cover 69 000ha - 170 500 acres, extending from Lake Constance to the Siebengebirge, from Trier to Würzburg. The growers produce a great variety of wines from a wide range of grapes – as the visitor may discover in most bars and restaurants, sampling them by the glass (offene Weine).

Notable among the **white wines** – 80% of production – are the vigorous Rieslings of the Middle Rhine and those of the Moselle, Saar and Ruwer rivers, aromatic and refreshing; the noble and delicate wines of the Rheingau; full-bodied and elegant Nahe wines; those of Franconia, potent, sometimes almost bitter; and the numerous and varied wines of Baden and Württemberg. Among the **red wines**, particularly choice examples come from Rheinhessen and Württemberg, not forgetting the ardent and thoroughbred reds of the Platinate and, above all, the red wines of the Ahr, paradise of the Spätburgunder.

SOME REGIONAL SPECIALITIES

Bavaria and Franconia

Leberknödel: Large dumplings of liver, bread and chopped onion, served in a clear soup.
Leberkäs: Minced beef, pork and liver, cooked as a galantine.
Knödel: Dumplings of potato or soaked bread.
Haxen: Veal or pork trotters.
Schlachtschüssel: Breast of pork, liver sausage and black pudding, served with pickled cabbage and quenelles.
Rostbratwürste: Small sausages grilled over beechwood charcoal.

Baden-Württemberg

Schneckensuppe: Soup with snails.
Spätzle: Egg-based pasta in long strips.
Maultaschen: Pasta stuffed with a mixture of meat, brains and spinach.
Geschnetzeltes: Slices of veal in a cream sauce.

Rhineland-Palatinate

Sauerbraten: Beef marinated in wine vinegar, served with potato quenelles.
Reibekuchen: Small potato pancakes with apple or blueberry sauce.
Hämchen: Pork trotters with pickled cabbage and mashed potato.
Saumagen: Stuffed pork belly with pickled cabbage.
Schweinepfeffer: Highly seasoned, spicy pork in the form of a ragout, thickened with blood.
Federweisser: Partially fermented new wine, customarily accompanied by an onion tart.

Hessen and Westphalia

Sulperknochen: Ears, trotters and tail of pork, served with pickled cabbage and pease pudding.
Töttchen: Ragout of brains and calf's head, cooked with herbs.
Pickert: Sweet potato cakes with raisins.

Thuringia

Linsensuppe mit Thüringer Rotwurst: Lentil soup with Thuringian sausages.

Saxony

Rinderzunge in Rosinen-Sauce: Calf's tongue in a grape sauce.
Dresdener Stollen: Raisin cake.

Lower Saxony and Schleswig-Holstein

Aalsuppe: Sweet-and-sour soup, made of eels, prunes, pears, vegetables, bacon and seasoning.
Labskaus: Favourite sailor's dish, basically beef, pork and salted herrings with potatoes and beetroot, the whole topped with cucumber and fried egg.
Buntes Huhn: Salt beef on a bed of diced vegetables.

Sights

Neuschwanstein Castle

Michelin map **412** B 14

Aachen, situated among the northern foothills of the Ardennes, is the most westerly town in Germany. Its hot springs, already famous in the time of the Celts, were transformed into thermal baths by the Romans ("Aquae Grani"). Under Charlemagne, Aachen became the capital of the Frankish Empire.

Coal seams and rich veins of lignite in the vicinity allowed the town to develop into an important industrial centre with a renowned college of technology.

Charlemagne (747-814) – King of the Franks from the year 768, Charlemagne chose Aachen as a permanent site for the Frankish Court – which had previously been held, as it was in the time of his ancestors, wherever war or the chase led him. In AD 800, Charlemagne was crowned Holy Roman Emperor. He then conquered the Saxons and the Bavarians, consolidating his frontiers north of the Pyrenees to resist invasions by Moors, Slavs and Danes. The Court became a fountain-head of wisdom, culture and Christianity, which spread throughout his realm. He brought to the West the treasures of Latin civilization and culture as well as the advantages of a centralized government.

The sovereign was buried at Aachen, in the Octagon of the Palatine Chapel.

The Imperial City – Between 936 and 1531, thirty princes were crowned King of Germania in the cathedral at Aachen. In 1562 the town lost the status of Coronation City to Frankfurt.

SIGHTS

★★ **Cathedral** (Dom) ⊘ – Shortly before the year 800, Charlemagne organized the building of a domed octagonal basilica on the lines of the churches in the Eastern Roman Empire – the first time this type of construction had been seen north of the Alps. The Gothic chancel, started in 1355, was consecrated in 1414, on the 600th anniversary of the Emperor's death.

Exterior – *Starting at the Katschhof (north side), walk around the cathedral.* Successively, the Chapel of St Nicholas, the Chapel of Charlemagne with its Flamboyant portal, and finally the chancel (19C statues between the clerestory windows) come into view.

From the Münsterplatz *(south side)*, there is a good view of the original Carolingian octagon, crowned now with a 16-sided cupola dating from the 17C. On this side are the Gothic Chapels of St Matthias and St Anne, together with the Hungarian Chapel. The Carolingian porch on the cathedral courtyard is closed by bronze doors embellished with lions' heads (c800).

Interior – The octagon is surrounded by a two-storey ambulatory with bronze grilles of the Carolingian period closing the openings on the upper level. Rich mosaics decorate the dome. From the centre hangs a magnificent **chandelier**★★ (Radleuchter) in copper, the gift of Frederick Barbarossa (12C). To the right of the two octagon piers in front of the chancel is the venerated 14C statue of the Virgin of Aachen.

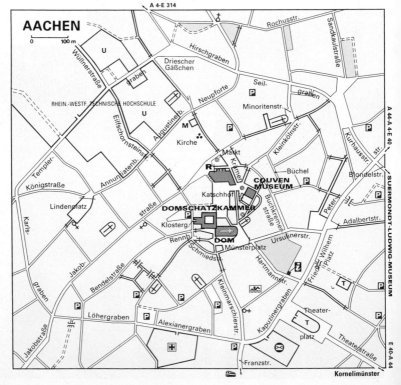

Modern stained-glass windows light the chancel. On the right, above the door leading to the sacristy, the **ambo of Henry II★★★** – a small pulpit in gilded copper, decorated with precious stones – can be seen (early 11C). The Carolingian high altar benefits from a **Pala d'Oro★★★** – a gorgeous, gold-faced frontal illustrated with scenes from the Passion and Christ in Majesty (c1020). Behind the altar is the **Charlemagne Shrine★★★** (Karlsschrein: 1200-1215), a reliquary where the Emperor's bones are preserved. This marvellously hand-worked silver shrine is gilded and embossed. On the upper floor of the octagonal ambulatory (west side) is the **Throne★** of Charlemagne (only visible during the guided tour). Made of simple, close-fitting marble slabs, this royal seat was where the German sovereigns installed themselves after their coronation to receive the homage of their subject princes. After the canonisation of Charlemagne in 1165, pilgrims were permitted to slip through the narrow passage below the throne.

★★★ **Treasury (Domschatzkammer)** ⊘ – Access via Klostergasse. The Treasury is one of the richest in Germany.

Basement: the gold **Cross of Lothair** (Lotharkreuz) (990), encrusted with precious stones and set with a fine Roman cameo of the Emperor Augustus, is on display here. Note also a 2C marble sarcophagus with a bas-relief illustrating the abduction of Proserpine, which contained the bones of Charlemagne while the Karlsschrein reliquary was being completed.

Ground floor: among other ecclesiastical reliquaries is a **Bust of Charlemagne** (1350) in silver and gold, which was presented by Karl IV together with the crown worn by the Emperor when he reigned. A blue velvet chasuble embroidered with pearls recalls the visit of St Bernard de Clairvaux to Aachen in 1147.

Cross of Lothair, from the Cathedral Treasure, Aachen

Town Hall (Rathaus) (R) ⊘ – The town hall was built in the 14C, on the site of Charlemagne's palace, of which the squat Granus Tower may still be seen on the corner of the Krämerstrasse. The façade of the tower, decorated with statues of the kings and emperors crowned at Aachen, overlooks the market place, with its **fountain** and statue of Charlemagne.

The Peace Treaty of 1748, which ended the War of Austrian Succession, was signed in the **White Room** (Weisser Saal), embellished with Italian stuccowork (c1725), on the right of the entrance. On the left, the **Council Chamber** is clad with panelling executed in 1727 by a master woodworker of Liège. From the staircase, there is a fine view of the cathedral.

On the upper floor, the Coronation Chamber, with its ogive vaulting, was used for the royal banquets when kings were crowned. Of the eight 19C frescoes of Charlemagne by the local painter Alfred Rethel, only five remain. In a showcase on the eastern side of the chamber, **copies of the crown jewels** can be seen, along with valuable Gospels and Charlemagne's crown, weapons and accoutrements. Each year in this chamber, the International Charlemagne Prize is awarded to those who have worked best for the unification of Europe.

★ **Couven Museum** ⊘ – A reconstitution of upper-class domestic life in the 18C and 19C. On the first floor is a large reception room with a chimneypiece in carved wood. Furniture, toys, and a Holy manger with many figurines are displayed on the second. An 18C dispensary has been reconstructed on the ground floor of the building, which was once a pharmacy (note the faience tiles from the Netherlands).

★ **Suermondt-Ludwig Museum** ⊘ – Wilhelmstrasse. On the first floor are **sculptures** from the Lower Rhine and southern Germany, from medieval times to the Baroque period. Admire the carved St Peter altarpiece and the graceful Gothic Virgins (Swabian Robed Madonna, 1420). The first-floor gallery exhibits German and Flemish primitives, including Christ Taken Prisoner (School of Cologne, 15C); Dutch and Flemish painting of the 17C; and both modern and Impressionist works. Apart from 20C stained-glass windows, the second floor displays an important collection of religious art.

Ludwig International Art Forum (Ludwig Forum für Internationale Kunst) ⊘ – Jülicherstrasse 97-109. Leave via the Peterstrasse.

A former umbrella factory – in its time the biggest in the world, and a splendid example of the Bauhaus style, moreover – is the unexpected site for this remarkable collection of modern art. Founded by a local industrialist named Ludwig and his wife, both connoisseurs and patrons of the arts, the exhibition includes works by Nam June Paik and Horst Antes (The Seven Monuments of Desire). Also represented are Duane Hanson (Supermarket Lady), Roy Lichtenstein, Georg Baselitz, Jonathan Borowsky (Ballerina Clown) and Jörg Immendorf (Brandenburger Tor). Theatrical performances and a park displaying sculptures add to the interest of the Forum.

EXCURSION

Kornelimünster – *10km - 6 miles to the southeast.*
This suburb of Aachen in the valley of the Inde is typical, with its slate-roofed, blue and grey stone houses, of small towns in the Eifel. In the centre is the old abbey church of **Kornelimünster★**, an unusual construction with five naves (14-16C), which dates back to a Benedictine church of the Carolingian period. The galleries above the chancel (east side) were added in the 17C, the octagonal Kornelius Chapel in the early 18C. The Gothic interior (ogive vaulting, painted ceilings) is essentially Baroque; note particularly the Baroque **high altar**, subsequently modified (*c*1750) by J J Couven in the Rococo style. On the left there is a stone statue of St Kornelius (*c*1460).
The richness of the relics belonging to the church (valuable ancient cloths, a 1360 bust of the saint in embossed silver, etc) attract a large number of pilgrims in September of each year. There is a fine **view** of the church, the abbey and the town from the Romanesque-Gothic Church of St Stephen (in a burial ground on a height to the north).

★★★ German ALPINE ROAD (Deutsche Alpenstrasse) Bavaria

Michelin map **413** folds 38 to 43

From Lindau to Berchtesgaden, from Lake Constance to the Königssee, this splendid scenic route runs through the foothills of the Allgäu and the Bavarian Alps, passing on the way such heights as the Zugspitze (2 962m - 9 718ft) and the Watzmann (2 712m - 8 898ft). One of the attractions of the trip is the fact that it allows the traveller both to enjoy the splendours of mountain scenery and visit such renowned monuments as the Church of Wies and the castles of Ludwig II of Bavaria, near Füssen. To cover the whole itinerary, allow three days.

★ ① THE ALLGÄU

From Lindau to Füssen *112km - 70 miles - half a day*

The landscape at this stage of the tour is not so much Bavarian as Allemannian. The farmers of the region have made their mountain countryside into the great cheese manufacturing area of Germany.

★★ Lindau – *See under Lindau.*

Paradies – Between Oberreute and Oberstaufen, engineers have given this name to a viewpoint built halfway around a sweeping curve, from which, far off to the southwest, the distant Alpenzell Alps in Switzerland (Säntis and Altmann) can be seen.

Oberstaufen – This charming resort, at the foot of the Hochgrat massif (1 834 m - 6 017ft), has some interesting ski slopes.
The route continues up the Alpine valley of the Iller river, which is dominated by the Grünten, "Guardian of the Allgäu".

★ Hindelang – Together with its neighbour, Bad Oberdorf, this flower-decked village is a holiday centre and spa (sulphur waters) from which mountain walks can be enjoyed in summer, and skiing on the slopes of the Oberjoch in winter.
Above Hindelang, the **climb★** of the Jochstrasse affords a variety of views over the jagged limestone summits of the Allgäu Alps. From the **Kanzel★** belvedere, almost at the summit, admire the panorama embracing the Ostrach Valley and the surrounding mountains.
Descending on the far side, the road traverses the valley of the Wertach, skirts the Grüntensee and passes near the large Pfronten ski resort before it arrives at Füssen.

★ Füssen – *See under Füssen.*

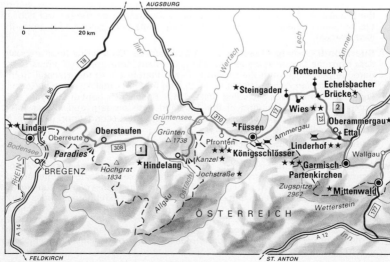

★ ② THE AMMERGAU

From Füssen to Garmisch-Partenkirchen
95km - 59 miles - one day

★★★ The Royal Castles of Hohenschwangau and Neuschwanstein (Königsschlösser) – *About 3 hours walking and sightseeing. See under Royal Castles of Bavaria.* This itinerary bypasses to the north the salient of the Ammergau Alps and then crosses a stretch of country that is seamed and broken up by the moraines deposited when the ancient Lech Glacier withdrew. The "onion" domes crowning the belfries of village churches punctuate this rolling countryside.

Steingaden – The former Abbey of the Steingaden Premonstratensians, founded in the 12C, still retains its remarkable minster, though this **abbey church★** was modified in the 18C in the Baroque style. Only the outside, with its massive towers and Lombardy arcading, has preserved the original thick-set Romanesque appearance. The Gothic entrance is enriched with a painted genealogy of the House of Welf, the original founders of the Abbey. The sobriety of the stucco-work embellishing the whole of the chancel is in sharp contrast to the lightness of that in the wide nave, which is enhanced by finely painted motifs. Furnishings in both the Baroque and Rococo style – pulpit, organ loft, altarpieces, statues – lend the ensemble a certain theatrical quality, symbolizing the triumph of decoration over architecture.

★★ Wies Church – *See under Wies Church.*

Rottenbuch – First built as an Augustinian monastery, the **Church of the Nativity of the Virgin★** (Mariä-Geburts-Kirche) was entirely remodelled in the Baroque and Rococo styles in the 18C. The stuccowork here exemplifies the virtuosity of the School of Wessobrunn, of which Joseph and Franz Schmuzer were among the masters. Frescoes by Matthäus Günther harmonize perfectly with this exuberantly sculpted decor. The pulpit, organ loft and altars are overburdened with statues and giltwork in the pure Rococo tradition.

★ Echelsbach Bridge (Echelsbacher Brücke) – Since 1929, this audacious reinforced concrete structure has spanned the Ammer gorge, which at this point is 76m - 250ft deep. Walk on foot to the middle of the bridge to get the most impressive view of the gorge.

★ Oberammergau – This small town of peasants and craftsmen, hemmed in by the wooded foothills of the Ammergau, owes its fame to the internationally-known **Passion Play**, which is performed only once every ten years (next performance: AD 2000). The play, involving 1 100 amateur actors drawn from the local population, lasts an entire summer's day. The tradition derives from a vow made by the inhabitants in 1633, after a plague epidemic had miraculously been cut short.

★★ Linderhof – *See under Linderhof Castle.*

Ettal – A blossoming of the Benedictine tradition, added to local veneration of a statue of the Virgin attributed to Giovanni Pisano, explain the vast dimensions of Ettal Abbey, founded by the Emperor Ludwig of Bavaria in 1330.
The sole example in Germany, the abbey church was based on a Gothic building with a polygonal floor-plan, the present elevation being due to the Baroque architect Enrico Zucalli, who built the façade and the chancel (1710-1726). Joseph Schmuzer of the school of Wessobrunn *(see above)* added the dome after the church was gutted by a fire in 1774. The painted decorations on the inside of this dome are the work of Johann Jacob Zeiller.
The road now rejoins the Loisach Valley. In the south, the Wetterstein range appears, with the summits of the Zugspitze, the Dreitorspitze and the pyramid peak of the Alpspitze. Continue to Garmisch-Partenkirchen.

★★★ Garmisch-Partenkirchen – *See under Garmisch-Partenkirchen.*

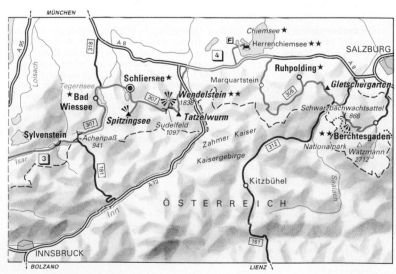

★ **3** **THE LAKE DISTRICT AND THE UPPER ISAR VALLEY**

From Garmisch-Partenkirchen to Schliersee
105km - 66 miles - half a day

★ **Mittenwald** – *See under Garmisch-Partenkirchen: Excursions.*
At Wallgau, the route joins the upper valley of the Isar (toll road as far as Vorderriss), a wild, bleak stretch of open country.

Sylvenstein Dam (Sylvenstein-Staudamm) – Controlling the excessive flooding of the Isar, this earthwork dam with its waterproof core has created a huge artificial lake whose waters power an underground power station.
The road crosses the wooded Achenpass *(going 2km - 1.2 miles into Austria)* and then plunges down towards the Tegernsee.

★ **Bad Wiessee** – An elegant resort, both a fashionable holiday centre and a major spa (iodized sulphur springs), Bad Wiessee is admirably placed on the shores of the Tegernsee lake in cultivated, green semi-Alpine surroundings.

★ **Schliersee** – Beside the lake of the same name, this small town – together with the neighbouring municipalities of Fischhausen, Neuhaus and Spitzingsee *(see itinerary below)* – offers interesting possibilities for a short stay. The **Parish Church★** (Pfarrkirche) is a former Collegiate of the Chapter of Notre-Dame in Munich, rebuilt in the Baroque style between 1712 and 1714. Both the painted vaulting and the delicate stuccowork were executed by Johann-Baptist Zimmermann (1680-1758), brother of the architect of Wies *(qv)*.

★ **4** **THE SUDELFELD AND THE CHIEMGAU MOUNTAINS**

From Schliersee to Berchtesgaden
172km – 107 miles - one day

Spitzingsee – A little less than a mile from the summit, the steeply-climbing access road offers a fine **overall view★** of the Fischhausen-Neuhaus plain and the Schliersee lake. Soon afterwards, the road ends by the Spitzingsee, a small lake around which a mountain resort is developing.
3km - 1 3/4 miles before Bayrischzell, the route passes the lower terminal of a cableway leading to the summit of the Wendelstein *(the climb can also be made by train, starting from Brannenburg-Waching – description below)*.

Falls of Tatzelwurm – *1/4 hour Rtn on foot.* From the "Naturdenkmal Tatzelwurm" car park, a footpath leads to this impressive cascade.

★★ **Wendelstein** ⊙ – *5 hour Rtn, of which 2 hours on a funicular railway and 3/4 hour on foot. Leave from the lower station at Brannenburg-Waching.*
Daringly forcing a passage up increasingly steep slopes, the little train finally reaches an altitude of 1 738m - 5 702ft. The rest of the climb is via a footpath carved out of the bedrock. The summit (1 838m - 6 030ft) is crowned by a solar observatory and a chapel built in 1718.
The **panorama★★** visible from there encompasses, from east to west, the mountains of the Chiemsee and the Alps of Berchtesgaden, the Loferer and the Leoberger Steinberge, the Kaisergebirge range with its jagged peaks, and the glacial crests of the Hohe Tauern.
The road winds down the valley of the Inn and then follows the Munich-Salzburg motorway, which skirts the southern shore of the **Chiemsee** *(qv)*. After Marquartstein, the route lies through a succession of tortuous, steep-sided valleys, running out finally above the Reit Basin, at the foot of the Zahmer Kaiser. Turning back towards the east, the Alpine itinerary traverses a long corridor which passes near a series of shallow, dark lagoons.

★ **Ruhpolding** – The locality, very popular with holiday-makers, is well known for upholding local traditions, crafts and folklore. The life of the town centres around the parish church of St George, where there is a Romanesque Virgin.

Gletschergarten – *1/4 hour on foot.* Opened up by the building of the road, this "garden of glaciers" forms a natural museum of glacial erosion. A prolongation of the Tauern glacier, moving along the Saalach valley *(see Michelin Green Guide Austria)*, once transported huge blocks of crystalline rock which striated or excavated the rolling, rocky surface of the land.
After the Schwarzbachwacht Pass (alt 868m - 2 848ft) there is a sharp contrast between the severe, wooded valley of the Schwarzbach river and the open pastureland on the Ramsau side. At a number of places, the descent offers an opportunity to appreciate fine panoramas, revealing the "teeth" of the Hochkalter biting into the white surface of the Blaueis (along with the Höllentalferner, in the Zugspitze massif, the only glacier in Germany) and the bulk of the Watzmann.
The Alpine Road ends at Berchtesgaden.

★★ **Berchtesgaden** – *See under Berchtesgaden.*

*When driving in German towns use the plans in the **Michelin Red Guide Deutschland** which are updated each year; they show*

- through-routes and by-passes
- new roads and one-way systems
- car parks.

A situation on the main route linking Hessen and Thuringia – in which, until the middle of the 13C, the town was administratively incorporated – brought prosperity to Alsfeld in olden times. Today the charm of the town lies in the half-timbered houses grouped around the picturesque old market place.

SIGHTS

★ **Market Place** (Marktplatz) –
The northeast corner of the square, where the Rathaus and the Weinhaus (recognizable by its stepped gable) are overlooked by the church tower, is quite delightful. Twin, spired turrets surmount the façade of the 1516 **Town Hall**★ (Rathaus), half-timbered above stone arcades that once served as a covered market. Diagonally opposite stands a solid stone house with a two-storey oriel window at one corner. Known as "the Wedding House" (Hochzeitshaus), this interesting building dates from 1565. Its two gables, set at right angles, are embellished with festoons and scroll-work typical of the First Renaissance in Germany.

The Market Place, Alsfeld

Rittergasse – This street, leaving the square on the side opposite the Town Hall, has two of the most interesting **old houses**★ in Alsfeld. The Neurathhaus at No 3 is a particularly fine example of projecting half-timbering in the Baroque style, while the Minnigerode-Haus at No 5, which is built of stone, conserves its original spiral staircase within. This masterpiece of carpentry rises without any support from the walls around a tall, twisted tree trunk.

Church (Stadtkirche) – The building is early Gothic, still with its original furnishings. Note the wooden galleries and, behind the altar on the left, a fine carved and painted panel of the Crucifixion between four scenes from the life of Jesus. In the small square to the north of the church there is a house adorned with modern graffiti and a fountain presided over by a goose-girl in Schwalm costume. Noticed in the neighbourhood of Alsfeld by the Brothers Grimm (qv), a costume of this type was used by them as a model for the clothes worn by Little Red Riding Hood.

AMBERG Bavaria   Pop 42 000

In the 14C and 15C, Amberg had an important role to play as a commercial centre on the route from Nuremberg to Prague. The large number of rich burghers' houses, tightly packed between the ramparts, testify today to that prosperity. A modern town has evolved around that ancient, picturesque nucleus, still very well preserved in its green setting.

The twin arches of the old fortified bridge, reflected in the water of the river below, form two perfect circles – reminiscent of a pair of spectacles. This image, which can be appreciated best from the Ring Bridge, in the south, and the footpath skirting the Arsenal (Zeughaus) to the north, is known as the **"Stadtbrille"** (Town Spectacles) and has come to stand as a symbol for Amberg.

Marktplatz – Closing off this square, the **Town Hall** (14C and 16C) displays a Gothic gable above a charming Renaissance balustrade. Opposite is the **Church of St Martin**, a powerful 15C Gothic construction to which a tower of almost 100m - 328ft was added in the 18C. Three huge naves, supported by elegant columns, make this the largest church in the Upper Palatinate.

★ **Salesian Church** (Deutsche Schulkirche) – This small church, built at the end of the 17C by Wolfgang Dientzenhofer (qv), is covered by graceful Rococo decorations, most of them the work of Amberg's own master craftsmen (1738-58). Original features include the curious position of the altar niches flanking the triumphal arch, and an organ loft in the form of a shell.

Chapel of Mary-the-Helper (Wallfahrtskirche Maria-Hilf) – This votive chapel was built as a thanksgiving gesture at the end of a plague epidemic which ravaged the region in 1634 (see also Oberammergau Passion Play). Vault **frescoes**★, painted by C D Asam in his youth, illustrate this tragic event and the subsequent pilgrimages.

Michelin map 987 fold 27 - Local map see under ERZEGEBIRGE

This locality, on the eastern slopes of the Erzgebirge was blessed with a sudden prosperity after the discovery, in 1492, of rich mineral lodes (silver and tin) in the mountain of Schreckenberg. When the seams ran out several decades later, Annaberg turned to the production of fine lace – a craft for which the town is still famous today.

Vaulting in St Anne's Church, Annaberg-Buchholz

★★ **St Anne's Church** (St-Annen-Kirche) – Built in a relatively short time (1499-1519), this church with three naves is one of the most successful and impressive examples of Saxony's Flamboyant Gothic style. Twelve tall pillars soar into the ribs of the vaulting so effortlessly, with such elegance, that they seem not to support it but merely to link it with the ground – perhaps only to anchor it there. The parapets of the galleries on the side walls are embellished with scenes from the Old and New Testaments.

At the far end of the church, in the left-hand wall, is the **"Schöne Pforte"**★★ (beautiful door), a brilliantly multicoloured portal originally designed for another church. It was made by Hans Witten in 1512. The **pulpit**★★ (1516) is the work of the sculptor F Maidburg. Note the relief figure representing a miner. A similar reference to Annaberg's old activity lies in the painted panels to be found behind the **Miners' Reredos**★ (Bergmannsaltar, c1520). Placed in the left-hand chapel of the chancel, these depict the various stages of work in a mine of that period.

The Frohnau Forge (Technisches Museum Frohnauer Hammer) ⊘ – Once a flour mill, this old building was turned into a workshop for the striking of coins when silver was discovered in the region; it was subsequently transformed into a blacksmith's forge. Hydraulically-operated bellows and power-hammers can be seen there today.

EXCURSION

★ **Erzegebirge** – See under Erzegebirge.

Gourmands or gourmets
Each year the **Michelin Red Guide Deutschland**
gives an up-to-date selection
of establishments renowned for their cuisine.
German gastronomic specialities
are described on page 34.

ANSBACH Bavaria   Pop 40 000

Michelin map 413 O 19

Ansbach, half medieval, half Baroque, is a peaceful Franconian town which owes its fame to the Hohenzollerns. The Margraves of the House of Hohenzollern's Frankish line settled in Ansbach and Bayreuth as early as the 13C. Since then the two towns have often been associated in history – the Ansbach-Bayreuth Dragoons, for example, fought under Frederick the Great.

On the feminine side, the cultivated Margravines of the 18C, one of whom was a sister of Queen Wilhelmina *(qv)*, made the life of the Ansbach Court almost as brilliant as that of Bayreuth.

SIGHTS

★ **Castle** (Residenz) ⊙ – This 14C fortress was enlarged and transformed in the Franconian Baroque style by Gabrieli, architect to the Court of Vienna, and Retti, at the behest of the Margraves of Brandenburg-Ansbach (1705-1750). The façade, with its sober lines and simple decoration, is imposing. The interior – symmetrical like the inside of most German Baroque palaces – is especially remarkable for: the princes' apartments (Fürstenzimmer); the **Porcelain Gallery★★** (Gekachelter Saal), which displays some 2 800 Ansbach pottery tiles, lightly and delicately designed with rural motifs; the **Hall of Mirrors★** (Spiegelkabinett) and its unbelievable profusion of china ornaments and gilded woodwork; the Red Salon, exhibiting portraits of the Hohenzollerns; and the Gobelins Gallery, with three tapestries woven after cartoons by Charles Le Brun. On the far side of the esplanade, the castle park extends away to the site of the Baroque Orangery.

St Gumbertus' Church (St Gumbertus-Kirche) – This church, with its 15C Gothic chancel, was transformed in the 18C into a huge preaching hall. The salient feature today is the Chapel of the Order of the Knights of the Swan (St Georgskapelle des Schwanenritterordens) a lay order founded by the Elector of Brandenburg in 1440. Through the glass door (on the left, behind the altar), emblems and funerary monuments of the Knights can be seen, along with a fine late 15C altarpiece of the Virgin in Glory.

ASCHAFFENBURG Bavaria   Pop 65 000

Michelin maps **412** and **413** K 17
Town plan in the current Michelin Red Guide Deutschland

Aschaffenburg, which has grown up at the foot of the wooded Spessart hills above a broad sweep of the River Main, has enchantingly beautiful parks – which makes it easy to understand why the Prince-Electors and the Archbishops of Mainz made it their second home in the 13C. The castle and the Schönbusch Park are reminders of this illustrious past. The town was re-attached to Bavaria in 1814. The proximity of Frankfurt's urban and industrial centres is largely responsible for the changing face of Aschaffenburg today.

SIGHTS

★ **Castle** (Schloss Johannisburg) – Built on the site of a medieval fortress destroyed in the mid-16C, this huge red sandstone palace is in the form of a hollow square quartered by lantern towers. The architect commissioned by the Bishops to design it was Georg Ridinger of Strasbourg. Constructed between 1605 and 1614, the castle was the pioneer example of the charmingly decorated style that came to be known as German Renaissance. Inside the walls, the steeply sloping roofs of the three-storey wings are dominated by the massive square towers and the 14C keep, retained from the old fort. The central portion of the three façades is topped by dormers adorned with shell niches, pilasters and obelisks – a typical Renaissance concept.

The **State gallery (Staatsgalerie)** ⊙ is on the first floor of the castle, in the wing nearest the river. Apart from 17C Dutch masters (Aert de Gelder), paintings are exhibited by – among others – Hans Baldung Grien (Golgotha) and members of the school of Lucas Cranach the Elder (qv). In the **Paramentenkammer**, vestments and liturgical objects used during the 17C and 18C in the Archdiocese of Mainz may be viewed. Between the West Tower and the old keep is the **Chapel** (Schlosskirche). The Franconian sculptor Hans Juncker was responsible for the splendid altar, richly decorated with motifs in relief and alabaster figurines.

On the second floor is a **collection of architectural models** of ancient buildings, made in cork. These formed part of the "Collection of Corkery" amassed by Archbishop K T von Dalberg between 1802 and 1806. The **Royal Apartments** in the riverside wing contain late 18C and early 19C furniture, landscape paintings and portraits of the princes who lived there. Finally the **Municipal Museum** (Städtisches Schlossmuseum) ⊙ displays prehistoric curios from archaeological digs, examples of religious art and craftwork from the 15C to the present day, and several collections illustrating the history of Aschaffenburg.

Walk through the castle grounds (Schlossgarten) to reach the **Pompeianum**. This is a reconstruction of the house of Castor and Pollux at Pompeii, built by Ludwig I of Bavaria on the bank overlooking the river.

Church (Stiftskirche) – Well situated at the top of a monumental Baroque stairway, this Romano-Gothic church has an oddly asymmetric appearance from the outside, owing to the overshadowing peristyle which flanks the west front and the northern aisle. The oldest part is the long 12C nave (the tower was not completed until c1490). The Romanesque west door (early 13C) has an interesting decoration with plant motifs; on the tympanum above, Christ in Majesty.

Inside, the major interest lies in the works of art. **Grünewald's The Lamentation** (1525), the praedella of an altarpiece now lost, is on display in a glass case: the artist-architect was Court Painter to the Prince-Electors at Aschaffenburg from 1516 until the Peasants' Revolt. The south transept contains a Resurrection (1520) by Lucas Cranach the Elder, that on the north a Romanesque Crucifixion (12C). In the **Chapel of Our Lady of the Snow** is a copy of Grünewald's famous painting of the Virgin, which was taken from the church in the 16C and is now at Stuppach (qv). The late Romanesque cloister is supported on 64 columns whose capitals are as varied as they are original.

EXCURSION

Schönbusch Park – *3km - 2 miles to the west.*
In the middle of this shady 18C park, which is laid out with ornamental ponds, canals, islets and follies (Temple of Friendship), there is a small and delightful **country house** (1780) built for the Archbishops of Mainz and decorated in the Empire style.
From the Hall of Mirrors on the first floor, there is a fine **view** of the castle, with the wooded heights of the Spessart massif in the background.

★★ AUGSBURG Bavaria   Pop 250 000

Michelin map **413** P 21
Plan of the conurbation in the current Michelin Red Guide Deutschland

Tacitus wrote of Augsburg that it was "the most brilliant colony in all the province of Rhaetia". Situated on the Romantic Road *(qv)*, the town today is both a busy industrial and commercial centre and an attractive reminder of life in the Renaissance period.

HISTORICAL NOTES

Founded in 15 BC by a kinsman of the Emperor Augustus, Augsburg is, along with Trier and Cologne, one of the oldest cities in Germany. It became a trading centre on the highway to Italy and, at the fall of the Roman Empire, an episcopal see. By the end of the 13C it was a Free Imperial City and the seat of the Diet.

The Fuggers – At the end of the 15C, Augsburg – which already had a population of 50 000 – became a centre of high finance and banking. This was due to the Fuggers and the Welsers, two local dynastic families who – so it was said – shared the known world between them so far as money and trade were concerned. History has preserved the name of Jakob Fugger the Rich (1459-1529), renowned as the Empire's banker and even better known as the financier of the Habsburgs. Charles V himself once received from this powerful man the rebuke: "It is well known that, without my help, Your Majesty would no longer wear the crown of the Holy Roman Empire." The debt of the Habsburgs to their Augsburg bankers, never settled, has been estimated at 4 million ducats.

The Augsburg Confession – In 1530 Charles V, disturbed by the growing strength of the Reformation in many states of the Empire, called an Imperial Diet at Augsburg with the hope of dissipating the religious troubles. The Protestants, inspired by Luther, thereupon proclaimed in a celebrated "Confession" the basic tenets of their belief. The statement was rejected, and it was not until the Peace of Augsburg in 1555 that Protestants in Germany won the freedom of worship.
The name of the town was once more inscribed in the history books in 1686 with the creation of the Augsburg League – directed by Austria and Prussia against Louis XIV following the Revocation of the Edict of Nantes.

The Pine Cone – This emblem, an ancient fertility symbol, appears on the city's arms, and indeed through the years Augsburg has flowered with the ideas and talents of artists and humanists. They include Holbein the Elder (d 1525), Hans Burkmair (1473-1541), Martin Schongauer and Konrad Peutinger. Augsburg's emergence as "the city of the German Renaissance" is due to the architect Elias Holl (1573-1646). Mozart's father was born in Augsburg, and some of the great composer's glory, too, has been reflected on the town.
By the 18C, the textile manufacturing industry was flourishing. The 19C was marked by the production (1893-7) of the first diesel engine.

SIGHTS

★ **Fuggerei** (Y) – This name was bestowed in 1519 on the quarter founded by Fugger the Rich to house the town poor. The eight streets in the Fuggerei are lined by 53 gabled houses. The district has its own church and its own administration. Each evening the four gateways to the quarter are closed, as they always have been. The social settlement, the first of its kind in the world, still welcomes citizens in need as it did in the 16C, charging them only a token rent but placing on them the moral obligation of praying for the souls of the founders.

★ **Maximilianstrasse** (Z) – Lined by mansions and private houses built by the wealthier burghers of Augsburg during the Renaissance, this street offers today one of the most majestic vistas of Old Germany. Many facades have been extensively restored. Three bronze Renaissance fountains adorn the street.

★ **St Ulrich and St Afra** (Z) – This former Benedictine abbey-church, founded *c*1500 by Maximilian, lies adjacent to a Protestant church of the same name. The core of the building, high and impressive, is separated from the three aisles by a fine Baroque screen. The caissoned vaulting is well lit by the clerestory windows and at the far end are three Baroque altars: in the choir, the Altar of the Nativity, to the right, the Altar of the Resurrection and to the left the Pentecostal Altar. At the transept crossing is a bronze group of the Crucifixion dating from 1607.
Among the chapels on the north side, St Simpert's is furnished with a Gothic baldachin and a balcony surmounted by terra-cotta **Statues of the Saints★**. Note also, above the pulpit, the sounding-board supported by two angels.

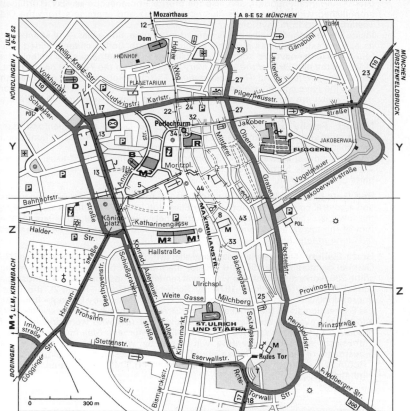

The juxtaposition of the two churches, one Catholic, one Protestant, each with the same name, is characteristic of Augsburg. The two **Churches of the Holy Cross** (**Y D**) are another example.

Municipal Art Gallery (Städtische Kunstsammlungen) ⊘ – *Entrance: Maximilianstrasse 46.*
The Schaezler Palais galleries (1767) are the first to be passed through (Deutsche Barockgalerie - **Z M¹**). Paintings by masters of German Baroque are on display here. The enormous **banqueting hall**★★ (Festsaal) is noteworthy for a ceiling lavishly decorated with Rococo frescoes and stucco-work, and wall panelling adorned in the same style.
Beyond this, a second gallery (Staatsgalerie Augsburg - **Z M²**) exhibits paintings by 15C and 16C Augsburgan and Swabian masters, including a votive portrait of *The Schwarz Family* by Hans Holbein the Elder and the famous *Portrait of Jakob Fugger the Rich* by Albrecht Dürer.
Works by Rubens, Van Dyck, Tiepolo and Veronese can be seen on the second floor.

Town Hall (**Y R**) – This vast Renaissance building is by Elias Holl. Two onion-domed towers frame a pediment adorned with the traditional pine cone. The **Perlach Tower** (**Y**), on the left, was originally a Romanesque watchtower. It was re-modelled in the 17C. When the Alps can be seen from the top of it, a yellow flag is flown.
Inside, the Town Hall's Golden Room (Goldener Saal), with its restored coffered ceiling, can be visited.

St Anne's Church (**Y B**) – This church was formerly part of a Carmelite convent where Martin Luther found sanctuary when he arrived in Augsburg in 1518. The Late Gothic architecture contrasts with the Rococo stucco-work and frescoes.
The **Fugger Funeral Chapel**★ (Fuggerkapelle) is considered to be the first example of the Italian Renaissance style in Germany. It dates from 1518.
Blind arcades at the back of the chapel frame four sculptured scenes: centre, above the recumbent figures, The Resurrection, and Samson Wrestling with the Philistines after Dürer, at each side, the arms of the House of Fugger, from which the fleur-de-lys is reproduced on the pavement.
In the church there are paintings by Lucas Cranach the Elder: *Jesus, the Friend of Little Children* (at the high altar in the main chancel), a Portrait of Martin Luther and the Prince-Elector Johann-Friedrich of Saxony.
The Goldsmiths' Chapel (Goldschmiedekapelle), on the north side of the chancel, dating from the 15C, has retained its original Gothic structure and murals.

Maximilian Museum (Y M³) – Life in Augsburg in days gone by; examples of Swabian sculpture; work by local goldsmiths and silversmiths.

Cathedral (Dom) (Y) – The church was rebuilt in Gothic style in the 14C. Outside, note the Gothic south door to the chancel (Südportal des Chores) or **Virgin's Door**★★ (Jungfrauenportal), and also the bronze Romanesque **panels**★ (Türflügel) embellished with 32 bas-reliefs illustrating scenes and characters from the Old Testament and from mythology.
Inside the church, the tall nave is flanked by double side aisles. The chancel, at its eastern extremity, has a double ambulatory with Gothic chapels added. The four altars in the nave are adorned with **paintings**★ (Tafelgemälden) by Holbein the Elder (on the left: *Birth of the Virgin Mary* and *Entry Into the Temple*; on the right, *The Offering Refused* and *The Presentation*). The clerestory windows on the south side of the nave contain stained glass **Windows of the Prophets**★ (Prophetenfenster - 12C) which are very rigid in style. The alabaster panes surrounding them are modern.

Mozart Family House (Mozarthaus) (Y) ⊘ – *Leave by Frauentorstrasse.* Documents and exhibits emphasize the Swabian origins of the Mozart family and the artistic heritage which was to benefit the young prodigy.
From this house, by way of the Stephingerberg and the Müllerstrasse, the tree-lined promenade bordering the moats which follow the line of the ancient ramparts can be reached.

Red Gate (Rotes Tor) (Z) – This is a group of 16C fortified buildings with two vaults and a central courtyard, remodelled by Elias Holl in 1622. The tower overlooking the town is circled by bands of decoration between the engaged pillars. At the foot of the tower, an open-air theatre has been laid out *(operatic performances late June to late July).*

★ **State Gallery** (Staatsgalerie in der Kunsthalle) (M⁴) ⊘ – *Leave by Imhofstrasse* (Z). German painters of the 19C and 20C for the most part fill this museum. Among some 200 works displayed, the visitor will remember those of the New Landscape school (*Mills by Moonlight*, 1874, by Schleich the Elder - Room 2), the Post-Impressionists (Corinth's *Three Graces*, 1904, and canvases by Slevogt - Room 3), the Expressionists of the Brücke Group (*Kirchner's Cows in the Forest* - Room 7) and the members of the Blauer Reiter movement *(qv)* who were precursors of modern art (Paul Klee's *Dance of the Sad Child*; Münter's *Man in an Armchair*). Enthusiasts of modern painting will linger by works that characterize the movements of the 1920s: Surrealism (*The Mathematics Room*, by Zimmermann - Room 12), Abstract and Concrete Art (Room 14), Informal Art and the New Figuration (Rooms 15, 16 and 17).

★★ BADEN-BADEN Baden-Württemberg   Pop 50 000

Michelin map ⁇⁇⁇ H 20 - Local map see under BLACK FOREST
Plan of the conurbation in the current Michelin Red Guide Deutschland

Sheltered between the Black Forest and the Baden vineyards, Baden-Baden is one of the most luxurious German health resorts, of which the latest asset is the "Caracalla" establishment (CY) *(premises open to the public).*

Spa and Casino – In Roman times the Emperor Caracalla came frequently to Baden-Baden to cure his rheumatism. In the 12C, the town became the seat of the Zähringer branch of the Margraves of Baden. In the 16C, the great Paracelsus, one of the founders of modern pharmacy, came to take care of the Margrave.
By the 19C, a casino launched by the Frenchman Jacques Bénazet, a theatre and opera house (opened in 1862), and a racecourse organized by the Paris Jockey Club had transformed the town into the summer capital of Europe.
In the gardens of the spa park, behind the white Corinthian columns of the **Kurhaus** (BZ), glittering balls and concerts are held, and the gaming rooms are always crowded. Nearby in the same park (Kurgarten) is the Pump Room **(Trinkhalle)** (BY), embellished with murals illustrating the legends of the Baden countryside.

SIGHTS

★★ **Lichtentaler Allee** (BZ) – This, the most beautiful promenade in Baden-Baden, runs beside the Oos river, flowing here over an artificial bed, and recalls irresistibly the 19C parades of carriages, complete with crinolines, parasols and gentlemen in tall hats. The esplanade has been the scene of many historical and political encounters. Queen Victoria rode along it; Napoleon III and Eugénie strolled beside the river; Bismarck was pursued by diplomats; the attempt on the life of the King of Prussia in 1861 took place in the shade of its trees.
Originally these were oaks, planted more than 300 years ago, but exotic species – azaleas, magnolias, silver poplars, tulip trees – have been added since. On the left, beyond the swimming-pool, is the **Gönneranlage** (BZ), a pretty park with fountains and pergolas flanking a rose garden.

New Castle (Neues Schloss) (CY) ⊘ – Built by the Margraves of Baden at the time of the Renaissance, the castle has been partly transformed into the **Zähringer Museum**, where local history can be traced through exhibits in the state rooms and salons.
From the terrace, there is a fine **view** of the town, with the Stiftskirche in the foreground.

BADEN-BADEN

Church (Stiftskirche) (CY) – The funerary monument of Ludwig the Turk (1754) stands in the chancel.

Roman Baths (Römische Badruinen) (CY) ☉   Beneath the **Römerplatz**, excavations have unearthed the ruins of a Roman bath house (note particularly the hypocaust under-floor heating system).

EXCURSIONS

⋏ **Yburg Ruins** – 6km - 3 1/2 miles to the southwest. Leave by Friedrichstrasse (BZ) From the tower (110 steps) there is a **vast panorama**★★ over the Rhine plain, with the Baden vineyards in the foreground.

★ **Motorway Church** (Autobahnkirche)   8km - 5 miles to the west. Leave by Langestrasse. Placed under the patronage of St Christopher, patron saint of travellers, this modernistic church is the work (1976-78) of the architect F Zwingmann and the painter-sculptor E Wachter. The design presents a harmonious blend of the plastic arts and architecture. Sculptures and stained glass panels are devoted to Biblical and symbolic themes.

Merkur – 2km - 1.2 miles to the east. Leave by Markgrafenstrasse (CZ).
From the upper terminal of the funicular, take the lift to the top of the Panoramic Tower; the immense view takes in the site of Baden-Baden, the Rhine valley to the west, the valley of the Murg to the east and (on a clear day) the Vosges.

Hohenbaden Ruins (or Altes Schloss); **Ebersteinburg Castle** – Round tour of 13km - 8 miles: about 1 1/2 hours. Leave Baden-Baden by the Schlossstrasse (CY). The parapet walk of the old castle of Hohenbaden commands a view over the town and valley. Afterwards, climb to the top of the Ebersteinburg keep, from which the foothills of the Black Forest can be seen.

★ **Baden Vineyards** – 30km - 19 miles: 1 1/2 hours. Leave by the Kaiser-Wilhelm-Strasse and then the Fremersbergstrasse. Once outside the town, follow the signposts "Baden Wine Road" (Badische Weinstrasse). The route twists sinuously from village to village as it winds through the vineyards on the lower slopes of the Black Forest.

Leave the Wine Road at Altschweir and return to Altwindeck.

★ **Altwindeck Castle** – This ancient castle, built on a circular plan, has been transformed into a restaurant with panoramic views. From its precincts there is a wide view★ of the plain.

Sasbach – 1/4 hour on foot Rtn. Leave the car opposite the Hotel Linde and walk into the park surrounding the Turenne monument. An obelisk and plinth with inscriptions in German, French and Latin mark the spot where, in 1675, a fatal cannon-ball ended the glorious career of Turenne – the French hero charged by Louis XIV with the defence of Alsace against the Imperial forces, during the conquest of Franche-Comte.

★★ **The Crest Road** – See under Black Forest.

Michelin map **413** G 23

In the southern foothills of the Black Forest, Badenweiler lies on a slope at the mouth of a valley with a view both of the Rhine Plain and the Vosges. The spa, noted for its curative treatments of rheumatism and disorders of the respiratory and circulatory systems, is surrounded by orchards and vineyards. Despite its limited population, Badenweiler boasts more than a score of good hotels.

★ **Spa Park (Kurpark)** – The rolling parkland abounds in tropical plants and splendid trees. Beside the lake, cedars and cypresses mingle with enormous sequoias. The park also includes extensive remains of Roman baths and a ruined castle from which there is a fine **view★** of the resort, the Rhine Plain and the Vosges.

EXCURSIONS

★ **Blauen** – *8km - 5 miles to the southeast, then 1/4 hour on foot Rtn.*
From the belvedere-tower, rising above the woods at the top of a hill, there is a remarkable **panoramic view★★** over the plain – the parallel ribbons of the Rhine and the Grand Canal of Alsace can easily be distinguished – and the tree-covered humps of the Vosges. The bare summit to the northeast is the Belchen. The Swiss Alps are also visible.

★ **Bürgeln Castle** ⊙ – *10km - 6.2 miles to the south.*
This gentleman's residence, set in beautifully kept, terraced gardens, was built in 1762 for the Abbots of St Blasien. The property overlooks the last undulations of the Black Forest, several reaches of the Rhine, and part of the city of Basle. Inside, there are beautiful examples of stucco-work in the Rococo style.

★ **Rötteln Castle** – *27km - 17 miles to the south*
The Oberburg, defensive nucleus of this fortress, is reached by a series of ramps and a drawbridge. The Green Tower (Grüner Turm), which overlooks the whole complex, has been restored and modified into a belvedere. From this, the view includes the Wiese valley (eventually lost among the outskirts of Basle), the wooded massif of the Blauen in the Basle Jura, the gentler slopes of the Black Forest and, far off on the horizon, the Swiss Alps.

*The current **Michelin Red Guide Deutschland** offers*
a selection of pleasant hotels in convenient locations.
Each entry specifies the facilities available (gardens,
tennis courts, swimming pool, beach facilities)
and the annual opening and closing dates.
There is also a selection of establishments recommended for their
cuisine – well-prepared meals at moderate prices; stars for good cooking.

Michelin map **412** M 14

The spa of Bad Hersfeld, noted for its mineral waters, is set in one of the craggiest, most convoluted parts of the Hesse forest. In the months of July and August, the town enjoys an additional popularity due to the Drama Festival staged in the majestic abbey ruins.

★ **Abbey Church Ruins (Stiftsruine)** ⊙ – The remains of the abbey, destroyed by French troops in 1761, reveal the imposing proportions of its church, which was more than 100m - 328ft long. The original building, which dated from the Ottonian period *(qv)* was designed with an expanded transept forming a single uncluttered chamber. In the 11C and 12C, while retaining the general plan, the church was modified in the Romanesque style, with two chancels. The western apse, constructed on a rectangular base and flanked by a single Romanesque tower, is impressive, particularly when viewed from inside.
St Catherine's Tower (1120), also in the Romanesque style, stands in an isolated position northeast of the church. Once part of the abbey complex, it houses the 900-year-old monastery bell.

Old Quarter – The blunt tower of the parish church emerges from a picturesque huddle of half-timbered burghers' houses near the market place (Marktplatz). Note especially the sacristan's house (1480) and the Baroque residence of the pastor (1714), with its beautiful entrance.

Town Hall – This Gothic building, modified at the end of the 16C, is surmounted now by gables in the style of the Weser Renaissance. From the forecourt, there is a good **view★** of the church.

EXCURSIONS

Rotenburg an der Fulda – *21km - 12 miles to the north.*
Situated in a steep, narrow section of the Fulda valley, Rotenburg has preserved its old-world charm. From the bridge spanning the river, the view of stone and half-timbered houses clustered against the cliff that drops sheer into the river here is quite breathtaking. The town hall boasts a Renaissance doorway and a Rococo staircase. The castle, now a School of Finance, recalls the period when Rotenburg was the official residence of the Landgraves of Hesse.

★ BAD KREUZNACH Rhineland-Palatinate Pop 39 800

Michelin map **412** G 17 - Town plan in current Michelin Red Guide Deutschland

This spa, whose origins go back to Roman times, is 15km - 9 miles from the Rhine, at a place where the Nahe flows out from the mountains of the Northern Palatinate. Bad Kreuznach is celebrated both for the health-giving qualities of its mineral waters and for the wines of the Nahe region – whose qualities lie between the fresh, strong taste of the Moselle and the softer appeal of Rhine wines. The centre of the thermal resort is on **Badewörth Island** – its downstream tip straddled by the **Old Bridge** (Alte Nahebrücke), whose piles support 15C houses which appear to defy the laws of gravity. From the **Kauzenburg** (café-restaurant on the Schlossberg), there is a fine view of the town and its surroundings.

★ **Römerhalle** ⊘ – Hüffelsheimer Strasse 11. The museum is on a former small-holding at the western end of the castle park. Items discovered during archeological excavations in Bad Kreuznach and the surrounding district are on display. There are two exceptional exhibits, both of them 13C **mosaic floors**★★: one depicts the Sea God in his element; the other illustrates wild animals and gladiators in combat. Below, a Roman central heating system has been unearthed (hypocaust). Nearby, a **Roman villa** has been uncovered.

EXCURSIONS

★ **Bad Münster am Stein - Ebernburg** – By car, 4.5km - 2 3/4 miles. Leave the car near the cure centre (Kurhaus); then 1 hour Rtn on foot.
Go into the thermal **park**★ and walk through the gardens to the Nahe. On the far side of the river is the **Rheingrafenstein**★★, a 136m - 446ft rock face surmounted by the ruins of an ancient castle.

> Take the ferry across and, from the Hüttental café-restaurant, climb to the panoramic platform on top.

From here, there is a **fine**★ view of the Bad Münster basin and, downstream, the Rotenfels, whose sheer porphyry cliffs tower 214m - 700ft above the river.

★ BAD MERGENTHEIM Baden-Württemberg Pop 21 000

Michelin map **413** M 18

Lying in the valley of the Tauber, the old town of Bad Mergentheim, chosen as a base for the Knights of the Teutonic Order in the 16C, owes its popularity today to its position on the Romantic Road (qv), its castle, and its spa specializing in the treatment of digestive disorders.

Castle of the Teutonic Order (Deutschordensschloss) ⊘ – The Order was founded as a Germanic hospitaller community in the Holy Land and became a religious order in 1190 after the collapse of the Kingdom of Jerusalem. Eight years later, the military wing was added. When the Knights returned home they fought against the Slavs and took part in the conquest of Prussia and the Baltic states.
In 1525, the Grand Master of the Order, a Hohenzollern, followed the advice of Luther and suppressed the religious side of the organization, converting the community's patrimony into a principality which became the cradle of the state of Prussia. Those Knights who remained faithful Catholics grouped themselves under the see of Mergentheim. This ambivalent situation continued until 1809, when the Order was dispossessed by Napoleon. Today, greatly reduced in power, the Order has resumed existence as a religious and charitable body, with the Grand Master a cleric.
The castle, built in 1565, was modified c1780. The armorial bearings of the Order are displayed above the main entrance, which was lavishly decorated in the 17C. The corner towers in the inner courtyard are furnished with Renaissance spiral stairways. Beside the local historic museum is a museum devoted to the Teutonic Order itself. The castle park was landscaped in the English manner in the late 18C.

EXCURSIONS

Stuppach – 6km - 3 1/2 miles on the Schwäbisch Hall road.
The **parish church** ⊘ of this village now boasts the central panel of the celebrated altarpiece from the Chapel of Our Lady of the Snow in Aschaffenburg (qv). The panel, known as the **Stuppach Virgin**★★ (1519), depicts a Virgin and Child and was the work of Matthias Grünewald.

★ BAD REICHENHALL Bavaria Pop 18 500

Michelin map **413** V 23 – Town plan in the current Michelin Red Guide Deutschland

Built where the last of the Saalach gorges finally opens out, Bad Reichenhall is the city of salt. The cures at the Spa are mainly for people with respiratory trouble. This thermal establishment extends for just over a mile along the busiest section of the **Ludwigstrasse**, the main street linking St Zeno's Church with the bridge over the Saalach river.
The town has produced domestic salt since Celtic times. The success of the industry is based on the fact that the concentration of the mineral (a maximum of 24%) is the highest in Europe - and the fact that the salt derives from abundant springs, not from rock brine as at Berchtesgaden or the mines of the Salzkammergut.

Until 1958 the waters were piped through a 79km - 49-mile conduit (Soleleitung) to extraction and refining plants at Traunstein and Rosenheim; today, together with brine from Berchtesgaden, they are treated in new saline works at Bad Reichenhall itself.

St Zeno's Church – *On the street that cuts across the northern part of the town.* This late 12C church (remodelled in the 16C and later decorated in the Baroque style) corresponds on the north side of the Alps to the well-known Romanesque church dedicated to the same saint in Verona. Lombard influence can be seen in the design and decoration of the main doorway, with its archstones of alternating shades and slender outside columns resting on couched lions. On the tympanum, a Virgin and Child are depicted between St Rupert, first Bishop of Salzburg, and the patron saint himself, invoked in the Alps against flooding.

Old Salt Works (Alte Saline) ⊙ – Ludwig I of Bavaria had this plant built in 1834 in the so-called "Troubadour" style in vogue at that time. Entering the huge machine-room, where two immense paddle-wheels operate the pumps, visitors could imagine themselves part of a mid-19C steel engraving in The Illustrated London News. Beyond this, caverns and galleries with marble cladding lead to different catchment areas where some of the archaic equipment still works - for example the 103m - 113yd transmission shaft which, thanks to five separate joints, actuates the pump at the Karl-Theodor spring.

★ BAD SÄCKINGEN Baden-Württemberg   Pop 16 000

Michelin map **413** G H 24

A small town on the fringe of the Black Forest and beside the Rhine – where the river forms the frontier with Switzerland. Much of the lay architecture shows Swiss influence.

★ **The Rhine Bridge** – Built to span the Rhine at the end of the 16C, this roofed bridge constructed of wood is the oldest of its kind still standing in the world. Restricted today to pedestrians and cyclists, the structure rests on pillars of stone.

★ **Church of St Fridolin** (Fridolinsmünster) – Named after the missionary who converted the Alemanni in the 6C, this 14C Gothic church is an example of how Baroque features were sometimes added to another architectural style – arcades of Gothic arches passing directly into groined vaulting; lowered vaults to make an easier decorating surface; tall windows transformed into rounded bays. The decoration includes fine stucco-work from the School of Wessobrunn *(qv)*.
The church Treasury contains the Shrine of St Fridolin (magnificent 18C work from Augsburg, in the form of a carriage chest).

EXCURSION

Waldshut – *26km - 16 miles to the west.* Halfway up a wooded, semicircular slope rising from a curve in the Rhine, this small town retains its two fortified gateways and its **Kaiserstrasse** – a street whose ordered lines are broken by houses with overhanging eaves in the manner of Bernese peasant homes.

BAD TÖLZ Bavaria   Pop 13 600

Michelin map **413** R 23

Bad Tölz is really two towns: on one side of the Isar is a modern spa, reputed for the healing qualities of its iodized water (at 41.5mg per litre, the richest in Germany); and facing it across the Alpine torrent is the picturesque old town, with its monuments to the Baroque and medieval eras.

★ **Marktstrasse** – Much of the character of this street derives from its wide curve and steep slope, bordered by multicoloured facades beneath overhanging eaves.

Calvary Hill (Kalvarienberg) – At the top of the Kalvarienberg pathway, which is flanked by the Stations of the Cross, a small chapel (1743) is dedicated to St Leonard, whose powers are still widely revered among the peasants of Bavaria and Austria. In this part of the country his intercession is sought not only for the deliverance of prisoners (note the chain surrounding the chapel), but also for the protection of horses. The saint's anniversary, November 6, is celebrated each year by a parade of rustic wagons and carts, colourfully decorated and drawn by teams of brilliantly harnessed horses *(see Calendar of Events)*.

EXCURSIONS

Benediktbeuern – *15km - 9 miles to the southwest.*
Built on the lower slopes of the Bavarian Alps foothills, this imposing complex dating from AD 739 is the oldest Benedictine abbey in Upper Bavaria. The **abbey church** ⊙ as it is now was remodelled between 1681 and 1686. On those parts of the cradle vaulting left free of stuccowork, Georg Asam – father of the famous Asam Brothers *(qv)* – painted the first complete cycle of frescoes dating from the beginning of the Bavarian Baroque period: the Birth, Baptism, Transfiguration and Resurrection of the Saviour, the Descent of the Holy Spirit and the Last Judgement.

Elegant frescoes and finely worked stucco make **St Anastasia's Chapel**★ (1751-53), a little to the north of the church, one of the most charming examples of Rococo art. The designer, J M Fischer, and the craftsmen who carried out the work for him, were commissioned a few years later to repeat their artistry at Ottobeuren *(qv)*.

★ **Walchensee** – *40km - 25 miles to the southwest.*
Framed by dense woods, this deep blue reservoir-lake is one of the beauties of the Bavarian Alps. Its waters serve the power station on the Kochelsee, some 200m - 600ft lower down. A chairlift rises to the Fahrenberg, from which a path leads in 30 minutes to the summit of the **Herzogstand** (1 731m - 5 679ft). From the observation deck, there is a superb **all-round view**★★ taking in the Walchensee, the Kochelsee, the Karwendel massif and the rock wall of the Wetterstein, which culminates in the Zugspitze.

★★ **BAD WIMPFEN** Baden-Württemberg Pop 6 000

Michelin maps 412 and 413 K 19 - Local map see under HOHENLOHE

Imperial residence of the Hohenstaufens in the 13C, this small fortified town, with its network of narrow streets lined with half-timbered houses, is built on a rise overlooking the River Neckar.
Along the foot of the hill extend the Ludwigshalle salt works, whose product once brought prosperity to the whole surrounding region, and especially the built-up area of Bad Wimpfen im Tal, which grew up around an old collegiate church.

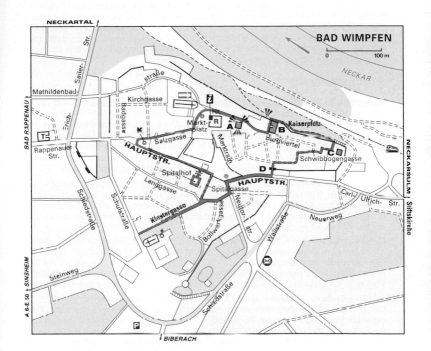

★★ **UPPER TOWN** (BAD WIMPFEN AM BERG) *time: 1 1/2 hours*

Follow the itinerary on the map, starting at the Marktplatz.

Remains of the Imperial Palace (Kaiserpfalz) – Standing on its own behind the Town Hall is the **Blue Tower** (Blauer Turm) (**A**), whose "neo-feudal" top dates only from the 19C. From the summit – occupied today as in medieval times by a watchman – there is a panoramic view of the town and the Neckar valley. A little further on is the Romanesque **Steinhaus** (**B**), with its 16C stepped gable, where there is a museum tracing the history of Bad Wimpfen since the Roman occupation.
Eight steps down from the Steinhaus terrace, on the right at the foot of the wall, note the twin-columned Romanesque arcading through which light entered the gallery of the old palace.
The decorative intricacy of the arcades demonstrates the building talents of the Hohenstaufens, under whose rule Romanesque civic architecture reached its peak.
Continue to follow the wall as far as a flight of steps, on the right, which leads to the tip of the spur on which the town is built, at the foot of the **Red Tower** (Roter Turm) (**C**), the fortress's final defensive point.
Return to the town centre, descending to pass beneath the **Hohenstaufentor** (**D**), which was the castle's main entrance in medieval times, and join the Klostergasse.

Old Streets – In the **Klostergasse**, which has considerable rustic charm, there are a number of half-timbered houses standing in their own gardens. On the left are the former spa bathhouses, recognizable by their outside galleries. To explore more of the town's old streets, return to the Langgasse crossroads and take a narrow alley on the right which leads to the **Hauptstrasse**. At No 45 is the courtyard of a former hospital (Spitalhof), one of the oldest buildings in Wimpfen. Return along the Hauptstrasse, with its many picturesque, finely worked signs, and pass the beautiful 1576 Eagle Fountain (Adlerbrunnen) (**K**) before regaining the Marktplatz via the Salzgasse.

The Upper Town, Bad Wimpfen

Church of St Peter and St Paul (Stiftskirche) – *At Bad Wimpfen im Tal.* This Gothic parish church has retained from an earlier Romanesque building a Westwerk *(qv)* which is strikingly crude. The **cloister**★★ (Kreuzgang) ⊘ shows the Gothic style slowly evolving towards an aridity of design, though the late 13C east gallery is an example of the period at its best: a true purity of line informs the sculpted decor and the tri- and quadrilobed windows. The north gallery (*c*1350), already more angular in design, marks the transition to the style of the west gallery, which is spindly and cold (late 15C).

EXCURSIONS

★ **Automobile and Technical Museum** (Auto- und Technikmuseum) ⊘ – *At* **Sinsheim**, *25km - 15 1/2 miles to the west.*
Mechanical vehicles of many types are brought together in this collection. In the first building are impressive early 20C tractors, steam locomotives, luxury motor cars (Bugatti, Mercedes), and a replica of the first hang-glider to be commercially marketed, the Lilienthal, which dates from the late 19C. A second building exhibits mainly military material (tanks, motorized artillery, aeroplanes).

★ **The Neckar Valley** (Neckartal) – *Round tour of 74km - 46 miles - about 4 hours.* Downstream from Bad Wimpfen, the Neckar, cutting once more through the sandstone massif of the Odenwald *(qv)*, runs through an area of wooded hills, many of them crowned by castles. Linked now with the great flow of navigation on the Rhine, river traffic is heavy.

★ **Guttenberg Castle** ⊘ – A massive defence wall protects this castle on the side facing the mountain. Inside, there are unusual **collections** of **objets d'art**★ and a series of archives. Note especially the odd 18C "Library-Herbarium", in which the plants are encased in 92 pseudo "books" made of wood. A 15C altarpiece, The Mantled Virgin, is on display. There is a fine view of the river from the keep.

Hornberg Castle ⊘ – *1.5km - about 1 mile outside Neckarzimmern.*
Crowning a hill planted with vines, this castle – now partly in ruins – can be recognized from far away by its cylindrical keep. In the part now turned into a **museum**, note the body armour of Götz von Berlichingen, who died here in 1562. From the high keep, the **view**★ extends a long way down the valley.

In the village of Hirschhorn am Neckar, turn right towards Beerfelden, then right again to reach the entrance to Hirschhorn Castle.

★ **Hirschhorn am Neckar** – The castle stands on a fortified spur. From the tower *(121 steps, a difficult climb)* the **view**★ extends over the meander and wooded slopes of the Neckar valley.

Neckarsteinach – Four castles dominate this site.

Dilsberg – *4.5km - 3 miles from Neckarsteinach.* Follow the Signposts "Burgruine" to reach the ruined castle. From the tower *(97 steps)* there is another **panorama**★ over the winding river Neckar.
The best way to arrive in **Heidelburg** is by the east bank road, which leads straight to the castle.

Jagst Valley (Jagsttal) – *See under Hohenlohe.*

Neckarsulm – *10km - 6 miles to the southeast.* The castle once belonged to the Teutonic Order. Today the castle houses the **German Cycle and Motorcycle Museum** (Deutsches Zweiradmuseum, NSU-Museum) ⊘. Nearby is the NSU motor factory which produced the first bicycles in Germany.

Michelin map **413** P 17

It was Emperor Henry II the Saint (1002-1024) who transformed this Imperial residence into a flourishing episcopal city.

From the 12C onwards, as was the case with all episcopal towns, the clergy, installed in the higher part, traded on their authority and came into conflict with the burghers who had settled in the valley, on the island, around the Grüner Markt and in the Sand quarter. The quarrel ended in the 16C with the ecclesiastics prevailing. Then gradually the schism healed and the 18C found both sectors profiting impartially from the prestige of the new Baroque style.

The sculptor **Tilman Riemenschneider** (1460-1531) and the **Dientzenhofer** family, architects of distinction, were the most brilliant of those responsible for the creation of this beautiful cathedral city whose art treasures have been spared by war.

Among Bamberg's many gastronomic specialities are carp prepared to a traditional local recipe, small Franconian sausages, and "smoked beer" (Rauchbier).

BAMBERG

Gruner Markt	**CZ** 13	Am Kranen	**BZ** 3
Hauptwachstraße	**CY** 15	Bischofsmühlbrücke	**BCZ** 5
Lange Str.	**CZ**	Dominikanerstraße	**BZ** 8
Luitpoldstraße	**CY**	Domstraße	**BZ** 9
Maximiliansplatz	**CY**	Geyerswörthstraße	**CZ** 12
Obere Königstraße	**CY** 34	Herrenstraße	**BZ** 18
Untere Königstraße	**CY** 55	Judenstraße	**BZ** 20
		Karollnenstraße	**BZ** 23
Außere Löwenstraße	**CY** 2	Luitpoldbrücke	**CY** 26

Mittlerer Kaulberg	**BZ** 30
Nonnenbrücke	**CZ** 32
Obere Karolinenstraße	**BZ** 33
Obere Sandstraße	**BZ** 36
Residenzstraße	**BZ** 40
Richard-Wagner-Str.	**CZ** 44
St-Getreu-Str	**BZ** 45
Schillerplatz	**CZ** 47
Schönleinsplatz	**CZ** 48
Untere Brücke	**BZ** 52
Unterer Kaulberg	**BZ** 61

CATHEDRAL PRECINCTS   time: 1 hour

The Domplatz is surrounded by the cathedral itself, the New (18C) Residence and the Old Residence, which houses the Historical Museum.

★★ **Cathedral (Dom) (BZ)** – Transitional Gothic in style, the building is characterized by its two apses. That to the east, the older, stands raised upon a terrace with a fine balustrade, its cornices worked in a chequered pattern; the western apse is entirely Gothic. Four towers quarter the two choirs. The design, inherited from the original Ottonian edifice, exemplifies the reticence of the Empire's powerful ecclesiastical institutions when faced with the innovations of French Gothic.

The finest of the cathedral entrances is the Princes' Doorway (Fürstenportal), on the Domplatz. It comprises ten recessed arches supported on fluted, ribbed or chevroned columns which alternate with statue-columns representing prophets with apostles on their shoulders.

Enter the church via the Adam Door, decorated with diamond and dogtooth carving (the statues are in the Diocesan museum). From east to west, the progression from Romanesque to Gothic is at once apparent. Two choirs, noticeably raised because of the crypts built beneath them, enclose a single nave whose walls – with neither triforium nor galleries – attest to the conservatism of the prevailing style. Underneath the eastern choir, the crypt is huge: three Romanesque naves with heavily ribbed vaulting supported on stout piers. The western choir is furnished with tall windows beneath diagonal rib vaulting.

The Knight of Bamberg

Masterpieces of German Gothic sculpture are on view in the cathedral.

1) Equestrian statue of **The Knight of Bamberg**★★★(Bamberger Reiter), a 13C representation of a non-identified king (possibly St Stephen, first King of Hungary and brother-in-law of Henry II), symbolizing an idealized view of the Middle Ages – much as Bayard, the "blameless and fearless knight" of France stands for the same chivalrous ideals.

2) Celebrated statuary group, The Visitation (note the features of St Elizabeth). The group, and the Knight on his horse, are the work of an artist strongly influenced by the French School, particularly that of Reims.

3) The **tomb**★★★ of Henry II the Saint and Cunegunda (St Heinrichs-Grab) stands in the centre of the nave, at the entrance to the eastern choir. It took Tilman Reimenschneider *(qv)* fourteen years to complete the tomb. The following scenes can be identified, circling the tomb: Cunegunda's ordeal by fire under suspicion of adultery; Cunegunda's dismissal of dishonest workmen; death of Henry II the Saint; the weighing of the Emperor's soul before St Lawrence; St Benedict miraculously operating on the Emperor for gallstones.

4) Reredos of The Nativity (1523) by Veit Stoss *(qv)*.

5) Funerary statue of a bishop (Friedrich von Hohenlohe).

6) Statue representing The Church.

7) Remarkable statue symbolizing The Synagogue, in the form of a blindfolded woman.

★ **Diocesan Museum (Diözesanmuseum) (BZ M)** ⊘ – The collections displayed include lapidary remains, among them statues of Adam and Eve, the former giving his name to one of the cathedral doorways *(see above)*, and the cathedral treasury, rich in imperial and pontifical vestments.

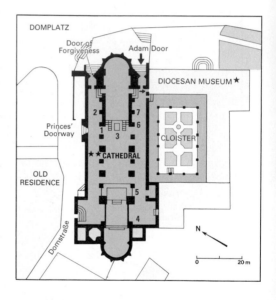

Old Residence (Alte Hofhaltung) (BZ) – *The courtyard is open until dusk.* This was formerly the episcopal and imperial palace. Its façade, with carved gables, oriel window and corner turret date, along with the doorway, from the Renaissance. The delightful **inner courtyard**★★ (Innenhof) is bordered by half-timbered Gothic buildings with steeply sloping roofs and picturesque, flower-decked wooden galleries. Opposite the entrance, take a covered alleyway which leads to a small square surrounded by houses once inhabited by the canons.

New Residence (Neue Residenz) (BZ) ⊘ – This palace, the largest building in Bamberg, comprises four main blocks: two, bordering the Obere Karolinenstrasse, were constructed in the early 17C and are Renaissance in style; the two wings on the Domplatz are Baroque. They were started in 1695 by the architect Leonard Dientzenhofer, on the orders of Lothar Franz von Schönborn, Prince-Elector of Mainz and Bishop of Bamberg.

(The palace boasts its own mystery. One morning in 1815, a corpse was found beneath the windows. It was the body of Marshal Berthier, retired to Bavaria after the return of Napoleon from the Isle of Elba. Accident, murder or suicide? The question has never been answered.)

On the first floor, works of the German masters are on **view**★ (Master of the Life of the Virgin, Hans Baldung Grien, etc). The Imperial Apartments on the second floor are among the finest in the Residence, with beautiful parquet floors, Baroque furniture and authentic Gobelins tapestries. The Emperors' Hall is outstanding for its portraits and its allegorical frescoes.

From the palace rose garden, there is a fine view of the town and the former Benedictine Abbey of St Michael.

Follow the Karolinenstrasse to the lay quarter of the old town, built on the banks of the Regnitz river (note the statues of the Virgin on the house corners).

★ **Old Town Hall** (Altes Rathaus) (BZ) – Standing alone on an islet in the river, this unusual building was remodelled in the 18C. In addition to the town hall proper, with its facades painted in trompe-l'oeil, there is a monumental Rococo gateway and a small half-timbered house, known as the Häuslein, balanced on a pierhead of the bridge leading to the islet. From the Untere Brücke – the bridge at the lower end of the isle – there is a good view of the old fishermen's cottages along the river bank.

Hoffmann's House (E T A Hoffmann-Haus) (CZ D) ⊘ – This tiny house in the Schillerplatz occupies a special place in the memory of the poet Hoffmann (1776-1822), whose tales, set to music by the Franco-German composer Jacques Offenbach *(The Tales of Hoffmann)*, made him a celebrity worldwide. Hoffmann lived here from 1809 to 1813, in two small rooms one above the other, communicating via a square trapdoor. This allowed the poet, at work in the attic, to talk and joke with his wife in the room below. It was here that he wrote one of his most famous fantasies, *The Golden Pot (Der Goldene Topf)*.

EXCURSIONS

★ **Ebrach** – *35km - 22 miles to the west.*
The **Old Abbey** (Ehemaliges Kloster - currently used as a prison), founded in 1127 and not completed until the end of the 13C, was extensively remodelled in the Baroque fashion, first by J L Dientzenhofer and then by Balthazar Neumann *(qv)*.
The design of the **abbey church★**, with its flat-ended chancel and square ambulatory, is directly inspired by that of Citeaux. A rose window 7.6m - 25ft in diameter illuminates the façade. Inside, there are fine Rococo railings, a Baroque organ in the choir, and a Renaissance altarpiece (north transept) illustrating the Vision of St Bernard.

★ **Pommersfelden Castle** (or Weissenstein Castle) ⊘ – *21km - 12 miles to the south.*
Designed by Dientzenhofer and Hildebrandt and built for Bishop Lothar Franz von Schönborn between 1711 and 1718, this castle is one of the most outstanding examples in Germany of a Baroque palace.
A rapid tour permits the visitor to admire the galleried **state staircase★** *(illustration p 25)*. The paintings on the ceiling represent the Olympian gods and the four quarters of the globe. On the ground floor, an artificial grotto opening onto the garden perpetuates a Renaissance tradition. The marble hall on the first floor, lined with stucco pilasters, is decorated with frescoes by Rottmayr.
A longer visit would include the Elector's apartments with their small painting gallery and a hall of mirrors.

Forchheim – *22km - 14 miles to the south.*
The **church** (Pfarrkirche) here stands amidst an imposing group of half-timbered houses. Inside are **eight paintings★** (15C), once part of an altarpiece. Seven of them illustrate on one side the legend of St Martin – commemorated with a procession each year on the 11 November – and on the other side scenes from the Passion. The **palace** (Pfalz), a crude Gothic edifice dating from the 14C, was built on the site of a former Carolingian castle.

★ **BAUTZEN** Saxony   Pop 50 000
Michelin map 987 fold 18

Bautzen owes much to a situation from which one can see as far as the horizon in three different directions – it is built on a rock outcrop skirted by the winding course of the Spree. There is an especially picturesque view of the town from the bridge (Friedensbrücke), combining St Peter's Cathedral, the castle (Ortenburg), a network of narrow streets and an ancient fountain which serves as an emblem for the municipality.

City of the Sorbians – There are many Sorbian families in Bautzen – descendants of a western Slav people settling between the Elbe and the Neisse after the migrations of the 6C. The Sorbian language is still taught in local schools and numerous folk traditions – the decoration of eggs at Easter, the wearing of tall embroidered headdresses, the use of Sorbian national costume for festivals and holidays – perpetuate the identity of this ethnic minority.

SIGHTS

Market Place (Hauptmarkt) – The old square is surrounded by fine burghers' houses and a three-storey town hall which had Baroque features added to it in 1732. There is a tourist information bureau on the Fleischmarkt, behind the town hall.

★ **St Peter's Cathedral** (Dom St Peter) – This hall-church with three naves (1213-1497) is the sole place of worship in the region to be used both by Catholics and by Protestants (Catholic masses in the chancel; Protestant services in the main nave).
The floor plan is distinguished by an "elbow" bending the central axis. In the middle of the 15C the southern part of the structure was enlarged, and the Late Gothic windows date from this period. In 1664, the 85m - 279ft tower was crowned with a Baroque cupola.

Inside the cathedral, note the large wood Crucifix (1714) by Balthazar Permoser, and the Princes' Loggia (1674) in the Protestant section. The Baroque (1724) high altar in the chancel (St Peter Receiving the Keys) is the work of G A Pellegrini.

Follow the road that runs past the cathedral as far as the monastery.

Those parts of the **monastery** that remain standing date from 1683. The southern façade with its imposing portal (1753-55) is particularly fine. The armorial bearings of the monastery are displayed between the rounded pediments.

Now follow the Schlossstrasse.

Ortenburg Castle – The construction of this fortress, built by the Margraves of Meissen to defend the frontier of the province of Upper Lusatia, was started in 1144. Originally known as Budusin Castle, it was remodelled between 1483 and 1486, then extensively damaged during the Thirty Years War. The tower of the north wing (1486) of that building is still standing. It is embellished with a bas-relief representing Matthias Curvinus, King of Hungary (Lusatia was a Hungarian province from 1469 to 1490). The later part of the castle, dating from the end of the Gothic period and subsequently transformed in the Baroque style, was garnished in 1698 with three Renaissance gables - already anachronistic for that period.

Museum of Sorbian History and Culture (Museum der Sorben) ⊘ – *In a building adjoining Ortenburg Castle.* Documents, costumes, photos, illustrating the history and development of this minority.

A walk around the town's ramparts gives the visitor an idea of what it must have been like in the Middle Ages. Note particularly the **old fountain** (Alte Wasserkunst) and, in the cemetery beside the northern sector of the city wall, the ruins of **St Nicholas' Church**.

★ # BAVARIAN FOREST (BAYERISCHER WALD) Bavaria

Michelin map **413** W 19

On the borders of Bavaria and Bohemia (Czechoslovakia), the crystalline massif of the Bavarian Forest, dark beneath its carpet of fir and spruce, reaches a height of 1 456m - 4 777ft at the Grosser Arber. A number of villages in the region have been developed as holiday centres which offer a variety of different excursions.

ROUND TOUR STARTING FROM BODENMAIS

66km - 41 miles - allow 4 hours

★ **Bodenmais** – The town lies in a pastureland depression at the foot of the Arber. A subsoil rich in sulphur and magnetic rock has been exploited since the 15C. From Kötzting onwards, the road mounts the pastoral Weisser Regen valley within sight of the peaks of the Osser.
Motorists continue climbing as far as the Lamer Winkel, a hollow of woods and upland meadows at the head of the valley. A panoramic drive across the mountainside, enlivened by a closer view of the Grosser Arber, terminates this part of the journey (highest point: Brennes-Sattel, at 1 030m - 3 380ft).

★ **Hindenburg-Kanzel** – A **belvedere**★ offers a fine view of the Lamer Winkel and the Arber.

★★ **Grosser Arber** ⊘ – *From the lower chairlift terminal, 1 hour Rtn, of which 20mn chairlift and 1/2 hour Rtn on foot.*
From the upper terminal, continue to climb on foot. At the top there are two rocky crags. That on the left (above a small chapel) overlooks the Schwarzer Regen depression, with an extended **view**★★ of the frontier region of the southeast. The right-hand rock (surmounted by a cross) affords a splendid view of the Lamer Winkel and the wooded undulations of the forest to the north.
The **Grosser Arbersee**★, a dark, romantic lake surrounded by pines, is passed on the right as the road goes down, winding through the tree-covered foothills on the southern slopes of the Arber. On the way, there are several magnificent **viewpoints**★ commanding the Zwiesel basin, the Falkenstein and the Grosser Rachel.

Lam – A most attractive small resort, at the bottom of a wide, open valley.

Help us in our constant task of keeping up to date.
Send your comments and suggestions to

Michelin Tyre PLC
Tourism Department
Davy House
Lyon Road
HARROW Middlesex HA1 2DQ
Fax: 081 863 0680

Michelin map 413 R 17

Bayreuth is the town of Wagner. Built between the wooded heights of the Fichtelgebirge and the curious, desolate landscape of Swiss Franconia, it existed peacefully for hundreds of years before a series of events starting in the 18C placed it once and for all on the world map. First of all, it was chosen as a residence for the Margraves of Brandenburg-Bayreuth, with all the prominence attached to the life of the Court; later it became one of Europe's architectural capitals of Baroque and Rococo; and today the town is the goal of Wagnerian pilgrims from the four corners of the globe.

HISTORICAL NOTES

Princess Wilhelmina – The Margravine Wilhelmina, daughter of the King-Sergeant *(qv)*, sister of Frederick the Great and lifelong friend of Voltaire, was one of the most cultivated women of the 18C. She could have been in line for the Prussian throne, but decided instead to marry the Margrave Friedrich of Brandenburg-Bayreuth. Finding him in fact rather a dull man, she allowed her talents to flower among the more cultured members of her entourage.

Her life (1709-1758) marked the most brilliant period in Bayreuth's history. A gifted artist, writer, composer, architect and decorator, dilettante and patroness of the fine arts, the Princess was responsible for the blossoming of "Bayreuth Rococo" – a highly personal style whose garlands and flowers differed markedly from the more rustic French Rococo then in vogue.

Wagner and Liszt – It is often said that many of Wagner's masterworks would never have seen the light of day if it had not been for the influence of Liszt. The two innovators of musical expression, stimulated by mutual admiration and drawn closer by family ties (Wagner married Liszt's daughter Cosima in 1870), were united again even in death: the tomb of Liszt, who died during one of the first festivals in 1886, is in the Bayreuth cemetery (Stadtfriedhof via Erlanger Strasse - Y), while the remains of Wagner, who died three years earlier in Venice, repose in the gardens of the Villa Wahnfried.

BAYREUTH

Bahnhofstraße	Y 4	
Kanalstraße	Y 15	
Kanzleistraße	YZ 17	
Ludwigstraße	Z 20	
Maximilianstraße	Y	
Opernstraße	Y 30	
Richard-Wagner-Str.	Z 32	
Schulstraße	Y 33	
Sophienstraße	Y 35	
Am Mühltürlein	Y 3	
Balthasar-Neumann-Str.	Z 5	
Bürgerreuter Str.	Y 7	
Erlanger Str.	Y 8	
Friedrich-Von-Schiller-Str.	Y 10	
Josephsplatz	Y 14	
Karl-Marx-Str.	Y 18	
Luitpoldplatz	Y 22	
Markgrafenallee	Y 24	
Muncker Str.	Y 26	
Nürnberger Str.	Z 28	
Wieland-Wagner-Str.	Z 36	
Wilhelminerstraße	Z 38	
Wittelsbacherring	Z 39	
Wölfelstraße	Y 40	

The Festival – Creator of a new musical form, Richard Wagner searched on his many wanderings for the ideal place to present his works. He chose Bayreuth in 1872. With the support of Ludwig II of Bavaria, he had the Festival Theatre (Festspielhaus) built to his own design. It was inaugurated in 1876 with a performance of *The Ring*. The tradition established by the maestro was continued after his death, thanks to the tenacity of Cosima and, subsequently, his son Siegfried, his grandson Wieland (d 1966) and Wolfgang Wagner today. Each year the world's greatest exponents of the Wagnerian ethos re-transmit the immortal message to an audience of spellbound enthusiasts.

SIGHTS

* **Margraves' Opera House** (Markgräfliches Opernhaus) (Y) ⊘ – The Margravine Wilhelmina was responsible for the building of this theatre between 1745 and 1748. The austere façade, hemmed in between 18C burghers' houses, is designed with a projecting centre-section, divided into three parts on its upper floors by four columns that stand on a balcony.
The interior, constructed entirely of wood, attains with the stage and apron an astonishing depth of 72m - 236ft. There are no seats in the stalls, as that part of the auditorium is reserved for dancing. The three galleries are subdivided into boxes, the most luxurious – beneath a canopy bearing the crown of Prussia and the arms of the local Margraves – being the Royal Box. The decoration, by Giuseppe and Carlo Galli-Bibiena, brilliant artists from Bologna, is of an exuberant richness. Their reds, greens and browns harmonize perfectly with the abundance of gilded stucco-work which winds around the columns, frames medallions and festoons the candelabra hanging over each box. This Baroque Court theatre is one of the best preserved in Germany.

Castle Church (Schlosskirche) (Y A) – The single aisle, painted rose-pink and decorated with stucco-work by Pedrozzi (1756), is a visual delight. A closed oratory beneath the organ contains the tombs of the Margrave Friedrich, the Margravine Wilhelmina and their daughter.

New Castle (Neues Schloss) (Z) ⊘ – Wishing to make Bayreuth into a second Potsdam, Wilhelmina created this palace between 1753 and 1754, unifying and remodelling a number of existing buildings.
The **interior decoration**, of a fascinating elegance, was executed by the stucco-master Pedrozzi, greatly influenced by the Princess, whose delight in the airy, flowered Rococo style is everywhere in evidence. Wilhelmina, whose private apartments were on the first floor of the north wing, concerned herself particularly with the decor of the Mirror Room, the Japanese Room and the old Music Room.
The solemnity of her husband's apartments in the south wing is alleviated by the decorative fantasy of the Palm Chamber, whose panels are carved to resemble exotic trees, and of another room designed to look like an arbour. On the ground floor of the central block a row of apartments, including a bathroom and a grotto, open directly onto a garden with access to the Italian Palace. This building, the residence of the Margrave Friedrich's second wife, is decorated in a less interesting style.

* **Richard Wagner Museum** (Z M¹) ⊘ – The Villa Wahnfried (Supreme Peace), which the composer lived in from 1874 onwards is still one of the main centres of Wagnerian pilgrimage. Collections on display in the museum evoke the maestro's life and work (furniture, manuscripts, pianos and death mask) as well as the history of the Bayreuth Festival (construction of the Festival Theatre, costumes and scenery).
At the end of the garden, in front of a rotunda, Richard and Cosima lie beneath a simple plaque on the edge of the Hofgarten.

Festival Theatre (Festspielhaus) ⊘ – *Leave by Karl-Marx-Strasse* (Y 18). The theatre is intended to concentrate all the attention on the dramatic action. Even the music, rising from a camouflaged orchestra pit, is no more than a fluid complement to the story. The acoustics have been worked out to the point where even the fabric of the seats (padding is forbidden) and the density of the human audience is taken into account.

* **Hermitage Castle** (Schloss Eremitage) ⊘ – *4km - 2 1/2 miles to the east by* ② *on the town plan.*
The park (Schlosspark), in which the unexpected and the fantastic manifest themselves in the manner of an English garden, is suffused with memories of Princess Wilhelmina. The **old castle** (Altes Schloss), surrounded by geometric flower beds, was built in 1715 and remodelled by the Margravine in 1736. Note the curious grotto opening onto the inner courtyard, and the "cells" in which guests could meditate and make believe they were hermits. Nearby is the artificial ruin of a theatre constructed in 1743.
The **new castle** (Neues Schloss), designed on a semicircular plan, was rebuilt after 1945. In the centre, mythological scenes are represented in the Temple of the Sun.

Carnival time
The Crazy Days (Tolle Tage) preceeding Ash Wednesday are the occasion for a series of boisterous, fun-loving carnivals. Parades, processions, decorated floats, street parties, painted faces and fancy dress are all part of the fun.

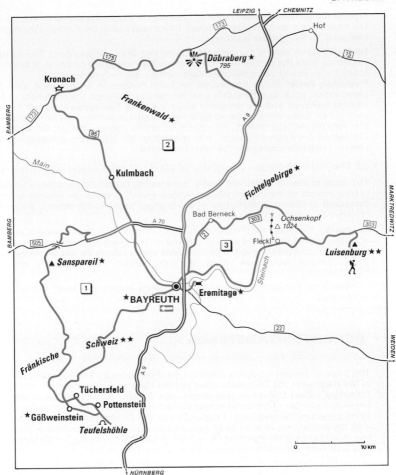

EXCURSIONS

★★ ☐ **Swiss Franconia** (Fränkische Schweiz) **and Sanspareil** – *Round tour of 125km - 78 miles - allow one day.*

Southwest of Bayreuth, far from the main road and rail arteries, an undulating plateau gashed by deep valleys forms the northern extremity of the Franconian Jura. Heavy erosion of this porous limestone shelf has resulted in a landscape of dolomitic relief, pitted with many caves.

Tüchersfeld – The houses of the village are dispersed among an astonishing series of rocky pinnacles.

Pottenstein – The castle, a former residence of the Elector-Bishops of Bamberg, overlooks the town. There are many natural curiosities (gorges, caves, etc) in the neighbourhood.

Teufelshöhle ⊘ – The **caves** here, particularly the one known as "Barbarossa's Cathedral", are endowed with fine stalactites and stalagmites. The exit through a maze of huge rocks scattered right and left is picturesque.

★ **Gössweinstein** – The Circuit of **Marienfelsen** *(about 3/4 hour Rtn on foot, leaving the castle to follow the signposts: Marienfels-Schmitt-Anlagen)* leads, through undergrowth strewn with picturesque rocks, to several fine **belvederes★★** above the deep valley of the Wiesent.
In the town, the **Pilgrimage Church** (Wallfahrtskirche), built between 1730 and 1739 by Balthazar Neumann, contains on the upper part of the high altar an early 16C Gothic group of the Trinity.

★ **Sanspareil** – Below **Zwernitz Castle** ⊘ (Fester Zwernitz) (there is a fine view from the keep), Princess Wilhelmina designed an impressive **rock garden★** with artificial grottoes and monuments theatrically disposed through a beech wood. "Calypso's Cave" opens onto the Theatre of Ruins, the most impressive feature of the garden.

★ ☐ **The Franconian Mountains** (Frankenwald) – *Round tour of 104km - 65 miles - allow 5 hours.*

★ **Döbraberg** – *3/4 hour Rtn on foot.* Climb to the belvedere tower (795m - 2 608.27ft). The majestic **panorama★** extends as far as the mysterious depths of the Thuringian Mountains in the north, and the Fichtelgebirge in the south. These massifs enclose the Hof Basin.

59

Kronach – Rosenberg **Fortress** (Festung) towers over the small town of Kronach and the wooded heights of the Frankenwald. Star-shaped bastions surround the nobly designed 16-18C fortress buildings.

Kulmbach – *Town plan in the current Michelin Red Guide Deutschland*. This industrial town, once the seat of the Hohenzollern Margraves of Franconia, is famous today for its strong beers (Aechtes Kulmbacher, Bayrisch Gfrorns).

Plassenburg Castle★ ⊘, an impressive medieval fortress in an excellent state of preservation, surprises the visitor with the contrast between the crudeness of its original buildings and the delightful elegance of its **Renaissance courtyard★★** surrounded on three sides by tiered galleries. Various collections are on display in the refurnished apartments, the most attractive being that of **tin soldiers★** (Deutsches Zinnfigurenmuseum), with more than 300 000 pieces grouped in dioramas. The battle scenes are the most successful.

★ ③ **The Fichtelgebirge** – *Round tour of 92km - 57 miles - allow about 5 hours.*

The route follows the Steinach valley, penetrating deeply into the pine-covered granite massif of the Fichtelgebirge. Above Fleckl, a cable car mounts to the **Ochsenkopf** (1 024m - 3 360ft), one of the highest peaks in the massif, which is crowned by a television tower.

★★ **Luisenburg** – This labyrinth (Felsenlabyrinth) of enormous granite boulders, in situ or fallen, eroded into round shapes or piled on top of each other, can be walked through along a pine-shaded, hilly path (**blue arrows indicate the way up, red the way down**). Several belvederes along the way afford varying views of the Fichtelgebirge.

> *Return to Bayreuth via Route No 303, which passes the small spa of Bad Berneck.*

★★ BERCHTESGADEN Bavaria   Pop 8 200

Michelin map 🗺 V 24 - Local map see under German ALPINE ROAD

The basin of Berchtesgaden is enclosed on three sides by the mountain chains of the Watzmann, the Steinernes Meer and the Hagengebirge, the whole complex forming a salient that penetrates deeply into Austria. Apart from these natural barriers, a number of historical events explain the unusual frontier situation. The development of the area, and of the small town of Berchtesgaden itself, is linked with the importance of a priory of Augustinian monks, which became a pivot of the Bavarian political machine at a time when the grasping Archbishops of Salzburg were becoming too demanding. Secularized in 1803, the priory and its lands were definitively incorporated into the kingdom of Bavaria six years later. Berchtesgaden was chosen as a holiday retreat by Adolf Hitler, who built his notorious "Eagle's Nest" sanctuary on the Kehlstein.

Journey's end on the German Alpine Road *(qv)* and departure point for many other tourist excursions, Berchtesgaden is intensely busy throughout the summer. The town is dominated by the bulk of the Watzmann (2 712m - 8 900ft).

SIGHTS

★ **Schlossplatz** – This square – it is in fact triangular in shape – is the heart of the old village. On the western side are the granary and a tax collector's office, remodelled and furnished with an arcaded gallery in the 16C. The church front and the façade of the old priory, now known as the castle, complete the picture.

Church (Stiftskirche) – The church, whose foundations are Romanesque, is interesting because of the comparison with St Zeno's at Bad Reichenhall *(qv)*, for it too was originally built for Augustinian monks. A Lombard influence manifests itself in the façade, where an alternation of stone in different colours makes a decorative pattern. The towers were rebuilt in the last century after a fire. The interior of the building is distinguished by early 16C network vaulting in the nave, and by a chancel some 200 years older, much higher and of a purer Gothic style.

Castle ⊘ – At the time of the commendatory prelates, the monks' priory did indeed become a sumptuous palace. From 1923 onwards, it was the home of the Crown Prince Rupert, former commander-in-chief of the Bavarian forces during the First World War and head of the House of Wittelsbach until his death in 1955. The Prince embellished the palace with furniture and art treasures, opening to the public his collections of weapons, French tapestries and Nymphenburg porcelain. German wood sculptures of the 15C and 16C, and examples of oriental art are also on view.

Cloister – Conserving its Romanesque galleries on three sides, the 13C cloister has a variety of columns – circular, polygonal or twisted, garnished with latticework, plant designs and capitals with foliated scrolls.

★ **Dormitory** (Dormitorium). – A fine Gothic hall with two aisles. Note among other examples of religious art, twelve magnificent busts from the stalls of Weingarten basilica (1487).

Museum – Worth special attention here are the two Renaissance rooms on the first floor (Italian furniture of the 15C and 16C), and the row of eight interconnected Seigneurs' rooms (Herrenzimmer) which offer an attractive glimpse into the 19C and its Biedermeier style *(qv)*.

Salt Mines (Salzbergwerk) ⊘ – Exploitation of the Berchtesgaden salt mines, started in 1517, brought prosperity to a region formerly very poor. The salt rock is washed by fresh water and the resulting brine (Sole), containing 27% of salt, is piped to Bad Reichenhall to be refined.

The tour, in miner's overalls, includes a trip through the galleries in a small train, the crossing by raft of an illuminated underground lake, and a documentary film show.

A room arranged as a salt museum exhibits the machinery, based on the hydraulic pump, invented by the engineer Georg von Reichenbach for raising the brine to the pipeline.

EXCURSIONS

★★ **Obersalzberg and the Kehlstein** ⊘ – *4km - 21/2 miles, there is a shuttle service by bus between Obersalzberg and the Kehlstein.*

After the abortive putsch of 1923 and the end of his prison sentence, Hitler, linked by friendships and family ties to the region, settled in Obersalzberg. When the Nazis seized power in 1934, the new Chancellor started an increasingly ambitious plan to enlarge and enhance the chalet (Berghof) which he had acquired. Subsequently, the sanctuary of "the lonely man of Berchtesgaden" became the stage for a number of expertly manipulated diplomatic receptions, notably that for the Austrian Chancellor, Dr. Schuschingg, on 12 February, 1938, and that for Neville Chamberlain on 15 September the same year.

The greater part of the Berghof buildings were destroyed in an American air raid on 25 April, 1945, prior to their capture on 4 May by a detachment of the French 2nd Armoured Division operating with the 101st U S Airborne Division.

Obersalzberg – With the exception of the Platterhof – a "People's Hotel" where the faithful could be lodged, at Hitler's behest, for the nominal sum of a single mark – the ruins of all the other buildings comprising the Nazi sanctuary have been razed. Only a few basement walls mark the site of the Führer's Berghof.

★★ **The Kehlstein** – The bus climbs an impressive **road**★★★ blasted from the bedrock on the craggy spur of the Kehlstein. At the end of the road (reserve seats for the return journey), a lift ascends the final 100m 328ft. On the summit there is now a tea-room (Teehaus) on the premises of the old Eagle's Nest – which, despite its name, was never a security refuge; Hitler himself only went there half a dozen times.

The **panorama**★★ (climb a little higher up the crest) extends over the neighbouring peaks and, on the far side of Salzburg, the rolling, rounded Pre-Alps of Salzkammergut, hard against the massif of Dachstein, glittering with small glaciers.

★★ **The Königssee** ⊘ – *5km - 3 miles to the south, then about 2 hours in a boat.*

This long, narrow lake, with its dark waters and steep banks, is one of the most romantic sites in Bavaria. Dominated on the west by the giant escarpments of the Watzmann, and the rocky base of the Steinernes Meer to the south, the lake narrows at St Bartholomä, where visitors can go ashore to admire the interesting **St Bartholomew's Chapel** with a triple apse and explore the hamlet nestling in a dense thicket of maples.

From the landing stage at Salet, a 15-minute walk brings the visitor to the Obersee, below the Teufelshörner at the circular end of the valley. From here the Röthbach falls, hurtling down from a height of 400m - 1 312ft, can be seen.

★★ **The Rossfeld Road** (Rossfeld-Ringstrasse) ⊘ – *Round tour of 29km - 18 miles (to be followed in an anticlockwise direction) to the east of Berchtesgaden- about 1 1/2 hours.*

The road reaches the lip of the crest and runs above the Austrian valley of the Salzach.

St Bartholomew's Chapel, Königsee

It overlooks the Golling Basin, hollowed out at the foot of the Tennengebirge, and the steep ridge linking the Hoher Göll to the Kleiner Göll. The Dachstein, still recognizable by its glaciers, fills in the background.

From the Hennenkopf car park, it is only a few minutes' climb to the beacon and the Hennenkopf Cross at 1 551m - 5 089ft. The road plunges down from the crest after the Rossfeldhütte (Inn) and winds through the charming, wooded valleys of the Oberau region.

★ **Hintersee** – *12km - 7 1/2 miles to the west*.
The road climbs the narrow Ramsau valley to reach this lake framed by the steep-sided domes of the Reiteralpe and the Teeth of Hochkalter. The eastern shore, and the "enchanted forest" (Zauberwald) bordering it, together with the shady banks of the rapids feeding the lake, are greatly appreciated by ramblers.

THE BERGSTRASSE Baden-Württemberg and Hessen

Michelin map **413** J 18 and I 17

This old road running at the foot of the low, scrub-covered mountains of the Odenwald *(qv)* has given its name to a strip of sunny hillsides sloping towards the Rhine valley. Orchards flourish on this fertile tract, and its ideal position assures the marketing of fruit earlier than anywhere else in the region. The old villages and small towns of the Bergstrasse are surrounded by typical Rhineland scenery.

FROM HEIDELBERG TO DARMSTADT
58km - 36 miles - about 3 hours

Weinheim – At the foot of the town, the picturesque half-timbered cottages of the tanners' quarter cluster around the Stadtmühlegasse. Take the Wachenbergstrasse to **Wachenburg Castle** (completely restored). There is a good view of the Rhine plain from the terrace. The **gardens★** of the castle in Weinheim itself, above the perched houses of the upper town, are planted with rare shrubs and trees.

Heppenheim an der Bergstrasse – The **Marktplatz★**, or Grosser Markt, owes its charm to two wooden buildings with corner oriel windows: the Liebig pharmacy and the 16C town hall. The square is dominated by a vast Neo-Gothic church, nicknamed "the Bergstrasse Cathedral".

Lorsch – Of the great abbey founded in 774, there now exist at the east end of the town only the church narthex and the **Torhalle★** ⊙, a triumphal arch in Carolingian style. Above the columns with their composite capitals is an impressive wall adorned with blind, cowled bays and ceramic marquetry in red and white. Behind the church, there is a wide view of the Rhine plain in the direction of the Odenwald.

Bensheim-Auerbach – In a sheltered valley is the **Fürstenlager★★**, once the summer residence of the Landgraves of Hessen. The park surrounding the building (Herrenhaus) is planted with tropical trees and studded with pavilions and symbolical monuments in the late 18C style. A little further north, **Auerbach Castle** ⊙ commands a view over the whole region.

Michelin map ▨▨▨ folds 17 and 18

Berlin, for so long a symbol of the world's division into two opposing camps, owes its economic and cultural dynamism today to the fact that both the Federal Republic and what used to be called East Germany have for thirty years been determined to use the city as a shop window for their respective ways of life.

HISTORICAL NOTES

In the 13C Cölln and Berlin were small towns built respectively on a sandy island and on the east bank of the River Spree, each inhabited by fishermen and travelling merchants. The first castle to be constructed on Cölln was completed in 1451. Nineteen years later it became the permanent residence of the Hohenzollern family – and it was the Hohenzollern Electors of Brandenburg who were politically responsible for the evolution of Berlin as a capital city.

The Great Elector (b 1620-1640-1688) – Friedrich-Wilhelm of Brandenburg found Berlin largely deserted at the end of the Thirty Years War. The great commander, who had in 1675 succeeded in beating the Swedish army at Fehrbellin, was also a very capable administrator. Emulating the Dutch (he had spent his youth in Holland), he constructed quays along the banks of the Spree and established many laws making Berlin a healthy and well-governed town.

The construction of a canal between the Spree and the Oder stimulated commerce, but Friedrich Wilhelm's most important contribution was to open Berlin to the French Huguenots after the Revocation of the Edict of Nantes in 1685. The arrival of a massive contingent – approximately one Huguenot for every five Berliners – transformed the city, strengthening its influence on its neighbours through the increased number of craftsmen, theologians, doctors, scholars and others now living there.

City Life in Berlin in the Age of Enlightenment (18C) – The first King of Prussia, Friedrich I, built the Palace of Charlottenburg for his wife, Sophie-Charlotte. He entrusted the work to Andreas Schlüter, a sculptor of genius (c1660-1714) who had worked mainly at the Royal Palace and the Arsenal.

Friedrich was succeeded by **Friedrich-Wilhelm I** (1713 40), known to history as the **King-Sergeant** because of his punctilious administration and a policy of systematic recruitment which laid the foundations of Prussian military power. He was less interested in the embellishment of Berlin than in making it more powerful. He ordered a new town, Friedrichstadt, to be laid out beyond the old city bastions. Commanding access to this were three monumental squares: the Quarré (Pariser Platz), the Oktogon (Leipziger Platz near the Potsdamer Platz - **GY**) and the Rondell (Belle Alliance, later Mehringplatz - **GY**). Draconian measures accelerated the development and peopling of the quarter, which is cut by such wide arteries as the Leipziger Strasse, the most lively street of pre-war Berlin, the Friedrichstrasse and the Wilhelmstrasse (now the Toleranzstrasse), the Whitehall of the Reich.

Frederick II the Great (1740-86) continued this civic effort, adding monuments along the famous Unter den Linden and the Forum Fredericianum (Bebelplatz). To fulfil his ambitions, he enlisted the aid of Knobelsdorff (1699-1753), an architect as much inspired by the Rococo tradition (Sans Souci) as by the Antique(Opera) The evolution towards Neo-Classicism continued until 1835. The monuments of Berlin were finally completed by the Brandenburg Gate (1789), the Neue Wache (1818), etc.

Towards Bismarck's Berlin – Berlin found its soul for the first time when the high patriotism inaugurated by the professors of the University, founded in 1810 by William Humboldt, was allied to the King of Prussia's call to arms in 1813 when he joined the Allies against Napoleon.

The city benefitted from the growing prestige of the Kingdom of Prussia and, as a favoured subject, developed its industrial life under the forceful direction of such great advisers as August Borsig, "the locomotive king", Werner von Siemens (1816-92), the pioneer electrical engineer and Emil Rathenau, the founder of the giant AEG. Although official projects like the Reichstag were pretentious, the number of open spaces increased as the residential suburbs moved westwards towards Grunewald Forest. By 1871, Berlin had become the capital of the Empire and numbered almost one million inhabitants.

Greater Berlin – In 1920 the city united, under a single administration, six urban suburbs, seven towns, 59 villages and 27 domains to form a unit of four million inhabitants. Despite the upheavals from which Germany was still suffering, "The Twenties" was an exciting period in Berlin, intellectually and artistically in particular. Berlin newspapers set the tone for newspapers all over Germany.

Films made in Berlin won international acclaim thanks to such directors as Ernst Lübitsch, Fritz Lang, Carl Mayer, Georg-Wilhelm Pabst and the actors Emil Jannings and Marlene Dietrich (*The Blue Angel, Maidens in Uniform*, etc.). The theatre, rejuvenated by Max Reinhardt (1873-1943), also flourished brilliantly. In 1928 Bertolt Brecht produced his famous *Threepenny Opera (Die Dreigroschenoper)*.

The blossoming of this talent was interrupted by the advent of the Hitler regime, when, along with the persecution of the Jews, a wealth of the country's artistic and literary heritage was forbidden or destroyed in the name of the campaign against "degenerate art" – that is to say all schools of writing, painting and sculpture judged by the Nazis as "decadent".

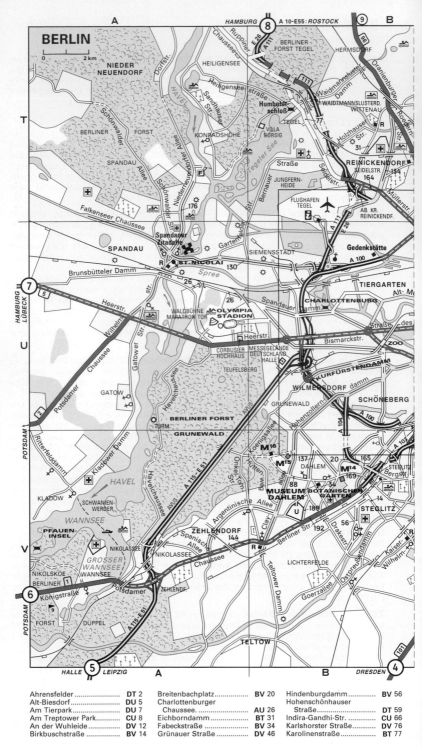

The Taking of Berlin – The final communiqué of the Yalta Conference in February 1945 announced that Berlin would be occupied after the war by the major powers.

From 21 April to 3 May, Berlin was a battlefield: the Red Army commanded by Generals Zhukov and Koniev against the remnants of the German army. The Soviet troops advanced through the defence lines, destroying everything above ground, including 120 of Berlin's 248 bridges. At last able to crawl out of their hiding places, the inhabitants learned of the final capture of the Reichstag and the suicide of Hitler (30 April 1945).

Berlin divided – After the German capitulation had been signed in Berlin on 8 May, the four victorious allies (the United States, the Soviet Union, France and Great Britain) took over the administration of Greater Berlin.

The political evolution of the (eastern) Soviet Sector, visualised by the occupants as the potential kernel of a future People's Democratic Republic, nevertheless hindered very rapidly the municipal administration as a whole.

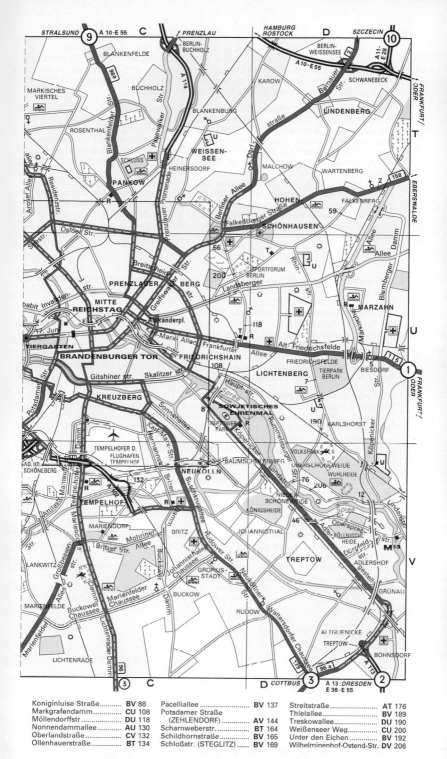

Political pressures, vetoes, and various incidents built up an increasing tension. Municipal Councillors unaligned with the concept of State Socialism walked out of the City Hall and formed a rival Council at Schöneberg. The Soviet representatives on the Allied Control Commission no longer took their seats. From 1948 onwards, the eastern sector found itself isolated.

The Berlin Blockade, provoked by Russian opposition to a currency reform introduced in the Western sectors, was beaten by the Berlin Airlift (26 June 1948 - 12 May 1949). The split was aggravated by the proclamation in 1949, in the east, of the German Democratic Republic, the popular uprising of 17 June 1953 and its suppression, the influx of refugees into West Berlin, and numerous other incidents.

On 13 August 1961 the eastern authorities ruled out all communication between the two parts of Berlin. A few days later the construction of the "Wall" began – following with implacable exactitude the theoretical borderline of the Soviet zone marked on the maps.

From then on, on either side of a concrete barrier 160km - 99.4 miles long and 4m - 13ft high, augmented by barbed wire, watchtowers and sentry posts, the two parts of the city evolved separately, each motivated by an ideological pattern opposed to the other. Attempts to pass from East to West through this hermetically sealed cordon ended more often than not in tragedy.

The "fall" of the Wall – A night of wild celebration, especially around the Brandenburg Gate, followed the official "opening" of the Berlin Wall during the evening of 9 November 1989: the eastern authorities, bowing to increased pressure from public protest movements, had finally agreed to re-establish the right of free passage between the two Germanys. And less than a year later, on 3 October 1990, the Treaty of Reunification re-established Berlin as the capital.

For a certain time, nevertheless, the two halves of the once-divided city will preserve certain particularities: "socialist" town-planning, for instance, with its broad avenues and grandiose residential units, is a constant reminder of the political climate and community which produced it. And the traces of the wall, in the mind as much as on the ground, will only fade slowly, as a scar that remains too long unhealed.

LIFE IN BERLIN

An outdoor city – Berlin, the biggest city in Germany, occupies an area eight times greater than Paris. Devastated in the last months of the war, the capital lost much of its historical heritage.

But thanks to the famous architects (Le Corbusier, Scharoun and others) involved in its reconstruction, a modernistic town, served by broad arteries linking different quarters separated by vast green belts, has emerged from the ruins of 1945.

The River Havel has been widened in its course through the woods to form lakes (Tegeler See, Stössensee, Grosser Wannsee). More than one third of the city's surface is covered by forests, parks and waterways.

A lively cultural scene – Before the Second World War, the centre of the city's life was concentrated around the Potsdamer Platz and the Friedrichstrasse. Today the liveliest part of Berlin is around the Kurfürstendamm, the memorial church and the Alexanderplatz complex. Nightlife centred on the **Kreuzberg hill (GZ)** has more of a cosmopolitan, anti-establishment flavour.

Deservedly, the city enjoys a worldwide reputation for the quality and diversity of entertainment it offers, particularly during the annual festivals of music, theatre and cinema.

During the past 300 years, Berlin has welcomed a large number of immigrants (French Huguenots after the Revocation of the Edict of Nantes, refugees from Poland, and Bohemia, all of whom have contributed to the emergence of a "typical" Berliner, lively, tolerant, with a sardonic sense of humour directed against the world around him.

After Theodore Hosemann in the Biedermeier period, Heinrich Zille (1858-1923) caught this character exactly in a series of spicy sketches satirising the everyday life of Berlin's "little people".

Because of this intermixture of populations, Berlin restaurants offer – along with such Brandenburger specialities as pig's feet (Eisbein) with sauerkraut and pease-pudding – a great variety of dishes from the international cuisine. Berliners term a tankard of lager beer a "Berliner Molle", and a dark beer with a dash of raspberry syrup a "Berliner Weisse mit Schuss".

★★ HISTORIC CENTRE

See plan opposite

The itinerary starts from the Reichstag and then follows the celebrated Unter den Linden, which until the war was the capital's busiest, most lively avenue.

Reichstag – In 1894 this massive Neo-Renaissance palace inaugurated in 1894 the sessions of the new Diet of the Empire (an Assembly elected through universal suffrage).

Gutted by a fire in 1933 and heavily damaged in 1945 during the Battle of Berlin, the building has now been restored. On 4 October 1990, it housed the inaugural session of the Parliament of reunified Germany.

An ambitious programme for the reorganization of Berlin's museums will entail the regrouping and relocation of many of the collections.
The descriptions of the museums are accordingly subject to change.

** The Brandenburg Gate

(Brandenburger Tor) – This triumphal arch, the very emblem of Berlin, was nevertheless for almost three decades the symbol of the city's division: the structure was integrated into the Wall, which followed a north-south axis here towards the Potsdamer Platz.

There is a vast perspective westward towards Strasse des 17 Juni and the Victory Monument, eastward towards the Unter den Linden.

Six Doric columns, incorporated into the stonework of the arch, support an antique-style entablature. Inspired by the Propylaea of the Parthenon, the gate

Berlin's Brandenburg Gate

was built by Carl Gotthard Langhans in 1789 and surmounted by the famous Victory Quadriga of Gottfried Schadow (1793).

The original group, reconstructed post-war, was removed to Paris after one of Napoleon's campaigns and returned to Berlin in 1814.

* **Unter den Linden** – The famous avenue "under the lime trees", conceived by the Great Elector Friedrich-Wilhelm in 1647, is bordered from the Friedrichstrasse onwards by monuments of the 17C and 19C.

Old Library (Deutsche Staatsbibliothek) (A) – Designed by Boumann in the Viennese Baroque style for the royal book collection, this library was inaugurated in 1780.

On the right, take the Charlottenstrasse to rejoin the Gendarmenmarkt.

* **Gendarmenmarkt** – In this square, the Schauspielhaus, an elegant theatre built by Schinkel in 1821, is bounded on the south side by the German cathedral (Deutscher Dom), and on the north by the French cathedral (Französischer Dom), both early 18C churches decorated by Karl Gontard during the reign of Frederick the Great.

St Hedwig's Cathedral – Situated behind the Opera House, this Catholic church (1747-1773) was modelled on the Pantheon in Rome by the architects Leguay and Boumann.

* **State Opera House (Deutsche Staatsoper)** – Built by Knobelsdorff between 1740 and 1743 on the site of the "Forum Fredericianum", the Opera House burnt down a century later. Langhans' reconstruction follows the original plans.

Humboldt University (U[1]) – The palace of Frederick II's brother, Prince Heinrich, built by Boumann in 1753, was transformed into a university in 1810. On the left side of the entrance, a statue of one of its founders, Wilhelm von Humboldt, faces that of his brother, the geographer Alexander von Humboldt, on the other. An **equestrian statue** of Frederick the Great stands in the centre of the avenue.

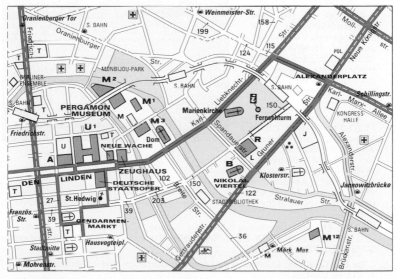

★ **New Guardhouse** (Neue Wache) – This small, exquisitely proportioned memorial, designed by Schinkel in 1818, is in the form of a temple with Doric columns. Wedged between two massive pillars, it was consecrated in 1960 as a Monument to the Victims of Fascism and Militarism.
A flame in their memory burns in the interior; two soldiers stand guard in front of the façade.

★★ **Arsenal** (Zeughaus) – Berlin's most important Baroque edifice, erected between 1695 and 1706.
Masks of dying warriors, sculpted by Andreas Schlüter, can be seen in the inner courtyard.

> *Crossing the branch of the River Spree here, you reach Museum Island (description below). Note, on the left, the imposing* **Protestant Cathedral** *(Dom) built at the beginning of this century.*
> *The promenade may be continued in the direction of the modern Alexanderplatz quarter.*

Alexanderplatz – The name derives from Tsar Alexander's visit to Berlin in 1805. Important public transport junction and immense commercial centre, the square acts as a focus of city life in the eastern sector of Berlin. **St Mary's Church** (Marienkirche) (end of the 14C: 15C Dance Macabre fresco in the tower; Baroque pulpit by Schlüter) looks flimsy indeed at the foot of the 365m - 1 198ft **Television Tower** (Fernsehturm).
The revolving sphere at the top of the tower houses a restaurant and a panoramic viewing platform.
South of the square, the **Town Hall** (Rathaus) **(R)**, built from 1861 to 1869 entirely of bricks, raises the red openwork of its tower 74m - 243ft above the surrounding roofs.

★ **St Nicholas Quarter** (Nikolaiviertel) – With its narrow cobbled streets and its old taverns, this quarter of restored period houses between the City Hall and the Spree seems like a country town transported to the heart of the city.
The quarter, which includes the Marx-Engels Forum and the Mühlendamm, is dominated by the Neo-Gothic bell-towers of **St Nicholas (B)**, the oldest church in Berlin.
The old Romanesque basilica, with its Gothic chancel (1379), was transformed into a brick-built Gothic hall-church after the great fire which ravaged the city in 1380. Inside, there is a **permanent exhibition** ⊘ from the March Museum *(see below)* outlining the history of Berlin from the city's foundation to the end of the Thirty Years War (models of Berlin and Cölln in 1440, weapons, jewels, domestic articles, manuscripts, letters patent). Polychrome statues in carved wood, gravestones and bells from the church (15C and 16C) can also be seen.

★★ MUSEUM ISLAND

Created at the instigation of Friedrich-Wilhelm III at the beginning of the 19C, this huge complex was the home until the last war of the fabulously rich collections of the National Museums of Berlin.

★★★ **Pergamon Museum** (Pergamon-Museum) ⊘ – The building, completed in 1930, is divided into five sections (we indicate, for each one, the main centres of interest; plan at the entrance).

– **Collection of Antiquities** (Antikensammlung): altar of Pergamon, a masterpiece of Hellenistic art, dedicated to Zeus (2C BC); richly ornate gateway to the Milet market (AD 2C); Greek and Roman sculptures.

– **Middle East Museum** (Vorderasiatisches Museum): processional way to the Gate of Ishtar in ancient Babylon, 580BC (Rooms 8 and 9); Plinth of Asachadon

The Babylonian Processional Way (detail) in the Pergamon Museum

(Room 3); brick façade of the Temple of the Goddess Irmin at Uruk (Sumerian period); bas-reliefs of the Temple of Assurnasirpal II at Kalchu, 9C BC (Rooms 10 and 11).

– **Islamic Museum** (Islamisches Museum): façade of Omayyade Castle, Mchatta (8C), 20 miles east of the Dead Sea; painted and lacquered panelling from a Syrian house (early 17C).

– **Far East Collection**: Chinese and Japanese porcelain and ceramics; statues of divinities, bronzes.

– **Museum of Popular Art** (Museum für Volkskunde): everyday life in working-class Berlin at the turn of the century.

* **National Gallery** (Alte Nationalgalerie) (M¹) ⊘ – This building (1867-1876), designed by Friedrich A Stüler *(qv)*, a pupil of Schinkel's, houses paintings and sculptures from the 19C and the first third of the 20C. Spacious canvases by **Adolf von Menzel** depicting life at the Court of Frederick II, but also the world of industry *(Iron Rolling Mill)*. The Prussian Army discovered its chronicler in **Franz Krüger** (paintings of parades). **Max Liebermann** distinguishes himself as a portraitist and observer of the life of the poor *(The Flax Weavers)*. The section exhibiting works from this century is rich in works from the Expressionist (Kokoschka) and Bauhaus (Schlemmer) schools. In the field of statuary, **Johann Gottfried Schadow** and **Christian Daniel Rauch** are especially to be noted. Here also are sculptures by Hildebrand, Kolbe *(The Dancer)*, Degas, Rodin and Maillol.

** **Bode Museum** (Bode-Museum) (M²) ⊘ – At the tip of Museum Island, the old Kaiser Friedrich Museum now houses five separate sections (see below for the most interesting exhibits in each).

– **Egyptian Museum** (Ägyptisches Museum): in the course of reorganization.

– **Collection of Byzantine and Pre-Christian Art** (Frühchristlich-byzantinische Sammlung): mosaic (6C) from San Michele Church, Ravenna; Coptic art.

– **Sculpture Collection** (Skulpturensammlung): Medieval religious sculpture (Naumburg Crucifix, 13C); Italian Renaissance sculpture.

– **Gallery of Paintings** (Gemäldegalerie): collections of works by Italian (Lippi), German (Cranach the Elder), Dutch Renaissance and Classical Age artists.

– **Numismatic Exhibition** (Münzkabinett): two halls trace the striking of coins at the Brandenburg mint from the 12C to the present day; a third is devoted to medals.

* **Old Museum** (Altes Museum) (M³) ⊘ – Berlin's first public museum, built by Schinkel between 1824 and 1830. The **colonnade** of the main façade (pleasure garden), 87m - 285ft long, is a masterpiece of Neo-Classical art. Inside, note particularly the frescoes decorating the cupola. The building, severely damaged during the war, was reconstructed between 1951 and 1966; today it exhibits mainly post-war works, and those from what was East Germany.
Ground floor (on the left): paintings from Eastern Europe (Poland, Hungary and the former USSR) and Italy (1920s and 30s). Behind: the Ludwig Aachen Collection, with important works by Renato Guttuso (*Wall Newspaper*, May 1968) and four heads by Picasso. Also on the ground floor: collection of prints and engravings and exhibition of drawings (*entrance on the Cathedral side*). Selection of treasures in reserve (15C-20C) in the study room.
The first floor is devoted to art from the ex-GDR. Works such as *Night Over Germany* by **Horst Strempel** or **Fritz Cremer's** study for a commemorative monument for Buchenwald express the engagement of artists in the struggle against Fascism and war. The paintings of **Willi Sitte**, often in the form of frescoes, use the workers' movement as their subject *(Leuna 1921)*. Waldemar Grzimek's sculpture *Futtermeister einer LPG (Farmers' Co-operative)* (1958) is typical of the Social Realism approach, which demands from the artist a moral stand in favour of the enlightenment brought by socialism.

* **TIERGARTEN QUARTER**

The oldest park in the city stretches almost 3km - 1 3/4 miles from Ernst-Reuter Square to the Brandenburg Gate. Originally a royal hunting reserve, it was transformed - thanks to the celebrated landscape architect Peter Joseph Lenné (1789-1866) - into a delightful park in the English style. The Hanse residential quarter (**FY**), a model of town-planning which lies to the north, was reconstructed in 1957 by 14 world-famous architects.

Victory Column (Siegessaule) (**FY C**) ⊘ – Sixty-seven metres - 222ft high, this landmark monument, surmounted by a Victory, commemorates the campaigns of 1864, 1866 and 1870. From the top (285 steps), there is an aerial **view★** of the Tiergarten, the Hanse complex, the Spree and the 12km - 7 1/2-mile perspective that extends to the shores of the Havel.

Bellevue Castle (Schloss Bellevue) (**FY**) – Built in the Neo-Classical style by Boumann in 1785, this was the summer palace of Frederick the Great's younger brother, Prince Augustus-Ferdinand. Today it is the official residence of the President of the Republic. The ground floor and first floor can be visited.
Behind the castle there is a 20ha - 50-acre park, the western sector laid out in the English fashion.

** **Zoological Gardens** (Zoologischer Garten) (**FY**) ⊘ – *Main entrance: Hardenbergplatz*. Situated in the heart of Berlin, this zoo, gathering together 16 000 creatures from more than 1 700 species, is one of the most important in the world. The **Aquarium** ⊘ (*entry via the zoo or directly from Budapester Strasse*) displays an important collection of approximately 650 species. The terrarium on the first floor is renowned for its crocodiles.

* **Museum of Decorative Arts** (Kunstgewerbemuseum) (**GY M⁴**) – *Tiergartenstrasse 6*.
This new three-storey building by the architect Rolf Gutbrod offers a broad survey of decorative art from the Middle Ages to contemporary industrial design.
Gallery I *(ground floor)* is devoted to the Middle Ages. Just inside the entrance, the Enger-Herford (Westphalia) **Treasure of Dionysius★** is displayed. This includes a remarkable reliquary-purse encrusted with precious stones (second half of the 8C). In the centre of the gallery, the **Guelph Treasure★★** is displayed. The reliquary here is in the form of a Byzantine church with a dome (Cologne *c75*).

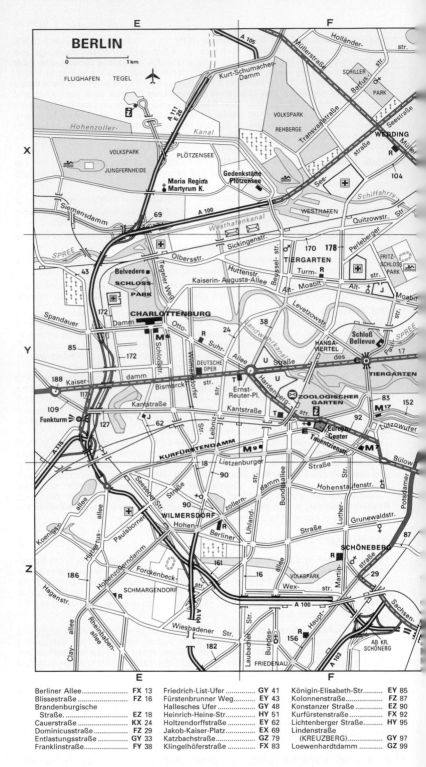

BERLIN

0   1 km

FLUGHAFEN TEGEL

It is thought to have held the head of St Gregory, brought back from Constantinople in 1173. The portable St Elbertus altar dates from the same period. The Guelph Cross (11C) almost certainly came from northern Italy.

Gallery II *(ground floor)*: Italian majolica from the 14C to the 16C, Venetian glassware from the 16C to the 17C; Gallery III *(ground floor)*: Lüneburg's **municipal plate★** (late Gothic and Renaissance) and jewellery from Nuremburg; Gallery IV *(first floor)*: the splendid **Pommern Cabinet★** and its contents (card games, draughts, measuring instruments, articles of toiletry from the 15C to the 17C); Gallery V *(first floor)*: porcelain from China and Germany (Meissen, Berlin), 17C and 18C, Chinese lacquer cabinets; Gallery VI *(first floor)*: Biedermeier glass, panelled glass from Wiesentheid Castle in Franconia (1724); Gallery VII *(first floor)*: porcelain, earthenware (glazed) and glass from the Jugendstil (Art Nouveau) and Art Deco periods. Galleries IX and X *(basement)* exhibit examples of industrial and domestic design from the 1920s to the present day.

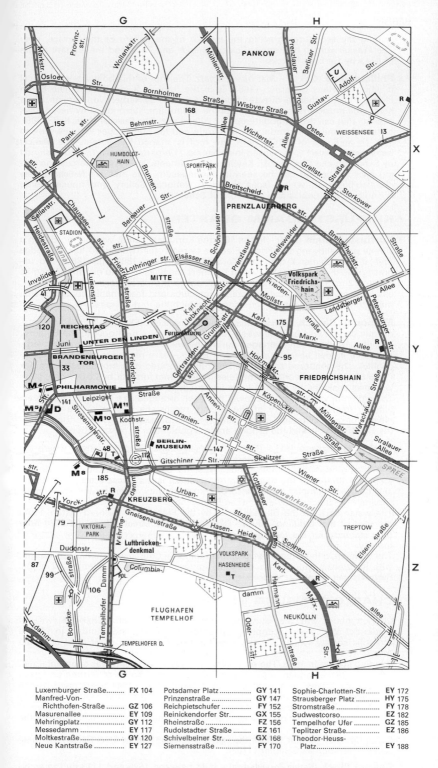

★ **New National Gallery** (Neue Nationalgalerie) **(GY M⁵)** ⊘ – *Potsdamer Strasse 50.*
This steel and glass structure, designed in 1968 by **Mies van der Rohe** *(qv)*, houses
paintings and sculptures from the 19C and 20C.
The collections include important work by the **Realists** (Leibl; *The Flute Concert*,
by Adolf von Menzel) and the **German Romantics** (Böcklin, Marées, Feuerbach). The
visitor can make interesting comparisons between the French Impressionists
(Manet, Pissarro, Monet, Renoir) and their German contemporaries (Liebermann,
Slevogt). The vivid and vital work of Lovis Corinth *(The Trojan Horse)* already
foresees the Expressionism of Beckmann, Nolde, Kokoschka *(Portrait of Adolf
Loos)* and the Brücke painters Kirchner, Schmidt Rottluff and Heckel. Modern
"classics" are represented by the **Bauhaus** painters (Schlemmer, Kandinsky),
Georges Grosz *(The Crutches of Society)*, **Paul Klee** *(Boats Leaving)* and the
Surrealist **Max Ernst**. Group Zero, the New Realists, and American painters provide
the high points of contemporary art.

Among the sculptures gracing the interior of the gallery or the terrace, note *The Washerwoman* by Renoir, Calder's *Heads and Tails*, and the elegant statue of *Maja* by Gerhard Marcks.

★★★ **Philharmonia** (GY) ⊘ – *Matthäikirchplatz*. The roof of this boldly asymmetrical building by Hans Scharoun (1963) is in the form of a giant wave. The Berlin Philharmonic Orchestra, directed from 1954 to 1989 by Herbert von Karajan, plays here – the musicians in the middle of the auditorium, surrounded by tiered rows of seats that can accommodate up to 2 200 people. The **Chamber Music Hall** (1988), built beside the Philharmonia by Scharoun and his pupil Edgar Wisniewski, can seat an audience of 1 150. Here, the roof is shaped like a tent. The **Musical Instruments Museum★** ⊘ is housed in an annexe *(Tiergartenstrasse 1)*, also designed by Scharoun and Wisniewski. Keyboard instruments, strings and percussion dating back to the 16C can be seen in this museum. The massive **National Library** (Staatsbibliothek), which faces the New National Gallery and houses some 3.7 million volumes, is also the work of Scharoun.

★ KURFÜRSTENDAMM QUARTER

★ **Kurfürstendamm** (EFY) – In the 16C, the Kurfürstendamm was no more than a simple path allowing the Prince Electors to reach the Grunewald hunting lodge *(qv)*. It was Bismarck who transformed it, between 1882 and 1886, into the prestigious thoroughfare known to Berliners today as the "Ku'damm". Along its 3.5km - 2-mile expanse, the boulevard unites the cafés, restaurants, theatres, cinemas, art galleries, luxury hotels, nightclubs and fashionable boutiques that make this area the centre of cosmopolitan high-life in the capital.

Memorial Church (Kaiser-Wilhelm-Gedächtniskirche) (FY E) – This Neo-Romanesque church was built between 1891 and 1895 as a memorial to the Emperor Wilhelm I. It was badly damaged during the war, but the ruins were preserved – and have indeed become a symbol of Berlin – as a reminder of the horrors of conflict. The shattered tower has been incorporated in a modernistic complex (1959-61) of pierced concrete modules in polygonal form, lit by 20 000 blue glass windows designed by Gabriel Loire and made in Chartres.
The old entrance beneath the tower has been arranged as a **Memorial Hall**. An exhibition traces the history of the church, recalls the victims of the war, and pleads for reconciliation. On the ceiling and walls, **mosaics★** (1906) to the glory of the Hohenzollerns and the Empire are in a good state of preservation.

Tauentzienstrasse (FY) – This is the fashionable shopping street where the "KaDeWe", said to be the largest department store in Europe, is situated. The abbreviation stands for Kaufhaus des Westens: Big Store of the West. Behind the Memorial Church at the beginning of the street is the **Europa-Center**, a shopping and business complex which also offers restaurants, cinemas and the famous cabaret "Die Stachelschweine" (The Porcupines).
The water-clock on the Blumenhof is by the Frenchman Bernard Gitton. From the roof of this building, 100m - 328ft above the street *(lift to the 20th floor then staircase for the last two storeys)* there is a fine **view★** over the centre of the city.
The fountain in the square between the Memorial Church and the Europa-Center, with its bronze sculptures and exotic figures, symbolizes the terrestrial globe. Berliners call it simply **"Wasserklops"**.

★★ CHARLOTTENBURG (EY) ⊘ *time: one day*

Charlottenburg was the favourite retreat of Queen Sophie-Charlotte, wife of Frederick I. With the philosopher-mathematician Leibniz she founded, in 1700, a scientific society which later became the Royal Academy of Science and Fine Arts.
Building started in 1695. The original castle was small, but it was soon enlarged, and a dome was added in 1710. The modern, gilded figure of fortune on top of this cupola serves as a weather-vane. Charlottenburg was abandoned by the King-Sergeant, but Frederick II had a new east wing (Neuer Flügel) added by Knobelsdorff, whose peristyled forefront was the sole decorative motif allowed the addition. Later, Queen Louise, the wife of Friedrich-Wilhelm III, lived in the castle.
In the Court of Honour stands the **equestrian statue★★ of the Great Elector**, the masterpiece of Andreas Schlüter (1703).

Central Block (Nering-Eosanderbau) – Built between 1695 and 1713 by the architects Arnold Nering and Eosander Göthe for Queen Sophie-Charlotte.

★ **Apartments of Frederick I and Sophie-Charlotte** (Historische Räume) **(1)** – *Guided tour: 1 hour*. The itinerary traverses several sombre galleries adorned with portraits of the Royal Family by **Antoine Pesne** (1683-1757), a French painter summoned to the Court by Frederick I, who remained its official portraitist for 46 years. Note particularly, in the apartments of Frederick I, his study, with the portrait of King Stanislas Leszcynski of Poland by Pesne. The room is decorated in red damask. See also the huge courtroom. In the apartments of Sophie-Charlotte, tapestries woven by Charles Vigne in Berlin and richly carved furniture (consoles, mirrors, fire screens with Chinese motifs) evoke the memory of the "Philosopher-Queen".

★★ **Porcelain Room (2)** – The visitor cannot fail to be impressed by the richness and beauty of the vases, figurines and plates on view here, most of them Chinese.

Charlottenburg

Chapel (3) – *Visible only during concerts*. Restored. Facing the altar, the enormous Royal baldaquin (canopy). Decorated pilasters frame medallions on the side walls.

1st Floor – Take the elegant staircase by Eosander Göthe. The salons on this floor contain several tapestries by Philippe Mercier of Berlin, views of the city by the painters Fechhelm and Gaertner, and large decorative vases. In the southeast arcade of the Oval Salon, a plate-glass window reveals the Insignia of the Prussian Crown (sceptres, globes) together with the swords of the Elector Princes (15C and 16C). To the north, there is a view over the park.

Knobelsdorff Wing – The eastern or new wing (Neuer Flügel) was built between 1740 and 1748 as a counterpart to the Orangery.

Summer Apartments (4) – *Ground floor*. The two Chinese rooms and the Etruscan room on the garden front were used by Friedrich-Wilhelm II. On the street side, Friedrich-Wilhelm III's apartments contain works dating from the Napoleonic Wars (Jacques Louis David: *Napoleon traversing the Great St Bernard Pass*; Ludwig Elsholz: scenes from the wars of liberation) in addition to Royal portraits and the death mask of Queen Louise.

★★ **Gallery of Romanticism** (Nationalgalerie) **(5)** – *Ground floor*. Works by the great Romantic painters of the early 19C can be seen to the right of the entrance hall. The collection of works by **Caspar David Friedrich** *(qv)* is the most significant in the world (23 canvases). Works such as *The Abbey in the Oak Forest*, *Woman at her Window*, or *The Watzmann* mark important stages in the development of this chief representative of German Romanticism. Important landscapes by the painter-architect **Karl Friedrich Schinkel** *(qv)* and by **Carl Blechen** can also be seen. One room is reserved for the Nazarenes (scenes from the Bible).
In the Biedermeier section *(restoration)* on the left of the entrance, pictures by **Carl Spitzweg** *(The Poor Poet)*, Moritz von Schwind and Ferdinand Georg Waldmüller are on display.

Royal Apartments and Banqueting Halls – *First floor*. The result of a collaboration between Knobelsdorff and the sculptor and interior decorator Johann August Nahl, these still present today the impact of "Frederician Rococo" manifested in equally grandiose style at Sans-Souci *(qv)*. The galleries exhibit masterpieces, essentially due to **French painters of the 18C★★**, collected by Frederick II.

Principal Apartment of Frederick II (6) – Some idea of the private life of a monarch can be gleaned from these rooms. A medallion portrait of the King himself hangs in the study. It was executed by Knobelsdorff.

CHARLOTTENBURG

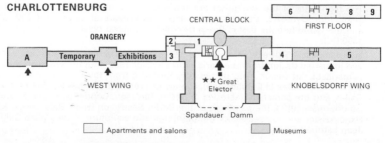

73

In the **library**, display cupboards contain works from Potsdam; in a glass case there is a selection from the King's priceless collection of snuffboxes. One room is embellished with Italian landscapes, another with Beauvais tapestries (cartoon motifs by François Boucher). In **Queen Louise's Bedroom** the pearwood sideboard for flowers and the bed itself were designed by Schinkel.

★ **White Room** (Weisser Saal) **(7)** – This huge salon in the central portion of the wing served as a banqueting hall and throne-room. The walls are clad with pink marble. The ceiling frescoes, painted by Hans Trier in 1973, express in abstract fashion the ethereal atmosphere of Pesne's original (destroyed) design: *The Marriage of Peleus and Thetis*.

★★ **Golden Gallery (8)** – In this superb example of Prussian Rococo, Knobelsdorff renounces the severe, purely architectural approach in favour of decoration.
The pink vaulting and spring green walls of the 42m - 138ft-long gallery recall the palette of Watteau, one of Frederick II's favourite painters. The Rococo ornamentation impresses above all in the gilded stucco surrounding the mirrors, along the walls and around the embrasures, above the doors and on the ceiling. Here, representations of cherubs, the elements and the four seasons are entwined with the decorative scrolls, garlands, foliage and cornucopia above.

Second Apartment of Frederick II (9) – The King appears to have had a preference for this series of rooms at the eastern extremity of the wing. It is here that the most remarkable examples of his collection of paintings are hung. **Watteau's** *Shop Sign* (painted for his friend, the art dealer Gersaint, in 1720) was acquired by Frederick the Great in 1745 to decorate the **concert hall**, where it remains today.
Also in the concert hall are two celebrated works by Jean-Baptiste Chardin: *The Letter Sealer* and *The Supplier (Die Köchin)*. The adjoining room contains one of Watteau's versions of the *Embarcation for Cythera* series.

West Wing (Orangerie) – This Orangery wing was built by Eosander Göthe between 1701 and 1707. The theatre at the far end is later. It was built by Langhans (1788-91).

Museum of Pre- and Proto-History (Museum für Vor- und Frühgeschichte) **(A)** – Dioramas and exhibits from archaeological digs evoke the pre- and proto-history of Europe and Asia Minor. The history of what was to become Brandenburg is particularly rich in artefacts. Famous dig by Schliemann at Troy.

★ **Park** (Schlosspark) **(EY)** – Landscaped in the English fashion under Friedrich-Wilhelm II, this green space is an oasis of tranquillity amidst the bustle of the city. To the west, at the end of a yew and cypress walk, is a small mausoleum in the form of a temple, built in 1810 by Heinrich Gentz. It contains the tombs of Friedrich-Wilhelm III, Queen Louise, the Emperor Wilhelm I and Queen Augusta. The **Schinkel Pavilion** *(between the east end of the Knobelsdorff Wing and the castle bridge)* was built by Schinkel in 1824 as a personal residence for Friedrich-Wilhelm III. It is carried out in the Pompeian style very popular in Berlin at that time. Almost all the interior decoration was also designed by Schinkel. The pavilion is a splendid setting for the two biscuit porcelain statuettes of Queen Louise and her sister Frederika (1796) and Queen Louise of Prussia (1802), by **Johann Gottfried Schadow**.
North of the lake, in the direction of the Spree, is a **Belvedere** designed by Langhans. It houses an **historic exhibition★** of the Royal Berlin Porcelain Manufactory founded in 1751 (Rococo tableware). Start the tour on the 3rd floor - view of the castle.

Auxiliary Buildings (EY M⁶) – The two blocks facing the Court of Honour, built by Stüler between 1851 and 1859, once lodged the Royal bodyguards. The building which adjoins the south side of the left-hand pavilion (1893) was once an infantry barracks.

★ **Museum of Antiquities** (Antikenmuseum) ⊙ – Ceramics, bronzes, weapons and the usual artefacts from Crete, Greece and the Etruscan regions.
The treasury (in the basement) contains a fabulous collection of antique **objects in gold and silver★★★**: thousand-year-old gems from the Mediterranean basin, superbly engraved Scythian jewellery (including a gold fish weighing more than 600gm - 1.3lbs), the fantastic Roman silverware unearthed near Hildesheim in 1868, extraordinary portraits painted on wood found with Egyptian mummies at the time when the country was a Roman colony, a multicoloured cameo depicting the triumph of Hadrian, insignia of Roman legionnaires, etc.

★ **Egyptian Museum** (Ägyptisches Museum) ⊙ – The collections here retrace, in the main, the historical and artistic evolution of Egypt in the time of the Pharaohs: bronze statuettes, terracotta vases, musical instruments, papyrus, jewels and tools, but also sarcophagi, pictures of mummies, masks and funeral offerings. The highlights of the exhibition are the impressive ebony head of the Queen Teje (18th Dynasty), the unusually expressive head of a priest (c300 BC), and the world-famous **Bust of Queen Nefertiti★★** (painted plaster over limestone - 1350 BC).

Bröhan Museum – This exhibition, based on a private collection, presents arts, crafts and industrial design from the Paris World Fair of 1889 until the nineteen-thirties (Jugendstil, Art Deco). Note particularly furniture from the French cabinet-makers in the twenties (J E Ruhlmann), the art of French glass makers (Marinot and Gallé), and the porcelain (factories in Berlin, Meissen, Copenhagen and Sèvres). Do not miss, either, the paintings of the Berlin Secession (Hans Baluscheck, Karl Hagemeister and W Jaeckel) or the paintings and sculpture of the Polish Cubist, Jean Lambert-Rucki.

★★★ DAHLEM MUSEUMS (BV)

Before the tour it is advisable to procure a map of the museum at the entry.

★★ Paintings Gallery (**Gemäldegalerie**) – *Entrance from Arnimallee. The Department occupies two floors in the right wing and one in the left wing of the old building* This important collection gives an overall view of European painting from its beginning in the 13C to the 18C.

Ground Floor – All the schools, up to the end of the 16C, are represented.

The section devoted to **German painting** begins on the right with the 14C *Madonna of Glatz*, from the School of Bohemia (large gallery). In the side galleries, German Renaissance paintings are exhibited. Note especially: the portraits of Jakob Muffel and Jerome Holzschuher, two masterpieces from **Albrecht Dürer's** final period; the admirable portrait of the merchant *Georg Gisze* by **Hans Holbein the Younger**; the luminous *Rest During the Flight into Egypt* by Albrecht Altdorfer, founder of the Danube School; and *Portrait of the Wife of Doctor Johann Reuss* by Lucas Cranach the Elder.

The section on Dutch and Flemish Primitives includes: Van Eyck's celebrated *Virgin in Church*; the delicate *Portrait of a Young Girl* by Petrus Christus; **A Sturdy Man** by the Master of Flemalle, and his pupil Rogier van der Weyden's **Woman in a Wimple**. Equally remarkable are the tumultuously animated *Adoration of the Shepherds* by Hugo van der Goes, and the phantasmagoric figures peopling **Brueghel the Elder's** *Proverbs*. *St John the Baptist (Geertgen tot Sint Jans)*, and *St John at Patmos* by Hieronymus Bosch testify to the religious fervour experienced by the Dutch Primitives. Jean Fouquet represents French art of the 15C with his splendid *Portrait of Estienne Chevalier*.

The French School of the 18C is represented in another room, with Watteau's graceful *Dance*, Antoine Pesne's *Frederick the Great as Crown Prince* and *The Designer*, by Chardin.

On the left, at the entrance, magnificent **Italian works** from the 13C to the 16C. The Florentines include **Giotto's** *Entombment of Mary* and *Virgin with Choir of Angels* by **Botticelli**. The School of Padua (early Renaissance) is illustrated by Mantegna's moving *Virgin and Child Sleeping*. To be admired also are Raphael's *Colonna Madonna* and *Young Girl with a Basket of Fruit* by Titian.

1st Floor Flemish and Dutch painting of the 17C. In the Rubens Room *Portraits* (separate) *of a Genoese Couple* by Van Dyck and **Rubens'** own *Andromeda Chained to the Rock* are on display. Side galleries, on the right, exhibit landscape and genre paintings: *Man and Woman Beside a Pitcher of Wine* by Vermeer, Pieter de Hooch's *The Mother* and works by Van Goyen, Ruysdel and Jan Steen *(The Inn Garden)*. The *Portrait of Malle Babbe* by Frans Hals impresses by the force of character it reveals.

Two other rooms are devoted to **Rembrandt** and his studio, notably the master's *Portrait of Hendrickje Stoffel* and the splendid *Man with the Golden Helmet*. The strong impression of power emanating from this canvas derives from the contrast between the rich, warm gold of the helmet and the menacing expression of the face, half hidden in the obscurity.

On the staircase leading to the gallery: 17C and 18C French and Italian paintings; note first of all Georges de la Tour's *Peasant Couple Eating*. Here, too, are such masters of Baroque in the Italian style as Caravaggio and **Annibale Carracci**. The 18C School of Venice is represented by Tiepolo, Canaletto and Guardi (views of Venice).

Finally, the visitor can enjoy works by those two great masters of classical landscapes, the Frenchmen **Poussin** and **Claude Lorrain**.

★★ **Sculptures** – *Entrance in Lansstrasse.*

Masterpieces of Byzantine and European sculpture from the 3C to the 19C.

Exceptional works such as the 4C *Pyxidus of Berlin* in ivory, and the glass mosaic Christ of Mercy (12C) garnish the section of primitive Christian and Byzantine art.

German medieval statuary is represented by work that is equally exceptional, in particular wooden sculptures from Swabia, Franconia and the Upper Rhine: the *Ravensburg Virgin with Mantle*, the *St John group*, *The Virgin of Dangolsheim*. Two superb works by **Tilman Riemenschneider**, *The Four Evangelists* and *Choir of Angels*, show the artist at the height of his powers. French Gothic is represented by a life-size Virgin as the Queen of Heaven (14C).

The Italian Renaissance section contains figures typical of the Quattrocento; the gracious *Pazzi Madonna* by **Donatello**, terracotta Virgins by Luca and Andrea della Robbia, small bronzes from the studio of Giovanni Bologna. Baroque and Rococo sculpture is well represented, including statues by the German masters of the 18C: Martin Zurn's St Sebastian and St Florian; Feuchtmayer's Assumption.

★ **Department of Prints and Drawings** (Kupferstichkabinett) *Entrance from Arnimallee.*

More than 35 000 drawings and 380 000 prints, from the Middle Ages to the present day, make this one of the most important collections of graphics in the world.

Among the European old masters (14C-18C) are works by **Dürer, Botticelli, Rembrandt** and **Brueghel the Elder**. Goya, Daumier, Menzel, Kollwitz and Picasso among others represent the 19C and 20C. The collection includes manuscripts, miniatures and illuminations from the Middle Ages, incunabula and illustrated books from the 15C to the 20C, and books of studies, sketches and designs (Knobelsdorff). Works from the large reserve collection may be consulted in the reading room.

★★ Ethnographic Museum (Museum für Völkerkunde) – *Entrance on Lansstrasse.*
Important collections from all over the world.

Central America and South America – Stone sculptures and **steles** from the Mayan civilization (Cozumalhuapa, Guatemala); **sacred and secular Aztec statuary** (human sacrifice cup); anthropomorphic ceramics and pre-Inca cloths in multicoloured designs from Peru. The **Gold Room★** displays magnificent jewels and exquisitely engraved cult objects dating from the 7C BC to the AD 11C.

Oceania Section (Südsee) – Among exhibits assembled since the end of the 18C – many of them due to the expeditions of Captain Cook – note the **painted masks** and **wooden sculptures** from New Guinea, the **Oceanian boats**, and the magnificent ochre and red feathered cloak of the King of Hawaii *(1st floor).*

Africa, Southern Asia, the Far East – The most interesting objects in this collection include **terracottas** from Ife (Nigeria), **bronzes** from the ancient kingdom of Benin, and carved and painted wood from Bali.

★ Museum of Indian Art – *Lansstrasse entrance.*
Sculptured stone; miniatures.

★ Museum of Islamic Art – *Lansstrasse entrance.*
Silver-encrusted bronzes (Asia Minor).

★ Museum of Far-Eastern Art – *Lansstrasse entrance.*
Chinese, Japanese and Korean ceramics. Intriguing ceremonial axe in bronze (China, 12C BC).

★ German Folk Museum (Museum für Deutsche Volkskunde) – *Im Winkel 6-8.*
Household items in everyday use in the Germanic countries since the 16C.

Ground Floor – The diversity of wardrobes, chests, beds, chairs, etc., on display permits an interesting comparison of the ornamentation – much more florid, for example, in Bavaria and Austria than in the north of Germany. Initially embellished with sculptures and inscriptions, the furniture was later to be decorated with floral motifs, then religious or geometric designs (cupboard from Alfeld, 19C).
There is a great variety of **traditional costumes**, mainly for women. Pictures hung in the "Herrgottwinkel" (God's Corner) testify to the piety of everyday folk. One section shows a selection of kitchenware – utensils, china, pots and pans – in different materials (wood, copper, stoneware and porcelain).

First Floor – An evocation of domestic life in country districts before the Industrial Revolution: recipients for the conservation of foodstuffs, baking tins for bread, beaters of many colours, threshing and combing machines used in the weaving of linen, of great importance in rural areas until the middle of the 19C.

ADDITIONAL SIGHTS

Berlin Museum of Post and Telecommunications (Postmuseum Berlin) (FY M7)
⊘ – *An der Urania 15.*
Documents, models and uniforms trace the evolution of Berlin's postal service during the past three centuries. Vintage machinery, explanatory diagrams and graphs explain the introduction and function of telegraphy, the telephone, radio and television.

★ **Transport and Technical Museum** (Museum für Verkehr und Technik) (GZ M8) ⊘
– *Trebbinerstrasse 9.*
Numerous models and original examples trace the evolution of different forms of transport. On the first floor, the **Railway Section★★** – particularly well represented – includes a selection of locomotives, some of them dating back to the middle of the last century. Visitors may operate working models and experiment with optical and electrical demonstrations.

★ **Käthe-Kollwitz Museum** (FY M9) ⊘ – *Fasanenstrasse 24.*
A broad survey of the works of the talented graphic artist and sculptress Käthe Kollwitz (1867-1945), in which – to quote Romain Rolland – "the trials and tribulations of simple folk are reflected". Her series of engravings *The Revolt of the Weavers* (1893-1897) and *The War of the Peasants* (1903-1908), the wood engravings titled *War* (1922-1923) and *The Proletariat* (1925), as well as the self-portraits and the late lithographs labelled *Death*, all mark milestones in the Kollwitz career. Well-known posters from the 1920s such as *Never Again War (Nie wieder Krieg)* underline the artist's political and humanistic engagement. The sculptures are exhibited on the upper floor, among them the *Muttergruppe (Mother Group)* in bronze (1924-1937). Also on display is a large bronze seated statue of the artist herself, by Gustav Seitz (1957).

★ **Martin-Gropius Museum** (Martin-Gropius-Bau) (GY M10) ⊘ – *Stresemannstrasse 110.*
This building in the form of a cube (1881) was originally conceived by Martin Gropius and Heino Schmieden as a home for the Royal Museum of Decorative Arts. Its reconstruction, after heavy war damage, began in 1978. The Neo-Classical style shows the influence of Schinkel. The interior, with its majestic columned hall, is a living proof of the expertise of Prussian designers during the Founders' Period or Gründerzeit *(qv).* There are several museums in the building.

Berlin Gallery (Berlinische Galerie) – *First floor.* Paintings and sculptures by Berlin artists of the 1920s can be seen here. But the highlights of the collection as a whole, from the turn of the century to the start of the 1930s, consist of works by **The New Secession** (Arthur Segal), **The November Group** (Walter Kampmann), founded in 1919, and the **Dadaists** (Hanna Höh, *The Journalists*).

One room is devoted to the Russian Constructivist working in Berlin, Naum Gabo. Special attention is paid to paintings concerned with emigration (Felix Nussbaum, *Prisoners' Camp*). The accent is placed also on the art of the immediately post-war period, notably the work of Carl Hofer *(qv)*, and that of the circle of artists centred on the Rosen Gallery (Alexander Camaro, Hans Uhlmann). The years 1960-1980 are represented by the Critical Realists (Fred Thieler, Bernd Koberling), by the Junge Wilde (Young Savages), and by Wolf Vorstell (collages).

Jewish Section, Berlin Museum – *Second floor*. Collections illustrating the history of Berlin Jews until their persecution by the National Socialists. By the end of the 1920s, 170 000 Jews lived in Berlin and there were 100 synagogues in the city. Documents stored in the museum retrace the activities of numerous Jewish organizations. The **Judaica Collection** exhibits tombstones from the old Jewish cemetery at Spandau, together with numerous religious cult items, mainly from Poland and Germany (18C and 19C): scrolls from the Torah, curtains, Sabbath lamps, Chanukka candelabra, Hawdala plates, etc.

"Topography of Terror" (Topographie des Terrors) ⊙ – Adjacent to the Gropius building lies an area known as the **Prince Albrecht Zone** (after the old Prinz-Albrecht Strasse). From 1939 on, this was the Reich security and secret police centre, grouping together the headquarters of the SS, the Gestapo and the SD (Sicherheitsdienst: Security Service). In the 1980s, on what had been considered just a stretch of wasteland, the foundations of the centre's prison building were unearthed. They have been left exactly as they are, silent witness to a **"Topography of Terror"**. Beside them, a documentation bureau explains the Nazis' power structure, the persecution of their opponents and the planned extermination of the Jews.

In the middle of this district is **Viktoria Park**, the highest "natural" piece of ground (66m - 216ft) in the city. The hillock is surmounted Schinkel's monument to the "Wars of Liberation". There is a panoramic view of Berlin from the terrace.

Airlift Memorial (Luftbrückendenkmal) (**GZ**) – The three west-facing arcs of this structure symbolize the three air corridors still open to the Allies during the Berlin Blockade.

★ **Berlin Museum** (Berlin-Museum) (**GY**) ⊙ – The exterior portions of this one-time administration building have been restored in the original Baroque style. On the pediment, allegorical figures representing Justice and Misery surmount the Prussian coat of arms. The interior – which is modern – houses interesting collections tracing the city's history and describing life in Berlin from the 17C to the present day.

Water-colours and prints (**scenes of Berlin** life from the 17C and 18C) are displayed on the ground floor, along with an architect's model of the city in 1688 and examples of porcelain and glazed earthenware from the Royal Manufactory *(qv)*. The first floor is devoted to Berlin in the 19C and 20C. Note the huge (8m - 264ft) lithograph of the Unter den Linden. Middle-class interiors by Biedermeier *(qv)* demonstrate how comfort can be allied with elegance of form. A portrait gallery shows Berlin's famous industrialists (Borsig, Siemens), scientists (Wilhelm von Humboldt) and writers (Fontane). **Berlin humour** is not forgotten: drawings and sketches, mainly by Zille, satirically lampoon the various types of Berliner.

On the upper floor, sections on arts and crafts, on fashion, and on toys can be seen.

Berlin Wall Museum (Haus am Checkpoint Charlie) (**GY M11**) ⊙ – Documentation on the building of the Wall and attempts to cross it.

March Museum (Märkisches Museum) *(See plan of city centre M12)* ⊙ – History of Berlin and the Brandenburg March.

Friedrichshain Park (**HY**) – Rubble from the battle-scarred city has enabled two artificial hills to be constructed in this leisure space. Homely characters from German folklore surround the fountains playing in the "Fairy Basin" (Märchenbrunnen).

★ **Soviet Memorial** (Sowjetisches Ehrenmal) (**CU**) – This monument in Treptow Park was erected in memory of the Red Army soldiers who fell during the Battle of Berlin.

★ **Museum of Decorative Arts** (Kunstgewerbemuseum) (**DV M15**) ⊙ – *In Köpenick Castle (Castle Isle)*. A visit to this museum takes the visitor into the old-world provincial charm of the Köpenick suburb, southeast of the city centre and far from the hectic bustle of international tourism.

The museum is situated in a Baroque mansion built by the Dutch architect Rutger von Langerfeld. The **furniture** is specially interesting (chests, cabinets, writing desks and tables, many of them inlaid with marquetry: 16C-19C). Note also the **panelled room★** from Haldenstein Castle (Switzerland, 16C) and the **writing desk★** by David Roentger (Neuwied, 1779), on which the marquetry represents the Seven Liberal Arts of Frederick II.

The **Treasury★** *(ground floor, on the left)* contains Gisela's jewels: bracelets, brooches, pins, necklaces and rings of the Ottonian period, together with 16C gold plate and Baroque silverware. In the Heraldry Room *(second floor, on the right)* 18C porcelain – including Frederick II's breakfast service – is on display. In the room behind is the great **silver sideboard★** from the Knights' Room in the old Castle of Berlin (made by J Ludwigg and A Biller, the famous silversmiths of Augsburg, between 1695 and 1698). Beside this, a **cask** (Münzfass, 1719) decorated with 688 talers (old German coins) and 46 medals.

Grosser Müggelsee – *Leave by the Lindenstrasse* (**DV**). The largest of the Berlin lakes. From the terrace at the top of the tower: broad view of the surrounding lakes and woods.

★★ **Botanical Gardens** (Botanischer Garten) (**BV**) ⊘ – *Königin-Luise-Strasse 6-8*. Vegetation from the temperate zone of the northern hemisphere, planted out geographically from mountains to plains. Rare species (trees and shrubs) in the Arboretum.

Botanical Museum (Botanischer Museum) (**M14**) ⊘ – The museum shows the evolution of flora in all its diversity. In addition to the "useful" plants, there are specimens of decorative species (offerings) discovered in Ancient Egyptian tombs. At the entrance, there is a cutting from an 800-year-old Sequoia tree.

Brücke Museum (**BV M15**) ⊘ – *Bussardsteig 6*. Works from the Brücke, the most important school of German Expressionists.
The movement was founded in Dresden in 1905, by a group of students who wished to create an expressive art by the deformation of lines and the use of violent colours. In 1911, the group moved to Berlin, where it disbanded two years later. The greater part of the oil paintings, water-colours, sculptures and drawings on display is the work of **Karl Schmidt-Rottluff** and Erich Heckel. Max Pechstein, Otto Mueller, Ernst Ludwig Kirchner and Emil Nolde are also represented.

★ **Grunewald** (**AUV**) – A hunting reserve of the Prince-Electors in the 16C, this forest of oak, pine and silver birch covers an area of 3 100ha - 745 acres. Wild boar, stags and deer still roam freely here.
The Grunewald is bounded on the east by a chain of small lakes, interspersed with residential areas. Beside one of these lakes, the Lake of Grunewald, is the elegant **Grunewald Pavilion★** ("Haus zum gruenen Walde" – **BV M16**) ⊘, built in 1542 by Caspar Theyss for the Elector Prince Joachim II. The building overlooks a courtyard surrounded on three sides by outbuildings (**Jagdzeugmagazin**) and bordered by 100-year-old beech trees. All that remains of the Renaissance original is the two-storey front and a hexagonal staircase tower. Among the paintings on view, note the nine gripping scenes of The Passion from the studio of Lucas Cranach the Elder, as well as Flemish and Dutch work of the 17C (Jordaens, Jan Steen, *Portrait of Caesar* by Rubens).
The western boundary of the Grunewald abords the **Havel lake★**. Beside this runs the picturesque Havelchaussee road, which leads, a little further south, to the beaches of the **Wannsee★★** (**AV**), a favourite place for Berlin bathers in the summer.

★ **Peacock Island** (Pfaueninsel) (**AV**) – *Access by boat, leaving from the landing stage at the end of Nikolskoer Weg (service on demand)*.
Landscaped gardens studded with small, picturesque buildings offer a perfect example of late 18C taste on this isle on the Havel.
The **castle** ⊘ (1794-1797), left incomplete in accordance with the taste for false "ruins" at the beginning of the Romantic period, displays souvenirs of Queen Louise in a number of salons panelled and floored with exotic woods.

Radio Tower (Funkturm) (**EY**) ⊘ – This 138m - 453ft structure, known to Berliners as the "Clodhopper", is indissolubly linked to the city and has become its mascot. At a height of 125m - 410ft there is a viewing platform offering a **panorama★** of Berlin. At the foot of the tower is the **German Radio Museum** (Deutsches Rundfunk-Museum) ⊘, which traces the evolution of the medium since its inception.

★ **Olympic Stadium** (Olympia-Stadion) (**AU**) – From the top of the campanile (77m - 286ft) (access by lift) there is an overall view of the former 132ha-316-acre Reich Sports Centre. The stadium, built for the 1936 Olympic Games, was used for propaganda reasons by the Hitler regime.

Bauhaus Museum (Bauhaus-Archiv Museum für Gestaltung) (**FY M17**) ⊘ *Klingelhöfersstrasse 14*.
Constructed in 1979 after the original designs of **Walter Gropius**, the founder of the Bauhaus *(qv)*.
The Bauhaus School is known predominantly for its work in the field of architecture (Walter Gropius, Mies van der Rohe), but it exerted a strong influence too on the plastic arts; through the everyday objects it designed (furniture, the first tubular steel chairs by Marcel Breuer, tapestries, ceramics), it was the precursor of contemporary design. Attempting to make art a component of day to day life through the uses of technology, the Bauhaus called into question the traditional function of art itself.
In this museum, apart from industrial products and craftwork, one can see sculptures and paintings (including montages) by Schlemmer, Moholy-Nagy, Feininger, Kandinsky and Klee, as well as models, experimental typography for posters and adverts, and drawings from the Bauhaus school at Weimar.

Church of Maria Regina Martyrum (**EX**) – Built in 1963 by Hans Schädel and Friedrich Ebert as a memorial to the victims of National Socialism, this church is entered via a Ceremonial Courtyard whose sombre walls of grey basalt evoke captivity and death. One of them is embellished by the Stations of the Cross, by O H Hajek.
Passing below *The Woman of the Apocalypse*, a sculpture by F König, one reaches the crypt, which is almost completely in the dark: only the front wall emerges, with a warm golden tint. Beneath König's Pieta is engraved the epitaph: "To all the Martyrs refused a grave – to all the Martyrs whose graves are unknown." Go to the upper part of the church.

A soft light indirectly illuminates one part or another of an immense coloured fresco by Georg Meistermann, representing the passage of night (death, evil) into day (the Redemption). To the right of the altar, there is a Gothic Madonna dating from 1320.

Memorial (Gedenkstätte) **of Plötzensee** (FX) ⊘ – The prison of Plötzensee, where many political prisoners were incarcerated, became a memorial to the German Resistance to Nazism after one hundred victims were hanged there following the failed coup against Hitler on 20 July 1944. The execution chamber may still be seen.

Tegel Mansion (Humboldtschloss) (BT) ⊘ – *Abelheidallee 19-20*.
A 16C manor house transformed by Schinkel for Wilhelm von Humboldt into a small Neo-Classical mansion (1821-1824). Bas-reliefs on the four corner towers represent the gods of the four winds. Inside: sculptures from Antiquity and family souvenirs.

Spandau Citadel (Spandauer Zitadelle) (AU) ⊘ – The citadel was built in the second half of the 16C on the site of a medieval castle (12C) at the confluence of the Havel and the Spree. Right-angled bastions occupy the four corners of the square, brick-built keep – a break with tradition in comparison with the old, round bastions used until that time. Spandau is the sole example north of the Alps of this so-called "Italian" system of fortification. In the course of its turbulent history, the citadel has been assaulted successively by Swedish, Austrian, French, Russian and Prussian troops, but it is best known as a state prison.
A drawbridge leads to the gateway. Armorial bearings painted on the pediment represent the different provinces of Prussia.

Julius Tower (Juliusturm) – *Skirt the right hand side of the building*. Sole remnant of the original castle, this 32m - 105ft keep has become the emblem of Spandau. It was here, in 1874, that the authorities stored the 120 million marks in gold demanded from France as war reparations after the defeat of 1870. The entrance is guarded by an impressive system of bolts. Inside the tower, 145 steps lead to a lookout point with a panoramic view. The external walls on the southern side of the citadel are studded with Jewish gravestones bearing 13C and 14C Hebraic inscriptions. They were salvaged from the Spandau Jewish cemetery sacked in 1510. A **Museum of Local History** has been installed inside the citadel *(entrance via the footbridge)*.

★ **St Nicholas Church** (Nikolaïkirche) (AU) – This hall-church is one of the last Gothic buildings in brick to remain in Berlin. The piers support ribbed barrel vaulting over the naves and star vaults above the choir. The entrance to the north chapel in the polygonal choir is surmounted by a handsome **Crucifixion Group** (1540) in polychrome carved wood. The magnificent **Renaissance altar★** (painted limestone and stucco) was a gift from the military architect, Count Rochus de Lynar. The central panel represents The Last Supper. Above it is a striking version of The Last Judgement. On either side there are likenesses of the donor's family. Note the gilded Baroque pulpit, which is finely carved, and the **baptismal font** cast in bronze (1398).

EXCURSIONS

★★★ **Potsdam** – *19km - 12 miles to the west. See under Potsdam*.

Oranienburg ⊘ – 31km - 19 miles to the north by ⑨ *on the plan*.
The **Concentration Camp of Sachsenhausen** (Nationale Mahn-und-Gedenkstätte Sachsenhausen) dates from 1936. More than half the 200 000 victims imprisoned there perished. A museum traces the resistance of European peoples to Hitlerism. A tour of the camp *(follow the plan distributed at the entrance)* gives some idea of the implacable organization of the Nazi concentration system, whose cynical approach is exemplified by the slogan still above the entrance gates: "Arbeit macht frei" (Work brings Freedom).

★★ **Chorin Abbey** (Kloster Chorin) ⊘ – *58km - 36 miles to the northeast by the Bundesstrasse no 2* (DT).
Constructed from 1273 onward by the Cistercian monks of Lehnin *(qv)*, the ruins of this abbey convey a fairly precise picture of primitive Gothic building in brick. The church is designed on the basilica principle with three naves, each preceded by a pedimented façade.

★ **BERNKASTEL-KUES** Rhineland-Palatinate   Pop 7 200

Michelin map **412** E 17 - Local map see under MOSELLE VALLEY

Bernkastel-Kues is in fact two towns, one on each side of the Moselle, at the confluence of the main river and a stream which has gouged a ravine through the Hunsrück schist. This is a famous wine-growing area, gay and animated during the first week in September, when the Wine Festival is held. Apart from the wine, which may be tasted in many specialized cellars, the local delicacy is smoked eel from the Moselle.

The Vineyards – Bernkastel-Kues boasts the largest single vineyard in Germany, spread over the slopes flanking a wide **bend in the Moselle** (Moselschleife) and continuing as far as Graach and Zeltingen. The grapes – 95% of the Riesling variety – produce a dry white wine of which the most sought-after is the fruity Bernkasteler Doktor.

SIGHTS

★ **Market** – Colour-washed houses, most of them half-timbered, surround this small, sloping square in the middle of which is the 17C **St Michael Fountain** (Michaelsbrunnen).

St Nicholas' Hospice (Cusanusstift) ⊘ – *On the Kues side of the river.*
Founded in 1447 by **Cardinal Nicholas of Kues** (or Nikolaus Cusanus) (1401-1464), a humanist and theologian, the hospice was built to house people in need. The number of lodgers was restricted to a symbolic 33 – the age of Christ at his death – a tradition still respected today.
Admire the late Gothic cloister, the chapel with its fine 15C reredos, and the copy in bronze of the Cardinal's tombstone (the original is in Rome, at San Pietro in Vincoli). On the left, entering the chapel, note the fresco depicting The Last Judgement – and, on the right, **the tombstone of Clara Cryftz**, the prelate's sister.
The **library** houses almost 400 manuscripts and early printed works, in addition to astronomical instruments used by the founder.

EXCURSION

Landshut Castle (Burg Landshut) – *3km - 1 3/4 miles to the southeast.*
The castle, built on a rocky promontory, was from the 11C the property of the Archbishops of Trier. It has been in ruins ever since the War of the Orléans Succession *(qv)*. From the ruin there is a fine **panoramic view★★** over the bend in the Moselle, above which even the steepest slopes are planted with vines.

★★★ BLACK FOREST (SCHWARZWALD) Baden-Württemberg

Michelin map **413** folds 23, 34 and 35

The Black Forest, stretching for 170km - 106 miles from Karlsruhe to Basle, is separated from the Vosges by the subsided plain of the Rhine. The two ranges, facing one another across this consequence of the Alpine Fold, have much in common. Each is densely wooded; each rises from a crystalline base in the south, sloping gently towards the north, where the massif is covered by limestone beds; both drop steeply in the direction of the Rhine, less abruptly on the far side of the crests – to the Swabian plateaux of the Upper Neckar in one case, to the plateau of Lorraine on the other. Even the highest points of each range correspond: the Feldberg at 1 493m and the Grand Ballon at 1 424m (4 899ft and 4 674ft respectively).
Unlike the Vosges, however, the Black Forest – the larger and denser of the two massifs – displays no marked north-south line of crests, and no coherent east-west arrangement of passes.
The economy of the region has always been linked to the **forest**, wood being practically the sole construction material and the base of all crafts. The trunks of trees, often 50m - 165ft long were floated away as far as the Netherlands, where they were much in demand by boat-builders. **Clock-making**, symbolized by the famous cuckoo clock, remains a fruitful activity.
Fruit farms and **vineyards** are cultivated on the foothills along the western limits of the forest.

Northern Black Forest – Drained by the Murg, the Nagold and the two Enz rivers, this sandstone area is almost entirely covered by conifers. The contrast, within a few miles, between the upper parts of the Grinde moors and the orchards and vineyards flourishing south of Baden-Baden, is remarkable.

Black Forest landscape.

Central Black Forest – The main axis of this region follows the valleys of the Kinzig and the Gutach – a gap through which the main road and rail arteries cut diagonally towards the Upper Danube and Lake Constance. The patchiness of the infertile sandstone topsoil is reflected in the forest's separation into groves, distanced by fields and pastureland. South of the Elz and Berg valleys, the Upper Black Forest, notably in the Feldberg region, forms a landscape that is almost Alpine in character.

Southern Black Forest – Gashed by the racing watercourses of the Wehra, the Alb and the Schlücht, the land drops progressively towards the Rhine. The climate, favourable to mountain cures, has led to the establishment of health resorts in the region.

★★ THE CREST ROAD (HOCHSTRASSE)

From Baden-Baden to Freudenstadt
80km – 50 miles - about 4 hours

Amply provided with viewpoints and car parks, the Black Forest Crest Road, the Hochstrasse, runs past many winter ski slopes with ski-lifts. Much of the route is at heights approaching 1 000m - 3 280ft.

★★ **Baden-Baden** – *See under Baden-Baden.*

Mummelsee – This small, dark glaciation lake is at the foot of the **Hornisgrinde** (1 163m - 3 816ft), the highest point of the Northern Black Forest.
At Ruhestein, the itinerary leaves the Crest Road temporarily to plunge towards the **Allerheiligen valley**★ and then climb back from Oppenau towards Zuflucht by way of an extremely steep mountain road.

★ **Allerheiligen** – The ruins of a late 13C church, built for a Premonstratensian monastery, add a romantic touch to this lonely dell. The vaulted porch and the walls of the transept are still standing, together with a polygonal Gothic chapel leading off them. A footpath leads from the ruins to the celebrated waterfall.

★ **Allerheiligen Waterfall** (Allerheiligen Wasserfälle) – *3/4 hour on foot Rtn from the car park at the foot of the falls (2km - 1 1/4 miles beyond the ruins).* A steep, stepped path climbs beside the torrent between rock walls overhung by huge trees.
From Zuflucht to Kniebis, the route crosses an upland plateau, most of it marshy moorland typical of the Grinde.

Freudenstadt – At the crossing of several routes, the town, built in the 17C by order of the Duke of Württemberg, was destroyed by fire in 1945. Rebuilt since the war, it now follows a checkerboard plan centred on the **Marktplatz**★, a huge square surrounded by houses with arcades.
The 17C **church** (Stadtkirche) is oddly placed: its two naves, arranged at right-angles, form one corner of the Marktplatz. The pulpit, supported by the four evangelists, and the carved 12C **lectern**★★, come from Alpirsbach, the most important Romanesque church in the Black Forest.

★★ CENTRAL BLACK FOREST

From Freudenstadt to Freiburg *152km - 94 miles - one day*

The itinerary follows the foot of the Kinzig and Elt valleys, passing through a number of busy villages before reaching the Upper Black Forest at Kandel.

★ **Alpirsbach** – The church, joined to the old **Benedictine abbey**★ buildings, has a 12C apse with unusual lines: the Romanesque lower floor supports a Gothic chancel in which the buttresses do not reach the floor but stand on free columns. Inside, at the apse's lower level, a hollowed-out niche – the central one out of three – bears traces of 12C **wall paintings**: Christ in Glory between the Chosen and the Damned on the vaulting; The Crucifixion on the hemispherical surface.
In the **cloisters** *(ring for the caretaker)*, the vault tracery and the bays, much restored, are in the Gothic Flamboyant style.

Gutach – The skills of the people of the Black Forest in matters of rural building, craftwork and agriculture are celebrated in the admirable **Black Forest Open-Air Museum**★★ (Vogtsbauernhof, Freilichtmuseum) in the Gutach valley. The Vogtsbauern farm, still in its original (1570) state, is surrounded by half a dozen reconstituted farmhouses with their outbuildings. At the **Hotzenwaldhaus**, replicas of a cowshed and interior furnishings are confined to an inner gallery to protect them from the weather. The **Hippenseppenhof** farm represents the commonest type, especially those found in the wilder upland valleys; its position on the slope allows farm carts direct access to the hayloft.
There is no trouble identifying the **Vogtsbauernhof** itself: the central portion is stone-built. Inside, note the timber roof framework, with the load-bearing beams set horizontally. Crafts connected with forest life are on display on the ground floor of the **Lorenzerhof** farm.
The road leading through the Landwassereck pass offers a number of fine **views**★ over the undulating landscapes of the Central Black Forest. Upstream from Oberprechtal, the beautiful cascades of the Elz border the route.

★ **Triberg** – This centre of the clockmaking industry is also a favourite health resort. The **Waterfall Walk**★ *(1 hour on foot Rtn)* follows the Gutach rapids in a natural setting of boulders and tall trees. The **Black Forest Museum** (Schwarzwald Museum) specializes in the exhibition of traditional costumes and local craftwork: watch and clockmaking, ceramics, wood veneers, etc.

The church, **Our Lady of the Firs** (Wallfahrtskirche Maria in der Tannen), one of the most popular pilgrims' sanctuaries in the Black Forest, displays carved and painted Baroque **furnishings**★ in an exuberant style that is wholly rustic.

Furtwangen – Cases and movements from all over the world, selected for their value, their artistic character or the ingeniousness of their conception are on display at the **Horological Museum** (Deutsches Uhrenmuseum) in this small clock-making town. Also on view are fantasy clocks, cuckoos, singing birds, wooden clocks and a reconstruction of a period watchmaker's workshop.

From the town it is only 6km - 3 3/4 miles to the **source of the Danube** (signposts "Katzensteig-Martinskapelle" and then "Donauquelle"), which feeds a tiny stream that ends its run 2 900km - 1 800 miles away when it flows into the Black Sea.

Soon after leaving Furtwangen, turn right for **Hexenloch**. Pass through a deep, steeply wooded gorge enlivened by many waterfalls. Between St Margen and St Peter, the twists and turns of the road allow plenty of clear **views**★★ of the Central Black Forest.

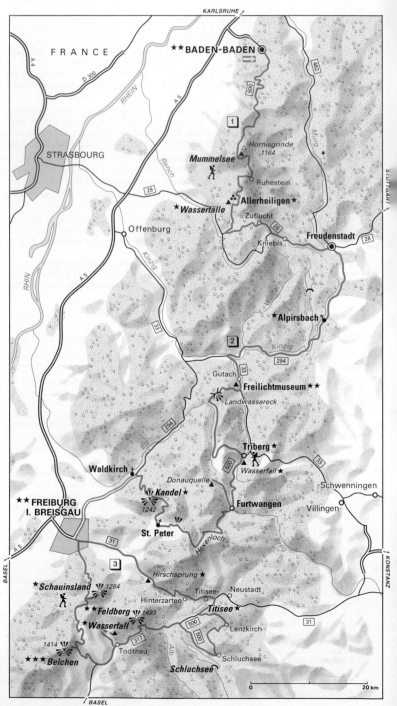

St Peter – A Baroque church attached to the huge **abbey** (1727) is the burial place of the Dukes of Zahringen, the founders of Freiburg-im-Breisgau (statues by the great sculptor J A Feuchtmayer). The extravagance of the Late Rococo style is exemplified in the high altar and the ceiling paintings. The elegant (restored) Baroque **library★** is decorated with delicate stuccowork.

★ **Kandel** – From the viewing table here *(1/2 hour Rtn on foot)* there is a splendid **panorama★** taking in the Vosges, the Feldberg, the Belchen, and the isolated Kaiserstuhl massif.

Waldkirch – Lovely 18C houses, once part of the chapter of canons, surround the former Collegiate Church of St Margaret in a tranquil, shady quarter of this small industrial town.

★★★ UPPER BLACK FOREST

Round tour leaving Freiburg-im-Breisgau *142km - 88 miles - one day*
This circuit, mountainous in the first part, passes the three principal summits of the Black Forest (Schauinsland, Belchen and Feldberg), and then the two best-known lakes (Schluchsee and Titisee) in the massif.

★ **Schauinsland** – The mountain road, extremely twisty, leads to the upper tele-feric station. From the car park, climb to the top of the belvedere tower *(91 steps)* after following the signs "Rundweg" and "Schauinsland Gipfel" *(1/2 hour Rtn on foot)*. The lookout point offers a **view★** across upland meadows to the Feldberg. Follow the road now for 1km – just over half a mile, and take the right-hand fork towards Stohen, and the Münstertal. Winding down through the meadows, the route finally plunges once more into the forest. At Wiedener Eck, turn right towards the Belchen.

★★★ **Belchen** – *From the end of the road, walk (1/2 hour Rtn) to the viewing table on the summit.* This rounded mountain with its steep, bare flanks, dominates the Wiesenthal and the valleys which, like the Münstertal, interlace the western fringe of the Black Forest. When visibility is good, it makes a magnificent **observation point★★★** from which to see the Rhine plain, the rounded heights of the High Vosges, and the Alps from Säntis to Mont Blanc. The Belchen summit is at a height of 1 414m   4 637ft.

★ **The Falls of Todtnau** – *1 1/2km - about 1 mile from Todtnau.* Climbing through a wooded combe, a footpath leads *(1 hour Rtn)* to an impressive series of cascades.

★★ **Feldberg** – A chairlift conveys sightseers to the Seebuck (1 448m - 4 750ft), which is crowned by the Bismarck monument. From here there is a **view★** of the symmetrically perfect, circular bowl of the Feldsee, a small lake at the bottom of a glaciated circus or amphitheatre. It is possible to reach the Feldberg summit at 1 493m - 4 897ft *(1 1/2 hours Rtn)*, to enjoy, again, a vast **panorama★★** stretching as far as the Alps.

Schluchsee – This lake, quite small to start with, has become - thanks to a dam - the most immense stretch of water in the Black Forest.
The Titisee is reached via Lenzkirch. During the final part of the descent, the road overlooks the lake.

★ **Titisee** – This pretty lake, formed by a moraine barrier, is at the junction of several tourist routes. Because of its position, it has developed both into a health centre (Titisee-Neustadt and Hinterzarten) and a departure point for many Black Forest excursions. The return to Freiburg *(qv)* is through the Höllental valley ("The Vale of Hell"), which - except perhaps in the **Hirschsprung Gorge★** - does nothing to justify its nickname.

★ **BONN** Rhineland-Westphalia   Pop 296 000

Michelin map **412** E 14
Plan of the conurbation in the current Michelin Red Guide Deutschland

This city is placed at a point where the Rhine flows out across Germany's great northern plain, at the foot of the Seven Mountains massif (Siebengebirge). The site has been inhabited since it was a camp for Roman legionaries, but it was not until the 16C that the town subsequently built there had any importance. At that time it became the fortified capital of the see of Cologne. In the 18C, the fortifications were transformed into a Baroque residence.
In 1949, what had grown into a peaceful, medium-size, riverside town was transformed again: Bonn was chosen as the "provisional" capital of the new West German Federal Republic – which gained it the nickname of Bundesdorf ("Federal Village"), but set it firmly on the road to civic advancement.
Bonn, whose status as German capital could never be more than provisional, has nevertheless for forty years fulfilled that role and become in the process a true seat of government – an administrative centre, some of whose institutions will still have a part to play in reunified Germany.
The whole town, including the Rhine and the surrounding countryside, can be seen from the **Atler Zoll (CZ)**. The **view★** of the river and the Seven Moutains (see below) is particularly attractive in late afternoon and early evening. From the foot of the bastion, riverside promenades beckon those with time for a leisurely stroll. (This is the departure point also for boat trips.)

BONN

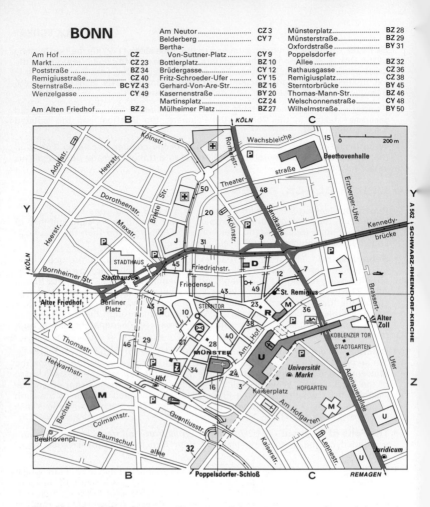

The Youth of Beethoven – Precursor of the great stream of romantic music, Ludwig van **Beethoven** (1770-1827) was born and grew up in the quarter around the **Church of St Remigius** (St Remigius-Kirche) (**CYZ**). At 13, Beethoven was already an accomplished musician, playing violin, viola and harpsichord in the orchestra attached to the brilliant Court of the Elector. When he was 22, a fervent admirer of Mozart and Haydn, he left Bonn for good, arriving in Vienna with only his virtuosity at the piano as an asset.

The **Beethovenhalle** (**CY**), a bold example of modern architecture, is the impressive setting for Bonn's biennial Beethoven Festival. The architect was Siegfried Wolske.

SIGHTS

Rhineland Museum (Rheinisches Landesmuseum) (**BZ M**) ⊘ – The history, culture and art of the Middle and Lower Rhinelands, from pre-history to the present day, is traced on the three floors of this building.

The **Prehistoric Section** *(1st floor)*, apart from the skull of the celebrated Neanderthal Man *(see under Düsseldorf: Excursions)*, shows interesting artefacts from the Stone and Bronze Ages and La Tène culture (weapons, metalwork, jewellery found in tumuli, etc.).

In the department of **Roman Antiquities★** (Römische Abteilung) *(also on the lst floor)*, note the **Altars to the Matrones**, a cult popular with Roman soldiers stationed in the Rhinelands. The fine votive stone (AD 164), discovered beneath Bonn Cathedral in 1928, clearly shows the distinguishing characteristic of these benevolent deities: a huge round headdress.

A masterpiece of Roman craft is the **Sun Mosaic** (*c*250 AD), which shows the Sun God in his chariot, surrounded by the circle of the Zodiac. Large **memorial stones**, such as that for Marcus Caelius found at Xanten (early 1C AD) and that for Firmus of Andernach (middle of 1C AD), illustrate the veneration of ancestors. Among the treasures of this particularly rich collection, admire also the delightful **bronze statuettes** (Venus, Diana, Hercules, etc.) and the **glassware**, often decorated with chased or spun motifs. Explanatory panels, illuminated illustrations and dioramas bring to life such facets of the Roman civilization as military service, building, water supply, traffic control and day-to-day existence in that period.

Pride of place in the **Frankish Section** *(2nd floor)* is reserved for a reconstruction of a chieftain's tomb (*c*600 AD). Gold pieces on display are decorated with serpents and the heads of birds. The two adjacent rooms are devoted to **medieval archaeology**. Among the exhibits are two 12C oakwood pirogues (canoes).

The section from the **Middle Ages to the Present Day** *(2nd floor)* displays arts and crafts from the Romanesque era to the 19C. Worth special attention: Romanesque sculpture (chancel parclose from Gustorf, 1130-1140); sculptures carved from wood; and above all the **Gothic paintings** (Master of the Life of St Ursula, Master of St Severin, Barthooomäus Bruyn the Elder, Derick Baegert, etc.). **Dutch painting** of the 16C and 17C is represented by Pieter Brueghel the Younger and Joos de Momper. Note also the selection of 19C views of the Rhine. The third floor galleries show art of the 20C. There is an interesting numismatic collection.

★ **Collegiate Church** (Münster) (BCZ) – This was originally a triple-aisle basilica, built on the site of a Roman necropolis. The present edifice – an excellent example of Late Rhineland Romanesque – was constructed after the fire of 1239.
Two rounded apses close off a transept surmounted by an octagonal tower. Tall, openwork flying buttresses support the nave. The eastern apse, flanked by two square towers, is circled by a miniature gallery topped by an upright gable.
Inside, the height of the nave at once proclaims a Gothic influence. The furnishing is essentially Baroque. Note the **lateral altars** at the entrance to the choir (1735), and the bronze statue of St Helen at the end of the nave. A fine Romanesque **cloister★**, the arcades supported by small columns, adjoins the southern part of the church.

Beethoven's Birthplace (Beethovenhaus) (CY D) ⊙ – Beethoven passed the first years of his childhood in this house in the old town. A genealogical tree of the family is displayed in the entrance. The bronze statue of the famous composer, at the foot of the small garden, is the work of N Aranson, a pupil of Rodin's.
The room in which Beethoven was born contains a simple marble bust. The larger room beside it houses souvenirs of the great man: a grand piano, an ear trumpet, a cast of his face at the age of 42. In the small rooms on the first floor one can see the organ on which Beethoven played when he was 10 years old, his violin, some original scores, a few pieces of furniture and mementoes of his friends, admirers and great interpreters.
In the house next door *(entrance two numbers further on)* are the Beethoven archives.

Town Hall (Rathaus) (CZ R) – A charming Rococo building (1738) with a pink and grey façade and a fine outside staircase with two flights.

Electors' Residence (Kurfürstliche Residenz) (CZ U) – The lawns of the Hofgarten park make a fine setting for this long Baroque building (1697-1725). Since 1818 the palace has housed the university.

Poppelsdorf Castle (Poppelsdorfer Schloss) (BZ) – The design of this building was entrusted to the French architect **Robert de Cotte**. It was built between 1715 and 1753. A splendid dual carriageway avenue, bordered by chestnut trees and divided by a broad grass strip (the **Poppelsdorfer Allee**, BZ 32), links it to the electoral castle.
The outer façade, with its three wings, reflects a classical French influence, while the inner courtyard, bordered by a semicircular colonnade, is more Italian in style. At the back, on level ground where a moat once flowed, are the university's **Botanical Gardens**.

Old Cemetery (Alter Friedhof) (BZ) – Artists, scholars and celebrities are buried here. One can visit the graves of Robert and Clara Schumann, Beethoven's mother, Ernst Moritz Arndt, August Wilhelm von Schlegel, and others.

THE OUTSKIRTS

★ **Schwarz-Rheindorf** – *Leave by the Kennedy bridge* (CY).
This **two-storey church★** in the Romanesque style was consecrated in 1151. The upper part, communicating directly with the palace, was reserved for the Elector and his immediate circle; the Archbishop's suite occupied the ground floor - where the walls are decorated with expressive frescoes illustrating the Book of Ezekiel.

Bad Godesberg – *Town plan in the current Michelin Red Guide Deutschland.*
With its comfortable villas and many parks (Redoute, Draitschbrunnen), this rich residential suburb south of the city is the seat of embassies, ministries and inter-national organizations. The **riverside walk** between the Rhine ferry landing-stages is very popular. The Petersberg Hotel and the Drachenfels ruins overlook the heavy flow of traffic on the river.
The ruins of **Godesburg Castle** ⊙, built in the 13C by the Prince-Electors of Cologne, stand on a basalt outcrop in the town centre. From the keep, there is a fine **panoramic view★** of Godesberg, the Bonn depression northwards as far as Cologne, and the Siebengebirge massif.

EXCURSIONS

★ **Siebengebirge** (The Seven Mountains) – This volcanic massif with an average height of 400m - 1 312ft rises opposite Bad Godesberg on the eastern bank of the Rhine. The whole range is classed as a national park with traffic circulation strictly controlled. Each of the seven summits, now heavily wooded, was once crowned by a castle. The slopes of the Siebengebirge form the most northerly point in Germany where vines are cultivated. The best known local wine is the Drachenblut (Dragon's Blood - *see below*).
At the foot of the range, bordering the Rhine, are the localities of **Bad Honnef-Rhöndorf** (house of Konrad Adenauer) and **Königswinter**, from where a funicular ⊙ rises to the jagged **Drachenfels★** ruins. It was here, so the legend has it, that Siegfried, the hero of the *Nibelungen (qv)*, slew the dragon and then bathed in its blood to render himself invulnerable.

From the terrace, near the ruins of the castle tower, the visitor can admire a vast **panorama**★★ comprising (from left to right) the Weserwald and Eifel plateaux, Bad Godesberg, Bonn, and finally Cologne.

Remagen – *23km - 14 miles to the south. Leave by the Adenauerallee* (**CZ**).
Passing Mehlem, one sees on the right the ivy-covered ruins of **Rolandsbogen**, and, on the left, the island of **Nonnenwerth**, linked to it by legend.
The origin of the small town of Remagen goes back to a Roman fortified camp. It became famous because of its **bridge** across the Rhine, which fell into American hands almost intact on 7 March 1945 – the first time they had been able to establish a bridgehead east of the river. Then days later, the bridge collapsed under the weight of armour. The remaining towers are today the site of a **Peace Museum** (Friedensmuseum) ⊘, tracing the history of the bridge and the battles of March 1945. In the town itself, see the **parish church**: its outer wall is furnished with **double Romanesque doors** – a carriage entrance and one for pedestrians. The reliefs which embellish the arches represent The Sirens and fantastic beasts.

★★ BREMEN Bremen   Pop 530 000

Michelin map **411** J 7
Town plan in the current Michelin Red Guide Deutschland and on Michelin map **411**

Bremen, at the inner end of the long Weser estuary, and Bremerhaven, its outer harbour 59km - 37 miles downstream, together form a remarkable port system. Bremen itself is Germany's oldest maritime city. It had market rights from 965; in 1358 it joined the Hanseatic League; in 1646 it was declared a Free Imperial city; and direct trading with America began as early as 1783. By tradition it is a cotton and coffee town, its Cotton Exchange ranks with Liverpool as a world authority. Bremen is also a town of culture, where the Weser Renaissance architectural style *(qv)* blossomed. For those interested in food, the city specialities are chicken ragout (Kükenragout), Vegesack herring (Vegesacker Matjeshering), and black pudding with cabbage (Braunkohl mit Pinkelwurst).

The Port ⊘ – It ranks second only to Hamburg in Germany and forty percent of the population works at the port. Bremen specializes in the importation of raw materials: timber, copper ore, wool, cotton, coffee, tobacco, cereals and cocoa. More than 10% of Germany's export trade (industrial and engineering products, cars, wine) is handled through Bremen.

OLD BREMEN *time: 2 1/2 hours*

★★ **Marktplatz** (**Z**) – The market square, its wide expanse surrounded by the finest buildings in the city, lies in the heart of the old town. The centre is marked by a giant 10m - 33ft **statue of Roland** beneath a Gothic canopy (1404). The knight bears the sword of justice and a shield adorned with the imperial eagle.
The **Schütting** (**A**), a restrained but elegant 16C building, formerly housed Bremen's Guild of Merchants. The decoration of its façade shows a Flemish influence.

★ **Town Hall** (**Rathaus**) (**Z R**) ⊘ – The main building is Gothic, its upper floors crowned by decorative gables – part of a 17C transformation made in the Weser Renaissance style. The three-storey principal façade rises from an arcaded gallery emphasized by a richly carved balustrade. Above this, tall windows alternate with statues of Charlemagne and the Seven Electors (copies: the Gothic originals are in the Focke Museum). Three Renaissance gables embellish the top floor.
At the corner of the west wing is a bronze group by the modern sculptor Gerhard Marcks representing the *Animal Musicians of Bremen* (a pyramid formed by an ass, a dog, a cat, and a cockerel) - characters from a popular fairy tale by the Brothers Grimm.

Interior – A splendid spiral **staircase**★★ (Treppe) in carved wood (1620) adorns the first floor Council Chamber. The room's Renaissance decoration recalls connections with the law courts *(The Judgement of Solomon)* and with the sea (models of boats). The **Guildhall** (Güldenkammer) - a small adjoining chamber renovated in 1905 - is noteworthy for its sumptuous leather wall hangings enriched with gold. *(It is open to groups of less than 12 people.)*
The Ratskeller (wine cellar) serves exclusively German wines from 600 different vineyards.

★ **Cathedral** (**St Petri-Dom**) (**Z**) – In general, the cathedral presents much the same massive appearance as it did in the 11C, but traces of the 16C and 19C rebuilding are clearly evident in the exterior detail.
Inside, against the first left-hand pillar of the raised chancel, stands a fine 16C **Virgin and Child**★. Among the 16C carvings on the organ balustrade can be seen, in the middle, the figures of Charlemagne and Willehad, the first Bishop of Bremen, who carries a small replica of the cathedral (16C). Beneath the organ loft, an 11C crypt houses Romanesque capitals and a magnificent bronze **baptismal font**★★ (Taufbecken - 13C).
At the end of the right-hand aisle, a gallery from the **Cathedral Museum** (Dom Museum) displays items recovered from tombs beneath the nave - in particular, medieval vestments and a priceless 13C bishop's crozier.

Church of Our Lady (**Liebfrauenkirche**) (**Z B**) – The bare interior of this church is relieved by 13C rounded ogive vaulting. The stained glass windows, on Biblical themes, were executed between 1966 and 1979 by Alfred Manessier.

BREMEN

Weigh-House (Stadtwaage) (Z D) – A lovely 16C building constructed with alternating layers of brick and embossed stone.

★ **Böttcherstrasse** (Z) – This narrow street, running from the Marktplatz to the river, was built between 1923 and 1933 by the industrialist Roselius, who had become wealthy through the marketing of a decaffeinated coffee. The tall, gabled, brick edifices, whose curious design was influenced by the Jugendstil (Art Nouveau) movement *(qv)*, house art galleries, museums, a theatre, bookshops and taverns. Between two of the gables, a porcelain carillon chimes at 12noon, 3pm and 6pm.

★ **Roselius (No 6) and Paula Becker-Modersohn (No 8) Houses (Z E)** ⊙ – Roselius House, an authentic 16C merchant's mansion, contains medieval furniture and items collected by Roselius, among them works by Cranach the Elder and a Pietà by Riemenschneider.
The small "Gothic Room" on the first floor is embellished with remarkable wood carvings (1430) from Wienhausen Abbey *(qv)* – on the right, The Visitation; at the far end, The Circumcision and The Annunciation. Hanging from the ceiling is an astonishing double figure by the Master of Osnabrück (1520): on one side, the Virgin in Majesty, on the other St Anne, the Virgin and Jesus.
Through a room displaying arms and armour, one arrives at the house of Paula Becker-Modersohn (1876-1907). Dedicated to the woman painter, who lived sometimes in Bremen but more often in Worpswede *(see below)*, the building was designed by Bernard Hoetger. Several of the painter's more important works are on view – canvases distinguished by simple forms, a hazy perspective and muted, refined colours.

Atlantis House (No 2) (Z F) – This 1931 block, decorated with the signs of the zodiac, has an unusual spiral staircase made of concrete and glass.
Not far from there, beyond the Martinistrasse, on the banks of the Weser, is the 13-14C **hall-church of St Martin** (St Martinikirche) ⊙.

ADDITIONAL SIGHTS

★ **Rampart Promenade (Wallanlagen) (YZ)** – The walk includes a delightful green belt where the ancient bastions used to be. There is also a working windmill.

★ **The Schnoor (Z)** – The cottages in this quarter, once the homes of fisherfolk, are all that remains of Old Bremen. In styles ranging from the 15C to the 19C, they have all been restored and are now used as art galleries, antique shops, restaurants and craft boutiques. The narrow streets of the quarter, popular with tourists, are very busy after dark.

★ **Art Gallery (Kunsthalle) (Z M¹)** ⊘ – An outstanding collection of 19C and 20C French and German art is the main attraction here. On display are works by: Courbet, Delacroix and the Barbizon School; Menzel, Leibl, Beckmann, the French Impressionists and their German counterparts, in particular Liebermann and Corinth; artists of the Worpswede School (below), notably Paula Becker-Modersohn and her husband Otto Modersohn. Earlier periods of European art are illustrated by 15C Old Masters, and by Rubens, Terborch, Rembrandt, Tiepolo, Maulbertsch, etc., up to Picasso.

Overseas Museum (Übersee-Museum) (Y M²) ⊘ – Well-displayed exhibits in this museum are devoted to Oceania, Japan, Southeast Asia, India, Africa, China and Australia. The best items, either original or in the form of scale models, relate to living conditions (a Papuan village, a Chinese house completely furnished), to occupations (fishing boats), and to customs and beliefs (legendary masks, effigies of ancestors, objects of worship). There is even a miniature Shinto temple and a Zen garden.
On the first floor there is a collection of masks from Black Africa. The second floor is concerned with the economic life of Bremen and in particular its port activities.

★★ **Focke Regional Museum (Focke-Museum) (Y M³)** ⊘ – Leave by the Rembertiring (Y). *See the plan of the conurbation.*
The quality of the exhibits here, and the spacious way they are laid out, make the visit particularly enjoyable.
In the main gallery, the power and wealth of Bremen in the Middle Ages and during the Renaissance are evoked through the original statues from the town hall façade, church furnishings, tableware and works of art from aristocratic houses. On the first floor *(staircase on the right, at the far end of the gallery)*, the 17C and 18C are illustrated by engraved goblets, portraits of merchants, stained glass windows, ceramics and the work of goldsmiths and silversmiths.

Return to the ground floor.

Two parallel galleries here are devoted, one to prehistoric, Roman and then Saxon antiquities from the Bremen region; the other to the local history of navigation and economic activities from the Middle Ages to the present day. Other examples of a city whose history is indissolubly linked with the sea include exhibits on whaling (harpoons, carved whalebone), on the transport of emigrants to the United States, on the famous steamers of the Norddeutscher Lloyd line, and on Bremen's shipbuilding yards.
A small tobacco museum recalls that the port has been one of Europe's major tobacco importers since the 17C. In the park outside, do not miss the typical Lower Saxony thatched farmhouse (Haus Mittelsbüren), with its barn (Tarmstedter Scheune) and well.

Riensberg House – *To the right of the lane leading to the Focke Museum.*
Once a farmhouse, this building was enlarged in 1768 for a noble family. Today it has been transformed into a museum showing mainly furniture from the 16C to the Jugendstil *(qv)* and 19C toys. One gallery is devoted to 19C women's fashions.

EXCURSION

Worpswede – *24km - 15 miles - about 1 1/2 hours. Leave Bremen by the Rembertiring* (Y).
Isolated at one time in a desolate landscape of peat moors, the village of Worpswede attracted at the end of the 19C a colony of artists, notable among whom were Paula Becker-Modersohn, her husband and the poet Rainer Maria Rilke. Since then, galleries, studios and craft workshops have mutliplied. Odd, asymmetrical buildings such as the Worpswede Café and the Niedersachsenstein First World War Memorial illustrate the avant-garde ideas and innovations of the architects allied to the group.

★ **BREMERHAVEN** Bremen   Pop 133 300

Michelin map ▥▥ I 6 - Town plan in the current Michelin Red Guide Deutschland

Bremerhaven, founded at the mouth of the Weser estuary in 1827, is Bremen's deep-sea port. The **Columbuskaje ship terminal**, once the home of transatlantic luxury liners, now handles ferries and cruise ships, while north of the town there is an immense specialized basin (Kaiser Wilhelm Container Terminal), protected from the tides, designed for the rapid turnaround of ore freighters and container ships. The **fishing port** (Fischereihafen), in the southern part of Bremerhaven, harbours half Germany's trawler fleet. Visit the famous fish auction, held in the Fischauktionshallen sheds from 7am, Mondays to Fridays.

★★★ **National Maritime Museum** (Deutsches Schiffahrtsmuseum) ⊙ – Facing the sea and designed by the architect Scharoun, this museum traces the history of the German merchant marine since olden times, and the navy since 1848. It was opened in 1975.

Basement – Liners after 1900; bridge and controls of the nuclear-powered ship Otto Hahn, built in 1968 (for reasons of security and of cost, the reactor has been replaced with a diesel unit); modern German port activities.

Ground floor – The age of the great sailing ships (from the 18C to 1918); different types of fishing; naval shipyards.

First floor – European fleets in antiquity (models); yachts and pleasure boats; navigation in the Elbe and Weser estuaries; cutaway display of a 1944 pocket submarine. At the back of the museum is a special chamber (Koggehalle) where a mixture of water and polyethylene-glycol assures the preservation of a medieval cog excavated in Bremen in 1962. This ancient craft, common in the Middle Ages, was able to serve the smallest of ports because of its shallow draught.
In the adjoining galleries: pre-12C German navigation; flat-bottomed Rhine skiff; Roman bireme; Viking drakkars; reconstitution, based on rock carvings, of the world's earliest ship (9 000 BC).

Wilhelm Bauer Submarine Museum (Technikmuseum U-Boot Wilhelm Bauer) ⊙ – Launched in January 1945, this submarine (U 2540) was scuttled on 4 May, shortly before the German capitulation. It was refloated in 1957 to serve as an experimental unit. A visit to the museum gives some idea of the technical complexity of a submarine as well as the life aboard one.

Open-Air Museum (Freilichtmuseum) ⊙ Six historic craft are preserved in the Old Port. Moored in the dock basin are: the sailing ship *Grönland*, which accompanied the first German polar (Arctic) expedition in 1868; the three-master *Seute Deern* (Germany's last wooden sailing ship, 1919); the lightship *Elbe III* (1909); the ocean-going tug *See-falke*; the small Antarctic whaler *Rau IX*; the high-speed patrol launch *Kranich*; and an experimental (1953) "sea spider" craft said to be a hydroplane prototype.

Deichpromenade – From the top of the breakwater (converted into a promenade) on the south side of the Geeste estuary, it is possible to see the mouth of the Weser and watch the cargo ships waiting their turn to pass up- or downstream.

North Sea Aquarium and Zoo Caves (Zoo am Meer mit Nordsee Aquarium) ⊙ – The aquarium makes a special feature of odible North Sea fish. Open-air grottoes in the zoo house bears, monkeys and seals.

EXCURSION

Cuxhaven – *39km - 24 miles to the north. Town plan in current Michelin Red Guide Deutschland.*
At the mouth of the Elbe, Cuxhaven is not only Germany's second fishing port but also a control point for navigation in the estuary and a seaside resort. There is an excellent **observation point★** on the **Alte Liebe** (Old Love) Pier (the name derives from a mispronunciation of Olivia – the name of a ship that sank close inshore in 1732, whose wreck was for a time used as a primitive landing stage). At the far end of the breakwater marking the geographic – if not the hydrographic – limits of the Elbe estuary stands the **Kugelbake**, a huge beacon no longer used but known to sailors the world over. From here there is a splendid **view★** of the river mouth and the open sea.
The **Wreck Museum** (Wrackmuseum) ⊙ displays – devoted to the techniques of lifesaving and salvage at sea – testify to the hazards of navigation in the dangerous waters off the Elbe and Weser estuaries.

★ **BRUCHSAL CASTLE** Baden-Württemberg

Michelin maps **412** and **413** I 19 - 17km - 11 miles north of Karlsruhe

Bruchsal, residence of the last four prince-bishops of Speyer, is blessed with a pretentious Baroque castle comprising something like 50 dwellings or annexes (reconstructed after the total destruction of 1945). Maximilian von Welsch was the architect of this vast complex, begun in 1720 on the orders of the Prince-Bishop Damian Hugo von Schönborn.

CASTLE (SCHLOSS) *time: 2 hours*

Central Block ⊙ – Pride of place here is held by a magnificent **staircase★★** with an oval well designed by Balthazar Neumann in 1731. Rococo stucco decorates the dome above it. The state apartments (**Regional Museum**) have items from the original furnishings on display. Apart from silver and porcelain tableware, portraits of the prelates can be seen and, above all, **tapestries** from the 16C to the 18C. These, fabricated in the renowned workshops of Holland and France (Beauvais), include a series representing scenes from ancient Greece.
At the west end of the castle's main block, the Gartensaal – a vaulted room with a marble floor – opens onto the **park** (Hofgarten). When they were at their best, blazing with formal flowerbeds in the French manner, the gardens boasted a broadwalk that extended as far as the river, ten miles away.

★★ Mechanical Musical Instruments Museum (Museum Mechanischer Musikinstrumente) ⊙ – *In the main building.*

This department of the Regional Museum derives from a private collection and includes about 200 instruments ranging from the 18C to the present day, most of them worked by cylinders, by pricked-out metal or cardboard, or rolls of paper. Cinema organs, "Barbary organs", and pianolas (mechanical pianos operated by perforated "piano-rolls") are also represented. Note particularly the "household" **organs** and **orchestrions** (in 19C England Aeolian Orchestrelles – machines resembling an oversize upright piano, complete with manual keyboard and stops for different "voices" – wind-operated by means of pedals). Orchestrions were often conceived as two-part instruments, imitating both piano and violin via their organ pipes. Before the arrival of the phonograph, such machines usually provided the music in taverns and at fairs. Examples from Leipzig and the Black Forest are well represented here.

Municipal Museum (Städtisches Museum) ⊙ – *Southern part of the main block, on the attic floor.* Apart from a palaeontology section and a collection of coins and medals (struck in Baden, the Palatinate and the see of Speyer), the museum houses a department of archaeology. Interesting exhibits include a finely-worked flint dagger (c1800 BC) from the centre of France, evidently brought this far north by way of trade, and 51 iron bars or rods excavated from riverside gravel beds - part of the cargo of a boat which foundered in the Rhine in the late La Tène period.

BRUNSWICK (BRAUNSCHWEIG) Lower Saxony   Pop 260 000

Michelin map **411** O 10
Town plan in the current Michelin Red Guide Deutschland

Brunswick's prosperity today is linked to the development of modern industries (electronics, optics, office equipment) and to the fact that the town is a centre of scientific research. The monuments to its illustrious past have nevertheless been restored.

HISTORICAL NOTES

The Lion of Brunswick – In 1166, having boosted the House of Guelph to the summit of political power in Germany, Henry the Lion, Duke of Bavaria and Saxony, settled permanently in Brunswick. Frederick Barbarossa, offended at Henry's meteoric rise, summoned him before the Diet. When "the Lion" refused to appear, he stripped him of everything except his personal properties between the Upper Weser and the Lower Elbe. Henry the Lion died in 1195.

Till Eulenspiegel Country – Memories of the famous jester and buffoon, Till Eulenspiegel, spread far and wide from the beginning of the 16C by storytellers and minstrels, are especially cherished in his native Brunswick. He was born c1300 in **Schöppenstedt**, 23km - 14 miles southeast of the city, where there is a small museum in his honour.

A Cultured Court – Brunswick ceased being a princely residence after the fall of Henry the Lion, but the Court was reinstated in 1753 by a younger branch of the House of Brunswick. In 1807, after its conquest by Napoleon, the region was added to the ephemeral kingdom of Westphalia. The young Stendhal (Henri Beyle) spent almost two years in Brunswick at this time, first as Commissioner for War, and subsequently as Steward of the Emperor's Domains.
Patrons of the arts were numbered among the later Brunswick princes: it was Karl II who invited Goethe to stage the first performance of *Faust* in the city in 1828.

SIGHTS

★ **Cathedral (Dom)** – The Westwerk *(qv)* supports two octagonal towers, linked the whole way up by a Gothic bell gable (1275) which acts as a campanile. This general design was later copied by other churches in the city.
The original Romanesque church built by Henry the Lion has groined vaulting with the weight reduced by sizeable cut-outs. The aisles were replaced in the Gothic period by four naves – those on the north side, in late or Flamboyant style, having spiral columns turned in alternate directions. The choir and transept are decorated with 13C painted murals. Note especially: the massive **candelabrum★** (Bronzeleuchter) in the choir; an impressive mid-12C **Christ Clothed★** by Imervard, in one of the north aisles; and, in the nave, the recumbent effigies of Henry the Lion and his second wife, Matilda of England, the daughter of Henry II Plantagenet. In the main crypt are the tombs of the Guelph princes.

Alstadtmarkt – One steps back in time when visiting this quarter, where the old municipal institutions of Brunswick's merchant quarter can be seen. The old **town hall** (Alstadtrathaus) is built with stepped gables, the two wings set at right angles to one another (13C-15C). The buttresses of buildings facing the square support statues of the Princes of Saxony and the House of Guelph. In the middle of the Poststrasse is the **Drapers' Hall** (Gewandhaus), the building with the town's most decorated gable (late Renaissance). Four principal floors rise above the street, and these are surmounted by four further pediment levels. The divisions of the gable are softened by inverted consoles, statuettes and globes topped by stone spikes.

St Martin's Church – Strongly influenced by the design of the cathedral, this was built in the mid-13C. In the 14C, the transept gables were adorned with statuary: on the north, the Resurrection of Christ in Glory, on the south, the Virgin, the Magi and the Saints. Inside, the first chapel on the south aisle (statues of St Anne and the Virgin) has a bronze Gothic baptismal font with a Baroque cover. St Martin, in the uniform of a 17C officer, rides on horseback at the foot of the pulpit.

Duke Anton-Ulrich Museum (Herzog Anton Ulrich-Museum) ⊙ – The painting gallery is mainly devoted to Flemish and Dutch Masters of the 17C: Rembrandt *(Family Portrait, Stormy Landscape)*, Rubens, Vermeer, Ruysdael. Worth attention also are the 16C German painters (Cranach, Holbein the Younger, Adam Elsheimer), and the 15C Italians (Palma Vecchio, Giorgione).
Works ranging from the time of Dürer to the present day are on display in a gallery of drawings and engravings (Kupferstichkabinett). A department of Baroque and Renaissance decorative arts completes the museum collections (furniture, bronze statuettes, ivories and watches in the first case; majolica and Limoges enamels in the second).

★ **Medieval Art Collection** (Abteilung mittelalter Kunst) ⊙ – This collection of church plate, on display in the ducal castle, includes a reliquary of the arm of St Blaise (patron saint of the cathedral and protector of the Guelphs), the imperial robes of King Otto IV, and the Gospels from St Evidius' Church.

EXCURSION

Königslutter am Elm – *20km - 12 miles to the east.*
On the fringe of the lovely beech forests of the Elm, Königslutter is renowned for its ancient **abbey**★ (Abteikirche). This is a Romanesque basilica with three naves and five apses, of which the principal is embellished with a fine, Lombard-inspired, **carved decoration**★★. The north doorway is original: it comprises three lobes upheld by twisted columns, each supported by a grimacing lion. The **cloister**★ north gallery consists of two Romanesque naves with groined vaulting resting on elaborate fluted, trellised and chevroned columns.

BÜCKEBURG Lower Saxony   Pop 19 400

Michelin maps **411** and **412** K 10 - 10km - 6 miles southeast of Minden

Bückeburg retains certain Renaissance buildings, traces of the period when the town was a princely seat. The Schaumburg-Lippe princes ruled, until 1918, over a small but extremely well administered state in the Bückeburg region.

Castle ⊙ – Before visiting the castle proper, visitors are advised to walk into the park, on the right of the state entrance. From here, across velvet lawns beyond the moat, a splendid example of German First Renaissance architecture is visible in the gabled **façade**★ with its semicircular pediments. The overall effect is majestic.
Pass through the early 17C monumental gateway then, to the main courtyard and beyond that to a small inner courtyard surrounded on three sides by a Renaissance balcony. This is the earliest (16C) part of the castle.
During the tour, visitors see a number of different reception rooms and the castle chapel, adorned with fine late Renaissance woodwork. An arcaded framework with decorative pediments supports the pulpit – placed, in accordance with Lutheran traditions, in the middle of the nave, facing the sumptuous Princes' Gallery.

Church (Stadtkirche) – This was one of the first great religious buildings to be designed expressly for the Lutheran sect (1615). The massive façade is symmetrically divided, in Renaissance style, by an alternation of cornices and vertical elements, but several features – the false bull's-eye windows, for example – hint already at the Baroque. There is a fine 17C font inside.

★ **Helicopter Museum** (Hubschraubermuseum) ⊙ – *Sableplatz.*
From Leonardo da Vinci to the present day, first in theory and then in practice, the evolution of this flight technique is illustrated by numerous models and no less than 40 actual helicopters. Some, like the BO-46, designed to fly at more than 400kmph - 249 miles per hour, have yet to go beyond the experimental stage.

EXCURSION

Mining Museum (Besucherbergwerk) ⊙ – *At Kleinenbremen, 3km - 1 3/4 miles to the south. Be sure to wear warm clothing.*
Worked from 1883 to 1982, this mine had produced a million tons of iron ore by 1952. Visitors go through enormous excavations, supported by huge pillars, before being shown the different systems of extraction which were utilized.

GREEN TOURIST GUIDES

Architecture, Art,
Picturesque routes,
Touring programmes
Town and site plans.

The town, whose centre still retains its medieval aspect, lies within a curve of the Salzach river, where it forms the frontier between Bavaria and Austria. Above the old town is the castle, built on a quite exceptional **site★★** – a long, narrow, rocky spur separating the Salzach from the Wöhrsee.

The Dukes of Bavaria, seigneurs since the 12C, made Burghausen into the biggest fortress in Germany: the defence system, reinforced at the beginning of the 16C in the face of a threatened invasion by the Turks, stretches for more than half a mile.

★★ **Castle** – *Allow about 2 1/2 hours walking and sightseeing.*

Leaving the car in the Stadtplatz, follow the road which circles the cliff at the southern extremity of the spur and pass beneath the **Wöhrenseeturm**. Beyond the lake, a steep path leads to the outer line of fortifications. From here, the ramparts stepped up the Eggenberg hill, on the far side, are visible. A wooden footbridge – fine view of the old town below, and the Salzach – carries the path across a moat to arrive at **St George's Gate** (Georgstor). This is set in the innermost ring of battlements, which protect the last small courtyard at the castle's centre.

The full strategic value of Burghausen becomes apparent: the lower town with its main square lined with brilliantly coloured house facades, onion-domed churches and the fortifications linking the castle with the Eggenberg, and, as far as the eye can see, the Salzach valley winding through the hills.

There are two museums in the main block.

Painting Gallery (Gemäldegalerie) ⊙ – The former ducal apartments (furniture from the 15C to the 17C) house an interesting collection of paintings from the Bavarian School. On the first floor are works by, among others, the Master of the Passion of Freising (c1500). Battle scenes painted by Hans Werl (c1600) are noteworthy on the second floor – especially a huge canvas depicting the Battle of Ampfing (1322), at which the Emperor Ludwig of Bavaria vanquished his rival Frederick the Handsome of Habsburg. From the observation **platform** *(62 steps higher up)*, there is a splendid panoramic **view★** of Burghausen, the Salzach and the surrounding hills.

The Gothic chapel (in the same wing) has elegant star vaulting.

Museum ⊙ – This is installed in the apartments once reserved for the Duchess (west side of the main block). The main exhibit traces the history of Burghausen. It includes a scale model of the town and castle in the 16C. Also on display are examples of local folk art, craftwork and peasant furniture.

Returning directly to the Stadtplatz via the **Burgsteig** *(a ramp between the castle entrance and St George's Gate)*, there is a particularly fine view of the old town: the onion-domed church towers rising above brilliantly coloured house facades are typical of the regions watered by the Inn and the Salzach.

It is also possible to reach the castle by car: there is a parking space on the flat area to the north of the spur.

EXCURSIONS

Marienberg – *4km - 2 1/2 miles to the south.*
Here there is a Rococo pilgrims' church (1764) almost square in plan. Inside, the dome over the central part of the building is adorned with a fresco painted by Martin Heigel: a boat (symbol of the Church) lies beneath the Holy Trinity, surrounded by celebrated members of the Founding Fathers.

★ **Raitenhaslach** – *6km - 3 1/2 miles to the south.*
Red marble tombstones enshrining the memory of abbots from the 15C to the 18C can be seen in this 12C Cistercian church, which was modified in the Baroque style in the late 17C. The life of St Bernard of Clairvaux is illustrated in the fine **ceiling paintings★** (1739) by Johannes Zick of Lachen, near Ottobeuren (1702-1762).

Tittmoning – *16km - 10 miles to the south.*
On the west bank of the Salzach, across the water from Austria, Tittmoning preserves the remains of its medieval fortifications and a castle which was once the residence of the Prince-Bishops of Salzburg. Two old fortified gateways give access to the wide **Main Square**, which is bordered by houses with ridge roofs masked by perpendicular copings *(qv)*. Brightly painted façades, some decorated with gilded figures, wrought iron signs, oriel windows and emblazoned fountains add considerable style to the ensemble.

Altötting – *21km - 13 miles to the northwest.*
This pilgrimage centre consecrated to the Virgin is one of the oldest in Bavaria and draws more than 700 000 people to the town each year. The Miraculous Virgin stands in a silver niche on the altar of the octagonal **Holy Chapel** (Heilige Kapelle).

In the Late Gothic **Parish Church** (Stiftskirche), there are two fine pieces in the Treasury (Schatzkammer): a splendid Flemish ivory crucifix dating from 1580, and a masterpiece of goldsmith's work (c1400) – a small gold horse given to Charles VI of France by his wife, Isabella of Bavaria, which he subsequently pledged against a loan from his brother-in-law, Ludwig the Bearded, Duke of Bavaria-Ingolstadt.

Johann Tzerklaes, Count of Tilly (1559-1632), a famous general on the side of the Catholic League in the Thirty Years War *(qv)*, is buried in the crypt *(entrance through the cloisters)*.

Michelin map **412** folds 2, 3 and 4

The **Wasserburgen** ⊙ – literally "water castles" – occur all over the Münster region. Witness to the incessant fighting between rival nobles in order to protect their territories, they are built on the sites of temporary encampments set up by the Teutons. They first appeared in the 12C in the form of wooden strongholds erected on artificial hills ("Motten") which were protected at the base by a surrounding stockade or defensive wall and a moat full of water. The invention of firearms at the beginning of the 16C made this system of defence precarious, and it was replaced, little by little, with proper fortifications isolated still more by moats or lagoons.

Many of these fortresses spread over two islands, joined by a bridge. The first isle, or "Vorburg", would be used for the outbuildings; the second, or "Hauptburg" for the dwelling. Subsequently, two separate influences could be detected in their design: that of the Weser Renaissance *(qv)* from the east, and that of the Dutch architectural school coming from the west. Their defensive character became less distinct over the centuries, and especially after the Thirty Years War (1618-1648). After that, virtual palaces set in formal gardens began to appear. In the 18C, a taste for the Baroque manifested itself in the treatment of façades and gateways. Such water-surrounded castles, situated in pleasant landscapes, fascinate still with their old-world charm. Descriptions of several of them are given below.

★ **Anholt** ⊙ – Surrounded by extensive English-style parkland, this moated castle (12-17C) is built around a square inner courtyard. Inside, note the Great Staircase in oak, the Knights' Room with its portrait gallery, a reception room adorned with Flemish tapestries, the Japanese and Chinese porcelains, and a second gallery displaying paintings mainly by the Dutch Old Masters.

Gemen ⊙ – The towers, battlements and buildings of this **castle** (15C, remodelled in the 17C) are grouped on a fortified islet which arises from beautiful, shaded stretches of water. The original keep was later crowned with a Baroque roof. Today, the castle is a youth centre.

★ **Hülshoff** ⊙ – The massive square towers of the outbuildings (first island) complement a **manor house** (second island) constructed in 1545. The brick and stonework manor is distinguished by gable ends and a turret with cupola and lantern. A neo-Gothic chapel was added in 1870. The poetess Annette von Droste-Hülshoff was born here in 1797 (small museum).

★ **Lembeck** ⊙ – The approach to this castle is impressive – a long perspective of driveway punctuated by a series of Baroque gateways and flanked by the arched entrances to various parts of the central complex. The monumental edifice spread over two islands today was built at the end of the 17C on the site of a 14C fortress. Huge towers with Baroque roofs stand at every corner. A few salons inside can be visited. The biggest (Grosser Saal) is embellished with fine panelling and stuccowork.

Raesfeld – Picturesque 17C brick outbuildings, including a small church, still surround this castle. The main block (1643-1658), reduced to two wings, is joined to a tower whose spire and onion dome together are as tall as the tower itself.

★ **Vischering** ⊙ – The two parts of the **castle** are on two separate islands, surrounded by a high wall in a setting that is truly delightful. The semicircular "Hauptburg" was built by the Bishop of Münster in 1271. Subsequent modifications (addition of a central tower in 1550, and an overhang on the south side in 1620) have not noticeably altered the characteristic blunt, stocky silhouette.

Carved chests and cupboards are among the furniture of the period on display in the interior. Note the handsome chimneypieces framed in faience and, in the main hall, the impressive beams.

Not far from Vischering, 8km - 5 miles southeast of Lündinghausen, is the 18C **Nordkirchen Castle**, known as "Westphalia's miniature Versailles". It is now a school of finance.

★ **Vornholz** – *See under Münster: Excursions.*

Michelin map **411** N 9
Town plan in the current Michelin Red Guide Deutschland

From 1378 to 1705, Celle was the official residence of the Lüneburg branch of the Dukes of Guelph *(qv)*, who had been banished from their original ducal seat by liberated burghers. With its carefully preserved centre of 16-18C half-timbered houses, Celle retains today the air of an aristocratic retreat.

The Three Ladies of Celle – **Eléonore d'Olbreuse**, a beautiful Huguenot from the old French province of Poitou, seduced Georg-Wilhelm, last of the Guelph Dukes to live in Celle, and became the town's chatelaine in 1676. As Duchess, she opened the Court to influences from her own country. The beautiful French-style garden (Französischer Garten) in the southern part of the town stands as her memorial.

Sophia-Dorothy, Eléonore's daughter (1666-1726), was married for reasons of state to her cousin, the future George I of England *(qv)* – a union which produced, first, George II, and subsequently a daughter who became the mother of Frederick the Great. Sophia's love affair with Count Philip of Königsmark was discovered, and she was banished for the rest of her life to Ahlden Castle.
From 1772 to 1775, a third doomed adventuress, **Caroline Matilda of England**, wife of the eccentric Christian VII of Denmark, expiated in Celle Castle her ill-advised affair with Struensee, the all-powerful minister and King's favourite. There is a monument to her in the French Garden.

★★ **OLD TOWN** *time: about 1 hour*

The half-timbered houses of Celle are distinguished by a superpositioning of crow-stepped gables.
Well-preserved buildings of this type can be seen in the Rabengasse, the Zöllnerstrasse and the Poststrasse (note the richly carved **Hoppenerhaus**, which dates from 1532). A recess widening the narrow Kalandgasse allows more space for the 1602 **old college** (Lateinschule), remarkable for the luxuriant ornamentation of its posts and wooden beams engraved with Biblical slogans.

Town Hall (Rathaus) – Roughcast in a pale colour, this building pleasingly blends several different Renaissance styles. The north gable, built in 1579 by craftsmen who came from the banks of the Weser, is heavily scrolled and bristles with fantastic pinnacles (The Weser Renaissance *qv*).

ADDITIONAL SIGHTS

Castle (Herzogschloss) ⊙ – This rectangular fortress, flanked by massive corner towers, boasts roofs in the shape of ribbed helmets. The eastern façade, overlooking the town, is designed with dormer windows topped by rounded pediments – a characteristic of the Weser Renaissance style.
The **Chapel★** (Hofkapelle) is Renaissance in origin; the ogive vaulting dates from the late 15C. The castle chapel was modified in the late 16C by the Flemish painter Martin de Vos, whose Crucifixion adorns the altar. With galleries that are both open and glassed-in, colourful frescoes, and curious decorations hanging from the ceiling, the chapel is a strange mixture. Nearby is the **Schlosstheater**, built in 1674 to an Italian design and said to be the oldest court theatre in Germany.

Bomann Museum ⊙ – *Schlossplatz*. Day to day life and traditional activities in Lower Saxony are illustrated in this museum. Among other interesting exhibits, there is a reconstruction of a typical farm interior (1571) of the Lüneburg heath. Craft items and goblets in silver and pewter represent Celle's former guilds.

Church (Stadtkirche) – This dark and originally Gothic church was considerably renovated in the Baroque style by Italian stucco-workers between 1676 and 1698. The remains of dukes from the Celle branch of the House of Guelph lie in the princes' vault beneath the chancel. The commemorative stones are above in the chancel itself.

EXCURSION

★ **Wienhausen Abbey (Kloster)** ⊙ – *10km - 6 miles to the south*.
This Cistercian abbey, founded in 1233 by Henry the Lion's daughter-in-law, has been occupied since the Reformation by a small community of Protestant canonesses. Among the piously preserved relics are a stone statue (1280) of the founder, and 13C wooden figures of the Virgin of Wienhausen and Christ Resurrected. The **Nuns' Choir** is embellished with fine early 14C **mural paintings**. During restoration work in 1953, a collection of trinkets was discovered beneath the floor of the choir – penknives, spectacles, small notebooks, etc., hidden there by the nuns five hundred years before to keep them from the hands of the Reformers *(the trinkets are on display in a small museum)*.
Once a year, for 11 days only, starting on the Friday after Whitsun, the Convent holds an exhibition of its famous tapestries, woven by the nuns in medieval times *(the museum is closed during this period)*.

Information in this Guide is based on data
provided at the time of going to press.
Improved facilities and changes in the cost of living
make alterations inevitable; we hope our readers will bear with us.

Michelin map **987** fold 27

Situated on the edge of the Erzgebirge mountain range (qv), Chemnitz has been an industrial town since the Middle Ages, when it became a centre of textile production – a role it still fills today. Since the early 19C it has also developed an important engineering and heavy industry sector. Between 1800 and 1900, the population increased from 10 000 to 200 000 inhabitants, the great majority of them belonging to the working class.

From Fritz Heckert to Karl Marx – With such a history, it is hardly surprising that Chemnitz became one of the most militant centres of the German workers' movement. Fritz Heckert, born in Chemnitz in 1884 and co-founder of the German Communist Party after the failed revolution of November 1918, was one of the driving forces behind this movement. From 1953 to 1990, the town was known as Karl-Marx-Stadt.

SIGHTS

Brückenstrasse – With the Avenue of Nations (Strasse der Nationen), which it crosses, this fine street is one of the two main arteries around which the new city centre was conceived. It is in this quarter that the impressive apartment blocks and such modern buildings as the Hotel Kongress, the Conference Palace (Kongresshalle) and the central post office can be found. The imposing **Karl Marx Monument** (12.5m - 40ft high), designed by Lew Kerbel in 1971, stands in front of a huge plaque bearing in several languages the last words of the Communist Manifesto: "Workers of the world, unite!" Returning in a southerly direction, the visitor passes a series of panels decorated with bas-reliefs illustrating the history of the workers' movement.

Old Town Hall (Altes Rathaus) – At the southern end of the Strasse der Nationen. Painstakingly rebuilt after 1945, this building has a fine Gothic façade, remodelled at the beginning of the 17C. There is a Renaissance doorway at the foot of the tower.

Natural History Museum (Museum für Naturkunde) ⊘ – The main exhibit here is a "Petrified Forest"★, part of it in the open air, formed by the trunks of trees geologically turned to stone some 250 million years ago. There is a collection of regional geology.

Fine Arts Museum (Städtische Kunstsammlungen) ⊘ – German painting of the 19C and 20C. One gallery is devoted to Karl Schmidt-Rottluf, born in Chemnitz in 1884 and a member from 1905 to 1913 of the Die Brücke movement (qv).

Castle Church (Schlosskirche) – Approach via the northern part of the Strasse der Nationen, then the Müllerstrasse on the left. Once part of a Benedictine abbey founded in 1136, this building was transformed into a hall-church at the beginning of the 16C. There is an elegantly carved Late Gothic doorway (now transferred to the interior, on the south wall). In the chancel is a moving painted wood **Flagellation Group**★ by Hans Witten (1515), that is more than 3m - 10ft high.

EXCURSION

★ **Augustusburg Castle** – 15km - 9 miles to the east, via Erdmannsdorf.
The Elector of Saxony Augustus I built this hunting lodge (c1570) on top of Schellenberg Hill (515m - 1 690ft). In the chapel, the high altar is adorned with a painting by Lucas Cranach the Younger (1571), showing the Elector surrounded by his 14 children.

The Museum of Game and Ornithology★ (Museum für Jagdtier und Vogelkunde) ⊘ presents the fauna of the nearby mountains in reconstitutions of their natural habitat. A series of paintings in the "Hasensaal" illustrate (16C) The War of the Hares against Mankind.
The castle also houses a **Motorcycle Museum**★★ (Motorradmuseum) ⊘ with an extensive display of different models, some of them rare and some highly original – the Megola of 1922, for instance, which had a rotary engine turning on its own axis attached to the front wheel. In the Brunnenhaus, a water pump powered by two oxen draws water from a well 130m - 427ft deep.

★ CHIEMSEE Bavaria

Michelin map **413** U 23 - Local map see under German ALPINE ROAD

Known as the "Bavarian Sea", the Chiemsee (pronounced Keem-zay) is the largest of the province's lakes, with a surface area of 82km - 32 square miles. Its calm waters lie between gently sloping, rush-covered banks on one side, and the foothills of the Bavarian Alps, clearly visible to the south, on the other. Two islands, not far from the west bank, are worth a visit. They are named the Herreninsel (gentlemen's isle) and Fraueninsel (ladies' isle). On the former is an extraordinary castle, which took Versailles for inspiration; on the latter, an abbey.
Summer resorts popular with water sports enthusiasts line the banks of the lake, in particular **Prien**, the busiest, and **Seebruck**.
The Salzburg-Munich motorway runs close to the Chiemsee's flat, marshy southern extremity, but it is from the northern bank, between Rimsting and Seebruck, that the most interesting vistas – with the Alpine peaks as a colourful backdrop – can be seen.

THE ISLANDS

From the motorway (Bernau exit), approach the lake from the west, and make for the **Prien-Stock landing-stage**. ⊙ *Allow 1/4 hour for the trip to the Herreninsel, 1/2 hour for the Fraueninsel.*

Herreninsel – The island, for the most part wooded, is famous for its castle.

★★ **Herrenchiemsee Castle** ⊙ – The young King Ludwig II of Bavaria bought the whole of this island in 1873 to save it from a systematic deforestation, but also because he wanted to build a sumptuous château there. His visit to Versailles in 1867 had greatly strengthened his admiration for Louis XIV, "the Sun King", and his Court; the castle on his island would be a replica of Versailles. Building started in 1878 and continued until 1886 – by which time 20 million marks had already been spent and the royal coffers were empty. The death of the King, who had spent only one week in the castle, put an end to the dream.

The ressemblance between the original and the copy is striking: the Latona fountain stands in the middle of formal gardens in the French style; the huge façade is adorned with columns and crowned by a flat roof with balustrade in the Italian style; the apartments include a State Room and a Hall of Mirrors, both of which are magnificent.

Fraueninsel – Although it is small, this islet boasts a charming fishing village and an ancient Benedictine monastery whose 13C church was rebuilt in the Gothic style in the 15C.

★ COBURG Bavaria   Pop 44 000

Michelin map ⬛ P 16 - Town plan in the current Michelin Red Guide Deutschland

The town centre, lying between the Marktplatz, the Church of St Maurice and Ehrenburg Castle, still bears the Renaissance imprint given to it *c*1600 by the Duke Johann Casimir, most enterprising of the Saxe-Coburg dynasty, which married into half the illustrious courts of Europe (Albert of Saxe-Coburg was the husband of Queen Victoria).

FORTRESS **(VESTE)** *time: 1 hour*

This complex, which can be seen from afar, is one of the largest fortresses in Germany with a double ring of fortified walls. The original castle dated from the 12C, but the present structure is 16C, the epoch of Johann Casimir. The buildings, with high roofs punctuated by dormer windows, enclose an inner garden.

Princes' Palace (Fürstenbau) ⊙ – This half-timbered structure holds memories of Luther, who visited the palace in 1530. Four paintings by Lucas Cranach the Elder adorn the Music Room in the Royal Apartments.

Art Collections (Kunstsammlungen) ⊙ – In the **central wing** (Karl-Edward-Bau), there is a display of hunting weapons from the 16C to the 20C on the ground floor, glassware on the first floor, and prints on the second. A collection of autographs and paintings by Lucas Cranach the Elder can be seen in the Luther Room (first floor) of the **Kemenate wing**.

On the ground floor of the **Duchess's Building** (Herzoginbau), there is an interesting vehicle museum, which includes a 17C marriage carriage and 17-18C tournament sledges. Decorative arts from the 16-20C occupy the first floor. Most impressive is a display of armour, in parade order, on the attic floor.

ADDITIONAL SIGHTS

★ **Casimir High-School (Gymnasium Casimirianum)** – Opposite the Church of St Maurice, this building, with its Baroque turret and lantern (1605), is the finest example of Renaissance civil architecture in Coburg.

Ehrenburg Castle ⊙ – Prince Albert spent his childhood here. The castle is a Renaissance building, remodelled in the 19C in the English neo-Gothic manner on the side facing the Schlossplatz.

The most original rooms are the Giants' Hall, heavy with Italian stuccowork, and the neo-Baroque Throne Room. Rich French tapestries can be seen in the Gobelins Room. Also in the Italian style are the intricately carved galleries in the Baroque chapel.

EXCURSION

Banz Abbey ⊙ – *26km - 16 miles to the south.*
Banz is the holy mountain of Franconia. In the 6C, the Franks, having subdued the tribes of Thuringia, settled in the region and introduced the Cult of St Denis, protector of the Merovingian dynasty. In 1120 Bishop Otto of Bamberg declared the martyr saint patron of this abbey.

The abbey church, completed in 1719 according to plans by Johann Dientzenhofer, has interior roofing of bewildering complexity. The principal dome breaks down into a series of niches that frame a central, tapering space; the wide supporting arches, themselves out of true and springing from keys, emphasize the virtuosity of this layout. The Baroque abbey towers, looking out over the valley of the Main, are balanced by the silhouette of **Vierzehnheiligen Church** *(qv)*, built on the opposite slope. There is a fine **view**★ from the terrace.

Michelin map **412** D 14 - E 14
Plan of the conurbation in the current Michelin Red Guide Deutschland and on
Michelin map **412**

Cologne is the capital of the Rhineland and one of the largest cities in Germany.
On the Rhine's west bank, the old town forms a semi-circle between the river and
the Ring – a curving, 6km – 3 1/2 miles avenue, much of it dual carriageway, that
follows the line of the city's 13C fortifications. Vestiges of these still remain at a
few points, notably the **Severinstor** and **Ulrepforte (FX)**. In the Middle Ages, 40 000
people lived within these walls, and Cologne was not only the biggest but also
the most densely populated city in the whole country. At that time the two main
thoroughfares were the **Hohe Strasse (GYZ)** (north-south) and the **Schildergasse (GZ)**
(east-west), both of them busy pedestrian precincts today. The more modern
quarters, developed after the destruction of the ramparts in 1881, lie in concentric circles outside this ancient nucleus. A double **Green Belt** lends space and
perspective to this outer urban area.

Many bridges link historic parts of the city with the industrial zones on the east
bank of the river. It is here that the **exhibitions** and **fairs** which draw so many busi-
nessmen to Cologne are held (the Photokina, a good-housekeeping exhibition and
a salon of confectionery, for example).

Cologne's principal industries are mechanical (automobiles, machine tools), pharmaceutical, chemical and petro-chemical – not forgetting the perfumery business,
with its famous Eau de Cologne. The principal manufacturer of this toilet water,
first elaborated in the early 18C by an Italian who settled in the city, is the cos-
metic firm Muelhens KG 4711.

The Rhine Riverside – The most impressive view of the old city and its skyline
can be found on the river's east bank, south of the Hohenzollern Bridge
(Hohenzollernbrücke), at the level of Kennedy Quay - or even from the Deutz
Bridge (Deutzer Brücke) **(FV)**. From these points the Rhine frontage, dominated
by the bold cathedral spires and the square, steepled belfry of St Martin-the-
Grand, is majestically attractive.

Cologne's cathedral quarter, seen from the east bank of the Rhine

HISTORICAL AND ARTISTIC NOTES

Cologne in Roman Times – Once the Roman legions had extended the Empire
as far as the Rhine, General Agrippa, the coloniser of the region, allowed the Ubii,
a Germanic people, to occupy (38 BC) the west bank of the river. The settlement
was named the *Oppidum Ubiorum*. Then, in the year AD 50, Agrippina, the third
wife of the Emperor Claudius and the mother of Nero, obtained for her birthplace
the official title of Roman Colony - *Colonia Claudia Ara Agrippinensium* (CCAA).
"Colonia's" first defensive walls were then built, and the town became the
residence of the Governor of Lower Germania. Roman ruins still exist: in the
(restored) Zeughausstrasse, at the North Gate of the town in front of the
Cathedral, and at the **Praetorium**, beneath the present town hall. From its official
recognition onwards, the town flourished: it was the start of an era, rich in craftwork, trade and architecture, which did not end until the time of the Great
Invasions, in the 5C.

The Holy City Beside the Rhine – Cologne's political power in the Middle Ages
derived from the Church. The bishopric founded by the Emperor Constantine in
the 4C was upgraded to an archbishopric by Charlemagne. Until the Battle of
Worringen in 1288, the Archbishops of Cologne exercised powers that were not
only spiritual but also temporal. Churches, of which the cathedral was one,
monasteries and collegiates rose rapidly – more than 150 in all.

In the 13C and at the beginning of the 14C, the city became the enlightened religious, intellectual and artistic centre of the Rhine Valley. Eminent men came to preach: the Dominicans **Albertus Magnus** (the teacher of Thomas Aquinas) and **Master Eckhart**, as well as the Scottish Franciscan, **Duns Scotus**. It was the work of such religious scholars that led in 1388 to the creation of Cologne university by local lay burghers.

Trade and Commerce – Because of its favoured position on the banks of the Rhine and at the crossroads of important trade routes, Cologne soon became a power in the commercial world, imposing its own system of weights and measures over the whole of northern Germany. Such authority derived from a decree known as the **Stapelrecht** (Law of Stockage), under which all foreign merchants passing through the city were obliged to keep their goods there for at least three days, thus allowing Cologne residents a prior right to purchase. The town's first fair was held in 1360. Its elevation to the status of Free City in 1475 did no more than set an official seal on the preponderant role the burghers of Cologne had in fact been playing since the 13C.

The School of Cologne – Manuscript illumination and the decoration of altars were already blossoming local arts in Cologne at the beginning of the 14C. Painting attained its summit in the first half of the 15C, with the works of **The Master of St Veronica** and **Stefan Lochner**, a native of Meersburg. From 1450 onwards, under the influence of the Dutch schools, the artists of Cologne abandoned the idealistic mysticism of the Gothic period in favour of the more gracious realism of the Renaissance (Master of the Life of The Virgin, Master of the Reredos of St Bartholomew). This later work is characterized by a delicacy of colour and a certain suavity in the treatment of subjects.

Sculpture – Religious sculpture in Cologne reached its high point between the 14C and the 15C. The many **Madonnas** on display underline a particular sentimentality of approach: more than one can be classed in the so-called "style of tenderness" sweeping Europe around 1400 – the hinted smile, a softness of drapery, a lissom stance, these all mark the distinguishing traits of such Virgins of the Late Gothic school.

MODERN CITY

Industrialization in the second half of the 19C conferred on Cologne an expansion that was both rapid and remarkable. After the Second World War, **Konrad Adenauer** continued the process of modernization he had inaugurated while he was Mayor of the city between 1917 and 1933 - the year in which he was deposed by the Nazis. It was through the man destined to become the Federal Republic's first Chancellor (qv) that the university, shut down under the French occupation in 1798, was re-opened (1919); that the Deutz Palace of Festivals was built; and that the green belts girdling the city were established. Much of the aspect of Cologne today is due to Adenauer.

War and Reconstruction – Between 1942 and 1945, continual air raids that were more than usually devastating destroyed 90% of the old town and 70% of the surrounding areas. Rebuilding of the city, under the direction of the architect **Rudolf Schwarz**, involved considerable modification of the original town plan, retaining at the same time the historic kernel at the heart of Cologne. A good example is the **Fest-und-Tanzhaus Gürzenich (GZ A)** – a municipal hall for fairs and balls which has been incorporated in the ruins of the Church of St Alban-the-Old. The restored Gothic façade hides an ultra-modern interior. A copy (E Mataré) of **The Afflicted Parents**, by Käthe Kollwitz, is displayed in the church ruins as a memorial to the victims of war.

Roman Catholicism – Reverential, yet sumptuous and enormously popular, the **Corpus Christi Procession** ("Gottestracht") is an indication each year of the importance and vitality of the Church in Cologne. First winding around the cathedral, the procession subsequently embarks in boats plying between Mülheim and St Cunibert (**FU**) on the Rhine. The city's many modern churches testify equally to the strength of faith today. The most influential figures in this renewal of sacred art are **Dominikus Böhm** (qv) and his son Gottfried.

Art and Culture – Diversity is the keyword in any consideration of cultural life in Cologne today. Apart from music and drama, the plastic arts hold pride of place: no less than 80 galleries are devoted to the exhibition of contemporary work. Every year since 1967, the city has promoted an international fair titled "Cologne Art". Beside the Schnütgen Museum, the **Josef-Haubrich-Halle (EV N)** mounts important permanent exhibitions.
Heinrich Böll, one of the most eminent representatives of post-war writing and winner of the Nobel Prize for Literature in 1972, was born in Cologne – and his work, sparing neither the Church nor society, is inseparable from his Rhineland birthplace.

The Carnival – The Rhinelander's gaiety and sense of fun is evident everyday in Cologne, but it is during the carnival season that this proverbial good humour reaches its apogee. Celebrations start on the Thursday before Ash Wednesday with the **Women's Carnival**, the participants outdoing one another to disrupt everyday life in the streets and shops and offices. Two days later, clownish processions organized by the schools and the various quarters of the city start to parade. It is in these **"Veedelzöch"** (a dialect word) that the survival of Cologne's Roman past is best preserved, for the origins of the carnival can be traced back to the Roman Saturnalia.

"Rose Monday" (the day before Shrove Tuesday) is when the fun is most furious, with public dancing, fanfares, elaborately decorated floats and a cavalcade of giants, each in its own way caricaturing or parodying some aspects of current news or views.

Town Life – If a sense of humour is characteristic of the city, conviviality is not far behind in the life of Cologne. This party spirit is inseparable from the **"Kölsch"** – a word standing at the same time for the local dialect and a famous beer, brewed in the region and served in huge stemmed glasses.

There is a strong sense of neighbourhood – almost rural – unity in the relationship linking the Cologne locals with their **"Veedeln"**: the traditional quarters of the old town, each centred on a Parish Church, each preserving its own traditions. St Severinus is the oldest and most typical (see below).

But in addition to their particular corner, all Cologne citizens appreciate that part of the old town bordering the Rhine. Remodelled in the 1980s, this is now, night and day, one of the liveliest parts of the city – especially the **Martinsviertel**, where, according to legend, the number of taverns by far surpassed the norm in medieval times.

Since the riverside highway has been diverted through tunnels between the Hohenzollern and Deutz bridges, land has been freed for the establishment of attractive **gardens** (Rheingarten) **(GYZ)** where the inhabitants can walk or relax in calm surroundings immediately above the water. **Boat excursions** leave from this point.

The **Dance Fountain** (Tanzbrunnen), situated in the 40ha - 100-acre **Rheinpark** on the far (eastern) side of the river, continues nevertheless to be very popular. The best way to get there is to take the **cable-car** (Rheinseilbahn), which runs from Easter until the end of October from a terminal near the zoo. Leave by the Konrad-Adenauer-Ufer **(FU)**.

CATHEDRAL QUARTER (GY) *time: one day*

The heart of Cologne beats in the immediate vicinity of the central station and the **Hohenzollernbrücke** – the busiest railway bridge in the world, with a train crossing it every two minutes, day and night.

Since the 1970s, road traffic has been banished from the surroundings of the cathedral, to the west and the south, to allow construction of the new Germano-Roman Museum (Römisch-Germanisches Museum) and the Diocesan Museum (Diözesan-Museum).

Once those were completed, the land between the cathedral and the river, for long used simply as a car park, was incorporated in the so-called **"Rhine-Cathedral Project"**. Since 1986 this has included the Wallraf-Richartz and Ludwig Museums, housed in a complex designed by P Busmann and G Haberer – a piece of modernistic architecture whose saw-tooth roofing blends harmoniously enough with the Gothic spires of the cathedral and the silhouette of the railway station. The project also embodies, at basement level, the **Philharmonia** auditorium. From the Heinrich-Böll-Platz, where the museums are located, a series of terraces leads down to the northern part of Rheingarten.

★★★ **Cathedral (Dom)** – It took more than 600 years to complete this gigantic edifice. In 1164, when Frederick Barbarossa donated **relics of the Magi** to the town of Cologne, an accelerating influx of pilgrims began, and by 1248 the need for a new and larger place of worship had become pressing. Thus began the construction of a new cathedral, the first Gothic church in the Rhineland, its original design based on those in Paris, Amiens and Rheims.

By 1320 the chancel was completed. Work on the south front tower, however, was stopped in 1437 – and that on the nave and transept in 1560.

More than three centuries elapsed before the gap in the building was to be filled: it was not until 1842, when neo-Gothic fever shook Romantic Germany, that work on the original plans was resumed. In 1880 the cathedral was at last ceremoniously consecrated in the presence of the Emperor Wilhelm I.

At first, the modern visitor is overwhelmed by the sheer size of the building and the profusion of its ornate decoration. The **twin-towered western façade** marks the peak of achievement in the style known as Flamboyant Gothic. Stepped windows, embellished gables, slender buttresses, burst upwards, ever upwards, slimly in line with the tapering spires that reach a height of 157m - 515ft. The apse facing the Rhine, spined with a multitude of turrets and pinnacles is a bravura expression of architectural prowess and enthusiasm. The **bronze doors (1)** in the south transept entrance (1948-53) are by Mataré (Celestial Jerusalem above; Cologne in flames on the right).

Entering the church by the west door, one appreciates the sweep of the nave in a single glance, but until the transept is reached, the building's colossal proportions cannot truly be taken in. The nave, as far as the choir, is 144m - 472ft long, 45m - 148ft wide, and 43.5m - 143ft high. Seen from the nave, the choir appears to float at some infinite distance, while the vaulting arched far above seems to reach a height that is completely unreal.

The five Late Gothic **stained glass windows★** in the north aisle (1507-08) depict the lives of The Virgin and St Peter. The south transept houses a large Flemish polyptych of 1520 known as **The Altarpiece of the Five Moors (2)** (Agilolphusaltar).

The 10C **Cross of Gero★** (Gerokreuz) **(3)**, a unique example of Ottonian art, hangs in the first northern chapel (Chapel of the Cross) off the ambulatory. Behind, in the Chapel of the Holy Sacrament, is **The Madonna of Milan**, a Virgin and Child in the local "tender" style.

*** **The Shrine of the Magi**
(Dreikönigenschrein) – This magnificent piece of medieval work is in a glass case behind the high altar. Intricately decorated with different characters, the reliquary is in the form of a basilica with unusual dimensions (2.20m - 7ft long). It was started by the goldsmith **Nicolas of Verdun** in 1181 and completed c1220 by the master craftsmen of Cologne. The altar itself dates from 1320.

In the axial Chapel of the Three Kings **(4)**, there are splendid 13C stained glass windows; the last chapel off the southern sector of the ambulatory (Mary's Chapel) contains the celebrated **altarpiece***** painted c1440 by **Stefan Lochner** and illustrating The Adoration of the Magi (centre section). Side panels portray the patron saints of the city of Cologne: St Ursula and her Virgins on the left; St Gereon on the right.

Choir ⊙ – The finely carved **choir stalls**★ (Chorgestühl), the most extensive medieval example in Germany, contain 104 places. High up above the stalls, on each of the chancel walls, frescoes represent symbolically the powers of Church and State. The 14 **statues** incorporated in the pillars of the chancel (Chorpfeilerstatuen) are of Jesus, Mary and the 12 Apostles.

CATHEDRAL

★ **Treasury** (Domschatzkammer) ⊙ – *Enter via the north transept.* The cathedral treasury contains gold and silver liturgical plate as well as ancient vestments, episcopal crosses and accoutrements, manuscripts, miniatures and swords of justice.

South Tower (Südturm) – A very steep stairway *(509 steps)* leads to a **platform** from which, at a height of 97m - 318ft, a splendid panorama of Cologne and the surrounding country can be enjoyed. Do not neglect the **belfry** (Glochenstube). The largest of the nine bells, **St Peter's Bell** (Petersglocke) was cast in 1923. At an overall weight of 24 tons (the clapper alone accounts for 800kg - 1 763lbs) this is the biggest swinging church bell in the world.

*** **Germano-Roman Museum** (Römisch-Germanisches Museum) (M¹) ⊙ – Capital of the Roman province known as Lower Germania, Cologne enjoyed an intense prosperity between the 1C and the middle of the 5C, due largely to fruitful exchanges between the civilization of the colonizers and the Germanic culture of the Ubii. In this museum, such evidence of the period as has been from time to time discovered is on display in the new site south of the cathedral. The exhibits are presented thematically, accompanied by audiovisual commentaries.

In the basement is the **Dionysius Mosaic**, uncovered here during excavations for an air-raid bunker in 1941. The work, measuring 10.5m x 7m (34ft x 23ft) was once the floor of the dining room in a Roman villa. Against a background of geometric motifs, colourful medallions depict lively scenes from the life of Dionysius, the god of wine, pleasure and fecundity. Adjacent rooms evoke day-to-day life in Roman times through the display of pottery, games, keys, sewing materials, tombstones and an astonishing swastika mosaic.

Overlooking the Dionysian mosaic is the **Mausoleum of Lucius Poblicius**, an officer of the Roman 5th Legion who lived in retirement in Cologne. The tomb, 14.5m - 47ft high, extends over several floors. It was originally erected (c50 AD) on the route linking Cologne with Bonn. The harmony of the monument's proportions is particularly noticeable on the upper storeys, where the ornamentation includes both mythological and vegetal motifs.

The different levels of the museum introduce the visitor to Roman statuary as well as architecture (fortified gateway inscribed with the abbreviated Roman name for the town: CCAA). There are also examples of transport (four-wheeled chariot), port activity (piles from a Rhine bridge), coinage, Roman religion, and games. Among the colonials' domestic decorations, the **Philosophers' Mosaic** is especially noteworthy. Amazing in its geometric composition, this villa floor represents the Seven Sages of Greece. Wealthy Romans did not hesitate to order such luxuries from abroad, witness the Pompeiian-style frescoes exhibited, and features in different colours of marble imported from Egypt.

Imagination pushed to the limits of fantasy informs the precious collection of **glassware**. Note especially the unique 4C vasa **diatreta** blown several times before being decorated with an outer tracery in coloured relief and a Greek inscription in purple. Vessels in the shape of animals and 2C **bottles decorated with coils** are also on view. Roman jewellery and "barbarian" ornaments in cloisonné enamel or engraved gold are of inestimable archaeological worth.

★★★ **Wallraf-Richartz Museum and Ludwig Museum** (M³) ⊘ – This double museum on the banks of the Rhine boasts sixty rooms – a complex including not only the Philharmonia but also a whole series of cultural institutions: a museum of photography (Agfa Foto-Historama, *see below*), a graphics collection, the Cologne cinémathèque, and a library.

Wallraf-Richartz Museum – *First floor.* Works by German, Italian, Flemish, Dutch and French painters from the 14C to the 19C are on display here. The very valuable **Medieval Painters of Cologne** collection, culminating with the Late Gothic work of Stefan Lochner and his contemporaries, is unique. Note in particular the **Master of St Veronica** with the early 15C triptych *The Holy Family*; the **Master of Life of the Virgin** with an Annunciation triptych and *The Vision of St Bernard* (late 15C); and **Stefan Lochner's** own **Virgin and the Rose Bush** (*c*1450) – a masterpiece which impresses not only by its use of colour, the delicacy of yellows and golds, but also by the serenity of expression on the faces.

Works by the **Italian Old Masters** Martini and Lorenzetti show the pan-European dimension of religious painting in the Middle Ages. Display panels with text and illustrations explain the techniques of medieval painting, the use of Illustrative themes in those times, and the history of Cologne.

Bartholomäus Bruyn the Elder (1493-1555) was one of the rare painters who took orders for portraits from private individuals. Influenced by the mannerists of Antwerp, he was much esteemed and sought after by the patrician burghers of Cologne. Note, in this gallery, the portraits of *Gerhard Pilgrim* and *Heinrich Salsburg*.

Among the **German Old Masters** on view are Dürer (*The Fife Player* and *The Tambourine Player*) and Lucas Cranach the Elder *(Virgin and Child)*. The 16C Italians are represented by Titian and Tintoretto.

Dutch and Flemish Painting of the 17C offer such great names as Rubens (*The Holy Family* and *The Stigmata of St Francis*), Ruysdael *(View of a River)*, Frans Hals *(The Fisherman's Daughter)* and **Rembrandt**, with the famous self-portrait in which the artist, already old, wearing a turban, regards the spectator obliquely, a smile on his lips. After this comes the section featuring 17C and 18C painters: Spanish (Murillo), Italian (Tiepolo, Bordone), and French (Boucher: *Young Girl Resting*; landscapes by Claude Lorrain).

French and German artists dominate the section devoted to the 19C. The German Romantics are represented by, among others, C D Friedrich; the Realists by the Cologne-born Wilhelm Leibl (Portrait of *H Pallenberg*). The German Impressionist school offers work by Liebermann, Corinth and Klinger. With the Romantic movement (Delacroix) as a point of departure, French painting advances via Realism (Courbet) to the Impressionists: Renoir, Monet, Sisley, Cézanne, Van Gogh *(The Railway Bridge)* and Gaugin. Sculptures by Degas and Rodin are also on display.

Ludwig Museum – First and second floor (modern classics); basement. There is an important collection of 20C art in this museum, with the **Expressionist** movement particularly well represented. Among the painters of the **Brücke** group, Kirchner is noteworthy with his *Five Women in the Street*, as are his associates Heckel and Nolde. The **Blauer Reiter** movement is represented by Macke, Marc, Kandinsky and Jawlensky; Expressionism by Kokoschka and Beckman. A separate section is reserved for art between the two World Wars: Constructivism, the Bauhaus, the New Objectivity, the Cologne Progressionists.

One of the museum's strong points is embodied in a collection of **Russian Avant-Garde Art** (1910-1930). Paintings and "spatial constructions" by Gontscharova, Larinov, Malevitz and Popova vividly convey the strength of the country's artistic renewal before the cultural freeze under Stalin.

The department devoted to the Surrealists reveals that the **Dada** movement was in fact born in Cologne, just before the First World War. Apart from oil paintings, gouaches and collages by Max Ernst *(Friend's Meeting)*, who was born in Brühl, near Cologne, exhibits include work by Hans Arp, Schwitters, Miro, Dali, Margritte and Paul Klee (with his late masterpiece *Main Roads and Minor Roads*).

French modern art is represented by Modigliani, Maillol *(The Slender Bathers)*, and above all the **Cubists** Braque, Léger, Delaunay and Juan Gris. A separate room contains paintings and sculpture by **Picasso**. Arman, Klein and Saint Phalle *(Nanas)* are there to illustrate "the new realism".

Paintings by Baumeister and Nay introduce the visitor to post-war German art and the "renewal" of the 1960s, in which **Beuys** and the Group Zero played an important part. American abstract painting is well represented, particularly **Pop Art** – oriented once more towards the object - which had its heyday in the United States in the 60s. Among the museum's latest acquisitions are paintings by Baselitz and Penck, as well as truly large-scale artistic compositions such as *The Black Town* by Anne and Patrick Poirier.

Prints and Drawings – *First floor.* Drawings (by, among others, Leonardo da Vinci, Raphael, Dürer, Rembrandt), miniatures, water-colours and prints from the end of the 11C to the beginning of the 20C.

★ **Museum of Photography** (Agfa Foto-Historama) ⊘ – *Ground floor and first floor.* Compiled from various private collections (the Stengler Collection, the archives of the Agfa company, etc.), these three galleries present an overall view of 150 years of photography.

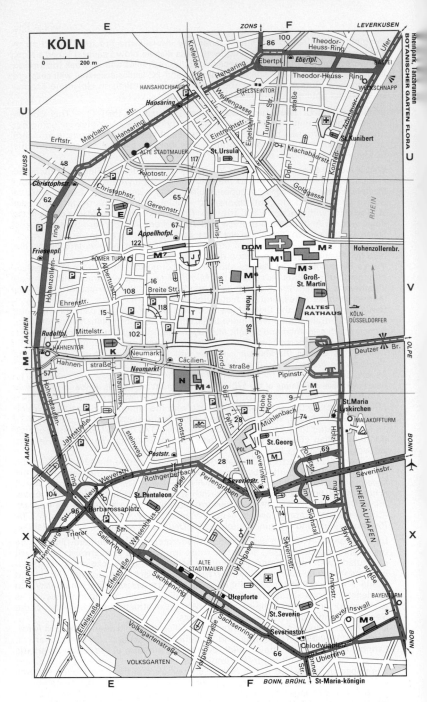

The impact of the displays derives from the juxtaposition of ancient exhibits and photographs of great historical or cultural value. Thus the history of photography can be followed through its various stages – magic lantern, Daguerrotype (1839), calotype (Talbot's negative process, 1841), amateur interest, spooled film (Eastman, 1888) – to the invention of microfilm and the small, high-tech cameras of today.

★ **Diocesan Museum** (Diözesan-Museum) (M³) ⊙ – Apart from rare religious objects (liturgical accessories, ecclesiastical vestments, chapelets, etc.), this small museum houses a collection, by no means minor, of sacred art in the Middle Ages – not least a series of statues once part of the cathedral décor.
The most famous piece is Stefan Lochner's **Virgin with Violets**, where each flower represents one of the virtues of Mary; the most priceless a length of Persian silk.
Discovered in the Shrine of St Cunibert, a 6C Bishop of Cologne, this piece of cloth dates from the era of the **Sassanians** (a Syrian dynasty reigning from the 3C to the 8C).
The weaving depicts a hunting scene, deployed with unique symmetry around a central palm tree.
Also on display are objects – including jewels set in gold – found in two Frankish tombs excavated beneath the chancel in 1959.

KÖLN

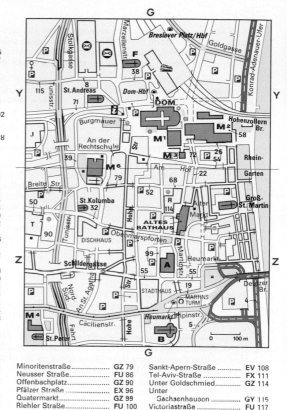

★ ROMANESQUE CHURCHES

The Romanesque period in Cologne, from the mid-10C to the mid-13C, saw the construction of numerous churches. In the old town alone, 12 churches from that era are still standing. Strolling through its old streets, therefore, the visitor gets a good idea of the different periods and varying styles of Rhineland Romanesque architecture. Certain concepts of religious design – the **trefoil chancel**, for instance – originated indeed in the city *(see the Introduction)*.

St Martin-the-Grand (Gross St Martin) (GZ) – This church, once a monastery, is built on what was once an island in the river, opposite the Roman port. The imposing square tower, rising 84m - 276ft above the transept crossing, lends with its four octagonal turrets a fortress-like aspect to the whole. In the forecourt, on the corner in front of the hostel, note the life-size bronze statues of eminent townsmen (**Tunnes** and **Schäl**).

St Mary of the Capitol (St Maria im Kapitol) (GZ B) – Another church which recalls a fortress. Situated on the river bank, this one too has a tall, square tower with four corner turrets above the transept crossing.

St Mary of the Lilies (St Maria Lyskirchen) (FX) – This triple-aisle basilica was built opposite the entrance to the Rhine port (c1220). The exterior is uninteresting, but there are splendid 13C **frescoes**★★ inside. A series of 24 Biblical scenes appears among the ribbed vaulting of the central nave.

St George's (St Georg) (FX) – A flat-roofed basilica with colonnades, this church dates from the 11C. Vaults above the choir and nave are 12C. The west end, where the walls are 5m - 16ft thick, is once more reminiscent of a fortified tower.

St Severinus' (St Severin) (FX) – The oldest Christian foundation in Cologne. There is a fine Gothic nave in the **interior**★. Note, in the two arms of the transept, paintings by the Master of St Severinus; a 13C forked Cross in the south transept; and behind the high altar, a shrine to the saint (restored in the 19C). His tomb is in the crypt.

St Pantaleon's (FX) – Built in the 10C, this church is an example of Ottonian art. The **rood-screen**★ is Late Gothic. The 10C tomb of Archbishop Bruno of Cologne lies in the crypt.

Church of the Holy Apostles (St Aposteln) (EV K) – Pure Rhineland Romanesque, this 11C church has a trefoil chancel and transept. Outside, the 13C **apse**★, flanked by two octagonal lantern turrets, is garnished with a beautiful Romanesque gallery.

St Gereon's (EV E) *Entrance via the Christopherstrasse.*
The unique design of this building is instanced by its elliptical plan and (in 1220) the addition of a decagon between the two towers. The crypt, floored with 11C mosaics, contains the coffins of St Gereon and other martyrs of the Theban Legion.

The frescoes are 13C, and the reredos above the altar Renaissance, with Gothic overtones. In the body of the church, on the north side, there is a tabernacle with bas-reliefs depicting The Last Supper (1608) as well as a fine Aubusson tapestry. A polychrome Virgin and Child stands on the south side (c1400).

St Andrew's (St Andreas) (GY) – This Romanesque church, with a very tall octagonal lantern tower and a widely projecting west transept, was transformed by the addition of a chancel in the Gothic era. The sarcophagus of Albert the Great lies in the crypt.

St Ursula's (St Ursula) (FU) ⊘ – In the south aisle, the **Treasury★** (Goldene Kammer) contains 14-17C reliquary busts and the 1170 Aetherius Shrine in hand-embossed copper. There are also collections of human bones arranged to spell out maxims and slogans.

St Cunibert's (St Kunibert) (FU) – The last wholly Romanesque church in Cologne. The twin towers flanking the chancel are intact. In the transept crossing, a group of over-life-size statues represents The Annunciation (1439; the folds of clothing and the gestures of the subjects suggest already an advance in the direction of realism). In a chapel on the north side of the choir, murals illustrate the life of the Virgin. The **stained glass windows★** (1230) above the choir stalls represent scenes of life at Court. Bells and clappers in the south aisle were once housed in the west tower, now in ruins.

OTHER MUSEUMS

★★ **Schnütgen Museum (GZ M⁴)** ⊘ – The 12C former Church of St Cecilia, one of the dozen Romanesque religious edifices still standing in the city, makes a suitable site for this museum devoted to sacred art from the 6C to the 19C, but essentially concentrated on the Middle Ages.

Numerous **Virgins in wood** illustrate the local "tender" style in statuary. **St Hieronymus and the Lion** (Erkelenz: 1460-70) is a masterpiece of Late Gothic wood carving. The Wassenberg choir stalls and a series of marble portrait statues from the cathedral (c1300-1310) are additional, important examples of work from the Gothic period. The gold altar panel (c1170) is from St Ursula's.

A collection of medieval items in **ivory**, most of them from Byzantium, France or other parts of Germany, is of particularly fine workmanship. It includes figurines, boxes, portable altars and copies of the Gospels. **Goldsmiths' and silversmiths' work** on display (reliquaries, busts, caskets, etc.) is equally impressive. Note, too, the items in bronze made by Christians from the East.

★★ **Museum of East Asian Art (Museum für Ostasiatische Kunst) (EV M⁵)** ⊘ – Universitätsstrasse 100.

Collections here comprise paintings, metalwork and ceramics from China, Japan and Korea, ranging from the earliest times to the 19C. Among the oldest exhibits are ancient **Chinese artefacts in bronze** (cauldrons, vases, ornaments) from the 1C and 2C BC, as well as **sandstone vessels** from the Shang dynasty (13C and 12C BC). Religious art is principally Buddhist.

Irresistibly fascinating are the ultra-delicate graphic works in ink or paints – on tapestry, fans, vertical or horizontal rolls, and above all **screens**. Do not miss the Chinese ebony screen (Ch'ing epoch, late 17C) with 12 panels illustrating life in the Imperial Palace – or, equally important, the Japanese screen dating from the beginning of the Edo epoch (mid-17C), which is decorated with aquatic birds (Japanese Screen Room).

★ **Museum of Applied Arts (Museum für Angewandte Kunst) (GYZ M⁶)** ⊘ – Here there is a general survey of the evolution of a functional aesthetic, from the craftwork of medieval artisans to post-modern design.

The Renaissance department displays splendid examples of marquetry furniture as well as **Italian majolica** from Faenza, Urbino, Genoa and Venice. The section reserved for Baroque and Rococo items contains **porcelain from Meissen** and other 18C manufactories, Dutch faience (Delft), a collection of "chinoiseries" and silver from southern Germany. Fine examples of neo-Renaissance French furniture (second half of the 19C) illustrate the emergence of "historicism", while ceramics from the France of the same period already foreshadow modernity. Among the furniture from the **Jugendstil period** (qv) note particularly a Viennese pear-wood desk (1914), a dining suite from Darmstadt (1910), and a semicircular work-table by Henry van de Velde (Berlin, 1901).

Metropolitan Historical Museum (Kölnisches Stadtmuseum) (EV M⁷) ⊘ – Cologne's eventful past is evoked here by arms and armour, pictures of battles, weights and measures, episcopal tombstones and portraits of eminent towns-people.

Rautenstrauch-Joest Ethnographic Museum (Rautenstrauch-Joel Museum für Völkerkunde) (FX M⁸) ⊘ – Pride of place is given to Thai and Khmer art from the 8C to the 16C (bronze, terracotta and stone statues; ceramics) and to pre-Colombian civilization in South America. Among the collection of metal artefacts from Peru (11C-15C), note the finely engraved bowls and vases in gold.

Carnival time
The Crazy Days (Tolle Tage) preceeding Ash Wednesday are the occasion for a series of boisterous, fun-loving carnivals. Parades, processions, decorated floats, street parties, painted faces and fancy dress are all part of the fun.

ADDITIONAL SIGHTS

★ **Old Town Hall** (Altes Rathaus) **(GZ)** – There are two separate sections to this building: the main 14C Gothic block, and a pavilion in the Italian Renaissance style which forms a porch to it. In 1953, beneath the new Town Hall, excavations revealed the Roman **Praetorium** – ruins of a palace (1C - 4C) of which the central octagon, the wells and the drainage system are still recognizable.

★ **Flora Botanical Park** (Botanischer Garten) ⊙ – *Leave by the Konrad-Adenauer-Ufer* **(FU)**.
An enormous **hothouse** (Gewächshaus) displays a variety of tropical species. The park includes an Italian "water stairway", formal terraces in the French style, and a vast English garden.

St Columba's Church (St Kolumba) **(GZ)** – This 1950 work by Gottfried Böhm is built on the site of a Gothic church destoyed during the war. Note the luminosity of the chancel with its blue stained glass windows, and a 15C statue of the Virgin, saved from the ruins.

St Peter's Church (GZ) – The Crucifixion of St Peter, by Rubens, is displayed in the entrance. Admire also the very fine late 14C stained-glass windows.

Church of the Assumption (St Maria Himmelfahrt) **(GY F)** – The spirit of the Counter-Reformation which inspired the building of this Jesuit church (1618-1678) led to a singular blend of Romanesque, Gothic and Baroque styles, inside as well as outside. Among Gothic elements borrowed by the Alsatian architect Christoph Wamser are the vaulting in the nave and the windows in the entrance façade. Rich Baroque decorations (restored) adorn the pillars which support galleries above the side aisles.

Church of St Mary the Queen (St Maria-Königin) – *Access via Bonner Strasse southeast of the plan* **(FX)**.
This modern church of vertically laid red brick was designed by Dominikus Böhm *(qv)* in 1954. Shades of grey predominate in the **glass wall★** (south) illuminating the interior.

EXCURSIONS

★ **Brühl Castle** ⊙ – *13km - 8 miles to the south.*
This castle, known as **Augustusburg** after its founder, the Elector Clement-Augustus, Archbishop of Cologne, was built between 1725 and 1768 by J K Schlaun and François de Cuvilliés. Inside, the splendid **staircase★** peopled by Rococo caryatids and atlantes is attributed to Balthazar Neumann *(qv)*.
The **gardens** are formal in the French manner.

★ **Altenberg Cathedral** – *20km - 12 miles to the northeast.*
This former Cistercian abbey church (still known locally as the Bergischer Dom - cathedral of the Berg Duchy) lies in a green valley much appreciated by the city dwellers of Cologne. Today it is a "parallel church", celebrating Catholic and Protestant rites alternately. Note especially the gigantic (18m x 8m - 59ft x 26ft) coloured glass canopy above the west entrance, and the **grisaille stained glass windows** in the chancel.

★ **Zons** – *24km - 15 miles to the north.*
A picturesque and delightful Rhineland fortified village, with a 14C **toll-house**.

*The diagram on the back cover shows the **Michelin Maps** covering the Guide; the chapter headings specify the appropriate map for the locality.*

★ **CONSTANCE** (KONSTANZ) Baden-Württemberg   Pop 75 000

Michelin map **413** K 23-K 24 – Local map see under LAKE CONSTANCE

A German enclave on the Swiss shore of Lake Constance and the southern bank of the Rhine, Constance occupies an agreeable **site★** opposite the narrows which separate the main body of the lake (Bodensee) from its picturesque prolongation (Untersee). The foundation of the town, long attributed to the Roman Emperor Constantius Chlorus (292-306), played a prominent part in the Great Schism of the West (1378-1429).

Constance, Capital of Christianity – From 1414 to 1418, a Council convened in the town attempted to re-establish the unity of the Church, compromised by the pretentions of three dignitaries, each elected in due form to the papal throne. After long negotiations, two of the three rival Popes, Gregory XII and John XXIII, agreed to stand down; only Benedict XIII, who had taken refuge in Spain, remained adamant. Then, in 1417, the election of Martin V, recognized everywhere as the true Pope, put an end temporarily to the schism.
Three years previously, the Council had summoned before it the religious reformer **John Hus**, Rector of the University of Prague. Hostile to German influence, Hus expounded his theses – which contested papal primacy and certain rites – was declared a heretic, and burned alive. This precursor of Protestantism remains a Czech hero today.

KONSTANZ

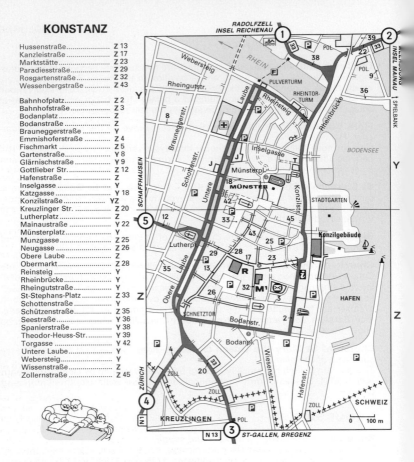

★ THE LAKE SHORE (SEEUFER) (Y)

The lakeside part of the town is the most attractive, with the port, shady public gardens, a casino (Spielbank), ancient defensive towers such as the Rheintorturm and the Pulverturm, and the quays – especially the Seestrasse – competing for the attention of the discerning tourist. The lake itself, busy with all kinds of water traffic, offers numerous opportunities for excursions. The Untersee, with its steep, indented shores, is particularly appealing.

ADDITIONAL SIGHTS

★ **Basilica** (Münster) (Y) – Since its construction was spread over a period from the 11C to the 17C, this former cathedral lacks any artistic unity.
The **panels** (Türflugel) of the porch doors in the main façade are decorated with bas-reliefs representing scenes from the life of Christ (1470).
The 17C vaulting in the central nave rests on the arcades of the original 11C sanctuary, achieving a visual harmony that is completely Romanesque. The decoration of the organ case and the loft itself preview the Renaissance. In the north transept, a spiral staircase turret (Schnegg), finely decorated in the French Late Gothic style, leads to the Treasury.
In the crypt are four plaques of gilded copper, each from a different period (11-13C). They represent Christ in Majesty, the symbolic Eagle of St John, St Conrad and St Pelagius, patrons of the diocese. A staircase to the right of the main door leads to a tower platform from which there is a fine view over the town and the lake.

Town Hall (Z R) – The façade of this Renaissance building is embellished with paintings that illustrate the history of Constance. In the inner courtyard – a quiet spot in the tourist season – is an elegant 16C house between two round towers.

Rosgarten Museum (Z M¹) ⊘ – This regional museum devoted to the lakeshore areas is housed in a former corporation building. It contains a famous Palaeolithic wall-carving of a reindeer as well as a copy of the 1440 Ulrich Richental Chronicle.
The latter is vividly illustrated with pictures of council meetings and daily life in Constance at that time.

Konzilgebaüde (Z) – *Not open to the public.*
This former warehouse, built at the end of the 14C, was used by the Conclave of 1417 which proclaimed the election of Pope Martin V. Across the road, in a garden bordering the pleasureboat harbour, is a monument to Count Zeppelin (1838-1917), the celebrated airship inventor, who was born in Constance.

EXCURSIONS

★★ Mainau Island (Insel Mainau) ⊙ – *7km - 4 1/2 miles. 2 hours sightseeing. Leave by ② on the plan.*
Tropical brushwood and exotic plants collected by the Baden princes and members of the Royal House of Sweden still flourish in this huge island park. Orange trees, hibiscus and the great trumpet-shaped blooms of daturas are living proof of the mildness of the climate. The castle, church and flower gardens are impressive.

★ Reichenau Island (Insel Reichenau) – *7km - 4 1/2 miles to the west. Leave by ① on the plan.*
In the 10C and 11C, this island was one of the most important monastic centres of the West. Today, lying as if anchored in the Untersee, it is devoted to market gardening, with floral glasshouses glinting among the crops. The late 9C Carolingian Church of St George of **Oberzell** – remarkable for the harmonious design of its stepped elements – contains a series of **wall paintings★★** (*c*1000 AD), depicting the miracles of Jesus.
At **Mittelzell**, the chief town on the island, there is an **old abbey★** (Münster) which was built between the 8C and 12C. The robust Romanesque tower of the Westwerk *(qv)* is lightened in appearance by a decorative band of Lombard pilasters and friezes. In the **treasury★** there is an early 14C reliquary of St Mark fashioned in beaten silver enriched with enamels.

★★ Lake CONSTANCE (BODENSEE) Baden-Württemberg

Michelin map **413** folds 36, 37 and 38

By the immensity of its horizons, sometimes lost in the summer haze, and a climate mild enough to permit tropical vegetation in the more favoured sites, Lake Constance attracts a multitude of German holidaymakers, who regard it as their local "Riviera".
With an area of 53 000ha - 210sq miles, the lake is only marginally smaller than Lake Geneva, biggest of the Alpine waterways. A wide choice of boat services provides many possibilities for cruises and excursions; most of these run from the ports of Constance, Überlingen, Meersburg, Friedrichshafen, Lindau and **Bregenz** *(see Michelin Green Guide Austria)*. The lakeside roads offer numerous vistas of the lake with the Alps, in clear weather, as an impressive background.
The islands of **Reichenau★**, on the Untersee, and **Mainau★★**, on the Überlingersee, are described in the Excursions of Constance *(see above)*.

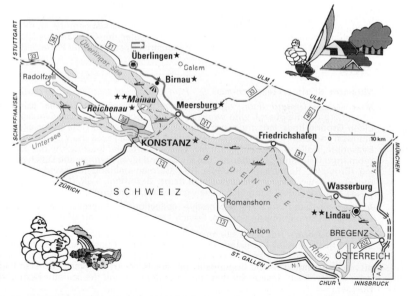

FROM ÜBERLINGEN TO LINDAU 56km - 35 miles - allow 4 hours

★ Überlingen – *See under Überlingen.*

★ Birnau – The present church was built between 1746 and 1750 on a terrace overlooking the lake, the Cistercians of Salem *(qv)* having entrusted the work to Peter Thumb, Master of the Vorarlberg school.
The building's Rococo charm is most evident in the architectural design, the painted decoration of the interpenetrating oval spaces and curved surfaces over the single aisle, the flattened dome above the chancel, and the cupola surmounting the apse. Halfway up the walls, an elegant gallery is supported on corbels the bosses of which are embellished with Rococo cartouches *(illustration p 108)*. Pilgrims venerate the early 15C Virgin above the tabernacle on the high altar.

★ Meersburg – Birthplace of the painter Stefan Lochner *(qv)*, Meersburg in an attractive town perched above the lake shore. The stylish upper town (Oberstadt) is centred on the **Marktplatz★**, from which the **Steigstrasse★**, bordered by half-timbered old houses, offers delightful views of the lake.

Apartments in the Old Castle where the great poet Annette von Droste-Hülshoff (1797-1848) spent the last years of her life may be viewed. From the terrace of the New Castle there is a **panorama★** of Lake Constance and the Säntis massif.

Birnau - The Church

Friedrichshafen – The lakeside areas have been furnished with attractive, wide promenade-quays. The town's **municipal museum** (Stadtmuseum) includes a section devoted to the history of Count Zeppelin's dirigibles, which were built here.

Wasserburg – This much-visited village is squeezed onto a narrow tongue of land jutting out into the lake. Appreciate it on foot, walking to the tip of the promontory.

★★ Lindau – *See under Lindau.*

DARMSTADT Hessen   Pop 139 000

Michelin map **413** I 17 - J 17
Town plan in the current Michelin Red Guide Deutschland

The former capital of the Grand Duchy of Hesse-Darmstadt, now a thriving industrial centre (machine tools, armoured glass, electronic equipment and chemicals) lies close to the Odenwald massif. It has long been renowned also as a cultural centre, thanks to the endeavours of a succession of princes who were enlightened amateurs – of Jugendstil notably, at the end of the last century. Numerous institutions continue the tradition today, in particular the German Academy of Language and Poetry, and the Institute of Industrial Design (Rat für Formgebung).

SIGHTS

★ Museum (Hessisches Landesmuseum) ⊘ – *Plan to different sections at the entrance.*

Main block – *Ground floor, right:* excellent choice of **medieval altar paintings** (Ortenberg and Reidberg), with works by Stefan Lochner and Lucas Cranach the Elder. Ground floor, left: craftwork and religious sculptures. Note especially the liturgical accessories, medieval enamels, and **sculptured ivory** from Syria, Byzantium, Holland, Italy and Germany itself (of particular interest: the marquetry room from Chiavenna, Lombardy - *c*1580). Second level: Flemish and Dutch painting (Brueghel, Rembrandt, Rubens), 19C German painting (Schwind, Böcklin, Stuck), and the famous **Werkkomplex of Beuys**. Basement: religious art (stained glass) and Jugendstil (ceramics, silver, glassware, furniture).

Annexe – *Ground floor:* representative collection of Expressionist painting. Basement: German Impressionism, French "New Realism", art of the 1980s.

Mathildenhöhe – This is the site on which the Grand Duke Ernst Ludwig founded in 1899 the colony of Darmstadt artists known as the Künstlerkolonie. It united painters, sculptors and architects anxious to work together in search of a "total art" corresponding to the Jugendstil *(qv)* ideals of Art Nouveau. Outstanding were the architects Joseph Olbrich and Peter Behrens and the sculptor Bernhard Hoetger.

The dwellings and workshops grouped near the Russian chapel formed in 1901 the centre of an exhibition titled "A Document on German Art". The ensemble, with its terraces and pergolas, is typical of this movement seeking new forms of expression. The **Wedding Tower** (Hochzeitsturm), built in 1908 to celebrate the marriage of the Grand Duke, overlooks the whole site. Inside are two mosaics (allegories on the subject of Love).

Castle (Schloss) ⊘ – The former residence of the Landgraves, in the town centre, comprises two separate buildings: the New Castle (Neuschloss, 18C), a Rémy Delafosse design with its symmetrical façade fronting the market place; and the Old Castle (Altschloss), an edifice with voluted gables and the family coat of arms on the gateway which leads to an inner courtyard.

In the Castle Museum (Schlossmuseum), family collections on view include carriages, furniture, silver and, in the picture gallery, Holbein the Younger's *Darmstadt Virgin*.

Prince George's Palace (Prinz-Georg-Palais) ⊙ – This onetime summer residence of the Landgraves (early 18C) houses the Grand Dukes' **porcelain collection★**. The services and ornaments come from Nymphenburg, Berlin, Frankenthal, Ludwigsburg, Meissen and the ducal factory at Kelsterbach; almost all the pieces were gifts from the royal and imperial families of Europe.

Symmetrical formations of clipped yews divide the formal flowerbeds planted around the castle; between them are attractive vistas of pavilions scattered through the park.

EXCURSION

Kranichstein Pavilion (Jagdschloss Kranichstein) ⊙ – *5km - 3 miles to the northeast.*

The **hunting museum★** in this small hunting-lodge has assembled an interesting collection of weapons, trophies and pictures.

*The **Michelin Red Guide Deutschland***
which is revised annually gives a selection of
establishments offering

- carefully prepared meals at reasonable prices
- simple meals at moderate prices
- prices including or excluding service
- car parking

DETMOLD Rhineland-Westphalia   Pop 68 000

Michelin maps ⁜ and ⁜ J 11
Town plan in the current Michelin Red Guide Deutschland

Until 1918, Detmold was the capital of the Lippe principality. It is a pleasant town, on the edge of the wooded heights of the Teutoburger Wald.

Castle (Fürstliches Residenzschloss) ⊙ – Dormer windows with semicircular pediments in the First Renaissance style adorn the façade of this fine 16C rectangular building. The interior courtyard is noteworthy for a very elegant corbelled gallery which links the corner towers. Souvenirs, the gifts of foreign royalty, enrich the apartments inside. Note particularly an outstanding porcelain service presented by the Empress Josephine, and fine 17C tapestries illustrating, after cartoons by Charles Le Brun, the life of Alexander the Great.

★ **Westphalian Open-Air Museum** (Westfälisches Freilichtmuseum) ⊙ – Peasant dwellings in which families lived alongside their beasts have been reconstituted, along with their outbuildings, furniture, etc., in this 80ha - 200-acre park which recreates rural life in Westphalia from the 15C to the 19C.

★ **Arminius Monument** (Hermannsdenkmal) ⊙ – This commemorates the victory in the year AD 9 of the local hero Arminius over the Roman legions, after he had united the tribes living in what are now Westphalia and Hessen. There is a **view★** of the surrounding forest, the town of Detmold and the Weser hills from the gallery *(75 steps)*.

EXCURSION

★ **Externsteine** ⊙ – In a forest setting beside a lake, this curious group of eroded sandstone rocks was once a place of worship for Germanic peoples, and subsequently, in the Middle Ages, a Christian pilgrimage. In the 11C a replica of the Holy Places of Jerusalem was constructed for the pilgrims. The most extraordinary sight is a **bas-relief★** of the Descent from the Cross, carved in the 12C from the living rock. Rare in Germany, this work is an example of Romanesque sculpture with a Byzantine influence.

DONAUESCHINGEN Baden-Württemberg   Pop 19 600

Michelin map ⁜ I 23.

This small town in the middle of the Baar, a fertile basin between the Black Forest and the Swabian Jura, stands at the confluence of two streams, the Breg and the Brigach. From this fact stems the German proverb "Brigach und Breg bringen die Donau zuweg" – roughly, "from small streams great rivers flow". This is because after the confluence the united streams are known as the Danube.

Donaueschingen is known as the **"official" source** of Europe's second-longest river (2 826km - 1 356 miles; the longest is the Volga, 3 895km - 2 292 miles), because of the confluence and because of the monumental fountain (Donauquelle) built in the Castle park in the 19C. The geographic source is in fact the source of the Breg, near Furtwangen *(qv)*.

Leading the way in music – The annual Festival of Contemporary Music, founded in 1921, soon became famous worldwide, thanks to the participation of such men as Richard Strauss, Schönberg and Webern. The concerts, relayed by the Südwestfunk radio station, gained a much wider public for composers like Boulez, Xenakis and Stockhausen.

SIGHTS

Princely Collections (Fürstenberg-Sammlungen) ⊘ – These are on display in a building on the Karlsplatz. The **picture gallery★** (Gemäldegalerie) on the second floor is the most interesting. In the large room on the right are works by 15C and 16C Swabian masters such as Bartholomäus Zeitblom and, above all, the very fine **Altarpiece of The Passion★★** (Passionsaltar) by Hans Holbein the Elder (note the pose of the Saviour). The gallery on the left is devoted to other Swabian painters, including the Master of Sigmaringen. Adjacent rooms exhibit pictures by Cranach the Elder and Younger, Kulmbach, the Master of Messkirch, etc.

Castle ⊘ – Remodelled in the 19C, the home of the Fürstenberg princes retains the luxurious amenities of the period, enriched now with gold and silver plate, porcelain and fine Beauvais and Brussels tapestries.

Parish Church (Pfarrkirche) – This was built in the Baroque style between 1724 and 1747. In the first (south) bay is the 1522 Madonna of Donaueschingen.

DORTMUND Rhineland-Westphalia   Pop 570 000

Michelin maps **411** and **412** F 12
Town plan in the current Michelin Red Guide Deutschland – Local map see under RUHR BASIN

Dortmund, an old Hanseatic town, is the most easterly industrial centre of the Ruhr. Producing 10% of the raw steel used by the former Federal Republic, it is also a thriving supplier of machine tools and electronics. But, for the visitor, it is above all the beer capital. The city's six breweries are responsible for more than 7% of the country's total output.

SIGHTS

★ **Westphalia Park** (Westfalenpark) ⊘ – The two main centres of attraction in this 70ha - 173-acre park are the **Television Tower** (Fernsehturm "Florian") and the **Rose Garden** (Deutsches Rosarium), which cultivates some 3 200 varieties from all over the world. The tower is 212m - 695ft high (75ft higher than the Telecom Tower in London). At a height of 450ft there is a revolving platform with a restaurant and a terrace from which there is a superb **panorama★** of the Ruhr and the Sauerland.

★ **St Reynold's Church** (Reinoldkirche) – *In the Ostenhellweg, near the market.*
This triple-aisle basilica dating from the early Gothic period has interesting furnishings, which include a 15C sculpted reredos that represents the Crucifixion. Note the 14C wood statue of St Reynold, patron saint of the town, on the north side of the chancel, and a 15C statue of Charlemagne on the south.

St Mary's Church (Marienkirche) – *Opposite St Reynold's.*
A Romanesque basilica with a Gothic chancel. The **Altarpiece of Our Lady★**, one of the finest works of Konrad von Soest, dates from 1420. The Madonna's face and hands are superbly expressive.

St Peter's Church (Petrikirche) – *In the Westenhellweg.*
This 14C hall-church is famous for its **carved reredos**, created in 1521 by members of the Guild of St Luke of Antwerp. Including the high altar itself, the work measures 6 x 7.5m - 20 x 25ft. It incorporates 633 carved and gilded figures and 54 paintings.

Priory Church (Propsteikirche) – *Entrance from the Westenhellweg, via Mönchenwordt.*
Another hall-church. This one, restored after the Second World War, contains a **triptych** by Derick and Jan Baegert (cl490). Open, this reveals, from left to right, the Holy Family, the Adoration of the Magi and the Crucifixion.

Brewery Museum (Brauereimuseum) ⊘ – *In the Dortmunder Kronen brewery, at no 85, Markische Strasse.*
A survey of the evolution of breweries during the 100 years from the middle of the 19C to the middle of the 20C. Two complete **brewing installations** (1928 and 1936) can be viewed at work on the ground floor.

Museum of Art and Civilization (Museum für Kunst und Kulturgeschichte) ⊘ – *At no 3, Hansastrasse.*
The exhibits here, displayed chronologically, cover such diverse subjects as the history of Dortmund (many items from archaeological digs); religious art at the end of the Middle Ages; houses and furniture in different periods; and 19C painting (Berlin Secession, C D Friedrich). The section devoted to the Romanesque epoch contains the **Dortmund Treasure★** (Dortmunder Goldschatz) - a collection of 444 gold coins, dating for the most part from the AD 4C.

Ostwall Museum ⊘ – *At no 7, Ostwall.*
Works by the greatest exponents of German Expressionism are on view here: paintings by Paula Becker-Modersohn, Jawlensky, Macke, Nolde, Müller and Rohlfs; sculptures by Barlach, Kolbe and Kollwitz. There is also a big display of international art from the years 1960-1980, in particular the installations of Wolf Vostell, Robert Filliou, Milan Knizak and Beuys.

Thanks to an exceptional artistic and architectural heritage and its position in the heart of Saxony, on the banks of the Elbe at and the gates of "Swiss Saxony" *(qv)*, Dresden has become one of the most popular and important tourist centres in Germany.

"The Florence of the Elbe" – Originally a Slav town, germanized in the 12C by the Margraves of Meissen, Dresden remained a possession of the Albertine succession from the partition of Saxony in 1485 until 1918.

The major development of the city took place during the first half of the 18C, in the reigns of the Electors Augustus II the Strong (Frederick-Augustus I) and Augustus III (Frederick-Augustus II). To them we owe the magnificent Baroque ensemble of the Zwinger, the Japanese Palace and the Hofkirche (the Court church), as well as outstanding collections of paintings and objets d'art. These, completed by the work of 19C and 20C German painters – Dresden was the cradle of German Expressionism – make the city one of Europe's most prestigious artistic centres. On the cultural side, the Staatskapelle and the Staatsoper orchestras enjoy a worldwide reputation.

The Night of the Apocalypse – A few months before the end of the Second World War, on the night of February 13-14, 1945, Dresden was the target of one of the Allies' most destructive air raids, designed to break the morale of the population. Three successive waves of heavy bombers left the blackened skeletons of the city's principal monuments emerging from a waste of smoking ruins, and a death-roll of over 100 000. The city was 75% destroyed.

Restoration of Dresden's historic patrimony – in particular the miraculous reconstitution of the Zwinger – and the rebuilding of residential quarters traversed by wide new thoroughfares have given the town a special quality marrying modern urbanism with this ancient heritage. The Prager Strasse (Z), linking the old town with the quarter around the railway station, is the most striking example of this contemporary town-planning, with imposing modern blocks on each side of a broad pedestrian mall.

HISTORIC CENTRE

★★★ **The Zwinger** – *The best view of the whole complex is gained if you go in via the Carillon Pavilion (Glockenspielpavillon) on Sophienstrasse.*

Augustus the Strong's original idea was to build, on the side of a former fortress, a simple orangery. But his architect, **Matthäus Daniel Pöppelmann** (1662-1736), brought such breadth of vision to the project that its conception changed in the course of construction and it ended up as an enormous esplanade surrounded by galleries and pavilions. On every side, an impressive succession of windows and arcades with rounded arches lends the composition as a whole its rhythmic unity. The main appeal of this jewel of German Baroque lies in the harmonization of architectural work with sculptures from the studio of **Balthazar Permoser** (1651-1732), a Bavarian artist strongly influenced by his visits to Italy.

The huge rectangular courtyard has two semi-elliptical extensions which include the **Rampart Pavilion**★★ (Wallpavillon) and the **Carillon Pavilion**. It is in the former that the intimate relationship between sculpture and architecture most admirably expresses itself. Not a single transverse wall breaks up the taut lines of these verticals animated by the exuberance and vigour of atlantes with the visage of Hermes, drowned in a sea of vegetation. Crowning the pavilion, **Hercules Carrying the World** is the only work personally signed by Permoser.

Steps from the Rampart Pavilion lead to the terrace on which Pöppelmann's **Bath of the Nymphs**★★ (Nymphenbad) can be seen. It was undoubtedly in Italy that the artist found inspiration for this marvellous set-piece, in which a subtle blend between the inorganic representation of nature – grotto work and fountains – and the grace of feminine forms creates an atmosphere that is irresistibly sensual.

The southwest side of the complex is closed off by the elegant **Zwinger Gallery** (Zwingergalerie), best seen from the outside, passing beneath the **Crown Gate** (Kronentor).

The Carillon Pavilion at the Zwinger

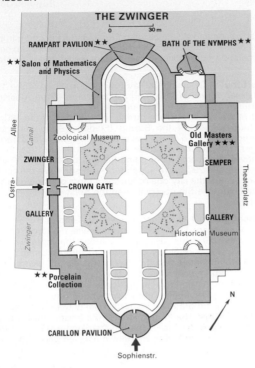

THE ZWINGER

0   30 m

RAMPART PAVILION ★★   BATH OF THE NYMPHS ★★

★★ Salon of Mathematics and Physics

Allee

Canal

Zoological Museum

Old Masters Gallery ★★★

ZWINGER   SEMPER

Ostra-   CROWN GATE

Theaterplatz

GALLERY   GALLERY

Zwinger

Historical Museum

★★ Porcelain Collection

N

CARILLON PAVILION

Sophienstr.

This latter, embellished with statues representing the four seasons, comprises two superimposed arcades surmounted by an onion-shaped dome, with terminates in four eagles supporting the Polish crown. The **Semper Gallery**, built in 1847 by **Gottfried Semper** (1803-1879), occupies the northeast side of the Zwinger reserved since 1728 for the exhibition of the royal collections. Of the Baroque ensemble as a whole – two-storey pavilions linked by one-storey galleries – the Anglo-German critic Sir Nikolaus Pevsner wrote: "What exultation in these rocking curves, and yet what grace! It is joyful but never vulgar; vigorous, boisterous perhaps, but never crude... of an inexhaustible creative power, with ever new combinations and variations of Italian Baroque forms placed against each other and piled above one another."

★★★ **Old Masters Gallery** (Gemäldegalerie Alter Meister) ☉ – *In the Semper Gallery*. Masterpieces on display here from the 15C to the 18C include paintings from Italy (Raphael, Botticelli, Titian, Caraveggio, Tiepolo, Tintoretto), Spain (Velasquez, Zurbaran, Murillo), Germany (Dürer, Holbein the Younger, Cranach the Elder), Flanders (Van Eyck, Van Dyck, Rubens, Rembrandt), and France (Poussain, Watteau, Lorrain).

★★ **Porcelain Collection** (Porzellansammlung) ☉ – *Entrance on Sophienstrasse*. This gallery displays not only the products of the famous factory at Meissen *(qv)*, but also porcelain acquired by Augustus the Strong from Japan and China (from the best period in the 19C). Do not miss the "giant animal room", including characters by Kirchner and Kändler of Meissen (first half of the 18C), and the room devoted to Böttger, a potter who profited from the discovery of kaolin deposits nearby to create (1708) in Europe a porcelain modelled on that of the Far East. His first attempts to colour glazes are particularly interesting. The largest room displays Meissen tableware of the 18C and a carillon of 52 porcelain bells.

★★ **Salon of Mathematics and Physics** (Mathematisch-Physikalischer Salon) ☉ – *Northwest corner pavilion* – A visit to this gallery recalls the inventive genius of scientists in past ages, with special reference to measuring instruments (thermometers, clocks, barometers); cartography (globes), and methods of observation. A collection of clocks on the first floor unites the most representative models since the 16C.

On the way to the **Theaterplatz (Y 52)**– note the equestrian statue of King John (1854-1873) in the middle – the road passes the **Old Town Watchtower** (Altstädter Wache), which was designed by Schinkel.

★★ **Opera (Semper-Oper)** – Built between 1871 and 1878 by Manfred Semper based on plans designed by his father Gottfried – Professor of Architecture at Dresden responsible for the previous edifice, destroyed by fire in 1869 – the present opera house owes its form to the Italian Renaissance.

The tiered façade, in plan a wide arc, comprises two storeys of arcades, surmounted by a third in recess. Each side wall is furnished with twin niches, occupied on the left by statues of Shakespeare and Sophocles, on the right Molière and Euripides.

★★ **Cathedral (Katholische Hofkirche)** – This enormous basilican edifice was built between 1738 and 1755 following the conversion of the Albertines to Roman Catholicism, the condition of their accession to the Polish throne. Its 5 000m^2 - 53 820sq ft floor area make it the largest church in Saxony. The building, strongly influenced by Italian Baroque, is dominated by an 85m - 279ft bell tower and decorated with statues of the saints and apostles, mainly on the attics.

The nave is separated from the side aisles by a semicircular ambulatory opening on to four oval chapels. Above the high altar, a fine painting (1750) by Anton Raphael Mengs depicts the Ascension. The pulpit was executed by Permoser in 1722, while the organ was the last work (1750-1753) of the master craftsman Gottfried Silbermann. The tombs of several kings and princes of Saxony can be seen in the crypt.

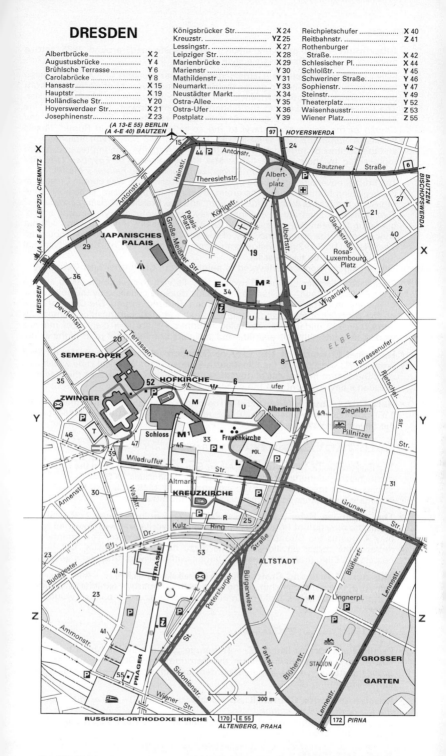

DRESDEN

Castle (Schloss) – Most of this Renaissance-style building, once the official residence of the Court, is in the process of restoration.

That part of the exterior façade linking the west wing to the Johanneum is covered by a colossal mosaic, **The Procession of Dukes★** (Fürstenzug, 1906). Composed in tiles of Meissen porcelain, the work represents a parade, in chronological order, of all the ducal members of the house of Saxe-Wettin. It measures 102m x 957m - 335ft x 3 140ft. The inner façade is formed by the **Langer Gang★**, a series of 22 Tuscan arcades enclosing the stable courtyard.

The **Johanneum (M¹)** (left of the entrance – Schöne Pforte, in the Renaissance style) was itself once used as the stables. It now houses a **Transport Museum** (Verkehrsmuseum), where collections of automobiles and powered cycles join a display outlining the evolution of public transport.

Leaving the Johanneum, cross the New Marketplace (Neu-Markt) towards the ruins of the **Frauenkirche**, preserved as a spine-chilling reminder of the destruction of the city in 1945. Visit the **Brühl Terrace (Y 6)**, laid out on the site of ancient fortifications, where there is a **view★** of the Elbe and the Neustadt quarter, on the river's east bank.

Albertinum – This one-time arsenal was transformed, around 1885, into a museum in the neo-Renaissance style.

★★★ **Gallery of 19C and 20C Painters** (Gemäldegalerie Neuer Meister) ⊘ – A visit to these rooms permits the visitor to gauge the richness and diversity of German art from the Romantics **(Casper David Friedrich**, *Two Men Contemplate the Moon*; **A L Richter**, *The Crossing of the Elbe*) to the Biedermeier **(Carl Spitzweg**, *The Hook and Line Fisherman*); from the Bourgeois Realists **(Adolf von Menzel**, *Sermon in the Old Church of the Berlin Monastery*) to the so-called "Germans in Rome" **(Arnold Böcklin**, *A Summer's Day*; **Wilhelm Leibl**, *Portrait of the Baron von Stauffenberg*) and the painters of Jugendstil **(Fritz von Uhde**, *The Nativity*). The Impressionists are represented by their leading lights: **Max Slevogt**, *Scenes of Egyptian Life*; **Max Liebermann**, *Portrait of Alfred von Berger*; **Lovis Corinth**, *The Painter's Model*.
The Brücke movement, spearhead of German Expressionism, was born in Dresden at the beginning of this century. The group, a spin-off from Fauvism, is notably represented by **Karl Schmidt Rottluff**, *After the Bath*; and **Max Pechstein**, *A Baltic Landscape*.
Two triptyches illustrate in a gripping way the "revolutionary" German school operating between the wars: *War* (1929-1932) by **Otto Dix**, a denunciation without concession of the cruelty and folly of the warlike mentality; and *The Thousand-Year Reich* (1935-1938), a vision both ironic and prophetic of the new National Socialist regime by **Hans Grundig**.
The remaining rooms are devoted to painters from the former East Germany.

★★★ **Green Vault Collections** (Grünes Gewölbe) ⊘ – To visit this exhibition is to enter a real "Ali Baba's Cave", for here is the artistic treasury collected by the sovereigns of Saxony, in particular Augustus the Strong. Centred around *The Court of Delhi on the Birthday of the Grand Mogul* – an extraordinary composition comprising more than 130 gilded and enamelled figurines – there is a display of marvels worked by goldsmiths, silversmiths and jewellers from different parts of the world.

★ **Historical Museum of the City of Dresden** (Museum für Geschichte der Stadt Dresden) **(YL)** – Installed in the Landhaus, a palazzo in the classical style which was once the seat of the provincial government, this exhibition retraces the stages of Dresden's development and the principal facts of its history.

★ **Holy Cross Church** (Kreuzkirche) – The original church, the city's oldest (early 13C), as it was remodelled in the Baroque style after its destruction (1760) during the Seven Years War.

NEUSTADT QUARTER (EAST BANK)

The **Hauptstrasse** (**X 19**), which joins Albert Square (Albertplatz) and the Neustadter marketplace – dominated by the gilded **equestrian statue** (**X E**) of Augustus the Strong – was the object after the catastrophe of 1945 of a tasteful restoration scheme which managed to preserve several 18C dwellings.

★ **The Japanese Palace** (Japanisches Palais) **(X)** – Built between 1715 and 1737 under the direction of Pöppelmann, this huge quadrilateral was designed to display Augustus the Strong's collection of Meissen tableware. The oriental-style roofs of the corner pavilions lend the place its Asiatic character. On the side nearest the Elbe, there is a pleasant garden with a **view** of the river's west bank.

★ **Museum of Arts and Crafts** (Museum für Volkskunst) **(X M²)** ⊘ – All the skill and taste of Saxon workmanship is apparent in the numerous exhibits displayed in this pretty Renaissance building (multicoloured furniture in painted wood, toys, ironwork, etc.).

ADDITIONAL SIGHTS

★ **Public Park** (Grosser Garten) **(Z)** – This huge park is traversed by a broad walk leading to a **Palace** (1678-1683) in the Baroque style. On either side there are groups of statuary, a zoo, botanical gardens and an open-air theatre, all in a pleasant sylvan setting.

★ **Russian Orthodox Church** (Russisch-orthodoxe Kirche) **(Z)** – *Leave to the south, to the left of the railway station.*
The designers of this colourful church, built in 1874, were inspired by Russian architecture of the 17C.

EXCURSIONS

Moritzburg Castle ⊘ – *14km - 9 miles to the northwest, via Hansastrasse* (**X**).
Built by the Duke Moritz on the Royal Reserve in 1546, this was originally designed to be no more than a simple hunting lodge in the Renaissance style. But it was considerably refashioned between 1723 and 1736 by Pöppelmann, at the request of Frederick-Augustus I (1670-1733), who had wanted to transform it into a Baroque château. The present striking edifice, with four wings and imposing ochre and white corner towers (the colours of the Baroque in Saxony), is surrounded by an artificial lake and a large park. The stone statues on the terrace, as well as the urns and cupids on the balustrades, are the work of JC Kirchner and B Thomae. Inside the castle there is a **Baroque Museum** (Barockmuseum) displaying furniture of the period, and a Stone Room with an impressive collection of trophies.
The castle chapel was built between 1661 and 1672 by WC von Klengel (1630-1691) and integrated by Pöppelmann into the remodelled building.
The small **Pheasantry Pavilion** (Fasanerieschlösschen) – a 30 minutes walk away – houses a museum of ornithology. It was built between 1769 and 1782.

* **Pillnitz Castle** ⊙ – *15km - 9 1/2 miles to the southeast, via the Bautznerstrasse* (**X**)
Pöppelmann, favourite architect of the Electors, was responsible for this pleasure palace too. Designed between 1720 and 1724, the **Riverside Palace** (Wasserpalais) was originally built on the east bank of the Elbe. The Late Baroque predilection for Chinese motifs is apparent in the roof treatment. A new castle, between the waterside structure and the **Upper Palace** (Bergpalais) was built between 1818 and 1826 under the direction of the architect Schuricht, following a fire which gutted the Renaissance building.
There is a **Craft Museum** (Museum für Kunsthandwerk) in the castle. Furniture, gilded bronzes, Baroque faience, silverware, glassware and Asiatic porcelain are on display.
The park was transformed into an English-style garden in 1778. A lagoon was added, a circular pavilion or gazebo a year later, and then a Chinese pavilion (one of the most perfect copies of Chinese architecture in Europe) in 1804. The banks of the Elbe offer attractive riverside walks. The islet opposite the gardens is a bird reserve, inhabited by grey herons.

*** **Swiss Saxony** (Sächische Schweiz) – *See under Swiss Saxony.*

* **Meissen** – *See under Meissen.*

---

* # DÜSSELDORF Rhineland-Westphalia   Pop 570 000
Michelin maps ⁢411⁢ and ⁢412⁢ D 13
Plan of the conurbation in the current Michelin Red Guide Deutschland

Once a fishing village on the east bank of the Rhine, Düsseldorf today is one of the most important economic centres of Germany. The development of the city, which lies at the confluence of the Rhine and the Düssel, has been given an added administrative importance since it was established, in 1946, as the capital of the Rhineland-Westphalia Land.

HISTORICAL NOTES

Düsseldorf first acquired city status in the 13C when it was chosen as the official residence of the Dukes of Berg. Four centuries later, the family of the Electors of the Neuburg-Palatinate settled there and the fame of the city spread. This was largely due to the energy and intelligence of the family's most famous member, Johann Wilhelm (Elector from 1690 to 1715). Patron and apostle of the Baroque, Jan Willem as he was known surrounded himself with a brilliant Court of musicians, painters and architects who transformed Düsseldorf into a true city of the arts.
After the French Revolution, Napoleon created the town capital of the Grand Duchy of Berg, and it became a minor Paris. Murat, and then Jerome Bonaparte were its first rulers. In 1815 it seceded to Prussia.

Heinrich Heine (1797-1856) – Heine, son of a Bolkerstrasse merchant, lived in Düsseldorf throughout his youth, deeply impressed by the presence of the French and the personality of Napoleon. In his *Memories of Childhood* he expressed his admiration of France with characteristic verve, at once biting and melancholic. A poet who was also a willing pamphleteer, eternal traveller, defender of liberalism, a Francophile and a genuine European, Heine once described himself as "a German nightingale which would have liked to make its nest in Voltaire's wig".

A Musical City – Among the musicians who have given Düsseldorf its enviable reputation as an artistic centre are Robert Schumann and Felix Mendelssohn. **Schumann** (1810-1856) was appointed conductor of the municipal orchestra in 1850. Living for four years in a house in the Bilker Strasse (**DZ**), he was already seriously ill mentally, attempting to drown himself in the Rhine in 1854. His friend **Mendelssohn** (1809-1847) brilliantly directed the city's Rhine Festival. He made his first journey to England in 1829, conducting his own *Symphony in C Minor* at the London Philharmonic Society.

LIFE IN DÜSSELDORF

The Head Office of the Ruhr – Seat of one of Germany's most important stock exchanges, Düsseldorf is not only the country's second banking and financial centre but also administrative capital for most of the Rhineland industries. All these functions are exemplified in the **Dreischeibenhaus** (the Thyssen Building) (**EY E**). Practically all business and commercial transactions concerning the Ruhr and surrounding cities are negotiated in an area between the Kasernenstrasse (**DZ**) and the Berliner Allee (**EZ**).

The World of Fashion – Exhibitions, fairs and collections of haute couture several times a year maintain Düsseldorf's reputation as a "minor Paris" and fashion capital of Germany. A walk along the **Königsallee** (**EZ**) (popularly known as "the Kö") demonstrates that the reputation is deserved. Everything that is elegant in the town centres on this graceful promenade. With its boutiques and arcades, its cafés and restaurants, built on either side of the old moat.

Food It is in the taverns typical of the old town that regional specialities can best be appreciated: a black pudding with onions; Halve Hahn – a caraway cheese eaten with strong local mustard; and Röggelchen (small rye loaves). On Friday evenings, there is a tradition of eating Reibekuchen, a kind of savoury potato cake. Alt-Bier, the still, dark, brown ale of the region, is brewed in Düsseldorf.

DÜSSELDORF

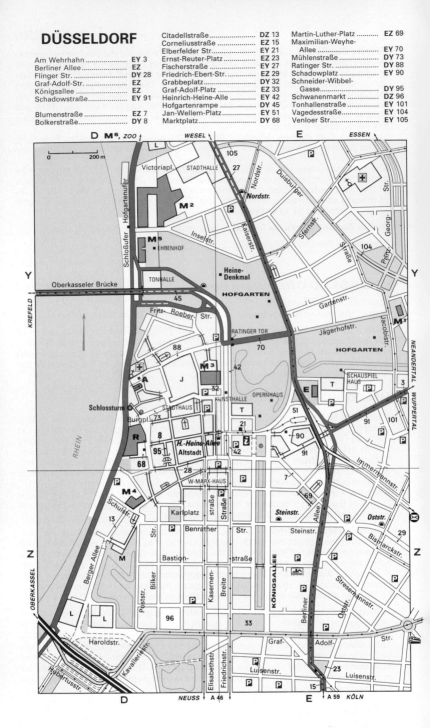

The Way Ahead – Düsseldorf plays an increasingly important role in economic relations linking Germany with the Far East. Japanese firms alone have 300 branches in the city.

This strong Oriental presence is reinforced by the existence of the **Japanese Cultural Centre** in the Immermannstrasse (**EYZ**) and the Taiwan Trade Centre, near the central station.

SIGHTS

Old Town (**DEY**) – This riverside quarter, with its taverns and bars jam-packed from the earliest hours of the evening, is known as **"the biggest boozer in Europe"**. It is here that the **"Radschläger"** – local street urchins and buskers who perform outdoor acrobatics for a few pennies – can be found.

The **Bolkerstrasse** (**DY 8**), birthplace of Heine (no 53), is the busiest and liveliest of the city's pedestrian precincts. The neighbourhood is equally linked with the story of the tailor Wibbel, who attended his own funeral after switching identities to escape a prison sentence. This folklore legend is recalled by the figures of the Schneider-Wibbel-Gasse carillon clock (**DY 95**), which operates at 11am, 1pm, 3pm, 6pm and 9pm.

Market Place (Marktplatz) (DY 68) – Separated from the Rhine only by the former **Town Hall** (DY R) (late 16C), this square is embellished with the bronze equestrian statue (early 18C) of the famous Jan Willem.

St Lambert's Basilica (DY A) – This huge 14C Gothic hall-church is distinguished by a spire that is both leaning and twisted. The interior decoration is basically Baroque. A finely-worked late Gothic ciborium – a canopy or baldachin above the altar – can be seen in the northern part of the chancel. The remains of 15C wall paintings are visible on the south wall.
At the far end of the nave there is a Pietà (cl420) in a modern (1975) setting. The bronze entrance door is by Ewald Mataré.

★ **Jägerhof Castle and the Hofgarten** (DEY) – The Hofgarten park forms a shady continuation of the Königsallee, northwest towards the riverside museum quarter and east as far as **Jägerhof Castle**. This delightful building, one-time home of the Electors Master of the Hunt, dates from the 18C. The French architect Nicolas de Pigage contributed to the plans. Today the mansion houses the **Goethe Museum**★ (EY M[1]), which displays the author's manuscripts, autographs, drawings and engravings, as well as busts and first editions of his works. On the second floor, a sumptuous apartment provides a perfect setting for the **Dr. Schneider Private Collection**: note especially the Augsburg gold and silver plate and the Meissen porcelain. Napoleon Hill, in the park, is crowned with a small Maillol bronze entitled *Harmony* - in fact a modest monument to Heine.

★ **Fine Arts Museum** (Kunstmuseum) (DY M[2]) ⊘ – Romantics of the Düsseldorf School (Cornelius, Shirmer, Achenbach, Rethel) dominate the important painting gallery in this museum. There is equal exposure for Impressionists and members of the German Expressionist movement (Corinth, Kandinsky, Jawlensky, Macke, Klee, Kirchner and Nolde). **Prints**, fabrics and glassware are displayed in other departments.

★ **Rhineland-Westphalia Art Collection** (Kunstsammlung Nordrhein-Westfalen) (DY M[3]) ⊘ – Designed by the Danish architects Dissing and Weitling, this modern building houses a 20C art collection including works by Picasso, Braque, Léger, Chagall, Ernst and **Paul Klee** – who was Fine Arts Professor in Düsseldorf from 1930 to 1933. Ninety-two of the artist's pictures are exhibited in rotation.

★ **Hetjens Museum** (Deutsches Keramikmuseum) (DZ M[4]) ⊘ – A collection of 12 000 ceramic objects from all over the world, covering a time span of 8 000 years, can be seen here.

★ **Land Economics Museum** (Landesmuseum Volk und Wirtschaft) (DY M[5]) ⊘ – Photographs, charts, comparative tables, graphs, maps and animated models illustrate in lively fashion the precepts of the science of economics. The process of extraction in a coal mine is demonstrated by means of a **diorama**.

★ **Löbbecke Museum and Aquatic Zoo** (Löbbecke-Museum und Aquazoo) ⊘ – *Kaiserwerther Strasse 380, in the North Park, via the Hofgartenufer* (DY M[6]).
This building houses under a single roof the Löbbecke Natural History Museum (butterflies, insects, molluscs, reptiles) and an aquatic zoo. No less than 78 aquariums, some of them huge, display aquatic creatures of every sort, including sharks and seals. Instructive explanations familiarize the visitor with all kinds of life in a marine element, and its ecological importance. A **Tropical Hall** in the middle of the building (crocodiles) can be crossed by means of a footbridge.

EXCURSIONS

Neuss – *10km - 6 miles to the southwest. Leave Düsseldorf via the Elisabethstrasse. Town plan in the current Michelin Red Guide Deutschland.*
The 13C **Church of St Quirinus**★ with its trefoil apse is one of the last Rhenish Romanesque constructions of importance. The octagonal tower above the transept crossing is flanked by four small square turrets with pointed diamond-shaped roofs. The shell form of the church's clerestory windows, as well as unusual mingling of round and pointed arches, marks the transition in Germany to the Gothic style. From the raised chancel there is a good view of the aisles.

Benrath Mansion ⊘ – *10km - 6 miles to the southeast. Plan of the conurbation in the Michelin Red Guide Deutschland.*
The stately home, built by Nicolas de Pigage between 1755 and 1770, is pure Louis XV in style. Two low wings flank a central pavilion designed for the Prince Elector of the Palatinate. The restraint of the original Rococo interior decoration foreshadows the formal Classicism which followed.
The wooded **park**★ extends to the Rhine, its normal vistas elongated by canals.

Neandertal – *14km - 9 miles to the east, via Am Wehrhahn.*
The deep and steep-sided valley of the Düssel owes its name to the Calvinist poet Joachim Neander (1650-1680), who liked to use it as a retreat. It was here, in a grotto since destroyed, that the famous skeleton of **Neanderthal Man**, 60 000 years old, was discovered in 1856. A plaque on a triangular rock (*on the right-hand side of the road, two miles beyond the motorway underpass*) marks the site of the cave.

Leave the car near the Neanderhöhle restaurant.

The **Prehistory Museum** (Urgeschichtliches Museum) ⊘ is on the edge of a wild animal reserve (Aurochs). It communicates some idea of the everyday life of prehistoric man, but only a few of the original bones are on view. The Neanderthal Man skull is in the Rhineland Museum in Bonn.

Michelin map **413** Q 20

Eichstätt is a small episcopal city embraced within a curve of the Altmühl river, in Germany's biggest natural park. It owes its Baroque character to the reconstruction following the sack of the town by the Swedes in 1634. Many of the roofs are covered with limestone slabs (Solnhofen) peculiar to the region.

EICHSTÄTT

Domplatz
Gabrielistraße 4
Luitpoldstraße
Marktgasse 12
Marktplatz
Ostenstraße
Westenstraße

Freiwasserstraße 3
Herzoggasse 5
Kapuzinergasse 8
Loy-Hering-Gasse 10
Pater-Philipp-
    Jeningen-Platz 13
Spitalbrücke 17
Walburgiberg 20
Weißenburgerstraße 23
Widmanngasse 25

★ **EPISCOPAL QUARTER** (BISCHÖFLICHER RESIDENZBEZIRK) *time: 1 1/2 hours*

Cathedral (Dom) – The building as a whole dates from the 14C, though parts of it are Romanesque, and others Gothic or Baroque. On the north side, facing the Domplatz, a sober Romanesque door opens into the transept, but the main entrance is via a Gothic door decorated with multicoloured statues. The west face is Baroque.

Inside, the most fascinating feature is the late 15C **Pappenheim Reredos★★**, almost 30ft high, in the north aisle. The representation of the Crucifixion with its attendant figures is a masterpiece of religious sculpture. In the west chancel is a seated statue of **St Willibald** (Bishop of Eichstätt in the 8C) as an old man, the major work of local sculptor Loy Hering (1514).

Go through the south transept to the Mortuarium.

★ **Mortuarium** – This funerary chapel, forming the west wing of the cloister, is a late 15C Gothic hall with two naves. Handsome tombstones pave the floor. A twisted column ends each line of pillars supporting the groined vaulting. The so-called "Beautiful Column" is very finely worked. Four **stained glass windows** in the east wall are by Hans Holbein the Elder (*c*1500). There is a 16C Crucifixion on the south wall.

Diocesan Museum (Diözesanmuseum) ⊙ – *Upper floor, above the Mortuarium.*
The long history of the Diocese is illustrated by means of pictures, maps, vestments, liturgical accessories and statues in stone and wood. In the Bishop's Room, note **St Willibald's Chasuble**, the oldest liturgical vestment in the See – a Byzantine work dating probably from the 12C.
Reliquaries, chalices, monstrances and other examples of religious art are on view in the **treasury**.

★ **Cloister (A)** – This element was a 15C addition to the cathedral. The stone tracery of the windows is richly decorated.

★ **Residenzplatz** – The southeast corner is the best place from which to obtain a general view of this irregularly shaped square which nevertheless displays a striking unity. Lawns carpet the centre; Rococo palaces surround it. The south side is bordered by four imposing houses with decorated gables and entrances guarded by atlantes. Facing them is the southern wing of the Residence and, on the west side, the former Vicar-General's mansion. The **Virgin's Column** in the immediate foreground (Mariensäule) rises from a fountain surrounded by cherubs.

Former Episcopal Residence (Fürstbischöfliche Residenz) **(B)** ⊙ – The main entrance opens on a magnificent staircase with a Baroque banister and painted ceiling.

The letter ß (eszett) which is to be found only in the German alphabet, appears in the text transcribed as "ss".

ADDITIONAL SIGHTS

Hofgarten – This park was designed in the style of an English garden by Eugene de Beauharnais, the son-in-law of Napoleon created Duke of Leuchtenberg and Prince of Eichstätt by King Maximilian of Bavaria. It extends in front of the summer residence of the Prince-Bishops. Three delightful pavilions adjoin the south wall. In the centre, the **Shell Pavilion★** (**D**), with its fountain and stuccowork, is a true shrine to the Rococo style.

Capuchin Church (Kapuzinerkirche) – One of the chapels in this 17C church contains a 12C copy of the Holy Sepulchre in Jerusalem.

St Walburg's Church – The interior of this Benedictine monastery church is discreetly decorated with Wessobrunn stuccoes. From the balcony outside the main doorway there is an attractive view over the roofs of the old town to the Altmühl valley.

St Willibald's Castle (Willibaldsburg) – *Access via route B13 and the Burgstrasse.* This 14C castle, unfinished until the beginning of the 17C, occupies a dominant position on a height overlooking the river in the western part of the town. Inside the castle, note the **well** (Tiefer Brunnen), 75m - 246ft deep *(access through the courtyard)*. From the top of the crenellated tower *(98 steps)* there is a **view** of the fortifications, the town and the river.

★ **Jura Museum** ⊙ – The geological history of the Franconian Jura is traced in this museum. Most of the fossils on display (ammonites, crustaceans, fish, reptiles and dragonflies) were discovered in the limestone beds of Solnhofen. An interesting comparison can be made between these fossil fish and those to be found in an aquarium. The museum's prize exhibit is the complete fossilized skeleton of an Archaeopteryx (prehistoric ancestor of birds). Halfway between the reptile and the bird in the evolution of species, this extremely rare example was found in 1951 near Workerzell, northwest of Eichstätt.

Historical Museum (Ur- und Frühgeschichtliches Museum) ⊙ – The exhibits here chart the history of settlers and settlements in the valley of the Altmühl from the epoch of hunters and crop-gatherers to the Middle Ages. Note especially the objects found in archaeological digs which relate to iron-working during the Hallstatt civilization and in Roman times.

EXCURSIONS

Weissenburg – *24km - 15 miles to the northwest.*
At the limit of the ancient Roman province of Rhaetia, Weissenburg was an important garrison town. The **Roman Baths★** (Römische Thermen) ⊙, discovered in 1977, and a **Roman Museum** (Römermuseum) ⊙ both testify to this significant past (in the museum, note particularly the fine collection of bronze **statuettes★**). The **Ellingen Tor**, to the north of the town, is an interesting gateway once part of the surrounding 14C ramparts. **St Andrew's Church** (Andreaskirche) has an elegant Late Gothic chancel built at the beginning of the 15C.

Ellingen – *3km - 1 3/4 miles to the north of Weissenburg.*
This locality owes its fame to the Teutonic Knights *(qv)*, whose Commander for Franconia was based in this small town from the 13C until Napoleon's dissolution of the Order in 1809. The castle (1708-1721) comprises an inner courtyard framed by four imposing wings, one of which is entirely occupied by the church. The huge twin-flight **main staircase★** links the different apartments with a frigid solemnity.

A number of Touring Programmes is given on pp 7-9.
Plan a trip with the help of the Principal Sights Map on pp 4-6.

★ **EIFEL MASSIF** Rhineland-Westphalia and Rhineland-Palatinate

Michelin map **412** folds 20 and 21

The Eifel, geographically an eastward extension of the Ardennes, is the largest and most complex of the four Rhineland schist massifs. An undulating plateau at an average altitude of 600m - 1970ft, the region is deeply gashed by the Ahr, the Rur and the Kyll rivers, which meander through picturesque wooded valleys.
The **Upper Eifel** (Hocheifel), in the centre, shows traces of ancient volcanic activity, with basalt crests (Hohe Acht: 747m - 2 450ft), tufa deposits, hot springs and lakes (Maare).
The **Schnee Eifel**, the most rugged and isolated of the four, forms a sombre barrier along the Belgian frontier, northwest of Prum. Much of it rises to 700m - 2 300ft.
The **North Eifel**, a landscape of moors and forests cut by deep valleys, is romantic and attractive. The touristic Seven Lakes sector extends in the northwest to the Upper Fagnes (Hohes Venn), a marshy tableland belonging more to the Ardennes than the Eifel.
The **South Eifel**, bordering Luxemburg's "Little Switzerland", is a region of picturesque valleys with small villages among the trees.

Ahr Wines – The vineyards bordering this river, planted with Burgundian stock on schistous slopes, produce dark red wines late in the season, designed to be drunk almost warm.

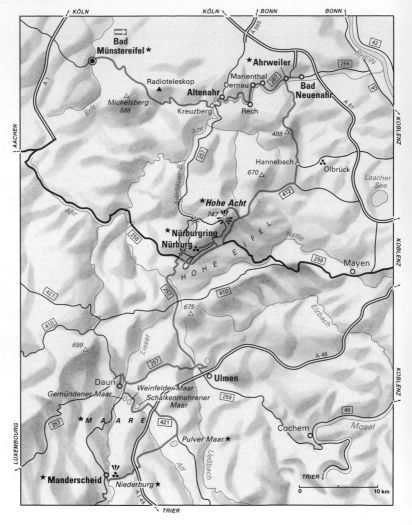

FROM BAD MÜNSTEREIFEL TO MANDERSCHEID
145km - 90 miles - one day

This excursion follows the busy valley of the Ahr, climbs to the rolling, forested immensity of the Upper Eifel, and then snakes between the volcanic lakes of the Maare.

★ **Bad Münstereifel** – Surrounded by massive **ramparts★** (Stadtbefestigunger), the town still boasts a quantity of old houses and monuments. **The Church of St Chrysanthus** (St Chrysanthus und Daria) is an outstanding abbey church recalling St Pantaleon in Cologne because of the two towers flanking its 11C Romanesque façade.

A few miles east of Münstereifel, the road leaves on the left a giant **radio-telescope**, rejoins the Ahr at Kreuzberg and continues along the winding valley. The telescope is 100m - 328ft in diameter and its parabolic depth is 21m - 69ft.

Altenahr – On a site between two bends in the river, Altenahr is an excursion centre dominated by the scattered ruins of the 12C **Burg Are**. There is an attractive view from the upper terminal of the chairlift.

The valley, in which vineyards now alternate with rock outcrops, plays host to a number of wine producing villages: **Rech**, on either side of its Roman bridge; **Dernau** with its "wine fountain"; **Marienthal** and its ruined convent.

Bad Neuenahr-Ahrweiler – The old town of **Ahrweiler★** still retains its medieval gates and its fortifications. Half-timbered houses line the narrow, pedestrians-only streets of the town centre. The spa at Bad Neuenahr, much favoured by diabetics, produces (as you leave the town, on the east) the celebrated "Apollinaris" sparkling mineral water.

Leaving Ahrweiler, the road climbs swiftly towards the forest before it runs out over a rolling highland area.

★ **Hohe Acht** – *1/2 hour on foot Rtn.* From the viewpoint at the top of the tower (*75 steps*) erected at the highest point of the Eifel (747m - 2 451ft), there is a superb **panorama★★** to delight the eye – a vast landscape slashed by deep valleys above which the only prominent points are Nürburg Castle to the southwest and, in the opposite direction, the ruins of Olbrück in front of the distant Siebengebirge (Seven Mountains).

Nürburg – *1/2 hour on foot Rtn.* A much-restored ruin in the middle of a rugged **landscape** which can be admired to the best advantage from the top of the keep.

★ **Nürburgring** – *See under Nürburgring.*

Ulmen – A pretty volcanic crater lake between the village and a ruined castle.

★ **The Maare** – The ancient volcanic region of the Maare starts at Daun. The lakes which distinguish it, of modest dimensions, mark the upheavals which occurred in the volcanic areas of the Upper Eifel in the Tertiary era. Gas pressure produced explosions, creating craters with neither cone nor lava but only a surrounding circle of cinders. The water which has gathered within these craters has formed lakes that are both deep and calm. *Follow the green signposts with the word "Maare".*

Gemündener Maar – A small, sombre green lake at the bottom of a wooded funnel, very popular in summer with bathers and canoe enthusiasts.

Weinfelder Maar and Schalkenmehrener Maar – These two lakes fill craters well clear of the road, one on either side.

★ **Pulver Maar** – A perfect circle in form, this is the most beautiful lake in the area. After the motorway underpass, the route leaves the plateau to follow the pretty, steep-sided valley that leads to Manderscheid.

★ **Manderscheid** – Arriving from Daun, stop at Niedermanderscheid and climb up to the **Niederburg★** ruins. From the top of the castle keep, there is a fine **view★** over the village to the Oberburg ruins and the Lieser valley. Return to the car and drive as far as the Pension Talblick. From here, take the footpath which leads to the **viewpoint★★** overlooking the Oberburg and Niederburg ruins.

*The **Michelin Red Guide Deutschland**
lists hotels and restaurants
which offer good meals at moderate prices;
consult the latest edition.*

EINBECK Lower Saxony   Pop 29 400

Michelin maps **411** and **412** M 11

In the Middle Ages, no less than 700 small breweries in this former Hanseatic town supplied the whole of Germany with "Einpöckisches Bier" (from which the modern name Bockbier is derived). Situated between the Harz mountains and the Weser, Einbeck still retains part of its medieval fortifications, but a more attractive heritage is a collection of almost 120 half-timbered 16C houses, richly decorated with multicoloured carvings.

★★ **Half-timbered Houses** – *Time: 1 hour.* Most of these half-timbered dwellings are near the old market.

★★ **Market Place** (Marktplatz) – Note first of all the two houses on the corner of the Münsterstrasse: the Brodhaus (1552), and especially the Ratsapotheke (1590), an impressive building which has - like most of the old houses - ventilated attics which served as lofts for hops and barley. Opposite is the town hall (Rathaus), its three projecting fronts crowned with unusual pointed roofs.

★ **Weigh-House** (Ratswaage) – The well preserved façade of this ancient weigh-bridge exhibits an embellishment typical of the burghers' houses in Einbeck: fan-shaped, palm-leaf motifs, beaded and twisted mouldings to frame doors and traverses, friezes festooned with garlands.

★★ **Tiedexerstrasse** – *Start behind the church tower (Marktkirche).* The gables and façades on either side of this street offer an especially pleasing perspective.

Marktstrasse – Note particularly the **Eickesche Haus★★** *(No 13 in the street, on the corner of the Knochenhauerstrasse).* Erected between 1612 and 1614, this wood-built construction ignores the traditional local style and imitates the stone mansions of the Renaissance. Carved panels represent the virtues and the artistic muses in an allegorical cycle; statues and expressive masks adorn the uprights and the beam-ends.

EXCURSIONS

Bad Gandersheim – *22km - 14 miles to the northeast.*
The birthplace of Roswitha von Gandersheim, Germany's first (10C) poetess, is today an appreciated hot spring and salt-water spa. The twin octagonal towers of the **cathedral★**, buttressing the 11C central façade, overlook the historic town centre. Inside are two very fine **altars**, one 15C and the other 16C. Around the market place are many well-preserved half-timbered houses (especially those dating from the 16C) and the **Renaissance Town Hall**, which adjoins the Moritzkirche.

Alfeld – *24km - 15 miles to the north.*
It is above all the **former college** (Alte Lateinschule) which makes a detour to this town on the banks of the Leine worthwhile.
Today this half-timbered building, which dates from 1610 and is adorned with carved figures, is the site of a **Regional Museum** (Heimatmuseum) ☉.

121

Eisenach was founded at the end of the 12C by Ludwig I, first of the Landgraves of Thuringia. The town, on the northwestern edge of the Forest of Thuringia, is indissolubly linked with the Fortress of Wartburg, which not only symbolizes but also externalizes the very spirit of German civilization.

At the Heart of Germany – At the beginning of the 13C, the Minnesänger (troubadours) took part in the famous jousts at Wartburg – a custom which inspired the theme of Wagner's opera *Tannhäuser*. It was at Eisenach that Luther studied before embarking on his translation of the New Testament under the patronage of the Duke of Saxony. **Johann Sebastian Bach** was born there in 1685, when the town was the seat of the Dukes of Saxe-Eisenach, who were obliged to relinquish it in 1741 to the house of Saxe-Weimar.

In 1817, the Wartburg fortress was the site of a manifestation by student corporations designed to stimulate patriotism and progressive ideas. Fifty years later (1869) the "Eisenach Declaration" marked the creation by August Bebel and Wilhelm Liebknecht of the German Social Democrat Party.

MARKET PLACE (MARKT)

Castle (Schloss) – The sober Baroque façade of the castle seals off the northern side of the market place. This former residence of the Dukes of Saxe-Weimar now houses the **Thuringian Museum** (Thüringer Museum) ⊙ (porcelain, faience and regional glassware of the 18C and 19C; Rococo banqueting hall).

Town Hall (Rathaus) – A three-storey 16C building in both Baroque and Renaissance styles, restored after a disastrous fire in 1636. Note the (slightly) leaning tower.

St George's Parish Church (Pfarrkirche St Georg) – This triple-aisle 16C hall-church contains the tombs of several Landgraves of Thuringia. Luther preached here on 2 May 1521, despite the fact that he was officially banned from the Holy Roman Empire *(qv)*, and Johann Sebastian Bach was baptized in this church on 26 March 1685.

Church of the Preachers (Predigerkirche) – The church, an Early Gothic (late 13C building), now houses the wooden **sculpture collection★** formerly in the Thuringian Museum *(see above)*. The carvings date from the 12C to the 16C.

Luther's House (Lutherhaus) ⊙ – It was in this fine late 14C house that Luther lived between 1498 and 1501, while he was a student at the School of Latin. Numerous documents and religious books are on view, as well as a complete collection of his theses.

> *Carnivals and Festivals.*
> *Germany's most important carnivals and festivals are listed in the Calendar of Events, in the Practical Information section at the end of the Guide.*

OTHER SIGHTS

Bach's House (Bachhaus) ⊙ – *From the Luther house, return along the Luther-strasse as far as the Frauenplan.*
Ambrose Bach, himself a musician and an eminent citizen of Eisenach, owned this discreet house believed to have been the birthplace of the great composer. The interior of the house provides fascinating insights into the life-style of a late 17C burgher. Manuscripts, scores and portraits recall not only Johann Sebastian Bach but several other members of the family, all of them composers.

Wartburg Automobile Museum (Automobil-Ausstellungs-Pavillon) ⊙ – On the Wartburgallee. Motor cars, from vintage models to the latest Wartburg made in Eisenach, are on display here.

Fritz Reuter and Richard Wagner Museum ⊙ – *Follow the Wartburgallee southwards as far as the Reuterweg.*
The apartment in which Fritz Reuter lived from 1863 to 1874 can be viewed. It was while he was living here that the poet, most of whose work is written in "Plattdeutsch" (Low German), excited the wrath of the Prussian authorities by participating in the Liberal Students' Movement.
The Richard Wagner Museum illustrates the life and work of the composer.

WARTBURG FORTRESS *time: 2 hours*

> *Leave the car in the Wartburgallee car park and take the shuttle (Pendlerbus). 15mn-walk.*

Perched on a rocky spur, the fortress shows clearly that it combines elements from several different periods. The visitor passes first beneath the porch of an entrance lodge, the oldest parts of which date from the 12C. Beyond this, the **outer courtyard** (Erster Burghof) is framed by half-timbered buildings erected in the 15C and 16C. A second, inner courtyard leads to the most interesting parts of the complex. On the left, the **Palais★**, where the Landgraves lived, piles three storeys one upon the other, the whole garnished with early 13C arcading.
At the far end of the bailey is the square castle keep (mid-19C), topped by a terrace with a panoramic view of Eisenach and the Forest of Thuringia.

Interior ⊙ – Successively, one passes through: the **Knights' Hall** (Rittersaal), where the vaulting is supported by an outsize central pillar; the **dining room**, with 11C capitals; **Elizabeth's boudoir and gallery**, with mosaics (1902-1906) and frescoes (Moritz von Schwind, 1854) recalling the life of the King of Hungary's daughter; the **Hall of the Troubadours**, with Von Schwind's huge mural illustrating episodes from *Tannhäuser*; the **Landgraves' Courtroom**, with a central capital illustrating the plunging flight of eagles; the **Great Banqueting Hall**, decorated in a style popular in the middle of the 19C.

Finally, the tour ends in the **Wartburg Museum**, which explains in detail the various stages in the construction of the fortress. There are several paintings by Lucas Cranach the Elder.

The Wartburg Fortress, Eisenach

Following the watchpath, the last thing to see is **Luther's Room** (Lutherstube).

EXCURSION

★★ **Forest of Thuringia** – *See under Forest of Thuringia.*

EMDEN Lower Saxony   Pop 50 000

Michelin map **411** E 6
Town plan in the current Michelin Red Guide Deutschland

The silting up of the Ems estuary in the 16C struck a fatal blow at the port of Emden. The subsequent construction of dykes, however, together with the opening of the Dortmund-Ems and the Ems-Jade canals, have enabled the town to regain its position as the chief maritime port of Westphalia, specializing in shipbuilding and the export of new cars. Large freighters sail into the inner harbour to tranship iron ore destined for the Ruhr, and there are now installations for the processing of North Sea gas.

Emden is the departure point for a daily service to the isle of Borkum, and for tours of the East Frisian islands *(qv)*.

★ **East Frisian Museum (Ostfriesisches Landesmuseum)** ⊙ – *In the former Town Hall.* Items excavated in peat bog digs, models of the port and fishing boats (Emden was the principal base of the German herring fleet), and paintings of the Dutch School evoke the colourful history of the town. Pride of place is given to the **Rüstkammer★★**, the old burghers' arsenal, which contains a splendid collection of 16-18C side-arms and armour, together with old reproductions illustrating the evolution of the arsenal.

From the bell tower, there is a view of the harbour and surrounding countryside.

Fifteen kilometers - 9 miles to the north is the picturesque fishing port of **Greetsiel**, a colourful sight when the boats are in.

★ ERFURT Thuringia   Pop 220 000

Michelin map **987** fold 26

In the year 742, Wynfrid, a missionary arriving from England who was later canonized as St Boniface, created a bishopric at Erfurt which was soon joined to that of Mainz.

From the Middle Ages onward, the town's position on the important trade route linking the Rhine with Russia lent it such commercial consequence that it was incorporated into the Hanseatic League in the 15C. Erfurt thus became an essential part of the connection uniting Central Europe with the powerful ports of the north.

Spirituality and Humanism – The numerous steeples and bell towers rising above the roofs of the town bear witness to the religious activity in Erfurt under the influence of the Archbishop-Electors of Mainz.

After the Dominican **Master Eckhart**, established in Erfurt from 1303 as Provincial of Saxony, the town was host two centuries later to the young **Martin Luther**. Eckhart was the instigator of what developed into the Rhineland spiritual mystique. Luther studied philosophy at the university – considered to be the cradle of German Humanism – entered the Augustine monastery in 1505 and left six years later to establish himself in Wittenberg (qv).

The Congress of Erfurt – With the aim of persuading the Tzar Alexander I to "neutralize" Austria while he progressed his Spanish campaign, Napoleon received the Russian ruler in Erfurt with great pomp and ceremony from 27 September to 14 October 1808. His plan, backed up with a demonstration of force, was only partly successful: all he could get was a promise of Russian military aid in the case of Austrian aggression. During the 17-day conference, Napoleon met Goethe several times, the two men sharing a mutual admiration, and subsequently created him a Chevalier de la Légion d'Honneur.

SIGHTS

★★ **St Peter's Cathedral (Petri-Dom)** – The original Romanesque basilica, built in 1154 on a hill occupied by the citadel, was added to in the middle of the 14C – a porch at the entrance to the north transept; a soaring Gothic chancel at the est end. A century later, the Romanesque nave was replaced by a nave in the Flamboyant Gothic style, with broad side aisles.

★★ **North Entrance** – The porch embodies two doors set obliquely and supporting elegant statuary groups – on the northwest side, the Wise and Foolish Virgins; on the northeast the Apostles at work, a group recalling the French cathedral master-masons.

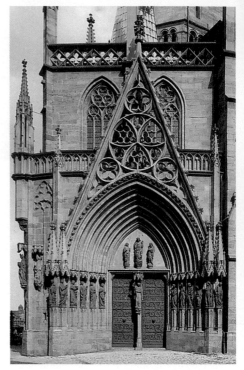

St Peter's Cathedral, Erfurt - the northwest door

Interior – There are several works of art worthy of attention: the Romanesque Altar of the Virgin (1160); the **statue-candelabra**★ known as "the Wolfram" (1160); the tombstone of the Count of Gleichen and his two wives; the intricately worked choir stalls (14C). Some of the **stained glass windows**★ above the choir (c1370-1420) show scenes of everyday life in the latter part of the Middle Ages.

★ **St Severin's Church (Severi-Kirche)** – Formerly the Augustinian monks' abbey-church, this Early Gothic building is of the hall type, with five naves. The **sarcophagus**★ of the saint (c1365) is in the southernmost aisle.

Cross the Domplatz and take the Marktstrasse.

Fischmarkt – Inside the imposing neo-Gothic Town Hall (Rathaus) are **frescoes**★ which illustrate the legends and the history of Thuringia. On the north side of the square (nos 13-16) there is a fine three-storey Renaissance building, "Zum Breiten Herd".

★ **Krämerbrücke** – Each side of this bridge, known as "the Grocer's Bridge", there are houses dating from the 17C to the 19C.

Augustinian Monastery (Augustinerkloster) ⊘ – *Entrance at Augustinerstrasse 10.* The monastery church, founded by hermits in the mid-13C, has a window (c1340) illustrating the life of St Augustine. The Gothic cloister leads to the abbey buildings where Luther lived and worked.

★ **Anger Museum** ⊘ – *Anger 18.*
In this museum, above all visit the Department of Medieval Painting and Sculpture (14, 15 and 16C altarpieces, a Pietà★★ by the Master of St Severin) and the gallery of German painting from the 18 to the 20C (CD Friedrich, Liebermann, Corinth and Slevogt).

Franciscan Church (Barfüsserkirche) ⊘ – The nave of this triple-aisle hall-church has been left in a state of ruin since 1945. The 14C chancel has been transformed into a **Museum of Medieval Art** (Museum für Kunst des Mittelalters): late 13C stained glass (Life and Passion of Christ, Life of St Francis); several altarpieces, among them the "Farbealtar" representing the Crucifixion (c1420).

EXCURSION

Arnstadt – *16km - 10 miles to the south.*
A small Thuringian town dating from the 8C, but known above all for the fact that
JS Bach stayed there from 1703 to 1707, when he was organist at the Parish
Church (An der Neuen Kirche) which todays bears his name. There is a **Local
History Museum** (Museum für Stadtgeschichte und Bachgedenkstätte) ⊘ outlining
the history of the town and displaying mementoes of the composer in the house
named "Zum Palmbaum" on one side of the market place (Am Markt).
In the old cemetery (Alter Friedhof, Bahnhofstrasse) are the graves of 20 members of the Bach family.
In the **New Palace** (Neues Palais, *August-Bebel Strasse*) ⊘, see the **collection of
marionettes and dolls**★ (Mon Plaisir Puppensammlung), the Brussels tapestries of
the Renaissance period, and the **porcelain**★ from Meissen and the Far East.

For a pleasant hotel in peaceful surroundings
Look in the current
Michelin Guide Deutschland
(Red Guide hotels and restaurants)

★ THE ERZGEBIRGE Saxony

Michelin map **987** fold 27

Known as the Ore Mountains, this medium-height massif owes its name to the
many veins and deposits of silver, tin, cobalt, nickel and iron distributed among
its strata – a natural wealth which has brought prosperity to a number of small
towns such as Zwickau *(qv)*, Annaberg *(qv)*, and Schneeberg.
The crest of the range marking the frontier with Czechoslovakia reaches a
modest 750m - 2 461ft, and the relatively high altitude of the valley floors
frequently gives the impression more of an upland plateau than a mountain
range. The most impressive single summit on the German side is the **Fichtelberg**,
at 1 214m - 3 950ft. Landscapes that are both open and wooded, reservoir lakes,
forests criss-crossed by footpaths and picturesque holiday villages combine to
make the region particularly attractive to visitors.
The itinerary described below,which explores the western part of the range, follows the Czech frontier to start with

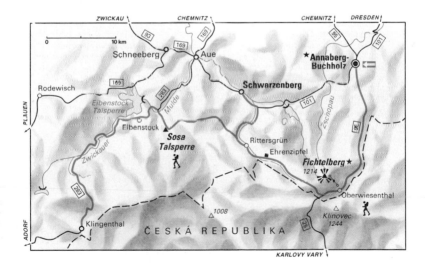

FROM ANNABERG-BUCHHOLZ TO KLINGENTHAL

81km - 50 miles (91km - 57 miles via Schwarzenberg) - time: 3 hours

★ **Annaberg-Buchholz** – *See under Annaberg-Buchholz.*

> *Leave Annaberg-Buchholz by Route 95 in the direction of Oberwiesenthal.*

★ **Fichtelberg** – Towering above the health and winter sports resort of
Oberwiesenthal. This peak is identifiable from far off by the meteorological equipment adorning its summit. The top is reached by ski-lift or on foot *(1/2 hour Rtn.
Leave the car in the car park 500 yards after the lower ski-lift terminal).* A vast
panorama★ opens out when the top is reached, showing all of the surrounding
country and, away in the south, the silhouette of Mount Klinovec in
Czechoslovakia. At 1 244m - 4 800ft, this is the highest peak of the Erzgebirge.

> *From Oberwiesenthal to Ehrenzipfel there is a pretty forest road which fol-
> lows the course of a river. At Rittersgrün, one can either take the detour via
> Schwarzenberg or continue along the direct route.*

Schwarzenberg – Beside a castle, built on the ruins of ancient fortress at the beginning of the 15C, is **St George's Church★** (Pfarrkirche St-Georg). This Baroque building (1690-1699) has a wide, very attractively decorated nave. Note the elegant pulpit, apparently supported by a statue, the wrought-iron chancel screen, and the cherubs on the ceiling.

Sosa Talsperre – *From the car park, walk to the kiosk and then the promontory.* This small lake and its dam are in an idyllic forest setting.

The road follows the northern bank of the reservoir formed by the Eibenstock barrage and then (Route 283) climbs the winding valley of the Zwickauer Mulde before it runs into **Klingenthal.**

★ **ESSEN** Rhineland-Westphalia   Pop 620 000

Michelin maps **411** and **412** E I2 - Local map see under RUHR BASIN

Essen is by no means the smoke-blackened industrial complex that many people imagine. On the contrary, the capital of the Ruhr has the air of a residential town, with attractive pedestrian precincts bordered by elegant shops, a lovely art gallery and pleasant suburbs in green surrounding (**Grugapark**, **RS**). Woods, extending southwards, border the tranquil Baldeneysee. Neither steelworks nor blast furnace has resumed activity since the end of the Second World War. The main industry is now the manufacture of machine tools, and there is a permanent exhibition of industrial design at the **Industrial Design Centre** (Design Zentrum Nordrhein-Westfalen) (**DZ B**) ⊘ in the centre of this altogether surprising town. The cathedral, one of the oldest places of worship in the Rhineland, is nearby.

SIGHTS

★★ **Folkwang Museum** (**R**) ⊘ – Paintings and sculpture of the 19C and 20C are displayed in profusion in these galleries. Alongside the German Romantics (Feuerbach, Trübner and Thoma) are numerous works by the French Impressionists (Pissaro, Sisley, Cézanne, Monet, Renoir and Gauguin). The diversity of German Expressionism is exemplified in works by the Brücke Group and artists of the Blauer Reiter movement (a fine painting in hot colours by Rohlfs; *Fashion House* by Macke). The art of the Bauhaus is represented by Feininger and Schlemmer, that of the Cubists by Léger, Delaunay and Miro. This outstanding collection also exhibits sculptures by Rodin and Minne, as well as diverse works by Chagall, Ernst, Manessier *(see below)* and Nay.

Cathedral (Münster) (**DZ**) – The 10C **west chancel★**, with three angled side walls, is the oldest part of the building. It was directly influenced by that in the cathedral at Aachen. The nave, a Gothic hall with ogive vaulting, dates from the end of the 13C; the Ottonian crypt now has stained glass windows by Manessier. Off the northern aisle, there is a lateral chapel housing a priceless work: **The Golden Madonna★★★**, said to be the oldest (980AD) statue of the Virgin in the West. In the western part of the church there is a gigantic seven-branch candelabra (*c*1000) decorated with geometric motifs. The **cathedral treasury★★** (Münsterschatzkammer) (**DZ M¹**) ⊘ holds four splendid **processional crosses★★★** (10 and 11C), the Golden Madonna's crown, monstrances, gospels, and the sword of the martyr-saints Cosmas and Damian.

St John's Church (Johanniskirche) (**DZ A**) – Originally a baptistry of the cathedral chapter – from which it is separated by an 11C atrium – this meditation chapel was transformed into a hall-church *cl*470. In the south aisle, an **altarpiece★** painted by Bartholomäus Bruyn the Elder (16C) represents scenes from the life of Jesus. The painting's composition, the facial expression, and the subtle shades of green and red foreshadow already the Renaissance.

★ **Villa Hügel** (**S**) – This mansion, an example of the pompous style of the Bismarckian era, was built for Alfred Krupp in 1872. Standing in an attractive park on the north shore of the Baldeney lake, it has been open to the public since 1953. The huge, darkly panelled rooms, scene of innumerable receptions and meetings of industrial tycoons, are used for art exhibitions today. The **Krupp Collections★★** (Historische Sammlung Krupp) ⊘ themselves are housed in an adjacent pavilion. They offer an insight into the extraordinary success story of this family business, which started in 1811 with Friedrich Krupp's construction of the first steel-casting crucible and subsequently reflected the entire growth and development of heavy industry in Germany.

Abbey Church of St Ludger (**S**) – *At Essen-Werden, 8km - 5 miles south of the city centre.*
The structure of this building is Romanesque (12C), but hints of early Gothic design are already evident, particularly in the ogive vaulting of the nave. The transept crossing is surmounted by a **dome on pendentives★**. In the treasury, note an 11C bronze **crucifix★** with a particularly pure line, as well as a 5C ivory pyx. In the crypt is one of the rare pierced galleries in Germany, from which pilgrims praying could at the same time venerate the tomb of St Ludger, lying in a central vault.

To find a pleasant country hotel
*consult the current **Michelin Red Guide Deutschland***

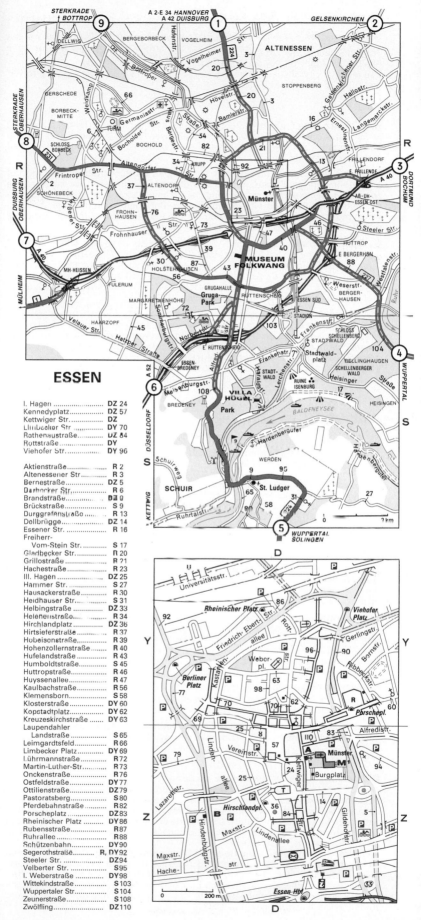

ESSEN

127

ESLINGEN AM NECKAR Baden-Württemberg Pop 91 000

Michelin map 413 K 20 - Town plan in the current Michelin Red Guide Deutschland

The old Swabian town of Esslingen, below the vine-covered slopes of the Neckar, retains, especially on the east bank of the river, all the atmosphere of a one-time free imperial city. Visually, the town is distinguished by belfries, the Burg tower, and ruins of the 13C fortifications.

SIGHTS

Marktplatz – The finest ornament to this picturesque, irregularly shaped square, which dates only from the 19C, is the Kielmeyer House. All the streets leading into the market are interesting, most of them bordered by old houses decorated with wood carvings.

★ **Former Town Hall** – This 15C and 16C building combines the severe charm of old half-timbering with the gracefulness of decorated Renaissance façades. The curvilinear stepped gable overlooking the Rathausplatz is surmounted by a double lantern (carillon) and vibrant with colour. But it is the south gable above all which must be seen – an outstanding feature typical of Swabian half-timbering, with heavy corbels and obliquely crossed beams.

St Denis's Church (Stadtkirche) – A Gothic building, its towers oddly linked by a footbridge, which overlooks the Marktplatz. The name of its patron saint recalls the fact that Esslingen, originally a hermitage, was given in the 8C to the great Frankish Abbey of St Denis. Inside the church, a rood screen divides the nave. Beyond this, a 15C Pietà adorns the lintel of a door on the south side. Fine 13C and 14C stained glass illuminates the chancel.

Church of Our Lady (Frauenkirche) – A pleasing architectural unity distinguishes this Gothic church, which stands on a hillside and can be reached from the Marktplatz via the Untere Beutau rise. From the west there is a fine view of the ornate church tower flanked by twin staircase turrets. The interior is richly decorated. The doorways are especially noteworthy – in the southeast, the Life of the Virgin (1350); in the southwest a 15C Last Judgement. Note the stained glass windows (1330) in the chancel.

★ # FLENSBURG Schleswig-Holstein Pop 87 000

Michelin map 411 L 2 - Town plan in the current Michelin Red Guide Deutschland

The port of Flensburg lies at the head of a sinuous arm of the sea, the **Flensburger Förde**★, appreciated by holidaymakers who can sail pleasure craft up numerous inlets shaded by beech trees. A glance at shop signs and newspaper kiosks along the quays or on the Holm, the Town's principal artery, will confirm the immediate proximity of the **Danish border** ⊙. Germany's most northern town, Flensburg lives mainly from its naval shipyards and its rum and spirit trade.

SIGHTS

★ **Municipal Museum** (Städtisches Museum) ⊙ – There is an attractive choice of antiques offering a perspective on the art and culture of Schleswig-Holstein (including that part of Schleswig that is now Danish). **The furniture and household items** on display include cupboards, trunks and marvellous wedding chests from the Gothic and Renaissance periods. Brass and copper gleam from the carefully reconstructed peasant and bourgeois interiors in the lower rooms.

Commercial and Warehouse Quarter (Kaufmannshöfe und Speicherhäuser) – Maritime trade with Norway, the Baltic and the East Indies, inseparable from Flensburg's prosperous past, is recalled by these buildings, mainly of the 18C, restored as part of an old town rehabilitation project. Note particularly the **Handelshof** (at no 86 Norderstrasse), the **Künstlerhof** (no 22 in the same street), and the **Westindienspeicher** at Grosse Strasse 24 (in the courtyard).

Church of St Nicholas (Nikolaikirche) – Overlooking the bustling Südermarkt, this massively proportioned brick building dates from the Gothic period (late 14C). There is a fine **Renaissance organ**★ (1609) inside.

North Gate (Nordertor) – This simply designed late 16C structure, with stepped gables over its brick façade, has become the symbol of the town.

EXCURSION

Glücksburg – 9km - 5 miles to the north.
The road offers glimpses of the Flensburger Förde, and then suddenly **Glücksburg Castle** (Wasserschloss) ⊙ swims into view, apparently floating on the waters of its own lake. Four corner towers link the three wings of the 1585 building, said to have been inspired by the French Château de Chambord, on the Loire. The castle is distinguished by a sobriety of decoration typical of northern Renaissance architecture.
A visit recalls memories of the House of Oldenburg-Schleswig-Holstein, to which the Danish Royal Family is related. Do not miss the great **banqueting hall** (Roter Saal) on the first floor. The heavy vaulting is delicately embellished with coffering, between which stars, rosettes and miniature busts are inserted. Note also the unusual **leather hangings**, embossed with designs in silver and gold, which were crafted in Mechelen (Belgium) in 1703.

Michelin maps 🆖 and 🆖 I 16 - J 16
Plan of the conurbation in the current Michelin Red Guide Deutschland

At the crossroads of the country's north-south and east-west communications, a truly cosmopolitan city rich in traditions, Frankfurt is the commercial capital of Germany. Owing to its central position, numerous government organizations, including the Federal Bank, are based there. Research institutes, the university founded in 1914, the opera, theatres and an ever increasing number of museums have made the city the scientific and cultural metropolis of the Hessen Land.

HISTORICAL NOTES

The historic centre of the town is the **Cathedral Hill** (Domhügel), on which there were already fortifications and a palace in Roman and Carolingian times.

When the Emperors Ruled – In 1152, Frederick Barbarossa engineered his election as King of Germania at Frankfurt, thus inaugurating a tradition which was to be ratified by the Golden Bull *(qv)* of the Emperor Charles IV in 1356. Two centuries later, in 1562, the town replaced Aachen as the **coronation place** of the rulers of the Holy Roman Empire – a privilege it retained until the dissolution of the Reich in 1806. In *Poetry and Truth ("Dichtung und Wahrheit")*, Goethe describes in great detail the sumptuous ceremonies and popular enthusiasm he witnessed as a boy when Josef II was crowned in 1764.

The Youth of Goethe – Johann Wolfgang von Goethe was born in Frankfurt in 1749, the son of a worthy Imperial Counsellor and a lively, charming, much younger woman. The great writer frequently described his debt to his parents, especially in his memoirs *(Aus Meinem Leben)*. To his father he owed his serious attitude to life, to his mother a happy temperament and a love of telling stories. At the age of 15 he fell in love for the first time, with a girl called Gretchen – who was later to serve as a model for the the character of Gretchen in **Faust**. After the tragic love affair at Wetzlar *(qv)*, where he was studying to be a young lawyer, Goethe returned to Frankfurt where, between 1772 and 1775 he enjoyed his most prolific period as a writer. It was during this period that **Werther**, based on the Wetzlar tragedy, was completed in four weeks.

Finance and Economy – In the 16C Frankfurt was granted the right to mint money. The money market rapidly flourished and the **stock exchange** was founded German banks dominated the economy in the 18C; in the 19C they acquired a worldwide reputation thanks to financiers such as **Bethmann** and above all **Rothschild** (1744-1812) whose sons, "the Five Frankfurters", established branches in Paris, London, Vienna and Naples. Profiting from such an economic climate, industries were not long to establish themselves in the city. Chemicals and pharmaceuticals (Hoechst) remain the most active today.
The first Autumn Fair was held in 1240. The Spring Fair was added in 1330. Since the war the Fur Fair, the Motor Show and the famous **Book Fair** (Buchmesse) have confirmed Frankfurt as the country's commercial capital.

Carnivals and Festivals.
Germany's most important carnivals and festivals are listed in the Calendar of Events, in the Practical Information section at the end of the Guide.

FRANKFURT TODAY

City Life – Despite its cosmopolitan character (one inhabitant in four is foreign), this "metropolis on the Main" has managed to preserve a typical Hessian atmosphere. It is around the **Hauptwache** (GY), a square dating from 1729 at the junction of the Rossmarkt and the **Zeil** (HY), that the life of Frankfurt is at its busiest. The Zeil is said to be the most important shopping street in Germany.
To the north, the quarter known as the Westend, a tranquil, shady residential area dating from the Bismarck era, fights to stave off the encroaching office blocks of the commercial centre. Cafés, cabarets, bars, and restaurants, often exotic, are grouped around the central station, while the taverns of the Alt Sachsenhausen quarter, on the south bank of the Main, specialize in the celebrated **Äppelwoi** (a very dry cider), and Handkäs mit Musik (small yellow cheeses in an onion sauce).

A General View – The old town, almost entirely destroyed in 1943-1944, lay within a green belt on the site of former fortifications razed in 1805. The **Eschenheim Tower** (Eschenheimer Turm) **(GHY)** still stands however as a well-preserved example of the medieval defence system. The tower dates from 1428.
After 1945, a small kernel of the **old town** was reconstructed around the Römerberg. The contrast between its modest silhouettes and those of the business quarter skyscrapers is at its most striking when seen from the southern end of the **Untermainbrücke (GZ)** river bridge. Between the apse of the old Carmelite church and the cathedral, one can see (from left to right) the dome of St Paul's Church, the sharply pointed roofs of the Römer, St Leonard's Church on the riverside, the soaring steeple of St Nicholas and finally, at the end of the Eiserner Steg (a metal bridge), the Saalhof, a one-time Imperial Palace of which only the Gothic corner tower remains. The most imposing skyscrapers are the Fair Tower, the Deutsche Bank and the Dresdener Bank.
From the 120m - 394ft **Henninger Turm (HZ)** ⊘, *(leave by the Paradiesgasse)* in the Sachsenhausen quarter, there is a **panorama★** taking in the town, the river, the sprawling forest of the Stadtwald and the wooded massif of the Taunus *(qv)*.

OLD TOWN *time: one half day*

Römer and Römerberg (HZ R) – The **Römer** is a disparate collection of (reconstructed) medieval burghers' houses. From 1404 the block served as a town hall, and subsequently as a coronation palace. The most characteristic façade, with three stepped Gothic gables, overlooks the Römerberg square. The name applied to the whole complex derives from the **Zum Römer house**, the centre of three and also the oldest and most richly decorated. The four statues of Emperors, above a balcony with a carved balustrade and beneath imperial eagles, are 19C additions. A graceful pierced Renaissance stairway adorns the small inner courtyard. In the 19C, to celebrate the thousand-year history of the Holy Empire, 52 statues of Emperors, from Charlemagne to Franz II (1806) were installed in niches hollowed from the walls of the **Imperial Hall** (Kaisersaal) ☉.

The southern side of the **Römerberg** is closed off by the **Church of St Nicholas (A)**, built in the 13C from the local red sandstone. The building is crowned by a gallery with four corner turrets, from which the city officials and their families would observe the lively popular fairs and fêtes. In the southwest corner is the **Wertheim House (B)**, a fine half-timbered structure in Late Renaissance (1600) style.

On the north side of the square, the 1464 **Steinernes Haus (C)** was clearly built in imitation of an Italian city mansion. A row of half-timbered houses dating from the 15C to the 18C (all reconstructed) flank the Römerberg to the east. In the centre of the square is the **Fountain of Justice** (1543).

The restored sector of old Frankfurt is hard up against the post-modern **Schirn Gallery** (Kunsthalle Schirn) **(D)** – a long, low, domed cultural centre, stark and uncompromising, where exhibitions of contemporary art are organized.

★ **Cathedral (Dom) (HZ)** – This church was designated a cathedral after it had been chosen first as the election and subsequently the coronation site of the Emperors (1356 and 1562 - *see above*). A Gothic hall-church with three naves and a wide transept, it was built between the 13C and the 15C on a hill previously occupied by a Carolingian edifice. Its outstanding feature is the tall **west tower★★** (Westturm), ornamented with a gabled polygonal crown topped by a dome and lantern, although this was not in fact completed until 1877, following the plans of the cathedral's original architect, Madern Gerthener.

In the columned peristyle erected in front of the tower in neo-Gothic style after the fire of 1867, note the outstanding grey sandstone sculpture of **The Crucifixion** (1509) – the work of the Mainz artist Hans Backoffen.

Inside, the finely worked **choir stalls★** are due to a master-craftsman from the Upper Rhine (c1350). The (restored) **mural paintings**, which date from 1427, are the work of a Master of the Cologne School *(qv)*. They illustrate the legend of St Bartholomew. In a niche on the south side of the chancel is the tombstone (1352) of Count Günther von Schwarzburg, unsuccessful rival to the Emperor Charles IV for the title of King of Germania. A door alongside leads to the chapel (Wahlkapelle: early 15C) where the seven Electors of the Holy Roman Empire in Germany *(qv)* made their final choice.

In the opposing chapel (north chancel) is the **Altar of Mary Sleeping** (Maria-Schlaf), which dates from 1434. Sole remaining altar from the church's original interior furnishings, this too is the work of the Cologne School. It represents the twelve Apostles grouped around the bed of the dying Mary. The large **Descent from the Cross** hanging on the west wall of the north chancel was painted by Anthony van Dyck in 1627.

★ **Cathedral Museum** (Dommuseum) ☉ – This has been installed in what remains of the Gothic cloister. Note the sumptuous **ornaments** worn by the ecclesiastic Electors at the coronation ceremonies. The oldest vestments date from the 15C. West of the cathedral is an **Archaeological Garden** (Historischer Garten), where the remains of Roman and Carolingian fortifications can be seen.

Historical Museum (Historisches Museum) (HZ M1) ☉ – The history of Frankfurt is presented under different headings: sacred art (sculptures, altars, stained glass windows); domestic life (interiors, utensils, clothes); trade and fairs (means of transport, colonial products); politics; justice; war (weapons); industrialization and industry.

A passageway leads to a 12C **chapel** (Saalhofkapelle) which is the oldest building in the city – in fact all that remains of the old Emperors' Palace.

St Leonard's Church (Leonardskirche) (HZ) – The outer aspect of this 15C Gothic church denies its Romanesque basilican origins. Two octagonal towers remain at the east end, along with the fine carvings of **Master Engelbert's Doorway** – although these can only be seen from inside (north aisle) now, as aisles were subsequently added on either side. The central nave, almost square, is surrounded on three sides by a gallery. Fine stained glass windows illuminate the chancel. Left of the chancel are a superbly carved reredos representing scenes from the life of the Virgin, and a painting by Holbein the Elder depicting the **Last Supper**. The baptismal chapel of the north aisle displays a very large hanging keystone.

St Paul's Church (Paulskirche) (HZ) – It was in this circular building dating from the beginning of the classic era (again, reconstructed) that the German National Assembly elected after the revolution of March sat from 1848 to 1849. The church houses an exhibition devoted to the history of the German democratic movement.

★ **Goethe's House and the Goethe Museum** (GZ) ☉ – "The house is spacious, light and tranquil, with freestanding staircases, large vestibules and several windows with pleasant views of the garden" – it was thus that Goethe described the paternal home.

An atmosphere lingers in these rooms today of ease and serenity, of a taste for the good things of life, of a love of Italy transmitted from the father to the son.

Paintings on the walls evoke memories of family friends, while details of the Goethes' day to day life are recalled by the pots and pans in the kitchen.

The room in which the poet wrote – reconstructed like the rest of the house after the war – is as it was in his lifetime, haunted by memories of Charlotte Buff. Even his old marionette theatre is in its place in the next room.

The **Museum (M²)** adjoining Goethe's birthplace displays documents and manuscripts relating to his life and work, as well as paintings by such artists as Tischbein, Fuseli and Hackert (note especially Fuseli's *The Nightmare*, 1781). The museum also houses temporary exhibitions devoted to contemporary artistic and literary life.

Liebfrauenkirche (HYE) – The church, today a Capuchin monastery, was built as a Gothic hall-church in the 14C. The interior was remodelled in the Rococo style in the 18C.

The early 15C tympanum of the south doorway (the Adoration of the Magi, inside) is attributed to the architect and sculptor Gerthener *(see above)*.

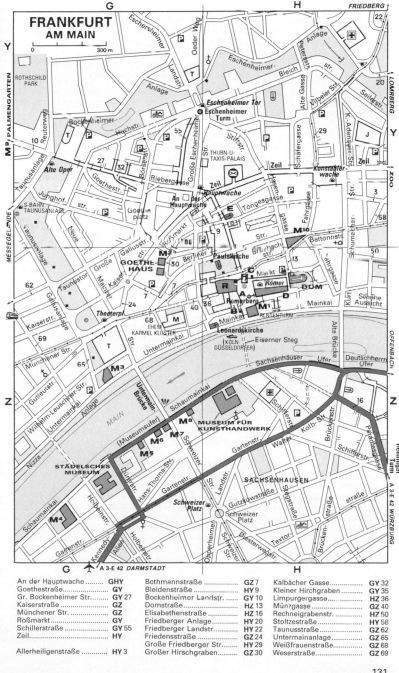

Modern Art Museum (Museum für Moderne Kunst) (HY M¹⁰) ⊘ – The Viennese architect, Hans Hollein, has achieved a spacious custom-built gallery in spite of the awkwardly-shaped site. The building in the form of a boat makes an interesting landmark in the cathedral quarter. The imaginatively designed interior is surprisingly large and makes an ideal setting for the mainly contemporary art collection. The New York school is represented by George Segal *(Jazz Combo)*, Roy Lichtenstein *(Brush-stroke)*, Claes Oldenburg and Andy Warhol. On the ground floor there is a work by Katharina Frische *(Tischgesellschaft)* remarkable in its disproportion. Also represented are Joseph Beuys with a monumental bronze installation, Mario Merz and one of his famous *Igloos* and Gerhard Richter and his oppressive *Stammhein Cycle (Stammhein Zyklus)*.

The modern art collection is complemented by a collection of photographs by Thomas Ruff (monumental portraits), the husband and wife team Becher and Blume and Jeff Wall.

Jewish Museum (Jüdisches Museum) (GZ M³) ⊘ – In the Rothschild Palace (1821). Organized according to the most modern of museographic procedures, the exhibits trace the history of Franfurt's Jewish community – one of the largest in Germany – from the Middle Ages to the present day.

SOUTH BANK OF THE MAIN

The south bank of the river, between the Eiserner Steg and the Friedensbrücke, is known to Frankfurters as the **Museum Bank**. An impressive series of museums does in fact stretch the length of the Schaumainkai in a middle-class residential area attractively interspersed with green spaces. The creation and development of projects such as the Museum of Applied Arts and the Museum of Architecture, started in the 1980s and now enjoying worldwide renown, has been skillfully integrated within this area of well-kept gardens and quiet streets.

★★ **Städel Museum and Municipal Gallery** (Städelsches Museum und Städtische Galerie) (GZ) ⊘ – On the second floor there is an important collection of **Flemish Primitives** and **16C German Masters**.

Room A: Van der Weyden, Hieronymus Bosch *(Ecce Homo)*, Hans Memling *(Man in a Red Cap)*, Jan van Eyck (the famous *Lucca Madonna)*; **Room B:** Altdorfer *(Adoration of the Magi)*; **Room D:** H Baldung Grien *(Birth and Baptism of Chirst)*. There are also remarkable altarpieces, most of them from Frankfurt churches, including the main reredos of the Dominican church which embodies *The Genealogy of Christ* by Hans Holbein the Elder. In **Cabinets 19 and 20** there are several works by the younger Brueghel.

Added to this collection are early Renaissance paintings from Italy (Fra Angelico, Botticelli), including the Mannerists (Tintoretto, Veronese); **17C Flemish work** with the Masters **Rubens** and **Rembrandt** *(The Blinding of Samson*, 1636); **French Baroque Painting** (Poussin, Lorrain, Watteau, Chardin); and the masterworks of **Adam Elsheimer**, an early Baroque painter born in Frankfurt, who lived at the beginning of the 17C in Rome (the Holy Cross altarpiece).

German works from the 18C and 19C dominate the first floor, among them the memorable meditation of *Goethe in the Roman Countryside*, painted by **JHW Tischbein** in 1787. French Impressionism is represented by **Renoir** and **Monet** *(The Luncheon Party)*.

German Expressionists exhibited include Beckmann, Kirchner and Marc. Matisse, Picasso and Braque represent that part of the modern movement influenced by Fauvism and the Cubists. Max Ernst, Paul Klee and Feininger introduce Surrealism and the art of the Bauhaus. Contemporary art is represented by Dubuffet, Bacon, Tapiès and Yves Klein.

★ **Museum of Applied Arts** (Museum für Kunsthandwerk) (HZ) ⊘ – The museum building (1985) was designed by the New York architect Richard Meier, a pupil of Marcel Breuer at the Bauhaus *(qv)*. Integrated within the design is the classically-styled Villa Metzler (1803).

Purity of line, richness of material and colour are all enhanced by the flood of light entering this airy, spacious building from every side. This is especially true of the furniture: medieval, 16C folding chairs, carved Renaissance and Baroque cupboards and chests, jewel-encrusted commodes and cabinets as well as Jugendstil items.

The **glassware collection** (15C and 16C Venetian work) is particularly interesting; and plenty of space is given to German stoneware from the 15C to the 19C, and faience from Delft, Hanau and Berlin.

The **Islamic Department** *(second floor)* contains carpets from Persia and Anatolia, furniture and weapons, and above all glassware and faience from 9C to the 15C.

The **Far East Department** *(also on the second floor)* displays bronze statues (14C to 17C) from China and Tibet; Chinese porcelain from the Ming and Ch'ing periods, including the white and the blue porcelain from the 17C and 18C; and a fine collection of lacquer.

Objects from the Rococo and Classic periods are exhibited in the former Villa Metzler. It is here that there is another remarkable **porcelain collection** assembled from the major European manufacturers in Meissen, Berlin, Fürstenberg, Nymphenburg, Vienna, Höchst and Sèvres.

★ **German Cinema Museum** (Deutsches Filmmuseum) (GZ M⁷) ⊘ – Here, the film buff may examine *(first floor)* the different inventions relating to the discovery of animation: stroboscopic discs, Emile Reynaud's 1882 Praxinoscope, a Thaumatrope, Edison's Kineto-scope (1889), and a copy of the Lumière Brother's Cinematograph (1894).

A reconstruction of the Meliès studio recalls the first film director. Daguerreotypes, a magic lantern and a dark room conjure up the beginnings of cinema. On the second floor, the visitor – introduced backstage, as it were, in both silent and talking studios faithfully reconstructed – can amuse himself composing different shots. Designs, drawings and models illustrate the techniques of special effects (*King Kong*, for instance). A small working cinema shows newsreels, publicity shots and shorts several times a day.

Liebig Museum of Sculpture (Städtische Galerie Liebighaus) (GZ M⁴) ⊘ – Here there are fine examples of sculpture and statuary from different civilizations, from **ancient Egypt** to the **Classical era**. Egypt: head of a dignitary (Middle Kingdom). Greece and Rome: statuettes; small bronze horse (8C BC); woman's head (2C BC); Tanagra figurines.

There are also Roman copies of the great Greek sculptures: Myron's Athena, the Torso of Polycletus, and the famous Praxiteles Satyr.

Equally interesting is the section devoted to the Middle Ages. A Virgin and Child (Trier, 11C), the Head of Bärbel von Ottenheim (NG van Leyden, 1463), the Rimini Reredos (c1430), another Virgin and Child (French, 14C) and the Riemenschneider Madonna – all these convey an idea of the wealth of talent working in that period. The genius of the Renaissance is exemplified by Andrea della Robbia's altarpiece of The Assumption (c1500) and a small Black Venus with Mirror (16C).

Postal Museum (Bundespostmuseum) (GZ M⁵) ⊘ – The transportation of mail – and of travellers – is illustrated from the mail-coach to the aeroplane, including the first omnibus. Also on display: a survey of the transmission of news, from antiquity to the present day.

German Architectural Museum (Deutsches Architekturmuseum) (GZ M⁶) ⊘ – For this museum, inaugurated in 1984, the architect Oswald Mathias Ungers designed an original and extremely controversial complex incorporating a magnificent villa of the Bismarck period into an ultra-modern construction.

Examples of modern architecture from all over the world are on display, as well as the best of interior design. The collection of architects' **plans and models** (19C and 20C) is presented in rotation organized by theme.

On the first floor a diorama illustrates the development of different types of houses from various civilizations.

Museum of Ethnography (Museum für Völkerkunde) (GZ M⁸) ⊘ – Different exhibitions explain the life and customs of primitive peoples in Africa, Asia, Latin-America and Oceania. Collections of masks, tools, jewels, domestic items and religious fetishes.

ADDITIONAL SIGHTS

★★★ **Zoo** ⊘ *Leave by Zeil* (HY).
The Frankfurt zoo is famous for its rare species (over 6 000 examples of 600 species), which are encouraged, successfully, to reproduce. The animals live in their natural habitat. The bird section, with its huge free-flight aviary, is particularly colourful, the occupants at liberty to fly around the visitors.

Penguins, reptiles, fish and insects inhabit the Exotarium. There is an amazing beehive with thousands of bees busily at work. In the **Grzimek-Haus**, darkened by day, night hunters such as fennecs and tapirs can be observed living their normal life.

★ **Senckenberg Natural History Museum** (Naturmuseum Senckenberg) ⊘ – *Leave by the Bockenheimer Landstrasse* (GY M⁹).
Founded in 1821, this museum is distinguished by its remarkable **Department of Palaeontology**★★ *(ground floor)*. Fossils from the Lower Jurassic (Lias) are on display in the entrance hall, most of them discovered near Holzmaden, in Württemberg. They include ichthyosaurus, sea crocodiles and crinoids – which despite their vegetal appearance were in fact marine animals.

In the **Hall of Dinosaurs** (Room 5), the skeletons of huge beasts from the Secondary Era are on view: diplodocus, iguanodon, triceratops, stegosaurus and plateosaurus (both original and in the form of mouldings).

In Room 6 there are impressive fossils including sea crocodiles, ichthyosaurus and the reptile with enormous teeth – placodus, which fed on whole crustaceans. In Room 8 there are turtles, tortoises, whales and an anaconda in the act of swallowing a sea pig.

Room 9 *(at the foot of the staircase)* displays objects found in **Jurassic digs** – most of them near Solnhofen, on the banks of the Altmühl, where the archeopteryx was found. See also an even older ancestor of the bird, the pterodactyl; a fish with circular teeth; and a dinosaur with a beak (Tracodon), which lived in North America.

The great land and sea mammals (elephants, whales) are in Room 10. Nos 12 and 13 trace the evolution of the human race (numerous implements, weapons, etc., found in digs). An interesting collection of stuffed animals (armadillo, apes), reptiles (python with 377 vertebrae) and birds can be seen on the first floor. On the second are insects, and marine vertebrates and invertebrates. Dioramas show mammals in their natural habitat.

★ **Tropical Gardens** (Palmgarten) ⊘ – *Leave by the Bockenheimer Landstrasse* (GY). A great variety of ornamental plants (roses), alpines and rare trees grow in this park. Unusual tropical and sub-tropical flora proliferate in the greenhouses.

EXCURSIONS

Offenbach – *7km - 4 1/2 miles to the east. Leave by the Deutschhern-Ufer* (**HZ**). *Town plan in the current Michelin Red Guide Deutschland.*
This town on the south bank of the Main is the centre of the German leather industry (International Leather Fair twice a year).

★★ **Leather Museum** (Deutsches Ledermuseum) ⊙ – *At Frankfurter Strasse 86.*
The most interesting departments are those recording the history of the handbag (15-20C), of gloves, of shadow theatres, and those on leather coverings (embossed and gilded Venetian, French, Spanish and German leatherwork). Rare items on display include Marie de Medici's casket, a toy elephant which once belonged to Louis XV, and one of Napoleon's portfolios.
The **Shoe Museum** in the same building presents a history of foot fashion in all its variety, from Coptic sandals to 18C court shoes and 19C button boots.

★ **Friedberg** – *28km - 17 miles to the north by the Friedberger landstrasse* (**HY**).
This is an attractive example of a medieval community with two distinct centres: the town enclosed within the imperial castle and the bourgeois town grouped at the foot of the church, at either end of the main street (Kaiserstrasse).
The **castle** (Stauferburg) erected by Frederick Barbarossa in 1180 together with its outbuildings still has the air of a small, self-sufficient town. The ramparts, now a promenade, have been made even more attractive with bays of greenery and lookout points. **Adolf's Tower★** (Adolphsturm, 1347) overlooks the assembled buildings.
The **Jewish Baths** (Judenbad, 13C) – at Judengasse 20, in the bourgeois sector – is a deep, square well with a dome, which served originally for ritual ablutions required by Jewish law. Columns with Gothic capitals support the arches over the stairway (74 difficult steps) leading 25m - 80ft to the water.
The **Church** (Stadtkirche) is a 13-14C building with a typically Hessian exterior – transverse attics with separate gables jutting from the roof above the aisles. The façade is unusual, its towers resting on Gothic arches. Inside, an unusually tall **ciborium★** (1482) stands in the chancel. On the left of the rood-screen is the **Friedberg Virgin** (*c*1280).

★ **The Taunus** – *Round tour of 62km - 39 miles - 4 hours.*
The Taunus is limited in extent, but reaches at the Grosser Feldberg a greater height (880m - 2 997ft) than any of the other Rhineland schist massifs *(qv)*. The area is covered by magnificent forests, and there are many mineral springs which have been developed into spas.

★ **Konigstein im Taunus** – The fortress here, on a height isolated from the main Taunus slopes, is a **feudal ruin** (Burgruine) ⊙ with impressive foundations: round 16C bastions and 17C projecting defences. Climb the keep *(166 steps)* for a **bird's eye view** of the small town and the surrounding woods.

★ **Grosser Feldberg** ⊙ – The tower and antennae of an important telecommunications centre top this height. From the tower's observation platform visitors can enjoy an immense **panorama★★** including the Westerwald tableland to the northwest, the Wetterau depression to the northeast and, in the southeast, the plain of the Lower Main invaded by the outskirts of Frankfurt.

Saalburg – This is a complete Roman fortress camp in the middle of the forest, reconstituted on the orders of Kaiser Wilhelm II on the Limes (fortified lines marking the northern limit of Roman occupation). Note the external trenches and, in the inner courtyard, buildings which now house a Roman museum.

★ **Bad Homburg vor der Höhe** – *Town plan in the current Michelin Red Guide Deutschland.*
In 1840, the opening of a casino by the **Blanc Brothers** transformed this little spa into one of Europe's gaming capitals. But the establishment was obliged to close its doors in 1872. Today the life of most visitors centres on the **Spa Park★** (Kurpark), where pavilions containing the health-giving springs are dispersed over shady lawns. The **castle**, dominated by the tall White Tower – a survival of the original fortress – was successively the residence of the Landgraves of Hesse-Homburg, then the summer palace of the Prussian Kings (who became, after Wilhelm I in 1871, the Emperors of Germany). A well-known exhibit in the castle is the artificial limb of Friedrich II (1633-1708), known locally as "the silver leg" because the joints of the wooden limb are fashioned from the precious metal.

To plan a special itinerary

- consult the map of the region on pp 4-6 which shows the main towns, individual sights and recommended routes described in the guide;

- read the descriptions of the above which are described in the middle section of the guide in alphabetical order under their own name or are incorporated in the excursions radiating from a particular town or tourist centre;

- use the appropriate Michelin Maps which show places of interest, scenic routes, viewpoints and natural features...

Michelin map 🗺️ G 22 - G 23 - Local map see under BLACK FOREST

One of the most attractive cities in southern Germany, Freiburg was founded in the 12C by the Dukes of Zähringen, who conferred upon it a number of special privileges (Freiburg or "free town"). When the dynasty died out in 1388, the town passed under Habsburg rule. It was here, in May 1770, that the Archduchess Marie-Antoinette said farewell to Austrian territory and set out for Strasbourg, where she was greeted in the name of France by Cardinal Rohan as the bride of the future Louis XVI – and foredoomed victim of the guillotine in 1793.

Five centuries of Austrian rule, which was only ended by Napoleon, left the city with an agreeable, easygoing life-style appreciated by young and old alike. The climate can be hot, but a refreshing breeze blows gently from the Upper Black Forest at nightfall and, streams ("Bächle") from the nearby mountains sweeten the air – many of them running in open gullies beside the ancient streets between the cathedral and the Swabian Gate.

FREIBURG IM BREISGAU

SIGHTS

★★ **Cathedral (Münster)** (Y) – Of the original Romanesque building, started c1200, only the transept crossing and the two "Cock Towers" flanking it remain. The octagonal towers are surmounted by Gothic superstructures. The technical progress characterizing the Gothic period was reflected as building continued westwards culminating in the erection of the splendid tower which crowns the west façade.

This feature, with its multiplicity of planes interesting at sharp angles, is one of the few church towers in Germany to be wholly completed in the Middle Ages.

In 1354, work started on the construction of a new chancel, but the grandeur of the design and the severity of the times were such that this huge addition was not finished and consecrated until 1513.

The ambulatory, typically German in concept, has fan vaulting in keeping with its Late Gothic style.

North Side – Above the door which leads to the chancel, the tympanum, carved c1350, illustrates the theme of Original Sin, while the archivolt concerns itself with the Creation of the World according to Genesis. On the right of this, note the rare representation of the Creator resting on the seventh day.

★★★ **West Tower** – On the plain, square base of this stands a pierced octagonal belfry surmounted by a delicate openwork spire of stone. Four sharply jutting projections in the form of a star at the foot of the tower house the Sterngalerie. The gargoyles here are worth a second glance.

South Side – Statues of the Apostles and the Old Testament kings stand on the buttresses of this richly ornate façade. A Renaissance porch shelters the south door.

West Porch and Doorway (Vorhalle) - Late 13C figures crowd this main entrance. On the left wall, facing the door, Satan, beguilingly disguised as "the Prince of this world", leads a procession. He is followed by his victim, sparsely clothed in a goat-skin, the Wise Virgins, and a number of Biblical characters. The Foolish Virgins, their expressions bitter, decorate the right wall. Behind them are statues of the liberal arts (painting and sculpture), St Margaret and St Catherine, the patronesses of Christian wisdom.

The doorway itself, flanked by statues representing the Church (left) and the Synagogue (with eyes covered; right) is entirely occupied by the mystery of the Redemption. The tympanum is unusual in that it portrays scenes from Christ's earthly life and an interesting Last Judgement.

Nave – Moderately tall, the nave is embellished with graceful galleries, their blind, trefoil arcades decorating the aisle walls from end to end. Furnishings and statuary of particular interest include:

CATHEDRAL

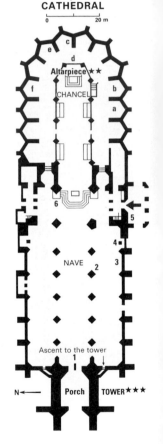

1) The Virgin at the pillar (1270-1280), worshipped by two angels (art from Ile de France);
2) A Late Gothic pulpit with rustic themes (1560); the sculptor himself is represented in a window beneath the stairway;
3) A statue (originally recumbent, remodelled in the 17C) of Berthold V, last of the Dukes of Zähringen, who founded the town;
4) The Holy Sepulchre, dating from 1340, behind a delicate Gothic grille;
5) In the three windows of the south transept, 13C stained glass medallions, the oldest in the cathedral, which were probably originally in the old Romanesque chancel;
6) A 1505 group sculpture, the Adoration of the Magi.

Chancel ⊘ – Very well lit, the chancel invites appreciation of the skilful design of the ambulatory vaulting combined with that of the widely-spaced side chapels. Among the many works of art note: the **altarpiece**★★ (Hochaltar) by Hans Baldung Grien (1512-16), which portrays the Coronation of the Virgin on the central panel.

a) A Rococo baptismal font by JC Wenzinger in the Stürzel Chapel;
b) The Oberried altarpiece (1521) in the University Chapel. The two side panels, the Nativity and the Adoration of the Magi, are by Hans Holbein the Younger;
c) In the Second Imperial Chapel: an altarpiece from Schnewlin depicting Rest during the Flight to Egypt by Hans Wydyz. The paintings are from the Baldung Grien studio;
d) Reverse of the large Baldung Grien altarpiece: a painting of the Crucifixion;
e) The Böcklin Chapel: the Romanesque Locherer Crucifix in beaten silver by Böcklin;
f) An altarpiece in the Locherer Chapel by Sixt von Staufen (1521-24). The carved part depicts the Virgin, with her cloak – held up by cherubim – shielding humanity.

Ascent of the West Tower (Turmbesteigung) ⊘ – The first section of stairway leads to the star-shaped gallery, and then, after a further climb, visitors reach the upper platform beneath the beautiful perforated spire. From here are **views**★ over the city, with distant perspectives of the Kaiserstuhl and the Vosges.

Münsterplatz (Y) – Facing the cathedral's south front across this square are buildings whose ostentation declares them to have been designed for municipal or ecclesiastical prestige. They comprise:

The Archi-episcopal Palace (Erzbischöflisches Palais) (**Y A**) – A fine wrought-iron balcony decorates the façade of this 1756 building.

★ **Old Kaufhaus** (**YZ B**) – A picturesque medieval atmosphere is lent to the square by this roughcast red structure. The watchtowers on either side have pointed roofs; covered with glazed tiles and supported by an arcaded gallery, the Gothic façade shelters statues of the Habsburg emperors (1530) on the first floor. The building is still used for official receptions and other city functions.

Wenzingerhaus (**Y D**) – Built for himself in 1761 by the famous local painter and sculptor Christian Wenzinger, this mansion completes the layout of the square. A magnificent Baroque staircase adorns the interior.

★ **Rathausplatz** (Y) – The Town Hall square is a pleasant sight, with its flowered balconies and its scented chestnut trees surrounding the statue of Berthold Schwarz, a Franciscan said to have invented gunpowder in 1350.

★ **New Town Hall (Neues Rathaus)** (Y R1) – Two 16C burghers' houses, once the heart of the old university, were linked in 1901 by a central arcaded portion to form the present Town Hall.
The oriel window at the Eisenbahnstrasse corner is decorated with carvings illustrating the *Lady and the Unicorn*.

Whale House (Haus zum Walfisch) (Y E) – Of the original 1516 construction, there remains today an oriel which forms a canopy above a richly ornamented Late Gothic doorway.

★ **Augustinian Museum (Augustinermuseum)** (Z M1) ⊙ – The most captivating part of this museum is the **Medieval Art Section★★** (Mittelalterliche Kunst), housed in the church of an old Augustinian monastery and adjacent ground-floor galleries. The works, destined originally for churches and abbeys in the Upper Rhine districts, came from Alsace, the Baden region and the country around Lake Constance. The statuary, in particular, includes admirable 14C and 15C pieces. Among the museum's treasures are a Grünewald altarpiece panel (once at Aschaffenburg - *qv*) depicting the miracle of the Snow, and an impressive 14C **Crucifix★** (Adelhauser Kreuz).

Swabian Gate (Schwabentor) (Z) – From this remnant of the town's medieval fortifications, sightseers can walk down through the picturesque but poor Insel quarter to the quays bordering the Gewerbekanal, once the preserve of Freiburg's fishermen and tanners. A small bridge spanning the canal offers a view of the cathedral spire.

★ **Schlossberg** (Z) – A wooded walk climbs this last foothill of the Black Forest. The pathway, which starts from the Swabian Gate, also offers fine views of the cathedral. A **cable-car** ⊙ operates from the Stadtgarten (Y).

EXCURSIONS

The Kaiserstuhl – *Round tour of 73km - 45 miles - allow 3 hours. Leave Freiburg by the Lessingstrasse (Z) and go to Breisach via Gottenheim.*
A small volcanic massif rising in the Baden plain, the Kaiserstuhl (the Emperor's Throne: 538m - 1 765ft) enjoys on its lower slopes a warm, dry climate particularly suitable for orchards and vineyards. The wines of Ihringen, Bickensohl and Oberrotweil are considered among the finest in the region.

★ **Breisach** – Breisach and its rock, crowned by a large church, tower above the Rhine, facing the twin town of Neuf-Brisach in France. The rock was the heart of one of the most redoubtable systems of fortification in Europe, the site serving at times as a French bridgehead, at times as an imperial advance post. French revolutionary troops sacked the town in 1793, and it was largely destroyed by the Allied armies in 1945.
As at Freiburg, the **Collegiate Church** (Münster) has a Romanesque nave, transept and two smaller twin towers, together with a Gothic chancel. The most important work of art is a carved **reredos★** (1526) with an extraordinarily complex decoration of loaves, flowing hair and billowing draperies from which emerge a crowd of cherubim and the figures of the Eternal Father and Christ crowning the Virgin. Murals depicting the Last Judgement (in the first bay on the west side) were painted in the late 15C by Martin Schongauer of Colmar.
A **viewing table★** in the Schlossplatz allows the visitor to identify the heights of the Black Forest to the south, the Sundgau and Lomont peaks, the Vosges from the Grand Ballon to Upper Königsburg Castle and, quite close, the Kaiserstuhl.

Burkheim – A village of wine growers, Burkheim is built on a gentle slope, rising in tiers above the roadway with three parallel streets giving access to the houses at different levels. The lowest of these, the Markstrasse, is delightful. Among the half-timbered buildings are a red, bow-windowed mansion and a town hall with a fine emblazoned doorway (1604).

Endingen – The Marktplatz in this village is surrounded by fine public buildings. The new Rathaus, a modified 18C burgher's dwelling, boasts a balconied frontage and an elegant mansard roof. The old (16C) Rathaus, in the northeast corner of the square, has impressive scrolled gables, while the gables of the long, low Kornhaus (the former granary), also dating from the 16C, are stepped.

Ettenheim – *33km - 20 miles to the north.*
Part of the Strasbourg bishopric until 1803, Ettenheim is worth seeing for the old residential quarter of Kirchberg, separated from the rest of the town by two 18C gates and clustered at the foot of the large parish church.
Facing the outer stairway of the Rathaus is the gable of the palace once owned by Cardinal Rohan, where the notorious "hero" of the celebrated affair of the diamond necklace lived out his eventful exile from 1790 to 1803. Higher up, where the Rohanstrasse bends towards the church, is the house owned by the Duke of Enghien, complete with coat of arms above the door. The Duke, fiancé of the Cardinal's niece Charlotte, was arrested on the orders of Napoleon in violation of the sovereignty of the State of Baden on the night of the 14-15 March 1804 and executed by firing squad six nights later in the castle moat at Vincennes.
Cardinal Rohan's tomb lies beneath the chancel in the church.

★★★ **Upper Black Forest** – *See under Black Forest.*

★ **FRIESLAND** Lower Saxony and Schleswig-Holstein

Michelin map **411** folds 2, 6, 10, 13 and 14

Scoured by the wind, scattered with stunted trees, with sea-birds crying over-head, Friesland forms the old Zuyder Zee to the Danish border; a single flat landscape crosshatched with dykes and canals. Offshore, the Frisian Islands, following the wide curve of the coastline, have existed since tempests destroyed the band of protective coastal dunes in the 5C BC. Twice since then, in 1362 and 1634, unusually catastrophic ocean assaults have laid waste the lowlands between the estuaries of the Weser and the Scheldt, reducing sizeable tracts of land to a string of tiny islets, as in the case of the Halligens.

Agriculturally, the consolidated silt deposits known as the **Marschen** have proved more fertile than the areas of **Geest**, which are slightly higher, with a sandy soil. The Frisian people, tall and fairskinned, with blond hair and blue eyes, speak a language related to ancient Anglo-Saxon. Fishermen and farmers – especially noted for their fine cattle – they fight the weather relentlessly for the preservation of their livelihood.

FRISIAN ISLANDS

Eastern Frisians ⊘ – Formed of dunes sometimes 20m to 30m - 66ft to 98ft high, these islands between the estuaries of the Ems and the Weser are constantly being re-shaped by winds and coastal currents. Their form, indented on the west, tapering to the east, is symptomatic of this process. An extensive system of dykes preserves them from too rapid an erosion.

These islands now are oriented towards seaside holidaymaking. In the summertime, the beaches of fine sand blossom with brightly-coloured bathing tents, pitched in sandy gullies out of the wind. The area is a paradise for bird-watchers, and large colonies of seals live in the shallows, particularly between Borkum and Sylt.

Borkum, the largest, most westerly island, and **Norderney**, the nearest to the main-land, are the most popular vacation centres in the summer. **Wangerooge**, **Langeoog** and **Juist** (where motor cars are not permitted) are equally well equipped for restful holidays. A favourite activity, on the islands as well as the coast, is the lowtide ramble, on foot or on horseback (a local guide is indispensable). The immense stretches of hardened silt glitter with huge banks of shellfish and are scattered with colourful seaweeds and starfish.

Northern Frisians – These are divided into two geologically different groups. Sylt *(qv)*, Föhr and Amrum, the three most northerly islands, are blocks of Geest which escaped drowning when the sea-level rose after the melting of Europe's Quaternary glaciers; the **Halligen archipelago★** *(qv)*, on the other hand, is all that remains of an area of Marschen inundated and destroyed during the storms of 1634.

As in the Eastern Frisians, the pleasures of the beach abound. But an atmosphere rich in iodine and the opportunities for nudism, mud baths, sulphur inhalations and sea-water therapy have led to the installation of successful climatic and thermal cures such at those as **St Peter-Ording** (on the mainland coast) and **Wyk**.

★ **FRITZLAR** Hessen   Pop 15 000

Michelin map **412** K 13

The placid waters of the Eder reflect the medieval towers and belfries of this small town.

A General View – From the end of the bridge that leads to the station on the south bank of the river's main stream, there is a fine view of the old town, its fortified walls overlooked by the towers of the collegiate church. The **ramparts** (Stadtmauer) retain almost all their ancient defence towers, in particular the impressive 13C spur structure, known locally as the **Grey Tower★** (Grauer Turm).

SIGHTS

★ **Marktplatz** – The original half-timbered gables, some faced with wooden shingles, have been preserved in all their variety. Note especially the small, elongated, 15C Kaufhaus (now the Reformhaus store), which is crowned with a turret.
The stem of the fountain (1564) supports a statue of Roland – here, as in Bremen, the symbol of public liberty.

★ **Collegiate Church** (Dom) ⊘ – The present building was constructed in the 13C on the site of an earlier church of which only the west face, the lower parts of the towers and the crypt remained. A typical Rhineland feature is the dwarf gallery, adorned with blind arcades, which encircles the apse. The church's individuality lies in the interplay of the many gable roofs and the graceful half-timbered design of the chapter house, built onto the north side of the apse.
Enter the church by the main door on the west side. The interior is noteworthy for an outstanding Gothic ciborium, and, on either side of the chancel opening, two Romanesque statues carved in wood. One of these represents the Virgin, the other St John. Below ground, the crypts are vast. The most important, with three aisles, has fine, Romanesque cushion capitals with a simple, ribbed decoration. It houses the tomb of St Wigbert, the first abbot of Fritzlar.

Museum and Treasury (Domschatz und Dommuseum) ⊘ – Enter via the cloister on the right of the chancel. Among the ritual objects, liturgical vestments and statues, the treasury displays the pearl-encrusted 12C Cross of the Kaiser Heinrich IV, as well as cameos, precious stones and a Romanesque reliquary plaque.

FULDA Hessen

Pop 56 500

Baroque palaces, towers, monumental doorways, balustrades and flights of stairs in the heart of Fulda bear witness today to the town's religious past, from the time of the prince-bishops who were guardians of the tomb of St Boniface. An overall view can be enjoyed from the top of the steps leading to the Frauenberg Church.

St Boniface, the Apostle of Germany – Wynfrid, an English missionary from a monastery in Exeter, was sent in the 8C to preach the gospel in Germany. In 751, anointing Pepin the Short as king, he confirmed the union of the Church with the Frankish monarchy, a bond that was to last for centuries. Wynfrid, who had changed his name to Boniface, was on a mission to Friesland when he was murdered at Dokkum in 754. He lies buried in a monastery, founded on his orders, at Fulda. The Benedictine abbey, especially under the rule of Abbot Raban Maur (822-842), subsequently became a centre of religious devotion, art and scholarship. The abbey in fact was responsible for the production of Germany's earliest literary works (*The Lay of Hildebrand* was copied by two monks c820).

SIGHTS

Cathedral (Dom) – From the beginning of 1704, this church was rebuilt in a style inspired by Italian Baroque by the architect Johann Dientzenhofer. Pilgrims still worship the tomb of St Boniface, which lies in a crypt (Bonifatiusgruft) beneath the high altar. At the base of the **funerary monument★**, an 18C alabaster bas-relief represents Boniface, in his priestly vestments, raising the lid of his tomb on Judgement Day.

The reliquaries of the saint, the head reliquary and his sword, are conserved in the **Museum** (Dommuseum) ⊙, which also displays an important collection of liturgical vestments from the Baroque period (access to the museum and treasury is via the crypt).

★ **St Michael's Church** – This church, built around an early 9C rotunda, with a stout, square tower, overlooks the cathedral forecourt. The crypt, in which the vaulting rests on a single pillar, is Carolingian. The rotunda itself is supported on eight columns marking the outline of an impressive well-head.

Castle – Here, only the outbuildings and dependencies are of interest. It is however pleasant to walk through the park (Schlossgarten), surrounded by terraces and balustraded walls, to the main staircase leading to the Orangery (1724). Halfway up there is a monumental **"Flora-vase"**, a superb Baroque masterpiece by Humbach dating from 1720, depicting the plant goddess Flora atop a basket overflowing with flowers, garlands and cherubs.

EXCURSIONS

Petersberg Church – *4km - 2 1/2 miles, plus 1/2 hour walking and sightseeing. Leave Fulda by the Petersberger Strasse and road no 458, on the east of the town plan. Follow the Petersberg signposts to the foot of the rock on which the church is built, and leave the car there.*
A vast **panorama★** is commanded from the summit: to the east is the Rhön massif (see below), the Milseburg spur and the rounded dome of the Wasserkuppe; southwest, behind Fulda, lies the Vogelsberg.
The Romanesque sanctuary built on this impressive **site★** was largely remodelled in the 15C. It contains five 12C **bas-reliefs★★** – Christ in Glory and the Virgin on either side of a triumphal arch; St Boniface, Carloman and Pepin the Short on the walls. Mural paintings from the 9C decorate three niches in the Carolingian crypt.

Pheasantry Castle (Schloss Fasanerie or Adolphseck) ⊙ – *6km - 4 miles to the south.*
Completed in 1756 by a prince-bishop of Fulda, this Baroque mansion owes to the Landgraves of the Electoral House of Hesse its interior style, decoration and furnishing – which today serve as an example of aristocratic taste from 1740 to 1850. Among other items of interest on display are a mirror that once belonged to Marie-Antoinette and a portrait (1859) of the Landgrave Anne, a masterpiece from the studio of Winterhalter, the celebrated painter of court beauties (including the family of Queen Victoria) at the time of the Napoleonic Second Empire.

★ **The Rhön** – *Round tour of 104km - 65 miles to the southwest of Fulda - allow 4 hours.*
The remnants of an enormous extinct volcano, the Rhön massif's craggy summits tower above the bleak moorlands clothing it up to a height of 1 000m - 3 28lft. These heights, swept by strong winds, have made the area a favourite among the organizers of gliding clubs.

Gersfeld – The most central resort in the Rhön district, Gersfeld has a Protestant church (1785) with interestingly placed furnishings: the grouping of organ, altar and pulpit in a single compact ensemble symbolizes liturgically the Lutheran reform.

★ **Kreuzberg** – From the Calvary - at 928m - 3 044ft after a steep uphill climb – there is a splendid **view★** of the massif. The Wasserkuppe can be seen to the north.

★★ **Wasserkuppe** – From the gliding centre, climb to the summit (950m - 3 116ft), following the fencing on the left. The **panorama★★** extends as far as Fulda and the Vogelsberg.

Michelin map ⁴¹³ OP 24 - Local map see under GERMAN ALPINE ROAD
Town plan in the current Michelin Red Guide Deutschland

The importance of Füssen as a tourist centre lies in its position – at the foot of the gorge where the Lech river cascades down from the Alps, the town serves as a gateway to the Tyrol and departure point for trips to the Royal Castles *(qv)* built by Ludwig II of Bavaria. A number of small lakes downstream, as well as the **Forggensee** reservoir, offer opportunities for boating, bathing and sailing.
Below the **castle** (Hohes Schloss), which rises high above the roofs of the old town, are the remains of ancient fortifications and defensive towers.

SIGHTS

Former Abbey (Ehemaliges Kloster) of St Magnus – A former Benedictine foundation set up by the followers of St Gall, this abbey was built on the site where St Magnus, the Apostle of the Allgäu, died in his hermitage in the year 750. It was rebuilt in the Baroque style during the 18C and secularized in 1803, when the abbey church was given to the parish.

Parish Church (Stadtpfarrkirche) – Rebuilt between 1701 and 1717, this church displays a remarkable unity, for Johann-Jacob Herkomer, born in the parish, was not only the architect but also the painter and stucco-worker. The Romanesque crypt was remodelled in 1971.

St Anne's Chapel – *The last door on the left before the church porch.* Within the chapel, there is a curious **Dance of Death**★ (Totentanz, *c*1600) by a local painter. There is also a group in the Gothic style portraying the Holy Family.

Abbey Buildings – The main quadrangle, which boasts three ante-chapels with scrolled gables, is a fine example of Baroque architecture. The complex (Klosterhof) is also attributed to Herkomer. In the former state apartments of the abbey – Hall of the Princes, library, the Pope's Room – there is a **regional museum** (Heimatmuseum) ⊙ displaying an admirable collection of musical instruments.

Castle (Hohes Schloss) – The ramp leading up to the entrance starts behind the parish church.
In the late 15C, the castle was the summer residence of the Prince-Bishops of Augsburg. The surrouding property has been transformed into a **public park** (Baumgarten), picturesque and peaceful, affording unexpected views of the Säuling escarpment. The apartments housing the local museum, in particular the Knight's Hall (Rittersaal) with its sumptuous octagonally-coffered ceiling, display a collection of Swabian painting from the 15C to the 18C.

Lech Falls (Lechfall) – *0.5km - a quarter of a mile to the south.*
The river hurls itself tumultuously over a ledge in a small, rocky gorge. The site, 500 yards north of the Austrian frontier, is known as the **Step of St Magnus** (Magnustritt). The falls are spanned by a footbridge which allows sightseers to return to Füssen by another route.

MICHELIN GUIDES

The Red Guides (hotels and restaurants)
Benelux – Deutschland – España Portugal – main cities Europe – France – Great Britain and Ireland – Italia

The Green Guides (fine art, historic monuments, scenic routes)
Austria – Canada – England: The West Country – France – Germany – Great Britain – Greece – Italy – Mexico – Netherlands – New England
Portugal – Scotland – Spain – Switzerland
London – New York City – Paris – Quebec – Rome – Washington

and 9 regional guides to France

Michelin map 🔢 Q 24 - Local map see under German ALPINE ROAD
Plan of the conurbation in the current Michelin Red Guide Deutschland

This is Germany's great winter sports resort, famed as the site of the fourth
Winter Olympics in 1936 and the World Alpine Ski Championships in 1978.
Worthy of its reputation internationally, the resort lies in an open mountain basin
at the foot of the Wetterstein range, from which two massive silhouettes stand
out. These are the Alpspitze and the axe-shaped Waxenstein, itself masking the
Zugspitze.

Despite its modest altitude (720m - 2 362ft), favourable meteoric conditions
assure the resort of a regular winter snowfall – from 12 to 20 inches in January
and February, anything up to six feet in the areas served by the ski-lifts. This is
complemented by the Zugspitzplatt snowfield, accessible in autumn and springtime via a rack railway.

Summer visitors are offered numerous mountain walks (Höhenwege), crisscrossing the lower slopes of the Wank and the Kramerspitze. Although more lively
and sophisticated than the twin town of Partenkirchen, Garmisch nevertheless
maintains certain customs and traditions. Thus, every evening around 6pm, there
is the communal Return of the Herds – with cattle frisking through the streets to
bring traffic to a standstill.

GARMISCH-PARTENKIRCHEN

Bahnhofstraße	X 10		
Ferdinand-Barth-Straße	X 15	Parkstraße	X 32
Hindenburgstraße	X 18	Promenadestraße	X 35
Mittenwalder Str.	X 27	Rießerseestraße	X 37
Münchener Str.	X 30	Von-Brug-Str.	X 46
		Wildenauer Str.	X 48

SIGHTS

Ice Stadium (Olympia-Eisstadion) – *At Garmisch.*
Open all the year round, this comprises three separate skating rinks with a total
surface of 6 500m2 - 7 800sq yds. The covered stands allow 12 000 spectators to
watch skating competitions and ice hockey matches.

Ski Stadium (Skistadion) – *At Partenkirchen.*
A ski-jump and a slalom course here are equipped for 80 000 spectators.

Old Church (Alte Kirche) – *At Garmisch.*
The parish church stands on the west bank of the Loisach river, in a picturesque
neighbourhood where the old chalets have been carefully preserved. The
interior embraces two equal naves, where a single central column supports
16C Gothic vaulting with liernes and tiercerons (ancillary ribs). A large number
of 15C and 16C murals have been uncovered and restored as far as possible
(note especially a huge representation of St Christopher and scenes from the
Passion).

St Anthony's Church (St Anton) – *At Partenkirchen.*
To the octagonal nave of this 1708 pilgrim's sanctuary, a second nave, oval in
shape, was added in 1738. The dome above this is decorated with frescoes by JE
Holzer.

The Philosophers' Way (Philosophenweg) – *At Partenkirchen.*
St Anthony's Park (St Anton-Anlagen) is the departure point for this panoramic walk
which offers fine, clear **views★** of the surrounding massifs – with the Zugspitze
visible this time behind the Waxenstein.

EXCURSIONS

★★★ **The Zugspitze** – *For access and description, see under Zugspitze.*

★★ **Wank** ⊙ – *20 minutes in a cable car. Leave from the Schützenhaus inn, on the northern fringe of Partenkirchen.*
From the summit (1 780m - 5 840ft) there is a comprehensive view of the Wetterstein chain - and a vertiginous appreciation of the Garmisch-Partenkirchen basin far below. A panorama of the surrounding mountains can be enjoyed from many of the footpaths crossing the Alpine meadows and skirting the forest.

★★ **Partnachklamm** – *About 1 1/2 hours Rtn, of which 5 minutes are in a cable car. (Remember to take rainwear).*
From the Partenkirchen ski stadium, go to the lower terminus of the Graseck cable car. The upper station is at the Forsthaus Graseck hotel, and from here a footpath leads up to the **gorges**. The route, carved from the solid rock, passes two spectacular bottlenecks amid the thunder of falling water and clouds of spray. At the Partnachklamm inn, the path rejoins the upward route. It is possible to make the same trip in wintertime, when the route will be decorated with a huge frieze of icicles.

★ **Eibsee** – *8km - 5 miles to the west.*
The calm waters of this lake occupy a superb forest site. It lies at the foot of the Zugspitze, at an altitude of 1 000m - 3 881ft. A footpath (2 hours' walk) circles the lake.

★ **Mittenwald** – *2km - 12 1/2 miles to the east.*
An old frontier town on the Augsburg-Verona trade route, Mittenwald still suffers from heavy traffic today. This due to the large number of excursions possible in the nearby Kranzberg and Karwendel massifs, and to the beauty of the town itself. The **painted houses**★★ lining the pavements of the main street are especially noteworthy.
If Mittenwald, as Goethe said, is "a living picture-book", a monument outside the church recalls that the town also has a place in the world of music. The memorial honours Matthias Klotz (1653-1743), who returned from Cremona in 1684 with a lute and, as an ex-pupil of Stradivarius, introduced the manufacture of stringed instruments to Bavaria despite the fact that it was then in the midst of an economic depression. A dozen artisans, a technical school, and a **museum** (Geigenbau-und-Heimatmuseum) carry on that tradition today.

GELNHAUSEN Hessen   Pop 19 000
Michelin maps **412** and **413** K 16

On the sunny slope of the Kinzig valley, Gelnhausen was built as a military installation by the Emperor Frederick Barbarossa, and is encircled to this day with fortifications. The most noticeable building is the Church of St Mary, whose towers overlook the rural Untermarkt at the highest point of the town.

★ **St Mary's** (**Marienkirche**) – Enter via the small south door that looks out over the valley. This solid, red sandstone building, with its spires and gables, is typical of the Rhineland Romanesque style *(see introduction)*. The **choir**★★ (Chorraum), adorned with trilobed blind arcades and heavily worked consoles, is considered to be one of the masterpieces of 13C religious architecture.

Imperial Palace Ruins (**Kaiserpfalz**) ⊙ – The ruins stand amidst the greenery of an island in the river. They comprise an entrance hall with two aisles, a colonnade with sculptured capitals, traces of the old perimeter wall, the chapel, and a watch-tower – all remarkable for the perfection of their Romanesque decoration.

EXCURSIONS

Büdingen – *17km - 10 1/2 miles to the north.*
The 15C and 16C **fortified perimeter**★ (Stadtmauer) has fine decorative details. Arriving via the Bahnhofstrasse, note the 1503 Jerusalem Gate, with its squat towers and Gothic embellishments.
The **castle** ⊙ of the Ysenburg Princes is one of the few Staufen residences which is still inhabited. From the entrance arch, moving in a clockwise direction, the buildings around the inner courtyard decrease in age from the 12C to the 15C. The **choir stalls**★ of the 15C chapel are decorated with saints' effigies and coats of arms.

Steinau – *25km - 15 1/2 miles to the northeast.*
The Brothers Grimm *(qv)*, sons of a magistrate, grew up in this small town. They lived from 1791 to 1796 in the massive **Tribunal House** (Hanauisches Amtshaus), which stands back behind a courtyard at No 80, Brüder-Grimm-Strasse. There is a **memorial** ⊙ to them in the castle, a fortified Renaissance ensemble with defensive towers and a square keep.

Each year
the Michelin Red Guide Deutschland
presents a wealth of up-to-date information in a compact
form. It is the ideal companion for a holiday,
a long weekend or a business trip.

★ GÖRLITZ Saxony Pop 82 400

Michelin map **987** fold 19

Founded in the middle of the 13C and incorporated in Bohemia a century later, Görlitz has spread out along the west bank of the Neisse, which has formed, since 1945, the frontier with Poland. A busy town, famous for its mechanical and optical industries, it boasts many excellent Renaissance and Baroque buildings, recently renovated and displayed to their best advantage around the Obermarkt and Untermarkt.

SIGHTS

Obermarkt – On the north side of this square, fine Baroque houses have been preserved between the **Reichenbacher Turm**, a fortified 14-15C gateway to the west, and **Trinity Church** on the east. Flamboyant Gothic **stalls★** are worth looking at inside the church. At no 29 (the tourist information centre), the façade, including an entrance framed by sculpted columns, is adorned with impressive stuccowork.

★ **Untermarkt** – Formerly the town's chief trading centre, the market place is overlooked by the tower (1378) of the **Town Hall** (Rathaus). Note, on the corner of the Brüderstrasse, the outside staircase (1537-38) encircling an elegant statue (a copy) representing Justice. To the right of the building's Renaissance doorway, a Late Gothic (1488) sculptured plaque displays the arms of Matthias Corvinus, King of Hungary. The central part of the Town Hall dates from Renaissance times, while the neo-Gothic additions are less than a century old.

In the middle of the market, the **former money exchange** (Alte Börse), with its entrance surrounded by allegorical figures, is the oldest Baroque monument in the town. Dating from 1706, the exchange is adjacent to the **Weigh-house** (Alte Waage), which combines three Renaissance upper storeys with a Baroque base at street level.

Arcaded houses bordering the southern side of the Untermarkt evoke the lives of the gentry and eminent burghers living there in the past.

Municipal Museum (Städische Kunstammlungen) ⊙ – At Neiss-Strasse 30.

This imposing Baroque mansion (1739) at the southeastern corner of the market houses an interesting exhibition of art and furniture from the Renaissance to the Baroque. Note especially the displays of glassware, and the painting (c1515) by Marco Palmezzano of the Holy Family. A collection of 18C rustic cupboards and cabinets on the second floor is distinguished by the variety of polychromatic treatment decorating the items on view.

In this Guide the length of time indicated
- for sightseeing is the average time required for a visit
- for touring allows one to enjoy the views and the scenery.

★★ GOSLAR Lower Saxony Pop 46 000

Michelin map **411** O 11 - Local map see under HARZ MOUNTAINS

This town, built around an 11C imperial palace on the northern fringe of the Harz Mountains (qv), retains a singular grouping of half-timbered houses and important monuments around its medieval centre.

A Mining Town – A former Free Imperial City, Goslar owed its prosperity to the mineral wealth of the Harz, and particularly to the Rammelsberg mines, worked during the Middle Ages for lead and silver. The city's commercial importance reached its height in the 15C and 16C, when profit accrued also from the vast surrounding forests which provided timber to fire the metal refineries. It was during this period that the fine houses of the city guilds were built.

Religious controversy between the Free City and the Dukes of Brunswick, who owned the mines, brought an economic decline in the mid-16C. Today, although the Rammelsberg mines are still worked, tourism is Goslar's principal industry. From the terrace of the **Georgenberg** (Y) there is a fine view of the town packed tightly against the mountain slope.

★★★ OLD TOWN (ALTSTADT) *time: 3 hours*

★★ **Marktplatz** (Z) – The market square, dignified and austere in appearance, is surrounded by houses protected by slate cladding. Its architectural prestige derives from two Gothic buildings: the Kaiserworth and the Town Hall (Rathaus), behind which soar the spires of the 12C **Marktkirche**. In the centre of the square there is a **fountain** (Marktbrunnen) with two bronze basins (1230) surmounted by the crowned imperial eagle with outstretched wings. On the gable of a house opposite the Town Hall there is a **chiming clock** ⊙ which animates four different scenes *(at 9am, noon, 3 and 6pm)* representing the history of mining in the Harz Mountains from the Middle Ages to the present day.

★ **Town Hall** (YZ R) – Following the medieval custom, this 15C building was designed with an open hall at street level, an arcaded gallery opening onto the Marktplatz.

On the south side, an exterior staircase leads to the first floor **State Room** (Diele). The lower part of the roof is masked by a balustrade and decorative gabling.

Goslar Town Hall

★★ **Chamber of Allegiance** (Huldigungssaal) ⊘ – This room, transformed into the **Municipal Council Chamber** in 1450, was magnificently decorated *c* 1510. Along the walls, beneath delicately carved upper panelling, Roman Emperors alternate with Sybils in Renaissance costume; on the ceiling, scenes from the childhood of Christ are surrounded by figures of the prophets and evangelists. Concealed behind a door is a tiny chapel containing paintings of the Passion and an arm-reliquary (*cl*300) of St Margaret. A display case on the west wall exhibits an embossed silver-gilt goblet (1477) and the **Goslar Gospel**, a rare manuscript dating from 1230.

Kaiserworth (Z S) – Built in 1494, this Gothic edifice, today a hotel, is embellished with a turreted oriel and Baroque statues of emperors beneath baldachins. On a gable ridge, at the foot of an allegorical statue of Abundance, a grotesque figurine of **The Ducat Man** (Dukatenmännchen) vividly illustrates Goslar's ancient right to mint coins.

★★ **Carved, timbered houses** (Fachwerkhäuser) – The **Schuhhof** (Y 76), a small square to the northwest of the Town Hall, is entirely surrounded by half-timbered buildings, those on the right resting on arcades. Further on, a passageway on the left leads to the narrow Münzstrasse, which in turn passes an old staging inn, **Am Weissen Schwan** (Y A) and then the **Old Mint** (Alte Münze) (Y Z). Transformed today into a restaurant, this timbered building dates from 1500. The fine house on the corner of the Münzstrasse and the Marktstrasse (Z V), with its splendid two-storey oriel, was constructed in 1526.
Facing the Marktkirche is the huge pointed roof of the **Brusttuch** (Z B), also dating from 1526, which was built for a rich mineowner and decorated, according to Renaissance taste, with a host of biblical, mythological and legendary characters and motifs. Not far away, the tall gable of the **Bakers' Guild Hall** (Bäckergildehaus) (Z Y), built between 1501 and 1557, rises into view.
The **Renaissance Houses** at the Marktstrasse-Bäckerstrasse crossroads are adorned with friezes of the fan motif so often found in Lower Saxony (no 2 Bäckerstrasse) or a row of blind arcades (no 3 Bäckerstrasse) (YZ W).

Siemens House (Siemenshaus) (Z C) ⊘ – An impressive half-timbered house built in 1693 by Hans Siemens, ancestor of the founder of the celebrated industrial firm of the same name. There is a particularly fine entrance hall (Däle), floored with small tiles, which serves as a living-room in summer.

Hospice of the Great Holy Cross (Stift zum Grossen Heiligen Kreuz) (Z K) – This former almshouse, founded in 1254, is on the banks of the Gose river, which has given its name to the local beer (Gosebier). The Gothic gable, beneath overhanging eaves, overlooks the Hoher Weg. Inside, the galleried **Great Hall** (Diele) communicates with an unadorned chapel.

ADDITIONAL SIGHTS

★ **Neuwerk Church** (Klosterkirche Neuwerk) (Y) – This former Cistercian church (12-13C) stands alone in what was the convent garden. The tall polygonal towers are among the most elegant ever built for a Romanesque church. The exterior decoration of the apse is exceptionally elaborate.
Heavily ribbed, pointed vaulting characterizes the interior. In the central bay, the columns carrying the transverse arches, two of which have a stone ring, are hollowed in their upper parts to form a curious handle. The balustrade of the organ is decorated with six bas-reliefs (Christ, the Virgin, the four Apostles) which came from the original rood-screen and are already manifestly, elegantly Gothic.

★ **St Peter and St Paul** (Pfarrkirche Peter und Paul) (Z F) – *Entrance on the Frankenberger Plan.*
The Plan, a square originally inhabited by miners, lends its name to the whole tranquil quarter. The 12C church was extensively remodelled and received, in the 18C, a Baroque roof and a lantern tower.
Inside, note the Nonnenempore (nuns' gallery), where the blind arcades rest on capitals adorned with acanthus leaves and small columns with a plaited decoration borrowed from those at Königslutter *(qv)*. On the north and south walls are traces of huge murals painted in the early 13C.

★ **Imperial Palace** (Kaiserpfalz) (Z) ⊙ – The castle, originally built for Kaiser Heinrich III in the 11C and reduced to ruins with the passage of years, was rebuilt and restored between 1868 and 1879. The impressive proportions of the whole give some idea of the power and prestige enjoyed by the imperial rulers. Ambitious historical paintings in the gigantic **Reichssaal** *(on the first floor)* chart the significant events affecting Saxony when Goslar was still an imperial residence.
Beyond the Reichssaal is the early 12C **Palatine Chapel of St Ulrich**, where the plan passes, in elevation, from that of a Greek cross to that of an octagon. Inside the chapel is the tomb of Heinrich III, whose heart is preserved in the plinth. The recumbent effigy of the ruler dates from the 13C.

Domvorhalle (Z) ⊙ – Of the cathedral built in the 11C by Heinrich III and demolished in 1822, all that remains is this de-consecrated chapel in the Romanesque style, which houses the late 11C imperial throne.

★ **The Wide Gate** (Breites Tor) (Y) – This massive construction with its round towers, its barrack quarters and its two huge doors (only the inner one remains) is in fact a fortress in the form of a gateway. It was built c1500.

★ **Monks' House** (Mönchehaus) (Y M1) – A museum of modern art, housed in an ancient half-timbered house, displays works by Beuys, Hundertwasser, Serra and de Kooning. In the garden are sculptures by Ernst and Rennertz, and an interesting Calder mobile.

Goslar Museum (Goslarer Museum) (Z M2) ⊙ – Particularly noteworthy displays outlining the history of the town include models of old Goslar and collections of domestic furniture from the 17C to the 19C, as well as examples of local arts and crafts, both secular and religious.
Also on view is the **Krodo Altar** (Krodoaltar), a large bronze reliquary dating from the 11C from which the jewelled decorations and precious stones have sadly been stolen. One room in the museum is devoted to the Rammelsberg mines.

The Zwinger (Z) – Built in 1517 as part of a defence ring, this fortified tower stands on the **ramparts** (Wallanlagen) south of the city centre. From the top of the tower, there is a fine view of the old town.

GOSLAR

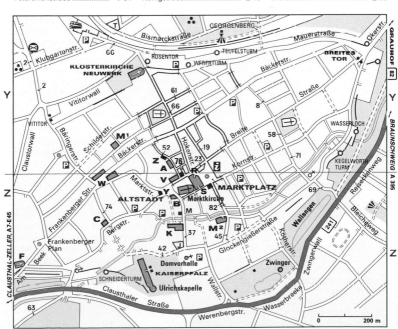

EXCURSIONS

★★ **Harz Mountains** – *See under Harz Mountains.*

★ **Grauhof Church** – *3km - 1 3/4 miles. Leave Goslar by the Okerstrasse* (**Y**).
Augustinian friars from Grauhof monastery (founded in 1527) employed an Italian architect to build this church in 1701. It was completed in 1717. The interior is remarkable both for its huge size and the restrained use of colour. Of particular interest are: a pulpit in the form of a boat (1721); the splendid organ case, which dates from 1737; and the **choir stalls** in exotic woods, where 56 separate scenes represent the life and philosophy of St Augustine.

GÖTTINGEN Lower Saxony   Pop 131 600

Michelin maps **411** and **412** M 12
Town plan in the current Michelin Red Guide Deutschland

Along with Heidelberg, Tübingen and Marburg, Göttingen is one of the four German towns most deeply imbued with the university tradition. Student life, often noisy and highly coloured, lends a particular vivacity to the scene, especially at examination time and on Foundation Days (Stiftungsfeste). The streets of the old town, with their Gothic churches and neo-Classical university buildings, are frequently bustling with squads of students cycling to dispersed lecture halls and libraries.

Two Centuries of University Life – The university was founded in 1737 by George II of England in his capacity as Elector of Hanover. At first it tended to be an aristocratic institution, frequented by the sons of important English and Russian families and Hanoverian gentry. While lawyers and philologists studied, champion horsemen exercised their skills at the enormous riding school. In 1807, however, the nomination of **Carl Friedrich Gauss** (1777-1855) as Director of the Observatory and Professor of Astronomy ushered in a period of great learning and scientific achievement.

A mathematical genius even more precocious than Pascal, Gauss had, at the age of 16, envisaged the possibility of a non-Euclidian geometry. His name was later given to the international unit used in the measurement of magnetic field intensity, and to a society of learned researchers. Members of this body even today are still trying to distil the quintessence of Gauss's scientific testament, embodied in 145 enigmatic pronouncements which are condensed into only 19 pages.

Since the end of the war, Göttingen has become the headquarters of the Max Planck Society (successor to the Kaiser-Wilhelm-Gesellschaft), which groups together some 50 scientific research organizations in Germany. Author in 1900 of the revolutionary Quantum Theory, Max Planck himself (1858-1947) is buried in Göttingen.

SIGHTS

Town Hall – Students, tourists and citizens combine to make the market place and the wine cellars beneath the Town Hall (Ratskeller) the animated centre of social life in Göttingen. The 14-15C building is constructed on the classic medieval pattern (introduction). In front of it is the modern **Goosegirl Fountain** (Gänselieselbrunnen) end goal of student processions after the annual examinations.

The Four-church View (Vierkirchenblick) – A church is visible at each point of the compass from the southeast corner of the market: east, the countrified dome of St Alban's; south, St Michael's; west, the octagonal towers of St John's; and north, the lofty belfry of St James's – at 72m - 236ft the tallest tower in town.

Half-timbered Houses (Fachwerkhäuser) – Most of these are in the eastern part of the old town. Note particularly the ancient **Junkernschänke inn★** (near the Rathaus, at the junction of the Barfüsserstrasse and the Judenstrasse). Medallions with portrait heads adorning this half-timbered Renaissance building are surmounted by biblical characters such as Adam and Eve, Samson and Delilah, etc. The master and mistress of the house when it was built are depicted on the corner-post.

Municipal Museum (Städtisches Museum) ⊙ – Largely devoted to regional religious art, the museum also possesses a historical department outlining the development of the town and university.

EXCURSION

★ **Duderstadt** – *31km - 19 miles to the east.*
Once known as "the Nuremberg of the Eichsfeld", Duderstadt retains from its colourful past more than 500 half-timbered houses, most of them displaying sculpturing of the exposed beams. Overlooking the Marktstrasse are the pointed turrets of the **Town Hall**, built at the beginning of the 13C and enlarged between 1432 and 1533. Not far away is **St Cyriacus's** (Cyriakuskirche), an enormous eight-bay hall-church built in the 15C. Among the works of religious art inside are 15 Baroque statues – including the twelve Apostles – joined to the supporting columns.

The key explains the abbreviations
and symbols used in the text or on the maps.

★ HAIGERLOCH Baden-Württemberg   Pop 10 100

Michelin map **413** J 21

The **site**★★ of this tiny town on the northern fringe of the Swabian Jura is extremely attractive. It lies cradled between two steeply enclosed and wooded horse-shoe bends of the Eyach river. When the lilac is in flower at Whitsun it looks delightful.

SIGHTS

Start at the Marktplatz in the lower town. Climb the slope or stairway, both of which rise to the castle, built along the clifflike promontory on the downstream bend of the Eyach.

Castle Church (Schlosskirche) – Built on the end of the spur, this early 17C church is impressive with the splendour of its Baroque furnishings, which date from 1748.

Continue up the rise, cross the castle courtyard diagonally, and follow the signposted path to the Kapf.

Kapf – From the lookout point there is a view of the upstream river bend where it hugs the upper town, overlooked by the Roman Tower (Römerturm).

Return to the Marktplatz and take the Pfluggasse, on the left.

The Atom Museum (Atommuseum Haigerloch) ⊘ – This small museum explains, with the help of display panels and three-dimensional material, how Professor Heisenberg and his colleagues constructed, deep inside the cliff in the closing months of the Second World War, Germany's first experimental nuclear reactor.

Return once more to the Marktplatz and the car. Take the Oberstadtstrasse and park opposite St Anne's Church at the top of the hill.

★ **St Anne's Church** – At the end of a shady avenue, St Anne's looks across the Eyach gorge at the Castle Church, high up on the far side of the river. To get a clear **view**★, walk back a little down the approach road.
A pilgrims' sanctuary built by Johann Michael Fischer in 1755, St Anne's, together with its chaplain's house (Kaplaneihaus), forms a remarkably elegant Baroque site. Inside, note on each side of the altar the enveloping reredos by Johann Michael Feuchtmayer.

HALBERSTADT Saxony-Anhalt   Pop 47 500

Michelin map **987** fold 16

Seat of a bishopric as early as the 9C and later a member of the Hanseatic League, Halberstadt was for hundreds of years one of northern Germany's most active commercial centres, trading mainly in linen and woollen goods. Sadly, a large part of the town's architectural heritage was destroyed in 1945, but the cathedral, despite the tremendous amount of restoration necessary after the war, remains one of the most interesting Gothic buildings in the country.

SIGHTS

★★ **St Stephen's Cathedral** (Dom St Stephanus) ⊘ – In its opulence and the spirit of its design, this church recalls the Gothic cathedrals of France. Building began in 1240 with the base of each tower and the western bays. A second stage of the work extended from 1354 to 1402. During this period, the chancel was erected, prolonged by the small Chapel of St Mary and the ambulatory, where the High Gothic influence resulted in lower walls and the installation of stained glass windows in the space thus freed. The nave, completed towards the end of the 15C, has no triforium. Owing to the size of the chancel, the transept occupies an almost central position on the cathedral floor-plan.
The **rood-screen**★, its lower part closed, is finely worked in the High Gothic style (c1510). Above it, a group representing the **Triumphal Cross** is a splendid example of late Romanesque sculpture. Dating from c1220, it is a relic from the Ottonian cathedral which once occupied the site of the present building. The figures of the Virgin and St John, together with two seraphim, are represented on either side of the Saviour. The 15C choir columns are adorned with 14 statues of saints and the Apostles. A cloister decorated with 13C Stations of the Cross opens off the southern part of the nave.

★★ **Treasury** (Domschatz) ⊘ – Rare liturgical vestments and religious vessels from the 12C to the 16C are displayed here with a precious collection of 12C tapestries, in particular the Abraham Tapestry, which is more than 9m - 30ft long.

Church of Our Lady (Liebfrauenkirche) – *To the west of the cathedral, at the far end of the square.*
The choir screen of this 12C Romanesque basilica is embellished with **high-reliefs**★ representing Christ, the Virgin and the Apostles. The workmanship, once again, rates them among the finest examples of late 12C Romanesque art.

Municipal Museum (Städisches Museum) ⊘ – *At no 36 Domplatz.*
Local furniture, craftwork and sacred statuary can be seen here. In an adjacent building is the "Heineanum", where there is a splendid ornithological display.

St Martin's Church (Marktkirche St Martini) – The saint is represented in a basrelief on the south door of this 13-14C church. A bronze baptismal font inside, dating from the beginning of the 14C, is decorated with scenes from the life of Christ.

Halle, on the banks of the Saale between the great northern plain and the first heights of central Germany, is a "two-faced town": on the one hand it is an important industrial centre specializing in mechanical engineering and chemical manufacture; on the other hand, an intellectual enclave whose university traditions go back to the 17C.

The Salt City – As early as 806 a fortress was built to safeguard the sources of salt extraction which formed the base of Halle's prosperity. The high-point of this era was between the 14C and the 16C, after which – especially during the Industrial Revolution – local lignite mines formed the commercial base on which the town's commercial development relied. Halle never, however, attained the status of an Imperial City.

A Musical Tradition – The creation at the end of the 13C of the Brotherhood of Musicians and Fife Players (Spylleuten und Pfeiffern), and the foundation of an opera in 1654 by the Duke Augustus, illustrate the age-old support of music shown by the municipality. George Frederick Handel was born in Halle in 1685. Organist at the cathedral in 1702, he composed many sonatas and cantatas before moving to north Germany and then London. It was nevertheless at Halle, in 1803, that his famous *Messiah* was performed for the first time.
In 1713 Johann Sebastian Bach attempted – unsuccessfuly – to obtain the post of organist at Halle's Market Church (a position, ironically enough, that went to his son Friedmann 30 years later). The city pays a tribute to the master of German Baroque music in the annual **Handel Festival**.

SIGHTS

★ **Market Place** (Marktplatz) – This huge square is dominated by the belfries of the Market Church and by the Red Tower (Roter Turm), built in the 15C and almost 80m - 262ft high. An 1859 statue of Handel surveys the square from the centre. The market and the tramway junction there make this the most animated part of the town.

★ **Market Church** (Marktkirche) – A triple-aisle hall-church with no chancel, this building was constructed during the first half of the 16C on the site of two ruined Romanesque churches of which nothing but the towers remains. Inside, admire the delicate interlacing of ribs beneath the barrel vaulting, unusual in the absence of transverse arches corresponding to the bays – a feature which seems to confer on the vaulting its own existence independent of the columns supporting it. The side aisles are fitted with stone galleries. The **reredos★** of the high altar carries a Virgin and Child painted by a pupil of the Cranach school (1529).

Church of St Maurice (Moritzkirche) – *On the Hallorenring.*
This, another triple-aisle hall-church, built between 1388 and 1511, displays a network of star-vaulting characteristic of the Flamboyant Gothic style. **Works★** by the sculptor Conrad of Einbeck are on view in the church, masterpieces distinguished at the same time by a naive realism and a great power of expression. Note in particular *The Man of Sorrows*, a statue (1411) of St Maurice, and a *Pietà* (1416).

★ **Handel's House** (Händelhaus) ⊘ – *Grosse Nikolaistrasse 5.*
The great composer's birthplace has been transformed into a museum outlining both his life and his work. One section of the museum exhibits period musical instruments, including several harpsichords dating from the 16C and 17C.

Cathedral (Dom) – *Am Domplatz.*
The original, simple edifice (early 14C) was modified c1520 by Cardinal Albert of Brandenburg, who transformed it into a Gothic hall-church with three naves. The interior columns are decorated with statues of Christ, the Apostles and the saints, executed in the studios of Peter Schroh, one of the most talented sculptors of the time. Along with the pulpit (c1525), they show signs already of a Renaissance influence.

Saltworks Museum (Technisches Halloren-und Salinenmuseum) ⊘ – *Mansfelder Strasse.* The history of the exploitation of local salt mines by the Halloren – the corporation or guild of Halle salt merchants.

★★ **Moritzburg National Gallery** (Staatliche Galerie Moritzburg) ⊘ – *On the Schlossberg.* The museum occupies several rooms in a fortress built at the end of the 15C to overlook and guard the town. There is an excellent collection of **German painting of the 19C and 20C**. The fine works on display embrace the periods of Romanticism (Hans von Marées, Caspar David Friedrich), **Impressionism** (Slevogt, Corinth, Liebermann), and **Expressionism** *(Bouquet of Wildflowers* by Paula Becker-Modersohn). The movement known as **Die Brücke** *(qv)* is represented by works by its most eminent members: Otto Müller, Ludwig Kirchner, Erich Heckel and Karl Schmitt-Rottluff. Finally, the visitor can admire works by the precursors of abstract painting, Kandinsky and Feininger.
German sculpture of the 19C and 20C. In this department there are works by, among others, Wilhelm Lehmbruck and Ernst Barlach *(The Bather)*.
Numismatists will enjoy a fine collection of moneys and medals in the fortress tower.

EXCURSION

Eisleben – *34km - 21 miles to the west.* Martin Luther was born – and died – in this small mining town within sight of the lower ranges of the Harz Mountains. Memories of the religious reformer are evoked in his **birthplace** (Luther Geburtshaus, *Lutherstrasse 16)* and the house where he died (Luther-Sterbehaus, *Andreaskirchplatz 7).*

Michelin map **411** M 6 - N 6
Plan of the conurbation in the current Michelin Red Guide Deutschland

Hamburg, Germany's second largest city after Berlin, is one of the most important ports in Europe. Its old title of "Free and Hanseatic Town" and its status as a "City State" (Stadtstaat) testify to its eminence and influence through the centuries.

Each year, on May 7, there is an anniversary celebration (Hafengeburtstag) in the port of Hamburg, commemorating Frederick Barbarossa's concession in 1189 of the right to free navigation on the lower Elbe. The exercise of this right, menaced by piracy and the feudal pretensions of neighbour states – especially Denmark – demanded a continual watch by the city authorities which could not be relaxed until the 17C.

The Hanseatic Town (13C-15C) – Originally a modest settlement on the banks of the Alster, a small tributary of the Elbe, Hamburg enjoyed its first taste of prosperity when it became a member of the Hanseatic League (qv), headed at that time by Lübeck. It was then that merchants started to organize the banks of the Elbe itself for warehousing and the berthing of ships. The town profited from the particular conditions then of Baltic-North Sea trade: in those days only heavy cargoes of grain and timber took the long sea passage through the Kattegat and the Skagerrak; more valuable material was landed at Lübeck, transported overland to Hamburg, then re-embarked.

Liberty and Neutrality – The great geographic discoveries of the 16C, and the new sea routes they opened up, destroyed existing trade patterns and dislocated the Hanseatic monopoly. Hamburg traders were thus forced to become intermediaries in warehousing and distribution. The foundation of the first German Stock Exchange in 1558 reflected the intense business activity which resulted – a situation in no way worsened by the city's policy of strict neutrality, which kept it out of the Thirty Years War.

In 1618 Hamburg became a Free Imperial City. One year later the Bank of Hamburg was founded. From 1806 to 1814 French troops occupied the town. In 1842 it was ravaged by a disastrous fire.

But American independence and the emergence of Latin America lent an added impetus to the extraordinary expansion of the later 19C. By 1913, the Hamburg-Amerika steamship line was the largest in the world, and shipbuilding was the city's key industry. Today, port traffic in Hamburg has reached an annual turnover of 57 million tons.

General view of Hamburg

LIFE IN HAMBURG

Business and Leisure – Like so many big ports, Hamburg has a reputation for night-life. This is mainly centred on the St Pauli quarter, to the west of the city centre, where in the side streets flanking the **Reeperbahn** (**EZ 70**) and the Grosse Freiheit, in the gaudy illumination of multicoloured neon signs, bars, discothèques, exotic restaurants, clubs and the Eros Centre function day and night. Many Hamburg residents are a little diffident about the fact that their city is known worldwide for the garish Reeperbahn district. They point to the elegance and attraction of the residential area around the northern end, and the business quarter around the southern part, and of the Alster lake which lies like a jewel in the heart of the city. Between the Opera House (Staatsoper) (**FY**) and the Town Hall, pedestrian precincts and covered malls form an almost uninterrupted labyrinth of art galleries, fashion shops, boutiques, jewellery stores and restaurants.

HAMBURG

The Mönckebergstrasse (**GHY**), which links the Town Hall with the railway station, is the city's other commercial artery. Antique shops around the Gänsemarkt (**FY**) specialize in oriental art. Between the Rathaus and the station, an impressive variety of old maps, prints, travel works and tourist guides can be found in a number of different booksellers', while philatelists and tobacco lovers will go to the small shops in the printing and counting-house quarter.

The people of Hamburg are said to be very "British" Germans, as they tend to be more reserved and serious than their lively southern copatriots. For visitors, Hamburg is among the most welcoming of German cities, and English is spoken in many of the restaurants, stores and wine cellars.

Food Specialities – These often mix local produce with Eastern spices, sometimes combining in one dish meat, fruit and sweet-and-sour sauces. Typical are Aalsuppe – eel soup – and Labskaus, a seamen's dish of minced meat, herring, chopped gherkins and mashed potato, topped with fried eggs.

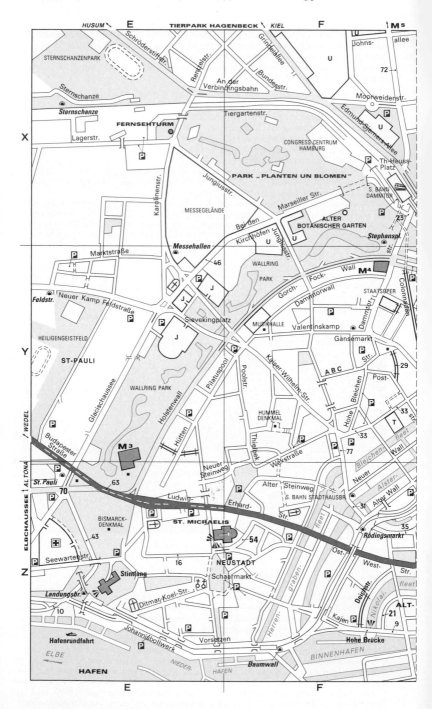

The main shopping streets are printed in red
at the head of the street list accompanying town plans.

CITY CENTRE *time: one day*

★★★ **Aussenalster** (GHXY) ⊘ – This beautiful stretch of water offers sailing and canoeing in the centre of the city. A fleet of Alsterschiffahrt motorboats ferries passengers regularly between a series of landing stages.

A **boat trip**★★★ (Alsterrundfahrt) on the lake allows the visitor to get far enough away to appreciate the city skyline punctuated by Hamburg's famous five towers, all of them over 100m - 328ft high. They stand above the four main churches and the Town Hall.

It is equally pleasant to make a circuit of the Alster by car, driving clockwise around the long shaded avenues with blocks of luxury flats on one side and immaculate stretches of greensward between the water and the roadway on the other. Their use as **viewpoints** has conferred names on such quays as the **Fernsicht** (View. *Leave by the Alsterufer* - GX) and **Schöne Aussicht** (Beautiful Vista. *Leave by An der Alster* - HX).

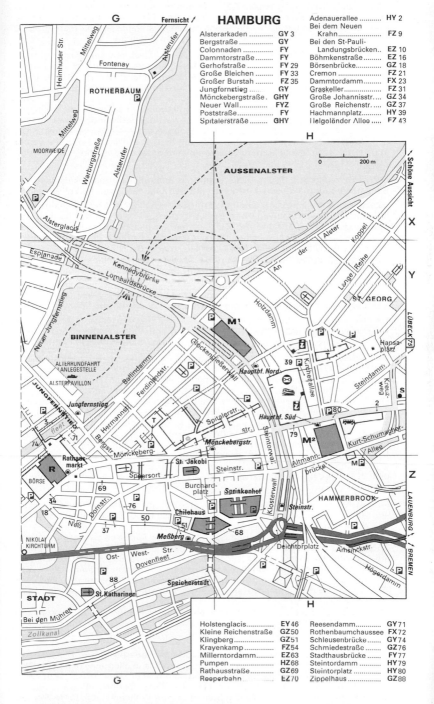

HAMBURG

Alsterarkaden	GY 3		Adenauerallee	HY 2	
Bergstraße	GY		Bei dem Neuen		
Colonnaden	FY		Krahn	FZ 9	
Dammtorstraße	FY		Bei den St-Pauli-		
Gerhofstraße	FY 29		Landungsbrücken..	EZ 10	
Große Bleichen	FY 33		Böhmkenstraße	EZ 16	
Großer Burstah	FZ 35		Börsenbrücke	GZ 18	
Jungfornstieg	GY		Cremon	FZ 21	
Mönckebergstraße.	GHY		Dammtordamm	FX 23	
Neuer Wall	FYZ		Graskeller	FZ 31	
Poststraße	FY		Große Johannisstr.	GZ 34	
Spitalerstraße	GHY		Große Reichenstr.	GZ 37	
			Hachmannplatz	HY 39	
			Helgoländer Allee	FZ 43	

Holstenglacis	EY 46		Reesendamm	GY 71	
Kleine Reichenstraße	GZ 50		Rothenbaumchaussee	FX 72	
Klingberg	GZ 51		Schleusenbrücke	GY 74	
Krayenkamp	FZ 54		Schmiedestraße	GZ 76	
Millerntordamm	EZ 63		Stadthausbrücke	FY 77	
Pumpen	HZ 68		Steintordamm	HY 79	
Rathausstraße	GZ 69		Steintorplatz	HY 80	
Reeperbahn	EZ 70		Zippelhaus	GZ 88	

Except where otherwise stated, all itineraries in town are designed as walks.

★ **Jungfernstieg** (GY) – Bordering the southern end of the Binnenalster (inner) basin, this famous street is perhaps the city's most cosmopolitan thoroughfare: the crowded terraces of the waterfront Alsterpavillon café-restaurant, the craft busily crossing and recrossing the basin, the presence nearby of one of the world's most famous hotels, and the imposing new office blocks lining the Ballindamm above the eastern quay all contribute to the general animation.

Rathausmarkt (GYZ) – This square, replanned after the fire of 1842, is dominated by the high campanile of the **Town Hall** (R), built in the neo-Renaissance style in 1887 and supported by no less than 4 000 piles.

The bridge (Schleusenbrücke), which forms part of the lock controlling the level of the Alster, crosses the Alsterfleet, a final relic of the complex canal system once characteristic of the city. The monument at the end of the bridge with a plinth carving by Barlach is the First World War memorial. On the far bank the colonnade of the Alsterarkaden shelters elegant shops.

St James's Church (St Jakobi) (GZ) – Among the numerous treasures of this 14-15C hall-church are the reredos of St Luke and the Fishers' Guild; a triptych of the Coopers' Guild on the high altar; Georg Bauman's alabaster and marble pulpit (1610); and finally the famous 1693 organ by Arp Schnitger.

Counting House Buildings (Kontorhäuser) (GHZ) – Massively constructed of sombre brick, these stand in the printing, press and business quarter around the Burchard-platz. The **Chilehaus**, built in 1924, stands against the sky like the prow of a ship. The **Sprinkenhof** (1930) is a town within the town, an office complex complete with roadways that can be used by motor cars.

To the south, the squat **Speicherstadt** (GZ) warehouses rise above the Zoll (customs) Canal and its secondary channels. The severity of these dark brick masses is relieved only by an upper decoration of stepped gables and turrets. Built in the late 19C for the free trade zone, they store in their 373 000m² - 447 000sq yds of floor space such valuable merchandise as coffee, tobacco, spices, raw silk and oriental carpets.

Old Town (Altstadt) (FGZ) – This quarter is bounded by the Nikolaifleet, the Binnenhafen (docks reserved for river craft and tugboats) and the Zoll Canal.

Deichstrasse (FZ) – Former 17C and 18C houses once inhabited by merchants have today been converted mainly into bars and taverns. It was in the Deichstrasse that the great fire of 1842 started. The restored façades of warehouses opposite, lining the curve of the Nikolaifleet Canal, recall the Hamburg of yesteryear.

The best view is from the **Hohe Brücke**, which crosses the Nikolaifleet and lies parallel with the Binnenhafen. Pulleys once used for the transhipment of cargoes from ship to shore and vice versa can still be seen on the warehouse gables. Traces of the severe floods of 1962 and 1976 are visible on the walls.

Cremon (FZ 21) – From no 33 to no 36, this street is lined by warehouses and former lodging houses, each with dual entrances – one from the street, one from the canal.

St Katharinen Church (GZ) – Brick-built in the 14C and 15C; a Gothic church with a bulbous openwork tower that rises above the narrow streets of the old port.

★ **St Michael's Church** (St Michaelis-Kirche) (EFZ) – Another brick construction, designed in 1762 by the architect Sonnin, this is one of the finest examples of the Baroque tradition in northern Germany. Intended for the Lutheran sect, the church is surprisingly spacious, well proportioned and well lit. Its famous **tower** (1786), rising high above the Elbe with a lantern turret in the form of a rotunda, is known by local people simply as "Michel" and has become the emblem of the city. The **view**★ from the **platform** ⊙ takes in all of the town centre, but most particularly the river, zebra-striped with the wake of ships, and its docks, basins, warehouses and wharves.

Near the east end of the church, pass through the porch at no 10 Am Krayenkamp (FZ 54). The blind alley beyond is lined with astonishing brick and timber houses built in 1670 as almshouses (**Krameramtswohnungen**) and today transformed into art galleries.

★★ **Fine Arts Museum** (Kunsthalle) (HY M1) ⊙ – The ground floor is devoted to 19C and 20C sculpture. Works by Rodin, Renoir, Maillol and Matisse are on display. The pictures mentioned below are all on the first floor.

Created in 1379 for St Peter's, Hamburg, the **Grabow Altarpiece** by Master Bertram of Minden is one of the largest and most touching examples of primitive painting in north Germany. Its 24 separate panels are related to the concept of Salvation and comprise a variety of scenes from the naive to the animated, with beautiful colour effects and attitudes. It is fascinating to compare this altarpiece with the one by the same artist at Buxtehude and the polyptych of St Thomas of Canterbury by Master Francke.

The 17C Dutch school is represented by an early Rembrandt *(Simeon in the Temple)*, and by land- and sea-scapes by Avercamp, Van Goyen, the Ruysdaels and Van de Velde. Genre paintings by Jan Steen and Pieter de Hooch are also exhibited.

19C German painting, well served with works by Feuerbach, Von Marées, and Böcklin, leaves plenty of space also for the portraits and allegories of Philipp Otto Runge (1777-1810), a Hamburger by adoption. Equally on view are Romantic compositions by Caspar David Friedrich *(The Ice Field, Rambler Above a Sea of Clouds)* and a canvas by the Realist School painter Wilhelm Leibl, *Three Women in Church*. Interesting 19C French works include paintings by Corot, Daubigny, Courbet *(Bouquet of Flowers)*, Manet (**Nana**), Renoir, Cézanne and Gaugin.

Not long before the First World War, the Frenchmen Bonnard and Vuillard dis-
covered interesting subjects for landscapes around Hamburg, some of which are
here. And, finally, together with paintings by Max Liebermann *(Women Repairing
Nets)*, Lovis Corinth and Edvard Munch *(Madonna)*, the museum possesses an
outstanding collection of works reprsenting the Brücke and Blauer Reiter (Blue
Knight) movements *(qv)*. Among these are a triptych of *St Mary the Egyptian* by
Nolde, Kirchner's *Self-portrait with Model* and *Frieze With Monkeys* by Franz
Marc. One of the galleries exhibits Paul Klee's enchanting **"Goldfish"**.

★ **Museum of Decorative Arts** (Museum für Kunst und Gewerbe) (HY M2) ⊘ –
Thousands of arts and crafts exhibits are displayed chronologically in this
museum. Among the most fascinating are the medieval statuary, gold and silver
plate (Reliquary of St George by Berndt Notke), sumptuous Renaissance furniture
and fine examples of north German clockmaking as well as delicate 18C porcelain. There is a generous display of ornaments, furniture and artworks from the
Jugendstil *(qv)* and separate departments for Chinese, Japanese and Islamic art.

★ **Historical Museum** (Museum für Hamburgische Geschichte) (EYZ M3) ⊘ – Here the
visitor can browse over models of Hamburg in days gone by, and a brilliant scale
model of the city's present railway system. There is a huge department devoted to the
port and navigation on the Elbe, including more than 100 model ships, among them
a cutaway section of 1901 steamer and the impressive 1722 *Wapen von Hamburg*.

★★ THE PORT (EZ)

Apart from St Michael's Tower, the best **viewpoint★** from which to see the port as
a whole is the Stintfang (**EZ**) – a raised terrace below the youth hostel.

A few statistics – The Hamburg docks comprise 60 basins and more than 68km
- 42 miles of quays, in addition to a great number of mooring buoys. Thanks to
a relatively small tidefall (3m - 10ft average), no locks are necessary in the basins
accessible to ocean-going traffic able to navigate the Elbe (displacing up to
110 000 tons and drawing no more than 13.5m - 44ft). The port's reputation relies
on a speedy turn-around and on the wide variety of equipment, warehousing,
transport and offloading machinery available for every kind of cargo. Three hundred and forty shipping lines call regularly (about 650 departures a month) to
transport merchandise to 1 000 ports all over the world.

Boat trip around the port (Hafenrundfahrt) ⊘ – *Boats leave from landing stage
no 2 in the St Pauli district (St Pauli-Landungsbrücken)* (**EZ**).
The visitor will be astonished by the sheer size of the dockyards – 5 separate ship-
builders, 26 floating docks – and by the extraordinary activity on either side of
the Elbe, where every type of vessel is constructed: tankers, lighters, tugs, cargo
ships, containers, refrigerator craft and pleasure boats as well as police and customs launches. Motor ferries ply back and forth all day long, transporting south
bank workers back to the city during the rush hour. Before 10am on Sundays and
public holidays, do not leave the quays in the St Pauli district without visiting the
lively Fischmarkt.

CITY OUTSKIRTS

★ **Postal Museum** (Postmuseum am Stephansplatz) (FY M4) ⊘ – This museum, in a
square named after the Prussian director-general who inaugurated the World
Confederation of Postal Services, outlines the evolution of mail transport and dis-
patches from the 16C to the present day. It has a particularly fine collection of
transmitting equipment, concentrating especially on the pioneer period of long-distance communications. There are many examples of early telegraphic equipment,
telephones invented by Bell and Siemens, instrument panels with warning lights,
exchange keyboards, fax machines and radio installations.
Some of the modern instruments are displayed in working order and may be tried
out by visitors to the museum.

★ **Television Tower** (Fernsehturm) (EX) ⊘ – A slender steel and concrete plinth
whose highest aerials are 272m - 890ft from the ground, the tower soars above
the Planten un Blomen park to the west of the Alster. There is an observation
platform at the top and, a little higher still, a revolving panoramic restaurant
affording a fine **view★★** of the entire city.

★ **Planten un Blomen Park** (Erholungspark) (EFX) ⊘ – Part of a green belt replac-
ing the old fortifications which ran in an arc between the Elbe and the Alster to
the west and north of the town, this park was laid out in 1936. Its geometrically
arranged gardens are used as a proving ground for new species of flowers and
trees. An artifical cascade tumbles into the main pool (Grosser Parksee), where
after dark the fountains act as background to a Son et Lumière performance
(Wasserlichtkonzert). Nearby are the city conference centre (Congress Centrum)
and the Hamburg Plaza hotel.

★ **Ethnographic Museum** (Hamburgisches Museum für Völkerkunde) (M5) ⊘ –
Rothenbaumchaussee 64 (**FX**). The collections in this museum – remarkable in
their variety and rarity – are directly due to the commercial relations between this
Hanseatic town and the rest of the world, Hamburg having been the departure
point at the turn of the century for explorers' expeditions to Oceania and elsewhere. Well represented are the civilizations of Europe, Asia (including the
former Soviet Union and Turkey), Africa (Benin bronzes and cult objects from
what is now Zaire), the Americas and the Pacific isles.

The **Golden Room** (Goldene Kammer), on the ground floor, has an exhibition of pre-Colombian jewellery. On the first floor, note the wand puppets used in shadow theatres from Bali and Java, a gallery of **Oceanian Masks★**, and the **Boat Hall★** (Bootshalle), which is devoted to Polynesian canoes and other craft. Symbolic figures decorate a fine **Maori Meeting Hall** from New Zealand, which is on the same floor.

★★ **Hagenbeck Zoo** (Tierpark) ⊘ – *Leave by the Grindelallee* (**FX**).
Founded in 1907 in the Stellingen suburb, the zoological gardens maintain a century- old tradition of capturing, breeding, selling and training wild animals for circuses. 2 500 creatures of 3 655 species from five continents live in relative freedom in 25 hectares - 62 acres of grassland, woods and artificial rocks. In recent years the zoo has saved from extinction the onager, a rare species of Persian wild ass.

EXCURSIONS

Altona; Klein Flottbek; Wedel – *22km - 14 miles - allow 1/2 day.*

★★ **Altona and Northern Germany Museum** (Altonaer Museum-Norddeutsches Landesmuseum) ⊘ – *Leave by the Reeperbahn* (**EZ**).
Day-to-day life and traditional activities in the lower Elbe valley and Schleswig-Holstein are illustrated here. Note the exceptional collection of **ships' figureheads** from the 18-19C, the models explaining the different types of fishing and boats to be seen in the North Sea, and the displays of ceramics, Frisian embroidery and period toys. An authentic thatched cottage from the Vierlande, a region southeast of Hamburg, has been transformed into a small restaurant. The upper floor is devoted to the history of Altona, the richest of the city's outlying areas.

Altona Balcony (Altonaer Balkon) – From a terrace south of Altona's Town Hall, there is a **view★** of the confluence of the two branches of the Elbe which marks the limit of Hamburg's industrial and port zone. The amount of shipping which passes each hour is astonishing.
Follow the **Elbchaussee★**, a spacious avenue bordered by great houses and superb properties developed since the beginning of the 19C by the grand Hamburg shipowning and trading dynasties.

> *At Klein Flottbek turn right and drive along the Baron-Voght-Strasse as far as Route 50.*

Villa Jenisch (Jenisch-Haus) ⊘ – A fine landscaped park planted with exotic trees surrounds this pleasant neo-Classical villa built between 1831 and 1834. The luxuriously furnished rooms illustrate the style of German bourgeois interiors from the late Renaissance to the beginning of the Jugendstil period. Note the splendid marquetry flooring of the ground floor state rooms, and the Danish style furniture upstairs manufactured in Altona.

Ernst Barlach House (Ernst-Barlach-Haus) ⊘ – *Baron-Voght-Strasse 50A.*
Designed to house the private collection of the tobacco tycoon Herman F Reemstma, this building contains sculpture, wood engravings and drawings *(displayed in rotation)* by the artist Ernst Barlach, a native of Wedel. Among the works exhibited in chronological order, note *The Frieze of the Listeners*, murals carved in oak, *Moses* and *Three Men Brandishing a Sword*, all of them showing a powerful expressive talent.

> *Continue along the Elbchaussee, then head for Wedel after driving through the pleasant suburban resort of Blankenese.*

Wedel – *Follow the Willkomm-Höft signposts to the café-restaurant beside the Elbe known as the "Schulauer Fährhaus".*
Above the terrace is a saluting base for passing ships (Schiffsbegrüssungsanlage). The ceremony – which many people come to watch – involves running up the flag and then playing the national anthem of the country of origin of every single vessel sailing upstream or downstream past the base.
There is an **Ernst-Barlach Museum** in the house where the artist was born *(Mühlenstrasse 1)* which displays drawings and lithographs as well fine bronzes, among them the impressive *Old Men Dancing*.

Ahrensburg Castle ⊘ – *23km - 15 miles to the northeast. Leave Hamburg by B25, the Lübeck road.*
The white bulk of this moated castle is framed by the green, leafy banks of the Hunnau. Built, like Glücksburg Castle *(qv)*, by Peter Rantzau, it comprises three main blocks flanked by corner towers surmounted by lantern towers. Scrolled gables framed by obelisks decorate the castle, which was the last true Renaissance creation to be built in Schleswig-Holstein (1595).
The interior recalls the family of Count HC Schimmelmann, who bought the castle in 1759 and refurbished it. Note the stairwell, the oak-panelled dining room, and the Emkendorf Room with its elegant Louis XVI furnishings.

Michelin maps ⬛⬛⬛ and ⬛⬛⬛ L 10
Town plan in the current Michelin Red Guide Deutschland

Built on the east bank of the Weser, Hamelin glories in fine old houses, of which the most typical belong to the **Weser Renaissance** (late 16-early 17C) period *(qv)*. The style is distinguished architecturally by ram's-horn scrollwork and pinnacled gables. Other characteristics include delicately worked stone bands encircling the building, forward projecting pavilions (Utlucht) treated as smaller extensions of the main façade, and large, well-developed lucarnes (Zwerchhäuser) with decorated gables at the base of the roof.

Hamelin is also a town with a special place in European folklore; it is the home of the celebrated ratcatcher immortalized by Goethe, and by Robert Browning as the Pied Piper in English. In the summer, a dramatic version of the legend is performed each Sunday at noon on the terrace of the Marriage House. As souvenirs, toys or sweets, the rats are still to be seen in many of Hamelin's shop windows.

The Pied Piper of Hamelin – In 1284, a mysterious man in multicoloured clothes promised the townspeople that, for a substantial reward, he would free Hamelin from a plague of rats and mice. He played his pipe, and all the rodents emerged to follow him to the banks of the Weser, where they drowned.

But the reward was not forthcoming, so the piper returned on Sunday, when everyone was at church, and played again in revenge. This time it was the children who emerged from their houses. There were 130 of them, and they too followed him, never to be seen again. Only two escaped; one was dumb, the other blind.

The historical version of the tale is that overpopulation in the 13C was such that a troop of young people were sent by the authorities, without any hope of return, to colonize far-away lands to the east.

SIGHTS

★ **The Ratcatcher's House** (Rattenfängerhaus) – It is a large, well-proportioned building dating from 1603. The symmetrical decoration of the façade involves differently sculpted bands of stonework, further adorned with carved busts and masks. Typical Weser scrolls and pinnacles enrich the gable.

★ **Marriage House** (Hochzeitshaus) – The building, constructed between 1610 and 1617, acted as a reception centre for burghers' weddings. Three elegant gables break the horizontals of the façade, themselves emphasized by cornices and lateral bands of stonework.

Dempter House (Demptersches Haus) – *In the market place.*
An outstanding building, dating from 1607, noteworthy especially for its fine Weser Renaissance projecting pavilion (Utlucht - see above).

Canons' House (Stiftsherrenhaus) – *Osterstrasse 8.*
Another remarkable house, this one half-timbered and built in 1558. The sculpted consoles represent biblical figures.

Lücking House – *Wendenstrasse 8.* This is a rich, half-timbered house of 1639 with a rounded doorway centred in a rectangular recess.

Rattenkrug – *Backerstrasse 16.* A projecting pavilion (Utlucht) and a tall gable of no less than five floors distinguish this 1568 building.

Collegiate Church (Münster) – From the public gardens to the south, the church appears to cower beneath the protection of the massive polygonal tower over the transept – once part of a 12C Romanesque basilica which was transformed a century later into the existing Gothic hall-church. Inside, the layout of the columns and their capitals, checkered or carved with palm leaves, draws attention once more to the raised transept.

EXCURSIONS

★ **Hämelschenburg** – *11km - 7 miles to the south.*
The **castle★** (Schloss) ⊙, which boasts both a moat and a lagoon, was built in the shape of a horse-shoe between 1588 and 1616. It is one of the masterpieces of the Weser Renaissance style.
The wing overlooking the road is the most ornate, with typical alternations of smooth and embossed stone bands, an oriel immediately above the moat, and four decorative gables. Weapons, trophies, paintings and furniture are on view in the interior.

Fischbeck – *7km - 3 3/4 miles to the northwest.*
The **abbey** ⊙ here was officially recognized by Otto I in the year 955 (photocopies of the original documents can be seen in the church). It is still used as a home for elderly Protestant women. The church itself dates from the 12C. It was equipped in the 19C with partitioned boxes, which allowed the female residents to take part in the services.
The **crypt** is in a pure Romanesque style, with each column topped by a capital embellished with a different motif. Left of the chancel is a moving Ecce Homo! in sculpted wood; to the right of it hangs a 16C tapestry illustrating the foundation of the abbey. The cloister, in its present state, dates from the 13C and 14C.

Michelin maps **411** and **412** LM 9
Plan of the conurbation in the current Michelin Red Guide Deutschland and also on Michelin map **411**

Hanover, capital of Lower Saxony, is one of the main economic centres of northern Germany. Its two annual international fairs, held in special pavilions southeast of the town, stimulate an enormous amount of business.

The city centre has been rebuilt to allow free movement of traffic and there is a pedestrian shopping area near the station. On the periphery are residential zones, waterways (Maschsee), and a green belt started as long ago as the 17C with the creation of the famous Herrenhausen gardens. There is a good view over the whole district from the dome of the **Town Hall** (Rathaus) (**Z R**) ⊘.

HISTORICAL NOTES

The House of Hanover – The principality of Hanover fell in the 17C to a branch of the House of Brunswick and Lüneburg. The Court moved to Hanover. The transformation of Herrenhausen began. And, under the aegis of the cultured Princess Sophia, a period commenced in which literature and the arts flourished. Handel, who composed his first operas in Hamburg, was frequently invited to give concerts. The philosopher Leibniz arrived in 1676 to take up the position of Court Librarian, a post he held for forty years. In 1692 the principality became the Electorate of Brunswick and Lüneburg, the ninth in Germany.

From the Hanoverian Court to the Court of St James – The marriage in 1658 of the Duke Ernst-Augustus with the Palatine Princess Sophia, grand-daughter of the Stuart King James I, had given the Hanoverian succession a claim on the throne of England.

In 1714 the Elector Georg-Ludwig, son of Princess Sophia, did indeed find himself heir to the crown and became George I of England. The Court left Hanover and Herrenhausen. It was not to return until 1837, when the union of Hanover and England under a single sovereign was abrogated because the Salic Law (forbidding the accession of women to the throne) applied in Hanover. Victoria therefore became Queen of England, while in Hanover it was her uncle Ernst-Augustus who succeeded.

Installing his Court in Hanover, the new monarch set about restoring the town to its former glory. But the year 1866 saw the fall of the House of Hanover and the annexation of the kingdom by Prussia.

★★ HERRENHAUSEN GARDENS (HERRENHÄUSER GÄRTEN)

*Leave by the Leibnizufer (**Y**) time: 1 1/2 hours*

This beautiful 17C development, in the northwestern part of the city, comprises four separate and quite different gardens: the Grosser Garten, the Berggarten, the Georgengarten and the Welfengarten. They are linked by an avenue of lime trees, the Herrenhäuser Allee, laid out in 1726 (drivers of cars are obliged to take the Nienburger Strasse).

HANNOVER

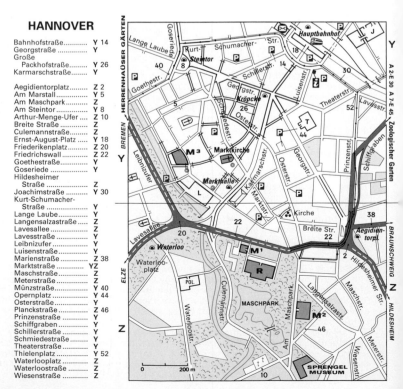

** **Grosser Garten** – Creation of the garden started in 1666. Between 1680 and 1710 Princess Sophia took it over, transformed it, and enlarged it for – as she wrote more than once – "that garden is my very life". The oldest part is a formal French pleasure garden divided into flower borders punctuated by statues of allegorical figures and Roman gods. On one side is an open-air theatre, on the other a maze. At the southern end a mosaic of clipped hedges is cut by pathways between ornamental ponds. The powerful central fountain jets a plume of water no less than 82m - 269ft into the air (as a comparison, Nelson's Column, in London, is 170ft high).

In the southeastern corner of the garden is the small **Wilhelm Busch Museum** ⊙, which is devoted to the local poet, illustrator and humorist (1832-1908) considered to be the originator of the strip cartoon . Busch's "Max und Moritz" was very popular among 19C German youth.

Berggarten – The greenhouses of this botanical garden display cactus plants and other succulents, as well as 2 500 varieties of orchid and flora native to the Canary Islands. At the far end of the garden's principal walk is the mausoleum of the Royal House of Hanover.

ADDITIONAL SIGHTS

Market Church (Marktkirche) (Y) – A four-gabled tower crowned by a sharp pinnacle presides over this church, rebuilt after 1945 in the style of the 14C original. An interesting contrast to the restored Gothic style are the modern bronze doors by Gerhard Marcks, depicting scenes from recent German history. Inside, note the 15C sculpted polychrome **reredos** at the high altar, which represents the Passion. Also noteworthy are the stained glass windows (14C) in the choir and the 15C baptismal font in bronze.

* **Kestner Museum** (Z M1) ⊙ – This valuable museum was founded by Charlotte Kestner, better known, thanks to Goethe, as Charlotte Buff. On the ground floor there is a fine collection of antique coins (Greek, Roman and pre-Islamic Persian) as well as European numismatic examples from the 16C to the 20C. Five thousand years of history are recalled on the second floor, where there is a splendid exhibition of antiquities from Egypt (magnificent head of Amenophis IV-Akhenaton) and ancient Rome (glassware and bronzes). European decorative art is amply represented on the first floor, where German porcelain and faience is on display along with interesting silverware and ceramics embellished in the Jugendstil fashion. Do not miss the 12C head-reliquary – said to be that of John the Baptist – a masterpiece of goldsmithing.

* **Museum of Lower Saxony** (Niedersächsisches Landesmuseum) (Z M2) ⊙ – This huge regional museum has a special **prehistoric section** (Urgeschichtliche Abteilung) which illustrates the evolution of primitive civilizations in northwest Germany. In the Fine Arts section an important **picture gallery** (Niedersächsische Landesgalerie) exhibits works ranging from medieval times to the present day. Primitives from Italy and Lower Saxony (Master Bertram; the Master of the Golden Table) are followed by German Renaissance artists (Holbein; Cranach) and Italian painters from the 16C to the 18C (Botticelli; Pontormo; Tiepolo; Piazetta). Flemish and Dutch work of the 17C is emblazoned with such names as Rubens, Van Dyck, Bruegel, Kalf and the Ruysdaels.

German artists of the 19 and 20C are represented by CD Friedrich, F von Lenbach, the Impressionists Liebermann, Slevogt and Corinth, and Paula Becker-Modersohn of the Worpswede School. French painters exhibited include Poussin, Lorrain, Corot, Courbet and the Impressionists Monet, Renoir, Sisley and Pissarro. The **Department of Sculpture** displays works ranging from the Middle Ages, through the Renaissance (Riemenschneider), to such "moderns" as Rodin, Degas and Maillol.

* **Sprengel Museum** (Z) ⊙ – Not far from the Maschsee, a stabile by Calder indicates the entrance to the museum, which concentrates on art of the 20C. Among the Cubists who experimented with form and volume are Picasso (*Three Women* - 1908), Léger (*The Village* - 1912), and the sculptor Henri Laurens (*Head of a Young Girl* - 1920). Expressionism, starting with Edvard Munch *(qv)* (*Half-Nude*), developed in intensity with Karl Schmidt-Rottluff *(Four Bathers on the Beach)*, Otto Mueller *(Lovers)* and Ernst Ludwig Kirchner of the Brücke movement, as well as members of the Blauer Reiter movement, whose research into different uses of colour is remarkable in the works shown here. They include Kandinsky's *Diagonal*, Jawlensky's *Turandot II*, Macke's *Nude With Coral Necklace*, a fascinating *Floral Myth* by Paul Klee, and *Horse with Eagle* by Marc. In a similar vein are Nolde *(Flowers and Clouds)*, Rohlfs *(Birch Forest)*, Kokoschka and Feininger. A key position in reserved for the portraits of Beckmann *(Woman with a Bouquet of Carnations)*. Research in the Surrealist direction is represented by the pictures of Max Ernst *(Fascinating Cypress)*, by Salvador Dali and above all by Kurt Schwitters, Hanoverian by birth and the author of many different kinds of work *(Merz-Bau)*. Contemporary tendencies have their spokesmen in Tapiès, Dubuffet, Lindner and W Baumeister.

Historical Museum (Historisches Museum) (Y M3) ⊙ – One section of this museum illustrates the history of Lower Saxony, and Hanover in particular, together with mementoes of the Hanoverian Royal House and a collection of carriages and harness (note the sumptuous golden coupé of the Prince of Wales, dating from 1783). Beautiful chests and cabinets from Lower Saxony are on view in the Ethnology section, as well as peasant interiors reconstructed with faience tiles and inlaid panelling.

Zoological Garden (Zoologischer Garten) ⊙ – *Adenauerallee 3. Leave by the Schiffgraben* (Y). The most attractive section is that devoted to the antelopes, kangaroos and giraffes.

Michelin map **987** fold 16

The wooded heights of the Harz form the northern foothills of those mountains of central Europe resulting from the Hercynian upthrust in the Primary Era. Standing at the southern extremity of the vast Germano-Polish plain and almost entirely covered in forests, they break the moisture-laden winds sweeping across from the west to create a hilly region plentifully supplied with watercourses. Numerous dams have transformed the Harz into an exceptional reservoir supplying the nearby areas.

The highest point of the range, the Brocken (alt 1 142m - 3 747ft), site of the legendary Witches' Sabbath (introduction), attracts a great number of walkers to its windswept slopes. The Harzquerbahn, a narrow-gauge railway with steam locomotives, penetrates the region from north to south, from Wernigerode to Nordhausen. This provides – especially between Wernigerode and the resort of Eisfelder Talmühle, but also from Schierke to the Brocken – an excellent way of exploring the heart of the eastern Harz.

① **THE UPPER HARZ** *81km - 50 miles - allow 1/2 day*

This itinerary follows an admirable road network, passing through huge tracts of rolling country with rounded hills covered in conifers.

** **Goslar** – *See under Goslar.*

Clausthal-Zellerfeld – This is the former mining capital of the Harz. At Zellerfeld, there is the **Upper Harz Mine Museum** (Oberharzer Bergwerksmuseum) ⊙ which illustrates the different mining techniques (once for gold and silver, later for lead, zinc and barium oxide) used until the last mine closed down in 1931.

At Clausthal, in the Hindenburgplatz, the **Church of the Holy Spirit** (Pfarrkirche zum Heiligen Geist), built in 1642, is one of the largest wooden churches in the whole of Europe. Note the majestic positioning of the galleries and the light falling obliquely from windows placed just below the panelled vaulting.

Oker Dam (Okertalsperre) – From the top of the barrage there is a fine **view** over the widely dispersed waters of the reservoir.

St.Andreasberg – The road leads first to an **old silver mine** (Silberbergwerk Samson) ⊙ at the bottom of the valley. This was closed in 1910 but has been reopened for tourists.

The Fahrkunst, a machine of ingenious simplicity which sent down and brought back the miners, can be seen at work. The device comprises two poles set side by side, each with steps cut into it, and a steady backwards and forwards movement. All the miner had to do was mark time with a foot on each pole.

Braunlage – An important tourist resort, high up on a plateau overlooked by the wooded slopes of the **Wurmberg** (971m - 3 186ft).

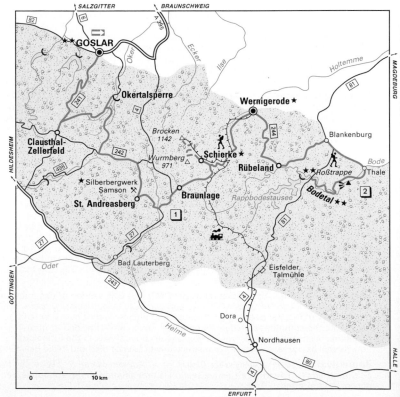

★ **Schierke** – A magnificent site here: a holiday centre from which many footpaths and ramblers' routes start - most of them leading towards the summit of the **Brocken**.

★ **Wernigerode** – *See under Wernigerode.*

② **THE EASTERN HARZ** *89km - 55 miles - allow 1/2 day*

In this part of the Harz, the forests have a greater proportion of deciduous trees. Even if it is on a smaller scale, the landscape is at times more spectacular.

★ **Wernigerode** – *See under Wernigerode.*

Rübeland – In this area, where the chief activity is the exploitation of limestone, tourists enjoy exploring the many caves and grottoes formed by the erosion of the rock. In **Hermann's Grotto** (Hermannshöhle) ⊘, note particularly the Chamber of Crystals and the small pool stocked with "cave fish" (Grottenolmen) – blind creatures, living out their whole lives in darkness.

Continue via Blankenburg and Thale to reach the Bode Valley (Bodetal).

★★ **The Bode Gorge (Bodetal)** – The river here has gouged a passage as best it could through a maze of rock masses and now flows along the foot of impressive cliffs. The most spectacular site, without doubt, is the **Rosstrappe**★★ (The Charger's Hoofmark).
This is ten minutes' walk from the parking place. From the lookout point, which projects vertiginously over the void, there is an incredible **view**★★★ of the sheer cliffs, the stream tumbling between crags at the foot of the chasm, and the distant woods. The place owes its name to a legend, according to which a horse ridden by a princess being chased by a giant pushed so hard while readying itself to spring across the gulf, that it left an imprint in the rock.
Following the course of the river, the road twists and turns through the rugged forest landscape. Until the junction with Route 81, the beauty of the scenery, the bumpy road and the undulating nature of the country all impose a reduced speed on drivers.

★★ **HEIDELBERG** Baden-Württemberg   Pop 132 000

Michelin maps **412** and **413** J 18
Plan of the conurbation in the current Michelin Red Guide Deutschland

Heidelberg, since 1386 seat of Germany's most famous university, lies on the banks of the Neckar river. It was here, in the early years of the 19C, that the poets Brentano, Eichendorff and Von Arnim united their talents to form the foundation of Germany's Romantic movement. Today, the city owes its liveliness to the presence of 27 000 students and innumerable foreign tourists, Anglo-Saxons in particular.
From the quays on the right bank of the Neckar, on either side of the picturesque **Old Bridge** (Alte Brücke or Karl-Theodor Brücke, **(Y)**, there are splendid **views**★★ of the castle ruins, their red sandstone ramparts distinct against the green of the forest, and of the old town clustered around the Church of the Holy Spirit (Heilig-Geist-Kirche).
Further superb views of the castle and the city can be seen from the **Philosophers' Walk** (Philosophenweg) **(Y)** – reached by crossing the Old Bridge and climbing the **Schlangenweg** steps **(Y)**.

Heidelberg Castle and the Neckar

HISTORICAL NOTES

The Rhineland Palatinate, of which Heidelberg was the political centre, owes its name to the title "palatines" given to the highest officers in the Holy Roman Empire who were in the sovereign's confidence. These functions and dignities disappeared in the 14C, except in the hereditary family ruling a group of territories whose appropriate centre was the confluence if the Neckar with the Rhine. Through the wise government of these palatine-electors (Kurfürsten), the **Electoral Palatinate** (Kurpfalz) became one of the most advanced states of Europe.

The "Orléans War" (1688-97) – In the 16C, the electors, who had become Protestant, were continually reinforcing and embellishing their castle at Heidelberg. The Elector Karl-Ludwig restored his states in an exemplary manner after the Thirty Years War. In the hope of ensuring peace in the Rhineland and extending the influence of his house he married his daughter Liselotte (**Elizabeth-Charlotte**) to "Monsieur", Philip of Orléans, brother of Louis XIV. The **Palatine Princess** did not pass unnoticed at the Court of France. Saint-Simon in his Memoirs returns frequently to her loud voice, her endless chatter and her intractable dislike of Mme de Maintenon. When the son of Karl-Ludwig died without an heir in 1685, the marriage alliance, which was invoked by Louis XIV to assert his claim to the territories on the left bank of the Rhine, proved disastrous to the Palatinate and to Heidelberg. The town was laid waste and the castle sacked in the brutal campaign of 1689. Total disaster followed in 1693, when the town was completely destroyed by fire. This catastrophe led to the rebuilding of the town in an uninspired Baroque style on the same foundations and with no thoroughfares. Before long the electors abandoned the ruined castle, turning their attention to their residences at Mannheim and Schwetzingen.

★★★ CASTLE (SCHLOSS)

Cars approach via the Neue Schlossstrasse (Z).

The route marked on the plan leads to the **Rondell** promontory, once the site of a battery of cannons and now a **viewpoint★** looking out over the town, the Neckar valley and the Rhineland plain. After this comes the **Great Tower** (Dicker Turm), and then the **Elizabeth Gate** (Elizabethentor), which Friedrich V had built in a single night in 1615, as a surprise for his wife Elizabeth Stuart, daughter of James I of England.

The castle's southeast corner is formed by the **Shattered Tower**. A mine laid by French sappers in 1693 gutted one side of the edifice and destroyed the gun emplacements radiating from a solid central core.

The **Gardens★** were laid out in terraces under Friedrich V, after an enormous amount of earthworks lasting from 1616 to 1619. The east face of the castle, with its three towers, is visible from the Scheffel Terrace.

The courtyard and buildings

The courtyard is on the far side of a fortified bridge guarded by the **Gate Tower** (Torturm). Immediately on the right is the fine Gothic hall of the **Well Wing** (Brunnenhalle), whose granite Roman columns came from Charlemagne's palace at Ingelheim, near Mainz.

Library (Bibliotheksbau) (6) – This Gothic building, set well back from the castle's west wing, is able thus to receive light from windows on all four sides. At one time it housed the personal library, art collections and treasure of the princely family. The loggia is worth looking at.

★★ **Friedrich's Wing** (Friedrichsbau) (10) – The façade design of this wing, with its two festooned gables, retains in its columns the classical orders of antiquity – Doric, Ionic and Corinthian – rediscovered during the Renaissance. But the composition of pilasters and cornices, creating contrasts of light and shade, presages already the subsequent taste for the Baroque. The statues (copies) represent the ancestors of Friedrich IV, who added the wing, among them princes of the house of Wittelsbach.

The rear of the building, the sole decorated wall directly facing the town, can best be seen from the **Great Terrace** (Altan). Looking down on the roofs of Old Heidelberg, this is approached via a vaulted passageway to the right of the palace.

Hall of Mirrors Wing (Gläserner Saalbau) (8) – Only a shell remains of this building, which retains, nevertheless, a series of tiered galleries in the Italian Renaissance manner.

Otto-Heinrich Wing (Ottheinrichsbau) (9) – This palace was built by the Elector Otto-Heinrich, one of the most enlightened rulers of the Renaissance. During the three years of his reign (1556-1559), the sovereign opened the Palatinate wide to innovative ideas, notably on religious and artistic matters. The wing inaugurated the fruitful late Renaissance period in German architecture.

Horizontals predominate in the composition of the façade. In line with contemporary taste, the ornamentation combines biblical and mythological symbols. The famous sculptor Alexander Colin of Mechelen collaborated in the design of the entrance, which is in the form of a triumphal arch displaying the Elector's armorial bearings: the Palatinate lion and the heraldic lozenges of the House of Wittelsbach framing the globe surmounted by a cross symbolizing the Empire.

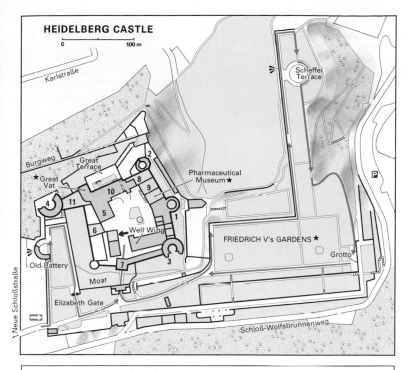

HEIDELBERG CASTLE

0   100 m

End of Feudal Period (and subsequent alterations).
1) Apothecary's Tower (14C) – 2) Bell Tower (14C) – 3) Shattered Tower (15C)
Gothic-Renaissance Transitional Period
  (Ludwig V. – 1508-1544).
4) Great Tower (1533) – 5) Ladies' Wing – 6) Library – 7) Gate Tower
Renaissance.
8) Hall of Mirrors (1549) – 9) Otto Heinrich Wing (1566)
Renaissance-Baroque Transitional Period
10) Friedrich Wing (Friedrich IV. – 1592-1610), and below, Great Terrace (Altan)
11) Englisch Wing (Friedrich V. – 1610-1632)

Interior ⊙

Two architectural models allow a comparison between the castle as it is today and as it was in the 17C. So far as the Renaissance decoration of the Friedrich's Wing is concerned, this is largely due to a felicitous restoration (c1900). Statues originally ornamenting the façades can be seen in the corridors. Baroque features were added to the chapel around 1720

★ **Great Vat (Grosses Fass)** – This colossal cask, with a capacity of 221 726 litres - 48 780 gallons – was installed in the reign of Charles Theodore at the end of the 18C. Wine from it can be drawn, with the aid of a pump, in the royal banqueting hall (in the Ladies' Wing). The platform above the vat is large enough for dancing as well as wine tasting. The guardian of this Bacchic extravagance – today an idol of local folklore – was the dwarf court jester **Perkeo**, celebrated himself for the astonishing amount he could drink. The memory of Perkeo lives on in a wooden figurine and in the ingenious "surprise" clock he invented.

★ **German Pharmaceutical Museum (Deutsches Apotheken-Museum) (Z M1)** ⊙ – *Entrance beneath the steps leading to the Otto-Heinrich Wing.* Interesting 18C and 19C apothecaries' equipment. Collection of contemporary chemists' prescriptions. An alchemist's laboratory, complete with instruments, has been reconstituted in the Apothecary's Tower.
There is an excellent **view★** of the castle from the **Molkenkur (Z)** restaurant, reached via the Molkenkurweg or by funicular railway. The restaurant is built on the site of an ancient fortification.

ADDITIONAL SIGHTS

★ **University Library (Buchausstellung der Universität) (Z A)** ⊙ – Valuable collections of books, manuscripts and miniatures are on display here in the exhibition gallery. Note especially the **Manesse Manuscript** (Manessische Liederhandschrift), an early 14C anthology collecting songs by 140 different poets in Old High German. The manuscript, which includes 137 full-page masterpieces of illumination, is considered a jewel of medieval literary and graphic art. Another important work, compiled almost a century later, is the **Mirror of the Saxons** (Sachsenspiegel), Germany's oldest legal work, still in use in several regions (Anholt and Thuringia) as recently as 1900.
Also to be found in the Library is **Des Knaben Wunderhorn** *(The Child with the Magic Horn)*, published in Heidelberg in 1805 by Achim von Arnim and Clemens Brentano – a compendium of popular songs marking the incursion of demotic poetry into German literature.

Königstuhl \ Molkenkur

★ **Electoral Palatinate Museum** (Kurpfälzisches Museum) (Z M²) ⊘ – *Haupt-strasse 97.*
The galleries consecrated to the history of the Palatinate exhibit a cast of the jaw of the prehistoric "Heidelberg Man" (500 000 BC). The department of German Primitives displays the **Altarpiece of the Twelve Apostles★★** (1509) by Tilman Riemenschneider *(qv)*. The collection **Works from the Romantic Period★★** is devoted essentially to the iconography of the town and castle.

★ **The Knight's House** (Haus zum Ritter) (Z N) – This magnificent bourgeois mansion owes its name to a bust of St George in knightly armour which adorns the rich, scrolled pediment. Built in 1592 for the Huguenot merchant Charles Bélier, it was the only late Renaissance masterpiece to be spared the devastations of 1689-1693.

Students' Gaol (Studentenkarzer) (Z B) ⊘ – From 1712 to 1914, students who were too rowdy or obtrusive ran the risk of incarceration here. Many of them left on the walls inscriptions, outlines darkened with soot or coats of arms as a reminder to future generations of what they considered a particularly estimable episode in their career.

Church of the Holy Spirit (Heilig-Geist-Kirche) (YZ E) – The church is an example of the late Gothic style. As in earlier times, covered stalls hug the walls between buttresses. The nave and chancel are of the "hall" type *(qv)*, though galleries above the aisles reduce the height on either side. The well-lit chancel was formerly the sepulchre of the Palatine Electors, but since 1693 only the tomb of Ruprecht III remains.

Church of the Jesuits (Jesuitenkirche) (Z F) – This Baroque church was built at the beginning of the 18C from plans drawn up by the Heidelberg architect J A Breunig. The main façade, based on the Jesuit Church in Rome, was the work of the Palatinate court architect F W Rabaliatti (1716-1782). The luminous triple nave is supported by robust pillars whose capitals are decorated with Rococo stuccowork.
The **Museum of Sacred and Liturgical Art** ⊘, which is reached through this church, houses religious artefacts (madonnas, altar crosses, liturgical objects). In the museum treasury are examples (chalices, monstrances) of the goldsmith's and silversmith's art.

EXCURSIONS

Schwetzingen – *10km - 6.2 miles to the west by the Friedrich-Ebert-Anlage* (Z). The castle, built between 1700 and 1717 (Rococo theatre and semicircular auditorium by Lorraine architect Nicolas de Pigage, mid-18C) served as a summer residence for the Elector Princes. The **park★★** (Schlossgarten) ⊘ was laid out stage by stage during the second half of the 18C. The French Garden, with its rigorous geometric design, is also the work of Pigage (1723-1796). At a later date an English Garden, with waterfalls, ponds and shrubberies, was added.

Königstuhl ⊘ – *5km - 3 miles to the southeast, via the Neue Schlossstrasse, the Molkenkurweg, and then the Gaisberger Weg; or take the funicular (stops: Stadt - near the Kornmarkt* (Z) *- Schloss, Molkenkur, Königstuhl).*
From the television tower on the summit (568m - 1 864ft) there can be seen a fine **panorama** of the Neckar valley, from the Odenwald to the plain of the Rhine.

★★ **HELGOLAND ISLAND** Schleswig-Holstein

Michelin map **411** G 4

Attracted by the idea of a short sea cruise, thousands of tourists each year head for the red sandstone cliffs of the island of Helgoland, just 70km - 43 miles out from the estuary of the Elbe. English for many years, the island was exchanged for Zanzibar in 1890.

A fantastic rock – Undermined for centuries by the sea, the island today covers an area of less than 1km² - 1/2sq mile. In 1947, in accordance with the Potsdam Agreement, German military installations, including a submarine base, were totally destroyed by British sappers using 6 000 tons of high explosive. Helgoland was returned to Germany in 1952, since when – thanks to a complete reconstruction of twin built-up areas divided by the form of the cliff (Unterland and Oberland) – it has once more become a tourist centre. An aquarium, an ornithological observatory and a marine biology station make the site of great scientific interest. The island has many attractions to offer the visitor: cliff walks, sea bathing from the lonely but sheltered sands of Düne Beach, even tax-free chocolates, cigarettes and spirits.

Access ⊘ – There is a daily car ferry service from Bremerhaven and Cuxhaven (passengers only), or a train-bus-boat linkup operated by the Sectouristik company from the main railway station (Hauptbahnhof) in Hamburg. A day excursion allows approximately four hours on the island.

★ **HILDESHEIM** Lower Saxony   Pop 105 000

Michelin maps **411** and **412** M 10
Plan of the conurbation in the Michelin Red Guide Deutschland

Hildesheim is the capital of the Romanesque art which flowered in Germany during the Ottonian period (qv).

The thousand-year-old Rose Tree – One evening in the year 815, as the legend goes, Louis I the Pious, exhausted after a day's hunting, hid his personal reliquary in a rose bush before he lay down to sleep. When he awoke the following morning, the precious casket was nowhere to be found. Interpreting this as a sign from Heaven, he founded a chapel – and subsequently a bishopric – on the spot. Around this, the town of Hildesheim developed.
In the winter of 1945, the famous rose tree – although apparently incinerated in an air raid – burst suddenly into flower. The town has likewise been re-born.

HILDESHEIM

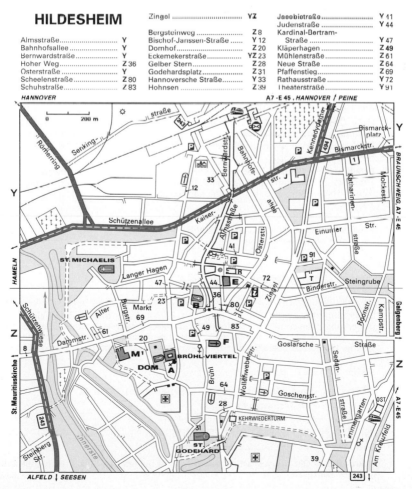

SIGHTS

* **Cathedral** (Dom) (Z) ⊙ – The present building is a reconstruction, based on the original plans of an 11C Romanesque basilica, with later side chapels faithfully reproduced in the Gothic style and the dome above the transept modelled on the cupola added in the 18C. The interior retains the simplicity of the original. The alternate use of a single pillar and two columns in the nave is typical of the architectural school of Old Saxony.

Fine **works of art**★ can be seen in the cathedral. A huge chandelier dating from the 11C hangs above the transept crossing. On the north side, the last chapel contains a rare carved baptismal font (13C) supported by four figures representing the rivers of Paradise. In the south transept, an 11C bronze column depicting the life of Christ is displayed.

The two-storey Romanesque **cloister** abuts the eastern extremity of the cathedral. The legendary rose is trained along the outer wall of the apse.

Scenes from the Old and the New Testament are illustrated in the panels of the bronze doors beneath the west front porch - superb examples of early Romanesque sculpture.

Close to the cathedral, a magnificent Renaissance **rood-screen**★ can be seen in the St Anthony Chapel (Z A).

* **Museums** (Z M¹) ⊙ – The **Pelizaeus Museum** houses one of the richest collections of Egyptian antiquities in Germany. Worth special attention: the chapel containing the coffin-tomb of the royal officer Uhemka; funerary monuments of the Ancient Empire (dating back to the 3rd millenium BC), including the famous statues of Prince Hem On and the scribe Heti.

The **Roemer Museum**, apart from a section devoted to local history, exhibits an interesting collection of Chinese porcelain.

* **St Michael's Church** (St Michaeliskirche) (Y) – Dating from the beginning of the 11C, this basilica is typical of Ottonian architecture in Old Saxony, with its double chancel and its alternation of pillars and columns. Note also the 13C painted ceiling in the nave, the two-tier galleries in the transepts, and the simplicity of the cushion capitals – again characteristic of Lower Saxony. Of the original decoration, an Angel Screen remains to the right of the west chancel (on your left as you enter). Above is a balustrade embellished with 13 angels.

* **St Gothard's Church** (St Godehardkirche) (Z) – This 12C church has an elegant silhouette marked by the slender spires crowning its three towers.

St Andrew's Church (St Andreaskirche) (Z B) – Built at the end of the 14C, this church is all that remains of the medieval quarter it once dominated. Huge Gothic windows pierce the impressive **façade**★. The tower, rising with its spire to a height of 118m - 367ft, is constructed on an asymmetrical base in the form of a trapezoid.

Templars' House (Tempelhaus) (Y E) – A fine 15C building with a Gothic façade adorned by a Renaissance oriel window.

The Brühl (Z) – Spared by the ravages of war, this quarter is typical of old Hildesheim.

Holy Cross Church (Heiligkreuzkirche) (Z F) – Behind the Baroque façade of this building hides an early (11C) Romanesque church originally refashioned from a fortified gateway. Gothic, Baroque and Ottonian elements jostle each other within.

St Maurice's Church (St Mauritius-Kirche) – Leave by the Bergsteinweg (Z).
This 11C church, with its 12C cloister, lies in the Moritzberg quarter, on the west side of Hildesheim. The interior has had Baroque features added to it.

*The **Michelin Maps** which accompany this guide
are shown on the back cover.*

THE HOHENLOHE Baden-Württemberg

Michelin map 🖽 K 19 - L 19

Separating the heights of the Swabian Forest from the Tauber valley, the Hohenlohe plain remains a profoundly rural area traversed by the valleys of the Jagst and the Kocher - the former swift-running and tortuous, the latter more serene. Numerous castles along the way recall the German Renaissance period.

THE JAGST VALLEY

① From Bad Wimpfen to Schwäbisch-Hall
114km - 71 miles - about 4 hours

The route follows the sinuous course of the Jagst, along whose lush banks orchards, and sometimes vineyards, flourish.

★★ **Bad Wimpfen** – *See under Bad Wimpfen.*

Neudenau – Old houses with wooden-walled gables overlook the elegant and gracious **Marktplatz**.

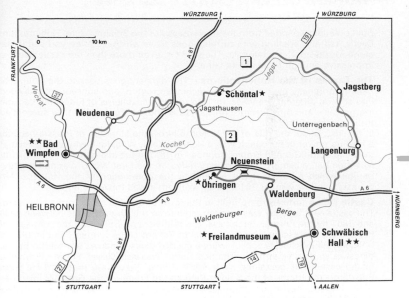

Schöntal – The whole town lies within the precincts of an ancient Cistercian abbey ⊙. The 1727 **hall-church★** is built in the Baroque style, although the soaring flight of free-standing pillars suggests a certain Gothic spirit. Four rare alabaster **altarpieces★★** (17C) stand against the pillars nearest the transept crossing. Among the old abbey buildings, the abbot's antechamber, or **Orders Room★** (Ordensaal) is especially noteworthy for its cladding of small panels painted to represent some 300 different costumes worn by the various religious orders.

Jagstberg – The village, sprawling over the crest of the valley's western slope, is dominated by a **church** (Pfarrkirche St Burkhard) built at the beginning of the 17C to which Baroque features were added in 1765 by the stucco worker Joseph Hell.

The route passes close by the famous wooden bridge of Unterregenbach.

Langenburg – This fortified town has been built along a crest encircled at its base by a bend in the river and crowned by the **castle** ⊙ of the Hohenlohe family. The **inner courtyard★**, kernel of the original 15C fort which was enlarged in the 17C and again in the 18C, is framed by tiered galleries and overlooked by scrolled pediments. Many souvenirs of the House of Hohenlohe can be viewed within.

★★ **Schwäbisch-Hall** – *See under Schwäbisch Hall*

🔢 FROM SCHWÄBISCH-HALL TO JAGSTHAUSEN
73km - 45 miles, about 3 hours

★ **Hohenlohe Open-Air Museum** – *See under Schwäbisch Hall: Excursions.*

Waldenburg – Situated on a spur projecting from the low ranges of the Swabian Forest, this fortified town enabled the Hohenlohes to command the plain below. There are three distinct fortifications separated by moats.

The road passes through the woods of the Waldenburger Berge before continuing downhill towards Neuenstein.

Neuenstein – Massively constructed, the 16-17C **castle** ⊙ here is built with scroll-worked Renaissance gables. A visit to the town gives the impression of day-to-day life in a small German court, in this case that of the Hohenlohes. A precious goblet fashioned in the form of a stag, richly encrusted furniture, ivories and glassware are among the curiosities on view.

Öhringen – The late 15C **church★** serves as a necropolis for the House of Hohenlohe. Enter through the Gothic hall-church's cloister and note in the chancel a monument to Philip of Hohenlohe (d 1609), son-in-law of William of Orange. Scenes from the Netherlands War of Independence are illustrated in relief at the base of the statue. The **Altarpiece of St Margaret★** (Margarethen-Altar) in the large north chapel is a delicate late 15C work.

The final section of the route follows the Kocher valley before coming to Jagsthausen.

*Each year the **Michelin Red Guide Deutschland** revises its 150 town plans which show*

- through-routes and by-passes
- new roads, one-way systems and car parks
- the exact location of hotels, restaurants and public buildings.

This up-to-date information makes town driving less stressful.

★ HOHENZOLLERN CASTLE Baden-Württemberg

Michelin map **413** fold 25 - Local map see under SWABIAN JURA

Built on a hill separated from the main massif of the Swabian Jura, Hohenzollern Castle, tall and bristling with turrets, looks from whichever side you see it like some fortress out of a fairytale. The **site★★★**, even more than the castle itself, is impressive enough to justify its fame.

The Cradle of the Hohenzollerns – The dynasty goes back to the Counts of Zollern, originally overlords of the Hechingen region, and subsequently divided into several different branches. In 1415, the Hohenzollerns of Franconia became Margraves – and thus Elector-Princes – of Brandenburg. In 1618 they succeeded to the Duchy of Prussia.

In the 18C, under the rule of the Hohenzollerns, the kingdom of Prussia became a leading power in Europe. It was a Hohenzollern, Wilhelm I, who was placed at the head of the German Empire, founded in 1871 at the instigation of Prussia. But less than half a century later, military defeat in the First World War and the revolution which followed it put an end to the domination of the Hohenzollern dynasty: on 9 November 1918, Kaiser Wilhelm II was forced to abdicate.

Castle ⊙ – A fortified ramp built in the form of a spiral leads to the courtyard. The castle as it is today was reconstructed from the original plans between 1850 and 1867 by the Prussian architects Von Prittwitz and Stüler. All that remains of the ancient fortress built by the Counts of Zollern is the Roman Catholic Chapel of **St Michael** (Michaeliskapelle), whose stained glass windows are said to be the oldest in southern Germany. The neo-Gothic **Protestant Chapel**, in the north wing of the castle, has contained since 1952 – when they were moved there from Potsdam – the tombs of the Soldier-King and of Frederick the Great. Mementoes of the latter (uniforms, decorations, snuffboxes, flutes) can be seen in the collections of the castle treasury (Schatzkammer).

Before leaving the castle, make a tour of the ramparts *(start on the left, after the drawbridge)* and enjoy the **panorama** of the Swabian Jura and the Upper Neckar depression below.

HUSUM Schleswig-Holstein   Pop 20 000

Michelin map **411** K 3

The birthplace of the writer Theodor Storm (1817-1888), who wrote several of his principal works here, is a small fishing port which also serves as a terminal for boats plying between the mainland and the Halligen Isles *(see below)*.

★ **North Frisian Museum** (Nissenhaus-Nordfriesisches Museum) ⊙ – *Herzog-Adolf-Strasse 25*. The ground floor display illustrates the different types of German coastal landscape (Geest, Marsch, Polder, etc.), as well as the life and culture of its inhabitants. Natural catastrophes (the cataclysms – "Manndränken" – of 1362 and 1634, the high tide of 1962) are evoked in exhaustive detail, as are the construction of dykes and the reclamation of land by Polders. A **dyke** made of wood (Stackdeich), restored after archaeological excavations, illustrates the technique of containment in the Middle Ages. Modern methods are illustrated by a model of the Eider Dam (see below). On the floor above, there is an exhibition of Frisian paintings (landscapes and scenes of everyday life).

EXCURSIONS

★ **The Halligen Isles** – These numerous flat islets, created, altered, submerged or once more re-formed over the centuries by the play of the tides, are scattered through the shallows off the coast of Schleswig-Holstein. The archipelago comprises a total population of around 400, mainly farmers and fishermen, who live in thatched cottages built on what are called **Warften** (hillocks of habitation). The seals, and an infinite variety of sea birds, are protected by law. On Langeness, the largest isle, salt is farmed. A tour of the Halligens (field-glasses recommended) is well worthwhile.

★ **Nolde Museum at Seebüll** ⊙ – *56 km - 35 miles to the north*. Known under the pseudonym of Nolde, the painter Emil Nansen (1867-1956) built himself a house of his own design in the solitude of the Seebüll marshes, between 1927 and 1937. Each year now, a different selection is displayed there of the works of Nolde – one of the most significant masters of German Expressionism. **The Life of Christ**, a series of nine canvases, is on permanent exhibition.

The psychic anxiety and religious emotion of the artist is expressed in thick masses of colour, aggressive and incandescent, which totally destroy any sense of form.

Friedrichstadt – *15km - 9 miles to the south*. Dutch refugees, hounded from their country for religious reasons and given sanctuary here by Duke Friedrich III of Holstein, founded this locality in 1621 and bestowed on it the name of their protector. The settlement – a rectilinear grid of tree-shaded canals criss-crossed by streets of identical houses with scrolled or curvilinear gables – seems never to have changed since then. A calm and attractive retreat.

★ **The Eider Dam** – *35km - 22 miles to the south*. Skirting a bird sanctuary, the road arrives at the mouth of the Eider river, closed off by a dam constructed between 1967 and 1972, after the catastrophic tidal wave of 1962. The five colossal steel sluice gates remain open when meteorological conditions are normal, permitting the customary rise and fall of tides. But they are closed when storms or abnormally high tides are threatened, preventing the sea from surging up the Eider to invade the low-lying country inland.

IDAR-OBERSTEIN Rhineland-Palatinate   Pop 38 000

Michelin map **412** EF 17

Twin towns here form a single built-up area – picturesque Oberstein lying along the foot of a gorge carved by the river Nahe, Idar spread out around a tributary beyond. The abundance in earlier times of nearby agate, jasper and amethyst deposits has left Idar-Oberstein a centre for the cutting and polishing of precious stones.

★ **Felsenkirche** – *Return trip 1/2 hour on foot. Access via a stairway (214 steps) rising from the Oberstein Marktplatz.*
Framed by a rock overhang in the cliff 60m - 197ft above the river, this church, restored several times, is worth a visit for the high-altar **reredos** (beginning of the 15C) alone. The scenes of the Passion represented depict with a ferocious realism, the hatred, the suffering and the annihilation involved.

★★ **German Museum of Precious Stones** (Deutsches Edelsteinmuseum) ⊙ – *At Idar, in the Diamond Exchange, Hauptstrasse.*
The gems, cut and uncut, in every known variety, are classified according to their geographical origin, their cultural importance or their industrial use. Note the dental instruments in agate.

Local Museum (Museum Idar-Oberstein) ⊙ – *At Oberstein, in the Marktplatz (at the foot of the Felsenkirche stairway).*
Collections of minerals and precious stones, notably "Landschaftsachate" – paper-thin flakes of agate exhibiting in transparency the appearance of phantasmagoric landscapes; also fluorescent stones and crystals.

New Castle (Burgruinen) – *At Oberstein.* Ruins with a view of the Nahe valley.

Old Stonecutting Centre (Weiherschleife) ⊙ – *On the outskirts of Idar.* The different stages in the facetting and polishing of gems can be seen. Skilled craftsmen still work in traditional fashion here, face down before sanded grindstones powered by a water-wheel.

EXCURSIONS

The Hunsrück – *Excursion 141km - 88 miles - allow about 5 hours. Leave Idar-Oberstein to the northwest by Route 422.*
The Hunsrück forms the southern rim of the Rhenish schist massif *(see introduction).* It is a region of low mountains and game-stocked forests, gashed by deep and steep-sided valleys.

Erbeskopf – Topping 818m - 2 660ft, this is the highest summit of the massif. From the wooden tower, there is a panoramic view over the undulating, wooded countryside.
After Thalfang, the **Hunsrückhöhenstrasse**★ going northward offers fine views of the valleys, the forest-covered hills and numerous villages with ancient houses roofed by slabs of schist. The road passes the Stumpfer Turm, an old Roman watchtower.

Kirchberg – Perched on a hillside, this village retains many pretty half-timbered houses, especially around the market-place. St Michael's Church dates back to the pre-Romanesque era, although the present building was constructed in the 15C.

Simmern – The farming centre of the Hunsrück. Tombstones from the Renaissance period can be seen beneath the vaults of the Church of St Stephen (15C). Behind the church, explore the old town.

Ravengiersburg – Hidden away at the bottom of a valley, this village boasts a Romanesque church built on top of a spur. The imposing west front has a sculptured cornice and a miniature gallery. Above the porch: Christ in Majesty.

Dhaun – The castle here is built on a remarkable **site**★ on top of a sheer rock outcrop. On the esplanade, behind the statue, a staircase leads down to the gun positions.

The road on the final section of the excursion follows the valley of the Nahe before returning to Idar-Oberstein.

INGOLSTADT Bavaria   Pop 100 000

Michelin map **413** R 20
Town plan in the current Michelin Red Guide Deutschland

Once famous for its university, Ingolstadt became in the 19C one of the most powerful strongholds in Europe.
Today the town owes its economic prosperity to a privileged geographic position which puts it at the heart of a rich agricultural area and at the same time at the junction of three important oil pipelines.

★ **Our Lady of Victories** (Maria-de-Victoria-Kirche) – This plain, single-nave chapel was transformed in 1/32 by the Asam brothers *(qv).* The huge ceiling fresco (490m1V2 - 5 200sq ft) illustrates the spreading of the Faith, through the intercession of the Virgin, to the four quarters of the earth. The perspective effect is astonishing.
The high altar, with a particularly rich canopy, is adorned by four statues representing Medicine, Theology, Law and Philosophy.

Church of Our Lady (Liebfrauenmünster) – The interior of this church is in the form of an extended Gothic hall. It was built in the 15C, and the fine reredos★ of the high altar (1572) is a transitional work linking the Gothic with the Renaissance. The Virgin, patron saint of Bavaria, appears in the central panel in the form of a cloaked Madonna.

★ **Bavarian Army Museum** (Bayerisches Armeemuseum) ⊘ – Installed in the huge chambers of a 15C fortress (Herzogschloss), the rich collections of this museum trace the military history of Bavaria from the 14C to the present day. Numerous firearms illustrate the evolution of weaponry; an enormous diorama (17 000 model soldiers) stages the battle of Leuthen, which saw the victory of Friedrich II over the Austrians in 1757.

Kreuztor – This hexagonal, battlemented keep with six pointed turrets at the angles of the walls is the finest relic of the town's 14C and 15C fortifications.

EXCURSION

Neuburg an der Donau – *23km - 14 miles to the west.*
This small Renaissance Baroque town is built on a limestone ridge above the south bank of the river.
The **castle**, constructed between 1530 and 1545 by the Palatine Count Otto-Heinrich, comprises a courtyard surrounded by a two-tier gallery, in the style of the early German Renaissance. The east wing, with its two towers, dates from 1665-68.
The courtyard's western façade is decorated with murals representing scenes from the Old Testament. The arched gateway leads also to the **chapel**, which is embellished with frescoes (1543).
There is a **museum** (Schlossmuseum) ⊘ in the east wing, where neolithic remains, examples of sacred art, and exhibits charting the history of the princely House of Pfalz-Neuburg may be viewed.
West of the castle is the **Hofkirche**, which was built at the end of the Renaissance (1607-1627). The richly decorated **stucco ceiling★** dates from the Counter-Reformation. The Baroque **reredos★** (1752-1754) is the work of J A Breitenauer, to whom the pulpit is also attributed.

JENA Thuringia	Pop 105 000

Michelin map **987** fold 26

Northeast of the forest of Thuringia, midway along the course of the Saale, the town has developed steadily ever since the foundation of its university in 1588. From then on, numerous scientists and intellectuals such as the philologist Wilhelm von Humboldt, his brother Alexander, a geographer, Goethe and Schiller, contributed to Jena's importance.

Optics – In the middle of the 19C, Carl Zeiss and Ernst Abbe, both members of the university, established an optical industry developed from their invention, the microscope. Since then the **Zeiss** works have acquired a worldwide reputation in the domain of optics and precision instruments.
The tower of the university, 120m - 394 ft high, dominates the town.

SIGHTS

St John's Gate (Johannistor) – *Johannisplatz.* Together with the Pulverturm (on the other side of the square), this is all that remains of the town's 14C fortifications.

Local Museum (Stadtmuseum Alte Göhre) ⊘ – *Am Markt.* The four floors of this Gothic building illustrate the history of Jena since its foundation.

St Michael's Church (Stadtkirche St Michaelis) – *Am Kirchplatz.* This ancient collegial church of the Cistercians was completely transformed in the Gothic mode in the 15C. Note, on the south side, the canopied porch.

Goethe Museum (Goethe-Gedenkstätte) ⊘ – *Fürstengraben 26.* The famous writer always said that it was in Jena that he found the tranquillity essential for literary creation. The house in which he lived when he was in the town contains numerous mementoes of the poet.

Schiller Museum (Schiller-Gedenkstätte) ⊘ – *Schillergässchen 2.* A collection of the poet's personal memorabilia is on view in the house he lived in between 1797 and 1802.

★ **Planetarium** ⊘ – *Am Planetarium 3.* Built next to the botanical gardens by the Zeiss firm, this scientific spectacle permits visitors to voyage through the cosmos via the artful manipulation and movement of planets and the stellar systems.

★ **Optical Museum** (Optisches Museum der Carl-Zeiss-Stiftung) ⊘ – *Carl-Zeiss-Platz.* Very interesting collection of optical instruments.

For details of working hours and public holidays
in Germany see the Practical Information section
at the end of the Guide.

Karlsruhe is one of the "new towns" designed on a geometric plan in the 18C by the princely building enthusiasts of southern Germany. After the devastations of 1689 and the destruction of his family seat at Durlach, the Margrave of Baden decided to build a castle a little further west, among the trees of the Hartwald, his favourite hunting ground. The idea, put into operation in 1715 with the construction of an octagonal tower, was for the castle to be the hub of a network of radiating streets (hunting rides to the north, fan-shaped development for a future town to the south). This **"town fan"** was eventually fully realized in the 19C, when Karlsruhe became the capital of the Grand Duchy of Baden (1806).

The architect **Friedrich Weinbrenner** (1766-1826), a native of the town, was responsible for its neo-Classical aspect. From this period dates the **Marktplatz**, along with the Town Hall, the Protestant church (Evangelische Stadtkirche), and the modest pyramid of the founder's mausoleum. The Kaiserstrasse (Pedestrian precinct), today the city's commercial centre, was also designed by Weinbrenner. Cutting through the "fan" on an east-west axis, it follows the course of the old road from Durlach to the Rhine.

The former seat of the Grand Dukes today houses Germany's supreme courts (Court of Appeal and the Constitutional Court), together with the country's oldest School of Technology (1825). Among the eminent graduates of the latter are Hertz, who discovered electromagnetic waves, and Carl Benz *(qv)*, the motorcar pioneer. Karlsruhe is also the birthplace of the Baron Drais, inventor in 1817 of a vehicle – ancestor of the bicycle – known as the Draisienne.

KARLSRUHE

SIGHTS

★ **Fine Arts Museum** (Staatliche Kunsthalle) ⊙ – The building, erected between 1838 and 1846, houses a remarkable collection of **German Primitives★** (Gemälde Altdeutscher Meister). Among them the focal point in the Grünewald Room is a terrifying Crucifixion by the painter of the same name. The golden age of Flemish and Dutch painting is represented by Rubens, Jordaens and Rembrandt *(Self-Portrait)*. Still-life pictures by Chardin highlight a collection of 17C and 18C French paintings. There is a selection of **works by Hans Toma★**, who occupies a special place in German painting of the 19C. *Children's Dance* and *Rain on the Black Forest* are among the best-known canvases by this regional artist.

Modern art is displayed in the neighbouring **Orangery**. Noteworthy here are French Impressionist works by Monet, Degas and Cézanne; German Expressionist paintings *(Deer in the Forest* by Marc*)*; and Cubist-inspired pictures by Léger and Delaunay. Sculptures from the studios of Rodin, Barlach and Lehmbruck are also on view.

* **Castle** – Of the original building, only the tall octagonal tower that marks the centre of the city's radiating road system now remains. Today it houses the **Baden Regional Museum★** (Badisches Landesmuseum) **(M)** ⊙, where the visitor may view a sizeable collection of Egyptian, Greek and Roman antiquities; examples of local folk art and craftwork from the Middle Ages onward; and a numismatic display. The first floor is devoted to the Margrave Ludwig Wilhelm, known as Ludwig the Turk, who governed Baden from 1677 to 1707. Rare items here include war equipment and **trophies** brought back from the battles against the Turks between 1683 and 1692: banners, ceremonial harnesses, chased and inlaid arms, etc.

From the castle park – which gives way, in the north, to a vast wooded area – there is access to the **Botanical Gardens** (Botanischer Garten) ⊙, where the **greenhouses★** (Pflanzenschauhäuser) offer a magnificent display of cactuses.

★ # KASSEL Hessen   Pop 197 000
Michelin maps **411** and **412** L 12-13

Once the seat of the Landgraves, today the economic, administrative and cultural capital of North Hessen, Kassel is situated on the banks of the Fulda river *(boat trips from Fuldabrücke)* **(Z)**, in the heart of a hilly, lush and wooded countryside. To the west, at the foot of the Habichtswald heights, Wilhelmshöhe Castle and its park overlook the town. A natural spring at Wilhelmshöhe feeds the **Kurhessen thermal baths (X)**.

Famous for its musical and dramatic activities, Kassel is nevertheless known best of all for the **Documenta**, an international exhibition of contemporary art which has been held every four or five years since 1955. The main centre for this event is the **Fredericianum (Z)**, a pre-classical building in the vast Friedrichsplatz designed by Simon Louis du Ry to be both museum and library for the Landgrave Frederick III.

An industrial tradition – The Landgrave Karl of Hessen (1670-1730) welcomed a large influx of Huguenots into his province – industrious folk who soon started workshops and factories all over the region. Subsequently he encouraged the research into steam power initiated by **Denis Papin**, who lived in Kassel from 1695 to 1707 after he had been granted a professorial chair at Marburg University. In 1690, the inventor designed a prototype steam engine, and in 1706 he perfected a high-pressure steam pump.

The Brothers Grimm – **Jakob** (1785-1863) and **Wilhelm Grimm** (1786-1859) lived in Kassel from 1805 to 1830, both employed as Court Librarians. Through their shared work on literature and linguistics (a German basic grammar, the first volume of a German language dictionary) they can be considered the inaugurators of the science of German philology. Fascinated by legends and folklore, the brothers collected from all over the province a wealth of stories which they published between 1812 and 1822 under the general title of *Kinder und Hausmärchen* (Stories for Children and the Home, in English simply: *Grimms' Fairy Tales*).

★★ ## WILHELMSHÖHE **(X)** *time: half a day*

★★ **The Park** – *West of the town.* The landscaping of this huge 350ha - 865 acre park was started in 1701 under the Landgrave Karl. It was based on a design by the Italian architect Guerniero. The Baroque-style park, in which almost 800 different species of trees grow, was transformed in the second half of the 18C into English-style gardens, complete with temples, pavilions, grottoes and artificial ruins. The ruins of **Löwenburg (A)**, a fantasy castle built between 1793 and 1801, is an excellent example of the taste for sentimental romanticism current in that period (note inside the furnishings and the valuable collection of arms and armour).

At the highest point of the park stands **Hercules★** (Herkules), emblem of the city of Kassel. This gigantic statue is a copy (1717) of the Farnese Hercules at the National Archaeological Museum in Naples. It is 72m - 236ft high (the Nelson monument in London's Trafalgar Square measures 52m - 170ft). In the Wilhelmshöhe park, the figure is placed on top of a pyramid, itself standing on a huge eight-sided pavilion, the Oktogon. From the base of the statue, there is a very fine **view★★** over the park and the castle to Kassel.

Below the Oktogon is the great **Water Staircase** – an enormous **cascade★** (Wasserkünste) with huge amounts of water falling in a sequence of steps to the Neptune Pool, before continuing past the rocks of the Steinhöfer waterfall, beneath the Devil's Bridge and along an aqueduct to the Fountain Pool (very high jets) in front of the castle. The Water Staircase falls 200m - 656ft from top to bottom.

Wilhelmshöhe Castle (Schloss) ⊙ – This building in the classical style was completed in 1803. From 1807 to 1813, Jerome Bonaparte, the King of Westphalia, held a brilliant Court here. The historic salons of the South Wing **(Castle Museum)**, with their paintings and their Louis XV and Empire furniture, still recall the splendours of that period. Another famous guest was Napoleon III, held prisoner here after the Battle of Sedan in 1870. Today the castle houses important sections of Kassel's National Art Collection (Staatliche Kunstsammlungen) *(central entrance)*.

★ **Antiquities** – *Ground floor.* In the entrance hall, 5C and 6C vases evoke echoes of Classical Greece. The Roman Empire is represented by an Apollo – referred to as the Kassel Apollo – a 2C work by Phidias; by a series of busts, a sarcophagus and some urns. Statuettes of gods and sacred animals in stone and bronze complete the section as examples of ancient Egyptian art.

★★★ **Old Masters Gallery** – The exhibits here are derived from collections amassed by the Landgraves.

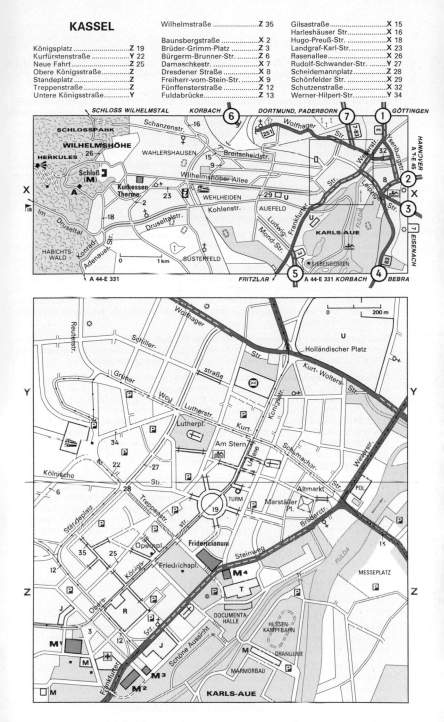

First floor: Flemish and German Primitives and paintings from the School of Antwerp: Altdorfer's Crucifixion, a triptych by Cranach the Elder, Dürer's *Portrait of Elizabeth Tucher*, *Hercules at Antioch* by Hans Baldung Grien and Mor's *William I of Orange*.

Rembrandt's *Old Man With a Gold Chain* has pride of place among Dutch painters of the 17C. Also displayed are *The Blessing of Jacob* (1656), a *Portrait of Saskia van Uylenburgh* (the painter's first wife), *The Holy Family at the Screen*, *A Winter Landscape* and various self-portraits. Among the Flemish painters of the 17C, note Rubens (*Crowning of a Hero; Mary and the Infant Jesus as a Refuge for Sinners*), Van Dyck (*Sebastian Leerse with his Wife and Son*), and Jordaens, who pictures himself as a lutenist in *The Painter's Betrothal*.

Second floor: landscapes and scenes of rustic and bourgeois life by Jan Brueghel, Ruysdael, Metsu and Jan Steen show an extraordinary sense of observation and attention to detail.

Third floor: works by painters from Italy (Belluci, Titian, Reni), Spain (Ribera, Murillo) and France (Poussin's *Love's Victory Over the God Pan*).

In the Art Library reading-room on the first floor (Kunstbibliothek), pages from the rich **collection of prints and drawings** can be seen.

171

ADDITIONAL SIGHTS

★ **Karls-Aue Park** (Z) – The most popular parts of this 18C riverside park are the steeply sloping gardens below the Schöne Aussicht terrace, and the Siebenbergen – an artificial island on the Fulda.

★ **Hessen Museum** (Hessisches Landemuseum) (Z M1) ⊘ – The street level is devoted to collections concerned with prehistory. On the mezzanine, the **Astronomy and Physics Room**★★ contains rare and ancient scientific instruments: a large planetary clock made in 1561 and designed by the Landgrave Wilhelm IV; a celestial globe with an astronomic clock and calendar (c1600); a small astronomic clock (late 16C) which functions on Copernicus's heliocentric theory.
On the first floor is the **German Tapestry Museum**★★, where more than 600 pieces chart the evolution of wall coverings from the 18C to the 20C: wallpapers with near- or far-eastern motifs, embossed leather, panoramic murals, printed papers with designs from famous workshops in Germany and France (Réveillon, Paris). The techniques of printing are also illustrated.
The second floor is concerned mainly with decorative art.

★ **New Gallery** (Neue Galerie) (Z M2) ⊘ – Works ranging from the 18C to modern times are on display here, particularly those by German painters. Note the series of 18C portraits by the Tischbein family, among them *The Woman in Blue* (Amalie). More classical in their approach are the mythological scenes by Nahl the Younger. The works of Liebermann, Trübner, and above all Corinth *(Walchensee Landscape, Woman with a Mask)*, are close to those of the Impressionists, while Schlemmer and Kirchner *(Café at Davos)* are veering towards Expressionism. Contemporary art is represented by the extravagant *Das Rudel* of Josef Beuys.

Brothers Grimm Museum (Brüder-Grimm Museum) (Z M3) ⊘ – This is housed in Bellevue Palace. Portraits, original manuscripts, letters, drawings and illustrations evoke the life and times, as well as the works of the two scholars.

Natural History Museum (Naturkundenmuseum) (Z M4) ⊘ – Divided into three sections – Geology, Botany and Zoology – this museum is in the former Ottoneum, Germany's oldest (1606) theatre. Note the remarkable Ratzenberger Herbarium (late 16C), also said to be the oldest in Germany, and the late 18C Schildbach'sche Holzbibliothek on the second floor. This comprises a series of small boxes, each made from the wood of a different tree – and each containing an example of the corresponding leaf, flower and fruit that tree produces.

EXCURSIONS

★ **Wilhelmsthal Castle** ⊘ – *12km - 8 miles to the north by the Rasenallee* (X).
This Rococo edifice (1743-1770), surrounded by a park in the English style, was built by François Cuvilliés. Interior decoration in the then current style, with fine panelling, elegant furniture (mother-of-pearl inlaid commode), Chinese porcelain and a gallery of beauties painted by J H Tischbein the Elder exemplify the taste of the Court in that period.

★ **KIEL** Schleswig-Holstein   Pop 245 000

Michelin map **411** N 4
Town plan in the current Michelin Red Guide Deutschland

Kiel owes its economic development to its position at the mouth of the maritime canal linking the Baltic with the North Sea. A former naval base, the city is still known principally for its busy shipyards.

★★ **The Roadstead** (Kieler Förde) – The shores of this deep inlet are brightened by a series of sheltered resorts and bathing beaches, among them Schilksee, Strande, Laboe, Heikendorf and Schönberger Strand. In the northern part of the bay, regattas have been held for more than a century, and more than 3 000 yachtsmen from all over the world congregate here each year for **Kiel Week**.

★★ **Hindenburg Quay** (Hindenburgufer) – This promenade extends for almost two miles along the shore, with shady parks on one side and extended **views**★ of the roadstead on the other.

Town Hall (Rathaus) ⊘ – Built between 1907 and 1911, the building is noteworthy for its 106m - 348ft tower. From the upper gallery of this, there is a splendid **view**★ of the roadstead as far as the tall Laboe Memorial.

EXCURSIONS

★★ **Schleswig-Holstein Open-Air Museum** (Schleswig-Holsteinisches Freilichtmuseum) ⊘ – *6km - 4 miles to the south.*
Sixty rural buildings and farms typical of the country north of the Elbe are grouped here in the form of hamlets, arranged according to their geographic origin. Those from the south, half-timbered, colour-washed or embellished with skilful designs in brick, resemble – inside as well as out – the rustic houses of Lower Saxony. The brick-built farms of the north Frisian area are more austere.
A forge, a potter's workshop, an old-fashioned bakehouse, flour mills and weavers' looms are all operated by local craftsmen in traditional manner.

★ **Laboe** – *20km - 12 miles to the north.*
The memorial tower, 85m - 279ft high, offers a **wide** view of the outer part of the roadstead and, on a clear day, the Danish archipelago. Together with its underground galleries, the tower – which is built in the form of a ship's stern – constitutes the **German Naval War Memorial★** (Marine-Ehrenmal) ⊙. It includes a museum of navigation. Also on display is the U-995, a submarine launched in Hamburg in 1943, which operated in Norwegian waters and in the Barents Sea.

Kiel Canal – This link between the Baltic and the North Sea was inaugurated by Wilhelm II in 1895. From Kiel to Brunsbüttel, its 100km - 62-mile length is the world's busiest waterway: 46 000 vessels pass through it annually (although from the point of view of tonnage transported, it is relegated to third place).
From the **Prinz-Heinrich-Brücke** *(5km - 3 miles to the north, via Holtenauer Strasse and Prinz-Heinrich Strasse)* one overlooks the **Holtenau** locks, which control the junction of the canal and the Baltic. Among the structures crossing the canal, the most impressive are the **Rendsburg Railway Viaduct★** *(see below)*, the **Grünenthal Bridge** on Route 204 (Itzehoe-Heide), and the new bridge north of Brunsbüttel.

★ **Holstein's "Little Switzerland"** (Holsteinische Schweiz) – *51km - 32 miles - allow 2 1/2h.* Between Kiel and the Bay of Lübeck (Lübecker Bucht), not far from the Baltic Sea, Holstein's "Little Switzerland" region is scattered with lakes separated by wooded hills formed from the glacial moraine. (Highest point: Bungsberg, 168m - 550ft.)
In the middle of the region, beside the biggest of the lakes (Grosser Plöner See) is the town of **Plön**. From the terrace of its castle, there is a pretty **view★** of the surrounding lakes. Further east, **Eutin**, birthplace of the composer Carl Maria von Weber, has retained its 17C, brick-built town centre. The moated castle (1723) is surrounded by an English-style park bordering the lake.
Malente-Gremsmühlen, a small resort built on a wooded isthmus, is a departure point for boating trips.

Rendsburg – *36 km - 22 miles to the west.*
Rendsburg occupied one of the strategic points of northern Germany, where the main highway from Denmark crossed the Eider. The old town, tightly packed around its 16C town hall and the 13C Church of St Mary, is built on a former island in the Eider. It is now hemmed in on either side by fortifications built in the 17C to defend the bridge. The **Neuwerk Quarter** in the south, between the Kiel Canal and the old town, is notable for its huge central esplanade (Paradeplatz), from which streets ray out in different directions.
South of Rendsburg, the Kiel Canal can be crossed by a **railway viaduct★** (Eisenbahnbrücke), a **tunnel for road traffic** (Kanalbrücke) and a pedestrian footway. The viaduct is 42m - 138ft above the water, with a transporter bridge below it. The tunnel beneath the canal is 640m - 656yds long; the footway, in a second tunnel parallel with the first, is equipped with 1 278m - 1 397yds of escalators and moving walkways.

★ **KOBLENZ** Rhineland-Palatinate   Pop 107 000

Michelin map 412 F 15 - Local map see under MOSELLE VALLEY
Plan of the conurbation in the current Michelin Red Guide Deutschland

The prosperity of Koblenz (from the Latin confluentia) derives from its position at the confluence of the Rhine and the Moselle. Placed under the jurisdiction of the Archbishops of Trier, the city came under French influence immediately after the Revolution, when refugees led by the Counts of Artois and Provence, brothers of Louis XVI, fled there. But in 1794 troops of the Republic occupied the east bank of the Rhine, and four years later Koblenz became the Prefecture of the French Rhine-and-Moselle Department. Subsequently the Prefect Lezay Marnésia decided to beautify the city, and in 1809 he gave it the impressive **Rheinanlagen** (Z), a splendid riverside promenade.
The tomb of Hoche, at Weissenturm, and the Marceau cenotaph in the French cemetery at Lützel *(north of the town plan, via the Balduinbrücke* – **Y**), evoke memories of those young generals who fell during the first coalition.
Departure point for numerous excursions on both the Rhine and the Moselle, Koblenz also offers a summer festival, when the Rhine is set ablaze with flaming torches, many open-air concerts, and the celebrated taverns in its "wine village" (Weindorf).
The old town (Altstadt) is centred on the Church of Our Lady.

SIGHTS

★ **The Deutsches Eck** (Y) – Only the base remains of the gigantic equestrian statue of Wilhelm I, which once presided over the tongue of land marking the confluence. From the gallery crowning the base *(107 steps)*, there is a fine **view** of the town, the port, the Moselle bridges and the east bank of the Rhine, overlooked by the fortress of Ehrenbreitstein.

St Castor's Church (Stiftskirche St Kastor) (**Y**) – This Romanesque church succeeded an earlier basilica in which the Treaty of Verdun, dividing Charlemagne's empire, was drawn up in 843. Heavy fan vaulting covers the nave and chancel. The furnishings are interesting: the tombs of two archbishops lie at the back of multicoloured Gothic bays and, in the south transept, there is a series of 16 painted wood panels, once part of a rood-screen, with a picture of St Castor (bottom left).

KOBLENZ

Church of Our Lady (Liebfrauenkirche) (Y) – This Romanesque edifice, remodelled in the 13C, was given a Gothic chancel in the 15C and Baroque belfries in the 17C. The carved keystones which ornament the vaulting tracery are worth examining.

Jesuitenplatz (Y) – In the courtyard of a 17C Jesuit College, now serving as the town hall, is the "Schängelbrunnen" – a fountain evoking the mischief perpetrated by the street urchins of the city.

EXCURSIONS

★★★ **Rhine Valley** – See under Rhine Valley.

★ **Ehrenbreitstein Citadel** – 4 1/2 km - 3 miles. Cross the Rhine by the Pfaffendorfer Brücke (Z) then turn left.
This strategic stronghold, commanding the confluence of the two rivers, was the possession of the Archbishops of Trier from the 10C until 1799, when it was destroyed by the French. Between 1816 and 1832 the Prussians, who had ruled the Rhineland since the Congress of Vienna (1815), constructed the powerful existing fortress.
From the terrace, there is a **view** of Koblenz, Stolzenfels Castle (qv) to the south, the wooded plateau of Hunsrück and the volcanic massif of the Eifel.

★ **Maria Laach Abbey** – 20km - 12 1/2 miles to the west.
The vast crater lake beside which this abbey stands emphasizes the monumental air of poise and solidity characterizing the abbey buildings. The 12C abbey church is a Romanesque basilica with three naves, whose exterior is reminiscent of the cathedrals of Worms, Speyer and Mainz.
The cloister-type entrance portico, added in the early 13C, has intricately worked capitals. An unusual hexagonal baldachin – perhaps suggesting a Moorish influence – is stretched over the altar. The crypt is the oldest part of the church.

Andernach – 18km - 11 miles to the north.
This small town on the west bank of the Rhine retains a strongly medieval atmosphere. Enter the old town through the **Rheintor**, a fortified double gateway whose oldest part dates back to the 12C, and continue to the **castle ruins** (14C and 15C), which command the southern entry to the town.
The beautiful twin-towered façade of the **Parish Church** (Pfarrkirche) is a fine example of the early 13C Rhineland style – a transition between the Romanesque and the Gothic.

LAHN VALLEY (LAHNTAL) Hessen and Rhineland-Palatinate

Michelin map **412** folds 22 and 23

The winding course of the lower Lahn, with its wild scenery and steeply wooded banks, makes an effective introduction to Romantic Germany. Above its sombre waters – the river is canalized but largely deserted – the ruins of perched castles and such small towns as Weilburg and Limburg offer a rich choice of historic souvenirs.

FROM BAD EMS TO WETZLAR *89km - 55 miles - about 4 1/2 hours*

Bad Ems – The Lahn Valley, separating the Westerwald and the Taunus-Rhine schist massif, is rich, like all areas on the fringe of a volcanic region, in mineral springs. Bad Ems, treating mainly rhino-pharyngeal affections, is one of the oldest spas in the area. In the 19C Emperor Wilhelm I of Germany was a familiar figure in the town. A flagstone (Benedettistein) bearing the date 13 July 1870 and set into the quay-promenade by the pump room between Wilhelm and the French Ambassador, Benedetti. The Emperor categorically refused the French request that the Hohenzollerns renounce "forever" their claims to the throne of Spain. A report of the meeting, distorted and then leaked by Bismarck, hastened the Franco-Prussian war of 1870.

Nassau – The small city of Nassau was the cradle of the Counts of Laurenburg, who adopted the name of Nassau in the 12C. The Orange-Nassau branch, still reigning in the Netherlands, was the House of William of Orange, King William III of England.

Arnstein Abbey – *1km - 1/2 mile by a steep uphill road from the Obernhof Bridge.* The church of this former Premonstratensian monastery stands alone on a wooded spur. The Romanesque west chancel contrasts with that in the east, which is Gothic.

Balduinstein – Ruins of a castle built in 1320 by Baudouin of Luxemburg, Archbishop of Trier, to rival that of Schaumburg.

Schaumburg Castle ⊙ – A neo-Gothic reconstitution after the English manner. There is a fine view from the tallest of the crenellated towers overlooking the valley.

Diez – Dominating the small town clustered around its ramparts, the tall mass of the 17C **Castle of Oranienstein** ⊙ contains souvenirs of the House of Orange-Nassau. The gardens open onto the valley.

★ **Limburg** – *See under Limburg.*

Runkel – The picturesque **setting**★★ of the castle, built into the rock face, and the ancient village below it, can best be appreciated from the 15C bridge over the river.

Weilburg – Once the residence of the Counts of Nassau, this Baroque town is built on a promontory enclosed by the Lahn. Of the many different structures which comprised the Renaissance **castle** ⊙, note especially the turreted clock tower and the elegant 1573 gallery, where the twinned Ionic columns of the arcades are topped by a glazed gallery with Corinthian columns. Vaulted **rooms** on the ground floor may be visited. The **museum** (Bergbau- und Stadtmueum Museum) ⊙ is devoted to the Upper Lahn and to souvenirs of the princely House of Nassau.

Braunfels – The castle, seen unexpectedly after a fork in the road, has a superb and exciting feudal outline. The perimeter wall encloses the whole village.

Follow the road as far as **Wetzlar** *(qv).*

★ ## LANDSBERG AM LECH Bavaria   Pop 20 000

Michelin map **413** P 22

A fortified frontier town between Swabia and Bavaria in the Middle Ages, Landsberg – on the old road from Salzburg to Memmingen – prospered through trade and the levying of tolls. Fortress gates, towers and perimeter walls still preserve a most attractive medieval atmosphere as one approaches the place.
There is a fine view of the tiered **site**★ from the shady riverside promenade on the west bank of the Lech, where it meets the Karolinenbrücke *(the best place to park if the Marktplatz below is full).*

SIGHTS

★ **Marktplatz** – Triangular in shape, this market place is surrounded by a remarkable group of gaily coloured roughcast houses. **St Mary's Fountain** (Marienbrunnen), in the centre, falls into a marble basin surmounted by a statue of the Virgin.

Town Hall – The façade of this building was executed *c*1720 by Dominikus Zimmermann, one of the greatest artists of the Wessobrunn School *(qv)*, who was burgomaster of Landsberg at the time. The gable of the elegant structure is ornamented with finely worked stucco. The rest of the town hall was built between 1699 and 1702. In the far corner of the square stands the **Schmalztor**, through which the upper town can be reached. Hemmed in on all sides by old houses, the 14C tower-gate is topped by a lantern turret roofed with glazed tiles.
The Alte Bergstrasse climbs steeply to the Bavarian Gate.

Bavarian Gate (Bayertor) – With its projecting porch flanked by turrets and sculptures, this 1425 town gateway is one of the best preserved of its period in the whole of Germany. Outside the ramparts, which continue on either side, the gateway is embellished with carved and painted coats of arms and with a Crucifixion.

Michelin map **413** T 21
Town plan in the current Michelin Red Guide Deutschland

Landshut on the Isar, once capital of the Lower Bavaria dukedom, has kept its medieval centre practically intact.

Memories of the Ingoldstadt and Landshut branches of the House of Wittelsbach, whose members until the 16C outshone even their extravagant Munich cousins, remain very much alive in the valleyed countryside surrounding the town. Every four years, Landshut commemorates with great pomp the marriage in 1475 of the son of Duke Ludwig the Rich with Hedwige, daughter of the King of Poland *(see Calendar of Events)*.

SIGHTS

★ **St Martin's Church** – Designed by Master Hans von Burghausen and built of rose-coloured brick, this 14-15C church impresses above all by its outstanding elevation. The **tower★★**, square at the base, slims and becomes octagonal as it soars to a height of more than 130m - 426ft. Circle the outside of the building, which is adorned with tombstones. The five Flamboyant doorways show an early Renaissance influence.

The well-lit interior shows a splendid unity of design. Octagonal pillars, deceptively fragile in appearance, support in a single thrust vaulting which rises to 29m - 95ft. There is a delicate Virgin and Child by Leinberger (1518) on the altar in the south aisle.

★ **Altstadt** – The town's most important monuments are to be found in this wide, slightly curving main street with its arcaded 15C and 16C houses, between the town hall and St Martin's. Note especially the variety and inventiveness of the gables, which can be seen again – though perhaps to a lesser extent – in the Neustadt, which runs parallel to the Altstadt. The façades in this second street have had many Baroque featyres added.

Palace (Stadtresidenz) ⊙ – Two main blocks linked by narrow wings comprise this palace, which faces the town hall. The German building is on the Alstadt (18C furniture, decorations, etc); the 16C Italian Renaissance one looks onto the courtyard (large rooms with painted, coffered ceilings).

Trausnitz Castle (Burg Trausnitz) ⊙ – Of the fortress decorated during the Renaissance with arcaded galleries, the chapel, the Gothic hall known as the Alte Dürnitz, and several rooms furnished or embellished in 16C style are open to the public. The chapel is remarkable for its Romanesque statuary. Note also the Jesters' Staircase (Narrentreppe), painted in the 16C with scenes from the Commedia dell'Arte.

From an upper loggia (Söller), there is an exceptional **view** across the roofs of the town to the spire of St Martin's.

★ **LEIPZIG** Saxony   Pop 530 000

Michelin map **987** fold 17
Plan of the conurbation in the current Michelin Red Guide Deutschland

Leipzig stands at the confluence of the Weisse Elster and Pleisse rivers. The city is famous for its trade fairs (spring and autumn) and its numerous publishing houses.

HISTORICAL NOTES

The Leipzig Fairs – The first mention of the locality historically was in the Chronicle of Bishop Thietmar of Merseburg (975-1018), who noted the death of the Bishop of Meissen in "urbs Lipzi". The township of "Lipzk" was granted a city charter *c*1165. Subsequently, a situation at the crossing of several important trade routes, plus the bestowal by the Margrave Otto the Rich of the right to levy tolls – one of the oldest feudal privileges enjoyed by burghers – established Leipzig as a commercial centre of more than local influence. From the 12C onwards, markets were held over the Easter period and on the Feast of St Michael. A third event – during the New Year celebrations – was added in 1485. The Spring and Autumn international trade fairs, symbolized by the famous "Double M", have been held since 1896.

Leipzig, the Book Town – One of the world's earliest books, the Glossa Super Apocalipsim, was printed in Leipzig in 1481 by an itinerant craftsman. The German Book Exchange was founded in 1825, and this was followed in 1912 by the German Library (Deutsche Bücherei) and the Museum of Books and Literature. More than 35 established publishers are based in Leipzig today, among them Göschen, Brockhaus and Reclam.

The city also enjoys a fine reputation in the musical world, thanks to the Choir of St Thomas **(Thomanerchor)**, the Gewandhaus Orchestra, and the Mendelssohn-Bartholdy National College of Music.

Science and Industry – The "Alma Mater Lipsiensis", founded in 1409, the present university, and numerous colleges of higher education testify to the importance of intellectual and scientific activity in Leipzig. The industrial basin in which the city lies is one of the most productive in the eastern part of Germany, with special emphasis on chemicals, machine tools, and the extraction of lignite.

MARKET PLACE (MARKT) (AY)

★ **Former Town Hall** (Altes Rathaus) **(AY)** – This long, low building with its fine Renaissance façade is crowned with gables which are pierced by windows – one of the earliest examples of an architectural style typifying town hall design during the German Renaissance. It was completed in 1556 after plans drawn up by Hieronymous Lotter, architect and burgomaster of Leipzig. Today the building houses the **Town History Museum** (Stadtgeschichtliches Museum) ⊙.

While in this neighbourhood, note the interesting Baroque burghers' houses in nearby **Katharinenstrasse (AY 18)**, in particular the **Romanushaus**, which was built for the burgomaster F C Romanus between 1701 and 1704 by the architect J G Fuchs. Opposite the Naschmarkt opens the **Mädlerpassage (AZ 24)**, immortalized by Goethe because the Auerbachs tavern is there, where some of the scenes in Faust were set.

St Thomas's Church (Thomaskirche) **(AZ)** – Erected between 1212 and 1222 as a collegial for canons of the Augustinian order, this triple-aisle hall church was not given its present form until the end of the 15C. On Whit Sunday in 1539, Martin Luther gave a sermon here to inaugurate the Reformation.

The church became famous through Johann Sebastian Bach, who was cantor for 27 years and who is buried here, and through the celebrated **Thomanerchor**. Originating at the School of St Thomas, founded in 1212, this choir at first had no more than 12 singers. Today, at Vespers every Sunday, it can be heard singing Bach cantatas and motets.

Opposite the church, in the 16-17C Bosehaus, the **Johann Sebastian Bach National Research Centre** (with a museum and the Bach archives) has been installed since 1985.

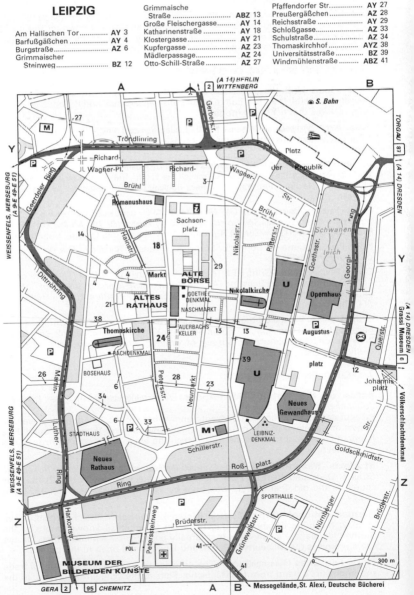

★ **Former Produce Exchange** (Alte Börse) **(AY)** – *On the Naschmarkt.* Built between 1678 and 1687 after plans by Johann Georg Starcke, this one-time commodity market was Leipzig's first Baroque edifice. It is used today for fairs and festivals. The statue outside (by Carl Seffner - 1903) represents **Goethe** as a student.

St Nicholas Church (Nikolaikirche) **(BY)** – *Nikolaistrasse.* Originally built in the Romanesque style, this church was transformed into a Gothic hall *c*1520. A double gallery surrounds the triple nave.

AUGUSTUSPLATZ (BYZ)

The 142m - 466ft-tall tower of the **university building (BYZ U)** dominates this wide square. The Schinkel Gate (Schinkeltor), designed by F Schinkel and E Rietschel in 1836, has been incorporated in the amphitheatre wing. A monument to the memory of **Leibniz** is on the south side of the university.

Egyptian Museum (Ägyptisches Museum) **(AZ M¹)** ⊙ – *Schillerstrasse 6.* Five thousand years of the Pharaohs' civilization, represented by more than 5 000 separate exhibits, are covered by the splendid collections in this museum, which is attached to the university.

New Concert Hall (Neues Gewandhaus) **(BZ)** – This superb auditorium was inaugurated in 1981. More than 1 900 enthusiasts can be seated to hear the famous Gewandhaus Orchestra. The statue of Beethoven (1902) was executed by Max Klinger.
The **Opera House** (Opernhaus) **(BY)** (1956-1960) and the swan lake (Schwanenteich) are on the north side of the square.
The **main station** (Hauptbahnhof) **(BY)**, to the north of the square, is the largest railway terminus in Europe.

Grassi Museum ⊙ – *Johannisplatz. Take the Grimmaischer Steinweg* **(BZ 12)**. A museum of arts and crafts, one of the oldest and most important in Europe. The exhibits illustrate the history, culture and way of life of the peoples of Asia, Africa, America, Australia and Oceania.

SOUTHWESTERN DISTRICT

New Town Hall (Neues Rathaus) **(AZ)** – Built on the foundations of the old Pleissburg Castle, the town hall marries both Renaissance and Baroque elements with features that are more modern.

★★ **Fine Arts Museum** (Museum der Bildenden Kunsten) **(AZ)** ⊙ – Art in Europe from the Middle Ages to the present day is outlined in the important collections here.

German Primitives: *The Man of Agonies* (*c*1425) by **Master Francke**; *Portraits of Luther and Junker Jörg* (1521) by **Lucas Cranach the Elder**; *The Seven Ages of Woman* (1544) and *Martin Schongauer* by **Hans Baldung Grien**; and works by **Cranach the Younger**.

Flemish Painting: *Portrait of an Old Man* (1430-40) by **Jan van Eyck**; *Visitation* (*c*1434) by **Rogier van der Weyden**; *Self-Portrait* (*c*1653) by **Rembrandt**; *The Mulatto* (*c*1630) by **Frans Hals**; and works by Gerard Honthorst, Van Goyen, Van Ostade, Van Ruisdael.

Italian Painting: Cima da Coneglio, Francesco Francia, **Tintoretto** (*The Resurrection of Lazarus* - *c*1565).

German Painting: Anton Graff, **J F A Tischbein**, J A Koch, **C D Friedrich** (*The Ages of Life* - *c*1835), Spitzweg, von Schwind, Arnold Böcklin (*The Island of the Dead* - *c*1886), Max Liebermann (*The Bottlers* - 1879), Max Klinger (*Blue Hour* - 1890) and W Leibl.

In the **Sculpture Department** there are works by, among others, Balthazar Permoser, Berthel Thorvaldsen, Auguste Rodin and Max Klinger. The Museum's **Collection of Drawings** offers a panoramic survey of graphic art that goes back as far as medieval times.

ADDITIONAL SIGHTS

Battle of the Nations Monument (Völkerschlachtdenkmal) ⊙ – *Take the Johannisplatz* **(BZ)**.
Inaugurated in 1913, on the hundredth anniversary of the Allied victory over the armies of Napoleon (Battle of Leipzig), this memorial took 15 years to build. Five hundred steps lead to a terrace from which the entire city and its surroundings can be seen.

St Alexis Memorial Church (St Alexi-Gedächtniskirche) – *Philipp-Rosenthal-Strasse.* Dedicated to the 22 000 Russian soldiers who fell in that battle, this church in the old Tzarist style was built by W A Pokrowski between 1912 and 1913.

German National Library (Deutsche Bücherei) – *Deutscher Platz.* Founded, again, in 1912, the huge library attempts to group together all known books in the German language – a collection that already comprises 7.5 million titles. On the same premises the Museum of Books and Literature is open to the public.

Trade Fair Sites (Messegelände) – The emplacements for Leipzig's annual trade and book fairs extend from the Deutscher Platz to the Wilhelm Külz Park, in the eastern part of the city.

Michelin maps **411** and **412** J 10

Flourishing trade relations with England and with Flanders in the 15C and 16C brought the Hanseatic town of Lemgo a prosperity still apparent today in its well laid out avenues of wealthy private homes.

★ OLD TOWN

From the East Gate (Ostertor), approach the Mittelstrasse, which is the main street. Note especially the fine façades of no 17 (with wood carving on all four floors) and no 36, known as the House of Planets.

★★ **Town Hall** (Rathaus) – Comprising eight buildings side by side, the civic centre of Lemgo is exceptional for its oriel windows, its arcades and its unique gables. The elegantly worked façade of the old apothecary's shop on the corner of the Marktplatz displays, on the first floor, the sculpted portraits of ten famous philosopher-physicians, from Aristotle to Paracelsus. Beneath the central arcades, witchcraft trials were held in about 1670.

Bear left into the Breite Strasse.

House of the Witches' Burgomaster (Hexenbürgermeisterhaus) ⊙ – Dating from 1568, this splendid patrician house has one of the finest façades in the town. Inside, a local museum (Museum für Stadt-und Rechtsgeschichte) has an exhibition of historical documents and instruments of torture used in the trials.

St Mary's Church (Marienkirche) – A Renaissance organ with a finely carved case, among the oldest in Germany (1587-1613), adorns this triple-aisle Gothic church constructed at the end of the 13C and the beginning of the 14C. Admire too the baptismal font (1592), the pulpit (1644) and the Cross Triumphant (1490).

Return to the Papenstrasse, following it to the right.

St Nicholas' Church (Nikolaikirche) – Appropriately dedicated to the patron saint of merchants, the church combines features that are both Romanesque (a three-figure tympanum in the south aisle; a stone triptych in the north) and Gothic (frescoes and vault keystones). The pulpit and the font are late Renaissance (c1600).

The Papenstrasse leads back to the starting point.

ADDITIONAL SIGHT

★ **Karl Junker's House** (Junkerhaus) ⊙ – *Hamelner Strasse 36.*
Karl Junker (1850-1912), painter, sculptor and architect, a contemporary of the blossoming Jugendstil *(qv)*, left in his own house a memorial to his highly personal style. His design is organized around a spiral which relies for its effect on an arcane play of movements alternately balanced and opposed. Surprise in this concept is everything: the visitor's perception of Junker's sculpted and painted décor (note the pointillist medallions adorning the ceilings) is of an infinite diversity, constantly changing with each different point of view.

EXCURSION

Herford – *20km - 12 1/2 miles to the west.*
The **Evangelical Church** (Johanniskirche) is garnished with fine 17C **wood carving**★, both sculpted and painted. Galleries, stalls and pulpit were all donated by different city corporations, whose shields and emblems can be recognized in the design. The chancel has interesting 15C stained glass windows.

★ **LIMBURG AN DER LAHN** Hessen   Pop 31 100

Michelin map **412** H 15
Town plan in the current Michelin Red Guide Deutschland

On the banks of the Lahn, between the Taunus heights to the south and the Westerwald to the north, this small medieval town is an excellent centre for excursions. The outline of its cathedral, at the same time lofty and compact, dominates everything else as it rises above the river.

★ CATHEDRAL (DOM) *time: 1/2 hour*

Built on a rocky spur, St George's Cathedral is in a picturesque **setting**★★. Apart from that, it is remarkable for the style of its architecture: a classic example of Gothic Transitional, which was widely known in Germany between 1210 and 1250.
The outside remains Romanesque and closely resembles the Rhineland cathedrals *(see introduction)*, but the interior is already Gothic, with a structure directly inspired by the cathedral of Laon, in Picardy.
Here we find superimposed galleries, a triforium and clerestory windows as typical of the early Gothic period as the distinctive crochet capitals. Diagonal ribs characterize the vaulting. The transept crossing lies beneath a domed lantern tower. The original multicoloured decoration has been uncovered and restored.
From the **cemetery terrace** (Friedhofterrasse) on the north side of the church, there is a good **view**★ of the river, the old bridge, and a new motorway viaduct.

★ Diocesan Museum (Diozesanmuseum) ⊘ – *Domstrasse 12.*
The 10C Byzantine reliquary-cross known as the Limburger Staurothek is the jewel of the religious art collection displayed in this restored building dating from 1544. The sheath encasing the reliquary Staff of St Peter, of the same period, derives from the School of St Egbert of Trier. Among the sculptures on view, is an admirable terracotta Lamentation of Christ, a moving work that dates from 1410.

ADDITIONAL SIGHT

Old Town (Alstadt) – Clustered around the southern part of the cathedral, the oldest part of Limburg offers a wealth of half-timbered medieval houses with festooned gables.

★★ LINDAU IM BODENSEE Bavaria   Pop 24 000

Michelin map **413** M 24 - Town plan in the current Michelin Red Guide Deutschland

Lindau is popular with visitors. The former Free Imperial City (1275-1802) adds to the charm of its old streets an island setting *(photograph p 348)*, harbour lights, and a magnificent panorama visible from the windows of all its hotels. Lindau – im Bodensee (in the lake) and not am Bodensee (by the lake) like its neighbours Überlingen and Meersburg – boasts a number of churches with belfries crowned by an onion dome. The gabled burghers' houses in the old town testify still to the prosperity of bygone days when it was an important trading centre, particularly for commerce with Italy. There is an almost Mediterranean quality to life in this lakeside Swabian resort at the gates of Austria - a retro charm which can be savoured to the full during an evening stroll between the port and the Maximilianstrasse.

SIGHTS

Municipal Museum (Städtische Kunstsammlungen) (Y M1) ⊘ – Installed in Cavazzen House, a typical example of bourgeois Baroque architecture (1729), the museum exhibits ancient documents relating to Lindau. There is a gallery of painting and sculpture.

Maximilianstrasse (Z) – This, the main highway leading through the old town, is a picturesque street lined by old houses and inns. Narrow, half-timbered façades with the oriel windows characteristic of the Alpine Rhine Valley and the Vorarlberg huddle together with the stepped gables of Old Swabia (the former **Town Hall** (A) – Altes Rathaus – is a fine example of the latter style).
Turn right into the Zeppelinstrasse and walk to the **Brigands' Tower** (Diebsturm), a well-known Lindau silhouette with its crown of bartizans.

Port (Hafen) (Z) – Tourists crowd the quays, many of them waiting to embark on one of the large white Bodensee pleasure boats. In the centre of the activity stands the Mangturm, a fortified 12C tower once used as a lighthouse. The present small lighthouse commands, along with a monument to the Lion of Bavaria (1856), the entrance to the roadstead. A few steps lead up to the **Römerschanze★** viewpoint – a pleasant, shady place from which to admire the Rhine Gap and the Alpine landmarks surrounding the "Bodan" (the ancient form of Bodensee).These are: Kanisfluh, the Hoher Freschen, the Drei Schwestern and (in Switzerland) Säntis and Altmann.

LINDAU IM BODENSEE

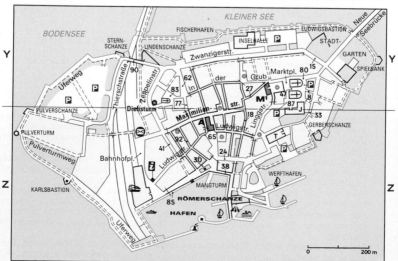

Michelin map **413** P 24 – Local map see under German ALPINE ROAD

Deep in the forest, in one of the wildest valleys of the Ammergau Alps – a region the royal hunters of the House of Bavaria reserved for their own use – Ludwig II had this small cream-coloured palace built. Designed in the style of the 18C, it served as a background, along with its Moorish pavilion and its grotto, for the romantic fancies of the young king, obsessed by oriental fables and the heroic legends of Germany. The extraordinary contrasts provided by a Rococo building surrounded by gardens and terraces inspired by the Italian Renaissance, set in the middle of a park landscaped in the English manner – the whole planted in an Alpine valley – lend the project its own peculiar charm.

Linderhof Castle

TOUR ⊘ *about 2 hours*

Castle – Built between 1869 and 1879, in a style intermingling the second Italian Renaissance and the Baroque, Linderhof was intended by the king to achieve a certain intimacy. Inside, nevertheless, one finds a state bedchamber surpassing in luxury even those of Versailles, a hall of mirrors, cloth panels painted to resemble tapestries, pastels and statues of Louis XIV, Louis XV, Madame de Pompadour, Madame du Barry and others. A similarity in the sheer extravagance of these decorative excesses does however impose a particular harmony on the concept.

★★ **Park** – The natural slopes of the valley have been used to lay out a vista in line with the castle in which pools, cascades and terraced gardens in the style of an Italian villa have been devised. Fountains of water and the blaze of formal flower beds strike yet another bizarre note in this wooded Alpine landscape. The east-west lateral borders, on the other hand, with their beech hedges and boxwood trained in pyramids, suggest a more placid approach in the French manner. Climb to the Temple of Venus rotunda, which closes off the perspective above an ornamental lake (a fine view, especially when the fountains play). Then descend, keeping to the right of the castle, and climb the opposite slope to reach the Moorish pavilion and the grotto. It is here that the skill of the landscape gardener, Karl von Effner, is most in evidence, with plantations of oak, maple and decorative beech placed with consummate art against clumps of conifers gradually retiring to form their sombre natural density.

Moorish Pavilion (Maurischer Kiosk) – Acquired by Ludwig II after the 1867 Exposition Universelle in Paris (which was really the world's first International Fair), this metallic structure was used by him when he wished to play the oriental potentate.

Grotto of Venus – A cavern, fashioned with the aid of artificial rocks and intended to recreate the atmosphere of the Venusberg sequence in the Wagnerian opera Tannhäuser, the conceit here instances once more the king's taste for theatrical effect: by the royal throne is a rock evoking the Loreley, which is set beside a lake, illuminated by the play of coloured lights, on which floats a golden skiff in the form of a huge conch shell.

★★★ **LÜBECK** Schleswig-Holstein   Pop 216 000
Michelin map **411** P 5
Town plan in the current Michelin Red Guide Deutschland

Girdled with canals, crowned by belfries and towers, Lübeck has retained much of its medieval character as business centre of the Hanseatic League; many of its buildings and monuments are still decorated with alternating bands of red and glazed black brick courses. Today the city remains the busiest German port on the Baltic and a focal point for shipbuilding and heavy industry.

At the head of the League – The 14C marked the summit of Lübeck's power as Hanseatic capital – the most influential town of that association of Dutch and north German cities which from the 12C to the 16C monopolized trade with Scandinavia and Russia. In the 16C, the business acumen of merchants and shipowners combined to extricate the port from a long period of decline, thanks largely to the establishment of new relations with Holland, and also with France and the Iberian countries, who sent cargoes of wine. For a long time, Dutch architecture was the preferred style for the rich burghers on the banks of the Trave.

In the 19C, Lübeck's seaport status was menaced by the Prussian port of Stettin (now Szczecin) and the opening of the Kiel canal. But the construction of a canal linking the Trave with the Elbe, plus an influx of almost 100 000 refugees in 1945, have together permitted the city to maintain its importance in present-day Germany. Among other assets it has the reputation of being the country's chief importer of the red wines of France, which are matured in the celebrated **Lübeck Cellars** beneath the river Trave.

★★★ OLD TOWN (ALTSTADT) *time: 3 hours*

Leave from the Holstentor (follow the itinerary marked on the plan)

★★ **Holstentor** (Y) – This fortified gate with its enormous twin towers was built between 1469 and 1478, before the construction of the city's perimeter wall, more as a matter of prestige than protection. The most impressively designed façade, that towards the town, has three tiers of blind arcades with ornamented ceramic friezes. The building houses the **municipal museum** (Museum im Holstentor).

St Peter's Church (Petrikirche) (Y A) – The triple nave of the original Romanesque church (completed *c*1240) was modified in the Gothic style in the first half of the 14C. A fourth aisle on the south side was added in the middle of the 15C, and then a fifth, on the north, at the beginning of the 16C. From the tower platform *(lift)*, there is an aerial **view★** of the port and the town - unique in its central nucleus surrounded by a double ring of canals separated by a circle of narrow islands.

★ **Town Hall** (Rathaus) (Y R) – Built from 1250 onwards, on two sides of the Marktplatz, the town hall is an elegant edifice in dark glazed brick raised, in accordance with municipal tradition, on a gallery of arcades. Note the high protective walls, sometimes pierced with blind arcades or by gaping round openings decorated and strengthened by slender turrets with "candle-snuffer" roofs.

In front of the north wing, a Renaissance superstructure in ornately carved sandstone has been added. The building at the extremity of the east wing, the Neues Gemach (1440), is interesting for the heightened effect lent to it by an imaginative openwork wall. Pass beneath the arcades to see, on the Breite Strasse, a stone staircase (1594) in Dutch Renaissance style.

Continuing the circuit of the Rathaus, arrive at the foot of the north façade.

The wall here displays an impressive layout, with immense bays lined up across almost its entire height.

The Holstentor at Lübbeck

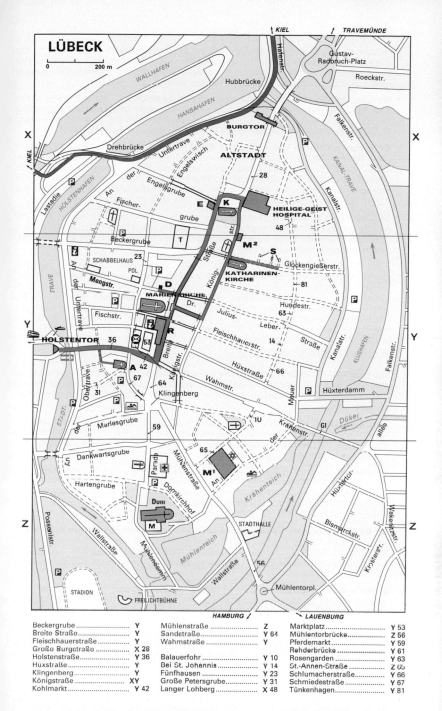

LÜBECK

0   200 m

KIEL   TRAVEMÜNDE

WALLHAFEN
HANSAHAFEN
Hubbrücke
Gustav-
Radbruch-Platz
Roeckstr.

BURGTOR

X   X

Drehbrücke   Untertrave   ALTSTADT

KIEL

der Engelsgrube   28

An Fischer-   E K   HEILIGE-GEIST
HOLSTENHAFEN   HOSPITAL
grube   48
Beckergrube   T

SCHABBELHAUS 23   M² S
POL   Str.   Glockengießerstr.
Mengstr.   D   KATHARINEN-
                           KIRCHE   81
MARIENKIRCHE
                Dr.   Hundestr.   63
Fischstr.   Julius-   Leber- Straße
R   Fleischhauerstr.   14
HOLSTENTOR 36   53   Breite   Hüxstraße   66

A 42
67   64   Wahmstr.
31   Klingenberg   Hüxterdamm
Marlesgrube   59   Krähenstr.   61   Düker

65   10

Dankwartsgrube Mühlenstraße   An   Krähenteich

Hartengrube   M¹

Dom   Hüxtertor-
Dom   STADTHALLE
M   Bismarckstr.
Wallstraße
Z   Z

Wallstraße   56

STADION FREILICHTBÜHNE Mühlentorpl.

HAMBURG   LAUENBURG

St Mary's Church (Marienkirche) (Y) – One of the finest brick-built Gothic churches in Germany. The original designers in 1250 planned a hall-type church without a transept, but the concept was changed while work was in progress. Subsequently, under the influence of French cathedral architecture, the main buttress-supported vaulting was raised to a height of 38.5m - 126ft. The 125m - 410ft spires were completed in 1350. The composer Buxtehude (1637-1707) was the church's official organist. The interior, audacious in concept, has grandiose proportions. A fire, started by an air raid in 1942, exposed the original polychromatic 13C and 14C decoration. At the end of the south aisle is an elegant 14C chapel, the **Briefkapelle**, with tall lancet windows recalling the High Gothic style. The star vaulting rests on two monolithic columns of granite. Inside the south tower, two huge church bells, which were brought down during the raid, remain embedded in the ground.

The ambulatory vaulting covers in a single sweep both the radial apsidal chapels and the axial Lady Chapel, which contains an altarpiece to the Virgin made in Antwerp in 1518.

Outside the church, walk around the east end and go through the arcade of the former Town Hall Chancellery (15C and 16C) to the Mengstrasse. Here, the Volksbank is installed in the Baroque **Buddenbrooks (Y D)** house, immortalized by the author Thomas Mann in the novel of the same name. Mann himself (1875-1955) was born in the house.

LÜBECK

★ **House of the Seamen's Guild** (Haus der Schiffergesellschaft) **(X E)** – Behind the stepped Renaissance gable, the **interior★★** (now a restaurant) still preserves the picturesque furnishings of a seamen's tavern, with rough wooden tables, copper lamps and ships' models hanging from the beams.

★ **Hospice of the Holy Spirit** (Hospital zum Heiligen Geist) **(X)** – Since the end of the 13C, the three turret-bordered gables of this almshouse have stood above the Koberg. The chapel, a large Gothic hall embellished with 13C and 14C paintings, is just outside the even bigger Great Hall of the hospice (Langes Haus).

★ **St James's Church** (Jakobikirche) **(X K)** – The magnificent woodwork of the two **organ lofts★★** (16C and 17C) in this small Gothic hall-church is noteworthy. A chapel on the south aisle contains an altar known as the "Brömbse" (15C), with bas-reliefs of very fine workmanship. The first side chapel on the north aisle is arranged as a memorial to the shipwrecked, and displays a lifeboat from the Pamir, the full-rigged Lübeck training ship lost with all hands in 1957.

★ **St Catherine's Church** (Katharinenkirche) **(Y)** – The lower niches of the 14C façade contain modern **statues★**, the first three on the left being by Ernst Barlach *(qv)*. Inside *(the museum is being restored)*, note, on the right side as you enter, *The Resurrection of Lazarus* by Tintoretto.

The "Höfe and Gänge" – At the corner of the church, turn left into the Glockengiesserstrasse, on which open the courts (Höfe), set back from the street, which are typical of Lübeck – social amenities donated in the 17C by local benefactors. Note, successively, the delightful **Füchtingshof★** (no 25 – **Y S**), with its Baroque doorway dating from 1639; the Glandorps-Gang, a simple alignment of small houses along an alley (no 41); and, from nos 49 to 51, the Glandorps-Hof.

ADDITIONAL SIGHTS

★ **Burgtor (X)** – This fortified gateway defended the narrow isthmus – now cut by a canal – which was once the only land approach to Lübeck. The structure is a fine example of military architecture (13-15C) with a design of superimposed tier-cepoint bays.

Mengstrasse (Y) – Much of the original character remains in this street, with its varied brick gables at the lower end recalling the rivalries of rich neighbours in years gone by. The two houses now occupied by the Schabbelhaus restaurant have been restored with great care.

Cathedral (Dom) (Z) – The 14C reconstruction of the chancel in the Gothic style transformed this Romanesque church. A covered entrance and a very fine porch were added to the north transept in the middle of the 13C. A gigantic Bernt Notke Crucifix (1477) stands on the rood-beam. On the left of the rood-screen is the altarpiece of the Merchants of Stecknitz (1422).

★ **St Anne's Museum** (St Annen-Museum) **(Z M¹)** – Installed in a former monastery, this museum devoted to the past history of the town has a rich department of religious sculpture, in particular works by Bernt Notke, the master sculptor of Lübeck in the 15C. Note also an altarpiece depicting the Passion, painted by Hans Memling in 1491.

Behnhaus and Drägerhaus (XY M²) ⊘ – The Behnhaus, an 18C mansion, exhibits works of the Romantic movement, of the Norwegian Edvard Munch (1863-1944), the Expressionist Ernst Ludwig Kirchner (1880-1939) and the local painter A Aereboe.
The Drägerhaus, formerly a merchants' meeting place, displays paintings by Friedrich Overbeck (1789-1869), the leader of the Nazarene movement, and evokes the life and work of the Mann brothers, Thomas (1875-1955) and Heinrich (1871-1950), writers born in Lübeck.

EXCURSION

★ **Travemünde** – *20km - 12 1/2 miles to the northeast. Plan in the current Michelin Red Guide Deutschland.*
On the Trave estuary, this resort with its casino and its pleasure beaches has become the playground of Lübeck and something of an international favourite. North of the town the low cliffs of the **Brodtener Ufer** offer wide views over the Baltic.
To the northwest is the important and popular seaside resort of **Timmendorfer Strand**.

GREEN TOURIST GUIDES

Architecture
Fine Art
History
Geography
Picturesque scenery
Touring programmes
Town and site plans

Guides for the holidays

Michelin map 413 K 20
Town plan in the current Michelin Red Guide Deutschland

An enormous Baroque palace built at the beginning of the 18C by a Duke of Württemberg, dreaming of another Versailles, was the start of Ludwigsburg – a town whose artificial character is emphasized by its grid of dead straight streets. Visitors today are more attracted by the park than the palace.

★ PALACE ⊙

This monumental quadrilateral has no less than 452 rooms, 75 of them open to the public.

Tour of the Apartments – *Entrance: 1st courtyard on the right on the road from Stuttgart (access also through the park).* Inside, the "best rooms" (on the 1st floor of the New Building, facing the park), in the Empire style, are arranged to illustrate life at Court in the Baroque period. Through the Ancestors' Gallery (Ahnengalerie) and the castle's Catholic Church (Schlosskirche), decorated with lavish Italian stucco, visitors arrive at the Fürstenbau state apartments. These are in the oldest and highest part of the palace, which closes off the north side of the court.

★ **Park** (Blühendes Barock) – Green Baroque arbours and terraces clothed with an embroidery of flowers have been reconstituted in the southern part of the park, in front of the newest part of the palace. The terrain to the north and east, more broken up, has been landscaped in the English manner. Fountains have been installed.

★★ **The Fairy-tale Garden** (Märchengarten) – Fairy stories, legends and folk tales from Germany (the Brothers Grimm) and elsewhere (Hans Christian Andersen) are illustrated here with performances by mechanical figures, some actuated by the sound of children's voices.

EXCURSIONS

Marbach am Neckar – *9km - 5 miles to the northeast.*
This small town cultivates the memory of the poet Schiller *(qv)*, its most illustrious son. The huge **Schiller National Museum** ⊙, rising like a castle above the valley, displays portraits, casts, engravings and manuscripts, not only of Schiller (1759-1805) but also of many other Swabian literary figures who lived between the 16C and the 20C. A visit to the writer's **birthplace** (Schiller-Geburtshaus) completes the pilgrimage.

Monrepos Castle – *2km - 1 1/4 miles to the northwest.*
Built in 1767 on a site bordering a small lake, this gracious Rococo castle encircles a rotunda.

Markgröningen – *5km - 3 miles to the west.*
The 15C **Rathaus★** in this picturesque small town is, by virtue of its impressive size and its skilful construction, a monument to German half-timbering craftsmanship. Many wood-framed houses still exist in Markgröningen.

Gourmets should look in the current **Michelin Red Guide Deutschland** *for the restaurants with stars.*

Michelin map 411 NO 7

The Salt Town – The town of Lüneburg is built on a salt deposit. The prosperity of Lüneburg, from the 10C onwards, was also built on salt. In the Middle Ages it was the principal supplier of the mineral to many places, notably Scandinavia, where, because of the Baltic's low saline content, it was always in short supply. Traffic followed the **Old Salt Route**, via Lauenburg, Ratzeburg and Lübeck.
The traditional architecture of Lüneburg is distinguished by stepped and scrolled gables, cornices with rounded or tiercepoint blind arcades, and the "Tausteine" – a local twisted brick feature producing an effect like a cable stitch.

SIGHTS

★★ **Town Hall** (Rathaus) (Y R) ⊙ – The municipal headquarters is an assembly of different buildings dating from the 13C to the 18C. Go in through the Gothic doorway on the Ochsenmarkt. The **Great Council Chamber★★** (Grosse Ratsstube), on the right of the entrance hall, is a Renaissance masterpiece (1566-1584). Panelled throughout, it is adorned with intricate wood sculptures by Albert von Soest: note the wealth of expression in the small heads rhythmically animating the frieze beneath allegorical paintings. The fine door frames also are worth attention.
The **Princes' Apartment** (Fürstensaal), on the first floor, is equally rewarding. It is Gothic, with lamps fashioned from stags' antlers and a superbly beamed and painted ceiling. The **Hall of Justice** (Gerichtslaube), with its cradle vaulting, is decorated on walls and ceilings with paintings inspired by the etchings of Hans Burgkmair and Heinrich Aldegrever.

LÜNEBURG

★ **Old Town** – The houses here are characterized by the traditional brick architecture. Typical are those lining the long, narrow square known as **Am Sande★** (Z),
especially no 1, the 16C **Black House** (Schwarzes Haus), which was once
a brewery.

In the Grosse Bäckerstrasse (**Y 30**) stands the **Rathsapotheke** (pharmacy) (**Y A**),
which dates, with its fine twisted brick gables, from 1598. The Reitende-Diener-
Strasse (**Y 40**) comprises a double row of identical low houses, each embellished
with medallions and, again, twisted brick cornices.

A sudden contrast is provided at no 14 Rotehahnstrasse (**Y 43**), the **Haus Roter Hahn**
(**Y D**), a former convent whose three 16C gables are half-timbered in a rustic
style.

St John's Church (St Johanniskirche) (**Z E**) – The robust **west tower** (108m - 354ft
high) is deliberately inclined to counter the pressure of violent winds blowing
from the west. Displacement from the vertical at the top of the tower is 2m - 6ft
6in. The tower has been refurbished several times to combat subsidence. The
church itself dates from the 14C. The huge interior, with five naves and two rows
of side chapels, forms a perfect square, closed at the east end by plain polygonal apses.

The most valuable item of the furnishings is the sculpted reredos of the high altar,
which has painted panels depicting scenes from the lives of John the Baptist,
St Cecilia, St Ursula and St George (1482). The 16C **organ**, modified several times,
is one of the oldest in Germany.

★ **Old Port Quarter** (Wasserviertel) – From the bridge across the Ilmenau, looking
downstream, there is a fine view of the old galleried houses on the west bank
and, on the right, a **crane** (Alter Kran) (**Y**) dating from the 14C (restored in the 18C).
A **brewery** (Brauhaus) (**Y F**) stands at the corner of the Am Werder square and the
Lünertorstrasse. This is a Renaissance building, its gables once more decorated
with medallions and twisted brick motifs. Further on, at the corner of the
Lünertorstrasse and the Kaufhausstrasse, is a house (Staatshochbauamt) (**Y K**)
built in 1574 with remarkable rusticated half-pilasters in sandstone and a solid
cornice. Beside it, note the Baroque façade (1745) of an old warehouse (Altes
Kaufhaus).

EXCURSIONS

Lüne Convent (Kloster Lüne) – *2km - 1 1/4 miles via ① on the plan.*
The Gothic cloister and its fountain are the outstanding features of this old 15C abbey and its dependencies.

Lauenburg an der Elbe – *25km - 15 1/2 miles via ① on the plan.*
A sleepy township today, Lauenburg commands a point where the ancient salt route from Lüneburg to Lübeck crossed the Elbe. The old sailors' houses lie clustered at the foot of a steep, wooded slope, at the top of which is a round clock tower, all that remains of a ruined ducal castle. The summit (Schlossberg) offers a clear view of several reaches of the Elbe. The **Elbe Navigation Museum** (Elbschiffahrtsmuseum) – in the Lower Town, at no 59 Elbstrasse – relates the history of river traffic between Dresden and Hamburg with the help of models, documents, illustrated panels and even ships' engines (demonstrations).

LÜNEBURG HEATH (LÜNEBURGER HEIDE) Lower Saxony

Michelin map **411** folds 23 and 24

The great expanse of Lüneburg Heath lies in an area bounded by the sweep of the Hamburg-Bremen motorway, the valley of the Aller, and the road from Brunswick to Lüneburg.
The region, picturesque but austere, is at its best from mid-August to mid-September, when the heather flowers and thickets of birch, pine and juniper add shades of varying green to the mauve and purple landscape. To preserve the heath from the increasing advance of agriculture and forestry, a 200-sq km - 77-sq mile **nature reserve** has been created in the neighbourhood of the **Wilseder Berg**, where the flora and fauna are protected and motor cars only permitted on the main roads which cross the heath. Considerable effort is being made to preserve the rural character of Lower Saxony housing, and even outside the reserve villages on the heath have retained much of their old world charm – notably in the case of their wooden belfries, separated from the church and half hidden in plantations of trees.

TOWNS, LANDSCAPES AND SIGHTS

Bergen-Belsen – *7km - 4.3 miles southwest of Bergen.*
The **memorial** (Gedenkstätte) raised to the victims of the Bergen-Belsen concentration camp – erected in 1946 on the orders of the British Military Government stands in solitude in a clearing on Lüneburg Heath surrounded by pines and birch trees. There is a **documentation centre** (Dokumentenhaus) at the entrance, with a permanent exhibition retracing the history of the camp.

The Monument – *From the car park, 3/4 hour Rtn on foot.* The monument is beyond the tumulus which marks the site of the mass graves. It is a simple obelisk in pale volcanic tufa, with inscriptions in 13 languages honouring the memory of those who fell victim to the Nazis' "extermination" policy.

★★ **Celle** – *See under Celle.*

Ebstorf – *26km - 16 miles south of Lüneburg.*
Do not miss the former **Benedictine abbey** (Ehemaliges Benediktinerkloster) ⊙ in this small town, where the 14C and 15C cloister and nuns' gallery (Nonnenchor) are the most impressive features among the ruins. A life-size wooden statue of St Maurice (1300) and several Romanesque and Gothic Virgins can be seen in the gallery. Visitors interested in cartography can see a reproduction **Mappa Mundi**★ (Ebstorfer Weltkarte). The famous 13C original, once preserved in the abbey, was destroyed by fire during the Second World War.

Lönsgrab – *Between Fallingbostel and Walsrode.* The memorial tomb of the poet **Hermann Löns** (1866-1914), who celebrated the beauties of the heath with extravagant lyricism, can be seen here in a setting of junipers.

Lönsstein – *1/2 hour on foot Rtn. Midway between Baven and Müden, leave the car and climb a footpath on the left which follows a line of birch trees.* On the crest is another monument to Herman Löns in a typical pine, heather and juniper landscape.

Suhlendorf – Windmills and watermills, both actual size and scale models, are on display in the Suhlendorf **museum** ⊙. There is also an exhibition illustrating 600 years of navigation.

★ **Undeloh** – A most charming village, with its old houses sheltered beneath huge oak trees, Undeloh is the departure point for the

4km – 2 1/2-mile trip to Wilsede, a nature reserve village which has been kept apart from the onward march of a mechanized civilization *(cars are not allowed: there is a service of horse-drawn vehicles from Undeloh).*

Walsrode – Follow the itinerary sign: Rundgang. Four thousand six hundred birds (900 species, from all parts of the world) live in this fine 22-hectare - 54-acre **ornithological park★** ⊙, most of them in their natural habitat and at semi-liberty. Waders and web-footed birds, as well as parrots and budgerigars, are particularly well represented.

★ **Wienhausen** – *See under Celle: Excursions.*

★ **Wilseder Berg** – From the summit (there is a marker post: 169m - 554ft), a vast **panorama★** of heath and woodlands is visible. On a clear day, the spires of the Hamburg churches can be seen, 40km - 25 miles away to the north.

★★ MAGDEBURG Saxony-Anhalt   Pop 287 000

Michelin map 987 fold 16

Ideally situated mid-way along the 1 100km - 683-mile course of the Elbe, on its journey from northern Bohemia to the North Sea, this town in the German heartlands was an important trade centre before the Middle Ages. Sadly, the architectural witnesses to this former glory did not survive the bombardments of 1945. Only a few ecclesiastical buildings remain, notably the cathedral - a grandiose example of Gothic evolution in Germany.

From Tilly to the Allied Bombers – It was a flourishing commercial city, converted to the Protestant faith, which fell into the hands of the **General Graf von Tilly**, head of the Catholic League, during the terrible Thirty Years War *(qv)*. The carnage inflicted by the Walloon general's troops was appalling: more than two-thirds of the population perished when the town was sacked and fired.

Slowly, Magdeburg rose again from its ruins, enjoying once more an economic and cultural boom of which the most remarkable representatives were **Otto von Guericke** (1602-1686), burgomaster and physicist famous for his experiments on vacuum, and **Georg Philipp Telemann** (1681-1767), one of the luminaries of Baroque music.

From 1850 onwards, the city was in the throes of an industrial expansion largely based on the manufacture of machine tools and mechanical components, a situation favoured by its position at the junction of important rail links. It was thus one of the richest and economically most active towns in Germany that the Allied bomber force overflew on the night of 16 January 1945. Half an hour later, virtually nothing was left of the city centre and the Baroque façades of its ancient streets.

★★★ CATHEDRAL (DOM ST MAURITIUS UND ST KATHARINA)

Am Domplatz. Entrance via the cloister.

At a time when the Romanesque style in Germany was losing its impetus, the construction of Magdeburg cathedral at the beginning of the 13C marked the first attempt to impose a Gothic style derived from the architectural precepts of the great French cathedrals. The decision was taken by the Archbishop Albert II following a visit to France, and several of the architects commissioned to work on the project were French.

If certain alterations which supervened at different stages of the construction denied the building as a whole a stylistic unity, Magdeburg cathedral can nevertheless be considered the first great German Gothic religious edifice, well ahead of its time.

Outside, the three levels of the east end (absidioles, ambulatory, apse) at once give an impression of power.

On the north side, the **Paradise Doorway** (reached from inside the cathedral) displays **statues★★** of the Wise and Foolish Virgins. Dating from *c*1245, these, in common with statuary at Strasbourg, Bamberg and Naumburg, mark a stage in the evolution of Gothic sculpture, more and more inclined towards the expression of emotional feeling.

Statue of Otto I and the Empress Edith in the Cathedral of St Maurice and St Catherine at Magdeburg

A statue of the Emperor Otto I stands at the late 15C west door. In the cloister's west gallery, the **Chapel of the Fountains** is remarkable for the elegance of its rib vaulting.

Interior – Slender divided pillars framed by columns of Italian porphyry distinguish the polygonal chancel. The upper gallery, built between 1232 and 1240 by Cistercian workers from Maulbronn, combines forms of great simplicity not unlike those characterizing the monastic style of Burgundy.

A 1240 modification of the original plan having suppressed the intermediate pillars, the tall nave with its wide bays admits an abundance of light to illuminate the works of art displayed.

Sculpture – A southeast transept pillar incorporates a sandstone **statue★** (c1240) of St Maurice, with African features. In the ambulatory, there are **bronze funerary plaques★** of the Archbishops Friedrich of Wettin (d 1152) and Wichmann of Seeburg (d 1192). Seated **statues★** said to represent Christ and the Church are more likely in fact to be Otto I and his wife, the Anglo-Saxon princess Edith. Dating from c1245, they are housed in a small 16-sided chapel off the north transept. In the western part of the nave there is a **bronze tomb★** of the Archbishop Ernst, which was cast in 1495 in the foundry of Peter Vischer of Nuremberg.

ADDITIONAL SIGHTS

★★ **Abbey of Our Lady** (Kloster Unser Lieben Frauen) ⊙ – *Regierungsstrasse*. Founded in 1015 by Augustinian monks on the fringe of the Germanic lands – separated from the Slav countries at the time by the Elbe – this abbey was designed to participate, at least spiritually, in an eventual expansion towards the east.

The buildings, largely restored after 1945, date from the second half of the 11C and form a homogenous Romanesque ensemble with the exception of the Gothic-inspired ogive vaulting of the abbey church, which was not completed until c1230. Groined vaulting covers the three-aisle crypt.

On the north side of the church, the **cloister★** remains one of the best preserved in Germany. Outside, the façade of the church comprises a squared fore part between two round towers with lateral stairways.

Town Hall (Rathaus) – In front of this two-storey Baroque building (1691-1698) stands the famous statue of **The Magdeburg Knight** (c1240 – copy), one of the oldest equestrian sculptures in Germany. On the left, is a monument to Otto von Guericke *(see above)*.

St Peter's Hill (Petriberg) – North of the town hall, on the banks of the Elbe. Three churches stand on the riverside rise: The **Chapel of Mary Magdalene**, with a single Gothic nave; St Peter's, a Gothic hall-church with three aisles (1380 1490); and the **Wallonerkirche**, a former abbey church (1285-1366) built by a community which came from the Netherlands (thus its Walloon name).

★ **MAINZ** Rhineland-Palatinate   Pop 180 000

Michelin maps **412** and **413** H 16-17
Plan of the conurbation in the current Michelin Red Guide Deutschland

Formerly the episcopal seat of the influential Prince-Electors, Mainz – elevated in 1949 to be the capital of the Rhine-Palatinate Land – is ideally placed for trade. Situated at the confluence of the Rhine and the Main, the city is Germany's largest and most important wine market. It is also the site of a famous annual carnival, the gaiety and colourful buffoonery of which are televised all over the country *(see Calendar of Events)*. **Gutenberg** (c1394-1468), the father of modern printing, is the city's most prominent son.

Bird's eye view – The restaurant An der Favorite, at the highest point of the **Stadtpark** (**BY**), affords a general view of the city on either side of the Rhine.

CATHEDRAL QUARTER (Z) *time: 2 hours*

> *Leaving the Liebfrauenplatz, walk down the Domstrasse and then left around the cathedral.*

From the Leichhof square, the cathedral in its **entirety★★** can be seen, the west chancel and transept rising loftily, their complex ridge roofs overlooked by the lantern tower which crowns the transept crossing. Baroque as well as Gothic elements adorn the upper part of this tower, which rests on a Romanesque base showing a Lombard influence.

The adjoining square, known as the Höfchen, is extended towards the south by the Gutenbergplatz (statue of the craftsman printer, theatre, House of German Wines) and to the northeast by the market square, embellished with a **Renaissance fountain** (Marktbrunnen) (**Z A**).

> *Enter via the doorway opening onto the market (Marktportal).*

★ **Cathedral** (Dom) – The cathedral is an enormous reconstructed Romanesque building – a basilica with two chancels, one in the west, leading off a wide transept whose crossing is illuminated by a fine Rhenish dome; one in the east of simpler architectural style.

Fixed to the massive Romanesque columns is a collection of archiepiscopal **funerary monuments★** (Grabdenkmäler der Erzbischöfe).

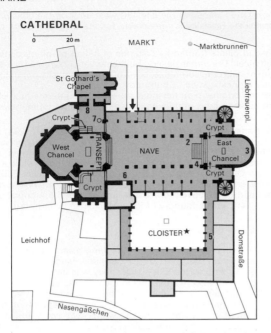

CATHEDRAL

0 — 20 m

MARKT

Marktbrunnen

Liebfrauenpl.

St Gothard's Chapel

Crypt

8 7

West Chancel

TRANSEPT

Crypt

NAVE

1

2

4

East Chancel

3

Crypt

6

Crypt

CLOISTER ★

5

Leichhof

Domstraße

CLOISTER ★

Nasengäßchen

Turn left into the north aisle on entering the church. In the second chapel (**1**), there is a moving late 15C Entombment. A multi-coloured Gothic funerary monument is attached to one of the main pillars (**2**).

In the east crypt, beneath the chancel, a modern **gold reliquary** (**3**) of the Saints of Mainz stands upon the altar.

A pillar (**4**) on the south side of the east chancel steps bears another Gothic funerary monument in many colours, surrounded by statuettes of St Benedict, St Catherine, St Maurice and St Clare.

A door in the south aisle leads to the **cloister★** (Kreuzgang). In addition to the tombstones, there is a bas-relief (**5**), remodelled in 1783, of the master-singer Heinrich von Meissen, known as "Frauenlob" – a man who, having sung the praises of women all his life, was finally laid to rest by the burgesses of Mainz in 1323.

Fine statues adorn the doorway (**6**) of the former Chapter House, built in the 15C in an elegant Rhineland style. Cross the transept below the west chancel steps and go into the opposite arm, where there is a fine 1328 baptismal font in pewter (**7**), ornamented with delicately worked figures. Beyond, a Romanesque doorway (**8**) leads to St Gothard's Chapel, built in the same style with a square plan and a two-storey elevation.

★★ **Gutenberg Museum** (Gutenbergmuseum) (**Z M¹**) ⊘ – The visitor to this museum is reminded how, over the centuries, men of taste and discrimination have nurtured the art of the printed word, regarding it as one of the most precious treasures of civilization, to be guarded and passed on as a sacred trust as its usage developed and spread.

Gutenberg's original hand press is in the basement of the building, along with reconstructions of early print-shops. On the first floor, along with incunabula and ancient presses, there is a collection of editions published between the 16C and the 19C. The museum's prize exhibit, the world-famous **Gutenberg Bible★★★** (1452-55), with 42 lines to the page, is on display in a second floor strong room.

Polychromatic wood engravings and printed works from China, Japan and Korea can be seen in the Far East Department on the third floor.

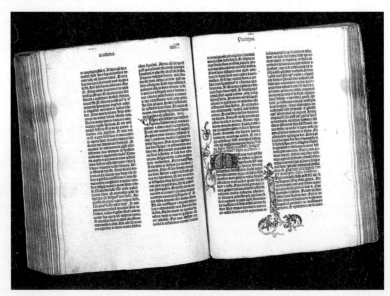

The Gutenberg Bible, Mainz

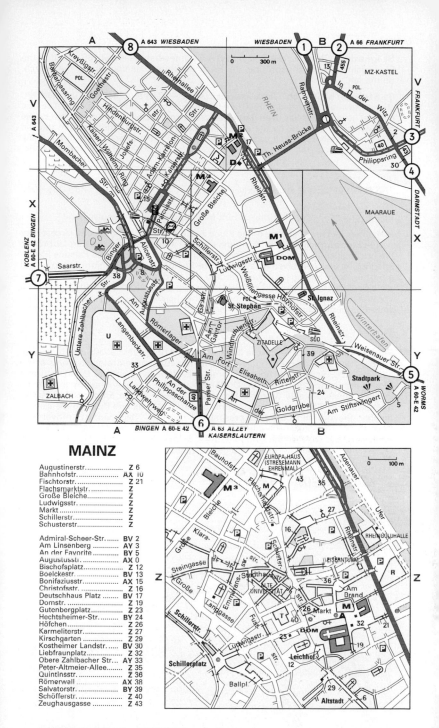

MAINZ

ADDITIONAL SIGHTS

★ **Romano-German Museum** (Römisch-Germanisches Zentralmuseum) (BV M²) ⊘ – Installed in the one-time Electors' Palace (15-17C), this museum unites collections dealing with the Mediterranean civilizations, prehistory and the Barbarians.

★ **Central Rhineland Museum** (Landesmuseum Mainz) (Z M³) ⊘ – The Department of Antiquities traces Rhineland civilization, and especially that of Mainz, from pre-historic times onwards. On display here too is Jupiter's Column (Jupitersäule), the most precious relic of the Roman colonization of Germany. A copy stands in the Deutschhaus Platz (BV D).

Schillerplatz and Schillerstrasse (Z) – The Baroque mansions in this square and street now house (after restoration) the Land's ministries. In the centre of the Schillerplatz, a fountain is decorated with scenes illustrating the carnival.

Old Town (Altstadt) (Z) – Off the Augustinerstrasse, the chief thoroughfare of the old quarter which is virtually intact, opens the picturesque Kirschgarten square, lined with pretty half-timbered houses. The Kapuzinerstrasse (note several houses with sandstone door frames and Rococo panels) leads to the Church of St Ignatius.

St Ignatius' Church (Ignazkirche) (BY) – A somewhat theatrical 16C group of the **Crucifixion**★ (Kreuzigungsgruppe), by Hans Backoffen, stands outside the church, on the left.

St Stephen's Church (Stephanskirche) (ABY) – All that remains of this late 13C church, severely damaged in 1945, are the outside walls and Gothic pillars. The east chancel nevertheless has been garnished with a remarkable series of modern **stained glass windows**★★. These, by the artist Marc Chagall, illustrate themes from the Old and New Testaments. Built against the south wall is a **cloister**★ of which the architecture, especially the vaulting, expresses all the virtuosity of Late Gothic design.

MANNHEIM Baden-Württemberg   Pop 305 000

Michelin map 🔢 H 13
Plan of the conurbation in the current Michelin Red Guide Deutschland

Mannheim, at the confluence of the Rhine and the Neckar, is the second largest river port in Europe (motorboat trips around the port area start from the Kurpfalzbrücke, the bridge spanning the Neckar). The town, founded in 1606 by the Palatine Elector Friedrich IV, was conceived as a fortified residential enclave. Conforming to a rigid plan, the centre comprises a checkerboard of 144 identical blocks (**Quadratstadt**), each identified only by a letter and number according to its coordinates on the city plan. Local enthusiasm for the arts – especially the theatre, where the works of Schiller were first performed – soon made Mannheim a cultural as well as a trade centre.

SIGHTS

★★ **Fine Arts Museum** (Städtische Kunsthalle) (DZ M1) ⊘ – Installed in a Jugendstil building designed by H Billing in 1907, the museum concentrates on works of the 19C and 20C. Statues by Rodin, Lehmbruck, Barlach, Brancusi, Giacometti and Moore occupy the ground floor. On the floor above are paintings by the French Impressionists, notably Manet's famous *Execution of the Emperor Maximilian* and Cézanne's *The Pipe Smoker*. Works by Corot, Monet and Pissarro are also on display. Slevogt and Corinth represent the German "Secessionist" movement. Expressionist paintings include Heckel's *Woman Sleeping*, Kokoschka's **View of Amsterdam**, and work by Beckmann and the Belgian Ensor. Post-1945 art and New Objectivity works are in a separate department.

MANNHEIM

Bahnhofplatz	**DZ** 7	Kurpfalzbrücke	**DY** 31
Bismarckplatz	**DZ** 10	Moltkestraße	**DZ** 38
Dalbergstraße	**CY** 15	Reichskanzler-Müller-Str.	**DZ** 49
Heidelberger Str.	**DZ**	Freherstraße	**CY** 20	Schanzestraße	**CY** 53
Kaiserring	**DZ**	Friedrichsplatz	**DZ** 23	Schloßgartenstraße	**CZ** 56
Kurpfalzstraße	**CDYZ**	Goethestraße	**DY** 25	Seilerstraße	**CY** 61
Planken	**CDYZ**	Konrad-Adenauer-Brücke	**CZ** 30	Spatzenbrücke	**CY** 62

★ **Reiss Municipal Museum** (Museum für Stadtgeschichte im Reiss-Museum) (**CY M²**) ⊘
– *In the Arsenal (Zeughaus: 1777-1779)*. Municipal history and the decorative arts
have pride of place here, but note the 17C Dutch paintings and 18C porcelain.
Writing desks (mainly 18C Baden work) and a collection of 19C bicycles are also
worth seeing.

★ **Museum of Archaeology and Ethnology** (Museum für Archäologie und Völkerkunde im Reiss-Museum) (**CY M³**) – *In a new building opposite the Arsenal*. The
archeological collections here came from the Antiquarium founded in 1763 by the
Prince-Elector Karl-Theodor. They include objects from archeological digs, stone
commemorative monuments from Roman provinces and Greek and Etruscan
vases dating from the Mycenean epoque to the 3C AD. The ethnologic exhibits
concern mainly Indian and Pacific civilizations.

Palace (Schloss) (**CZ**) ⊘ – The building of this Baroque palace, the biggest in all
of Germany (400 rooms, 2 000 windows), lasted from 1720 to 1760. Restored after
heavy damage sustained in the Second World War, the main body of the palace
is occupied today by departments of the university. Two wings at right-angles to
the central block enclose an enormous main courtyard. The palace church terminates the right wing, the former palace library the left.
From the state staircase inside, there is a view down the entire perspective of the
Kurpfalzstrasse, the street that bisects the chessboard centre from one end to the
other, as far as the River Neckar.
The painted ceilings have been restored after the original work of Cosmas Damian
Asam *(qv)*. The same artist was responsible for the ceiling of the church
(Schlosskirche) and the frescoes in the **Knights' Hall** (Rittersaal). The most inter-
esting apartment is the green and rose **Rococo library** in the university wing, which
is embellished with stucco-work, panelling and camaïeu (monochrome) paintings.

Jesuit Church (Jesuitenkirche) (**CZ**) – Founded at the same time as the palace
(building in fact lasted from 1733 to 1769), this massive edifice is said to be the
biggest Baroque church of the Upper Rhine. The façade is classical with the three
orders superimposed. The well-lit interior, faced with stucco-marble, is a little
cold. **The Silver Virgin with her Crown of Light** (Silbermadonna im Strahlenkranz), in
the northern aisle, is the work of the Augsburg silversmith J I Saler (1747).

Boat Museum (Museumsschiff Mannheim) (**DY M⁴**) ⊘ – This museum is installed in
the paddlesteamer *Mainz*, which was built in 1929 and is now moored beneath
the Kurpfalzbrücke, on the Neckar.
The engine room and galley are well worth a visit. Many models are on display,
along with river charts, photographs and equipment illustrating the history of
navigation on the Rhine and Neckar.

★ **Regional Museum of Industrial Techniques** (Landesmuseum für Technik und
Arbeit) ⊘ – *At Museumstrasse 1* (**DZ**). Two hundred and fifty years of industrial
development in southwest Germany are retraced in this modernistic building,
which impresses with the elegance, lightness and transparence of its architecture.
Over 81 000sq ft of floor space, the museum, which was opened in 1990, exam-
ines the relationship between industrialisation and the evolution of society,
together with innumerable demonstrations of the techniques involved (weaving,
papermaking, printing, steam locomotives, etc.).

★★ **MARBURG** Hessen   Pop 75 000

Michelin map **412** J 14
Town plan in the current Michelin Red Guide Deutschland

Marburg was once one of the great pilgrimage centres of the West, crowds being
drawn to the town by the relics of St Elizabeth of Hungary. Since the Reformation,
and still maintaining the magnificent Gothic cathedral dedicated to the Saint,
Marburg has become through its university a centre of Protestant scholarship and
theology.
Wandering through twisting medieval alleys that climb through the old quarters
massed around the castle hill, the visitor is still likely to meet country folk in traditional peasant costume – especially on the Wednesday and Saturday market
days.

St Elizabeth (1207-31) – Princess Elizabeth, daughter of the King of Hungary and
the intended bride of the Landgrave Ludwig of Thuringia, was brought to the
Thuringian court at Wartburg Castle at the age of four. Early in her life she
became known for her kindness to the unfortunate, and there are many stories
concerning the ruses she employed to help them.
In 1227 her husband Ludwig died of the plague, and Elizabeth resolved to with-
draw from the world. She installed herself below Marburg Castle in a house
adjoining the hospital for incurables, of which she took charge. She died of
exhaustion at the age of 24. Canonized four years later (1235), she was to have
her remains exhumed the following year to be immortalized in the superb Gothic
church built by the members of the Teutonic Order *(qv)* to receive them.
In 1527 her descendant, the **Landgrave Philip the Magnanimous**, converted publicly to
Protestantism and decided once and for all to abolish the cult of relics. Personally
forcing the shrine, he had his ancestor's bones removed and buried in a nearby
cemetery.

★★ OLD MARBURG and THE CHURCH OF ST ELIZABETH
time: 2 hours

★★ **St Elizabeth's (Elisabethkirche) (BY)** ⊙ – The first truly German Gothic church, this was built between 1235 and 1283. Its regional character derives from the stylistic unity of the chancel and transepts, each terminating in an apse, and from its three aisles of equal height – making it in fact the first hall-church *(qv)*. Transverse roof timbers covering the side aisles are typically Hessian. The towers, surmounted by stone spires, rest on massive buttresses.

Enter through the main doorway. The chapel beneath the tower immediately on the left contains the tomb of Field-Marshal von Hindenburg (1847-1934).

Nave – Note the following works:

1) A statue of St Elizabeth (*c*1470) wearing an elegant court gown.

2) An openwork Gothic rood with finely decorated consoles; on the altar (nave side), a modern Crucifix by Ernst Barlach.

Chancel and Transepts – A collection of exceptional items★★★:

3) Altarpiece of the Virgin; 1360 Pietà before the predella.

4) Tomb of St Elizabeth (after 1250). The 14C bas-relief on the sarcophagus represents the Saint's burial.

5) The remains of frescoes visible in the niches date from the 14C and 15C. On the right, a scene evoking St Elizabeth's charitable activities (the Landgrave sees in his imagination the Saviour, in a bed in which Elizabeth placed a sick man); the formal exhumation of 1236.

6) St Elizabeth's Shrine★★ (Elisabethschrein) in the old sacristy. This masterpiece of the goldsmith's art was completed by craftsmen from the Rhineland *c*1250. Scenes from the Saint's life enrich the casket's sloping panels.

7) St Elizabeth's Window. Assembled from a collection of 13C medallions, this illustrates the charitable works of the Saint.

8) Above the former priest's seat, a statue of St Elizabeth as the personification of Charity (the work, dating from 1510, is attributed to Juppe, one of the most illustrious Marburg artists).

9) "The Landgraves' Chancel" (in fact the south transept). Necropolis of the Landgraves of Hessen descended from St Elizabeth.

Leaving the church, climb up into the old town by way of the Steinweg – an unusual ramp with three different levels, which continues as the Neustadt and then the Wettergasse. Banners of the various student societies are draped from the windows of the houses in June and July.

Turn right into the Marktgasse.

MARBURG

★ **Marktplatz** (AY) – Only the upper part, the Obermarkt, has retained its ancient half-timbered houses, outstanding among them nos 14 and 21, dating from 1560, and no 23. The market fountain, dedicated to St George, is a popular student's meeting place.

Rathaus (AY R) – A Gothic building built in 1524. Above a door in the staircase tower is a fine Juppe carving representing Elizabeth bearing her arms of the House of Hessen-Thuringia. A mechanical cock crows the hours from an animated clock.

Past the Gothic ossuary (Karner), the Nikolaistrasse now leads to the forecourt of St Mary's Church (Marienkirche - late 13C), from which there is a fine view over the roofs of the old town to the valley beyond. Past the church façade, at the top of a steep slope, there is a glimpse of the castle above.

At the end of the esplanade, a passage leads down to the Kugelkirche, a fine small church in the Late Gothic (end of the 15C) style. Climbing again, the route leads past the Kalbstor fortified gate at the top of the Kugelgasse, turns right into the Ritterstrasse, and finally passes above the Marienkirche to rejoin the Marktplatz. In the Ritterstrasse, at no 15 (**B**), is the house which belonged to the famous legal historian Friedrich Karl von Savigny (1779-1861).

ADDITIONAL SIGHTS

★ **Castle** (AY) ⊙ – From the 13C to the 17C, the castle was the home of the Landgraves of Hessen, descendants of St Elizabeth and Ludwig. From the terrace beside the first entrance esplanade on the south side, there is a view along the Lahn valley to the Taunus heights.

Passing through the historic buildings on top of the spur, the visitor sees the Landgrave's study, a small Gothic chapel with a ceramic floor, and the Gothic Knight's Hall with its double nave, all of them dating from the 13C and 14C.

The **Regional and Art History Museum★** (Museum für Kulturgeschichte), housed in the 15C Wilhelmsbau wing, displays among other things precious artefacts from St Elizabeth's Church (fragments of stained glass, 15C tapestries depicting the story of the Prodigal Son etc.). There is also an exhibition of medieval shields.

There is a pleasant walk through the park at the foot of the buttress.

Fine Arts Museum (Marburger Universitätsmuseum für Bildende Kunst) (BZ M) ⊙ – German paintings from the 16C to the present day are on view here.

★★ MAULBRONN Baden-Württemberg

Michelin map **413** J 19

This was one of the earliest Cistercian foundations in Germany, an enormous abbey complex, very well preserved, with all its outbuildings and dependencies enclosed within a perimeter wall. The school established here since the Reformation (1556) has seen the flowering of such diverse literary and philosophical talents as those of Hölderlin and Hermann Hesse.

★★ ABBEY ⊙ time: 3/4 hour

The abbey was founded in 1147. Embracing the Protestant faith at the time of the Reformation, the abbey escaped any Baroque transformations.

★ **Abbey Church** – This was consecrated in 1178.
The early 13C Paradise Porch (**1**) is the first German example of the Romanesque-Gothic transition.

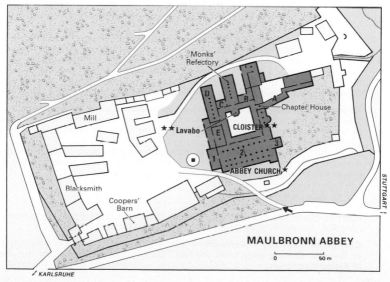

MAULBRONN ABBEY

Inside, the fan vaulting of the nave and south aisle, which was not added until the 15C, spoils the homogeneity of the original Romanesque design. The ten-bay nave is separated into two sections – one for the monks, the other for the lay brothers – by a Romanesque rood-screen (2) of exceptionally pure line, which is topped by a dog-tooth frieze. A large Crucifix (1473) stands before the screen. The chapels off the transept are all that remain of an earlier church. Note a beautiful 14C Virgin to the left of the high altar (3).

★★ **Cloister (Kreuzgang) and Monastery Buildings (Klosterbauten)** – A stroll through the galleries and adjoining rooms unites the pleasures of ancient stones with the poetry of the cloister garden.

The south gallery, running between the church and the close, is designed with slender columns grouped in clusters, a feature noticeable also in the church porch and the monks' refectory.

Opening off the east gallery are the chapter house, whose 14C groined vaulting springs from central pillars, and the parlatory (A), which has fan vaulting.

The early 13C monks' refectory is flanked by the calefactory (B) and the kitchens (C). The massively built refectory seems crushed beneath the early Gothic vaulting with its heavy ribs, despite the fact that this rests on ringed columns that are quite tall. Opposite the entrance door, a charming lavabo★★ (Brunnenkapelle, c1350) with quadri-lobed blind arcades juts out into the cloister garden.

The west gallery leads to the (restored) lay brothers' refectory, where groined vaulting arches low over the two aisles (D), and to the store-room (E). The store-room vaulting is square-ribbed.

Avoid visiting a church during a service.

★ **MEISSEN** Saxony   Pop 36 000

Michelin map ███ fold 18

To understand the development of Meissen, only 15km - 9 miles northwest of Dresden, the foundation of the town has to be placed in the military and historical context of the campaigns waged against the Slav tribes east of the Elbe and the Saale by the King Heinrich I. In the year 929, he fortified a height commanding a strategic ford crossing the Elbe. The fortress was built on a rocky plateau where a tributary, the Triebisch, precipitated itself into the main river. And the town grew up around the foot of the castle hill from the 12C onwards. Since the 18C, of course, Meissen has been famous worldwide for its porcelain.

THE PORCELAIN OF SAXONY

It was in the reign of Augustus the Strong *(qv)* that the alchemist **Johann Friedrich Böttger** (1682-1719) revealed that he had discovered the formula for creating the white hard-paste porcelain until then made only in China. The formula is based on kaolin (china clay), large quantities of which could be – and still are – mined only a short distance northwest of Meissen.

Böttger made the discovery in 1708, although he did not reveal the secret until 29 March 1709. A year later, Augustus, Elector of Saxony and King of Poland, founded the Royal Saxon Porcelain Manufactory, which he installed in the castle – an isolated, well-guarded site well suited to the protection of secrets. Böttger, who had until then produced only hard red stoneware, was its first director.

The Motifs – Initially, the lavish decoration imitated Chinese and Japanese models. The period of plant designs, red and green dragons, a yellow lion, flowers, birds and mythical creatures dates from the directorship of Böttger's successor, Johann Gregorius Höroldt (1720-1755), who was responsible for the factory's first flush of prosperity (Old Saxony).

It was Höroldt who produced the famous **"Blue Onion"** (Zwiebelmuster) tableware design, based on the use of cobalt, which was to become one of the most celebrated glazed designs in the world. Innumerable elegant services, along with individual vases, pots, giant animals and "conversation pieces", were also created by Johann Joachim Kändler (1706-1775). The Ceramic Mark distinguishing Meissen Porcelain is a pair of crossed swords in blue.

★ **National Porcelain Factory** (Staatliche Porzellanmanufaktur) ⊙ – In 1865, the studios and workshops of the Meissen factory were transferred from the castle (Albrechtsburg) where they had been for more than 150 years to a site in the Triebisch Valley.

Today the history of the industry is retraced here via a large number of superb exhibits. In a demonstration workshop, the preparation of paste and the processes of painting, fabrication and firing can be observed.

OLD MEISSEN

Market Place (Markt) – The Late Gothic Town Hall (1472-78) is surrounded by burghers' houses in both Gothic and Renaissance styles.

Church of Our Lady (Frauenkirche) – This three-aisle Late Gothic hall-church with its fine star-vaulting dates from the late 15C. The bells of the carillon are made of Meissen porcelain.

CASTLE HILL (BURGBERG)

The castle, the cathedral and its subsidiary buildings are all grouped on this hill which was the original site of the town.

★ **Castle** (Albrechtsburg) – Arnold von Westfalen, one of the most esteemed architects of late medieval times, was commissioned to build this castle in 1471 by the Margrave Albert. The finished work is considered to be one of the finest civic examples of the Late Gothic style.
The **spiral staircase** (Grosser Wendelstein) adorning the façade is a model of its kind. Although the castle housed the porcelain factory from 1710 to 1865, most of the exhibits on view in the elegant, frescoed apartments are purely historical or concerned with other types of art – principally German painting of the 16C.

★ **Cathedral** (Dom) – Another Gothic hall with a transept and three naves, this church was built from 1260 onwards on the remains of a Romanesque sanctuary and not completed until the end of the 15C. Early 16C sketches for bronze **funerary plaques★** in the Dukes' Chapel (Fürstenkapelle) are said to be due in part to Albrecht Dürer and Lucas Cranach the Elder, and came from the famous Peter Vischer studio in Nuremberg. In front of the rood screen, sculpted between 1260 and 1270 in Naumburg, is the **Lay Brothers' Altar★** (Laienaltar), which is again due to Cranach the Elder. The **Benefactors' Statues★★** (Stifterfiguren) in the chancel, from the same studio, represent the Emperor Otto I and his second wife, the Empress Adelaide. In style, they are reminiscent of the statues in the chancel of Naumburg Cathedral.
The Cathedral Square (Domplatz) is surrounded by **monastic buildings**. The Dean's residence, at no 5, dates from 1526; next door at no 6 is the Canons' House (1728); and the Priory (c1500) is at no 7.

MEMMINGEN Bavaria   Pop 38 000

Michelin map 413 N 23
Town plan in the current Michelin Red Guide Deutschland

Medieval gateways crowned with "helmet" roofs and traces of earlier fortifications still survive in Memmingen, a former imperial town in the Allgäu Pre-Alps.

Old Town – This lies on either side of the stream canalized through the city centre. Its character is exemplified by such ancient buildings as **The House with Seven Roofs** (Siebendächerhaus), once the tanners' headquarters. Interesting buildings also surround the Marktplatz: the **Steuerhaus**, dating from 1495, with its ground floor opened by arcades; the 1589 **Town Hall**, which was remodelled in the Rococo style in 1765. The design of this is unusual, with three oriel windows on different floors, each with an onion dome.

St Martin's Church – Gothic in origin, this church had its chancel elegantly modified at the end of the 15C. Inside, the **choir stalls★** (Chorgestühl), dating from 1507, are intricately carved with figures of the prophets, sybils and church benefactors.

Kreuzherrenkirche – *On the Hallhof Square*. The final octagon on the 1617 belfry surpasses the town's other towers in the refinement of its decoration.

MERSEBURG Saxony-Anhalt   Pop 50 000

Michelin map 987 fold 17

An episcopal town since the end of the 10C and seat of the Dukes of Saxe-Merseburg from 1685 to 1738, Merseburg has enjoyed a substantial industrial development during the present century. Symbolizing the commercial success of this small town is the gigantic Buna petro-chemical complex (synthetic rubbers, hydro-carbon derivatives), which was built in 1936 a little way to the south. The most interesting historic monuments, the cathedral and the castle, stand on a hill (Domberg) overlooking the Saale river.

SIGHTS

★★ **Cathedral** (Dom) – Three separate styles can be distinguished in this church. The crypt testifies to the Romanesque origins of the earliest structure; the porch, transept, apse and chancel owe their early Gothic character to remodelling carried out in the first half of the 13C; and the three-aisle nave, originally Romanesque, was transformed between 1500 and 1517 into the purest of High Gothic, with reticulated vaulting and slender octagonal pillars.
The **pulpit★** (1514-1526) is richly carved in a fashion distinctively Late Gothic. The bronze **funerary plaque★** plaque of King Rudolph of Swabia (d 1080), which is in the choir, is remarkable for the elegance of its workmanship.

Castle (Schloss) – This building, frequently modified, offers a variety of styles: Late Gothic in the east wing; Renaissance in the north and west wings; and Baroque on the upper part of the west wing.

EUROPE on a single sheet: Michelin Map no 970.

Michelin maps 🔢 and 🔢 J 10
Town plan in the current Michelin Red Guide Deutschland

An important junction at the Porta Westfalica gap, the last point on the Weser before the river, the road and the railway branch out across the north German plain, Minden has long been a key crossroads on Europe's trade routes.

SIGHTS

★ **Cathedral (Dom)** – The Romanesque **Westwerk★★** *(qv)* is beautiful. It is preceded by a porch and fretted with delicate blind arcades, above which rises the great wall of the belfry.
The interior is notable for the rounded Westphalian-style vaulting which covers the transept, and for the chancel's tiered Romanesque blind arcades in the Rhineland tradition. A copy of the celebrated Minden Cross hangs on the left-hand pillar of the transept crossing (the original is in the cathedral treasury). An altarpiece by a Westphalian master representing the Crucifixion (1480) is in the chancel. The Frieze of the Apostles (c1250), now in the south transept, once crowned the cathedral rood-screen.

★ **Cathedral Treasury (Domschatzkammer)** ⊙ – *On the right-hand side of the West-werk.* Under cover. Aside from the **Minden Cross★★** masterpiece (a Crucifix dating from the second half of the 11C), a very fine Virgin in Majesty (the Silberne Madonna: 1250) is on display along with a beautifully worked gold reliquary dating from 1070. Episcopal awards and liturgical items (13C-18C) are on view in glass cases.

Local History Museum (Mindener Museum für Geschichte, Landes- und Volkskunde) ⊙ – *Ritterstrasse 23-31.* Apart from prehistoric and archeological departments, this museum offers a fine selection of traditional regional costumes, interiors in the Biedermeier style, and reconstituted craft workshops and studios (shoemakers, photographers, leatherworkers, cobblers, etc.). In the department of military history there is a diorama model of the battle of Minden in 1759, when the English, allied with the Prussians, beat the French during the Seven Years War.

By way of the Marienstrasse, drive out of town in the direction of Bremen. Soon after the bridge over the canal, turn right and continue around the dock basin after crossing the Great Lock. There is a visitors' car park after the bridge.

★★ **Great Lock (Schachtschleuse)** – This engineering marvel, 85m - 280ft long and 10m - 33ft wide, lowers or raises shipping between the canal and the Weser, 14m - 46ft below. A small museum explains the operation of the Weser basin, the management of its course and the current work on the Mittelland-Kanal.

Return to the car and continue around the port. After the exit from a tunnel beneath the canal, it is possible to climb, on foot, up the embankment and reach the aqueduct towpath.

★ **Aqueduct (Kanalbrücke)** – This 375m - 410yd aqueduct has enabled canal traffic to treat the 211km - 131 miles separating Münster from Hanover as a single reach, obviating the necessity of any more locks.

Return to Minden via the Werftstrasse.

EXCURSION

Porta Westfalica – *Tour of 28km - 17 miles. Leave Minden via the Portastrasse, ④ on the town plan. At Barkhausen, take a right turn towards Porta Denkmal.*

Wilhelm Denkmal – There is a fine view of the Weser Gap from the foot of this enormous statue, raised to the memory of the Emperor Wilhelm I in 1896.

Return to Barkhausen, take Route 61 on the right and cross the Weser in the direction of the Porta Westfalica. Follow the signs: Fernsehturm.

Television Tower (Fernsehturm) – Built on the site of the former Bismarckturm, the tower has 129 steps which lead to a viewing platform. The panorama visible from this terrace embraces the Porta Westfalica gap with its intense road and rail traffic, the Wilhelm I monument, the town of Minden and the north German plain. The horizon is blocked on the east by the Wesergebirge, and towards the south by the Lippisches Bergland.

Return to Minden via Route 482.

Michelin map 🔢 C 13
Town plan in the current Michelin Red Guide Deutschland

A Benedictine abbey founded in 974 was at the origin of this thriving industrial town. The oldest part, bordered on the south by the Parish Church of the Assumption (Hauptpfarrkirche St Mariä Himmelfahrt), lies around the **Alter Markt**, behind which are the cathedral and the ancient abbey buildings. The former Prelate's residence, dating from the 17C, is well preserved and serves today as the Town Hall. To the southwest of the old market, stepped alleys and cobbled streets lead down to the park through a quarter where there are still traces of the old medieval fortifications, notably the **Dicker Turm** (Great Tower).

SIGHTS

Abteiberg Municipal Museum (Städtisches Museum Abteiberg) – *At no 27 Abteistrasse*. The use of space and light in this modern building, with its complex, overlapping and interlinked storeys, makes it an ideal site for the exhibition of 20C art. Expressionism is represented by Pechstein, Kirchner, Heckel and Rohlfs; Constructivism by Willi Baumeister. But above all it is the post-1950 avant-garde who predominate: Pien, Mack and Uecker of the Group Zero, Warhol's and Palermo's Pop Art, and exponents of Op Art, the New Realism, Conceptual Art and Process Art (many exhibits by Beuys and sculptures by Richard Serra).

Cathedral of St Vitus (former Abbey Church) – The church, a marriage of the Gothic and the Romanesque, overlooks the southern flank of the hill (Abteiberg). The powerful three-tower ensemble of the Westwerk *(qv)* dates from 1183, while the three aisles of the long nave, with their quadripartite vaulting supported on massive pillars, were constructed between 1228 and 1239. The Gothic chancel (1256-1277) was designed by Master Gerhard, the chief architect of Cologne Cathedral. The oldest part of this particular building is the great Romanesque **crypt-hall** (*c*1100) which lies beneath the choir. A Romanesque baptismal stone remains in the Apostles' Chapel. The **treasury** (Schatzkammer) is reached through the northern part of the cloister.

Rheydt Castle – *Leave the town centre southwards via Theodor-Heuss-Strasse and then take a left turn into the Breite Strasse-Ritterstrasse*.
A moated Renaissance castle, Rheydt was originally built with four wings, of which only two survive. Inside, a **museum** displays arts and crafts from the 16C to the 18C, along with archeological collections relating to the history of Mönchengladbach and a department illustrating the development of weaving.

EXCURSION

★ **Dyck Castle** ⊙ – *9km - 5 miles to the east*.
The buildings of this small 17C castle are arranged around a square central courtyard with a tower surmounted by an onion dome at each corner. The ground floor rooms inside are embellished with magnificent Chinese hangings originally ordered by the Empress Maria-Theresa of Austria. There is a remarkable **arms collection** (from the workshops of armourers employed by the Counts of Dyck).
A 20ha - 50-acre park invites the visitor to stroll among plantations of many rare species of bushes and trees.

★★ **MONSCHAU** Rhineland-Westphalia   Pop 12 000

Michelin map **412** B 15

From a **belvedere**★★ lay-by on Route 258, coming from Aachen, there is a superb view of this ancient Eifel village, with its tall, narrow, slate-roofed houses huddled together at one end of a winding gorge carved from the rock by the Rur river. The **half-timbered façades**★★ (Fachwerkhäuser) of the old buildings overlook the stream and crowd the twisting streets.
Leaving the market place via the Unterer Mühlenberg slope, on the right of the Kaular café, turn right again along the Knieberg and climb to the chapel (Friedhofkapelle) which lies beyond the cemetery. From here, again, there is a good **view**★ of the town, the castle, and the ruins of the Haller watchtower.
The oldest part of Monschau is in the Kirchstrasse quarter (note especially the period house at no 33, which is faced with slate).

Troistorff House – *Laufenstrasse 18*. A solid, well-preserved house built by a linen merchant in 1783.

Red House (Rotes Haus) – Originally inhabited by a rich draper, this 1762 building retains its full 18C **interior decor**★, which forms part of the **local museum** ⊙ now installed there. Note the magnificent carved oak staircase.

EXCURSION

The North Eifel Lakes – *85km - 53 miles - allow 1/2 day*.
Still on Route 258, leave Monschau. The road rises rapidly, and after 1 mile there is yet another **belvedere** from which a bird's-eye view of the village can be enjoyed. From Imgenbroich onwards, particularly between Strauch and Schmidt, there are attractive glimpses, on the right, of the Rur lake region. Leaving Schmidt, the Nideggen ruin lies straight ahead.
Nideggen – Until the 15C the rose-coloured sandstone **castle** ⊙ – a true "eagle's nest" site – was the residence of the Counts and Dukes of Jülich, after which it fell into disuse. From the 12C keep (partially restored and turned into a **museum** – Burgenmuseum – devoted to the castles and fortresses of the Eifel), there are fine **views**★ to the south of the Rur valley cutting into the Eifel plateau, and of the Aachen basin to the north. The restored 12C church has a Romanesque chancel with frescoes.
★ **Rur Dam** (Rurtalsperre) – In a wild stretch of country, the Stausee artificial lake, known also as the Schwammenauel, forms with the Urft reservoir to the south the largest stretch of water in the Eifel. **Motorboat services** operate on each of them.
The road crosses the dam to enter the Kermeter forest. From Einruhr, the route skirts the southern end of the Rursee, which is overlooked from a viewpoint laid out at the top of the hill beyond.

Michelin map **412** folds 20 and 21

The wide, peaceful curves of the River Moselle flow between two massifs of Rhineland schist, the Eifel to the west and the Hunsrück to the east. Most of the steep slopes are planted with wonderful vines, producing dry white wines largely from Riesling stock. Here the schistous subsoil plays a vital part in the maturing of the grapes, the decomposed rock absorbing heat during the day and breathing it out at night among the vines. The harvest is late and sometimes continues until the Feast of St Nicholas (6 December).

The wines are light, sometimes pungent, but with an extremely delicate bouquet. The further north the vines are planted, the more acid the wine becomes.

The river, canalized from Thionville onwards, comprises twelve separate sectors, the locks beside each dam taking barges of up to 1 500 tons, or towed convoys of 3 200 tons. On this navigable part of the Moselle popular cruises ⊙ between Trier and Koblenz are available.

FROM TRIER TO KOBLENZ *195km - 121 miles - one day*

★★ **Trier** – *See under Trier.*

Neumagen-Dhron – This town is known for its Roman discoveries, which have been transported to the Rhine Museum at Trier. A copy of the famous *Wine Ship* can be seen beside the chapel opposite the Weinhaus café.

★ **Bernkastel-Kues** – *See under Bernkastel-Kues.*
One magnificent vineyard follows another on this route. Note the oversize sundials (Sonnenuhr) fixed here and there to bare rock outcrops, which have given their names to some of the better-known vintages (Wehlen and Zeltingen, for instance).
The road passes through many villages typical of this wine-growing region: **Ürzig**, **Kröv**, **Enkirch** and **Pünderich** among them. From Enkirch, make a 5km - 3-mile detour to **Starkenburg**. From the terrace there, there is a splendid **view**★ over the river's lazy Mont-Royal meanders.
3km - 1 3/4 miles after the bridge at **Zell**, which offers a fine perspective of the riverside houses lining the bank on the far side of the water, take the left turn in the direction of Marienburg.

Marienburg – The old convent here stood in an exceptional **setting**★★ overlooking the narrowest stretch of land enclosed by the river bend at Zell. From the restaurant terrace and the wooden tower *(follow the footpath: 3/4 hour Rtn)*, there are impressive **views**★★ of the various curves in the course of the river, and the vineyards on either side.

Beilstein – This tiny fortified town, whose last squire was the Chancellor Metternich, is huddled at the foot of a huge church and an enormous castle. From the ruins of the **castle** ⊙ *(1/2 hour Rtn on foot, from the Liesenich road)* there is, again, a splendid **view**★ of the ever-curving valley.

Cochem – Leave the car on the outskirts and follow the river bank to discover one of the most celebrated **sites**★★ of the Rhineland: towering above the river, the castle crowns a conical hill entirely covered with vines.

Of the original **castle** (Reichsburg) ⊙ *(1/2 hour on foot Rtn, from the Marktplatz)*, only the keep and the foundations of the walls remained after the destructions of 1689 – but the ruins were rebuilt in 14C style during the 19C, bristling with turrets and pinnacles. The **interior** has been re-furnished in an opulent "feudal" manner.

Treis-Karden – The **Church of St Castor**, in the Karden quarter, exemplifies a transitional style halfway between Rhineland Romanesque (the "dwarf gallery" in the apse) and Gothic (ribbed vaulting). Inside, there is a 1420 high-altarpiece in carved wood representing the Three Magi and, in the chapel on the left-hand side of the chancel, small wooden shrin to St Castor in the Gothic style (1490).

Cochem

★★ **Eltz Castle** ⊙ – *10km - 6 miles from Hatzenport, plus 1/2 hour on foot or 5 min by bus*.

From the promontory at the first hairpin bend after the car park, there is an awe-inspiring view looking down on this romantic **site**: the fortress, spined with towers and turrets, pinnacles and spires, rises majestically above the trees at the far end of the wild Eltz valley. There are period furnishings inside, as well as weapons and armour.

Returning to the main road, the visitor soon sees the twin-tower silhouette of Thurant Castle on the east bank of the river. At **Kobern-Gondorf**, not long before the final twist in the river, the road passes right through an enormous restored 15-17C castle – one of two overlooking this stylish small town and blending remarkably well with the landscape. The upper castle, a plain square keep, adjoins the polygonal Romanesque Chapel of St Matthias.

★ **Koblenz** – *See under Koblenz.*

★ # MÜHLHAUSEN Thuringia   Pop 43 000

Michelin map **412** O 13

The name of Mühlhausen figures in a manuscript dated as early as 775. Established as a Free City of the Holy Roman Empire in 1180, the town was incorporated in the Hanseatic League from 1418 onwards. Its prosperity was based on a trade in leatherwork, beer and cotton goods.

Mühlhausen had a more historic role to play in the 16C when **Thomas Müntzer**, a local preacher, fomented a peasant rising against the feudal overlords. He was beheaded in the town's main square once the insurrection was put down (1525). Spared the fate of so many German towns at the end of the Second World War, Mühlhausen today still conserves the flavour of its restoration after the terrible fire which ravaged it in 1689. The houses in the best state of preservation are to be seen along the **Herren-Strasse**, the **Holzstrasse**, and in the quarter around **All Saints' Church** (Allerheiligenkirche), by the Steinweg.

SIGHTS

★ **Town Walls** (Stadtmauer) – Built in the 13C, this peripheral fortification is still largely intact, the passageway crowning its ramparts turned into a promenade. Start the tour at the Frauentor, at the end of the Herren-Strasse.

★ **St Mary's Church** (Marienkirche) – Apart from Erfurt Cathedral, this is the largest church in Thuringia. Its tower reaches a height of 86m - 282ft. The 14C exterior is notable for the exuberance of its decoration: gargoyles, statues, cornices, pinnacles and gables rival each other in the elegance and inventiveness of their design. Oddly placed on the south porch balustrade are the statues of the Emperor Karl IV and his wife. Fashioned between 1360 and 1380, these came from the Parler studios in Prague.

Inside the church, with its five aisles, the **folding altarpieces★** are finely crafted, especially the one depicting the life of St Nicholas and that relating to the Crowning of the Virgin. The latter, dating from 1530, betrays in its treatment of faces the strong influence of Lucas Cranach the Elder. On the western pillars of the transept crossing, note The Adoration of the Magi (early 16C): the treatment of draperies and the bearing of the figures already hints at the Renaissance. Thomas Müntzer, who preached in this church, lived nearby, at no 1 Herren-Strasse.

Town Hall (Rathaus) – *Ratsstrasse*. This comprises blocks built at different times between the 14C and the 19C. The main block (16C) houses the former prison, a wine cellar (Ratsstube), and the local council chamber.

St Blaise's Church (Blasiuskirche) – *Johann-Sebastian-Bach-Platz*. In 1707 and 1708, Bach was organist at this church, which was built between 1235 and 1260 and transformed into a three-aisle Gothic hall in the first half of the 14C. Worth seeing: the mid-14C stained glass windows in the choir; the Late Gothic central reredos, executed by craftsmen from Erfurt.

★★ MÜNDEN Lower Saxony   Pop 28 000

Michelin maps **411** and **412** L 12
Town plan in the current Michelin Red Guide Deutschland

Once known as Hannoversch Münden, this town with its numerous **half-timbered houses★★** lies where the Fulda and the Werra converge to flow on as the Weser. The most interesting buildings are to be found in the streets between the town hall and the Werra.

★ **Town Hall** – The main façade of this building is a typical Weser Renaissance design *(qv)*, its gables adorned with scrollwork, pyramids and statues.

St Blaise's Church – Modified into a Gothic hall in the late 15C, this church with its steep slate roof is overlooked by a hexagonal tower. Inside, the south aisle contains the tomb of Wilhelm of Brunswick (d 1503), and there is an epitaph to his son in the northern part of the chancel. In the north aisle: a 14C baptismal font.

EXCURSION

★ **Upper Weser Valley** – *67km - 42 miles - allow 2 hours.*
From Münden to Bad Karlshafen, the Weser twists through a heavily wooded valley. In this otherwise deserted stretch of country, French Huguenot refugees gathered together in the 18C by the Landgraves of Hessen founded a number of villages baptised with such symbolically pious names as Gottstreu (Fidelity to the Creator) and Gewissensruh (Conscience in Repose). The valley is still without industry or railway.

Wahlsburg-Lippoldsberg – The old abbey church of Lippoldsberg (Ehemalige Klosterkirche) was one of the first vaulted Romanesque churches erected in northern Germany.

Take the ferry across to the other side of the river.

Gewissensruh – Visit the tiny temple (1779) here. Note French inscriptions on the houses.

Bad Karlshafen – The town was founded in 1699 by the Landgrave Karl of Hessen and peopled with French refugees. It lies around a shipping basin at the confluence of the Weser and the Diemel. A regular plan and uniform building design lend the place something of a monumental air. There is a small **Huguenot Museum** ⊙ (Deutsches Hugenotten-Museum, Hafenplatz 9a).

Fürstenberg – Since 1747, world-famous porcelain has been created at the castle-factory here. Particularly fine pieces can be admired at the **porcelain museum** ⊙, along with an explanation of the manufacturing techniques (film video).

Höxter – Renaissance and Baroque unite in the gay, colour-washed houses of this town, with their decorated wooden side walls and roofs of pink sandstone tiles. The most picturesque and pretty line the **Westerbachstrasse**. In St Kilian's Church, there is an outstanding **Renaissance pulpit★★** (1597) adorned with rare alabaster motifs.

Corvey – The only part of the original Carolingian **abbey church** that remains is the impressive Westwerk *(qv)*. The lower parts can be traced back to the 9C. Above the pre-nave entrance is a square church, two storeys high, into which opened – according to unconfirmed tradition – a gallery reserved for the Emperor. The history of Corvey is outlined in a **museum** at the castle.

★★★ MUNICH (MÜNCHEN) Bavaria　　　　Pop 1 300 000

Michelin map **413** R 22
Plan of the conurbation in the current Michelin Red Guide Deutschland

The Bavarian capital, one of the largest, most important cities in Germany, lies not far from the Alps. Munich is not only a first-class cultural centre but also the most flourishing economic zone in the southern part of the country. Especially in recent years, the development of high-tech industries allied to the production of automobiles, locomotives, rubber, chemicals and machine tools has enormously increased the commercial influence of the town. Nor have such trades as printing, publishing and craftwork been ignored: exhibitions such as the International Crafts Fair (Handwerkmesse) attract almost 2 500 exhibitors each year, and the products of Munich's Breweries are known worldwide.

The choice of Munich as seat of the European Patents Office (opened in 1980) recognizes the city's illustrious scientific past, resounding with such famous names as Fraunhofer, Liebig, Ohm and Sauerbruch.

Among writers working in Munich were Lion Feuchtwanger, Thomas Mann, Frank Wedekind and Ludwig Thoma – the last two also being collaborators in the production of the satirical weekly Simplicissimus. It is however in the absurd, surrealistic logic of the comedian Karl Valentin that the spirit of Munich most popularly expresses itself.

With the foundation of the review Jugend in 1896, the city became the centre of the Jugendstil movement *(qv)*; and then, after the Blauer Reiter *(qv)* exhibition in 1911, one of the meccas of modern art.

Munich's cultural wealth, its special atmosphere – a blend of gaiety, tolerance and respect for tradition – and the beauty of the surrounding countryside have combined to make it one of the most appreciated German cities.

General view of Munich

HISTORICAL NOTES

The foundation of the town – A small village founded in the 9C near a Benedictine abbey identified itself by taking the name of the monks – in German Mönch, in Old High German Muniche. Ever since, the town's emblem has been a little monk (Münchner Kindl).

In 1156 the Emperor Frederick Barbarossa ceded a part of Bavaria to Henry the Lion, Duke of Saxony. Two years later, the Duke decided to take for himself the salt trade taxes formerly levied by the Bishop of Freising, and to this end destroyed the bridge, warehouse and customs building set up six miles from the town. He then built a new bridge over which traders had to pass, forcing all commercial transactions into the town. The stratagem, subsequently legalized by Barbarossa, proved to be the beginning of a long and flourishing history for Munich, which until then had been no more than a cluster of unimportant houses.

The Rise of the Wittelsbachs – In 1180 Henry the Lion was stripped of his titles and banished from his lands in southern Germany. Barbarossa replaced him with the Palatine Count Otto von Wittelsbach, and from then on that house became closely linked with Bavaria. In 1225 Munich became the ducal seat. In 1314 one of the Dukes, Ludwig the Bavarian, became King of Germany, and then Emperor (1328). After the demise of the Wittelsbachs of Landshut in 1503, Munich was created the sole capital of the Bavarian Duchy, rivalling as a trade centre both Augsburg and Nuremberg.

In 1623, Duke Maximilian I exercised the function of Prince-Elector and made the town, during the Thirty Years War, the bastion of German Catholicism. During the 17C and 18C, religious and civil architecture sprang up everywhere: the Theatine Church, Nymphenburg Castle, the Church of the Holy Spirit, the Asam Brothers' Church and the Ducal Theatre among them. The ramparts were demolished and replaced by spacious, well-laid-out gardens, the finest of them in the English style.

203

The Kings of Bavaria – It was under the enlightened rulers of the 19C that Munich reached its artistic zenith. **Max Joseph** (1799-1825), who had at first remained neutral in the conflict opposing Napoleon and the European coalition, finally took sides with the latter – a ploy which rewarded him in 1806 with the crown of Bavaria under the name of **Maximilian I**. Despite the Napoleonic wars, in which large numbers of Bavarian troops were involved, Munich continued to flourish, embellished now with monuments in the classical style, such as the Palace of Prince Karl and the buildings of the Karolinenplatz and the Brienner Strasse.

Maximilian's son, **Ludwig I** (1825-48), a great admirer of classical antiquity, welcomed to his court the best of Europe's architects, painters and sculptors. In his desire to make his capital the most beautiful in Europe, he enriched the city with the Old and the New Pinakothek, the university, the Glyptothek and the Propylaea. He cut a swathe through the old town with the construction of the Ludwigstrasse and greatly enlarged the ducal residence. But in 1848, faced with a rebel movement provoked by the scandal of his liaison with the Spanish dancer Lola Montez, he was obliged to abdicate in favour of his son, Maximilian. A younger son, Otto, had already become King of Greece (1832).

Maximilian II (1848-1864) continued the artistic traditions of his father, founding in 1855 the Bavarian National Museum.

In the history of the Wittelsbach dynasty, a special place must be reserved for **Ludwig II** (1864-1886). This tormented romantic, a passionate admirer of Wagner, succeeded to the throne at the age of 18. Beloved by his subjects, he was nevertheless restless and unpredictable, a young man a prey to extreme depression – especially in the face of political setbacks. After his disastrous choice of an alliance with Austria (their combined armies were beaten by the Prussians at Sadowa in 1866), he switched sides a year later and supported the proclamation of Prussia's Wilhelm I as Emperor of all Germany. But the young ruler, craving solitude and living in a fantasy world, largely withdrew from his court and built himself the three extravagant and isolated castles of Neuschwanstein, Linderhof and Herrenchiemsee. Mentally unstable, Ludwig II (whose tragic life has been the subject of books and films) was deposed in 1886 and confined to Berg Castle, on the shores of Starnberg Lake. He was found drowned there shortly afterwards.

In the absence of a direct heir – and in face of the fact that the younger brother Otto, the King of Greece, was also mentally deranged – the son of Ludwig I, **Prince Luitpold**, assumed the Regency. An able and inventive man, always open to new ideas, the Regent improved the Bavarian capital with a zoological garden, an ethnographic museum, a new town hall, the German Museum and the impressive avenue named after him, the Prinzregentenstrasse. His son, crowned as **Ludwig III** (1912-1918), was the last King of Bavaria: under pressure from a workers' revolutionary movement after the defeat of Germany in the First World War, he was forced to abdicate.

In between two wars – The months following the cessation of hostilities were turbulent with strife, nowhere more so than in Munich. In February 1919 Kurt Eisner, the social democrat Bavarian President, was assassinated. A month earlier, Adolf Hitler's **German Workers' party** had been formed and its aims announced by the leader at the Munich Hofbräuhaus. Meanwhile, a republican **Council of State** had been proclaimed, only to be annihilated by Imperial troops in May of the same year.

In 1923, Hitler and Ludendorff fomented a popular uprising, but it was unsuccessful, the party was dissolved and Hitler imprisoned. Released before the sentence had run its term, he reorganized the group as the National Socialist (Nazi) Party. After he had become Chancellor, it was Munich that Hitler chose in 1938 for the notorious meeting with Chamberlain, Daladier and Mussolini at which the annexation by Germany of the Sudetenland was agreed.

LIFE IN MUNICH

The most animated part of the town is concentrated in the pedestrian precincts of the Neuhauser Strasse and the Kaufingerstrasse, between the Karlsplatz (or "Stachus") and the town hall. The most elegant shops, however, are to be found along the Maffeistrasse, the Pacellistrasse, the Maximilianstrasse and the Brienner Strasse. Beneath the colonnades of the Hofgartenstrasse are the art galleries, and most of the antique dealers congregate near the Maximilianplatz, in the Ottostrasse. The Schwabing quarter (via the Ludwigstrasse **KLY**), deployed around the Leopoldstrasse, enjoyed its hour of glory as the city's artistic and intellectual hub at the turn of the century – but with its boutiques, its pavement cafés and its nightspots remains one of the most brilliant and lively after-dark centres in Germany.

Munich Food – Local specialities include the white sausages known as Weisswurst, roast knuckle of pork (Schweinshaxe) and Leberkäs, a meat and offal pâté which can be bought in slices, hot, from most of the butchers any time after 11am. Customarily these dishes are accompanied by Semmelknödel, a bread-based dumpling. At the beer festivals, a favourite offering is Steckerlfisch (small fish grilled on a skewer). Black radishes (Radi), bretzels and Munich Salzstangen (small salt rolls) are often served with beer.

Carnival time
The Crazy Days (Tolle Tage) preceeding Ash Wednesday are the occasion for a series of boisterous, fun-loving carnivals. Parades, processions, decorated floats, street parties, painted faces and fancy dress are all part of the fun.

Beer – Five million hectolitres - 110 000 000 gallons of beer are brewed in Munich every year, most of it being drunk in the brasseries, taverns and beergardens of the town itself. There is a season of strong beers, starting in March. The names of these more alcoholic drinks ("Which at least" – as the local people say – "help us to get through Lent!") are distinguished by the suffix "-ator". The arrival of the month of May is celebrated by the drinking of Maibock.

Holidays and Feast Days – The term Fasching is the Munich name for a carnival traditional throughout western Germany and the southwest (where it is known as Fastnacht). Starting in early January, it is a period of unbridled and uninhibited public merriment, frequently involving masked costume balls, both indoors and outdoors.

Munich beer tankard

The origins of the famous early autumn **Oktoberfest**, which is held on the **Theresenwiese** (via the Mozartstrasse **JZ**) goes back to the official engagement of the heir to the throne, Prince Ludwig, and Princess Theresa in 1810. Almost 7 million visitors flock to Munich each year for this gigantic public fair, for which the local breweries produce a special drink, the Wiesnbier, delivered in the old style by horse-drawn drays. Under canvas marquees and in stands ranged around the base of a huge statue representing Bavaria, nearly 5 million tankards of this beer are handed out during the festivities. The party is complemented by roasts of poultry and beef (two entire oxen are cooked on a spit each day). The Oktoberfest goes on for 16 days. **Corpus Christi** (Fronleichnam) is the most important religious holiday of the year. An immense procession winds its way through beflagged streets garlanded with branches of young birch trees, the vast crowd preceded by the clergy and members of the religious orders, Roman Catholic personalities, Catholic student organizations and representatives of the various city guilds.

★★ OLD TOWN (ALTSTADT) allow one day

The tour indicated starts at the Karlstor.

Richard Strauss Fountain (Richard-Strauss-Brunnen) (KZ A) – Bas-reliefs on the central column illustrate scenes from the opera *Salome*, which the famous Munich composer wrote in 1905.

St Michael's Church (Michaelskirche) (KYZ B) – This Jesuit sanctuary was built between 1583 and 1597 on the model of the society's Roman church (Gesù). Each tier of the Renaissance façade is decorated with pilasters; the niches contain statues of those Bavarian sovereigns most devoted to the Roman Catholic cause. Between the two entrances, St Michael vanquishes the dragon.
The single nave – which inspired many builders of the Vorarlberg Baroque school – is covered by a colossal cradle vault resting on massive pillars abutting the walls. The tomb of Eugène de Beauharnais is in the north transept. Thirty of the Wittelsbach princes, including Ludwig II of Bavaria, are buried in the **crypt** (Fürstengruft).

★ **German Hunting and Fishing Museum** (Deutsches Jagd- und-Fischereimuseum) **(KZ M1)** ⊘ – The museum, housed in a disused Augustinian church (1618-1621), displays on three different levels a splendid collection of ancient and modern arms, trophies (including the skeleton of a giant Irish stag from the Stone Age), paintings and drawings of hunting scenes, and stuffed animals. Different species of freshwater fish, stuffed and mounted, are shown in their separate groups against a diorama.

★ **Church of Our Lady** (Frauenkirche) (KZ) – The architect of this vast Late Gothic hall-church (1468-1488) was **Jörg von Halspach**, who also designed the old town hall. The exterior of the church, in dark red brick, is extremely sober; only the side entrances and tombstones built into the walls break the monotony of the tall façades. The onion domes, which since 1525 have crowned the two towers at the west end (99 and 100m - 325 and 328ft), have become the symbol of the city.

Interior – In striking contrast to the exterior, the nave, a dazzling white, impresses at once with its simplicity and its height. Eleven pairs of powerful octagonal pillars support the reticulated vaulting. Seen from the entrance, the perspective of these columns forms a continuous line, effectively hiding the aisles.

MÜNCHEN

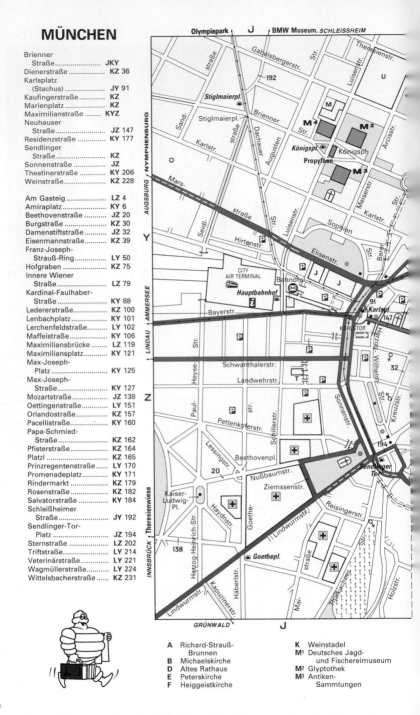

A	Richard-Strauß-Brunnen	**K**	Weinstadel
B	Michaelskirche	**M¹**	Deutsches Jagd- und Fischereimuseum
D	Altes Rathaus		
E	Peterskirche	**M²**	Glyptothek
F	Heiggeistkirche	**M³**	Antiken-Sammlungen

Furnishing and works of art blend the old and the new. Thus the 24 carved wood busts representing the Apostles, the Saints and the Prophets, attributed to the early 15C sculptor **Erasmus Grasser**, are placed immediately above the modern **choir stalls**. The axial chapel in the apse contains a fine Robed Madonna, and that to the south, the old Chapel of the Holy Sacrament, a 15C altarpiece (a Crucifixion and scenes from the life of Christ). The original stained glass windows (medallion of the Annunciation, 1392) have been restored to the north chapel, the chapel of the Baptism of Christ, which is also furnished with a 1510 **altarpiece**. The central panel of this, which illustrates the baptism, is by **Michael Pacher**, a native of Salzburg, while the lateral panels are the work of **Jan Polack**, the greatest Munich painter of the Gothic period.

A staircase to the left of the choir leads to the **Bishops' and Princes' Crypt**, with the burial vaults of certain Cardinals of Munich and Wittelsbach princelings. A lavishly-built early 17C mausoleum dedicated to the Bavarian Emperor Ludwig (1287-1347) stands in the south aisle. In the **south tower**, there is now a lift taking visitors to the platform, from which there is a fine **view★** of the town.

★ **Marienplatz** (KZ) – This square is the heart of Munich. In the centre rises the **Virgin's Column** (Mariensäule), which was erected by the Prince-Elector Maximilian in 1638.

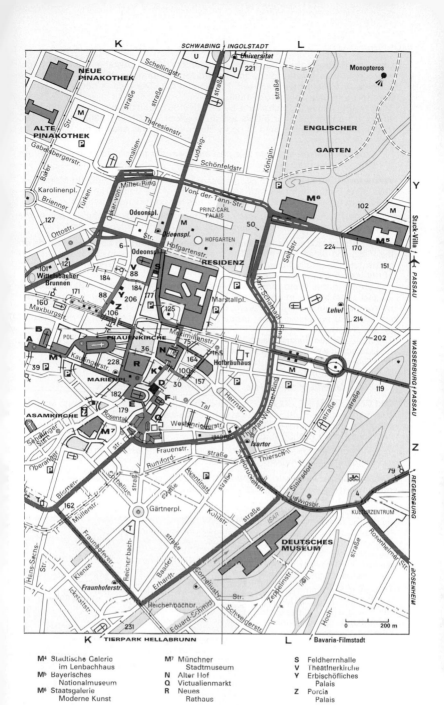

M⁴	Städtische Galerie im Lenbachhaus	M⁷	Münchner Stadtmuseum	S	Feldherrnhalle
M⁵	Bayerisches Nationalmuseum	N	Alter Hof	V	Theatinerkirche
M⁶	Staatsgalerie Moderne Kunst	Q	Victualienmarkt	Y	Erbischöfliches Palais
		R	Neues Rathaus	Z	Porcia Palais

The north side is occupied by the neo-Gothic new town hall (1867-1908) (**R**), whose **carillon** (Glockenspiel) installed in the tower's oriel window, is a favourite tourist attraction. When the mechanism is activated *(at 11am, noon and 5pm)*, brightly coloured figures in enamelled copper emerge and enact the Dance of the Coopers (Schäfflertanz- below) and (above) the Tournament which accompanied royal weddings in the 16C. From the town hall tower (85m - 279ft: lift) there is another lovely **view** of the city. The façade of the **old town hall** (**D**), with its stepped gables and bell turrets, occupies the eastern side of the square.

St Peter's (**KZ E**) – Baroque vaulting remodelled this 13C, three-aisle Gothic church in the 17C and 18C. The centre section of the enormous high altar is occupied by an Erasmus Grasser statue of St Peter (1492). Slightly lower down, the flanking figures representing the four Fathers of the Church were sculpted by Egid Quirin Asam in 1732. The church's 1386 bell tower is affectionately nicknamed "Old Pete" by the people of Munich. Visitors braving the climb to the top (294 steps) are rewarded with a splendid view.

Food Market (**Viktualienmarkt**) (**KZ Q**) – The permanent daily market and an adjoining beergarden *(the open-air beergarden operates only during the summer months)* make this square one of the city's liveliest. Two fountains recall the famous comedian Karl Valentin and his partner Liesl Karlstadt.

Church of the Holy Ghost (Heiliggeistkirche) (KZ F) – Another Gothic original which paid later tribute to the local taste for the Baroque, this hall-church was completely transformed between 1723 and 1730. The façade however is neo-Baroque, and dates only from 1885.
The painting above the **high altar** is by U Loth (1661), and the two angels with large wings in front of the altar pillars are the work of J G Greiff (1730). The mid-15C Virgin in the north aisle, said to be by Hammerthal, was once in the Benedictine abbey at Tegernsee.

Cross the Talstrasse, take the passage beneath the old town hall, and turn right into the Burgstrasse.

Weinstadel (KZ K) – At no 5 Burgstrasse. The oldest house (1552) in Munich, in days gone by the municipal office of the Clerk of the Court. The façade is decorated in trompe l'oeil. The fine doorway has a basket-handle arch.

At no 10 in the Burgstrasse, take the vaulted passageway to reach the Ledererstrasse, then cross diagonally (left) into the Orlandostrasse.

Hofbräuhaus (KZ) – The best-known of the famous Munich beer halls stands on the Platzl and dates from 1589. The present building was constructed at the end of the 19C, the original brewery having already been transferred to the east bank of the Isar through lack of space.
Every day, in this great temple of beer, perspiring waiters serve 100 hectolitres (17 500 pints) of beer in one-litre (1 3/4 pints) tankards (Masskrug). In many of the rooms and in the shaded courtyard, orchestras add to the festive atmosphere with renditions of popular songs – frequently with additional help from the drinking public.
The huge vaulted **Bierschwemme**, on the ground floor, where the odours of strong tobacco mingle with those of sausages and beer, is the rowdiest part of the building. Customarily there is a police presence to ensure that high spirits do not degenerate into brawls.

At the far end of the square, turn left into the Pfisterstrasse.

Old Castle (Alter Hof) (KZ N) – This building, a quadrilateral opening onto an inner courtyard, was the official Wittelsbach residence from 1253 to 1474. The south wing has an elegant tower with half-timbered corbelling (late 15C). The courtyard with its fountain is charming.

The Hofgraben leads to the Max-Joseph-Platz, enclosed on the north and east by the imposing mass of the palace.

★ **Palace** (Residenz) (KY) – In 1385, the Wittelsbachs started the building of this new residence (Neuveste) which, with the passing of time, expanded into a complex that grew ever more vast.
Work was well advanced in the Renaissance period (Antiquarium, Kaiserhof, the Residenzstrasse façade) and the subsequent classical era (Festsaalbau, Königsbau).

★★ **Treasury** (Schatzkammer) ☉ – The magnificent exhibits here – crowns, diadems, illuminated prayerbooks, ciboria, cameos, reliquaries, etc – are enticingly set out. On no account miss the superb chased cross executed at the beginning of the 11C for Queen Gisela of Hungary, or that dazzling example of the goldsmith's art showing St George slaying the dragon (1590). Note, too, a marvellous ivory crucifix,

Wine Cup from the Palace Treasury

swords with diamond - and ruby - encrusted pommels, vases and plates in jasper, agate and lapis lazuli, exotic works of art from Turkey, Persia and Mexico.

Palace Museum (Residenzmuseum) ☉ *(Successive morning and afternoon guided tours are necessary if nothing is to be missed).*
Morning Tour – A room embellished with marvellous gilded stuccoes houses the Wittelsbach **Ancestors' Gallery**, where Charlemagne has the place of honour. The enormous **Antiquarium** (1570), the oldest part of the palace, impresses with its painted ceilings and innumerable Roman busts. The **State Rooms** (Reichen Zimmer – 1730-1737), decorated by Effner and Cuvilliés, illustrate in great style the French version of the Rococo.
Afternoon Tour – Masterpieces from the workshops of Meissen, Nymphenburg and Sèvres ("Bird Service" of 1759) are on display in the **Porcelain Rooms**. The 17C **Court Chapel** (Hofkapelle) has a fine compartmented ceiling. On the first floor is the **Reliquary Room** (Reliquienkammer), where the gems of the Wittelsbach Chapel Treasure are on view (note the outstanding Passion shrine) as well as various examples of 16C and 18C gold and silver plate.

★ Palace Theatre (Altes Residenztheater) ⊙ – This enchanting Rococo theatre was built by Cuvilliés between 1751 and 1753, with four tiers of Court boxes, each different from the others in design and decoration. The Prince-Elector's box, in the centre, is set apart by the elegance and richness of its hangings and the fine decorations in marble and stucco. The harmonization of colours in red, gold and ivory is particularly beautiful.

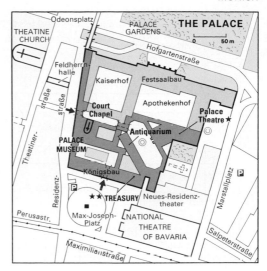

National Theatre of Bavaria (Bayerisches Nationaltheater) – Built between 1811 and 1818, this national theatre was endowed with one of the largest stages in the world, on a par with the Scala in Milan or the Viennese Opera. The five-tier auditorium can seat 2 100 spectators.

Odeonsplatz (KY) – A fine square dominated on the west by the lofty silhouette of the Theatine Church. To the south, the **Feldherrnhalle** (S) portico, erected in the 19C by F von Gärtner in imitation of the Loggia dei Lanzi in Florence, closes the long perspective of the Ludwigstrasse. The far (northern) end of this splendid avenue leads in a straight line to a triumphal arch.

Theatine Church (Theatinerkirche) (KY V) – A fine example of Baroque ecclesiastical architecture, this church was built between 1663 and 1688, first under the direction of the Italian Barelli and later by Zuccalli, who came from Graubünden. The façade was added a century afterwards, by Cuvilliés.
Inside, the dome of this very tall building, which rises to a height of 71m - 233ft, emphasizes a grandiose impression of space. The stuccowork is particularly rich, the Italian stuccodore having paid especial attention to the smaller load bearing arches and the pendentives. The wreathed double colonnade of the monumental high altar is also very generously embellished. The dark wood of the pulpit, designed in 1681 by Faistenberger, makes a striking contrast with the whites and greys in the nave and elsewhere. More princes from the Wittelsbach dynasty are buried in the crypt beneath the chancel.

From the Salvatorstrasse turn into the Kardinal-Faulhaber-Strasse.

Episcopal Palace (Erzbischöfliches Palais) (KY Y) – *At no 7 Kardinal-Faulhaber-Strasse.*
An elegant building, one of the masterpieces by the Rococo architect **Cuvilliés**, constructed between 1733 and 1737.

Porcia Palais (KY Z) – *No 12 Kardinal-Faulhaber-Strasse.*
This mansion, originally designed by Zuccalli in 1694, was transformed in the Rococo style by Cuvilliés in 1735. The façade, in tones of pink and grey pargetting, is charming.

Regain the Marienplatz via the Maffaistrasse and Weinstrasse.

OLD PINAKOTHEK QUARTER (KY) *time: half a day*

★★★ Old Pinakothek (Alte Pinakothek) ⊙ – This colossal building (the word Pinakothek means art gallery) was destined to house the collections of paintings amassed by the House of Wittelsbach from the beginning of the 16C onwards. It was built between 1826 and 1836 by the architect Leo von Klenze, in the Venetian Renaissance style. The collection was started by Duke Wilhelm IV, who commissioned historical scenes from the most eminent painters of his time, Altdorfer and Burgkmair. The Duke's great grandson, the Elector Maximilian I, continued the tradition by founding a home for the collection, the Kammergalerie, in the 17C. And this, under King Ludwig I, developed into the finest exhibition of art in the whole of Europe. Today, the Old Pinakothek can boast a sublime and unequalled range of European painting from the 13C to the 18C.

First Floor

Galleries I, IIa – Dutch and Flemish Primitives. Note an extraordinary triptych by **Rogier van der Weyden** (1400-1464), known as *The Three Kings Altarpiece*. Painted for the Church of St Columba in Cologne c1460, the work impresses above all by its clear, precise drawing, the harmony of the composition, the admirable organization of colour and the expressive qualities of the different characters. Works by Hans Memling (c1435-1495) and Dieric Bouts the Younger (1448-1490) are also on view.

OLD PINAKOTHEK

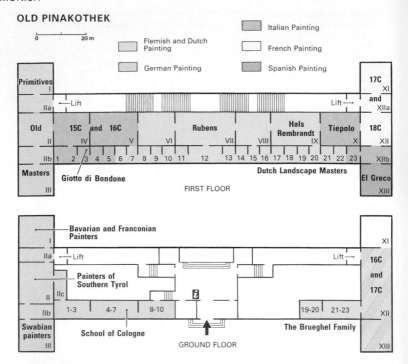

Galleries II, IIb, III – German Old Masters. *St Erasmus and St Maurice*, by **Mathias Grünewald** (*c*1480-1528), is a perfectly executed work, full of expression. **Albrecht Dürer** (1471-1528) is particularly well represented here: the famous *Self-Portrait In A Fur-lined Coat* (1500) is complemented by **The Four Apostles**, painted when the artist was at his greatest in 1526. In *The Battle of Alexandria* (1525), **Albrecht Altdorfer** (1480-1538), a master of the Danube School, paints with infinite and unbelievable detail the thousands of protagonists involved in the action.

Galleries IV, V – Italian painting of the 15C and 16C. Here is a brillant collection of works by Fra Filippo Lippi, Perugino, Botticelli, Bassano, Veronese and Tintoretto.
Raphael, painter of the High Renaissance, is represented by *The Madonna of the House of Tempi*; **Titian** (1490-1576) by a late work, *The Crowning With Thorns*, notable for its splendid colour effects. Superb colour again, added to a love of detail in the painting of draperies, distinguishes the *Virgin and Child* by **Leonardo da Vinci** (1452-1519).

Rooms 1 to 5 – Do not miss, in this part of the museum, three small pictures by Giotto (1266-1337) illustrating scenes from the life of Christ, one of which depicts The Last Supper.

Galleries VI, VII and VIII – Flemish painting. Works by two of Rubens' pupils can be seen here: *The Satyr and the Peasant*, by **Jakob Jordaens** (1593-1678); and *Susanna Bathing* and *The Rest During the Flight into Egypt* (which shows also the influence of Titian), by **Van Dyck** (1599-1641).
Paintings by the master himself are in Gallery VII. The extraordinary talent of **Rubens** (1577-1640) manifests itself here in works as diverse as the huge *Last Judgement*, the *Rape of the Daughter of Leucippus* and *Meleager and Atlanta*; in domestic scenes like *Hélène Fourment and her Eldest Son Francis*, exceptional for its colouring and the subjects' graceful attitudes; or again in *Isabella Brant* and the *Artist in a Honeysuckle Bower*, in which Rubens himself is represented.

Rooms 6 and 11 – German painting of the 16C and 17C. Beside Flegel, who inclines towards the Dutch tradition, and Rottenhammer, a disciple of Tintoretto and Altdorfer, **Adam Elsheimer** (1578-1610) impresses with small canvases devoted to idyllic landscapes in which the art of chiaroscuro predominates (*The Flight into Egypt* is a good example).

Rooms 7 to 10 and 12 – Popular scenes by the Flemish artist Adriaen Brouwer (1605-1675).

Gallery IX – Dutch painting. Noteworthy among the works of **Frans Hals** (1580-1666), chronicler of the bourgeois life of his time and specialist in group portraits, is the single *Portrait of Willem van Heythuysen*. Also exhibited: *Still Life with Lobster* by Abraham van Beyeren (1629-1675).
Scenes from the Passion treated in chiaroscuro by **Rembrandt** (1606-1669) are on display in this gallery, in the first two of which the artist himself is represented (in the centre, dressed in blue).

Rooms 13 to 22 – Works by the great Dutch landscape masters **Jakob van Ruisdael** and **Jan van Goyen** *(Village on the River)*. There is also a Rembrandt self-portrait.

Galleries X, XIIb, Room 23 – Italian painting. Works by Giordano, Carracci, Guardi, Canaletto and Calgario; a luminous *Adoration of the Magi* by the Venetian **Tiepolo** (1696-1770).

Galleries XII and XIIa – French school of the 17C and 18C. *Seaport at Sunrise* by **Claude Lorrain** (1600-1682); *The Lamentation of Christ*, an early work by **Nicolas Poussin** (1593-1665); *Portrait of Madame de Pompadour* by **François Boucher** (1703-1770), and elegant paintings by Chardin, Greuze and Fragonard.

Gallery XIII – Spanish painting. A remarkable *Christ Despoiled* by **El Greco** (1540-1614) demonstrates the artist's genius for rendering the intensity of expression. From the studio of the court painter **Velasquez** (1599-1660): *Young Spanish Nobleman in Black*. Famous for his Seville street scenes, **Murillo** (1617-1682) contributes *The Grape and Watermelon Eater*. Pictures by Zurbaran and Ribera can also be seen.

Ground Floor

The arrangement and numbering of galleries is identical to that on the 1st floor.

The east wing and corresponding rooms are reserved for German and Dutch Mannerists of the 16C (the transition period between the Renaissance and the Baroque); the west wing for German Primitives.

Gallery I – Bavarian and Franconian painters. There is a spellbinding *Crucifixion* by the Master of the Tegernsee Altarpiece (c1440-1460).

Gallery IIa – Gothic and Renaissance portrait painters. Among them is a **Hans Baldung Grien** (1484-1545) Portrait of *Philip the Bellicose, Count Palatine*.

Gallery II – Painters of the Southern Tyrol. Note especially a superb Fathers of the Church altarpiece by **Michael Pacher** (1435-1498).

Gallery III – Swabian painters.

Rooms 1 to 10 – The School of Cologne. Early 15C: works by the Master of St Veronica; late 15C: a very fine painting on wood by the Master of the Altarpiece of St Bartholomew. On the central panel, the saint is shown with St Agnes and St Cecilia, and the benefactor on his knees nearby.

Gallery XII and XIII – Paintings of the 16C and 17C. *The Tax Collector and his Wife* by Marinus van Roymerswaele (c1493-1547); *Landscape with Farm* (on which hints of the Romantic approach are already discernible) by Cornelis van Dalem; *The Death of Lucretia* by **Lucas Cranach the Elder** (1472-1553), which it is fascinating to compare with the Dürer painting of the same subject *(Gallery II on the first floor)*.

Rooms 19 to 23 – Numerous paintings by the Brueghel dynasty. From **Pieter Brueghel the Elder** (1520-1569), famous painter of landscapes and scenes of rustic life, there is the celebrated *The Land of Milk and Honey* with its near-surrealistic accents. His son, **Jan Brueghel the Elder** (1568-1626) is represented by *A Bouquet of Flowers*.

★ **New Pinakothek** (Neue Pinakothek) **(KY)** ⊘ – A modern building, completed in 1981, which replaces the original museum, constructed under Ludwig I and so badly damaged in the Second World War that it had to be demolished. It houses important collections of 18C and 19C painting and sculpture.
The Romantic movement started in Britain by Turner and Gainsborough found its way to Germany at the beginning of the 19C, in particular in the hands of Caspar David Friedrich, whose dreamlike evocations of nature nevertheless reveal an ethos that is typically Germanic *(A Riesengebirge Landscape)*. It gathered impetus with the vast old style landscapes painted by Rottmann and the Italianate scenes conceived by the Nazarenes *(Italia and Germania*, by **Overbeck**). The portrait of Goethe in this museum is the work of the Bavarian Court painter J Stiele. The Biedermeier school is represented by **M von Schwind**, the Realists by **Leibl** and his circle *(Portrait of Mme Gédon)*. **Liebermann** and **Corinth** once again stand for German Impressionism *(Portrait of Count Edmund von Keyserling)*. The art of Marées, Feuerbach and Böcklin links up with mythological themes and the classical tradition. In the work of G von Max there is already a pre-echo of Expressionism *(The Ecstasy of Katharina Emmerich)*. **Jugendstil** *(Art Nouveau)* makes its appearance with the paintings of the Viennese Gustav Klimt.
Late Romantics and Realists are included in the **Collection of French Painting** – Corot, Courbet, Manet *(Luncheon in the Studio)* and Daumier *(The Drama)* – as well as the Impressionists and neo-Impressionists Monet *(The Bridge at Argenteuil)*, Cézanne, Gaugin *(The Nativity)* and Van Gogh *(View of Arles)*.

★ **Glyptothek** **(JY M²)** ⊘ – One thousand years of Greek and Roman sculpture are gathered together under the roof of this museum, built with its classical porch and Ionic colonnade, by the architect **Leo von Klenze** (1816-1830). The **Tenea Apollo**, with his handsome, smiling face, is typical of the Kouros – those large naked figures, half human, half divine, who spread through Greece in the 6C BC *(Gallery I)*. The **Barberini Faun** *(Gallery II)*, which appears sated with drink and half asleep, dates from the Hellenistic epoque (c220 BC). The Classical period is represented by Roman copies of ancient Greek statues and funerary stones (5C and 4C BC): here the **bas-relief by Mnesarete** displays a magisterial harmony of proportion, and the sculptor's handling of the draperies swathing Irene, the Goddess of Peace, is equally fine *(Gallery V)*.

Note too, in the original works from the east and west pediments of the Temple of Aphaia on the island of Aegina, which were sculpted from Paros marble, how finely detailed is the shaping of the warriors' musculature. These statues *(Galleries VII-IX)* date from the end of the Archaic era (500-480 BC).

Finally *(Galleries X to XIII)*, the visitor can judge to what state of virtuosity the Romans had brought the arts of portraiture and the decoration of sarcophagi.

★ **Collection of Antiquities** (Staatliche Antikensammlungen) (JY M³) ⊘ – *Opposite the Glyptothek.*

A building by G F Ziebland (1838-48) which, with its Corinthian colonnade, forms an architectural counterpart to the sculpture museum across the road.

An important display of **ceramics** on the ground floor traces the evolution of pottery and the painting of vases in Greece, which reached its zenith during the 6C and 5C BC. Geometric decoration was succeeded by the representation of black figures on a red background – illustrated by an amphora and a goblet by the painter Exekias. The amphora depicts Ajax carrying the body of Achilles; Dionysius decorates the goblet, in a boat escorted by dolphins *(Gallery II, showcases 10 and 12)*. The transition towards the use of red figures against a background of varnished black can be seen on another amphora, where a single subject – Hercules' banquet in the presence of Athena – is treated in the two styles *(Gallery III, showcase 6)*.

Certain vases (loutrophora and lecythus on a white ground) were destined for funerary worship; others – such as the elegant canthare (drinking vessel in the shape of a female head) – for domestic use (*Gallery II, showcase 7 –* 540 BC).

Bronzes on the first floor (ceremonial vessels, engraved plaques, statuettes), and particularly the **Etruscan jewellery** in the basement *(Galleries VII and X)* testify to the enormous craftsmanship enjoyed by these workers in metal: necklaces, fibula, rings, in filigree or with granulations, rival each other in the delicacy and elegance of their execution.

★ **Villa Lenbach Collections** (Städtische Galerie im Lenbachhaus) (JY M⁴) ⊘ – Built between 1883 and 1889 in the style of a Florentine villa, the house containing the Lenbach collections is devoted mainly to the works of **Munich painters of the 19C.** Among these are the landscapes of E B Morgenstern *(Starnberg Lake)* and portraits by F A von Kaulbach and F von Defregger. There is also a set of powerful **portraits** by Franz von Lenbach himself *(King Ludwig I, Bismarck, Wagner)*.

But the gallery's international reputation is built above all on the avant-garde **Blauer Reiter collection** *(qv)*. Born in the tumultuous period just before the First World War, the movement is represented by its founder members, Kandinsky, Marc *(Blue Horse)* and Kubin, as well as by paintings from the hands of Jawlensky, Klee and Macke. Contemporary art is also displayed in the Lenbach villa.

★★★ **GERMAN MUSEUM** (DEUTSCHES MUSEUM) (LZ) ⊘

Allow at least half a day

Opened in 1925, this museum – one of the most important in the world for scientific and technical matters – is built on an isle in the Isar (Museuminsel). It traces the history of science and technology from the beginning of time to the present day.

Apart from a large number of original items and reconstructions, most of them of great value, the exhibits comprise dioramas, synoptic tables, scale models and examples of working apparatus. In line with the expressed wish of the museum's founder, the Bavarian electrification pioneer **Oskar von Miller**, the display system is pedagogic: the visitor is there to inquire, to touch, and to discover. Thus there are innumerable **working models** and workshop and laboratory **demonstrations** to explain the relevant techniques in a way that even a beginner can understand. Such physics experiments as Faraday's Cage and Foucault's Pendulum, for example, are reproduced. And there are regular performances illustrating such manufacturing processes as papermaking, glassblowing, smelting and the fabrication of tiles. Some of the demonstrations are accompanied by a commentary on film.

A library endowed with 700 000 different volumes is associated with the museum, as well as privately donated collections and archives including documents, plans, maps, blueprints and drawings.

> *In view of the huge scope of subjects covered, visitors are advised to choose a particular theme to follow. There are some 16 000 exhibits displayed over an area of 40 000m2 - 394 000sq ft. A brochure in English and a plan of the museum's layout are obtainable at the entrance.*

Ground Floor – Natural resources (including oil); metallurgy; machine tools; machines powered by different types of energy (wind, water, steam); applications of electrical current; bicycles and barouches; civil engineering (roads, bridges, tunnels, railways, canals, etc.). In the **Railway Hall**, there are famous steam engines, including the 1912 S-3/6 which powered the Bavarian Express, and the first electric locomotive (*Werner von Siemens*, 1879). The **Aeronautical Section** (Modern Division) exhibits early jet planes, including the Messerschmitt Me-262, the first jet fighter made on a production line, helicopters, gliders and vertical take-off machines.

An Elbe sailing ship (1880) and an Italian steam tug (1932) stand at the entrance to the Navigation Department *(continued in the basement)*.

Basement – Among many other displays, the **Navigation Section** highlights naval construction, warships (including U-1, the first German submarine, built in 1906), methods of navigation, fishing techniques, and the sphere of Jacques Piccard's 1958 bathyscaphe.

A section on **mining** details the working of a coal mine, the extraction of salt, and the treatment of ores. There is a model salt mine.

The **Automobile Department** shows an 1885 carriage with a Benz motor, an 1891 steam-driven Serpollet, luxury cars of the 1920s and 1930s (Daimler, Opel, Horsch, Bugatti), utility vehicles, racing cars (1936 Auto-Union Grand Prix Type-C), an assembly line, and motorcycles. Note the 1885 Daimler-Maybach (a replica, built in 1906).

First Floor – The most interesting section here is perhaps Aeronautics. Gliders built by the engineer Lilienthal (c1885), the pioneer of this form of flight, can be seen. Also a **1917 Fokker Dr. I Triplane**, of the type made famous by Baron von Richthofen's "circus" in the First World War (a replica including parts from the original). Note also the Wright Brothers' Type-A Standard (USA, 1909), a Blériot Type XI (1909), a Junkers F-13 (the first true air-liner, 1919), and the legendary Junkers Ju-52 (built under licence in France, 1947). Military aircraft of the 1930s and 1940s are on show, including the Messerschmitt Bf-109.

From this most recent gallery devoted to aeronautics, there is direct access *(by escalator)* to the second floor section on space flights. Technologies from the earliest attempts at rocketry (Hitler's V2, code-named A4) to the current Spacelab are illustrated.

Department of Physics – Physical laws and their application: optics, mechanics, electronics, thermology, nuclear physics; chemistry: alchemy, Liebig's laboratory, pharmacy, biochemistry; techniques of information; musical instruments.

Second Floor – Manufacture of glass and ceramics (beautiful 17C earthenware stove from the Thurgau area in Switzerland); paper printing; photography (Daguerre's apparatus, 1839); textile processes (Jacquard's 1860 loom).

Third Floor – Weights and measures; climatic forecasts; agriculture (dairy farming, flour milling, breweries); data processing and computer science, robotics and microelectronics. Access to the fourth floor observatory *(it is necessary to book a visit in advance)*.

Fourth Floor – *See above.*

Fifth Floor – Astronomy (celestial globes, sundials, astrolabes, quadrants, etc.).

Sixth Floor – Planetarium.

ENGLISH GARDEN QUARTER

★ **English Garden** (Englischer Garten) (LY) – Not far from the city centre, this park, with its broad sweeps of tree-bordered lawn, its streams and its lake, was designed in the late 18C by **Friedrich Ludwig von Sckell** and the British-American scientist **Sir Benjamin Thompson**, Count von Rumford. It is particularly popular in summer, when an open-air beergarden seating 7 000 people operates near the **Chinese Tower** (Chinesischer Turm). From the **Monopteros**, a circular temple built on a knoll by Leo von Klenze, there is a fine view of the belfries in the Old Town.

★★ **Bavarian National Museum** (Bayerisches Nationalmuseum) (LY M⁵) ⊘ – Maximilian II created this museum in 1885 with the aim of preserving Bavaria's artistic heritage. The 47 rooms on the ground floor offer a survey of Bavarian **arts and crafts** from the Great Invasions (5C and 6C) to the 19C, including silver and gold plate and religious statuary, tapestry, furniture, altarpieces and stained glass windows.

The Italian Renaissance is evoked in other sections by jewellery, costumes, bronzes, glazed earthenware, and pewter work.

On the first floor, ceramics and porcelain are exhibited, along with gold, silver and glassware. Everyday crafts – including a collection of Christmas cribs – are illustrated in the basement.

State Gallery Modern Art Collection (Staatsgalerie moderner Kunst) (LY M⁶) ⊘ – In the west wing of the Haus der Kunst, built between 1933 and 1937 in the heavy, pompous "National Socialist" style.

The ground floor concentrates on "classic" modern art: Matisse, Picasso, Braque, Léger and Juan Gris represent Cubism and Fauvism; Kirchner *(Interior)*, Schmidt-Rottluff, Marc, Kandinsky and Beckmann (remarkable self-portrait of 1943) the different tendencies of German Expressionism. Examples of the Blauer Reiter and Die Brücke *(qv)* movements are shown with paintings from the Bauhaus (Feininger's *Halle Church*). Surrealism is present with Ernst, Miró, de Chirico and Dali; sculpture with Lehmbuch, Barlach, Giacometti and Mario Marini. The upper floor is reserved for late 20C art (Abstract Expressionism, Pop Art, Photorealism, Group Zero, CoBrA and Vasarely).

Admission times and charges for the sights described
are listed at the end of the Guide.
Every sight for which there are times and charges
is indicated by the symbol ⊘ in the middle section of the guide.

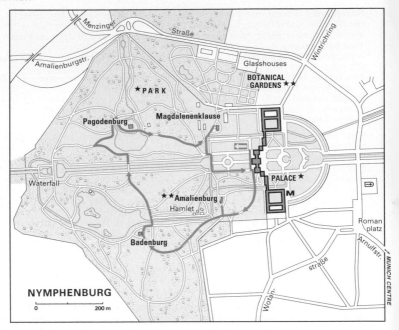

NYMPHENBURG

★★ NYMPHENBURG *time: half a day*

At 6km - 3 3/4 miles from the city centre, leaving Munich by the Marstrasse (JY). Plan of the conurbation in the current Michelin Red Guide Deutschland

The oldest part of the palace, once the summer residence of the Bavarian sovereigns, is the five-storey central pavilion, built by Barelli between 1664 and 1674 in the style of an Italian palazzo. The Prince-Elector Max Emmanuel, who reigned from 1679 to 1726, added two lateral pavilions on either side which were linked to the main building by arcaded galleries. At the same time he remodelled the central block, accentuating the verticals by the addition of pilasters. His successors, Karl-Albrecht (1726-1745) and Max III Josef (1745-1777), then constructed a semicircle of outbuildings and dependencies, which underlined the castle's resemblance to Versailles.

From 1701 onwards, the surrounding park too was enlarged under the direction of Carbonet and Girard, the pupils of Le Nôtre. The formal French gardens date from this period, as do the various park pavilions: Pagodenburg (1719), Badenburg (1721), Magdalenenklause (1728) and Amalienburg (1739).

★ **Palace** ⊙ – The splendid **banqueting hall**, a symphony of white, gold and pale green, was richly adorned with coloured stuccowork and frescoes by Johann Baptist Zimmermann and his son Franz. A musicians' gallery is placed beneath the high windows looking out over the park.

The rooms in the north wing of the central block – antechamber, bedroom, study – are panelled, with tapestry hangings and paintings displayed. Beyond this the north pavilion contains views of the castle and park in the early 18C.

The most fascinating room in the main block's south wing is the one devoted to a collection of **Chinese lacquer**. In the south pavilion, the apartments of Queen Carolina contain the famous **Gallery of Beauties** conceived by Ludwig I. Commissioned by the King to immortalize the most seductive women of the epoch, these paintings were executed by the portraitist Josef Stieler (1781-1858).

★ **Park** – *See itinerary on Nymphenburg map.*
Most of the park can be seen from the top of the steps in front of the palace's main entrance. Below the steps, beyond the formal rectilinear flower gardens lined with white marble urns and the statues of gods, the Grand Canal, which ends in a waterfall, flows straight as an arrow away into the distance.

★★ **Amalienburg** ⊙ – This charming little hunting lodge by **Cuvilliés** is one of his most accomplished designs – a model for the many Rococo country pavilions which so delighted the Courts of 18C Germany. The simplicity and sobriety of the exterior is in vivid contrast with the extraordinary richness of the interior. Beyond the curious Kennel – a panelled central room surrounded by the quarters of hunting dogs – are the Blue Room and a beautiful bedchamber, with silver woodwork on a background of lemon yellow.

In the centre of the building is the **Hall of Mirrors** rotunda. Here the combination of blue walls and ceiling, silver stucco and wood-framed glass forms a marvellous ensemble. A Hunting Room, the Pheasant Room, and kitchens whose walls are tiled with blue Delft complete this masterpiece of Bavarian Rococo.

Badenburg – A luxurious heated swimming-pool, with a ceiling decorated by mythological motifs, is the centrepiece of this 18C bath-house. A dressing room, and an antechamber serving as games and rest room are also included in the pavilion.

Pagodenburg – The 18C taste for exoticism and the Far East is exemplified in the design of this octagonal tea-house. A drawing-room, a Chinese room and a boudoir occupy the first floor.

Magdalenenklause – A "hermitage" or folly built in the then popular style of "artificial ruins", this pavilion is dedicated to St Mary Magdalene.

Carriage Museum and Porcelain Collection (Marstallmuseum und Porzellansammlung) (M) ⊘
– The museum is housed in the castle's former stables. Besides superb 18C and 19C harnesses, broughams, coaches, carts, sledges and sedan chairs used by the Wittelsbachs are on display. Note especially the coronation coach of the Emperor Karl VII, and the state coach and personal sleigh of Ludwig II, all of them equipped with quite incredible luxury.

Above the old stables, a series of rooms exhibits the **Bäuml Collection of Nymphenburg Porcelain**. Painted figurines by Franz Anton Bustelli, master modellist of the factory between 1754 and 1763, are particularly fine. The **reproductions in porcelain★** – miniature copies in extraordinary detail of paintings in the Old Pinakothek – were commissioned by Ludwig I.

★★ **Botanical Gardens** (Botanischer Garten) ⊘ – Reputed to be among the finest and most richly stocked in Europe. A stroll through the Schmuckhof *(opposite the main building)*, the Spring Garden and the Rosery, past masses of rhododendrons shaded by pines and around the Alpine Garden by the Great Lake is not only a feast for the eyes but a horticultural lesson in itself. There are marvellous orchids among the tropical and subtropical species flowering in the greenhouses.

ADDITIONAL SIGHTS

Propylaea (Propyläen) **(JY)** – This imposing gateway by Leo von Klenze (1784-1864) was completed two years before the Munich architect died. Inspired by the Propylaea of the Acropolis, it stands on the west side of the Königsplatz (which is thus flanked on three sides by monuments in the classical style). The frieze represents the war of liberation against the Turks; Otto I of Wittelsbach, King of Greece from 1832 to 1862, is commemorated in a statue on the pediment above the Doric colonnade.

Villa Stuck ⊘ – *Leave by the Prinzregentenstrasse* **(LY)**.
Professor at the Munich Academy of Fine Arts from 1895 and one of the founding members of the Munich Secession, Franz Stuck (1863-1928) built this Jugendstil villa with an Italian influence after his own plans. The interior of the house is magnificent: it was Stuck himself who made the furniture, the panelling, the bas-reliefs and coffered ceilings, and some of the sculpture. Note also the famous canvases by the artist, including *The Guardian of Paradise* and *The Sin*.

★ **City Historical Museum** (Münchner Stadtmuseum) **(KZ M7)** ⊘ – *In the stables of the old Arsenal.* A collection of arms and armour is among the exhibits recalling the history of Munich. Do not on any account miss the **Moorish Dancers★★** (Moriskentänzer), ten carved wooden figures painted and gilded in 1480 by **Erasmus Grasser** (ground floor). **Specialized collections** consecrated to the marionette theatre, the cinema, musical instruments, photography and brewing are also on view.

★ **Church of St John of Nepomuk** (Asamkirche) **(KZ)** – The church, built in 1733, is always referred to locally under the name of the men who constructed it, the Asam Brothers: Cosmas Damian Asam, who specialized in the painting of frescoes, and Egid Quirin Asam, sculptor and stucco-worker. The church's remarkable unity of style is due to the fact that the two brothers drew up the plans themselves, and both executed and supervised every stage of the work.

The design of the interior is strikingly harmonious. A curved gallery links the choir, the nave and the organ loft; above, supported on pillars, a second gallery is adorned with stuccowork and statues of angels or cherubim. The frescoed ceiling, lit by windows concealed behind mouldings, depicts episodes in the life of St John of Nepomuk.

Wittelsbach Fountain (Wittelsbacher Brunnen) **(KY)** – *Between the Lenbachplatz and the Maximiliansplatz.* **Adolf von Hildebrand** *(qv)* built this neo-Baroque fountain in 1895 to mark the completion of a water canalization programme which provided the city with clean drinking water.

★ **Hellabrunn Zoological Gardens** (Tierpark Hellabrunn) ⊘ – *6km - 3 1/2 miles from the city centre, leaving via the Wittelsbacherstrasse* **(KZ)**. *Plan of the conurbation in the current Michelin Red Guide Deutschland.*
Munich's zoo, laid out in 1911 on the east bank of the Isar, is at the same time a nature reserve. Its 5 000 inhabitants live in their natural habitat. See particularly the Elephant House (1913), the monkey reserve and the huge free-flight aviary, where the visitors are not separated from the birds.

Bavaria Film Studios (Bavaria-Filmstadt Geiselgasteig) ⊘ – *10km - 6 miles from the centre via the Hochstrasse* **(LZ)**, *the Grünewalderstrasse and the Geiselgasteigstrasse. Plan as above.*
The first film shot in these studios was made in 1919. Since then, the Bavaria Film Studios can pride themselves on a long line of successes in the great tradition of the cinema, including such famous features as *Cabaret*, *The Boat* and *Neverending Story*.
Once through the gates, the visitor is immediately backstage behind the cameras, free to ease himself into a space capsule, lower himself into a submarine, or sit astride a dragon. There are demonstrations of trick photography and special effects.

Olympiapark ⊘ – *5km - 3 miles from the centre, via the Dachauer Strasse* (**JY**).
Munich was host to the XX Olympic Games in 1972. The many swimming-pools, gymnasia, training fields and tracks, as well as an open-air theatre, a cycling circuit and an artificial lake which remain on the site are used today as a leisure centre by the people of Munich. The 1968 **Olympiaturm** (television tower) is no less than 290m - 951ft high. At the 190m - 623ft level *(lift)*, there is a terrace with **panorama**★★★, which offers an exceptional view over the city to the Bavarian Alps.

BMW-Museum ⊘ – *At Petuelring 130.5km - 3 miles to the north, via the Schleissheimer Strasse* (**JY**) *and the Lerchenauer Strasse.*
This strange silver building shaped like a cup lies at the foot of the administration tower – which in no way detracts from the futuristic effect by being built in the form of four linked cylinders. The guided tour, which progresses in a spiral, retraces the history of the famous firm founded in 1916 and specialized in the construction of motorcycles and cars (Dixie-Roadster, 1929; R-32, 1923) – and, since the Second World War, of high-performance sports models and luxury automobiles.

EXCURSIONS

★ **Schleissheim Castle** ⊘ – *15km - 9 miles to the north. Leave by the Schleissheimer Strasse* (**JY**).
The so-called "new" castle (Neues Schloss), which was built between 1701 and 1727, extends majestically for 330m - 1 083ft in geometric precision with the strictly formal gardens laid out in long perspective by the Frenchmen Carbonet and Girard *(qv)*. The great staircase leads to the first floor State Apartments: a huge banqueting hall in dazzling white, and a Hall of Victory, adorned with paintings of battle scenes, gleaming with gold stucco. The princely apartments and galleries, now hung with 16C and 17C Dutch and Flemish paintings, are open to the public. On the ground floor, a second series of galleries has been opened beyond the music room.

★ **Ammersee** – *Circuit of 116km - 72 miles - allow 4 hours.*
Lying at an altitude of 533m - 1 749ft, this lake of glacial origin is cradled in a pretty landscape of wooded hills. Swimming, sailing and **boat trips** can be enjoyed at small resorts such as Diessen and Herrsching. Enthusiasts of the Rococo style must not miss a visit to the abbey church at Andechs.

Follow the western lake shore to reach Diessen.

Diessen – The **church**★ (Stiftskirche) was built between 1732 and 1739 to replace a former monastery collegiate. The architect was J M Fischer, one of the most celebrated of the Upper Bavarian Baroque school. The delicacy of the white, gold and rose-pink stucco, the remarkable painting of the dome, the nave vaulting and the side altars contrasts vividly with the slightly theatrical character of the high altar, which was designed by François Cuvilliés.

The climb from Fischen to Andechs offers fine views of the lake.

★ **Andechs** – Crowning the "holy hill" (Heiliger Berg), this **Benedictine abbey** overlooks the Ammersee by more than 200m - 656ft. Its **church**★★ ⊘, erected on a Gothic base, was remodelled as a Rococo building between 1751 and 1755. The architect J B Zimmermann (1680-1758), then at the height of his powers as a mature artist, was responsible both for the frescoes and the stuccowork. An elegant gallery, its balustrade decorated with painted panels evoking the history of the abbey, surrounds the main body of the church. The treatment of the vault frescoes, in various shades of pastel, shows an exceptional talent in the handling of colour.
A brewery, installed in the abbey outbuildings, produces an annual 70 000hl - 1 540 000 gallons of a very high quality beer.

Return to Munich via Hersching and Seefeld.

Dachau Concentration Camp – *19km - 12 miles to the northwest.*
Nazi Germany's first concentration camp was organized near the pleasant, terraced town of Dachau on the orders of Heinrich Himmler in 1933. Originally designed for the detention of German political opponents, the camp was soon flooded by tens of thousands of deportees, the majority of them Jews of diverse nationalities. More than 32 000 died there – without counting the 6 000 Russian prisoners-of-war shot dead on the nearby SS firing range. The system was described by Joseph Rovan, one of the few who escaped from the camp, as "implacable, perverted, an organization that was totally murderous, a marvellous machine for the debasement and de-humanizing of man".

Ruins, Commemorative Monuments, Museum ⊘ – *Follow the signposting "KZ - Gedenkstätte".* A Jewish memorial, a Protestant commemorative sanctuary and a Catholic expiatory chapel in the form of an open tower have been built within the precincts of the old camp. Behind, outside the perimeter, is a Carmelite convent with a chapel which may be visited. The huts were razed, but two, complete with their interior layout, have been reconstructed. On the Appelplatz (roll-call square), where prisoners were forced to muster morning and evening whatever the weather, a monument has been erected by the International Community.
The Museum, which outlines the punitive penal system established there by the Nazis, is housed in the former camp administration buildings. Land surrounding the cremation ovens, outside the camp, has been turned into a park-necropolis. The bodies of other victims have been buried in the cemeteries of Dachau (Waldfriedhof) and Leitenberg, 2km - 1 1/4 miles to the northeast.

Michelin maps ⁴¹¹ and ⁴¹² FG 11 – Local map see under CASTLES OF MÜNSTER-LAND - Plan of the conurbation in the current Michelin Red Guide Deutschland

Münster, the historical capital of Westphalia, where the local lords used to stay in winter, lies in the middle of a wooded plain studded with castles and manor houses. The city, one of Germany's most important university centres, has been carefully restored to give full value to its many Gothic and Renaissance façades.

The Peace of Westphalia – This treaty, signed on 24 October 1648, ended the Thirty Years War. During the five years of negotiations, the Emperor shuttled between the plenipotentiaries of the Protestant states in Osnabrück *(qv)* and those from the Catholic states in Münster, where the documents were finally agreed. As a result, much of Germany was carved up, to the detriment of Imperial prestige. The treaty recognized or confirmed the cession to France of Alsace and the bishoprics of Metz, Toul and Verdun, guaranteed the independence of Switzerland and the Netherlands, and favoured the development of Prussia. Three religious faiths were recognized, the Calvinists receiving the same rights as the Lutherans.

SIGHTS

★★ **Cathedral** (Dom) (Y) – A squat building with two towers, two chancels and two transepts, this church is in the transitional style typical of Westphalia in the 13C. Entering via the 16C south porch, the visitor sees that the inner door is surrounded by 13C statues and overlooked by a Christ in Judgement. A 16C statue of St Paul, patron saint of the Cathedral, looks down from the pier.

Visit the interior anti-clockwise.

The wide central nave and its bays lie beneath rounded vaulting. The side aisles are very low. In the ambulatory there is a 1540 **astronomic clock**★ in which the hours are struck by metal figurines wielding hammers. The spectators' gallery, high up in the church, was painted by Tom Ring the Elder.

The Chapel of the Holy Sacrament, left of the entrance to the cloister, is **richly furnished**★ (note especially an 18C silver tabernacle, made by a craftsman in Augsburg). The cloister entrance is reached through the left transept crossing.

★★ **Treasury** (Domkammer) (M²) ⊘ – *Off the cloister.* This is a modern building, blending perfectly with the structure of the cathedral, to which it is indirectly attached by the cloister.

MÜNSTER

On the ground floor, fourteen 15C reliquary-busts of the prophets in copper and silver, the 11C head-reliquary of St Paul, together with a 13C Virgin – both of them in chased gold – surround the **Processional Cross** of the Chapter. And this, due to superimposed openings adjusted on the three levels, becomes the focal point of the whole treasure house. In the basement there is a fine collection of liturgical vestments (copes, stoles, chasubles), particularly from the 17C and 18C, and ritual items. In the centre stands a portable altar (12C) hung with a cloth embroidered in pearls.

Noteworthy on the first floor, amidst a collection of Gothic and Baroque statuary, is the 1520 **Altarpiece of St John**.

★ **Fine Arts Museum** (Westfälisches Landesmuseum für Kunst und Kulturgeschichte) (YZ M¹) ⊙ – The medieval art of Westphalia lives on, thanks to the Gothic statuary of the cathedral and churches of Münster, to a series of stained-glass windows in this museum, and the sculptures of Johann and Heinrich Brabender. There is a remarkable collection of **altarpieces★★** by Konrad von Soest, Koerbecke and the Masters of Liesborn and Schöppingen. Flemish influence is noticeable in the works of the Tom Ring family (Ludger Tom Ring was a precursor of the still-life). Interesting portraits of Luther and his wife are by Lucas Cranach. The Thirty Years War in Westphalia is evoked in one department; another exhibits 20C art.

★ **Prinzipalmarkt** (YZ) – Running in a semicircle to the east of the Cathedral, this is the busiest – and at the same time the most historic – street in town. The elegant, gabled Renaissance houses, starkly restored in a style shorn of ornament, were once the homes of rich burghers. Under the arcades, attractive shops compete for space with restaurants and beer halls. The northern end of the street opens into the Bogenstrasse, a wide space equally inviting for window-shoppers and strollers (the statue halfway up, a pedlar with his basket, is known as the Kiepernkerl).

Town Hall (Rathaus) (YZ R) – The late 14C gabled façade, adorned with pinnacles and fine stone window tracery, is one of the most impressive examples of Gothic civic architecture.

★ **Peace Hall** (Friedenssaal) ⊙ – A former council chamber, named after the treaty. The Gothic and Renaissance woodwork is original and intact. At the far end, symbolic scenes hide the archive compartments. Behind the councillors' bench, the fine panelling is carved with niches containing figures, and there is a frieze in which the heads of eminent burghers can be distinguished. The paintings show rulers of the treaty's signatory countries: the Emperor Ferdinand III, Philip IV of Spain, the young Louis XIV of France, and their delegates. Note the beautiful 1520 wrought iron chandelier.

★ **Palace** (Residenzschloss) (Y) – Once the Prince-Bishops' residence, this Baroque palace is now part of the university. The red brick of the elegant three-part façade is variegated with sandstone facings which enliven any monotony of style. At the back, surrounded by water, lies a park (Schlossgarten) with an adjoining botanical garden. This green space is continued south of the castle by the Rampart Walk (Wallpromenade), from which there is a view of the Aasee lake.

St Lambert's Church (Lambertikirche) (Y) – Groined vaulting over the centre nave and star vaults above the side aisles distinguish this Gothic hall-church. Its elegant perforated **spire★** (99m - 325ft), built in the 19C, crowns a tower from which hang three iron cages. It was in these that the bodies of the three Anabaptist leaders (chiefs of a sect advocating baptism for adults only) were exhibited after the movement was crushed in 1536.

By the chevet of the church is a fine guild-house with a gable end (1588).

Church of St Ludger (Ludgerikirche) (Z) – Modern stained glass windows (1961) illustrating the life of Jesus have been added to the well-lit chancel.

Erbdrostenhof (Z) – This palace, dating from 1757, was built with a majestic concave façade and a triangular forecourt.

★ **Westphalian Museum of Natural Science** (Westfälisches Museum für Naturkunde) ⊙ – Sentruper Strasse 285. Entrance signposted from the Hüfferstrasse (Y). Departments of geology, palaeontology, mineralogy, botany and zoology, all beautifully laid out, offer a huge, panoramic survey of our environment and its evolution. Note especially the collection of naturalized birds. The highlight of the palaeontology department is the largest **ammonite★** ever found in the world. The displays in the **planetarium★** provide an excellent introduction to astronomy.

Open-Air Windmill Museum (Mühlenhof Freilichtmuseum) ⊙ – Signposted from the Hüfferstrasse (Y), south of the palace gardens.

In a peaceful setting on the shores of the Aasee, a 1748 windmill and a large farm dating from 1619 are surrounded by such traditional rural features as a forge, a Westphalian chapel, different kinds of barn, a bread oven, a local well, etc.

EXCURSIONS

Telgte – 12km - 7 1/2 miles to the east by Route 51.

A Marian pilgrimage worships a 1370 Pietà housed in an octagonal Baroque chapel in this small town. The **local museum** (Heimathaus Münsterland) ⊙ nearby displays a folk art masterpiece on cloth, **The Veil of Hunger★** (Hungertuch – 1623), which measures no less than 32m² - 344sq ft.

Freckenhorst – *26km - 16 miles to the east by Route 51.*
The **Collegiate Church★** (Stiftskirche) with its fortified façade, is a fine example of pre-Romanesque German architecture *(see introduction)*. Note the magnificent **baptismal font★** in the north aisle, inscribed with the date of the church's consecration (1129). On a tomb in the crypt is the recumbent statue of Geva, the church's founder.
Fine twinned columns support the remaining (west and south) galleries of the cloister.

Ostenfelde – *36km - 22 miles to the east by Route 51.*
The graceful **Vornholz Castle★** (1666) stands in a rolling landscape forested with ancient oaks. Built on two islets, its tall, roofed main block flanked by two wings, this is a typical Münsterland Wasserburg (water castle – *qv*).

★ **NAUMBURG** Saxony-Anhalt　　　　　　　　　Pop 34 000

Michelin map **987** fold 16

In the Middle Ages, this town built at the intersection of several trade routes was so important that its annual fair rivalled that of Leipzig. Seat of a bishopric since 1028, Naumburg retains as evidence of its former prosperity and religious rôle a magnificent cathedral.

★★ CATHEDRAL OF ST PETER AND ST PAUL
(DOM ST PETER UND PAUL)
Access by the Domstrasse

This two-chancel church is a perfect example of the architectural evolution from Late Romanesque to Early Gothic. The nave and the east chancel were built in the former style at the beginning of the 13C. Ten years later, the western section was completed by a chancel already displaying certain Early Gothic features. The east chancel, under which there is still a Romanesque crypt, was itself transformed into a Gothic structure in the 14C.

Benefactor's statues,
Naumburg Cathedral

West Chancel – The Master of Naumburg, sculptor of the celebrated **statues of benefactors★★★** deployed around the choir, undoubtedly took medieval sculpture in Germany to the summit of its glory. The individual personification of these figures, the profundity of their expressions, the overall impression of seriousness all add up to an exceptional effect of humanity and grandeur. The best-known are those of the founders of the town, Margrave Ekkehardt and his wife Uta (centre, right).
The rood screen bears a series of haut-relief scenes representing the Passion, which were executed by the same studio.

ADDITIONAL SIGHTS

★ **Church of St Wenceslas** (St Wenzel) – The proportions of this Late Gothic church are extraordinary: the nave, for instance, built between 1517 and 1523, is 11m long by 33m wide (36ft x 108ft). The 18C organ, which was played by Johann Sebastian Bach, is the work of Zacharias Hildebrand. There are two fine paintings by Cranach the Elder: *The Adoration of the Magi*, facing the choir, in which the artist himself is represented on the right (1522); and, on the right side of the choir, *The Blessing of the Children* (1529). In this painting, Katharina von Bora, the wife of Luther, is shown surrounded by her sons and daughters.

Market Place (Markt) – The town hall, a Late Gothic building erected between 1517 and 1528, has six gables. It stands in the middle of a cluster of 16C and 17C houses.

Each year
*the **Michelin Red Guide Deutschland***
revises its selection of hotels and restaurants
in the following categories

- pleasant, quiet, secluded
- with an exceptionally interesting or extensive view
- with gardens, tennis courts, swimming pool, beach
  facilities.

★ NENNIG ROMAN VILLA Saar

Michelin map 🔢 C 18 – 3km - 1 3/4 miles southeast of Remich

The foundations of this immense Roman villa ⊙ were excavated in 1852. Built on a splendid site overlooking the Moselle Valley in the 2C or 3C AD, the façade was no less than 120m - 394ft long.
The superb reception hall **mosaic★★**, in a fine state of preservation, measures 16m x 10m (52ft x 33ft). It comprises eight cartouches, framed by intricate geometric designs, illustrating gladiatorial combats between men and beasts in the arena of the Trier amphitheatre.

★ NÖRDLINGEN Bavaria   Pop 19 700

Michelin map 🔢 O 20
Town plan in the current Michelin Red Guide Deutschland

Lying along the Romantic Road, the fortified, former Imperial Town of Nördlingen was founded in the middle of the Ries Basin *(qv)* in the 2C BC. Its development throughout the centuries has been by concentric extension, witnessed by the street pattern and the ring of fortifications. Occupying an important position at the gates of the Bavarian Plateau, Nördlingen saw the armies of the French subdue the Austrians in 1796 and 1800.

SIGHTS

★ **St George's Church** – *Am Obstmarkt*. This late 15C hall-church, built in volcanic stone, is surmounted by a majestic, flamboyantly decorated tower 89m - 292ft high. Fan vaulting covers the interior in splendid style. The late 15C pulpit is reached via a corbelled staircase. At the high altar, the original Friedrich Herlin reredos (now in the local museum) has been replaced by a Baroque altarpiece, although the Crucifixion group and the statues of St George and **Mary Magdalene★** by Herlin still remain. Note the expression of the Saviour, moving in its sweetness and acquiescence.

★ **Town Walls** (Stadtmauer) – The wall is reinforced by fortified gateways and watchtowers, the most elegant of which (Reisturm, Löpsinger Tor, Deininger Tor) are capped by helmet roofs. A walk around the parapet from the Berger Tor to the Alte Bastei and the Reimlinger Tor is recommended.

★ **Municipal Museum** (Stadtmuseum) ⊙ – The panels from the original altarpiece at St George's Church were painted by Herlin, who was born in Nördlingen, between 1462 and 1477. Dedicated to the patron saint, the works display an extraordinary freshness of colour, particularly that representing women benefactors at prayer.

EXCURSION

★ **Neresheim Abbey** – *19km - 12 miles to the southwest.*
The huge white buildings of the Benedictine abbey stand out in the largely undeveloped landscape east of the Swabian Jura. The abbey church (Klosterkirche), started in 1745 under the direction of Balthazar Neumann *(qv)*, was the last work of the great Baroque architect. Inside, the decorations painted in 1755 by Martin Knoller, admirably spaced, complement the exceptional size of the building.

When driving in Great Britain
*use the **Michelin Motoring Atlas Great Britain***
Scale – 1:300 000.

★ THE NÜRBURGRING Rhineland-Palatinate

Michelin map 🔢 D 15 – Local map see under EIFEL MASSIF

This motor-racing track, laid out over a stretch of wooded, undulating country, has taken the name of the Nürburg ruin *(see under Eifel Massif)*, which stands inside its northern loop. The new circuit, opened in 1984, is used for such prestigious events as the World Championship for Sports Prototypes and the Nürburgring 24-hour Race for Touring Cars. The 4 1/2km - 3-mile lap includes 14 corners, with a height differential of 56m - 184ft. Aside from competitions and practice sessions, the circuits are open for normal use (apply at the Information Bureau B258). The old northern loop is 20km - 12 miles long.

Motor Racing Museum (Rennsportmuseum) ⊙ – Many different models, some of them unique examples, recall the great days of motor sport and of the Ring. Note in particular a **Bugatti Type 35A** (1925), one of the cars responsible for the success of this famous make; a 1934 **K3 MG** with splendid lines; a **Mercedes-Benz W-196** single-seat Grand Prix racer capable of 171 mph (1954); and more recent Formula 1 types such as the Ferrari B3 (1973) and the 1976 McLaren M-23.
In the upstairs gallery, motor-cycling history starts off with the Belgian **FN** (1910), equipped with a shaft drive of which this company was the pioneer, and also a belt-driven **Stehermaschine-Anzani** of the same period. Dozens of other exhibits remind the spectator of the great variety of European production this century, before so many different makes disappeared.

Michelin map **413** Q 18
Plan of the conurbation in the current Michelin Red Guide Deutschland

Before the Second World War, Nuremberg was one of the most beautiful medieval cities in Germany. Whole blocks of half-timbered burgher's houses with embellished gables made a setting so typically "Germanic" that the city was chosen by the Nazi party for its huge annual rallies each September. Some of the buidings used for the rallies still stand in Luitpoldhain Park in the southeast suburbs. It was in this "ideological capital" of the Reich that the notorious anti-semitic laws were promulgated in 1935; and it was here that the Allies held the war crimes trials when the fighting was over.

Today, with many of those medieval quarters completely destroyed, the old bronze-caster's and gold-beaters' town, together with its neighbour Fürth, is one of the main industrial centres of southern Germany. Machine tools, tractors, electrical and electronic apparatus, motorcycles, typewriters and toys are among its principal manufacturing products. Gastronomically, the Franconian capital offers a number of specialities: carp, either fried or poached in wine; Bratwurst (small grilled sausages); and **Lebkuchen** – fragrant gingerbread sold in attractive coloured boxes. From the last Friday in November to the end of December the market place is occupied by the famous Christmas market, known locally as the Christ-child Market **(Christkindlesmarkt)**. A wide choice of Christmas tree decorations and gifts are on offer.

The Golden Age – It was in the 15C and 16C that the fame of Nuremberg was at its height. At the crossroads of main trade routes and a shop window for Franconian craftsmanship, the city at that time rivalled Augsburg in importance. Nor was its renown purely commercial; literature and the arts and sciences flourished. The first German science university was founded in Nuremberg in 1526. At the same time the local humanist Willibald Pirkheimer (1470-1530) was translating texts from Latin and Greek. From 1510 onwards the locksmith Peter Henlein manufactured fob watches. In the world of art, the audacious sculptors **Veit Stoss** (c1445-1533) and **Adam Krafft** (c1460-1508); the talented bronze-caster **Peter Vischer the Elder** (1460-1529); **Michael Wolgemut** (1434-1519), the painter of altarpieces – and above all his pupil **Albrecht Dürer** *(qv)* – all profoundly influenced the German scene with their works.

Finally, the Nuremberg **Mastersingers** *(qv)* brought new life to German poetic form.

★★★ GERMAN NATIONAL MUSEUM

(GERMANISCHES NATIONALMUSEUM) (JZ) ⊘ *time: half a day*

This temple to German art and culture, as rich in treasures as it is enormous, lies around a former 14C Carthusian monastery. Map available at the ticket office.

Sculptures – First floor *(In galleries 5 to 14, centred on the old monastery church)*: valuable examples of statuary bearing witness to artistic styles from the 13C to the 16C. Here are statues of the Saints and Apostles, stone angels, canopies and carved consoles that adorned the façades of Nuremberg churches in days gone by. In the figure groups, altar decorations and Gothic madonnas, pure mysticism gives way little by little to a kind of pathos that is typically Germanic. Among the most remarkable works are those by Adam Krafft, Tilmann Riemenschneider (*The Lamentation of Christ*, c1500 – Gallery 13), and Veit Stoss (*The Archangel Raphael and the Young Tobias*, 1516 – Gallery 10).

Paintings – Ground floor: 14C and 16C works. Almost all the important schools are represented here. Particularly noteworthy are *Christ Crucified and The Saints* (c1445) by Stefan Lochner *(qv)*; Derick Baegert's *Christ Before Pontius Pilate* (c1480); an extremely severe *Golgotha*, dating from 1445-46, by the Master of the Tegernsee Altarpiece; and an *Adoration of the Magi* (c1470) from the studio of the Masters of the Life of Mary. Twelve paintings depicting Christ, Mary and the Saints were originally part of the high altar decoration in St Guy's Church, Nuremberg (1487). *(All the above paintings can be seen in Gallery 13.)*
First floor: this is where the works of **Dürer** and the other German Renaissance masters are to be found – artists who are often at the same time painters and engravers on copper. From Dürer himself one can see vigorous portraits of his teacher, Michael Wolgemut, and Charlemagne in coronation robes *(Galleries 33 and 34)*. Dürer's own influence is visible in the works of Albrecht Altdorfer and Hans Burgkmair *(Virgin with a Bunch of Grapes)*, in the religious scenes of Hans Baldung Grien, and the splendid portraits of Hans Holbein the Younger. From the hand of Lucas Cranach the Elder, turbulent partisan of the Reformation, there is a portrait of Martin Luther *(Gallery 48)*.

Decorative Arts – Ground floor: the exhibition of **craftsmanship** is in Gallery 27. Furniture from the 15C to the 19C can be seen here along with silverware and pewter, glassware, porcelain and ceramics, some from China.
First floor: more furniture; tapestry and hangings; stoneware; and again porcelain and objects in gold, silver and glass, give an idea of the interior decoration of patrician houses between the 16C and 18C. The skill of workers in silver and gold in Dürer's time can be gauged from an examination of **The Schlüsselfeld Nef**, a fully-rigged, three-master designed as a table decoration (1503), on display in Gallery 66.
One of Peter Henlein's fob watches (c1510) is among a collection of scientific instruments in Gallery 65 next door.
In addition to these treasures, the museum boasts an exhibition of **arms and hunting pieces** from different eras *(Ground floor)*; a Department of **Ancient Musical Instruments** *(Ground floor)*; and a section devoted to **folk art** (1st, 2nd and 3rd floors). The display of **copper engravings** on the Ground floor is superb.

* **Dürer's House** (Dürerhaus) (JY) ⊘ – This (restored) 15C burgher's house with jutting eaves lies at the base of the fortifications. Dürer bought it in 1509 and lived here until his death in 1528. The interior, soberly furnished, gives some idea of the life of the artist. Apart from eight sculptures in wood on the second floor, the works on view are copies.

Castle (JY) ⊘ – Symbol of the city, the castle stands proudly on a sandstone outcrop a little way to the north. The original **castle of the Burgraves** (Burggrafenburg), almost completely destroyed in 1420, had been completed in the 12C by the part known as the **Kaiserburg**; its appearance today dates from the 15C and 16C. From the outside terrace or the **Sinwellturm** (keep), which is 30m - 98ft high, there is an exceptional **view★** of the steeply sloped roofs and belfries of the old town. In an adjoining courtyard, the **well** *(under cover inside the building)* is impressive with its 53m - 174ft depth.

Among the dependencies, note particularly the two-storey Romanesque **Palatine Chapel**, which has a special Imperial Gallery from which the Emperor could survey his court assembled below.

* **Fortifications** (Stadtbefestigung) – Completed in the mid-15C, these have – uniquely for a large town in Germany – remained practically intact. They comprised an inner and an outer ring (Zwingermauer), the ramparts of the former with a covered parapet walk. A wide dry moat (in which today modern avenues run) lay outside the latter. No less than 67 defensive towers still exist. Among them are the four **Great Towers**, dating from the 16C and protected by colossal shells of cannon-proof masonry, sometimes 6m - 20ft thick (Frauentor – **KZ**, Spittlertor – **HZ**, Neutor – **JY**, Laufertor – **KY**).

The most interesting sector lies between the Kaiserburg and the Spittlertor (west side). An instructive half-hour **walk** starts from the castle gardens (Burggarten) (outside, below the Kaiserburg). From the ramparts it is possible to reach the watch path, which can be followed as far as the Neutorzwinger. Continue inside the ramparts. The Pegnitz river is crossed via a suspension foot-bridge beside the fortifications, before the promenade is concluded, once more on the outside (there is an attractive view of the castle from this point).

Fembo Municipal Museum (Stadtmuseum Fembohaus) (JY M²) – The museum is housed in a sandstone Renaissance mansion with a scrolled gable embellished by cornucopiae and obelisks. It is concerned with the history of Nuremberg, and in particular the homelife of the town's gentry between the 16C and the 19C.

St Sebald's Church (St Sebalduskirche) (JY) – A church with two chancels, built in the 13C and 14C. The sobriety of the west front, which is plain, with two Romanesque doorways framing the projecting chancel, is in vivid contrast with the huge Gothic east chancel, intricately worked and adorned with statues and pinnacles. Inside, the Romanesque and transitional Gothic western section (central and side aisles) is easily distinguished from the radiating High Gothic style of the east chancel and its ambulatory.

Works of Art★★:

1) St Peter Altarpiece (1485), painted on a gold background in the Wolgemut studio.

2) Richly decorated bronze baptismal font (Gothic, *c*1430), including a hearth – the oldest work cast in bronze in Nuremberg.

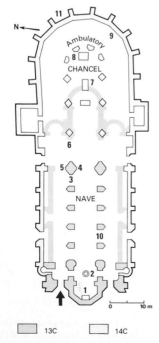

13C   14C

Non-extant parts

3) St Catherine (1310).

4) St Sebald (1390).

5) The Emperor Heinrich II (1350).

6) The Virgin in Glory (1420).

7) St Sebald's tomb. The Gothic shrine is part of a bronze display shelf by Peter Vischer (1519), supported by dolphins and snails and adorned with a host of statuettes. On the side panels, St Sebald is represented, and the artist himself in working clothes.

8) A Crucifixion group (1520) by Veit Stoss.

9) From the studio of the same artist: (above) Christ Transfigured and The Virgin In Sorrow (wood); (below) The Last Supper, The Garden of Olives and Christ Taken Prisoner (bas-relief in stone). Both groups date from 1499.

10) The Bearing of the Cross, by Adam Krafft (1506).

11) (Outside the church) Funerary monument of the Schreyer family: the Passion and The Resurrection, by Adam Krafft.

A fine series of **stained glass windows** (14C and 15C) illuminate the east chancel.

★ **Beautiful Fountain** (Schöner Brunnen) (JY C) – This 14C Gothic fountain in the old market place is one of the best-known sights of Nuremberg. Comprising 40 separate figures arranged in the form of a pyramid, the structure is 19m - 62ft high. At the top, Moses is surrounded by the prophets; around the base are the seven Electors and a series of nine Old Testament and medieval heroes: three forefathers, three Jews and three Christians. The figures decorating the fountain today are copies.

★ **Church of Our Lady** (Frauenkirche) (JY E) – A Gothic church on the east side of the market, built on the site of a destroyed synagogue, this sanctuary was erected during the reign of the Emperor Karl IV and served as a court chapel (1352-1361). The gable, with its pinnacles, niches and small oriel window, was designed by Adam Krafft (early 16C).

223

Dating from the same period, the clock above the balcony attracts visitors each day at noon, when a series of jacks appear to strike the hour. These colourful metal figures (Männlinlaufen) represent the seven Electors coming to swear allegiance to the Emperor after the enactment of the Golden Bull *(qv)* in Nuremberg in 1356.

The roof above the main body of the church, which is almost square in plan, is supported by four massive columns. On the north wall of the building is Adam Krafft's **Peringsdorffer Epitaph** (a robed Madonna), which dates from 1498. The **Tucher Altar** in the chancel, garnished with human figures, is a masterpiece of the Nuremberg school of painting: the triptych (*c*1440) depicts the Crucifixion, the Annunciation and the Resurrection.

Toy Museum (Spielzeugmuseum) (JY M³) ⊘ – *Karlstrasse 13-15*. The museum, housed in a 17C burgher's house, illustrates the important role played by Bavaria, and Nuremberg in particular, in the intricate skills of miniaturism. Dolls'-houses, tin soldiers, clockwork toys, and model cars, railways and aeroplanes here will delight children and adults alike.

Hospital (Heilig-Geist-Spital) (JKY F) – This 14-15C building, spread over two wide arches, spans a branch of the Pegnitz. Its graceful corbelled tower, and the oriel window embellishing the façade, can be seen from the Museumsbrücke. The central courtyard *(reached from an islet upstream)*, with its wooden galleries above wide sandstone arches, recalls a rich patrician's mansion of times gone by.

Banks of the Pegnitz – Parts of the old city still standing can be seen from here. Those crossing the Maxbrücke (**JY 90**) enjoy an attractive **view** of the ancient, half-timbered wine hall (Weinstadel) and its flanking tower, together with the Henkersteg covered footbridge.

★ **Church of St Lawrence** (St Lorenz-Kirche) (JZ) – A magnificent rose window enlivens the west face of this 13-14C Gothic church. The impressive hall-type chancel was added in the 15C. Inside (enter via the south door), once in the nave, the visitor is compelled by two outstanding works of art: the 1420 rood-beam Crucifix, with delicate medallions fashioned from its outer ends; and Veit Stoss's **Annunciation**★★ (Engelsgruss, 1517-18), which is suspended from the chancel vaulting. Marvellously sculpted in wood, the Virgin and the Angel appear to float in the interior of a circular space surrounded by six medallions depicting the other Joys of the Virgin after the Annunciation.

Left of the high altar, a Gothic **ciborium**★★ by Krafft (1493-95) rises to the level of the vaulting. In the lower part, the sculptor himself is represented supporting the balustrade.

The ambulatory is lit by superb stained glass windows from the workshop of the Alsatian Peter Hemmel of Andlau, notably that representing the Tree of Jesse (1487, second on the right, starting from the central window).

Transport Museum (Verkehrsmuseum) (JZ M⁴) ⊘ – The chief attraction in the **Railway Department**★ is the replica of the very first German train, drawn by an Adler locomotive, which linked Nuremberg and Fürth in 1835. There are a great many scale models. Note also the **postal section**, where there is a fine collection of postage stamps. On the far side of the Sandstrasse, all kinds of railed vehicles, ancient and modern, are on display in a special hall.

EXCURSIONS

Hersbrucker Alb – *Tour of 109km - 68 miles - allow half a day. Leave by the Sulbach-erstrasse* (**KY**), *then take the motorway A9 in the direction of Bayreuth, leaving at the Plech exit.*

★ **Neuhaus an der Pegnitz** – This charming locality comes suddenly into view after a bend in the road, with the tall tower of Veldenstein Castle dominating the town.

Continue following the course of the Pegnitz in the direction of Hersbruck. The valley is steeply enclosed, overlooked here and there by tall, pointed crags.

Hersbruck – A busy, bustling town, situated at a point where the valley of the Pegnitz opens out. Continue *(direction Happurg)* to the river bridge, from which, looking back, there is a fine view of the Wassertor fortified gate and the huddled roofs of the ancient quarter.

Return to Nuremberg, taking road no B 14.

Erlangen – *17km - 10 1/2 miles to the north.*
This residential town of the Baroque period, with its rows of uniform houses, was one of the places where the French Huguenots settled. The Protestant church marks the centre of the quarter built for them. Sharing with Nuremberg the functions of a university city, Erlangen was the birthplace of the physicist **Georg Ohm** (1789-1854), who formulated the law relating to the resistance of electrical circuits. In an early 18C **English garden** behind the castle stands the strange **Fountain of the Huguenots**, built by the French in 1706 as a gesture of thanks to their protector, the Margrave of Bayreuth.

*The **Michelin Green Guide France**,*
an informative travel guide,
aims to make touring more enjoyable
by highlighting the country's
natural features, historic sites
and other outstanding attractions.

Michelin map **413** N 24

The proximity of the Allgaü chain, one of the most popular with mountaineers, has led to the formation of a climbing school at Oberstdorf. Within easy reach are the Mädelegabel (2 645m - 8 676ft), the Hochvogel (2 593m - 8 505ft) and the Nebelhorn.

Nebelhorn ⊙ – *1 1/2 hours Rtn, of which 30 minutes are by cable car and chairlift.* From the summit at 2 224m - 7 295ft, there is a splendid **panorama**★★ extending from the Zugspitze *(qv)* in the east to the Säntis (the Swizz Appenzell Alps) in the west. In clear weather, beyond the bold outlines of the Allgaü itself, even the snows of the Bernese Oberland can be seen.

EXCURSIONS

★★ **Breitachklamm** – *6.5km - 4 miles to the southwest, plus a one and a half hour walk Rtn. (Recommended also in winter, when fantastic "curtains" of ice are formed.)*
In the lower gorge, galleries lead down to a cutting with sheer, polished walls, where the turbulent mountain stream has carved a course 100m - 300ft deep into the bedrock. At the foot of this path it is possible to turn back and re-mount by the long series of stairways that lead to the upper gorge (which is, however, less impressive). To return to Oberstdorf without a car, leave the gorge path at the top of these stairways. Walkers will then arrive at the Walserschanze, on the Kleinwalsertal road, from which there is a frequent bus service to the resort.

★ **The Kleinwalsertal** – *17km - 10 1/2 miles.*
The name identifies a high valley of the Breitach river, a mountain area some 100km² - 38 square miles in size, which was settled in the 13C by the **Walsers** – emigrants of Germanic origin from the Upper Valais. Cut off from the rest of the Vorarlberg by the peaks of the Allgaü, the Walsers found themselves Austrian subjects when national frontiers were established in 1453, although such culture and traditions as they had were oriented exclusively towards Germany.
In 1891 the area was granted a special status whereby, still under Austrian sovereignty, it was nevertheless economically regarded as part of Germany.
Today the Kleinwalsertal has Austrian police, German customs, a German postal service but Austrian stamps, and the only legal tender is the German mark. Until a modern road was built in 1930, the valley remained isolated and the Walsers, like other hardy pioneers, retained a reputation of grim individualism and dourness of character – traits still reflected in the sombre buildings of their scattered homesteads.
Having passed through the resorts of **Riezlern** and **Hirschegg**, tourists can turn down the steep hill at the entrance to **Mittelberg** that leads to the hamlet of Bödmen, which is interesting for its traditional Valaisian chalets.

★ **ODENWALD** Bavaria and Hessen

Michelin map **413** K 17-18

A popular excursion for the inhabitants of big cities nearby, this huge natural park lies between the Rhine, the Main and the Neckar, undulating and rural to the west, forested and with steeper hills east of the Mömling river.

EXCURSION FROM MILTENBERG

92km - 57 miles - allow 4 hours

★ **Miltenberg** – A remarkable row of half-timbered houses lines the main street leading to the **Marktplatz**★. This small town is overlooked by the wooded heights bordering the final curve of the Main.

★ **Eulbach Park** ⊙ – A romantic place, with ruins, Roman remains, a lake – and an adjoining reserve where European wild oxen (bison) can be seen.

Michelstadt – Ancient houses, a flowered 16C fountain, and the **town hall**★ façade, topped by a very steep roof flanked by two oriel windows, combine to form a striking ensemble in the market place. Follow the road beside the town hall and turn right into the Einhardtspforte alley: the **Odenwald Museum** ⊙ (rural activity, craftwork) is housed in a fine group of half-timbered buildings, the former **Municipal Cellars** (Städtische Kellerei) around an ancient courtyard.

> *Leave Michelstadt to the south in the direction of Erback. Shortly after Hetzbach, turn left to Kailbach and Amorbach. The road winds through the hills and wooded valleys.*

★ **Amorbach** – On the eastern slopes of the Odenwald, Amorbach is dominated by two pairs of belfries, those with a red stone courses belonging to the former **abbey church**★ ⊙ (Abteikirche).
This was built between 1742 and 1747, respecting the plan of the Romanesque building which preceded it. Even the old towers were left, the architect simply adding a Rococo sandstone façade. Note the **chancel grilles**★, the Rococo pulpit and the 1782 organ.
The abbey **library**★ has rich Baroque decorations (1789-99). The neo-Classic ornamentation in the **Green Room**★ is a rare feature for a German abbey.

Michelin map **411** H 7
Town plan in the current Michelin Red Guide Deutschland

Oldenburg is a widespread, open town chiefly concerned with agricultural shows and the processing of foodstuffs produced in the fertile hinterland where market-gardening, horticulture, cattle raising and horse breeding predominate. The river port is linked to the North Sea by the Hunte, a tributary of the Weser, and to the Netherlands by a coastal canal (Küstenkanal). From the Lappan Tower in the north to St Lambert's Church in the south, a pedestrian zone now follows the plan of the medieval city centre.

★ **Castle Park** (Schlossgarten) – A mild, moist coastal climate has encouraged in this landscaped garden the growth of magnificent trees and shrubs such as rhodo-dendrons and tulip trees. From the weeping willows on the lake shore there is an attractive view of the towers of St Lambert's.

Regional Art and History Museum (Landesmuseum für Kunst und Kulturge-schichte) ⊙ – The museum, housed in the former seat of the counts and grand dukes of Oldenburg, was built in the 17C and remodelled in the 18C and again the 19C.
Rembrandt's *Angel in the House of Tobias* is among the Old Masters in the state rooms on the first floor. There is also a pleasant series of **small pictures** (*Idylls*) by Johann Heinrich Wilhelm Tischbein (1751-1825), the most prominent painter of this name thanks to *Goethe in the Roman Countryside*, which hangs in the Städel Museum, Frankfurt (qv).
On the top floor are reconstructions: fine 16C and 18C peasant interiors from northern Germany; a late 18C pharmacy.

★ **Municipal Museum** (Stadtmuseum) ⊙ – Interesting here are rooms from the vil-las Francksen (1877) and Jürgens'sche (1863), furnished and decorated in the fashionable styles of the 19C and early 20C.

Augusteum ⊙ – *Elisabethstrasse 1*. Works by painters from the Worpswede colony (qv) are on show here along with such German Expressionists as Erich Heckel. Among the Surrealists, note Franz Radziwill – who classes himself as a "symbolic realist".

Natural History Museum (Museum für Naturkunde und Vorgeschichte) ⊙ – *Damm 40-44*. An interesting survey of the fauna found in North Germany's most typical regions: mammals, fish, birds and environment; plant civilizations, forest and marsh eco-systems. There is a model of a sea-wall organization to protect the low-lying coastal regions from high tides. In the prehistoric department 2 400-year-old bodies found preserved in the peat (Moorleichen) always attract attention.

EXCURSIONS

Cloppenburg – *31km - 19 miles to the south*.
In this town there is a **Museum-village** (Museumsdorf) ⊙ – 37 acres of farms, peas-ant houses and craft workshops in local style laid out around a church and a pond. In the **squire's house** (Burg Arkenstede) is a most attractive collection of furniture and decorative objects.

★ **Megalithic Monuments of Visbek** (Steindenkmäler) – *38km - 24 miles to the south*.
In this group collectively known as "The Intended", the **Bride** (Visbeker Braut) is a collection of granite blocks arranged in a rectangular pattern in a clearing that measures 80m x 7m (262ft x 23ft).
The **Groom** (Visbeker Bräutigam) comprises a dolmen, considered as a sacrificial altar (Opfertisch), and, again, an alignment of 80 blocks in a rectangle 108m x 10m (354ft x 33ft). At the western extremity of the site a funerary chamber recalls – it is thought – the dwellings of this period. The site is 30 minutes' walk, there and back, from the Engelmannsbäke inn.

Michelin maps **411** and **412** H 10
Town plan in the current Michelin Red Guide Deutschland

Lying between the Teutoburger Wald and the Wiehengebirge heights, Osnabrück developed around two separate centres: in the 9C the Old Town spread from the ancient market and the episcopal quarter; and from the 11C onwards, a New Town proliferated around the Church of St John. When they united within a single city wall (c1300), Osnabrück became an important commercial centre.
The all-important linen trade has now been supplanted by metallurgy (automo-bile coachwork; cables) and paper mills.

Before the Peace in 1648 – Preliminaries to the Peace of Westphalia started in Osnabrück between the Emperor and the Protestant belligerents (Sweden and the Lutheran Princes of Germany). On the other side, the Roman Catholic pow-ers negotiated with the Emperor in Münster. News of the treaties' final signature was announced in Osnabrück on 25 October 1648 to a crowd, at first incredulous and then bursting into a spontaneous hymn of thanksgiving.

SIGHTS

Town Hall ⊙ – This early 16C building had to be restored after the Second World War, but still retains its Gothic look beneath a wide pavilion roof. The peace of 1648 was announced from its steps. The statue of Charlemagne, above the entrance, is surrounded by the effigies of eight other Emperors and Kings.

★ **The Peace Chamber** (Friedensaal) – The hall in which the peace talks were held is adorned with portraits of the heads of state and their delegates. The floor and ceiling have been rebuilt; the carved wooden seats and the chandelier are authentic and date from 1554. Among the gold plate in the **Treasury** is the priceless 14C Kaiserpokal Goblet.

St Mary's Church (Marienkirche) – A 14C Gothic hall-church which, with its elegant transverse gables, closes off the northern end of the Marktplatz. Its most interesting work of art is the early 16C **Altarpiece of the Passion★**, originally from Antwerp.

St Peter's Cathedral (Dom) – The squat outline of this 13C Transitional Gothic church is distinguished by large towers differing both in shape and size. The north face boasts a fine Romanesque embellishment of blind arcades and cornices. The interior is equally unusual, with a flat chevet and squared-off ambulatory. The chapels leading off this contain a few works of art, notably a 15C Pietà and a 16C stone Crucifixion.
The ogive vaulting in the nave is rounded; from the triumphal arch hangs an early 13C Crucifix. There is a good view of the two towers from the asymmetrical cloister, entered via the south aisle.

St John's Church (Johanniskirche) – This Gothic hall-church, again dating from the 13C, served as a parish church for the New Town. Every architectural and decorative effect has systematically been reduced to the basic minimum. The dark wood **altarpiece** (high altar: scenes of the Passion) was carved in 1512. Outside, the long, narrow cloister once served as a burial place.

EXCURSIONS

★ **Tecklenburg** – *23km - 14 miles to the southwest. About 30 minutes. Leave the car in the park at the entrance to the town.*
Famous for its half-timbered houses and its position on the crest of the Teutoburger Wald, this is a very popular small town. Make for the main square and then head west, through the Legge gateway, to the oldest part, at the foot of the **castle**. Of this, nothing remains but a monumental Renaissance gateway and a lookout tower.

★★★ **OTTOBEUREN** Bavaria   Pop 7 300

Michelin map **413** N 23

Ottobeuren Abbey, the jewel of German Baroque, stands in a small town surrounded by pleasant, hilly country, with the dramatic outline of the Allgäu in the background.

The Climax of the Baroque Style – Founded in 764, the Benedictine Abbey prospered from the start, when its patron, Charlemagne, granted it extensive rights. The early 16C saw one of the first printing presses working here. Soon afterwards, a school was established whose fame spread far beyond Bavaria.
In the 18C the abbey was totally transformed into a Baroque style mingling the influences of Salzburg (rounded transept arms), the Vorarlberg school (dividing columns) and Rome (domes). In 1748, Johann Michael Fischer, the great architect of southern Germany, put the finishing touches on what was to be his masterpiece. But in the realms of Rococo decoration, the names of Zeillers must be associated with his (for the frescoes), and also that of Johann Michael Feuchtmayer (stuccowork and statues). Under their direction, a number of German and Italian artists helped with the church's interior ornamentation.
Secularized in 1802, the abbey was re-established as a priory in 1834 and regained its former status in the Benedictine Order in 1918.

ABBEY (KLOSTER) *time: 1/2 hour*

★★★ **Abbey Church** (Klosterkirche) ⊙ – The squat outside appearance of the church *(illustration p 24)* offers no clue to its actual size. The towers are 82m - 272ft high; the length of the nave is 90m - 295ft; and the transept is no less than 60m - 200ft wide. It is in fact an enormous building, with an overall length outside of 480m - 1 575ft. The secret of course lies in its perfect proportions (and it is here that the theory of certain German art critics can be tested: that the exterior of a Baroque church has no intrinsic value, but serves only to reflect in its arrangement of masses the powerful influences of the interior).
Once inside *(photograph see over)*, the visitor is struck by the luminosity of the nave: this astonishing church, in defiance of tradition, being oriented north-south, the light effects are often unexpected – particularly when the sun's rays slant low, in early morning and evening.
The colours are harmonious. Half-tones of rose, amber, violet and ochre predominate, while the vault frescoes adopt warmer tints. In the chancel, relatively shadowed, more sombre shades complement gold ornamentation and the patina of natural wood.

Transept Crossing (Vierung) – The impression here is of great strength. The transept – being angled of course east-west – could in fact be a church in itself. Every architectural element derives from the flattened central dome. Johann Michael Fischer has even furnished the crossing piers with cut-off corners. Noteworthy here are the altars of St Michael, patron of the Ottobeuren region and of the Empire; of the Saintly Guardian Angels; of St Joseph and of St John the Baptist. But the most interesting works are the pulpit and, opposite, a group above the font representing the baptism of Christ himself, the work of the sculptor Johann Joseph Christian. Paving designed by Johann Jakob Zeiller is based on the motifs of the cross, the circle and the star. Zeiller also painted the grandiose composition embellishing the interior of the cupola, The Miracle of Pentecost.

Interior view of Ottobeuren Abbey Church

Chancel (Chor) – At the entrance, the small altar of the Holy Sacrament is surmounted by a much venerated 12C Saviour, surrounded by stars symbolizing the sovereignty of the universe.

The high altar glorifies the Holy Trinity. At the foot of the reredos columns are statues of St Peter and St Paul; of St Ulrich, Bishop of Augsburg and patron saint of Swabia; and of St Konrad, Bishop and patron saint of the nearby diocese of Constance.

The walnut **choir stalls★★** (1764) form, with the chancel organ loft, a single artistic composition. The high backs of the stalls are decorated with gilded limewood bas-reliefs by Johann Joseph Christian depicting Biblical scenes and events in the life of St Benedict.

Karl Joseph Riepp (1710-1775), a pupil of Silbermann who worked for a long time in Burgundy (churches at Dijon, Beaune and Besançon), built the chancel **organ★★** (1766). The instrument's musical and decorative properties, already impressive, were supplemented in 1957 by a new Organ of the Virgin, installed in the same loft.

Abbey Buildings (Klostergebäude) ⊙ – These were constructed between 1711 and 1731. They include an abbatial palace (Prälatur), with the usual state apartments and an Emperor's Hall, together with such luxuries as a theatre and a manificent library.

PADERBORN Rhineland-Westphalia   Pop 123 000

Michelin maps 411 and 412 J 11
Town plan in the current Michelin Red Guide Deutschland

This old Hanseatic town, an important stage on the commercial and strategic route linking Flanders and Saxony, was one of the first episcopal sees of Westphalia (895). Almost one hundred years before, in 799, it was the site of a meeting between Charlemagne and Pope Leo III which sealed the union between the papacy and the western Empire. Each year in July, the town commemorates the transfer in 836 from Le Mans, France, to Paderborn of the relics of St Liborius, who later became the town's patron saint.

SIGHTS

★ **Cathedral** (Dom) – A massive tower, pierced with many Romanesque bays, overlooks the church, most of which dates from the 13C.

The entrance porch (Paradiesportal) is on the north side, where the doors are flanked by statues of bishops and saints (among them St Julian, the first Bishop of Le Mans), with the Virgin (c1250) above on the pier.

The 13C interior, modelled on Poitiers Cathedral, demonstrates the evolution from Romanesque (in the western part of the huge hall) to Gothic (in the east). Off the north chancel is a small atrium with three equal aisles and some arches dating back to the year 1000. The crypt, reached from the transept, houses the relics of St Liborius.

Cloister (access via the atrium) – Note the funerary chapel of the Westphalian Counts, with a graceful Gothic altarpiece (1517), and the amusing "Three Hares Window". The animals, visible from the outside only, each have a pair of ears and yet there are only three ears in all.

St Bartholomew's Chapel (Bartholomäuskapelle) – A Romanesque hall, built apart, a little way north of the main structure, by Byzantine masons in 1017. The slender columns with ornate capitals in Late Corinthian style support a domed vaulting.

Diocesan Museum (Diözesanmuseum) ⊙ – Note here especially the fine **Virgin of Bishop Imad★** (1050). The museum, devoted to sacred art, also displays the two small portable altars of Roger von Helmarshausen (c1100), and the 1627 St Liborius shrine.

Town Hall – A monumental 1616 building with three gables, of which the ram's-horn scrollwork (Late Renaissance) recalls the Weser style of architecture *(qv)*.

The Pader Springs (Paderquellen) – Below the cathedral, more than 200 springs bubble from the ground, merging to form streams strong enough to turn a water-wheel, before flowing into the Pader river.

★★ PASSAU Bavaria — Pop 50 000

Michelin map **413** X 21

Passau, a frontier town between Bavaria and Austria and known as the Town of the Three Rivers, lies in a marvellous **setting★★** at the junction of the Inn, the Danube (Donau) and the small river Ilz. The old town, with its Baroque churches and patrician houses, lies crowded onto the narrow tongue of land separating the Inn and the Danube. Northwards, on the far bank of the Danube, rises the wooded bluff on which the Oberhaus fortress is built.
Passau's cultural and economic influence on eastern Bavaria was reinforced in 1978, when a new university was opened. In summertime, the European Weeks attract a large number of music – and theatre – lovers.

A Powerful Bishopric – The see was founded in the 8C by St Boniface, the English-born "Apostle of Germany" *(qv)*. By the end of the 10C it had become so powerful that it rivalled that of Salzburg. In 1217 the bishops were created by Princes of the Empire. Until the 15C the diocese was so huge that it encompassed the entire Danube valley in Austria, even including Vienna.

A commercial base – The arrival of the Inn waters at Passau almost doubles the flow volume of the Danube; from there on it becomes a really big river. From the Middle Ages, river trade played an important role in the town's prosperity, including such essentials as cereals, wine and salt, for which the Passau merchants enjoyed the "right of storage". Business with Bohemia, which was conducted via the valley of the Ilz, was also important. Today, when barges can go upriver as far as Kelheim, the "town of three rivers" also offers excursions, cruises and passenger traffic to Vienna and Budapest.

SIGHTS

Oberhaus Fortress (Veste Oberhaus) (B) – Work on this imposing citadel, which served the bishops as a refuge against continuous rebellions by the burghers, started in 1219. It is linked with the **Fortress of Niederhaus** by a fortified road along the spit of land separating the Danube and the Ilz. From the belvedere marked Zur Aussicht, near the car park – or from the top of a tower inside the compound *(142 steps)* – there are magnificent **views★★** over the rocky promontory dividing the Inn from the Danube, with the town's churches and houses jumbled close together upon it. Some of the houses, following a former Inn Valley tradition, have ridge roofs behind façades – masking the many sloping angles from street level.
The history of the town and its craftwork, folk art, and religious past are traced in a small **museum (B M1)** which also displays paintings of the Danube School *(qv)*.

St Stephen's Cathedral (Dom St Stefan) (B) – Apart from the east chancel and the transept, the original Late Gothic building was destroyed by fire in the 17C. Once rebuilt, the greater part of it was in the Baroque style. The majestic west front is so severe in concept that the late 19C addition to the two towers of a final, octagonal stage seems almost frivolous.
The huge interior is overloaded with frescoes and stuccowork. There are four **lateral chapels** with fine paintings by the Austrian artist J M Rottmayr (1654-1730). The first on the south side shows *The Beheading of John the Baptist*. Opposite is *The Conversion of St Paul*. In the two remaining chapels are *St Sebastian Succoured by St Irene* (north) and *The Martyrdom of St Agnes* (south).
The pulpit, lavishly decorated with figures, is a Viennese work (1722-26). Henselmann's modern (1953) high altar represents the stoning of St Stephen (figures In silvered poplar wood). The organ, rebuilt in 1928 with 17 388 pipes and 231 registers, is the largest in the world.
From the Residenzplatz, visitors can admire the Cathedral's **east end★★**, a remarkable work in Late Gothic (1407-1530) whose slender outline is emphasized by the domed belfry which tops the transept cupola.

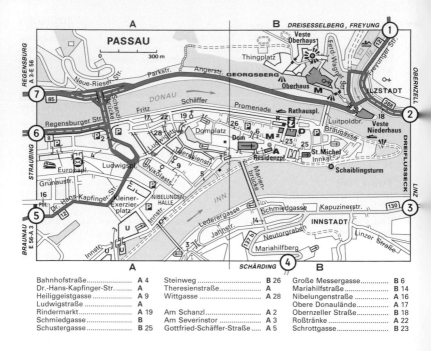

Residenzplatz (B) – The square is bordered on the south by the bishops' **New Residence** (A), which dates from the beginning of the neo-Classical period. The surrounding streets are still lined with many old houses above arcades, with corbelling and concealed Inn Valley ridge roofs.

Rathausplatz (B) – One of the town's most picturesque squares. The painted façade of the **town hall** (D) dates from the 14C; the building's tower was built in the late 18C.

★ **Glass Museum** (Glasmuseum) (B M²) ⊘ – Glassware from Bohemia, Bavaria and Austria, from the late 18C to the 1930s, makes up most of this fine collection. The most important display comes from **Bohemia** (Biedermeier, Historicism, Jugendstil); coloured glass, vases, pots and figurines attest to the great skill of the Bohemian glassblowers.

St Michael's Church (B) – This 17C church built by the Jesuits overlooks the north bank of the Inn. The over-rich gilding and stuccowork date from c1720. A reredos painted by Carlone hides the squared-off chevet.

★ **The Three Rivers Walk** (Dreiflusseck) (B) – *From St Michael's Church, go down to the Inn quayside.* The fast, at times almost torrential, river runs at the foot of the **Schaiblingsturm** (1481), which was once part of Passau's defence system. At the confluence, the green current of the Inn can be seen running alongside the brown Danube waters for a long time before they mingle. From the Danube bank, on the far side of the promontory, there is a fine **viewpoint**, looking across the river at the wooded, rocky height of the Georgsberg, on which the Oberhaus fortress is built.

EXCURSIONS

★ **Dreisesselberg** – *48km - 30 miles to the northeast.*
The drive to this curious group of granitic rocks, eroded into flat, saucer-like shapes, runs through some of the wildest forest regions of Bohemia. The inn at the foot of the formation is soon reached from the road. Green triangles bordered with white signpost the path leading to the lowest rock outcrop. From there, steps rise to the **Hochstein** (1 332m - 4 370ft). The viewpoint at the summit affords a splendid **panorama**★ which reveals the immensity of this Bohemian forest.

Osterhofen Church – *36km - 22 miles to the northeast. Leave Passau by ⑥ on the town plan.*
Three great names of the Bavarian Baroque style have given here the fulness of their talent: Johann Michael Fischer for the architecture and the Asam brothers for the decoration. The alternation of the convex lines of the balustrades and concave lines of the pilasters as well as the almost total absence of right angles gives many contours to the buildings. Note in particular the monumental high altar with its wreathed columns and its angels with enraptured smiles surrounding a radiant almond-shaped glory.

Danube School

The German painters working in the Danube valley in the 16C were among the first to depict landscape for its own sake. The best masters of this so-called school were Albrecht Altdorfer, Lucas Cranach the Elder, Wolf Huber and Jörg Breu the Elder.

Only a few miles west of Berlin, Potsdam was chosen at the beginning of the 17C as the official residence of the Electors of Brandenburg because of its ideal setting – a natural wooded site dotted with lakes and crisscrossed by canals and arms of the Havel river. Sacked by Swedish troops during the Thirty Years War *(qv)*, the town was revived by Friedrich Wilhelm I. After the Revocation of the Edict of Nantes, many French Huguenots emigrated to Potsdam, amongst them merchants and craftsmen who contributed to the subsequent economic development of the area.

A Prussian Versailles – Under the rule of Friedrich Wilhelm, "the King-Sergeant" (1713-1740), Potsdam became an administrative centre and above all a garrison town (to the extent that at one time three-quarters of the population were military).

The King's son, Frederick the Great (Friedrich II: 1740-1786), was on the contrary a patron of the arts and man of letters. Most of the prestigious monuments for which the city is famous today were due to him, notably Sans-Souci and the New Palace. Frederick, as eloquent in French as in his own language, welcomed many eminent Frenchmen to his Court, among them Voltaire, who lived in Potsdam for three years.

In 1991, 205 years after his death, the remains of Frederick the Great were reinterred in the crypt of his beloved palace of Sans-Souci in Potsdam.

The Potsdam Conference – The treaty defining the role of the victors in the occupation and future of Germany after the Second World War was signed here at Cecilienhof Palace on 2 August 1945 by the leaders of the Allied powers (Churchill – subsequently Attlee – Roosevelt and Stalin).

★★★ SANS-SOUCI PALACE AND PARK

Follow the itinerary suggested on the map.

Designed by Peter Joseph Lenné (1789-1866), the most talented landscape gardener in Prussia, the 300ha - 740-acre park contains several hundred different species of tree. The various castles and palaces occupying it were all built between 1744 and 1860. This huge complex marrying architecture with the landscape is undoubtedly the best example of its kind in Germany. Wandering here and there it is easy to understand why Frederick the Great, turning his back momentarily on affairs of state, took such delight coming here to steep himself in the arts, especially music.

Neptune's Grotto (Neptungrotte) – Laid out according to plans drawn up by Knobelsdorff *(qv)* between 1751 and 1757, the grotto houses a statue of the sea god.

★ **Great Gallery** (Grosse Bildergalerie) ⊘ – This is the oldest museum in Germany. It was built between 1755 and 1763. Amidst the pretentious Rococo décor of the great rooms it is possible to admire the works of the Italian schools (Bassano, Tintoretto and Caravaggio), the French (Simon Vouet and Van Loo), and the Flemish (Van Dyck, Rubens and Terbrugghen)

Sans-Souci Palace, Potsdam

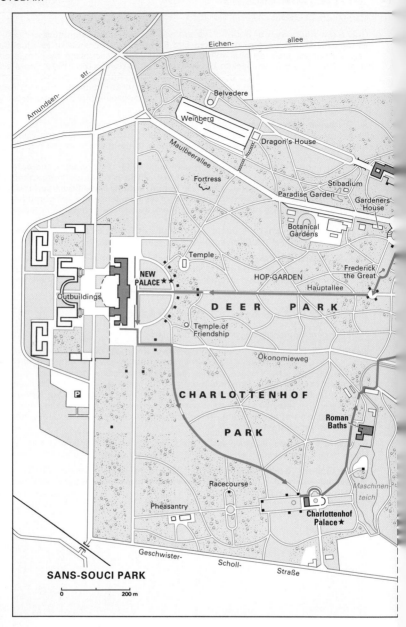

SANS-SOUCI PARK

0   200 m

★★★ **Sans-Souci Palace** (Schloss Sanssouci) ⊘ – It is impossible to remain unmoved by the progressive appearance of this majestic façade as one climbs the great staircase rising through the tiers of terraces before it. The original idea of the architect (Knobelsdorff again) was for the façade, adorned with 36 atlantes, to encompass the entire terrace area. But the king preferred a generous proportion of space which indeed became one of his favourite places to relax in. On the far side of the palace the state entrance is flanked by an elegant semicircular colonnade.

Interior – A walk through these rooms reveals the enormous skill and artistry in the Rococo mode of the craftsmen who decorated them.

Ante-chamber – Grey and gold, the decoration here is elegant and sober. The ceiling was painted by Harper in 1746.

Small Gallery – Paintings by Nicolas Lancret (1690-1743) and Jean-Baptiste Pater (1695-1736), both of them followers of Watteau. On the chimneypiece, busts of Frederick and his brother Henry.

Library – A relatively small room in the form of a rotunda. Decorations in cedar-wood and gilded bronze.
Bedchamber and Study of Frederick the Great – Portraits of the royal family as well as the King's table and the armchair in which he died.

Concert Hall – A painting by Menzel represents the King playing the flute. The décor here is rocaille, with Pesne murals on the theme of Ovid's *Metamorphoses*.

Reception Hall – Paintings by Coypel and Van Loo. Ceiling (*Zephyr and Flora*) by Pesne.

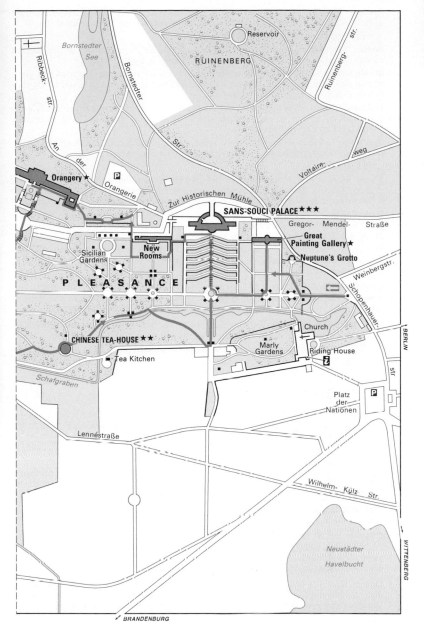

Hall of Marble – Beneath the cupola there is a Bernini bust of Richelieu, also statues of Apollo and Venus by François Gaspard Adam (1710-1761), who introduced French taste to the Potsdam Court. The decoration, in marbles from Carrara and Silesia, is superb.

Four Guest Rooms – The fourth was Voltaire's, from 1750 to 1753. There is a replica of the great writer's bust by Jean Antoine Houdon (1741-1828).

The New Rooms (Neue Kammern) – Designed in 1747 by Knobelsdorff in the form of an orangery, this block was in fact transformed into the palace guest house. Outside, the **Sicilian Gardens** (Sizilianischer Garten) were designed in the Renaissance style by Lenné.

★ **Orangery** – Built in the style of an Italian Renaissance palace between 1851 and 1860, the Orangery today houses the archives of the State of Potsdam.

★★ **New Palace (Neues Palais)** ⊙ – This imposing – and in fact rather pompous – building was ordered by Frederick the Great to demonstrate that the economic power of Prussia remained intact after the arduous Seven Years War. Some 400 rooms behind a frontage of almost 700ft, together with over-lavish decorations and a superabundance of sculpture, themselves alone testify to the over-ambitious nature of the project – which was nevertheless completed in a relatively short time, from 1763 to 1769. The style of architecture, an unrestrained Baroque, today seems both heavy and over-mannered, very far from the elegant simplicity of Sans-Souci.
Behind the palace, the outbuildings and servants' quarters take the form of small pavilions linked by a curved colonnade (1766-69).

Interior – *The number and nature of rooms open to visitors being subject to variations, what follows below is restricted to the most popular examples.*

Ground floor

Grotto – Sea-shells and minerals contribute to the exuberant décor of this fantasy room. The ceiling fresco, *Venus and the Graces*, is by J G Niedlich.

Marble Gallery – Red jasper and white Carrara marble decorate the floor and walls of this hall. The allegorical frescoes on the ceiling, based on the hours of the day, are by C B Rode, a pupil of Pesne.

Red Damask Room – The eight canvases depicting members of the royal family were executed by Pesne when he was the official Court Painter. Note especially *Frederick II as Crown Prince*.

Oval Office – A barrel-vaulted room with a magnificent parquet floor. The marquetry, in floral motifs, was laid by the Spindler Brothers.

First floor

Marble Room – The stone floor is an elegant grey-blue, enhanced by discreet gilding. Statues in the same stone represent the Electors of Brandenburg. The ceiling fresco, by Van Loo (1769), depicts *Ganymede and Hebe on Olympus*.

Upper Gallery – This is neo-Classical in style, with stuccowork antique heads on plinths. Seventeenth-century Italian paintings include Giordano's *Judgement of Paris* and *The Suicide of Lucretia* by Reni.

Theatre (Schlosstheater) – Designed as part of the palace's south wing, this is a fine example of Germany's Late Rococo style (1766-1768). The auditorium is encompassed by two galleries supported by gilded Hermes.

★ **Charlottenhof Palace** – Designed by Karl-Friedrich Schinkel (1781-1841), this was built in the Classical style between 1826 and 1829. Visitors can see, among other things, the bedchamber and office of Alexander von Humboldt.

Roman Baths (Römische Bäder) – Serving as outbuildings and an ablutions centre for the Court gardeners, these too were based on plans by Schinkel.

★★ **Chinese Tea-House** (Chinesisches Teehaus) – A circular pavilion decorated with gilded statues, this structure arose from the "Sino-mania" so popular in 18C Germany. There is an exhibition of Chinese porcelain inside.

ADDITIONAL SIGHTS

Brandenburg Gate (Brandenburger Tor) – *Platz der Nationen.*
A monumental gateway in the form of a triumphal arch, Roman style, built in the Baroque fashion in 1770.

★ **Hydraulic Waterworks** (Wasserwerk) ⊙ – *Take the Schoppenhauerstrasse, and then, on the right, the Wilhelm Külz Strasse.*
Installed in a most unusual building imitating a mosque, complete with minarets, this pumping station (1841-42) supplies water to the fountains, pools and cascades in Sans-Souci Park. The ingenious machinery can be seen at work.

★ **Old Stables** (Marstall) – *Wilhelm Külz Strasse.* Dating from 1675 and modified by Knobelsdorff in 1746. Groups of horse-trainers decorate the attics.

★★ **Church of St Nicholas** (Nikolaikirche) – Built on the site of an old Baroque church destroyed by fire in 1795, this is a perfect example of German Classicism as conceived by Schinkel. Construction of the squared nave and preceding porch was completed in 1837. The cupola was added two years later.

★ **Dutch Quarter** (Holländisches Viertel) – It is on each side of the **Mittelstrasse** that one can still see these gabled houses in varying colours, built by the Dutch architect Boumann around 1740 for Netherlands artisans working in Potsdam.

★ **Cecilienhof Palace** (Schloss Cecilienhof) ⊙ – *Leave the northern part of the Old Town via the Nauener Tor.* Designed as a residence for the heir to the throne and his familiy, this was built on the model of an English timber-framed manor house.

Museum – Visitors can see the workrooms used by the members of the Allied delegations and the conference hall where the Potsdam Agreements were signed (2 August 1945).
The **New Park** (Neuer Garten), surrounded by lakes, is embellished with a number of different follies: an obelisk, a pyramid, an **orangery** (1790) and the **Marble Temple** (an imitation of an antique ruin dating from 1787-91).

EXCURSIONS

Brandenburg – *38km - 24 miles to the west.*
It was in the 14C that this small town in the heart of the Havelland (an area of scattered lakes fed by the Havel river) began to prosper, mainly through the cloth trade. The **Cathedral of St Peter and St Paul**, founded in 1165 and remodelled in the 14C, is furnished with several Gothic altarpieces. In the two-aisle crypt there is a mausoleum in memory of the clergy murdered during the Nazi regime.
Rich exterior decoration distinguishes the 15C **St Catherine's Church**, which boasts a polygonal chancel. The ambulatory (in the process of restoration) is a typical example of brick-built Gothic.

Lehnin Abbey ⊙ – *28km - 17 miles to the southwest.*
Brick-built again, this three-aisle basilica, founded in 1180 by the Cistercian Order, has all the hallmarks of Early Gothic. Worth seeing: a Triumphal Cross dating from 1225 and the funerary stone of the Margrave Otto IV.

Nestling at the foot of a rock pinnacle crowned by a castle and an abbey church, the picturesque half-timbered houses and narrow, winding streets of Quedlinburg form a picture that corresponds to everyone's idea of a 17C German town.

The Abbesses of Quedlinburg – A convent for the daughters of the nobility was founded on this height by Otto I around AD 930. Thanks to certain privileges, and to the lands with which it was endowed, the religious community prospered to the extent that Quedlinburg was chosen as a residence by the Saxon kings, and six Diets, or Councils of State were convened there.

★ OLD TOWN

★ **Market Place** (Markt) – The early 17C Renaissance **Town Hall**, a two-storey building flanked by a gateway showing the town's armorial bearings, borders the northern side of the Market Place. On the left of the façade is a statue of Roland (c1420). Houses built in the 17C and 18C line the other three sides of the square.

★ **Old Streets** – Circle the Church of St Benedict via the Marktstrasse and the Kornmarkt to explore the cobbled lanes behind the Town Hall, then return to the Market Place along the Breitstrasse, which has several picturesque alleyways opening off it. On the far side of the square, stroll to the hill that leads up to the castle by way of the Wordgasse, the Hohe Strasse and the Blasiistrasse.

Klopstock Museum (Klopstockhaus) ⊘ – The poet Friedrich Gottlieb Klopstock was born in 1724 in this late 16C house (No 12) on one side of the charming **Schlossberg Square★**. Drawing on sources close to the German psyche, inspired by ancient Teutonic myths, he composed a saga glorifying the hero Arminius (qv), but he is best known for the huge religious epic, *Messias (The Messiah)*, said to be inspired by Milton's *Paradise Lost*. Various rooms in the house recall his life and his work.

Feininger Gallery ⊘ – *Behind the Klopstock Museum, entry at No 5A, Finkenherd.* There is an interesting collection of drawings and water-colours by the Expressionist painter Lyonel Feininger (1871-1956).

★ CASTLE HILL (SCHLOSSBERG)

The ramp leading up to the castle end in a wide terrace with a fine general **view★** of the town.

★★ **Church of St Servace** (Stiftskirche St Servatius)   On the site of the original 9C church, the present basilica, in the form of a Latin cross, was started in 1070 and consecrated in 1129. The **capitals★** and **friezes** above the central nave were sculpted by craftsmen brought especially from northern Italy. Beneath the chancel, the **crypt★★** is divided by three aisles with diagonal rib vaulting decorated by **frescoes★** depicting scenes from the Bible. Note the sarcophagi of King Heinrich I and his wife Matilda, interred here in the 10C, and the funerary stones of abbesses. The **treasury★★** (Domschatz) – manuscripts, 10C Gospel, and, above all, the **Quedlinburg Knotted Carpet★** – is kept in the sacristy.

Castle – Construction of this building, which formed part of the abbey, extended from the late 16C to the middle of the 17C. The irregularity of the floor plan was imposed on the architects by the nature of the rocky base onto which the castle was built.

In the **Castle Museum★** (Schlossmuseum) ⊘, 16C and 17C paintings from the Flemish and Italian schools are on display. The Abbess's Reception Room, a Throne Room and the Princes' Hall (mid-18C) can be visited.

Church of St Servace, Quedlinburg, the interior

EXCURSION

Gernrode – 7km - 4 1/2 miles to the south.
Here, the **Collegiate Church of St Cyriacus★**, built at the end of the 10C, was designed with the three-aisle nave and flat ceiling characteristic of the Ottonian basilica. The crypt was excavated and the west chancel added at the beginning of the 12C. Late 12C baptismal font in the Romanesque style, together with the funerary plaque of the Margrave Gero, one of the convent founders, can be seen in the crypt. Upstairs, in the south aisle, is the **Holy Sepulchre group★**, a handsome and rare example of Ottonian sculpture.

RASTATT Baden-Württemberg   Pop 40 000

Michelin map **413** H 20
Town plan in the current Michelin Red Guide Deutschland

Rastatt has never regained the prestige it enjoyed at the beginning of the 18C, when it was ruled by the **Margrave Ludwig of Baden** (1665-1707), known as **Ludwig the Turk** *(see under Karlsruhe)*. Faced by the threat of an invasion arising from the political ambitions of Louis XIV, the gallant captain abandoned the ruins of Baden-Baden and turned Rastatt into a stronghold, at the same time building a castle that was in line with his own ambitions.
The town is connected with two treaties between France and the Holy Roman Empire. The first, in 1714, ended the War of the Spanish Succession. The second in fact came to nothing: the congress discussing the enforcement of the Peace of Campo Formio, inaugurated in 1797, came to a tragic end two years later when two of the French plenipotentiaries were assassinated.

Castle ⊙ – Ludwig the Turk's enormous red sandstone palace was designed by D E Rossi, the architect to the Viennese court. It was built between 1698 and 1707, and was only just completed when Ludwig died. The three wings of the castle, based on Italian models, enclose a vast state courtyard on the town side.

Royal Apartments – The nucleus of the central block is the tall, sumptuous **Hall of Ancestors** (Ahnensaal), with the column capitals decorated will stucco figures representing Turkish prisoners. The Margrave's apartments are in the south wing, those of his wife in the north. Both are richly embellished with frescoes and stuccowork. The **Collection of Porcelain** (Porzellankabinett) is worth seeing.

★ **Church** (Schlosskirche) – *Enter from the Lyzeumstrasse*. This Baroque building constructed between 1720 and 1723 by the architect M L Rohrer is attached to the north wing of the castle. The centrepiece of the magnificently decorated interior is the high altar, the colums of which have been hollowed and can be illuminated from inside. The legend of the Holy Cross is represented in the ceiling paintings.

Military Museum (Wehrgeschichtliches Museum) ⊙ – *On the ground floor of the main block (south side)*. German military history from the end of the Middle Ages to the 19C. One of the most interesting sections concerns the war against the Turks.
While renovations are being carried out, the modern departments of the museum have provisionally been transferred to the Military History Research Centre (Militärgeschichtliches Forschungsamt) at No 1 Karlstrasse.

Liberty Museum (Freiheitsmuseum) – *Also on the ground floor of the main block, but on the north side*. The displays here evoke the history of the 19C German Liberation Movement. The exhibition is oriented around the struggles arising from the 1849 Constitution of the Empire (the Baden War).

EXCURSION

★ **The Favourite's Palace** (Schloss Favorite) – *5km - 3 miles to the southeast*.
This marvellous Baroque palace was built between 1710 and 1712 for the Margravine Sybilla Augusta, widow of Ludwig the Turk. The architect was again Rohrer, who had designed the church attached to her old apartments in the Rastatt castle. He coated the outside of this much smaller building with an unusual matrix of roughcast gravel and granite chips. The interior is particularly fine: floors of brilliant **scagliola** (stucco imitating encrusted marble), shiny as glass; mirror decorations; mosaics; chinoiserie. Note especially the **Florentine Room**, embellished with miniatures; the **Mirror Study**; Sybilla Augusta's apartments; sumptuous kitchen quarters with pottery from Frankfurt, Delft and Strasbourg; and a collection of Meissen, Nymphenburg and Chelsea porcelain.

Help us in our constant task of keeping up to date.
Send your comments and suggestions to

Michelin Tyre PLC
Tourism Department
Davy House
Lyon Road
HARROW Middlesex HA1 2DQ
Fax: 081 863 0680

Michelin map **411** P 5

The island town of Ratzeburg is built attractively in the middle of a **lake★**, the biggest of many in the morainal hills between the Elbe and Lübeck. The tower *(129 steps)* rising from the woods on the eastern shore of the lake *(access via the Hindenburghöhe Avenue)* provides the best **view★** of the town dominated by the squat outline of its cathedral.

★ **Cathedral** – Brick-built and Romanesque in style, this 12C construction lies in a stretch of parkland on the northern point of the island. Outside, note the lavish gable decorations of the south porch, remodelled as a chapel. The entrance now is through doors beneath the tower. Above the high altar is an altarpiece in the form of a triptych, illustrating the **Crucifixion★** (1430), on the superb central shrine. Beautiful ecclesiastic vestments embroidered with gold thread may be seen in a chapel off the north aisle.

Barlach Museum (Ernst-Barlach-Museum) ⊘ – *At No 3 Barlach Square, in the town centre, beside St Peter's Church (Peterskirche).*
Works of the sculptor Ernst Barlach (1870-1938), one of the leaders of the German Expressionist movement. They include *The Singer, The Avenger, The Doubting Thomas*, etc.

EXCURSION

Mölln – *11km - 7 miles to the southwest.*
A stage on the old Salt Road, this small town is famous for the memory of **Till Eulenspiegel** *(qv)*, whose tombstone is at the foot of the **St Nicholas' church tower** (13C and 15C). A statue of the celebrated jester, who died at Mölln in 1350, adorns the fountain in the market below. There are many lakes in the wooded countryside around Mölln (Seenlandschaft), the most popular of which is the romantic **Schmalsee★**, easily reached on foot from the Kurhaus Waldhalle.

RAVENSBRÜCK CONCENTRATION CAMP Brandenburg

Michelin map **987** fold 7 (south) - 1km - 1/2 mile north of Fürstenberg

Built in 1938 on the shores of Schwedtsee lake, Ravensbrück soon became Nazi Germany's largest camp for the detention of women: 132 000 women and children from 23 different countries were deported here. Conditions of work and the harshness of the imprisonment were so terrible that the camp had the highest mortality rate of any in Europe, with more than 90 000 deaths.

National Ravensbrück Memorial (Mahn-und Gedenkstätte Ravensbrück) ⊘ – Laid out even in the cells in which the deportees were herded, the **camp museum** evokes with horrifying realism the life (and death) of the victims. On the ground floor of the main block, evidence from more than 20 countries from which deportees were taken is exposed.
Nearby, the execution passageway and the original crematory death ovens are on view. At the lakeside, there is a monument in memory of the victims.

RAVENSBURG Baden-Württemberg — Pop 45 000

Michelin map **413** LM 23

Ravensburg remains to this day an ancient Swabian town, bristling with many towers, still sheltering behind a well-preserved rectangular city wall. The road from Wangen passes beneath the Obertor, a gateway with stepped gables near the Mehlsack *(see below)*. At the end of the Marktstrasse is a block of old buildings comprising the Rathaus and the Blaserturm, a square clock-tower with a polygonal coping and lantern.

The Mehlsack ("Sack of Flour") – In order to overlook and spy on the activities of the constables of Veitsburg, on a nearby hill, the burghers of Ravensburg erected this grey stone **tower** ⊘, which rises to a height of 50m - 164ft. Looking out over the city wall from the top *(240 steps)*, the view extends as far as the church at Weingarten.

Church of Our Lady (Liebfrauenkirche) – A 14C building which has been completely modernized. It is worth visiting for its best-known work of art, which is exposed on an altar in the south aisle. This is a copy of **The Ravensburg Virgin★★**, a moving 15C sculpture of the Madonna in a mantle (the original is in the Dahlem Museum in Berlin).

EXCURSION

★ **Wangen im Allgäu** – *23km - 14 miles to the east.*
Lying within sight of the first crests of the Allgäu Alps, this small Swabian town has been built with its colourful houses arranged in a simple cruciform plan, the two main streets crossing at right angles in the **Marktplatz★**. The Herrenstrasse, running as it were from side to side, is lined with attractive houses, many with decorative shop signs. At the far end is the Ravensburg Gate (Ravensburgertor or Frauentor), a square structure of which the 17C coping, confined by engaged turrets, is topped by an elegant ribbed roof. Perpendicular to this street, the other main thoroughfare ends at St Martin's Gate. Painted outside like the Ravensburg Gate, this entrance is crowned with a pyramidal roof, beneath which very finely worked gargoyles jut out.

Michelin map **413** T 19
Plan of the conurbation in the current Michelin Red Guide Deutschland

Regensburg, originally a Celtic colony *(Radasbona)*, later became a Roman garrison town *(Castra Regina)* guarding the natural frontier of the Danube at its most northerly point. It was converted to Christianity by St Emmerammus in the 7C, and St Boniface founded a bishopric there in 739. A 14C **fortified gateway** (Ostentor) is all that remains of the medieval stronghold. Napoleon was wounded beneath its walls in 1809 (a commemorative plaque can be seen at the corner of the Kräuter Markt and the Residenzstrasse), since when Regensburg has remained untouched by war.

Because of this, the city centre still has an extraordinary density of religious buildings, among which rise the 13C and 14C Italian-style towers erected by prosperous and ambitious merchants. Recent developments of navigation on the Danube are helping to bring new life to the economy.

The City of Diets – Once a Free Imperial City, Regensburg was privileged on occasion to be the seat of plenary sessions of the Royal Diet (Reichstag), which was charged with responsibility for the internal peace and external security of the immense and confused federation of states forming the Holy Roman Empire. From 1663 to 1806, date of the Empire's dissolution by Napoleon *(qv)*, the city was the seat of a **Permanent Diet** – the first indication of a continuing, overall German government.

OLD QUARTER *time: half a day.*
Follow the itinerary suggested on the map.

★ **St Peter's Cathedral** (Dom St Peter) (**E**) – Based on the design of certain French cathedrals, this pillared Gothic church has three naves and a non-projecting transept. Building began in 1250 and the major part of the work was completed by 1525, but the spires were not added until the 19C. The **Donkey Tower** (Eselsturm), above the northern part of the transept, is all that remains of the original Romanesque sanctuary built on this site.

The **west front**, richly decorated, is the work of a local family of sculptors named Roritzer. The main entrance, flanked by two neo-Gothic towers, is unusual, with a triangular, jutting porch. St Peter can be seen on the pier, and there are beautiful statues in the niches – particularly the meeting of the Virgin and St Elizabeth.

Go inside via the south porch.

The Late Gothic interior has impressive dimensions: 85m long and 32m high (279ft long and 105ft high). On each side of the nave, the aisles are encircled by a gallery, that on the south side supported by fine carved consoles. Two masterpieces of local Gothic statuary – the Archangel Gabriel, and Mary at the Annunciation, by the Master of Erminold (c1280) – stand in front of the west transept pillars. The three chancel windows are adorned with beautiful 14C **stained glass★★** (Farbfenster).

Treasury (Domschatz) ⊘ – *In the south wing of the former bishops' residence (Bischofshof), entrance via the courtyard.*
Liturgical items from the 11C to the 18C – vestments, chalices, monstrances, reliquaries – are on display here. Among rarest and finest, note the Ottocar Cross (c1430) and the Schaumberg Altar (1534-40), in the 12 Messengers' Chapel.

Cloister (Kreuzgang) ⊘ – *Access through the Cathedral garden.* This is divided by a central gallery paved with tombstones. On the right is the Romanesque **All Saints Chapel** (Allerheiligenkapelle), on the walls of which are traces of ancient frescoes. Another gallery leads to the Alter Dom – the old 11C **St Stephen's Church**, with its empty saint's confessional altar pierced by small openings.

★ **St Ulrich's Diocesan Museum** (Diözesanmuseum) (**E**) ⊘ – The museum is installed in **St Ulrich's Church** (Ulrichskirche), an early Gothic galleried building (c1225-1240) decorated with 1571 murals. Among other exhibits, visitors can see antique bishops' crosses (including the 12C Cross of St Emmerammus), fine medieval reliquaries, gold and silver plate, and religious paintings such as *The Legend of St Severinus* (a gift from the Regensburg Wool Merchants' Guild in 1456).

REGENSBURG

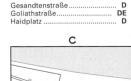

Gesandtenstraße .... **D**
Goliathstraße .... **DE**
Haidplatz .... **D**

Taking the covered passageway that links the Ducal Palace (Herzogshof) with the massive quadrilateral of the Roman Tower (Römerturm), visitors arrive at a wide, paved square where once a **grain market★** (Alter Kornmarkt) used to be held.

★ **Ancient Chapel** (Alte Kapelle) (E) – Originally Carolingian, this chapel was completely transformed in the Rococo style in the 18C. The two double oratories in the chancel, the splendid reredos, the painted ceiling and the gilded stuccowork executed by a Master of Wessobrunn combine to form a harmonious ensemble admirably set off by the light penetrating the tall windows.

St Cassian's Church (Kassianskirche) (E) – *Enter by the west door.* A Romanesque basilica with pillars and later (18C) Rococo decoration. On the left of the main doorway, a Gothic bas-relief represents the Visitation. On an altar in the south aisle is a Schöne Maria (Lovely Mary) sculpture by Hans Leinberger, the Master of Landshut (1520).

Hinter der Grieb (D) – In this ancient alleyway with its old burghers' houses, the visitor is transported back to the Middle Ages. From the far end, there is a fine view of one of the Cathedral spires.

★ **Haidplatz** (D) – A square surrounded by historic buildings, among which (at No 7) is an inn, **Zum Goldenen Kreuz**, with a grey stone tower and façade, and a crenellated pediment. In the centre of the square is the 1656 Fountain of Justice (Justitiabrunnen).

★ **Old Town Hall** (Altes Rathaus) (D) – The eight-storey tower dates from c1250. The Gothic western section (Reichssaalbau) was built c1360. The façade includes a gabled doorway and a pedestal supporting a charming oriel window which lights the Imperial Hall.

Imperial Hall (Reichssaal) – This splendid Gothic hall, the one where the "Permanent Diet" used to meet, now forms part of the **Reichstag Museum** ⊙. In the same building the Reichsstädisches Kollegium houses an exhibition tracing the history of all the Regensburg Diets.
On the ground floor, the interrogation room (Fragestatt) and the dungeons are open to the public.

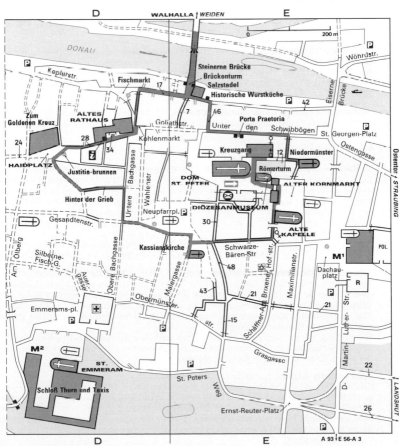

Fish Market (Fischmarkt) (D) – The market operates every morning. Note St George's Fountain (Georgsbrunnen, also known as Fischbrunnen) which dates from c1600.

Stone Bridge (Steinerne Brücke) (E) – Built between 1135 and 1146, this 310m - 1 017ft bridge rests on no less than 16 arches. From the middle, there is a fine **view★** of the old town, its medieval roofs dominated by the cathedral's spires. In the foreground is the 14C **Bridge Tower** (Brückenturm) gateway, flanked, on the left, by the huge roof of the **Salt Loft** (Salzstadel, early 17C). Beside this building, on the quayside, is the **Historische Wurstküche**, the oldest cooked sausage kitchen in Germany.

Porta Praetoria (E) – Near the Alter Dom *(see above)*, a little way south of the Danube, this arch and corner tower are all that remains of the old Roman fortified gateway that was once the northern entrance to Regensburg.

Niedermünster (E) – A Romanesque basilica with two towers that was originally the church of a convent of nuns. The interior was remodelled in the Baroque style in the 17C and 18C. The stuccowork is good. The tomb of St Erhard, surmounted by an altar and baldachin (c1330), is in the north aisle.

ADDITIONAL SIGHTS

★ **St Emmerammus' Church** (D) – This was once the abbey church of an 8C Benedictine monastery. A Gothic gateway on St Emmerammus' Square leads to a close from which visitors pass through the huge Romanesque **porch** (12C) to the double doors at the church entrance. The 11C **sculptures** by these doors (Jesus Christ, St Emmerammus and Dionysius) are among the oldest in Germany.
The original Romanesque aspect of the church was lost when the Asam brothers introduced a Baroque decorative scheme. Light from the clerestory windows highlights the ceiling's frescoes and stuccowork. Among the numerous tombs is the tombstone (c1280), by the north wall, of the sad looking Queen Hemma.

Thurn and Taxis Castle (Schloss Thurn und Taxis) (D) ⊘ – The Thurn and Taxis family – which until 1867 had the monopoly of German postal services – owns the St Emmerammus abbey buildings. The great Gothic cloister and the Abbot's halls, as well as the refectory and (separately) a **transport museum** (Marstallmuseum) (D M²) are open to the public.

★ **City Museum** (Städtisches Museum) (E M¹) ⊘ – A former Minorite monastery, now deconsecrated, houses this museum, which traces the cultural and artistic history of Regensburg and eastern Bavaria from the Stone Age to the present day. In the 13C building's **Roman section** is the town's "Act of Foundation" – a stone slab 8m - 26ft long on which an inscription recalls the implantation of the Roman garrison in AD 179. On the second floor there is an exhibition of paintings by **Albrecht Altdorfer** and other masters of the Danube School.

St James' Church (Jakobskirche) (C) – This sanctuary was built at the beginning of the 12C for Irish monks. The Romanesque **main entrance★** (north side) is famous for its statuary: on the tympanum, Christ is between St John and St James; above, on the frieze, the Saviour and the Apostles are flanked by Adam and Eve.

Dominican Church (Dominikanerkirche) (C) – A building that is bare to the point of severity – but nevertheless one of the oldest of all Gothic churches in Germany.

EXCURSIONS

★ **Valhalla** – *11km - 7 miles to the east. Leave Regensburg by the Steinerne Brücke.* Built between 1830 and 1842 by Ludwig I of Bavaria, this Doric temple – which seems strangely out of place in the Danube Valley – was intended to honour all the great men in German history (In Nordic mythology, Valhalla is the final resting place for the souls of heroes). Inside the memorial are 121 busts of famous soldiers, artists, scientists, etc., and, beneath a gallery, 64 plaques of older or lesser-known heroes.
From the peristyle there is a good view of the river bend above which the temple is built, the ruins of Donaustauf Castle, and the distant spires of Regensburg.

★ **Liberation Monument** (Befreiungshalle) ⊘ – *32km - 20 miles to the southwest.* The liberation is that of Germany from Napoleonic rule. It was, again, Ludwig I who conceived the idea of a memorial while returning from a visit to Greece in 1836. It takes the form of a huge rotunda, which was built between 1842 and 1863. The central hall is supported by 18 buttresses, each bearing an allegorical statue representing a Germanic people.
The coping, which partly hides the cupola roof, is adorned with trophies. Inside, 34 victory tableaux form a homogenous ring. From the outside gallery *(staircase)*, there is a fine view of the Altmühl Valley.

★ **Weltenburg Abbey** ⊘ – *30km - 18 1/2 miles to the southwest.* Cosmas Damian Asam *(qv)* built this abbey church in 1718, with an ante-nave – or narthex – and a nave proper, both of them oval. The attention is drawn immediately to a statue of St George, theatrically illuminated in the central arch of the reredos by light from a hidden source. Visible through an aperture in the lower dome is a trompe l'œil Asam composition in the upper dome on the theme of the Church Triumphant.

The Palatinate mountains are a continuation of the northern Vosges, with a similar forested aspect broken up by escarpments of red sandstone.
The **Pfälzer Wald**, densely wooded and sparsely inhabited, is a huge natural park in the northern part of the massif much favoured by walkers; further south lies the broken country of the **Wasgau**, where tree-clad heights crowned by ruins or rock outcrops overlook the valley clearings which shelter the villages.

The Wines of the Palatinate – The most extensive wine-growing region of the country, the Palatinate produces almost one-third of Germany's total output: a long reach of suitable country, calcareous, protected, facing the sun, stretches along the foot of the **Haardt** – the steep eastern flank of the massif overlooking the Rhine.
The highest point of the Haardt is the Kalmit, at 673m - 2 208ft. The strip below being almost flat, vines can be cultivated in the traditional way on low cordons. This permits late-harvested grapes to ripen more and produce fruity wines of fairly high alcoholic content, the most appreciated being the whites. The most famous vintages come from the villages of Bad Dürkheim, Forst, Deidesheim and Wachenheim. The itinerary suggested below follows part of the celebrated Deutsche Weinstrasse (German Wine Road), which begins at Schweigen, on the French frontier, and ends at Bockenheim, west of Worms.

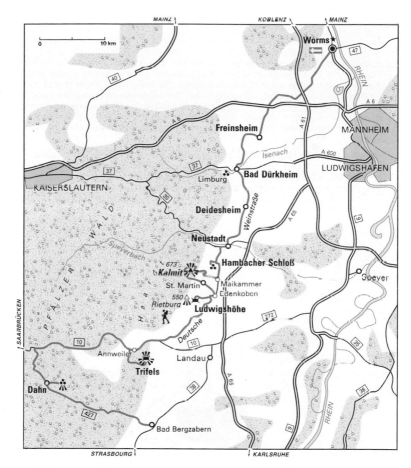

FROM WORMS TO BAD BERGZABERN

158 km – 98 miles - allow one day

South of **Worms★** *(qv)*, cultivation of the Rhine plain becomes progressively devoted to the vine. Soon, the steep barrier of the Haardt appears in the distance.

Freinsheim – A large wine town, encircled by ramparts. The town hall, beside a 15C church, occupies an elegant Baroque house with an overhanging roof that protects an outside staircase.
The road continues through vineyards, past pretty villages.

Bad Dürkheim – Sheltered by the Pfälzer Wald, this thermal cure town enjoys a mild climate in which fig, almond and chestnut trees in the **Spa Park** flower early. A couple of miles west (via the Schillerstrasse and the Luitpoldweg) are the ruins of Limburg Abbey. From here there are picturesque views – to the east across the vineyards of the Rhine plain; westwards along the Isenach Valley to the Hardenburg ruins.

Deidesheim – One of the most typical and prosperous towns on the German Wine Road.

Neustadt an der Weinstrasse – Narrow, picturesque lanes in this small town surround a pretty market place with a 16C town hall.

Hambach Castle (Hambacher Schloss) ⊘ – *On the outskirts of Hambach.*
The ruins of this old fortress are famous in Germany because it was here, in 1832, that militant patriots demanding a more liberal approach raised for the first time the black, red and gold flag adopted as the German national emblem in 1919, and again in 1949. Fine view over the vines.

The Kalmit – *8km - 5 miles, leaving from Maikammer, then 15 minutes on foot Rtn.*
There is a viewpoint at the summit. From the Kalmithaus terrace, a splendid **panorama★★** of the Rhine plain and, in the east, Speyer Cathedral. Return to the Wine Road through the charming village of St Martin.

Ludwigshöhe Castle ⊘ – *2km - 1 mile from Edenkoben.*
Built by Ludwig I of Bavaria in the "Italian villa" style, this castle now houses a gallery devoted to the works of the German painter Max Slevogt (1868-1932, *qv*). A chairlift carries sightseers to the Rietburg (550m - 1 804ft), departure point for forest walks. The return journey in the chair lift affords superb, plunging views over the vine-covered slopes.

Trifels Castle ⊘ – *7km 4 1/2 miles from Anweiler, plus 1 1/2 hour walking and sightseeing.*
On a superb site crowning the summit of a bluff in the Wasgau, rebuilt in 1937 in the style of the Romanesque palaces of the Hohenstaufens, this is one of the castles in Germany most steeped in history. It was once an imperial residence housing the crown jewels and the royal treasury – a fact lending credence to the poetic tradition that once it also contained the Holy Grail. What is true is that Richard the Lionheart, returning from the Third Crusade, was captured and held prisoner here by the Emperor Heinrich VI in 1193 (to be freed a year later on payment of an enormous ransom). The oldest part of the castle is built into the rock. From the chapel tower (Kappelenturm) there is a **panoramic view★** over the Wasgau region.

Dahn – The **ruins** (Burgruinen) of three separate castles – Altdahn, Grafendahn and Tanstein – lie within the same perimeter wall here. Among the ruins, there remain troglodytic halls shored up by monolithic columns, and two ancient towers. Once more, there are fine **views★** of the Wasgau.
Winding through a landscape scattered with rock outcrops, the road arrives at Bad Bergzabern.

Rhine-Main-Danube Canal
Ever since Roman times emperors, kings, engineers and visionaries have dreamed of linking the Rhine and Danube waterways. Charlemagne began the great enterprise, hence the name Charlemagne's Ditch (Fossa Carolina). Bavaria's Ludwig I made another attempt when he built the Ludwig Canal. However it was bargeloads of 20c dignitaries who were the first to cross the watershed between the Rhine and the Danube on the 25th September 1992.
The 177km - 110 mile-canal with its hundreds of locks takes the barges up and down the 245m - 800 ft climb. 12 centuries after it was orignally started the idea of a waterway linking Europe from the North Sea to the Black Sea has become a reality.

Michelin map **412** folds 21 and 22

The river, 1 320km - 820 miles long, flows through four different countries and has often been a source of controversy between neighbours: below Basle, for instance, no town has ever completely settled both sides of the stream. At the same time it has always been a unique highway for the exchange of commercial, intellectual, artistic and religious ideas, a vital artery of the West.

Shipping companies today organize many **excursions and Rhine cruises**, especially from Cologne, Koblenz and Rüdesheim or Bingen.

The Rhine Legends – There is not, along the whole length of the river, a castle, an island, even a rock without its tale of chivalry or legend. Lohengrin, the Knight of the Swan, appeared at the foot of Cleves Castle *(qv)*; Roland escaped from Roncesvalles to arrive too late before the island of Nonnenworth, where his fiancée, inconsolable at the rumour of his death, had taken the veil (Roland in despair withdrew to the neighbouring castle of Rolandsbogen); at the **Loreley**, the Rock of Lore, an enchantress bewitched boatmen with her song, leading their vessels to disaster. The outstanding legend however is the story of the Nibelungen, an inexhaustible source of inspiration from which Wagner borrowed both names and ideas for his opera tetralogy *The Ring (qv)*.

Inspired by Germanic and Scandinavian myths, the **Song of the Nibelungen** was probably composed towards the end of the 12C. It tells of the splendours of the 5C Burgundian Court at Worms, and of the passions scouring the hearts of its heroes, known also under the name of Nibelungen.

Brunhilde, proud wife of Günther, the Burgundian king, determines to take revenge when she discovers she has been tricked into the marriage by Siegfried, the husband of her sister-in-law Kriemhild. She persuades a fellow-conspirator, Hagen (so the story goes), to murder Siegfried during a hunting party and then throw into the Rhine the Burgundian treasure which had been Siegfried's wedding present to Kriemhild. This is to stop Kriemhild using the treasure to pay someone to avenge Siegfried in turn.

Kriemhild has to wait 13 years for her revenge. Then, having married Attila, the King of the Huns, she engineers an invitation to the Burgundians: they are to come to Etzelburg, in Hungary, for a special feast. But the fête turns out to be an ambush; the ambush turns into a general massacre. Hagen, decapitated by Kriemhild with Siegfried's sword, takes with him to the grave the secret of the treasure's whereabouts.

From the Alps to the North Sea – At the beginning of its journey to the north, the Rhine is a typical Alpine river, with little water in the winter and a full flood in summer when the snows melt. Lake Constance, through which the Rhine flows, and the lakes of the Swiss plateau which drain into its tributary, the Aar, help to moderate this irregularity.

Reception of the Neckar at Mannheim and the Main at Frankfurt, each with a more regular flow, tend to even out that of the main stream, and the process is completed with the arrival of the Moselle at Koblenz.

After the exit from Lake Constance, rock outcrops from the Black Forest and the foot-hills of the Jura impede the force of the current and produce the famous Rhine Falls *(see the Michelin Green Guide Switzerland)*.

Gutenfels Castle and the fortified isle of Pfalz on the Rhine

Further downstream, limestone strata result in rapids (Laufen). These obstacles, although they inhibit the use of shipping, do allow the installation of powerful hydro-electric projects. At Basle, the Rhine abruptly changes direction, veering north to follow and fertilize the subsidence fault separating the Vosges and the Black Forest. In Alsace, a canal draws off some of the excess water, but after Breisach this is fed only from power station dams.

From Bingen to Neuwied, north of Koblenz, the Rhine cuts its way through the Rhineland schist massif, where the hard rock – especially the quartzites exposed in the neighbourhood of the Loreley – can foment dangerous whirlpools. This so-called "heroic" stretch of river valley, with its alternation of vineyards, woods and impressive escarpments, punctuated by ruins perched on rock spurs, is the most picturesque part of what is known as the Rhine Gorge. Later, having passed through the industrial region around Duisburg, the river turns west and curls slowly across the plain towards the sea.

An Exceptional Shipping Lane – The traditional strings of Rhine barges, displacing anything from 1 000 to 2 000 tons each as they are towed, have been supplanted latterly by self-powered "auto-barges" and convoys towed or pushed by tugs which can comprise anything up to six 2 000 - or 3 000-ton freight carriers. Recent work carried out on the more difficult reaches upstream from St Goar have guaranteed shipping a uniform navigation channel 120m - 394ft wide.

Today, the Rhine, navigable over the 850km - 528 miles between Rotterdam and Rheinfelden (upstream from Basle), handles an annual traffic of 265 million tons. Linked both to Rotterdam and to Antwerp, it boasts also in Duisburg-Ruhrort the world's largest river port (18 million tons annually).

Next in order of importance, on the river's German sector, are Cologne-Godorf, Karlsruhe, Ludwigshafen and Mannheim.

** THE LORELEY

From Rüdesheim to Koblenz 75km - 47 miles - about 4 hours

This route, following the Rhine's east bank, passes through the wildest and steepest part of the valley, with splendid views of the castles and fortresses on the far side of the river.

After **Rüdesheim★** (qv), the road runs at the foot of terraced vineyards overlooked by the ruins of Ehrenfels Castle, built by the Archbishops of Mainz at the same time as the Mouse Tower on the opposite bank to supervise the collection of tolls from shipping on the river. After Assmannshausen, silhouetted high up on the west bank, the castles of Rheinstein, Reichenstein and Sooneck appear one after the other. The crenellated tower of Fürstenberg, on the wooded slopes facing Lorch, marks the start of a more open stretch. And then the vineyards and towers of Bacharach slide into view. After that comes the fortified isle of Pfalz.

★ **Pfalz** – The massive five-sided keep of this **toll castle** ⊙ rises from the river bed in the centre of the stream, encircled by a turreted fortress wall.

Kaub – One of the outstanding landmarks in the valley, this village dominated by the restored ruins of Gutenfels is worth exploring on foot by way of the picturesque main street, the Metzgerstrasse.

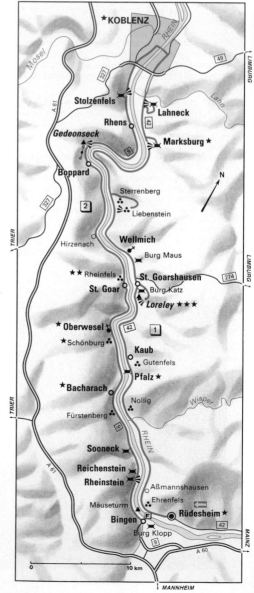

Before a sharp, almost right-angled bend in the river, admire the **setting**★★ of the towers of Oberwesel as they succeed one another at the foot of the Schönburg, on the far side of the water. The sharp bend, veering northeast and then northwest, leads to the most untamed stretch on this part of the Rhine.

★★★ **The Loreley** – This legendary spur, towering 132m - 433ft above the rock-strewn river, has become the symbol of the Romantic Rhine and has a very special place in German literature. Heine's poem, *I Know Not Whence Cometh My Sadness*, set to music by Silcher, is traditionally played aboard ship when the promontory appears around a curve in the valley.

From St Goarshausen, just beyond the famous rock, take the road signposted Loreley-Burgen-Strasse and drive up to the Hotel Auf der Loreley. From the car park, walk *(1/4 hour Rtn)* to the **Loreley Belvedere**★★. There are impressive **views**★★ plunging down into the "heroic gorge" from several accessible spurs here.

St Goarshausen – The town, strung out along the river bank (which makes a very pleasant walk), is dominated by the **Katz** (Cat) stronghold (*not open to the public*), said to have been built to neutralize that of another **Maus** (Mouse), a little further downstream.

Wellmich – In the church of this small riverside town, there are traces (restored) of 15C wall paintings. Note: in the nave, the Crucifixion and the Last Judgement; in the Gothic chancel, the Legend of St Mary the Egyptian.

The Rival Brothers – *At Kamp-Bornhofen, turn right towards Dahlheim, and then right again at the sign "Zu den Burgen".* The hill slopes become wild again. Beyond Kestert there is a fine **panorama**★★; from the ruins of the **Liebenstein** fortress, **Sterrenberg** and the valley below can be admired (the two castles are traditionally linked to an ancient legend concerning two rival brothers).

From Boppard onwards, where the Rhine swings lazily into a huge double loop, dense cultivation of vines appears and the landscape becomes less wild. Soon the fortress of Marksburg emerges on its promontory (At Braubach, take the road to Nastätten).

★ **Marksburg** – The **castle** ⊙, the only one in the whole Rhine Valley never to be destroyed, is built on a **site**★★ above the river that is almost aerial. Particularly notable are the fortress's great battery, a medieval garden with more than 170 different species of plant, and a collection of armour ranging from 600 BC to the 15C.

Lahneck – *3km - 2 miles from Lahnstein, near the confluence of the Rhine and the Lahn.* The ruins of this **fortress** ⊙, originally built in the 13C to protect neighbouring silver mines, were reconstructed in neo-Gothic style in the 19C. From the keep there is a view of the junction of the two rivers and the troubadour castle of Stolzenfels, on the far side of the Rhine.

Soon afterwards, the road arrives on the outskirts of Koblenz.

★★★ THE RHINE CASTLES

From Koblenz to Bingen *63km - 39 miles allow a whole day*

This itinerary in effect retraces the previous one, in the opposite direction, on the other side of the river. Soon after leaving Koblenz, Lahneck comes into view again, with its tower overlooking the river confluence. Above, on the right, is Stolzenfels.

Stolzenfels – This enormous **castle** ⊙ was reconstructed, with its many crenellations, by Friedrich-Wilhelm IV in 1842. The style is now neo-Gothic, inspired by certain English manor houses. The sumptuous **interior**★ is arranged as a museum. From the slope against which Stolzenfels is built, the terrace offers a view of Koblenz and the citadel of Ehrenbreitstein.

Rhens – A town of pretty colour-washed houses with half-timbered facades. The old town hall juts out into the main street.

Gedeonseck ⊙ – *1 hour Rtn, including 20mn on a chair lift.*
Southwards, there is a superb **view**★ of the great convex loop of the Rhine as it flows around the Boppard curve.

Boppard – A residential town where several small valleys meet. The **Rhine Path** (Rheinallee) makes a particularly pleasant riverside walk. Near the quay, the Gothic Carmelite church with its single tower still has its 15C choir stalls, and a very fine Renaissance funerary monument depicting the Eternal Father receiving the dead Christ.

The beginning of the "heroic" Rhine Gorge is marked by the two Rival Brothers fortresses *(see above)* on the opposite slopes. After Hirzenach, the Cat and Mouse towers are visible, standing above St Goarshausen.

St Goar – The village, clinging to the hillside at the foot of the impressive **Rheinfels fortress**★★ ⊙, commands with St Goarshausen the Loreley passage. The river here, obstructed and narrowed by the legendary rock, swirls and eddies dangerously as it races through the defile. Rheinfels, which threw back the assaults of Louis XIV, was until it fell to the French in 1797 the most powerful fortress in the whole valley. It is worth climbing to the top of the clock tower to get an overall view of the turbulent Rhine, the Cat and Mouse castles, and the maze of towers, gates, courts and casemates comprising the Rheinfels complex.

The banks of the river remain steep and heavily wooded until Oberwesel.

Oberwesel – South of the town, the Gothic **Church of Our Lady★** (Liebfrauenkirche) has a fine high-altarpiece, one of the oldest in Germany (early 14C), a Gothic rood-screen and, in the north aisle, a most unusual 1510 triptych illustrating the 15 cataclysms presaging the end of the world.

From the terrace of **Schönberg Castle★**, a little further on, there is a view of Kaub, on the far side of the river, and the fortified isle of Pfalz. Schönberg is in fact a block of three forts sheltered by a common – and impressive – defense wall.

Pfalz, with the Gutenfels ruins perched on the heights far above it, is an astonishing sight: a massive stone ship, anchored in the middle of the fast-running river.

★ **Bacharach** – Once the property of the Counts of the Palatinate, Bacharach – a town of vineyards and ancient towers, relics of medieval fortifications – is one of the most popular in the Rhine Valley. The houses in the **Marktplatz** and the **Oberstrasse**, wooden-walled and decked with flowers, are a delight. One of the last Romanesque naves built in Germany can be seen in **St Peter's Church** (Peterskirche), although its four-stage elevation (arcades, galleries, triforium and clerestory windows) sound already a pre-echo of French Gothic. The ruins of **St Werner's Chapel** are nearby.

The ruined towers of Nollig and Fürstenberg mark the end of the valley's most grandiose stretch; from here onwards it is less winding, the river running between the steep eastern bank, topped by a few vines, and the cliffs on the opposite shore.

The road on this side passes below castles whose sites are ever more audacious, from Sooneck to Reichenstein and finally Rheinstein.

Sooneck ⊘ – This **fortress** is much restored and tiered to suit the terrain with a maze of staircases, platforms and terraced gardens beneath the turrets.

Reichenstein – Well-situated at the mouth of a rural valley, this neo-feudal **castle** ⊘ has a fine collection of arms and hunting trophies.

Rheinstein ⊘ – The **castle** is perched on a perpendicular rock spur, in a commanding position above the Rhine. From the foremost watchtower there is a **bird's-eye view★★** of the valley.

Once past the second **Mouse Tower** (Mäuseturm), balanced on its tiny islet in the middle of the river, the valley widens out and the east bank becomes covered with terraced vines.

Bingen – Founded by the Romans at the confluence of the Rhine and the Nahe (Castel Bingium), this small river port today serves chiefly the wine-growing hinterland.

Burg Klopp, an ancient stronghold built by the Bishops of Mainz, has been razed to the ground more than once – in particular by the troops of Louis XIV in 1689, during the "Orléans War". Today it houses the town council, from the terrace of which there is a fine **view★** of the Binger Loch, between Hunsrück and the hills of the Rheingau, upstream from the Niederwald monument on the outskirts of Rüdesheim.

★★ ROMANTIC ROAD Baden-Württemberg and Bavaria

Michelin map **413** folds 5, 16, 17, 28, 29, 39

From the Main valley to the foot of the Bavarian Alps, by way of peaceful valleys and a poetic, rolling countryside, the Romantic Road itinerary recalls at every stage of its course some aspect of the past that could only belong to the history of Germany. One after the other, the tourist experiences evocations of life in the great medieval cities (Rothenburg, Nördlingen and Dinkelsbühl), the religious sensibility of artists like Tilman Riemenschneider *(qv)*, the prestige of German chivalry (Bad Mergentheim), the sumptuously Baroque character of the old episcopal courts and such imperial towns as Würzburg and Augsburg.

FROM WÜRZBURG TO ROTHENBURG

100km – 62 miles - about 4 hours

Leaving **Würzburg★★** *(qv)*, Route 27 winds down towards the valley of the Tauber, which it reaches at Tauberbischofsheim.

★ **Bad Mergentheim** – *See under Bad Mergentheim.*

Weikersheim – Once the seat of the Hohenlohe Princes, this small town has retained its 18C architectural unity, especially noticeable in the layout of the market, built in a semicircle on the palace side to provide a splendid vista.

The **castle** ⊘ was built between 1580 and 1680 on the banks of the Tauber, in a sober style divorced from Baroque influences. Two hundred years of decorative art (1550 to 1750 approximately) are illustrated by the remarkable collection of **furniture★★**. The magnificent **Knights' Hall★★** (Rittersaal), completed in 1603, is typical of the transition between the Renaissance style and the Baroque. Note the sculptured figures above the monumental doorway of emperors and empresses. The perspective of formal gardens (1710), peopled with statues in caricature in the style favoured by the Franconian courts of the period, ends in a charming perforated orangery.

The picturesque section of the run, in the narrow part of the Tauber Valley, begins above the attractive town of Bieberehren. The road rises and falls over slopes covered at times by natural woodland, at times by orchards, above the willow-fringed river banks. Occasionally the stream forms a loop to feed a sawmill or watermill. This countryside is at its loveliest in springtime.

Creglingen – The isolated **Chapel of Our Lord** (Herrgottskirche) – about one mile along the road to Blaufelden – contains the precious **Altarpiece of the Virgin**★★ sculpted by Tilman Riemenschneider. The theme of the Assumption in the central motif has permitted the artist to translate all his own sensitivity into the attitude and expression of the Madonna.

Detwang – In the church at Detwang another Riemenschneider **altarpiece**★ portrays the Crucifixion.

★★★ **Rothenburg** – *See under Rothenburg.*

FROM ROTHENBURG TO DONAUWÖRTH
105km – 65 miles - about 5 hours

Feuchtwangen – A small town with an attractive market place surrounded by pretty houses and overlooked by a parish church housing another **Altarpiece of the Virgin** – this time the work of Albrecht Dürer's teacher, Michael Wolgemut. Near the café Am Kreuzgang there is a Romanesque **cloister**. Installed in a 17C peasant house is a **Museum of Franconian Folklore** (Heimatmuseum) displaying fine rustic furniture with regional pottery and costumes.

A **Dinkelsbühl** – Ramparts and watch-towers still surround this medieval town which wakes up every year in mid-July with a colourful children's festival (Kinderzeche) commemorating the relief of Dinkelsbühl in the Thirty Years War *(see the Calendar of Events).*

St George's Church★ has retained its Romanesque tower. The interior, a Gothic hall-church *(illustration p 24)*, is a remarkable sight, with all three naves decorated with skilfully designed fan vaulting.

Among the many ancient buildings, note the **Deutsches Haus**★ *(Am Weinmarkt)*, and its richly decorated Renaissance façade, as well as the **Hezelhof** *(Segringer Strasse 7)*, remarkable for the long, two-tiered balconies hung with flowers that overlook its inner courtyard.

The undulating landscape of the Feuchtwangen-Dinkelsbühl region is supplanted, after Nördlingen, by the bleak wastes of the **Ries Basin**. This practically treeless depression amid the heights of the Swabian Jura forms a symmetrical bowl 20km - 12 1/2 miles across and a regular 200m - 656ft deep, which is thought by some geologists to have been caused millions of years ago by the fall of a gigantic meteorite.

Wallerstein – From the summit of the rock, reached by a pathway and then steps cut in the strata, there is a vast panorama over the Ries Basin *(access via the Fürstlicher Keller).*

★ **Nördlingen** – *See under Nördlingen.*

Harburg Castle ⊙ – A large fortified castle whose buildings, considerably enlarged and remodelled in the 18C, look down on the picturesque houses of a village tightly packed along the banks of the Wörnitz. On display are extensive **collections**★ of sculpture, ivory, enamel, tapestry and gold and silver plate.

Kaisheim – The former Cistercian **abbey church** (Zisterzienserkloster) was built at the end of the 14C in the full flower of the Gothic era. Around the chancel, very pure in style, is a 12-sided **ambulatory**★ with ogive vaulting, divided into two galleries. *(To visit, apply at the presbytery.)* The abbey itself is now used as a prison.

The valley of the Wörnitz, commanded by Harburg Castle, peters out after a final, narrow, twisting section, allowing the Ries to connect with the Danube Valley.

Donauwörth – On a hillside running steeply down to the Danube, the town is dominated by the **Holy Cross Church** (Heiligkreuzkirche). The large 1720 Baroque building, with its concave interior galleries, is decorated with Wessobrunn stuccowork *(qv).*

FROM DONAUWÖRTH TO FÜSSEN
148km – 92 miles - about 1 day

This drive along the ancient Via Claudia, one of the main arteries of the old Holy Roman Empire, owes its interest less to the route (which follows the Lech Valley, by now largely widened) than to the historical souvenirs evoked by the sites on the way. These include **Augsburg**★★ *(qv)*, **Landsberg** *(qv)*, the **Royal Castles**★★★ *(qv)* and (at the price of a small detour) the **Church of Wies**★★ *(qv).*

With this Green Guide
use the Michelin Maps no ▨▨▨, ▨▨▨ *and* ▨▨▨ *1:400 000 (1cm:4km)*
The map provides road and tourist information,
town plans of Berlin, Bremen, Hamburg and Hanover (Map no ▨▨▨*);*
Berlin, Cologne, Dortmund, Düsseldorf, Essen, Frankfurt am Main
and Hanover (Map no ▨▨▨*);*
Munich, Nuremberg and Stuttgart (Map no ▨▨▨*).*

Michelin map **987** fold 6

Rostock, with its widespread port installations, shipyards and huge fishing fleet, was until re-unification East Germany's only major sea outlet to the Baltic and the rest of the world. In order to get some idea of the scope of maritime activity in this city of half a million people, a **boat trip** ⊘ around the International Port is strongly recommended.

A Busy (and coveted) Port – A particularly choice situation on the wide Warnow estuary favoured the development of Rostock from the earliest days: by the beginning of the 13C, the town was already a member of the Hanseatic League, was minting its own money and was in the process of asserting its independence from the Princes of Mecklenburg. In 1419, Rostock founded the first Baltic university, which earned it the nickname of "Light of the North". Such a position and such a reputation soon excited the envy of powerful and covetous neighbours. The Danes and then the Swedes occupied the city during the Thirty Years War (1618-1648), returning for a second time while the Nordic countries were struggling for supremacy in the war raging from 1700 to 1721. Nor was the port spared during the Napoleonic Wars; it was occupied by French troops until 1813.

SIGHTS

★★ **Church of Our Lady** (Marienkirche) – *Am Ziegen Markt*. The building as it is today – an imposing basilica in the form of a cross – results from a transformation in the second half of the 15C of a hall-church built in the previous century. It is one of the biggest churches in northern Germany.
The massive tower, lightened by pierced sections, was not completed until the end of the 18C. From the top there is a **panorama**★ of the city and the dock area. Inside the church, the overriding impression is one of height, of verticality. Note especially the 1472 **astronomic clock**★★ (its face was remodelled in 1643), which comprises a calendar valid until the year 2017. The delicately worked bronze **baptismal font**★, decorated with scenes from the life of Christ, is supported by the figures of four men. The Baroque organ dates from 1770.

Town Hall (Rathaus) – *Neuer Markt*. This is composed of three 13-14C gabled houses topped by a brick-built arcaded gallery supporting seven towers. In front of the block is a Baroque façade added in 1727. Across the square are fine gabled houses.

★ **Navigational Museum** (Schiffahrtsmuseum) ⊘ – *At the corner of the August-Bebel-Strasse and the Richard-Wagner-Strasse*. Models, paintings and navigational instruments chart the history of maritime activity from the time of the Vikings to the present day. Note in particular the full-size reconstruction of a tramp steamer bridge, and a model of the present international port.

Kröpeliner-Strasse – This pedestrian precinct, crossing the old city from the Town Hall to the Kröpeliner Gate, has become the town's shop-window and commercial centre. It is bordered by the familiar gabled houses dating from Baroque and Renaissance times. At No 82, the brick façade of the old (late 15C) Holy Spirit Hospital presbytery is distinguished from the other buildings by a stepped gable.

★ **Kröpliner Gate** – The 14C brick gate, six floors high, closes off the western end of the Kröpeliner-Strasse. The interior has been turned into a **museum** evoking the history of the town (Stadtgeschichtliches Museum).

★ **Historical Museum** (Kulturhistorisches Museum) ⊘ – Collections of paintings and sacred art are displayed in this former Cistercian convent joined to the Holy Cross Church – a brick-built, triple-aisle hall dating from the late 13C. On the late 15C **Altarpiece of the Three Kings**★, the background gives a good idea of Rostock in the Middle Ages.

EXCURSIONS

★ **Warnemünde** – *11km - 6 miles to the north*.
This one-time fishing village, "bought" by the town from the Prince of Mecklenburg in 1323, has become Rostock's most popular holiday beach. From the ferry terminal, services run to Denmark.

Bad Doberan – *15km - 9 miles to the west*.
The prosperity of this area started with the foundation of a Cistercian abbey at the end of the 12C. The brick-built **Abbey Church**★★, erected between 1294 and 1368, is undoubtedly one of the most successful in north Germany. Ogive vaulting covers the three naves, and the chancel ambulatory is encircled by radiating chapels. Worth seeing: a 14C **Triumphal Cross**★, the high altar panelled **reredos**★, and a Late Gothic **tabernacle** in oak that rises to a height of almost 12m - 40ft.

★ **Kühlungsborn** – *30km - 19 miles to the west*.
Both a spa and a seaside resort, Kühlungsborn owes to its extensive pinewoods and a beach several miles long its position as one of the busiest holiday centres on the Baltic coast.

★ **Güstrow** – *41km - 26 miles to the south*.
There is an imposing late 16C Renaissance **castle**★ with a richly decorated façade in this town. Beside it are formal French gardens blazing with flowers. In the Cathedral (Am Domplatz), note the **Statues of the Apostles**★, sculpted in oak in a Rostock studio around 1530. The **Ernst Barlach Museum**★ (Ernst-Barlach Gedenkstätte) ⊘ is laid out in St Gertrude's Chapel. Several works of remarkable expressive power testify to the genius of the sculptor who twice lived for a time in Güstrow.

Michelin map 413 N 18
Town plan in the current Michelin Red Guide Deutschland

One of the oldest towns on the Romantic Road *(qv)*, Rothenburg overlooks from its rocky crag four ox-bow bends in the Tauber river. As well as being old, the town is both picturesque and unspoiled. Once behind the ramparts in the car-less central enclave, the visitor faced with Rothenburg's ancient houses, street signs, fountains and narrow, cobbled lanes seems all at once in some kind of time-warp plunged back into the middle of the 16C.

HISTORICAL NOTES

The Burggarten spur, whose steep-sided promontory is enclosed within the tightest of the ox-bow curves, was a strongpoint, according to tradition, as far back as the time of King Pharamund. What is certain is that, from the 12C onwards, two castles – the first imperial, the second belonging to a count – stood successively on this rock platform so ideally placed to command the winding valley below. At first the town itself was small; the outline of its earliest circle of fortifications can be seen, with two towers (Markusturm and Weisserturm), in the arc formed by the Judengasse and the Alter Stadtgraben.

In the 13C the town spread out... then lost both its castles, destroyed in an earthquake in 1356. From then on the ambition of the local Rothenburg worthies inclined more and more towards the building, and then the embellishment, of such public works as might enhance their own importance: the Town Hall, St James's Church, the long line of merchants' houses, with their impressive gables, on the Herrngasse.

But Rothenburg, now won over to the Protestant side, failed to recover from the recession and economic stagnation engendered by the rigours of the Thirty Years War *(qv)*. Reduced to the status of an obscure regional market, too poor even to rebuild its houses in line with the prevailing taste, the town vegetated ingloriously throughout the 17C and 18C, unable to expand beyond its own walls. In the 19C however this very antique-ness became an asset: strict preservation orders were placed on the steep-roofed houses with their tall gables, inherited from the Gothic period; no staircase turrets or corner oriels could be dismantled. Tourists of today, therefore, are granted a genuine glimpse into the past.

They will notice that half-timbering above a stone base or foundation is the general building rule, although roughcast or pebbledash usually hides the beams. In the hospital quarter, nevertheless, the woodwork of many lovely old houses remains exposed.

A Long Drink (Meistertrunk) – During the Thirty Years War, the Protestant Rothenburg fell to the Imperial army commanded by General Tilly *(qv)*. Tilly decided to raze the place to the ground. All pleas for mercy having been rejected, the Burgomaster as a last resort offered the victorious general a goblet of the very best local wine...and the miracle occured. His heart warmed by generosity, Tilly offered a way out. He would spare the town if some eminent local could empty in a single draught a hanap (a 6-pint tankard) of the same wine. A man named Nusch, a former Burgomaster, succeeded in this exploit and Rothenburg was saved (the after-effects on the courageous drinker are not recorded).

Every year now, on the three days of the Pentecost (Whitsun) weekend and certain other occasions, the population of Rothenburg takes part in a huge fête which is in effect a reconstitution of this event (see Principal Festivals).

★★★ OLD TOWN (ALTSTADT) *time: 3 1/2 hours*

Starting at the Marktplatz, follow the itinerary marked on the town plan.

★ **Town Hall** (Rathaus) – The Gothic part, its gable topped by a 60m · 197ft belfry, is 14C, while that facing the Marktplatz, with its octagonal staircase tower, is a Renaissance work, completed by an 18C portico. Visitors can inspect various state or council chambers, or climb the tower for a **view★** of the fortified town.

North of the Marktplatz is the gable of an ancient inn, the Ratstrinkstube, on which the figures of an animated clock re-enact mechanically *(at 11am, noon, 1pm, 2pm, 3pm, 9pm and 10pm)* the famous legend of the Long Drink.

Baumeisterhaus – The steps on the gables of this Renaissance house serve as pedestals for dragon motifs. Statues on the first floor represent the seven cardinal virtues, those on the second the seven deadly sins.

Museum of Medieval Justice (Mittelalterliches Kriminalmuseum) ⊙ – Medieval attitudes towards crime and dissidence are reflected in this museum installed in the former headquarters of the Knights of the Order of St John of Jerusalem. Law books, seals, engravings, along with instruments of torture, punishment and execution are exhibited on four different floors. Among the most typical are a spiked chair used in witchcraft trials, iron-collared yokes, and "masks of shame".

Plönlein – A picturesque corner formed by the bifurcation of two streets, one level, one descending – but both ending at the same fortified gateway.

Leave the town by the Koboldzell gate, on the right, turn sharp right again, and follow the path circling the spur some way below the ramparts.

In the valley below, there is a remarkable arched, two-storey, **fortified bridge** (Doppelbrücke) which crosses the Tauber. Return to the Old Town via the Burggarten.

Burggarten – All that remains of the double fortress erected on this promontory is the Chapel of St Blasius (Blasiuskapelle), which has been turned into a war memorial, and a fortified gateway, the Burgtor. The area is now a public garden with views of the river, the two-tier bridge, the Topplerschlösschen (a riverside tower oddly topped by apartments) and, some way to the north, the village of Detwang.

Herrngasse – The mansions of formerly well-known personages line this busy commercial street. Those interested should look into some of the courtyards, for instance No 15 (**A**), where the half-timbered gallery rests on embossed wooden pillars.

St James' Church (St Jakobskirche) – Building of the Gothic church's east chancel started in the mid-14C. The foundation of the west chancel is penetrated by a vaulted passageway that leads to the Klingengasse. This chancel also houses the most precious work of art: Tilman Riemenschneider's **"Holy Blood" altarpiece★★** (1504).

The composition of the main scene, the Last Supper, is original. Judas is shown from behind, facing Christ. The expressions are tense and perplexed, except for that of Jesus, which is full of compassion.

The east chancel overlooks a square on which stands the 1593 Renaissance building of the former college (Gymnasium).

Return to the Marktplatz.

ROTHENBURG OB DER TAUBER

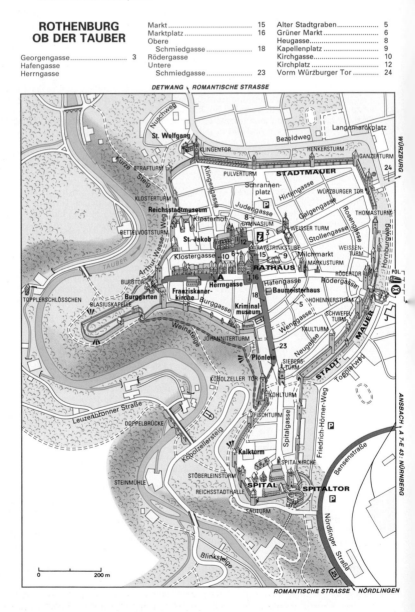

For a pleasant stroll in town
look for the pedestrian streets marked on the town plans.

ADDITIONAL SIGHTS

★ **Hospital (Spital)** – A picturesque group of buildings, mostly 16C and 17C, built on the southern extremity of the plateau known locally as the Kappenzipfel (peak of the cap). There are works of art in the Gothic chapel and, in the middle of the courtyard, the Hegereiterhäuschen – a graceful pavilion with a pointed roof and turrets.

From the hospital courtyards, the **Kalkturm** viewpoint can be reached (also accessible from outside), with its **view★** over the town centre and the watch-path linking the Stöberleinsturm and the Sauturm.

★ **The Ramparts (Stadtmauer)** – Constructed in the 13C and 14C, these, complete with gates and towers, are still in a state of perfect preservation. Long stretches are open to the public. Near the hospital, the southern entry to the town is defended by the **Spitaltor★**, a massive 16C bastion enclosing two inner courtyards, both oval.

St Wolfgang's Church – North of the Klingentor. A curious late 15C Gothic church, fortified and incorporated into the barbican doubling the defences of the gateway. The casemates and the parapet walk can still be viewed.

Franciscan Church – The rood-screen, as well as walls and columns in this church, is decorated with fine 15C and 16C sculptures. Note also, on the left above a funerary niche, the Creglingen Virgin (1400).

Museum (Reichsstadtmuseum) ⊙ – A Dominican monastery from 1258 to 1544, this building is now a local museum showing, among other collections in its spacious, oak beamed rooms, the Rothenburg Stations of the Cross (1494). Perhaps the most fascinating exhibit is the original hanap drained by ex-Burgomaster Nusch in front of General Tilly *(see above)*.

The tankard's design depicts the Emperor and the seven Electors. It was made in 1616.

★ **ROTTWEIL** Baden-Württemberg   Pop 24 000

Michelin map **413** IJ 22

Rottweil is a small, pleasant, fortified town on a spur circled by a bend in the Upper Neckar. The site, between the Swabian Jura and the Black Forest, is attractive. At carnival-time, Rottweil is renowned for its spectacular fools' procession (Narrensprung) *(photograph p 312)*.

SIGHTS

Leave the car near the gateway (Schwarzes Tor) at the main entrance to the upper town, at the junction of the roads from Oberndorf and Schramberg.

Hauptstrasse – From this street, dropping abruptly towards the river, the visitor can see what the old city must have looked like – between the old houses with their three-sided oriel windows, there is an appealing **view★** of the distant Swabian Jura.

Holy Cross Church (Heiligkreuzmünster) – On the left, past the Town Hall. A Gothic church remodelled in the 16C. Use the south entrance (the porch is neo-Gothic). Many **altarpieces★** are displayed in the side chapels.

Outside, on the Münsterplatz esplanade, St George's (Gothic) Fountain is ornamented with three charming sculpted groups: The Virgin, St George, St Catherine.

Turn right beyond the church on the far side of this square and pass another church, to come to St Lawrence's Chapel, which was built on the original rampart wall.

St Lawrence's Chapel (Lorenzkapelle) – Almost two hundred Gothic **statues★** have been collected from churches in the region and assembled in this former cemetery chapel. Among the masterpieces of Swabian art, note the Holy Women of Eriskirch.

Turn left, and take the Hauptstrasse back to the town's central crossroads.

Kapellenkirche – The **tower★** of this Gothic church, Baroque on the inside, is a splendid example of the Flamboyant style. The square base, quartered with graceful staircase turrets, supports on the façade an unusual pierced loggia. The upper part of the tower, in two octagonal tiers, is lit by windows with a fine tracery of stonework.

The three entrances retain their original Gothic carvings: the Last Judgement on the west face, and the Knight's Betrothal on the right corner turret are outstanding.

EXCURSION

★ **Dreifaltigkeitsberg (Trinity Hill)** – *20km - 12 1/2 miles to the southeast.*
A minor road leads up to the pilgrimage church here from Spaichingen, on the edge of the Swabian Jura. From the site of the church, a wide **panorama★** includes the Baar Depression and, a dark line in the distance, the sombre outline of the Black Forest*(qv)*.

(KÖNIGSSCHLÖSSER) Bavaria

Michelin map **413** P 24

The term Königsschlösser is generally reserved for Hohenschwangau Castle and its extravagantly romantic, neo-feudal neighbour, Neuschwanstein. The other royal residences of Upper Bavaria, equally examples of Ludwig II's passion for historical reconstruction, should not however be forgotten. They include Linderhof Castle and Herrenchiemsee *(qv)*.

HOHENSCHWANGAU★ and NEUSCHWANSTEIN★★

About 3 hour's walk and sightseeing

Leave the car in the special park at Hohenschwangau.

Circle the wooded spur crowned by Hohenschwangau Castle until you arrive at the shady promontory of the Pindarplatz, on the northern shore of the **Alpsee★**. At this point, there is a **lookout point** with a fine **view★** of the dark, pine-ringed waters of the lake and the Säuling escarpments above. Take the path on the right which leads to the castle.

★ **Hohenschwangau Castle** ⊙ – This castle, constructed from the ruins of a large 12C feudal fortress, was built between 1832 and 1836 on the orders of Maximilian II of Bavaria, when he was still Prince Regent.
The neo-Gothic style, strongly influenced by the traditional English manor house, satisfied the current taste for troubadour romanticism. It was in these surroundings that the unfortunate Ludwig II dreamed away his youth.
Compared with Neuschwanstein, and despite its many infelicities – excessive repetition in the décor of the etymological swan (Schwan) motif; accumulation of inelegant objets d'art offered to the Royal Family by Bavarian communities – Hohenschwangau retains the warmth of a palace that was once lived in. The presence over many years of Queen Marie, the mother of Ludwig II, goes a long way to explain the atmosphere of relative intimacy that still pervades the apartments. Having endured the mania for over-decoration characteristic of the period – in particular the High Gothic ceilings – visitors will welcome with relief the clean lines of the maple and cherrywood Biedermeier *(qv)* furniture. The place given to Oriental art is completely compatible with the ambiance of romantic chivalry instanced by huge murals depicting heroes of medieval verse chronicles, and based on cartoons by Moritz von Schwind.
The King's admiration for Richard Wagner is evoked on the second floor, where the old music room displays correspondance between the two men, and a piano which both played. Fantasy returns with the entry to the bedchamber of Ludwig II: the ceiling is painted to resemble the night sky, and the constellations can be illuminated at will. From his window, the King could observe through a telescope the progress of work at Neuschwanstein.

Take either the bus (leave from Hotel Liesl) or the horse-drawn cart (leave from Hotel Müller) to get to Neuschwanstein. Alternatively, take the wide, steeply sloping path (1/2 hour) from the car park.

★★ **Neuschwanstein Castle** ⊙ – Bristling with turrets and pinnacles, the cold grey granite mass of this fortress rises from a spur penetrating the eastern extremity of the Pöllat Gorge. As at Hohenschwangau, it was a designer of theatrical décor and not an architect who produced the original plans, which explains the dreamlike atmosphere of the place. Building began in 1869.
A tour of the interior, where gilded panelling, heavy tapestries and acres of marble proliferate, confirms the impression of unreality. Ludwig II stayed at the castle only 170 days: it was at Neuschwanstein on 10 June 1886 that he learned from a government commission hastily despatched from Munich that he had been deposed. He died three days later *(see under Munich)*.
The most revealing rooms are on the third floor. They include an artificial stalactite grotto with a small adjoining winter garden that recalls the Tannhäuser legend; the Great Hall, whose décor has for its theme the legend of Lohengrin (another invasion of swans); and the unfinished Throne Room, a Byzantine-Romanesque sanctuary whose apse was to have accommodated the Royal Throne.
Almost the whole of the fourth floor is taken up by the Singers' Hall (Sängersaal), which has a fine coffered ceiling and many impressive chandeliers and candelabra. The designer here was influenced by Wartburg Castle *(qv)*, the Thuringian fortress said to have been the site, in the early 13C, of the legendary poetical contest recalled in Wagner's opera Tannhäuser. Wartburg was later made famous by the visit of Martin Luther. Wagner, who was a guest at Hohenschwangau, never stayed at Neuschwanstein, Linderhof or Herrenchiemsee.
After the tour, visitors who still have the stamina can walk up the Pöllat Gorge to St Mary's Bridge (Marienbrücke), which spans the chasm *(allow an extra hour for this promenade)*. Sometimes at night Ludwig II would come to this bridge to stare down at the castle, silent, empty, and in darkness except for lights he had illuminated in the Singers' Hall.

★ RÜDESHEIM AM RHEIN Hessen Pop 9 600

Michelin map **412** G 17 - Local map see under RHINE VALLEY

The wine town of Rüdesheim lies at the southern end of the Rhine Gorge – where the river, deflected westwards through the Rheingau vineyards by the Taunus massif, decides to turn north again. Here at the Bingen Gap, gateway to the "Romantic Rhine", Rüdesheim has become the most popular tourist centre in the whole valley: the narrow streets, including the famous **Drosselgasse**, are crammed with visitors, attracted by the wine bars offering a taste of the celebrated local Riesling. There are also distilleries to be visited and cellars where sparkling wine can be drunk.

Brömserburg – Residence-cum-refuge for the Bishops of Mainz until the 13C, this stronghold passed into the hands of the Knights of Rüdesheim, and then became a meeting-place for brigands. It was re-taken in 1281 by Archbishop Wernherr. Today, it is arranged as a **wine museum**. The outstanding exhibits are 21 old wine presses and a collection of amphorae (vases, jars, bins for storage or transport of wine).

EXCURSIONS

Niederwald Monument – *Access by road (2km - 1 mile) or by cable car (terminal on the Oberstrasse: 20mn Rtn).*
Built (1877-83) to commemorate the re-establishment of the German Empire in 1871, the monument comprises a statue of Germania (which alone weighs 32 tons) on a plinth with bronze bas-reliefs showing Bismarck, the Emperor Wilhelm I, the German Princes and their armies. From the terrace there is a **view** of the vineyards, Bingen, and the confluence of the Rhine and Nahe. The heights of the Palatinate are visible in the distance.

★ **The Rheingau** – *23km - 14 miles - allow 2 hours.*
A southern exposure allows successful cultivation of vines high up on the foothills of the Taunus. Before passing through these vineyards to reach Eberbach Abbey, the road skirts or traverses the picturesque villages of Geisenheim, Winkel and Hattenheim.

Eberbach Abbey ⊙ – The Cistercian abbey lies at the foot of a small valley, at the upper limit of the vines. Vaulting with 16 ribs arches from a central pillar in the 1345 chapter house, which opens off a partly ruined cloister (only two galleries remain).
In the former refectory a magnificent collection of antique **wine presses**★★ is on view. The pillars are treated in a decorative fashion. On the upper floor of the Fathers' House, the dormitory comprises two 14C aisles, each 72m - 236ft long.
The old **abbey church** – with a flattened chevet and low rectangular chapels in the Cistercian tradition – retains an atmosphere of austere grandeur.

Kiedrich – The 15C church in this wine-growers' market town is still furnished in its original, rare Flamboyant form: the early 16C carved **pews**★ and choir stalls are still adorned with polychromatic embellishment; they still have their Gothic inscriptions. The 14C **Kiedrich Madonna**★, beneath the rood-screen, shows French influence.

Eltville – Built beside the Rhine, the castle here was the residence of the Prince-Electors of Mainz in the 14C and 15C. Living quarters in the tower can still be viewed. In the Church of St Peter and St Paul *(Rosengasse 5)*, there is a very fine baptistry from the Mainz studio of Hans Backhoffen, with the symbols of the Four Apostles worked into the base.

★ RÜGEN Mecklenburg-West Pomerania

Michelin map **987** fold 7

Joined to the mainland by a long bridge (2.5km - 1 1/4miles) straddling the straits opposite the town of **Stralsund**★ *(qv)*, Rügen is Germany's largest island. In a total area of 926km - 358 sq miles, the Baltic island offers a surprising variety of scenery. In the west, as the straits widen towards the open sea, the coastline is indented, following the irregular contours of many inlets. Chalk cliffs and sandy beaches in the east attract summer crowds; the wooded southern shores face the wide, shallow waters of the Greifswalder Bodden (Gulf); and to the north Rügen is cut almost in two by the deep, extraordinarily jagged penetration of the Jasmunder Bodden – which is practically an inland sea.

The Stubbenkammer, Rügen

MAIN SIGHTS

★ **Seaside Resorts** – These are mainly on the island's southeastern peninsula: **Binz, Sellin, Baabe** and **Göhren** add to their safe beaches the attraction of a forested hinterland.

Sassnitz – Beautiful beechwoods lie to the north of this small port, which is the terminal for ferries linking this part of northern Germany with Scandinavia.

★★ **Stubbenkammer** – Southeast of the town, the viewpoint of the Königsstuhl height ("The King's Seat") lies 133m - 436ft above impressive white chalk cliffs advancing into the Baltic.

★ **Cape Arkona** (**Kap Arkona**). – The chalk cliffs of this headland mark Rügen's most northerly point. Above the 50m - 164ft cliffs, not far from the lighthouse, a hillock or barrow pinpoints the site of the ancient fortress of Jarosmarburg, built by the Slavs and destroyed by the Danes in 1168.

THE RUHR BASIN (RUHRGEBIET) Rhineland-Westphalia

Michelin map **987** folds 13 and 14
Town plans in the current Michelin Red Guide Deutschland

Europe's largest single industrial centre, the Ruhr Basin (1 930 square miles) lies between three rivers: the Ruhr, the Rhine and the Lippe. The total population of the area is over five million, and almost 700 000 of these work in industry. But the Ruhr no longer merits its "Black Country" image, and today less than 2/5 of this workforce is employed by the mines and steelworks once characteristic of the Basin. The implantation of light industries, and an extensive "green belt" policy followed after the massive destructions of the Second World War, mean that a motorist today can cross certain sections of the region without seeing a single blast furnace or factory.

MINES, INDUSTRIES, LANDSCAPES

The Ruhr coal reserves are exceptionally well situated: seams run straight with few faults and little folding, dropping gently from south to north as they increase in thickness. All types of coal are present, from anthracite and slack to gas-bearing lodes. But since its beginnings in the 18C, the mining industry has moved its sites constantly towards the north. The original opencast outcrops in the Ruhr Valley were abandoned long ago. Richer deposits occur between the Ruhr and the Emscher, but in the century between 1850 and the beginning of the 1960s, no mine ever had to be sunk deeper than 400m - 1 312ft. Even here, however, rusting pitheads and deserted buildings testify to the large number of workings now shut down.

It is in the "new basin", a little further north, between the Emscher and the Lippe, that mining activity is concentrated today. Late 20C rationalization demands restriction of production to the most prolific source with the most efficient equipment, and since 1969 the existing Ruhr companies have been regrouped into a single development organization, the Ruhrkohle AG. Now, with a coalfield extending as far as Münster, with ultra-modern installations, fewer shafts and pits sometimes as much as half a mile deep, the exploitation yield has risen to 4 1/2 tons per day per man employed.

Costs nevertheless remain high: Ruhr coal is too expensive, competitive neither with the imported product nor with rival forms of energy. The mining industry is in recession and the workforce contracts every year. Two definitive changes have resulted from this situation, one geographical, the other social.

Each also depends upon two factors – the production of steel and heavy industry – inseparable from the use of coal and relatively affected in the same way today. Resettlement plans and environmental imperatives have thus combined to make profound changes in these aspects of the Ruhr.

INDUSTRIAL REORGANIZATION

In the southern zone, as mining moved north, the old ironworks have given way to the scattered introduction of metal workshops and the small, clean installations of modern light industry. These Ruhr Valley hillsides – the Bergisches Land – half industrial, half forested, without being idyllic nevertheless make a welcome stopping place.

In the middle zone – a 50km - 30 mile stretch between Duisburg and Dortmund – the pre-war concentration of steelworks, factories, mines and industrial towns had by 1950 produced an urban sprawl of such density that all traces of agriculture, market towns and rural life had long been submerged. Yet even here, following a plan put into operation in 1968, seven north-south green belts, lakes, parks, airy workers' resettlement developments and re-established woodland areas have wrought astonishing changes in the landscape.

With heavy foreign competition in the fields of metallurgy and steel, the industrial face of the Ruhr turns increasingly towards chemicals, electronics, textiles, glassware, petro-chemical derivatives and the manufacture of automobiles.

But the process is not complete: the establishment of "clean" new industrial patterns remains the prime concern of the Ruhr's economic policy. Efforts already made in the direction of town planning (green spaces, restriction of traffic flow), of education (the new university at Bochum), of new technology and the defence of the environment, demonstrate the scope of the reconversion envisaged. Together with intense activity in the field of culture and a publicity campaign presenting the Ruhr Basin as "Germany's Rising Star" it is hoped this will erase the "Black Country" image of the Ruhr once and for all.

MUSEUMS OF THE RUHR AND
THE BERGISCHES LAND (A SELECTION)

Technical Museums

★★ **German Mining Museum** (Deutsches Bergbau-Museum) ⊘ – At **Bochum** *(plan of the conurbation in the current Michelin Red Guide Deutschland).*
Founded in 1930, this museum is on the site of the old Germania mine (recognizable by its 68m - 223ft pithead frame). Over more than 100 000sq ft of floorspace it gives a complete picture of mining from antiquity to the present day. Models, reconstructions, graphics and original equipment cover every aspect of extraction, along with such techniques as drilling, ventilation and the use of explosives. Fifty feet underground, more than a mile of abandoned workings have been restored to illustrate coalface extraction and transport.

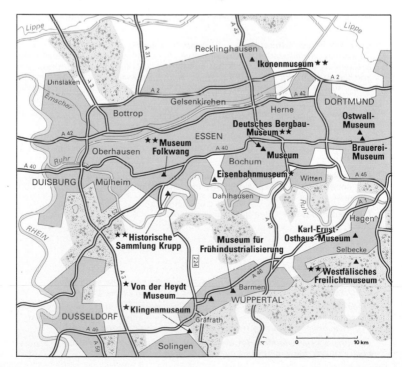

★★ Open-Air Technical Museum (Westfälisches Freilichtmuseum) ⊘ – At **Hagen-Selbecke**, *in the valley of Mäckingerbachtal. From Hagen (plan of the conurbation in the current Michelin Red Guide Deutschland), leave by* ④ *on the town plan. At Eilpe, turn right in the Breckerfeld-Halver direction and continue for just over a mile to Selbecke. From the museum car park (Museumsparkplatz), on the left of the road, 15mn on foot.*

Along one and a half miles of this valley, more than 70 installations or buildings have been reconstructed to illustrate the evolution of crafts and techniques in Westphalian industry. Traditional metalwork displays (at the foot of the valley) include giant iron and copper hammers activated by water from artificial lakes. A half-timbered 18C house has been turned into a **Blacksmith Museum** with a working forge.

There are also examples of James Nasmyth's steam hammer (*c*1840) and the zinc rolling mill of Hoesch (1841), both of which marked the start of true industrialization. Higher up the valley an 18C papermill houses a **Printing Museum**. Finally there is a whole village of traditional craftsmen, where not only saddlers and smiths and ropemakers and dyers, but also bakers and brewers ply their trade.

★ Railway Museum (Eisenbahnmuseum) ⊘ – At **Bochum-Dahlhausen**, *halfway between Essen and Bochum (C. Otto-Strasse 191).*

Founded by a society of railway enthusiasts, this museum is installed in a disused station and rolling-stock repair shop on the north bank of the Ruhr. Equipment dating from 1914 (an engine house, a turntable, a hydraulic crane) is for the most part still in mint condition. More than 100 machines that ran on rails retrace the evolution of this form of transport from the beginnings to the end of the steam era. The highlights of the collection are 15 steam locomotives, the oldest of which is a Prussian T-3 of 1882. A postal locomotive built by AEG in 1913 marks the start of electrification. Railcars, hand-operated gangers' trucks, many types of wagon and a rail-or-road motorbus can also be seen.

★★ Krupp Collection in the Villa Hügel – *See under Essen.*

★ The Blade Museum (Klingenmuseum) ⊘ – *At* **Solingen-Gräfrath**.

Known the world over for its knives and its scissors, Solingen is the centre of fine metalwork in Germany. The museum traces the history of side arms (magnificent dress swords), surgical instruments, razors and table cutlery.

Early Industrialization Museum (Museum für Frühindustrialisierung) ⊘ – *At* **Wuppertal-Barmen**.

Housed in a disused factory, this museum traces the economic and social history of the Wupper Valley since the middle of the 18C.

Brewery Museum (Brauerei Museum) – *See under Dortmund.*

Fine Arts Museums

★ Folkwang Museum – *See under Essen.*

★★ Icon Museum (Ikonenmuseum) ⊘ – *At* Recklinghausen, *Kirchplatz.*

The marvellous specimens exhibited here are classed by theme: the Holy Trinity and the Celestial Hierarchy (a theme rich in symbolism); the Virgin; the Saints and their Days (a splendid calendar of all the religious feasts). To these must be added a collection of iconostases (screens separating the sanctuary from the rest of the church).

★ Von der Heydt Museum ⊘ –. *At* **Wuppertal-Elberfeld**.

This museum, housed in a former Town Hall built between 1827 and 1842 and extensively remodelled in 1990, has an interesting collection of paintings: Flemish and Dutch from the 16C and 17C; French and German from the 19C to the present day. Sculptures from the 19C and 20C are also on display. The cafeteria was designed by Buren.

Karl-Ernst Osthaus Museum ⊘ – *At* Hagen *(plan of the conurbation in the curent Michelin Red Guide Deutschland), Hochstrasse 73.*

Housed in a building designed by Henry van de Velde in the Jugendstil *(qv)*, this displays for the most part the paintings and drawings of the artist Christian Rohlfs (1849-1938).

Bochum Museum ⊘ – *At* Bochum, *Kortumstrasse 147, opposite the park.*

The collections in this spacious, airy modern building concentrate mainly on **contemporary art from Eastern Europe**.

Ostwall Museum – *See under Dortmund.*

To plan a special itinerary

- consult the map of the region on pp 4-6 which shows the main towns, individual sights and recommended routes described in the guide;

- read the descriptions of the above which are described in the middle section of the guide in alphabetical order under their own name or are incorporated in the excursions radiating from a particular town or tourist centre;

- use the appropriate Michelin Maps which show places of interest, scenic routes, viewpoints and natural features...

★ SAALE VALLEY (OBERES SAALETAL) Thuringia

Michelin map **987** fold 26

Rising on high ground at the eastern extremity of the Forest of Thuringia *(qv)*, the River Saale flows 427km - 265 miles to the north before joining the Elbe upstream from Magdeburg. Its winding course forms a natural link between such towns as Jena and Halle, masterpieces of sacred architecture like Merseburg and Naumburg, and the innumerable castles – Heidecksburg, Weissenfels, Dornburg – built on its banks.

The itinerary suggested below heads south through a countryside of woods and fields and small market towns to an attractive upland region dotted with lakes, in a corner formed by the old East- and West-German demarcation line and the Czech frontier.

FROM RUDOLSTADT TO SAALBURG

61km – 38 miles - allow 4 hours

Rudolstadt – Once the seat of the Princes of Schwarzburg-Rudolstadt, this town is dominated by the fine silhouette of **Heidecksburg Castle★**, ⊘ which dates from 1737. Several **rooms★** magnificently decorated in the Rococo style are open to the public.

Saalfeld – In medieval times, Saalfeld was among the most important towns in Thuringia, thanks to local silver and copper mines and a position on the main trade route to Bohemia which assured its commercial prosperity.

The Renaissance **Town Hall** in the Marktplatz is designed around a façade that centres on a staircase tower with two oriel windows. On the other side of the square, the **Market Pharmacy** (Stadt Markt-Apotheke) is one of the rare Romanesque (restored) buildings in the area. **St John's Church** (Stadtkirche St Johannis) displays a late 14C Last Judgement above its main entrance. Several altarpieces from a Saalfeld studio (late 15C) can be seen in the **Museum of Thuringia** (Thüringer Heimatmuseum) ⊘, which has been installed in a former Franciscan abbey.

★ **Fairy Grottoes (Feengrotten)** ⊘ – *1km - 1/2 mile southeast of Saalfeld by Route No 281.*
Stalactites, stalagmites, concretions and petrifications... such near-magical subterranean décor can be found in the abandoned galleries of this disused mine.

Leave Saalfeld by Route No 85. Cross the Saale at the Hohenwarte dam.

The artificial lake at **Hohenwarte** (Hohenwarte-Talsperre) curves for half a dozen miles, in a series of wide arcs magnificently incorporated into the existing landscape. Woodland scenery alternates with crops as the road crosses the plateau.

Via Drognitz and Remptendorf, the suggested route arrives at the Bleiloch barrage. Driving across the dam, sightseers regain the river's east bank.

This reservoir, 29km - 18 miles long, with an enormous volume of water retained, is the largest of the five artificial lakes between Blankenstein and Saalfeld.

Saalburg – Now a lakeside town, Saalburg lost part of its outskirt when first the valley was flooded. Remains of the 16C fortifications, however, can still be seen.

SAAR VALLEY Rhineland-Palatinate and Saar

Michelin map **412** fold 29

Between Mettlach and Konz, the River Saar cuts its way through the crystalline Hunsrück Massif, the resistance of which reduces the valley to a winding defile at times visible only from the top of its steeply sloping sides.

FROM METTLACH TO TRIER

57km - 35 miles - about 2 hours

Mettlach – The Baroque, red sandstone façade of the old abbey – now the offices of a ceramics factory – rises above the trees bordering the road leading uphill towards Merzig. Downstream, in a public park nearby, stands the Alter Turm, a ruined octagonal funerary chapel dating from the 10C.

★★ **Cloef** – *7km - 4 miles west of Mettlach then 15mn on foot Rtn.* From a viewpoint high above the river, there is a view of the Montclair Loop, a hairpin curve enclosing a long, densely-wooded promontory.

Return to Mettlach.

From Mettlach to Saarburg, the road runs at the foot of the valley, forested on the lower slopes, with tall escarpments above. Vines appear as the valley widens.

Saarburg – The setting of this small town is typical of the valley's final section, with terraced vineyards now on every side. There is an attractive view of the town from a knoll crowned with the ruins of a 10C castle. In the old quarter, near the Markt, a 20m - 66ft cascade plunges between houses built on the rock.

After Konz, where the Saar joins the Moselle, follow the river to Trier (qv).

★★ **Trier** – See under Trier.

ST BLASIEN Baden-Württemberg Pop 4 400

Michelin map **413** H 23

The majestic domed church dedicated to St Blaise comes suddenly into view at the far end of a wooded valley in the Hotzenwald, in the southern part of the Black Forest. It stands in the grounds of a medieval monastery founded in 835 by a brotherhood of hermit monks who ranged all over the southern part of Germany. Although the air is bracing, the town – popular with holiday-makers – distils an air of great tranquillity.

★ **Church (Dom)** – The Baroque church, following a plan favoured in that epoque, is built within a rectangle of old abbey buildings.
The French architect, Pierre-Michel d'Ixnard (1726-1795), graced it with a central cupola, behind a peristyle, which rises 64m - 210ft from the ground. After St Peter's, Rome, and Les Invalides in Paris, this is the third largest dome in Europe. Within it, lit by deeply embrasured windows, is a false cupola. Despite the fact that it appears to rest on the columns of the central rotunda, this is in fact suspended from the true dome. The chancel, which has cradle vaulting, lies behind the high altar.

EXCURSIONS

The Hochkopf Massif – *45km - 28 miles to the west – 3 hours. Drive, via Todtmoos, to the Pass of Weissenbachsattel.*

Hochkopf – *1 hour Rtn on foot.* From the car park, on the right side of the road, a footpath leads to the lookout tower, from which there are superb **views**★★ of the barren peaks of the Belchen and the Feldberg, to the west, and – on clear days – the Alps to the southeast.

Bernau – In a lush pastural valley, the fine Bernau farms, hugging the fertile ground, are grouped in picturesque hamlets.
At Bernau-Dorf, the Town Hall houses an **exhibition** of paintings by the local artist Hans Thoma – notably landscapes of the Black Forest executed with great sensitivity.

The Valley of the Alb (Albtal) – *30km - 18 1/2 miles to the south - 1 hour.* The road runs high above the Alb Gorges, alternating sections along the edge of the cliffs with tunnels through the rock, before it rejoins the Rhine at Albbruck.

★ **SALEM ABBEY** Baden-Württemberg

Michelin map **413** K 23

This Cistercian abbey, founded in 1137, was at its most influential under the Abbot Anselm II (1746-1778), the builder of Birnau *(qv)*.
Part of the buildings are now occupied by a private school started by the educationist Dr Kurt Hahn and attended before the Second World War by Britain's Duke of Edinburg (Dr Hahn later emigrated to Scotland and founded Gordonstoun).

★ **Abbey Church** (Abteikirche) ⊙ – The building was constructed between 1299 and 1414. Outside, the extreme severity ot the Gothic façade is relieved by slender bays lightening the east and west gables.
Inside, the design is typical Cistercian Gothic, with a large chancel and flattened chevet, soaring vaults and side aisles supporting the nave through walls abutting on wide arcades.

★ **Abbey Buildings** (Schloss) ⊙ – These were remodelled in the Baroque style at the beginning of the 18C. Visitors can follow the evolution of the stuccowork entrusted to artists of the Wessobrunn School *(qv)* over a whole century.

Oratory (Betsaal) – Wessobrunn stucco still adorns the ceiling of this former summer refectory.

Library – Another superb ceiling, this time with basket-handle vaulting.

Emperors' Hall (Kaisersaal) – Completed in 1708, this was the first great State Hall in the Baroque style inaugurated in a German abbey. Statues of Emperors and medallions of Popes comprise the sculpted decoration.

Abbots' Apartments (Prälatenquartier) – Note among these discreetly charming rooms the green Rococo study (1764) with its swan motif – the emblem of Abbot Anselm II.

Lower Gatehouse (Untertor-Haus) – Between the pilasters of this strikingly elegant Baroque entrance, the decorative window lintels have a different design on each storey.

★ THE SAUERLAND Rhineland-Westphalia

Michelin map **987** folds 14, 24 and 25

The Sauerland, which forms the hinterland to the Ruhr Basin, is the most mountainous, if not actually the highest part, of the Rhineland Schist Massif.

It is crowned by the **Langenberg** (843m - 2 766ft), near Niedersfeld, which is already in effect a transitional area linking the Sauerland with the Waldeck heights.

Numerous artificial lakes in the region supply water and hydro-electric energy to the industrial towns of the Ruhr, serving also as centres for water sports. The Upper Sauerland, especially the Rothaargebirge, a range covered by forests of beech and fir, is very popular with tourists.

FROM SOEST TO BAD BERLEBURG

18km - 112 miles - allow one day

★ **Soest** – *See under Soest.*

★ **Möhnesee** – *See under Soest: Excursions.*

Arnsberg – The old town is built on a spur enclosed by a bend in the Ruhr river, rising in tiers above the waterside. To the north, a clock tower commands the approach to the Schlossberg ruins; to the south lies the former abbey quarter, where a superb Rococo gate, the Hirschberger Tor, still stands.

Beyond Arnsberg, the road skirts the right bank of the Sorpe artificial lake (water sports), then crosses the Lennegebirge massif. There are many attractive viewpoints, particularly near the pass. On the far side of Finnentrop, the Bigge Valley is punctuated by a number of rock-strewn passages.

★ **Attahöhle Grotto** ⊙ – *On the right-hand side of the road, just before Attendorn.* This strange cavern eroded from the limestone extends for no less than 3km - 1 3/4 miles into the bedrock. Apart from a multitude of stalactites and stalagmites, curious stone "draperies" are visible, some of them translucent.

Attendorn – The reputation of Attendorn was at its height in the Middle Ages, as witness the splendid 14C **Town Hall** (Historisches Rathaus) with its stepped gable, the open, arcaded hall of the old covered market (Alter Markt), and the **Sauerland Cathedral** (Sauerländer Dom). This Gothic hall-church has magnificent 14C interior decorations.

Southeast of Attendorn, on the other side of the Bigge, is **Schnellenberg Castle**, which dates, in its present form, largely from the 17C.

Bigge Dam (Biggetalsperre) – This dam, which has been in service since 1964, forms with the Lister barrage – which has flooded an adjacent valley – the largest reservoir in Westphalia.

About 2km - 1 mile before Olpe, fork left on Route B 55. Soon after Bilstein, on a small mountain road, take a right turn in the direction of the Hohe Bracht.

Hohe Bracht (584m - 1 916ft). – From the viewing tower (620m - 2 034ft), there is a fine panorama, including the hummocked Rothaargebirge massif as far as Kahler Asten.

After crossing the rural landscape of the Lenne Valley, the route passes **Grafschaft** and **Oberkirchen**, two villages with pretty half-timbered houses, and then the country becomes wilder and more hilly. Beyond **Nordenau**, a typical Upper Sauerland village where the houses are roofed with slate, is the ski station of Altastenberg. Finally, on the far side of an open upland plateau with splendid views all around, the road arrives at Kahler Asten.

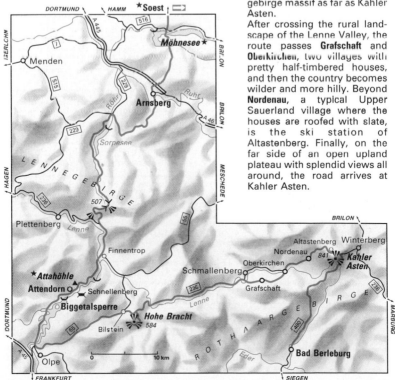

Kahler Asten – At 841m - 2 759ft, this is the highest point of the Rothaargebirge. From the lookout tower, as might be expected, there is a superb **view** all around. To the northeast is the spa and winter sports centre of Winterberg.
Slate quarries flank the road back down, which is twisty but well-made. There are many attractive views towards the south.

Bad Berleburg – The slate cladding which faces the houses lends this mountain village an air that is both sober and dignified. From the upper levels there is a good view of the 16-18C castle.

★ **SCHLESWIG** Schleswig-Holstein   Pop 26 000

Michelin map **411** L 3
Town plan in the current Michelin Red Guide Deutschland

Schleswig, an old maritime town of white houses, was built on low-lying banks at the inner end of an arm of the sea, the **Schlei**, which penetrates the coast for 43km - 27 miles.
From the car park on Route B 76, there is an attractive **view**★ of the old town below the cathedral, on the far side of the water.

The Vikings – Merchants were settled on the south bank of the Schlei at the beginning of the 9C. Their favoured position at the crossroads of the old north-south road to Jutland and the east-west route used to transport light loads from the Baltic to the North Sea soon made the settlement an important North European trade centre.
A century later, Vikings from Sweden invaded the region. They renamed the area **Haithabu** ("the town in the heather") and encircled it with a vast defence system of which the **semi-circular retrenchment** beside the Haddebyer Noor *(access by ② on the town plan)* remains today.
Near this lagoon, stones with runic carvings such as the **Busdorfer Runenstein** (access via the Busdorfer Strasse) are visible at another archaeological site. There are further Viking remains at Gottorf Castle.
In the 11C, the townspeople of Haithabu, seeking better defences against Scandinavian marauders, crossed to the north bank of the Schlei to found the town of Schleswig.

★★★ **THE NYDAM BOAT (NYDAM-BOOT)** ⊘ *time: 1/2 hour*

This oak-hulled long ship with its fine lines is the oldest Germanic vessel of any size that has ever been discovered. Dating from about the 4C, it was excavated in 1863 from the Nydam marshes, on Danish territory. Displayed in the Regional Archaeological Museum (Archäologisches Landesmuseum), the ship is 23m long by 3m wide (75ft [88] 10ft). It was powered by 36 oarsmen.
Other discoveries preserved for centuries in the peat, can be seen in the museum. They include weapons, footwear, the remains of clothing – mostly leather – and even human bodies.

ADDITIONAL SIGHTS

Gottorf Castle ⊘ – Two large museums devoted to the Schleswig-Holstein Land are housed in this 16-18C castle, once the seat of the Holstein-Gottorf ducal family, which in 1762 became the Imperial House of the Tsars of Russia. The **Schleswig-Holstein Regional Museum**★★ (Schleswig-Holsteinisches Landesmuseum) has representative collections of local arts, crafts and handiwork.
Note especially the Gothic Hall (sacred art of the Middle Ages), the galleries exhibiting furniture, and the **Renaissance Chapel**★★, complete with ducal loggia. The **Regional Archaeological Museum**★ *(see also above)* offers a systematic presentation of the area's pre-history, from Neolithic times to the era of the Vikings.

★ **St Peter's Cathedral** (Dom St Peter) – Thanks to its graceful spire, this brick-built Gothic hall-church can be seen from far off. Enter by the south (St Peter's) doorway, which is of stone, with a carved tympanum dating from 1170. The most remarkable work of art is the 1521 **Bordesholm Altarpiece**★★, which can be seen in the chancel. Northwest of the transept lies the 14C **cloister**, with stylized vine-leaf motifs painted on the vaulting.

The Holm – This is an old sailors' and fishermen's quarter. The low houses crowd around a quiet square, the **Friedhofsplatz**★, which contains a cemetery and a chapel.

Haithabu Viking Museum (Vikingermuseum) ⊘ – *Access via Route B 76, direction Kiel*. This annexe to the Regional Archaeological Museum is near the Haddebyer Noor lagoon, next to the old Viking site *(see above)*, whose history it traces.
A large number of objects unearthed in various digs (jewels, weapons, tools and domestic implements) are on display, along with graphics and models of the Viking settlement.
The galleries are very well laid out, with a wealth of information on the life and times of the Haithabu inhabitants. In the **Boat Hall**★ (Schiffshalle) there is a Viking longship, partly reconstituted from contemporary fragments dredged up in the ancient port site.

EXCURSIONS

Eckernförde – *23km - 14 miles to the east, again via Route B 76.*
The town lies at the inner end of the Eckernförder Bucht, a deep, wide inlet penetrated by the waters of the Baltic. It is a picturesque fishing port which existed already in the 12C (a document dating from that period mentions "fishermen's community"). Eckernförde is the home of a Holsteiner delicacy known as Kieler Sprotten (smoked fish).

St Nicholas' Church (Nikolaikirche), a sober triple-aisle brick building, stands in the market place. The **interior★**, supported by four massive columns, is lavishly decorated. The early Baroque **altarpiece** (1640) is said to be the most accomplished work of the wood carver Hans Gudewerdt the Younger, whose father sculpted the Renaissance pulpit with its Biblical scenes. The bronze **baptismal font** in the middle of the church, also richly decorated, dates from 1588.

SCHWÄBISCH GMÜND Baden-Württemberg   Pop 60 000

Michelin map **413** M 20
Town plan in the current Michelin Red Guide Deutschland

Traditionally, Schwäbisch Gmünd is a centre for the working of precious metals, and its silverware is seen on many German tables. The town is a good excursion centre, since it is near the **Kaiserberge** (Imperial Mountains), whose three conical peaks, the Hohenstaufen, Hohenrechberg and Stuifen, are clearly visible and characteristic of that part of the Swabian Jura.

★ **Holy Cross Cathedral** (Heiligkreuzmünster) – The cathedral was built in the 14C by Heinrich Parler, a Swabian master whose descendants designed cathedrals as far apart as Prague, Vienna and Milan. Surprisingly, it has no towers. The pinnacles, balustrades and exterior tracery are Flamboyant Gothic. The architect skilfully worked the decoration into a grid over the west gable, and both chancel doors are sculpted beneath porches which were once also fully decorated. The two-tier chevet is gracefully conceived.
The interior is a perfect hall, the chancel – which has a similar layout to the nave – profiting from more intricately worked ribbed vaulting. The early Renaissance choir stalls and radiating chapels are rich in statuary: note especially, in the axial chapel, an early 15C Holy Sepulchre watched over by the three Marys. The Baptismal Chapel contains the Tree of Jesse (1520), composed of 40 sculpted figures.

Marktplatz – A huge square whose Baroque character is emphasized by the prosperous-looking houses surrounding it and a twin-statue fountain dedicated to the Virgin. Several half timbered buildings, the hospital and the Gräth (old Town Hall) nevertheless recall the medieval existence of the town.

EXCURSIONS

★ **Hohenstaufen** – *14km - 8 1/2 miles to the southwest, plus 30 mn on foot Rtn.*
From the two churches at the top of the town, a shady footpath leads to the summit at 684m - 2 244ft. Nothing remains of the castle, the one-time seat of the royal Hohenstaufens, but the climb is worthwhile for the **panorama★** of the two remaining Kaiserberge and, on the horizon, the Swabian Jura. (The car should be left on the village's central esplanade.)

★ **Hohenrechberg** – *12km - 7 1/2 miles, plus 1 hour on foot Rtn.*
The castle ruins, again, command a vast **horizon**. Visitors can stroll around the ancient rampart walk or, higher up, walk around the ruined walls whose crests have been converted into a walkway. In the foreground is the massive cone of Hofenstaufen.

*The **Michelin Green Guide France**
aims to make touring more enjoyable
by suggesting several touring programmes
which are easily adapted to personal taste.*

★★ SCHWÄBISCH HALL Baden-Württemberg   Pop 31 500

Michelin map **413** M 19 – Local map see under HOHENLOHE
Town plan in the current Michelin Red Guide Deutschland

This old town, built in tiers up the steep flank of the Kocher Valley, grew up around salt springs known as far back as Celtic times. In the Middle Ages, it was famous for the Imperial silver coins, the Häller or Heller, minted there.
From the Mauerstrasse (the quay on the west bank), at the level of the Löwenbrauerei (brewery), there is a fine **general view★** of the old town, with its roofs stepped one above the other at the foot of St Michael's Church, and the imposing 1527 **Büchsenhaus** or Neubau (the former arsenal). Below, the arms of the river are spanned by attractive roofed wooden bridges. Still in the old town opposite, the two parallel streets of the **Obere-** and the **Untere-Herrngasse**, linked by stone stairways, are bordered by several 15C and 16C half-timbered houses.

★★ MARKET PLACE (MARKTPLATZ) *time: 3/4 hour*

Laid out on a slope, this square is dominated by the monumental stone steps of St Michael's Church (where actors, during a festival from June to August each year, perform a repertory of the world's theatre classics). In the square itself, only a characteristic alignment of half-timbered gables on the south side – spared by the great fire of 1728 – remains to remind us of what the town must have looked like in the early 18C.

★ **Town Hall** – An elegant building in the Late Baroque style.

Market Fountain (Marktbrunnen) – Dating from 1509, the fountain stands against a decorative wall adorned with statues of Samson, St Michael and St George. The rectangular design, unusual in a Gothic work, includes the old pillory post.

St Michael's Church (Pfarrkirche) – The church's position at the top of 53 steps is impressive. The octagonal porch, opening beneath a Romanesque tower with a Renaissance top, has a statue of its patron saint in front of its central pillar. The interior★, originally Romanesque also, was transformed into a Gothic hall-church in the 15C. The Flamboyant chancel was added in the 16C.

ADDITIONAL SIGHTS

Regional Museum (Hällisch-Fränkisches Museum) ⊘ – This historical museum is in a tall Romanesque tower ten storeys high, which was once inhabited. The collections include mementos of the region's past in general, and that of the town in particular (as an industrial salt centre, as a mint, etc.). Several rooms are devoted to Württemberg-Franconian regional art.

Gräterhaus – This beautiful half-timbered house, so exquisitely decorated, stands in the town's northern suburb. It dates from 1605.

Henkersbrücke – There is an attractive view from this bridge of the mass of half-timbered buildings of the Ilge quarter, and their reflection in the waters of the Kocher. The view is perhaps even better from the junction of the street named Am Spitalbach and the Salinenstrasse quay, from which the east end of the old Church of St John can also be seen.

EXCURSIONS

★ **Gross Comburg** – *3km - 2 miles to the south.*
The church of this old fortified **abbey** ⊘ still has its three Romanesque towers. The rest of the building was reconstructed in 1715, the interior taking the form of a Baroque hall. Along with those of Aachen and Hildesheim, the church's chandelier is one of the most precious in the West. Dating from 1130 and designed in the shape of a crown, the **chandelier★★★** (Leuchter) is made of iron subsequently copper-plated and then gilded. In front of the high altar is an **antependium★** of the same period, made of gilded beaten copper representing Christ among the Apostles. The framework supporting this is treated with cloisonné enamel and filigree work.

★ **Hohenlohe Open-Air Museum** (Hohenloher Freilandmuseum) ⊘ – *At Wackershofen, 5km - 3 miles to the northwest – local map see under Hohenlohe.* Thirty reconstituted buildings, barns and outbuildings faithfully recapture the rural life of this area from the mid-16C to the end of the 19C. There is an exhibition of furniture and agricultural implements.

The Hohenlohe – *See under Hohenlohe.*

★ SCHWERIN Mecklenburg-West Pomerania   Pop 130 000
Michelin map **411** R 6

Magnificently situated in a landscape of lakes and forests, Schwerin renewed its links with an administrative past by becoming a Land capital in 1990. The origins of the town go back to the 11C, when the Slavs built a fortress on what is now Castle Island. It was not long, however, before they were expelled by Henry the Lion, the Duke of Saxony *(qv)*, who used the emplacement as a base for the construction of the first German town east of the Elbe. For almost five centuries after that (1358-1918), Schwerin was capital of the Duchy of Mecklenburg.

★★ CASTLE ISLAND AND PARK *time: 2 hours*

The island, and the two bridges linking it with the town, separate the smaller Burgsee from the 21km - 13 mile stretch of Schwerin Lake.

★ **Castle** ⊘ – Built between 1845 and 1857 in the neo-Renaissance style – with certain elements borrowed from the Gothic and the Baroque – this is one of the most important civic constructions of 19C Germany. From the outside, it recalls the Château of Chambord on the Loire, by which in fact the architects Demmler and Stüler were inspired. The rooms inside are lavishly decorated, with particularly fine floors. Note especially the **Throne Room★** (Thronsaal), the Ancestors' Gallery (Ahnengalerie) and the Smoking Room (Rauchzimmer).

★ **Chapel** (Schlosskapelle) – This is much older; it was built between 1560 and 1563. The Renaissance galleries and vaulting rest on Tuscan columns.

★ **Park** (Schlossgarten) – Created in the mid-18C, this formal Baroque garden is organized around canals in the form of a cross and rectilinear walks. It is peopled with statues (copies) by Balthazar Permoser *(qv)*.

ADDITIONAL SIGHTS

★ **National Museum** (Staatliches Museum) ⊙ – *Werderstrasse.*
Important Flemish and Dutch paintings of the 17C (Breughel, Brouwer, Jordaens and Van Ruysdael) are on display in this museum, a neo-Classic block built between 1877 and 1882 beside an old public garden (Alter Garten) near the theatre. The outside is adorned with Italian Renaissance decorations.
A department of 18C and 19C European painting houses works by Houdon, Pesne, Friedrich, Liebermann, Corinth, etc.
Relics of Slav settlements established in the region in the Stone Age are on view in a Prehistoric section.

Market Place (Markt) – Four late 17C half-timbered houses with gables have been preserved next to the Town Hall. On the north side of the square, the so-called **New Building** (Neues Gebäude) was erected between 1783 and 1785 in the Classic style, with Doric columns and attics, to be used as a Chamber of Commerce.

★ **Cathedral** (Dom) – Brick-built in the Gothic style during the 14C and 15C, the church contains several works of art worth a visit. They include a Gothic altarpiece (from a Lübeck workshop, *c*1480); a number of 14C funerary plaques; and, in the Chapel of the Assumption, frescoes dating from *c*1335.

EXCURSIONS

★ **Wismar** – *31km - 19 miles to the north.*
Founded at the beginning of the 13C at the head of an inlet on the eastern side of the Gulf of Lübeck, Wismar has always based its prosperity on maritime trade. The enormous **Market Place★**, which covers almost 2 1/2 acres, is bordered by a Neo-Classic Town Hall (1817-1819), an ancient gabled house known as "The Old Swede" (Alter Schwede, c1380), and a late 16C installation named the Wasserkunst (Hydraulic Machine). Built in the Renaissance style, this was designed to supply the whole town with water. On the west side of the square, the Princes' Court (1533-1554) is noteworthy for the sculpted frieze crowning its façade.

St Nicholas' Church★ (Nikolaikirche) is huge too. Inside the tower of this Gothic brick sanctuary, there is a vast mural representing St Christopher. The panelled **high altar★** (*c*1430) is devoted to the Crowning of the Virgin.

★ **Palace and Park of Ludwigslust** – 36km - 22 miles to the south.
The palace, designed by J J Busch between 1772 and 1776, is one of the most beautiful examples of Baroque civic architecture. The façade, with a fine cladding of Elbe sandstone, is topped by an attic with 40 statues.

★ **SIGMARINGEN** Baden-Württemberg   Pop 15 000

Michelin map **413** K 22 - Local map see under SWABIAN JURA

The strong defensive position of Sigmaringen – a rocky spur rising from the valley at the mouth of the Upper Danube Gap – made the town an ideal choice as minor capital of the principality ruled by the Swabian (Catholic) branch of the Hohenzollerns *(qv)*. The castle rises in traditional style from the edge of the cliff, but the only feudal parts remaining are the site and its general appearance: all the buildings and their interior decoration are pastiches of different styles.

★ **The Castle and its Annexes** ⊙ – *Time: 1 hour.* The approach ramp starts at the highest point reached by the road cutting across the land enclosed by the loop of the Danube *(leave the car in front of the Stadthalle, the Rathaus, or the fortified gateway to the castle).*

Castle – The State Apartments adorned in 16C style with coffered ceilings and tapestries (Royal Bedchamber, Ancestral Hall, etc.) will be of most interest to those versed in the history of European royalty. Fine **collection of arms and armour**.

Church – Luminous with Rococo stuccowork, the church clings to the castle rock. A shrine in a transept chapel on the left contains the Cradle of St Fidelio of Sigmaringen (1577-1622), first Capuchin martyr, Patron of the Order and local patron saint.

Museums – On view here are paintings (Swabian Primitives) and an exhibition of means of transport (Marstallmuseum).

★ **SOEST** Rhineland-Westphalia   Pop 43 000

Michelin map **412** H 12 - Local map see under SAUERLAND.

Traditionally the agricultural market for the Westphalian Plain, Soest today looks much as it must have done in medieval times. The old ramparts still enclose a spider's-web of houses, gardens and narrow, twisting lanes that lend the place an almost village-like air. One of the most remarkable half-timbered buildings is the twin-gabled hotel, **Im Wilden Mann** (Y A), in the Market Place. Another, decorated with motifs in colour, is the **Haus zur Rose** (Z C), at the corner of the Marktstrasse and the Rosenstrasse. The well-preserved **Osthofentor** (East Gate) (Y), with its fine Gothic embellishments, formed part of later 16C fortifications. The past history of the town can be traced in the **Burghofmuseum** (Z M¹).

Pumpernickel, the black rye bread baked for 24 hours which is found on so many German breakfast tables, is made in Soest.

SOEST

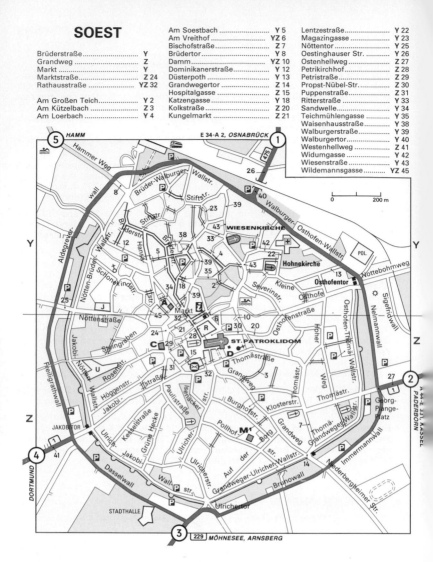

SIGHTS

★ **St Patroklus' Church** (Patroklidom) (Z) – The interest in this massive 11C and 12C Romanesque building lies entirely in the **Westwerk**★★ *(qv)* and its perfectly balanced square **tower**★★ austerely decorated with blind arcades and blind rose windows. The two tiers of arcades lightening the upper part of the tower are matched by two more at the base, the lower of which is furnished with very delicate small columns. The Romanesque frescoes in the apse of the north transept are original, having survived the Second World War. The others were restored to Romanesque designs in 1950. A fine 15C Crucifix stands on the altar. Parts of the original furnishings salvaged from the war damage can be seen in the Treasury.

St Nicholas' Chapel (Nikolaikapelle) (Z D) – In the chancel of this two-aisle chapel is the **St Nicholas Altarpiece**★, painted on a gold background in about 1400 by Conrad von Soest *(qv)*, a great name in Westphalian art. St Nicholas is shown as the patron of merchants and mariners.

★ **Church of Our Lady in the Fields** (Wiesenkirche) (Y) – Length, width and height are virtually identical in the nave of this beautifully lit 14C Gothic hall-church. A late 14C Virgin and Child can be seen at the pier of the south doorway.
The 1520 **stained glass window of the Last Supper**, above the north doorway, gave the artist the chance to advertise some local specialities: boar's head, ham, pitchers of beer and small loaves of rye bread can be recognized on the table. The most important work of art in the church is the 1525 **Aldegrever Altarpiece**★ – the Virgin between St Anthony and St Agatha, bathed in a halo of light – in the south apsidal chapel.

Hohnekirche (Y) – This bizarre, squat church of Romanesque origin was built with a flat chancel and dissymmetric apsidal chapels out of line with the main block. It was converted into a hall in the 13C. The whole interior, walls, vaults and roofing included, is covered with frescoes. In the chancel, the **Dance of the Angels** (c1280) depicts the Virgin in Majesty surrounded by a ring of 16 angels with stylized wings in the form of flames.
A **funerary niche** (Grabnische) with 13C frescoes faces the south entrance; on the left, half hidden by three short, thick columns, is the baptistry with its Romanesque font.

EXCURSIONS

★ **Möhnesee** – *11km - 7 miles to the south. Leave by ③ on the town plan.*
This artificial lake on the northern edge of the Sauerland is 10km - 6 1/2 miles long. The dam retaining the reservoir is 650m – over 700 yards across and almost 40m - 131ft high. To the north, the lakeshore is open to tourists and those practising water sports. The south bank, on the other hand, which is well forested, is a nature reserve harbouring many species of birds, some of them very rare.

★ **The Sauerland** – *See under the Sauerland.*

★ **SPEYER** Rhineland-Palatinate   Pop 46 000

Michelin maps **412** and **413** I 19 - Local map see under RHINELAND PALATINATE
Town plan in the current Michelin Red Guide Deutschland

The old imperial City, on an elbow of the river in the Upper Rhine Plain, can be recognized from far off by the silhouette of its belfries. Because of its exposed situation, however, few of the town's historic monuments have resisted the tides of war. As the seat of the Diet *(see Historical Notes)* and the Imperial Council, Speyer was annihilated by the troops of Louis XIV in 1689. Some idea of its past, nevertheless, may be gained from the group of buildings formed by the Emperors' Cathedral, the houses on the Maximilianstrasse and the Altpörtel, a tall tower that was once the town's main gateway.

The "Protestants" – The Edict of Worms *(qv)*, in fact never enacted, was confirmed by the Diet of Speyer in 1529. The Lutheran states then made a solemn protest against the Diet's decisions, from which derives the label "protestant" to identify partisans of the Reformation. The fact is commemorated in the existence of a neo-Gothic church, the Gedächtniskirche, built early this century on the Bartholomäus-Weltz-Platz.

SIGHTS

★★ **Cathedral (Dom)** ⊙ – This fine building, founded by Konrad II in 1030 and remodelled at the end of the 11C, is a Romanesque basilica with four towers and two domes.

Exterior – There is an interesting view★★ of the east end from the garden approach to the 13C **Heidentürmchen** (Pagan Tower). An elegant dwarf gallery circles the nave and transept just below the roof. The finely carved capitals display a wide variety of motifs on the garden side of the apse. On the lower part of one of the blind arcades, in the centre, a worn 11C relief depicting the Kingdom of Peace can be distinguished. The window arches of the east transept show Lombard influence and – especially on the south side – a lavish decoration of palm leaves and scrollwork. Similar motifs are repeated on the cornice below the roof.

In the gardens south of the cathedral is the **Ölberg** (1502-1512), once the centre of the cloisters. A large stone trough – the **Domnapf** – stands in the forecourt. In days gone by, each time a bishop was enthroned, it was filled with wine and anyone who wished to could drink until he dropped.

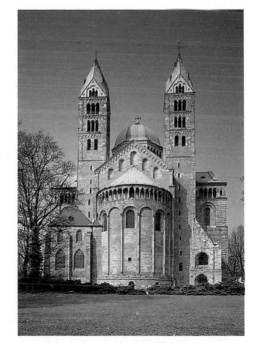

The east end, Speyer Cathedral

Interior – The most impressive way to enter is via the door in the west face (rebuilt in the mid-19C). On the right of the porch is a statue of Rudolph of Habsburg. The huge, well-lit nave has groined vaulting with prominent transverse arches. The half columns engaged in the main pillars are cut by rings and capitals with acanthus leaves.

The sobriety of the side aisles, also with groined vaulting, is remarkable. There is a good view of the building's harmonious proportions from the top of the south aisle stairway.

The raised **transept**★★ is a masterpiece of unity and balance. Note particularly, above the transept crossing, the octagonal cupola on squinches with its small lantern tower. The lack of texture and ornamentation on the walls emphasizes the natural decorative character of the architecture itself.

Chapel of the Holy Sacrament (Afrakapelle) – On the left, before the north transept – houses two 15C bas-reliefs: the Bearing of the Cross and the Annunciation. Opposite, before the south transept, eight groined vaults surround a two-tier central rotunda in which are the **baptistry** (Chapel of St Emmerammus) and, above, a chapel dedicated to St Catherine.

★★★**Crypt** ⊘ – This is the finest and largest Romanesque crypt in Germany. Beneath the chancel and the transept, whose crossing above is marked by four columns with splendid cushion capitals, Romanesque groined vaulting spreads out like a net supported by transverse arches of alternately pink and white sandstone.

Four Holy Roman Emperors and four German Kings are buried in the impressive **Royal Vault**. The 13C tombstone of Rudolph of Habsburg stands guard at the entrance.

★ **Jews' Baths** (Judenbad) – *Access via the Judengasse, southwest of the Cathedral (signposted)*. Ritual ablutions were performed here. The building (Judenhof), in the centre of the medieval Jewish quarter, was erected in the 12C, probably by workmen engaged in the construction of the cathedral.

A stairway with double doors leads down to the first chamber, which has groined vaulting and, on the left, an anteroom for changing. A second, semicircular staircase then descends to the level of the water-table, where the actual bath is situated.

Trinity Church (Dreifaltigkeitskirche) – *In the Grosse Himmelsgasse*.
The **interior**★ of this enormous Baroque church (1701-1717) is surrounded by a two-storey gallery with a balustrade adorned by paintings. The wooden capped vaulting is painted too.

Palatinate Museum (Historisches Museum der Pfalz) ⊘ – In Gallery 4 on the ground floor of this museum is the celebrated **Golden Hat**★ of Schifferstadt, the rarest, most valuable item in the Prehistoric Department. In the shape of a cone, this solid gold religious cult object dates from the 12C BC.

The collections on the first floor are concerned with the various arts and crafts, from the 16C to the 19C, and include outstanding examples of Frankenthal porcelain (1755-99).

Wine Museum – In the cellars. The round room beneath the tower boasts the oldest wine in the world. Still liquid in its bottle, this **Römerwein**★ (Roman wine) dates from the 3C.

SPREEWALD Brandenburg

Michelin map 987 fold 18

A network of more than 300 waterways criss-crosses this lush countryside – site of an ancient forest swamp painstakingly cleared and drained – lending it the appearance of a "Venice in the Woods". The region's special interest lies also in its **Sorabian minority**, descendants of western Slav people who settled in the Lausitz area of Germany after the migrations of the 6C, who remain fiercely proud of their language, traditions and culture today *(see the Sorabian Museum at Bautzen)*.

Basically agricultural, the Spreewald specialises in the cultivation of cucumbers and horseradish.

Barge Trip (Kahnfahrt) ⊘ – At **Lübbenau**, *leave the main road opposite the railway station and take Maxim-Gorki-Strasse to one of the car parks near the landing stage.*

From here, boat-men/guides organize excursions aboard flat-bottomed craft which ferry passengers to the heart of a leafy paradise shaped by man into a limitless garden. Only the ripple of water, the singing of birds and the quacking of ducks break the silence.

A stop at **Lehde**★, a tiny lagoon village with a population of 150 which boasts almost as many islands as houses, allows sightseers to visit the **Open-Air Museum** (Freilandmuseum Lehde). Here, three early 19C farms, complete with living quarters and outbuildings, display rustic furniture, agricultural implements and fishing gear, along with a generous selection of livestock native to the area.

Visitors preferring to make these discoveries on foot can choose between three different footpaths starting from Lübbenau: one leading towards Lehde *(time: 1 hour Rtn)*, another to Wotschofska and a third to Leipe *(time: 3 hours Rtn)*.

*Each year the **Michelin Red Guide Deutschland** revises its 150 town plans which show*

- *through-routes and by-passes*
- *new roads, one-way systems and car parks*
- *the exact location of hotels, restaurants and public buildings.*

This up-to-date information makes town driving less stressful.

STADE Lower Saxony Pop 45 000

Michelin map **411** L 6

Turned into a strongpoint when it was under Swedish rule from 1648 to 1712, this old Hanseatic town linked to the Elbe by a navigable channel has retained part of its original fortifications and its water-filled moats.

Old Port (Alter Hafen) – Traditionally handling wood on the ancient Hanseatic route, the winding basin is now almost deserted, leaving only a nostalgic stretch of still water bordered by rusting iron. An idea of how it must have looked in the 17C is nevertheless provided by the fine houses, meticulously restored, which stand on either side.

★ **Local Museum** (Schwedenspeicher-Museum) ⊙ – *Am Wasser West*. Built between 1692 and 1705 on one of the quays, this brick granary now houses a museum illustrating the town's commercial history and its old system of defences. There is also a prehistoric department exhibiting four magnificent **bronze wheels★** (*c*700 BC) from a funerary carriage, as well as antique jewellery, weapons and pots.
Not far from the museum *(at Wasser West No 7)*, the Kaufmann Collection, housed in a handsome building, displays paintings of the Worpswede School *(qv)*. The artists include Fritz Mackensen, Otto Modersohn (*Marsh, Barns and Silver Birches*, 1896), Paula Modersohn-Becker (*Peasant Woman with Red Scarf*, 1900) and Fritz Overbeck (*Flooding in the Marsh*, 1903).

Church of St Cosmas and Damian (St Cosmae und Damianikirche) – The Baroque spire of this 13-15C church, complete with onion bulb, rises above a picturesque old quarter where the wooden houses are bricked in between the beams. Inside, the fine 17C furnishings (organ, pulpit, copper chandeliers) are intact. The wrought iron grillework (1670) is imaginative.

EXCURSION

★ **Altes Land** – *Round tour of 51km - 32 miles to the southeast- about 2 hours. Roads narrow, twisting and cobbled. Take the main Hamburg road for Buxtehude.*
Between Stade and Buxtehude, the flat land beside the Elbe is a countryside of apple and cherry orchards, enchanting in the spring when the blossoms are out. Leave Buxtehude via the Jork road, which runs northwards beside the winding Este embankment. After the pretty village of Estebrügge, turn left in Königreich towards **Jork★**. Drive through to see, right at the far end, a series of thatched **farmhouses★** (Bauernhäuser) with decorative brickwork embellishing the gables in mosaic designs. At Mittelnkirchen, stay on the east bank of the canal, crossing further downstream at the Steinkirchen weighbridge. Return to Stade via Grünendeich (splendid view of the Elbe from the top of the embankment).

STENDAL Saxony-Anhalt Pop 50 000

Michelin map **987** fold 16

Founded *c*1160 by the Margrave Albrecht the Bear, Stendal soon developed into an important trade centre. The town was a member of the Hanseatic League from 1359 to 1518, and until the middle of the 16C remained the most influential in the Brandenburg March. The ravages of the Thirty Years War, however finally dealt it a death blow. Several monuments typical of Gothic brick architecture can still be seen from its period of prosperity still.
Stendal was the birthplace of **Johann Joachim Winckelmann** (1717-1768), considered to be the inaugurator of a scientific approach to archaeology. One of his admirers, the French novelist **Henri Beyle** (1783-1842) adopted as a pseudonym the name of the town (with a slightly different spelling: Stendhal).

SIGHTS

Town Hall (Rathaus) – *On the Market Place*. The oldest part, in exposed brick, dates from the beginning of the 15C. The gables are stepped. Added at the end of that century, the main wing was later remodelled in Renaissance style. On the square stands a copy of the statue of Roland destroyed by a hurricane in 1972.

St Mary's Church (Marienkirche) – Behind the Market Place. A triple-aisle hall-church, this was built between 1435 and 1477. The chancel, surrounded by an ambulatory, is separated from the nave by a delicately worked partition. The high altar (Crowning and Death of the Virgin) is in the Flamboyant Gothic style.

★ **St Nicholas' Cathedral** (Dom St Nikolaus) – The former Augustinian monks' church was supplanted in the 15C by a cathedral of much larger size, the square ground-plan recalling the hall-churches of Lower Saxony, in particular St John's Church in Lüneburg *(qv)*. The **stained glass windows★** (1420-1460) are remarkable. Note especially those in the chancel, which, because of the amount of wall they replace, suggest a huge conservatory.

★ **The Uenglingen Gate** (Uenglinger Tor) – *Northwest of the Old Town*. Dating from *c*1380, this is one of the most interesting fortified medieval gateways in the region. From the outside, the two lower storeys present an aspect that is purely defensive, while the upper part – added in the 15C – is much more decorative.

EXCURSIONS

★ **Tangermünde** – *10km - 6 miles to the southeast*.
Situated (as the name suggests) where the waters of the Tanger river join those of the Elbe, Tangermünde's history closely follows the history of Stendal. The small town, still enclosed within its late 14C ramparts, is crossed by two parallel streets, bordered by half-timbered houses with finely worked doorways. The brick-built 1430 **Town Hall**★ has a three-gable façade garnished with a superb lace-work of carved decorations.
The town's ancient gateways retain their monumental aspect, particularly the **Neustädter Tor**★, an imposing circular tower on the south side.

Havelberg – *46km - 29 miles to the north; cross the Elbe at Tangermünde*.
Overlooking this small, pretty town on the banks of the Havel river, **St Mary's Cathedral**★ (Dom St Marien) was founded at the end of the 12C but almost entirely rebuilt in the Gothic style between 1279 and 1330. The sculpturing of the chancel partition and the rood-screen **panels**★★ (*c*1400) is greatly to be admired. Illustrating scenes from the life of Jesus, these were probably the work of crafts-men from the Parler studio in Prague. Note also three **sandstone candelabra** and a **Triumphal Cross** (*c*1300). The early Gothic cloister dates from the 13C.

★ # STRALSUND Mecklenburg-West Pomerania   Pop 70 000
Michelin map **987** fold 7 - Local map see under RÜGEN

Separated from the island of Rügen *(qv)* by a narrow sea channel and surrounded by lakes, the Baltic town of Stralsund has developed since the earliest times as a centre of maritime navigation and long-distance trade. Its Gothic brick buildings, inspired by those of Lübeck, its more powerful neighbour, are among the best-known in northern Germany.

A Coveted City – From the moment of its foundation by Prince Jaromir of Rügen in 1209, Stralsund was subjected to assaults from envious neighbours: from Lübeck, from Denmark, from Sweden and even Holland they came with their troops to seize this port, so admirably situated. Protected by its massive rampart belt, the town was able during the Thirty Years War to beat off the forces of the all-conquering Imperial General Albrecht von Wallenstein. Subsequently taken – several times – by Sweden, it returned to Prussian rule after the Napoleonic Wars. Today, Stralsund's prosperity depends mainly on its shipyards and its fishing fleet.

SIGHTS

★ **Town Hall** *(Rathaus)* – *Alter Markt*. Built in the 13C and 14C, this splendid edi-fice comprises two separate, parallel blocks. The magnificent **north façade**★, crowned by a pediment with openwork gables – again, inspired by the Town Hall in Lübeck *(qv)* – was added *c*1450. The ground floor arcades open onto a covered market hall. From this a passageway leads to the west porch of St Nicholas' Church. Among the old houses bordering the market place, the **Wulflammhaus** (No 5), brick-built in the mid-15C, is noteworthy for its odd three-storey gable pierced by small windows.

★ **St Nicholas' Church** (Nikolaikirche) – *Alter Markt*. Modelled on St Mary's of Lübeck *(qv)*, this 13-14C hall-church has seen its central nave raised and its sin-gle tower replaced by a powerful façade with two towers. The relatively low ambulatory at the east end is dominated by solid buttresses.
Inside, there is a striking contrast between the modest height of the side aisles, flanked by low chapels, and the spectacular, soaring nave. Certain columns and several chapels still have late Gothic frescoes. Among the altarpieces, note the stone group figuring St Anne (*c*1290) and the central reredos, made at the begin-ning of the 18C based on designs by Andreas Schlüter.

★ **Oceanographic Museum and Aquarium** (Meeresmuseum) ⊙ – *Mönchstrasse*. Buildings which once belonged to the former St Catherine's Abbey have been transformed into galleries devoted to the Baltic Sea – its flora, its fauna, the exploitation and refinement of salt, etc – and to the fishing industry. Among the aquaria installed in the old church crypt is a huge 50 000-litre (11 000-gallon) tank stocked with tropical species.

Historical Museum (Kulturhistorisches Museum) ⊙ – *Mönchstrasse*. Sacred art from the Middle Ages, gold and silver plate from the isle of Hiddensee (Rügen), and the history of Stralsund itself are among the diverse exhibits displayed here.

★ **Church of Our Lady** (Marienkirche) – *Neuer Markt*. Apart from the impressive 104m - 340ft west tower, which was added between 1416 and 1478, this church was built towards the end of the 14C. Its originality lies in the fact that the flying buttresses of the chancel are concealed below the roof. The interior of the west tower comprises a central portion flanked by side aisles, in the manner of a transept.

The Ramparts (Stadtbefestigung). – The sections on the west side of the town are in the best condition, between the Kniepertor and the Kütertor, beside the lake.

Embraced by a loop of the Danube, this small market-town in the Gäuboden –
the "granary of Bavaria" – remains faithful to its agricultural traditions.

★ **Stadtplatz** – In the centre of the huge main square stands an original 13C tower
crowned by five pointed turrets, the remains of an old Town Hall. The tower lends
a final flourish to a vista which begins with the gabled houses of the
Theresienplatz, continuing with a beautiful Renaissance fountain and the Column
of the Trinity, adorned with swirling statuary. The whole is an elegant reminder
that Austria is not far off.

St James' Church – Just off the Stadtplatz, this large brick hall-church was built
in the 15C. The rib-less vaulting of interpenetrating ovals above the nave is supported on round, slender pillars. Unusual in this part of Bavaria is an almost total
lack of Baroque decoration.

The panels of the high altar reredos, bought in 1590 from a church in Nuremberg,
frame some 16C statuary. Note particularly the figure of the Virgin, in the middle, and – at the far left – Mary Magdalene. In the first chapel north of the axial
chapel is the admirable tomb of Ulrich Kastenmayer (1430), his effigy costumed
as a magistrate of the town. The features and expression are of a poignant
realism.

The church pulpit dates from 1753.

St Peter's Church – *1 1/2km - 1 mile. Leave the town in the direction of the
Danube by Route 20 (signposted Cham). Turn right before the bridge. St Peter's
is the second church.*

The old burial ground surrounding the Romanesque church contains many
crosses made of wrought iron, of which the town was once a manufacturing centre. Ask the caretaker to open the Chapel of the Dance of Death and the Chapel
of **Agnes Bernauer**, a touching and popular folk heroine in Germany.

Agnes, a young commoner from Augsburg, was secretly married to her love,
the son of a Duke of Bavaria. But she fell victim to the spite of her father-
in-law, who had her condemned for witchcraft and thrown into the Danube in
1435.

EXCURSIONS

The Abbeys of the Danube – *Round trip of 46km - 29 miles, downstream, on
the north bank of the river. Allow 2 1/2 hours.*

Oberalteich – *1km - 1/2 mile south of Furth.* Founded by Count Friedrich von Bogen,
Bailiff of Regensburg Cathedral *c*1100, this Benedictine monastery church was
transformed between 1622 and 1630 into a hall-church with five aisles. Note especially the hanging staircase that leads to the gallery, a technical feat at that time,
and the Rococo tabernacle with its furiously busy embellishments, realized by
Matthias Obermayer in 1759.

Metten – *4km - 2 1/2 miles northwest of Deggendorf.* The onion-domed towers of
the **Benedictine Abbey** ⊙ of Metten rise at the lower fringe of the Bavarian Forest
(qv). The church, whose foundations are pre-Romanesque, was remodelled in the
Gothic era but was given its final facelift between 1720 and 1729.

Tall windows illuminate the frescoes on the cradle vaulting. The high-altarpiece, a work due to Cosmas Damian Asam, represents St Michael slaugh-
tering the dragon. It is possible to visit the old abbey **library★**, decorated
in Baroque style by F J Holzinger from 1706 to 1720. There are no less
than 160 000 volumes on the shelves, among them one of the first Bibles to
be translated into German (1477) and the original Nuremberg Chronicle
(1493).

Niederalteich – *14km - 9 miles southeast of Deggendorf.*
The present **abbey church★** is the result of a Baroque remodelling of the original
Gothic hall-church, of which nothing but the nave columns were re-used. The
chancel was again rebuilt in 1726 with flattened vaulting. The upper parts of the
aisles are interrupted by galleries oddly pierced by lantern-windows which afford
an astonishing view of the vaulting.

From here it is possible to reach **Osterhofen Church**, *on the south bank of the
Danube (10km - 6 miles – see under Passau: Excursions).*

Michelin map 🔢 KL 20
Plan of the conurbation in the current Michelin Red Guide Deutschland and on
map 🔢

The capital of the Baden-Württemberg Land lies in a depression surrounded by
wooded hills opening in the northeast onto the Neckar. The site itself is undulating, with an encircling belt of trees separating the city centre from extensive suburbs. The finest overall **view★** of Stuttgart is from the upper platform of the
Television Tower (Fernsehturm) (access via the Hohenheimer Strasse – **LZ**), which
soars 400m - 1 312ft above the woods on the southern side of town.
The name of the city, originally **Stutengarten**, derives from a 10C seigniorial stud
farm which flourished in the region, the German word "Stute" meaning "mare".
By the 14C, the town which had grown up there was significant enough to be protected by fortified walls and had become the seat of the Counts of Württemberg.
Soon, supplanting such older burgs as Cannstatt, Waiblingen and Esslingen,
which were equally part of the Hohenstaufen heritage, it became also the home
of the Dukes and Kings of the realm.

Two Automobile Pioneers – An engineer who lived in Bad Cannstatt, **Gottfried
Daimler** (1834-1900) pioneered the adaptation of the internal combustion engine
to the powering of vehicles. Collaborating with the brilliant designer Wilhelm
Maybach, he developed a vertical motor which was patented in 1883.
Unlike Daimler, **Carl Benz** (1844-1929) was less concerned with the actual invention of a new motor than with its universal application. Born and educated at
Karlsruhe, he envisaged an entire motor vehicle, which he elaborated himself in
every detail at Mannheim. Soon he was able to start manufacturing in series and
put his cars on the market. In 1899 he sold his 2000th vehicle and thus became
the world's leading automobile manufacturer. Then, in 1901, Daimler's company
marketed a model baptized **Mercedes**, after the daughter of its most important foreign agent. The name was to make a fortune. And since the two firms amalgamated in 1926 Mercedes-Benz has been synonymous with luxury cars built to a
high standard of excellence and technical prowess. Today, above the roofs of the
city, the night sky over Stuttgart blazes with the illuminated three-point-star
within a circle that is the firm's world-famous trademark.

Urban Landscape – The former appearance of the city can only be found today
on the **Schillerplatz** (**KLY**), which is flanked by a collegiate church (Stiftskirche) and
the old castle (Altes Schloss). The **statue of Schiller** in the centre of the square is
the work of the Danish sculptor Thorwaldsen (1839). In front of the **New Castle**
(Neues Schloss) (**LY**) is the wide **Schlossplatz** (**LY 72**), off which a tree-lined avenue
leads through the castle gardens to **Rosenstein Park** *(access via the Heilbronner
Strasse* – **LY**) in the north. The New Castle was built between 1746 and 1807 after
a design by L Retti. It is now the home of regional ministerial departments.
Modern Stuttgart's business centre is based on the Königstrasse (**KLY**), in the
pedestrian zone.

CENTRAL SIGHTS

★★ **Linden Museum** (**KY M¹**) ⊙ – This museum consecrated to fine arts and folk arts
worldwide dates back to the foundation of the Württemberg Commercial
Geography Society in 1884. The exhibits, beautifully presented, fall under six
main headings: America; the Pacific (ground floor); Africa; the Middle-East (first
floor); Southern and Eastern Asia (second floor). Both ancient and modern civilizations are illustrated, and the accompanying explanations examine present-day
problems of development.

America – There is a display of ancient Peruvian ceramics, including an interesting collection of vessels decorated with human figures, and examples of fine
workmanship in silver and gold (note the death-mask in gold leaf, dating from
*c*400 AD). The section on North-American Indians (Apache, Pawnee, Crow, Cree,
Dakota, etc.) is perhaps the most fascinating. A rich variety of weapons, jewels,
clothing and everyday objects provides a comprehensive illustration of tribal life
as it once was.
Hunting and cooking implements, as well as a 19C kayak, a selection of toys, and
clothing made from furs and skins give the visitor an idea of existence among
the Eskimos.

The Pacific – Here the interest is concentrated on the inhabitants of New Guinea and
neighbouring isles in the Papuan archipelago (New Britain, New Ireland) where the
indigenous culture is centred on belief in spirits and the cult of ancestors.

Africa – Reconstitution of a typical North Nigerian market is the first thing to meet
the eye in this department. Gold body ornaments from Ghana and bronze reliefs
from Benin (Southern Nigeria) are examples of superb craftmanship. The traditions of African tribal life and its superstitions are evoked in fantasy masks representing, among animist deities, crocodiles, sawfish and sharks. Replicas of a
royal palace and an army post (Cameroon) exemplify forms of political and military organization.

The Middle-East – Visitors to this department pass through an oriental bazaar with
its potters, dyers, tinsmiths and jewel workers before being presented with different aspects of Islamic culture and beliefs. These include a mosque, the Koran,
ornaments and ceramics, the tomb of a 12C Ghaznavide dignitary, even
dervishes. Note also the varied examples of fine Arab cloth, splendid beaten metalwork ranging from the 11C to the 14C, and an exhibition of Persian arms (17C
to 19C).

The Far East – Initially, visitors to this department pass through a Japanese tea-house, a lacquer workshop and a traditional Japanese room (reconstructions). The Chinese sections give pride of place to porcelain and ceramics, including ancient ceramics used in funeral rites with human and animal motifs. One of the finest examples of Chinese pictorial art is a 12-panel folding screen decorated with scenes representing the Festival of Fishing (Ch'ing dynasty, 1707).

Southern Asia – Tibet is represented by bronze figurines, ritual instruments and replicas of ceremonial vestments and an altar used by the Dalai Lama.

An atmosphere of magic bathes the galleries showing examples of the Chinese shadow theatre and marionettes from Bali and Java. Bronze statues of the divinities (including Shiva, king of the dance) preside over the section devoted to Hindu India, and there are temple bas-reliefs in stone on display as well as religious items relating to the more rustic cultures (open-air altars from Rajasthan; an 18C ritual plough in silver from northern India).

The State Gallery, Stuttgart

★ **State Gallery** (Staatsgalerie) **(LY M)** ⊘ – Painting from medieval times to the Impressionists is on show here. Note especially the **Old Masters Section**★★, in which Swabian painting from the 14C to the 16C is pre-eminent. One of the masterpieces exhibited is the **Herrenberg Altar** of Jerg Ratgeb (1519), which portrays – from left to right – the Last Supper, the Martyrization Of Jesus, the Crucifixion and the Resurrection. Fourteenth-century Venetians and Florentines dominate an excellent collection of Italian painters. Among the Dutch Old Masters are Hans Memling *(Bethsheba Bathing)*, Rembrandt *(St Paul In Prison)*, Jacob van Ruisdael and Rubens.

An annexe designed by the British architect James Stirling houses the Department of Modern Art.

Among the "modern classics" on display are works by the Fauvists and French Cubists (Matisse, Braque, Juan Gris), the German Expressionists (a fine selection of Kokoschka paintings), the artists of New Objectivity or Verism (Dix, Grosz) and artists of the Bauhaus School *(qv)*.

A special place is reserved for the work of **Willi Baumeister** (1889-1955) and **Oskar Schlemmer** (1888-1843) of the Bauhaus, both natives of Stuttgart. Schlemmer's famous six-figure Triadic Ballet is on view, as well as certain enormous sketches for murals (the finished works, painted in 1929, were victims of the Nazi crusade against the so-called "degenerate art").

Another highlight of this museum is a collection of 12 **Picasso** works covering every period of his working life. Among them is the world-famous sculpture group in wood, **The Bathers**.

The section on contemporary art covers the half century since the Second World War, starting with Dubuffet and Giacometti and ending with the latest works of Baselitz and Kiefer, by way of American Pop Art (Warhol, Segal), Italy's Arte Povera and the "installations" of Beuys.

Old Castle (Altes Schloss) **(LY)** – Four wings flanked by round towers comprise this building, most of which dates from the 16C. The **Renaissance Courtyard**★ is surrounded by three floors of arcaded galleries. The interior now houses the **Württemberg Regional Museum**★ (Württembergisches Landesmuseum) **(M³)** ⊘.

On the ground floor and the mezzanine, the exhibits include rare tapestries, craftwork in ceramics, glass and silver tableware (from the 14C to the 19C), and clothes worn by the nobility (especially in the 18C). Ancient history and prehistory are also represented on the first floor, while the second contains an extremely interesting collection of **religious statuary**★★. Note above all the eight Scenes of the Passion (in the central octagon) executed by the sculptor Jörg Syrlin in 1515 for the church at Zwiefalten *(qv)*.

Funerary objects (weapons, jewels and household items) can be seen in the section devoted to the Franks and the Alemanni, which is also on the second floor, and gives some idea of the civilization of these peoples between the 5C and the 8C.

There is a fine collection of musical instruments and clocks on the third floor, which also houses a numismatic gallery.

STUTTGART

The Treasury Tower *(entrance on the ground floor or second floor)* contains items from the "Ducal Chamber of Arts and Marvels" (Herzogliche Kunst-und-Wunderkammer) which range from the 15C to the 18C. They include the crown jewels of the Kings of Württemberg (19C).

Collegiate Church (KY A) – The most impressive part of this church, built in the middle of the 15C, is the west tower belfry porch with superimposed polygonal copings (1490-1531). When the church was restored after the war damage of 1945, the nave and former aisles were combined into a single hall covered with panelled vaulting. A large funerary **monument★**, a memorial to the Dukes of Württemberg, stands in the chancel. Commissioned by Duke Ludwig III, this was executed by the sculptor S Schlör *c*1580. Eleven armoured figurines representing ancestors of the Duke are standing in front of a décor of Renaissance arcades.

Stuttgart City Gallery (Galerie der Stadt Stuttgart) (LY M4) ⊘ – Between-the-wars painting (1918-1939) figures prominently in this museum. Note particularly the **work★** of **Otto Dix**, famous for the ferocity of his criticism of modern society. Typical of his approach are the *Big City* (Grossstadt) triptych and the anti-war picture *Grabenkrieg*. Young Stuttgart artists of the 1980s are represented, and so too are the local painters Hölzel, Schlemmer and Baumeister *(see above)*.

ADDITIONAL SIGHTS

★ **Wilhelma Park** – *Leave by the Heilbronner Strasse* (**LY**).
This botanical garden laid out more than a century ago is furnished with hot-houses displaying many fascinating tropical plants and a celebrated exhibition of orchids. Worth seeing also: the aquarium and a terrarium.

National Museum of Natural Sciences (**Staatliche Museum für Naturkunde**) – *In Rosenstein Park.*
There is a Zoology Department in **Rosenstein Castle** which features a collection of stuffed creatures (especially mammals and birds) from all over the world, displayed in their natural habitat. The most imposing exhibit is a 13m - 43ft northern whale, reconstituted around a genuine skeleton.
The department consecrated to the origins of Planet Earth is now installed in the new **Museum am Löwentor★** (**LY M5**) ⊘ – a collection of spacious modern galleries in the same park. Here, through a fine assembly of Baden-Württemberg fossils, beautifully displayed, 600 million years of world history can be skimmed over. Fossil birds, fish, reptiles, tortoises and even dinosaurs can be seen. And there are actual skeletons of large prehistoric mammals, excavated bones, and a section dealing with man in the glacial period in different parts of the museum.

★ **Killesberg Park** (**Höhenpark Killesberg**) ⊘ – *Leave by Heilbronner Strasse* (**LY**).
A little way to the west of the Rosenstein, this park is a continuation of the green belt encircling the inner city. Laid out on a height to the north of the centre, it integrates perfectly with the undulating terrain. Terraced cascades, fountains and brilliantly coloured flowerbeds invite the visitor to relax and admire, and there is a miniature train on which a tour of the whole park can be made. A panoramic view of Stuttgart can be enjoyed from a lookout tower at the highest point (Aussichtsturm).

★ **Bad Cannstatt Spa Park** (**Kurpark Bad Cannstatt**) – *Leave by the Cannstatter Strasse* (**LY**).
The old town of Bad Cannstatt, now the city's largest residential suburb, has retained its function as a spa. The 18 thermal springs – feeding a fountain and three swimming-pools – have made the place, after Budapest, Europe's second largest producer of mineral water. The park (Kurpark) is attractive.

★ **Mercedes-Benz Museum** ⊘ – *Leave by the Schillerstrasse* (**LY M6**). *At 136 Mercedesstrasse, in a block of the company's main Stuttgart-Untertürkheim factory.*
Nearly 100 vintage and veteran motor cars are on show here, the models ranging from the earliest to the most recent, as well as video films tracing the history of engines and cars, especially at Daimler-Benz. The racing car collection testifies to the success of Mercedes worldwide until 1955. Engines powering aircraft, airships (Zeppelin) and rail-cars complete the exhibition.

A 1927 Mercedes Sportwagen "S" (Mercedes-Benz Museum, Stuttgart)

EXCURSIONS

★ **Solitude Castle** (**Schloss Solitude**) ⊘ – *Leave by the Rotebühlstrasse* **KZ**.
The former summer residence of the Württemberg Court stands on the edge of a plateau about five miles from the city centre, west of the Botnang suburb. Flanked by lateral wings, the castle is centred on an oval pavilion with a cupola, the whole being majestically raised on a base of open arcades. Around this, the lower outbuildings lie in an immense arc. The design was by the French Court architect, La Guépière, who supervised construction between 1764 and 1769. A certain restraint, tempering the sumptuousness of the concept, can be traced to the architect's admiration for the buildings of ancient Greece.
Inside, the decorations of the central rotunda (Weisser Saal) and the small marble room are in the neo-Classical tradition. The other apartments, which are panelled, are French Rococo. One of the more bizarre items on view is the desk used by Friedrich I of Württemberg – largely hollowed out because of the obesity of its owner, so cruelly ridiculed by Napoleon.

* **Swabian Brewery Museum** (Schwäbisches Brauereimuseum) ⊙ – *At 12 Robert-Koch-Strasse, Stuttgart-Vaihingen.*
Five thousand years of beer-making are traced in this museum. Objects discovered in Mesopotamian and Ancient Egyptian digs (some of them reproductions) prove that, even in the mists of antiquity, appreciation of this liquid with a base of hops and barley was not confined to Europe. The principles and techniques of brewing are explained in the lower basement. Well-chosen instruments and plants illustrate the different stages in the making of beer (malting, crushing, wort preparation, fermentation, filtering, bottling, etc.).

* **Porsche Museum** ⊙ – *Leave on Heilbronner Strasse (LY), in the direction of the motorway. Before the motorway, take the exit signposted Zuffenhausen-Industriegebiet, and then turn right into the Porschestrasse. Stop at No 42.*
In 1934, the engineer Ferdinand Porsche (1875-1951), already distinguished by his work at Daimler-Benz, produced a design for the famous "people's car" – the Volkswagen. His prototype evolved into the celebrated "Beetle". Porsche himself, from 1948 onwards, devoted himself to a sports model bearing his own name, which was developed from the original VW chassis and engine and subsequently manufactured at Zuffenhausen. In one of the factory buildings 30 different Porsches are now on show, along with a display of high-performance engines.

* **Tiefenbronn** – *38km - 24 miles to the west.*
The Gothic **church** (Pfarrkirche) in this village houses the well-known **Lucas Moser altarpiece★★** (1431) in its south aisle. On the outside of the various panels, the artist has illustrated, in a perfect unity of style, the legend of Mary Magdalene: on the tympanum is the Feast at Bethany; in the centre, the crossing of the Mediterranean from Palestine to Provence by Martha, Lazarus, Maximinus and Cedonius, then the homeless saints staying in Marseilles and Mary Magdalene appearing before the town governor in a dream and, finally, Mary Magdalene's last communion.

---

* # THE SWABIAN JURA (SCHWÄBISCHE ALB) Baden-Württemberg

Michelin map **413** folds 25 and 26

The high limestone plateaux of the Swabian Jura, watershed between the Rhine (Neckar Basin) and the Danube, lie between the Black Forest and the crystalline massifs of Bohemia and form in effect the "roof" of southern Germany. The highest point is at Lemberg (1 015m - 3 330ft). From this summit, the Jura drop no less than 400m - 1 312ft to the Neckar Basin in the northwest.
Mountain outcrops detached from the main block form natural fortresses, and some have been chosen as castle sites by familes subsequently to enjoy great glory and dynastic fame (the Hohenstaufens, the Hohenzollerns).

An ingenious population – As in many mountainous regions, the length and harshness of the winters have resulted in the formation of numerous small family businesses or cottage industries. In the 19C, through the philanthropic activities of pastors, schoolteachers and modest inventors, the whole northern fringe of the massif became covered with workshops, studios and small factories turning out toys, precision instruments, musical accessories, clothing, etc.

* 1 **FROM KIRCHHEIM UNTER TECK TO HOHENZOLLERN CASTLE**
125km - 78 miles - allow one day

Kirchheim – The pinnacled tower of the half-timbered **Town Hall** overlooks the main crossroads. The building dates from 1724.

Holzmaden – Follow the arrows leading to the **Hauff Museum★** (Urweltmuseum Hauff) ⊙: an astonishing assembly of saurian fossil skeletons immured in the local schists and dating back almost 160 million years.

Reussenstein Castle (Burgruine Reussenstein) – *Round tour 20mn on foot.* Make for the edge of the escarpment to appreciate to the full the **setting★★** of Reussenstein as it dominates the coomb of Neidlingen. From the lookout point built into the castle ruins, there is a **view★** of the whole narrow valley and, beyond it, the plain of Teck.
After Wiesensteig (half-timbered houses), the route follows one section of the **"Swabian Jura Trail"** (Schwäbische Albstrasse), which is marked by blue-green indication arrows.

Bad Urach – A pretty town, enclosed deep in the Erms valley, with half-timbered houses clustered round a central Marktplatz.

Urach Falls (Uracher Wasserfall) – *1/4 hour on foot Rtn. Leave the car in the park marked "Aussicht 350 m".*
Impressive **view★** of the valley and the waterfall (flow reduced in summer).

Lichtenstein Castle – Built on a rock spur protected by a natural cleft, Lichtenstein was completely re-designed and decorated in the "troubadour" style in 1842. Before crossing the entrance bridge, turn right and make for two viewpoints: one overlooks the Echaz valley, the other the castle itself.

Bärenhöhle – The biggest cavern in this "Bear Grotto" contains well-preserved stalactites and stalagmites.
At Onstmettingen, follow the signs "Nädelehaus" and "Raichberg".

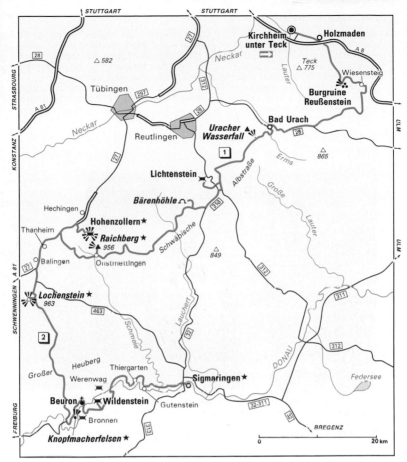

★ **Raichberg** – *1/2 hour on foot Rtn.* Leave the car at the hotel and walk past a brown stone tower, across the fields to the lip of the plateau. From here there is a fine **view**★ of the downward sweep of the Jura and, two miles away, Hohenzollern Castle *(qv)*.

Return to Hohenzollern Castle via Tannheim and Hechingen.

★ **2** **THE HEUBERG PLATEAU AND THE DANUBE GAP**

From Hohenzollern to Sigmaringen
89km – 55 miles - allow half a day

★ **Hohenzollern** – *See under Hohenzollern Castle.*

Lochenstein – *1/2 hour on foot Rtn.* Leave the car at the saddle (Lochenpass) and climb to the summit (altitude 963m - 3 160ft) of the Lochenstein, which is surmounted by a Cross. From here there is a **view**★ of the Balingen-Hechingen Depression, and still – away in the distance – Hohenzollern Castle.
Beyond the pass, the road sweeps downhill in tight curves and then crosses the bare, rolling uplands of the Grosser Heuberg plateau.

★ **Knopfmacherfelsen** – Below the car park, make your way to a viewpoint from which there is a **view**★ of the Danube valley as far as Beuron Abbey and, on the right, Bronnen Castle.

★ **Beuron Abbey** – A flourishing Benedictine congregation at Beuron contributed greatly to the revival of monastic life, the liturgy and the use of the Gregorian chant in Germany.
The Gnadenkapelle, abutting the Baroque abbey church, is treated in the "Beuron style" – derived from a late 19C school of sacred art much influenced by Byzantium.

Wildenstein Castle – *7km - 4 1/4 miles from Beuron via Leibertingen.*
This small citadel commanding the Danube was designed with two moats and a forward defence system on the plateau side comprising two towers linked by a long wall.
Below Beuron, the road follows the **valley**★ past the rocky fortresses of Wildenstein and Werenwag on the way to Sigmaringen *(qv)*. Approaching the town, the cliffs give way to curious rock needles which form a fantastic ensemble between Thiergarten and Gutenstein.

★ **Sigmaringen** – *See under Sigmaringen.*

Michelin map 987 fold 18

Lying between Dresden and the Czech frontier, the region known as Swiss Saxony is one of Germany's most popular – and most spectacular – natural wonders. It is an area of sheer sandstone cliffs, of table-shaped outcrops and isolated pillars, of deep gorges gouged from the rock and fantastically shaped formations through which the upper reaches of the Elbe flow in wide curves.

This huge depression can be explored by road, following the itinerary suggested below, or from the river, taking one of the "Weisse Flotte" boats plying between Dresden and Bad Schandau.

The Bastei Belvedere, Swiss Saxony

Geological Formation – The Elbe sandstone massif (Elbsandsteingebirge) resulted from the raising up – and subsequent decomposition – in the Tertiary Era of sedimentary limestones originally laid down over the Primary bedrock.

Vertical faulting of the horizontal sandstone beds, followed by the action of erosion, then produced over the millenia the flat-topped maze of fantasy formations through which the river today winds its way.

ROUND TOUR FROM DRESDEN *78km - 49 miles - 1 day*

★★★ **Dresden** – *See under Dresden.*

    Leave the city by the Pillnitzer Landstrasse (**CY**) *on the plan.*

★ **Pillnitz Castle** (**Schloss Pillnitz**) – *See Dresden: Excursions.*

★★★ **Bastei** – This magnificent viewpoint perched 200m - 656ft above the Elbe crowns a bleak spine commanding a lunar landscape carved from the rock. The superb **view** takes in the greater part of Swiss Saxony.

From the hotel nearby, a footpath leads to **Rathen Castle** (Felsenburg Neurathen), which is reached via a natural bridge spanning a deep ravine. Below the castle, an open-air theatre quarried from the rock can be seen.

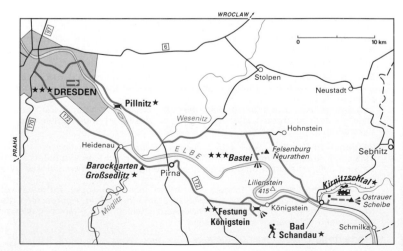

★ **Bad Schandau** – Apart from being the main tourist centre of the region, Bad Schandau is also a spa renowned for the properties of its iron-rich waters, which have been exploited since 1730. At the exit from the town, in the direction of Schmilka, a lift and a footpath lead to the Ostrauer Scheibe, from which there is a superb **view**★ of the Schrammsteine – a chaotic rock massif much favoured by amateur mountaineers. The **Kirnitzsch Valley**★ (Kirnitzschtal), which can be followed by mountain railway, is hemmed in by steep cliffs.

Cross the Elbe at Bad Schandau and turn right towards Königstein.

★★ **Königstein Fortress** (Festung Königstein) – The great sweep of the Elbe here is overlooked by the 415km - 1 362ft Lilienstein on the east bank, and the Königstein (360m - 1 181ft) on the west. The formidable fortress crowning the latter was built between the 13C and the 16C, strengthened and enlarged in the 17C and 18C, and served several times as a refuge for the Court of Saxony. Prisoners held there had very little chance of escaping. Among the most famous internees were Böttger, the inventor of hard-paste porcelain *(see under Meissen)*; August Bebel, founder with Karl Liebknecht of the Social Democrat party in 1869; and the Second World War French General Giraud. (Giraud was one of the few who did get away, a celebrated escape accomplished with the help of a rope tied to the bars of a loophole in the castle's outer wall.) From the old rampart walk, which follows the edge of the Erzegebirge, there are splendid **views**★★ of the Lausitz foothills and the distant mountains of Bohemia.

★ **Grosssedlitz Gardens** (Barockgarten Grossedlitz) ⊙ – This **Baroque pleasure ground** was partly laid out by Pöppelmann *(qv)* in the French style in 1719. It is still possible to see the Orangery, the Stille Musik – a double-flight stairway surrounding an ornamental pool – and statues of mythological Greek heroes sculpted by Kirchner and Thoma.

Continue the itinerary and return to Dresden.

★★ **SYLT ISLAND** Schleswig-Holstein

Michelin map **411** fold 2

The Frisian island of Sylt, the most northerly point of German territory, extends in a north-south direction for 40km - 25 miles, although in parts it is less than 500 yards across. Despite the reduced area of this long, narrow isle, however, the landscape is varied. Around Kampen, Westerland and Morsum, the agricultural aspect of the countryside testifies to its rich Geest *(qv)* origins. This is increased in area to the southeast by Marschen reclaimed from the sea.
On the west side, facing the open sea, an immense beach of fine sand runs for miles. Passing beneath low red cliffs (Rotes Kliff) between Kampen and Wenningstedt, this superb strand finally joins a continuous belt of dunes south of Westerland.
The island as a whole is a holiday paradise where sea, sand, sun and the magnificient northern light reign supreme. There are a number of official naturist reserves on the coast.

Speed should be reduced while driving along the island roads and through built up areas. Motor traffic is regulated in certain places.

Access by rail ⊙ – Train-car ferries depart from Niebüll and cross the arm of sea separating Sylt from the mainland via the Hindenburgdamm causeway.

Access by car-ferry ⊙ – There is a seaborne car ferry service between Havneby (*on the Danish island of Römö - accessible by road*) and List, on the northern tip of Sylt.

★★ **Westerland** – This is the most important seaside resort in the whole of Germany, meeting place for the elegant and fashionable, with a lively, popular casino. The 1 1/2-mile seafront promenade (Kurpromenade) is always busy – and when the tide is high, the sea hurls itself with relentless force against its foundations.
The therapeutic virtues of saltwater treatment have recently regained popularity, and in Westerland now there is a huge cure establishment specializing in marine and mud baths (Kurmittelhaus).

Keitum – This is the exact opposite of animated Westerland – and old, peaceful Frisian village with thatched roofs half hidden among trees and plantations of lilac. Behind the Louise-Schröder-Heim institution, a path leads to a low coastal bluff (Keitumer Kliff), a pleasant, shady **site**★ where visitors can sit and admire a view in which the horizon is lost in a limitless expanse of sea, sand, mudflats, and the sky above the low mainland shore beyond.

★★ **Forest of THURINGIA** (THÜRINGER WALD) Thuringia

Michelin map **987** fold 26

Much in the same way as the Harz *(qv)*, the Forest of Thuringia is a wooded massif, orientated northwest-southeast, with an average height of 1 000m - 3 300ft. Long known as "the green heart of Germany", the massif is scattered with charming villages whose inhabitants still retain their traditional skills and craftsmanship. A wealth of tourist amenities, particularly at Oberhof, and the development of several resorts have made the region popular with a large number of ramblers and summer holidaymakers.
Granite, gneiss and porphyry formations underlie the central nucleus of the forest, while the foothills are composed mainly of sandstone and limestone sedimentary deposits.

Forest of THURINGIA

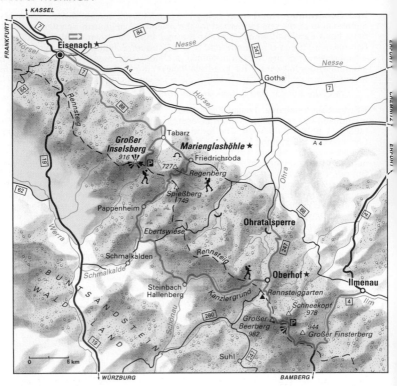

Flora and fauna – The forest covering practically the whole area is largely beech, pine and fir. Marshy plateaux have developed in some of the higher reaches, and there is moorland on the approaches to some crests. Among the larger varieties of game, stags, roe deer and wild boar are abundant.

THE THURINGIAN HIGH ROAD

From Eisenach to Ilmenau *110km - 68 miles - 1 day*

This fascinating route mainly follows the Rennsteig, a ramblers' path 160km - 100 miles long which keeps to the highest parts of the forest and includes such major summits as the Grosser Inselsberg (916m - 3 005ft) and the Grosser Beerberg (982m - 3 222ft).
Leave **Eisenach★** *(qv) in the direction of Gotha.*

Grosser Inselsberg – *1 hour Rtn on foot.*
The **panorama★★** extending from the summit takes in the greater part of the forest.

★ **Marienglas Cave** (**Marienglashöhle**) – Crystalline gypsum is extracted from this natural cavity. The use of this mineral in the decoration of church altars has led to the grotto's unusual name (Marienglas = Glass of Mary).
The route cuts across the Rennsteig and twists between the Regenberg (727m - 2 385ft) and the Speissberg (749m - 2 457ft), offering numerous possibilities for sightseeing and walks, especially in the direction of **Ebertswiese**, a zone of marsh and meadows.
Steinbach is overlooked by the Hallenburg ruins.
The road continues towards Oberhof via the Kanzlergrund, a valley beautified by wide stretches of grass and meadowland.

★ **Oberhof** – At 800m - 2 625ft altitude, this town is the most important leisure centre and winter sports station in the Forest of Thuringia.
In the **Rennsteiggarten**, a botanical park specializing in Alpines and the flora of Central European heights, more than 4 000 varieties of plant can be seen.

Ohratal Dam – *Follow Route 247 to the large car park.*
The reservoir dammed by this barrage, the surface of which extends over 88ha - 218 acres, supplies water to Weimar, Jena, Gotha and the Thuringian capital, Erfurt.
Leaving Oberhof in the direction of Schmücke, the country road winds once again sinuously between the Grosser Beerberg (982m - 3 222ft) and the Schneekopf (978m - 3 209ft). From the hotel car park at Schmücke, there is a fine viewpoint looking out over the valley. The 944m - 3 097ft Finsterberg is visible on the left.

Ilmenau – This locality on the northern fringe of the Forest of Thuringia has always been associated with the name of Goethe, who is said to have been particularly fond of its natural beauties. There is a plaque in his memory on the wall of the town's municipal headquarters (Amtshaus, in the Marktplatz), which has been transformed into a Goethe museum, and another in the Gabelbach hunting lodge. A pathway baptised **"In Goethe's Footsteps"** (Auf Goethes Spuren) links the places associated with the great writer.

Michelin map **412** C 17 - Local map see under MOSELLE VALLEY
Town plan in the current Michelin Red Guide Deutschland

This venerable episcopal city, whose ecclesiastical Electors ruled as far north as
Koblenz, is the first German town reached by the Moselle and an important wine-
growing centre. It can be regarded as the capital of Ancient Rome in Germany –
a situation emphasized by the richness and variety of the works of art that remain.
The philosopher and economist Karl Marx (1818-1883) was born in Trier.

A SECOND ROME

Trier became the meeting point very early on for the Celtic, Germanic and Latin
cultures which evolved to form Western civilization.
After the conquest of the Treveri, a Celtic tribe from the eastern part of Gaul, the
Roman Emperor Augustus founded on their territory the town of **Augusta
Treverorum** (c15 BC), which soon became a centre of intense economic, cultural
and intellectual activity, continuing to develop until the invasion of Germanic
tribes in AD 274. Essentially a civic and residential settlment, the town fell before
the onslaught.
Later, however, when Diocletian reorganized the Roman Empire, Trier was
retaken and became capital of the western territories (Gaul, Spain, Germania and
Britain). As the town regained its former eminence, the Emperor Constantine
(306-337) surrounded it with a defensive wall within which magnificent buildings
were erected. In this second period of prosperity, Trier was given the status of
imperial residence.
In the year 313, the Edict of Milan put an end to the persecution of Christians,
and a year later the See of Trier, the oldest in Germany, was created. But towards
the end of the 4C, renewed pressure from the Germanic tribes became so strong
that the imperial residence was transferred to Milan and the prefecture to Arles.
In 470, Trier finally fell into the hands of the Franks.
During the Middle Ages, the Archbishops of Trier wielded a great deal of power
as Prince-Electors.

OLD TOWN *time: one day*

★★ **Porta Nigra** (DX) ⊙   This magnificent four-storey structure – originally the northern entrance to the
walled town – dates from the 2C
and is the most important Roman
relic on German soil. Its name
derives from the dark patina forming over the centuries on the sandstone blocks used in its construction. The stones are fitted together
without mortar, held only here and
there with iron crampons. The gateway was designed for military use:
the double arcade of the central
block, flanked by two massive towers, leads to an inner court where
only the upper arcades are pierced
– and assailants forcing the outer
gates would find themselves
exposed here to attack from all
sides.
In the 11C, the fortified gateway
was transformed into a church on
two levels, dedicated to St Simeon.
The Romanesque apse can still be

The Porta Nigra at Trier

seen on the east side, and there are traces of additional alterations – Rococo dec-
oration, for example – in the upper galleries (on the inner courtyard side). It was
Napoleon who ordered the monument to be restored to its original form in 1804.
There is a fine view from the tower terrace.

Municipal Museum (Städtisches Museum Simeonsstift) (DX M²) ⊙ – This is installed
in the **St Simeon Convent**, built beside the Porta Nigra at the same time as the church
(11C). The history of Trier is illustrated with models, paintings, engravings, maps
and sculptures, among them the original figures surrounding the fountain in the
market place (the Four Virtues and St Peter, late 16C). Above the arcades, the old
cloister has been transformed into a lapidary museum.

★ **House of the Three Kings** (Dreikönigenhaus) (DX K) – This early Gothic town
house (c1230), with its arched windows, recalls the Italianate towers of the patri-
cians of Regensburg *(qv)*.

★ **Hauptmarkt** (DX) – One of the finest old squares in Germany. In the middle is
the **Market Cross★** (Marktkreuz), erected in the year 958 when the town was granted
the right to hold a market. The **fountain**, with its painted figures, dates from the
late 16C. Standing by the Cross (which was restored in the 18C), the visitor can
see fifteen centuries of history encapsulated in the monuments around the
square. To the north is the Porta Nigra, to the east the Romanesque cathedral, to
the south the Gothic **Church of St Gangolf**, whose early 16C tower was once used as
a lookout post.

TRIER

Picturesque half-timbered houses, both Renaissance and Baroque, stand on the west side. The **Steipe** (D), a medieval (15C) municipal building with a steep, tall roof, is elegantly built over an open gallery. Beside it, the 17C **Red House** (E), bears the proud inscription: "There was life in Trier for 1 300 years before Rome even existed".

Frankenturm (CX) – A heavily-built Romanesque tower (*c*1100) with small windows.

★ **Cathedral** (Dom) (DX) – Seen from its forecourt (Domfreihof), Trier Cathedral looks more like a fortress than a church. A rounded apse projects from a massive, austere façade which, with its squat, square towers, is a fine example of early Romanesque architecture.
From the north side, different stages in the construction are evident. A flattened gable and rectangular plan distinguish the 4C Roman heart of the building. West of this central block is the 11C Romanesque section; east of it the polygonal chancel, which is furnished with a dwarf gallery and dates from the 12C *(see introduction)*. Unfortunately, a Baroque axial chapel crowned by a dome was added to this in the 18C.
Entering the cathedral from the forecourt, note the fallen section (Domstein), near the main door, of a Roman column which supported part of the former church. Inside, the decoration is principally Baroque and includes some interesting altarpieces. In the west chancel (on the left of the entrance) there is a Gothic funerary monument of the Archbishop and Prince-Elector Baldwin of Luxembourg. A splendid **tympanum**★ in the south aisle depicts Christ between the Virgin and St Peter. Another Virgin, a graceful 16C example, stands in the stuccoed chapel on the right of the chancel.

★ **Treasury (Domschatz)** ⊙ – Silver and gold plate (portable altar of St Andrew, richly enamelled), valuable ivories, and magnificently illuminated Gospels are on view here, in the domed axial chapel.

Cloister (Kreuzgang) – From the Gothic cloister, there is a good **view**★ of the cathedral and the Church of Our Lady. In the northeast corner is the 15C Malberg Madonna.

★ **Church of Our Lady** (Liebfrauenkirche) (DX) – One of the earliest Gothic sanctuaries in Germany (1235-1260), this church was directly inspired by one in Champagne, with the ground plan in the form of a Greek cross. There are thus four apsidal chapels, between each pair of which two smaller, three-sided chapels have been interposed, giving the whole church the highly original form of a rose with 12 petals.

The **tympanum** over the west porch shows St Mary Enthroned, the Annunciation, the Adoration of the Magi, the Massacre of the Innocents and the Presentation in the Temple. The Coronation of the Virgin is represented at the north entrance.

The interior has an incomparable elegance, enhanced by rings of foliage carved around each column, by the finesse of the public gallery, and the richness of the high central vaulting. There is a fine 17C **funerary monument★** (north chapel) to Metternich's personal canon.

★ **Episcopal Museum** (Bischöfliches Museum) (DY M1) ⊙ – The most interesting exhibits here are the frescoes (Deckenmalerei, 4C) of the Palace of Constantine, discovered beneath the cathedral. It is supposed that they represent St Helen, the Emperor's mother, and his wife Fausta. The colours are extraordinarily fresh and the technique highly skilled.

The first floor of the museum is reserved for sacred art (note the original statues which once adorned the west face of the Church of Our Lady).

Basilica (Basilika) (DY) – Once the main hall of the building, this "Aula Palatina" is all that remains of the imperial palace built by Constantine c310. Remodelled and altered many times, it was finally restored to its original form in the 19C and early 20C. The basilica is used today as a Protestant church. The interior, restrained in decoration, nevertheless overwhelms with its sheer size.

★ **Palace Gardens** (Palastgarten) (DY) – A formal, French-style park, once belonging to the old Prince-Electors' Castle (17C and 18C), this still includes ornamental pools, exotic flowerbeds and Baroque statues.

★★ **Rhineland Museum** (Rheinisches Landesmuseum) (DY) ⊙ – At street level, a Department of Prehistory and a section on Roman antiquities are particularly interesting.

Palaeolithic Age: Stone Age implements, ceramics and weapons; objects found in Bronze Age tombs; jewels set in gold from Iron Age sepulchres.

Roman Period: marvellous mosaics; bronze statuettes; sculptures and bas-reliefs (including a school scene and one depicting the payment of farm rent). Among the sculpture discovered at Neumagen *(see under Moselle Valley)* is the representation of a ship sailing down the Moselle loaded with wine . Included in this **Neumagen Ship** carving is the figure of "the jolly sailor" – a mariner with a broad grin who has passed into the folklore of the Moselle. Regional ceramics and jewels and glassware found in Frankish tombs are also on display.

★★ **Imperial Roman Baths** (Kaiserthermen) (DY) ⊙ – Among the largest in the Roman empire, these baths date from the time of Constantine, but appear never to have been used. The construction of the rounded walls – alternate layers of brick and rubble – is typically Roman. The window openings are wide and arched. Inside, the hot water caldarium is preceded by a tepidarium (warm water baths), a frigidarium (cold) and a gymnasium for physical exercises. The two floors below ground where the heating and circulating plant were installed are particularly interesting to see.

★★ **Municipal Library Treasury** (Schatzkammer der Stadtbibliothek) (DY B) ⊙ – Fascinating exhibits are on view here. The collection includes rare ancient manuscripts, beautifully illuminated (medieval Bibles, homilies, fables, etc.); examples of the earliest books to be illustrated (Gospels, teaching manuals, legal volumes); and many old documents, treaties, letters of credit and safe conduct passes.

Karl Marx House (CY) ⊙ – *Brückenstrasse 10.* The birthplace of the socialist theoretician turned into a museum. Letters, manuscripts, first edition of Communist Manifesto, etc.

ADDITIONAL SIGHTS

★ **St Paulinus' Church** (Pfarrkirche St Paulin) – *Access via Thebäerstrasse* (DX).
Tall windows illuminate the single nave of this church designed by Balthazar Neumann *(qv)* and completed in 1754. The martyrdom of the Saint and members of the Theban Legion in AD 268 is illustrated in paintings on the ceiling, Rococo stucco decorates the vaulting.

St Barbara's Baths (Barbarathermen) (CY) ⊙ – 2C Roman baths, used for several centuries, now in ruins.

Roman Amphitheatre (DY) ⊙ – Once seating 20 000 spectators, this arena was used as a quarry in the Middle Ages, and became so damaged by the 18C that vines were grown on the terraces. The cellars below ground house theatrical equipment.

St Matthias' Church – *Access via Saarstrasse* (CY).
A 12C pillared Romanesque basilica, now a Benedictine convent church housing the St Matthias reliquary shrine. Apart from Romanesque, the façade shows traces of Baroque and neo-Classical influence.

The chapter on Practical Information
at the end of the Guide lists

- local or national organisations providing additional information
- admission times and charges.

Michelin map **413** K 21 - Local map see under SWABIAN JURA
Plan of the conurbation in the current Michelin Red Guide Deutschland

Built on the banks of the Neckar and overlooked by Hohentübingen Castle, this ancient medieval city boasts a university, founded in 1477, which has schooled – among many others – such poets as Hölderlin, Mörike and Uhland, the philosophers Hegel and Schelling, scholars like Kepler and theologians of the status of Melanchthon.

Today, with its animated student life, its steep and narrow streets rising between old houses from a pleasant riverside setting, Tübingen remains one of the most attractive towns in southern Germany.

From **Eberhards Bridge** (Z), there is a fine **view★** upstream of the Neckar, bordered by weeping willows, with time-worn roofs and the outline of the Hölderlin tower emerging through the greenery. On the left, the **Platanenallee★★** (Z) – an avenue of plane trees on a man-made island – is a delightful place for a waterfront stroll, especially in summer when the river at night is alive with lantern-lit boats and student songs echo beneath the lights of the old town.

TÜBINGEN

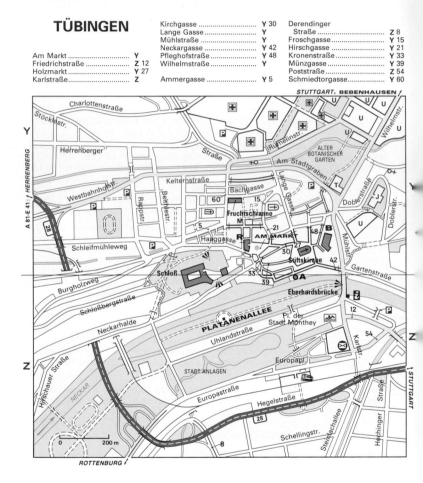

SIGHTS

★ **Market Place** (Am Markt) (Y) – An old square, very animated on market days (Mondays, Wednesdays and Fridays). In the centre, a Renaissance fountain and statue of Neptune.

★ **Town Hall** (Y R) – The outside decoration of this 15C building dates from 1876. The astronomic clock on the façade (1511) is the work of Stöfler.

Collegiate Church of St George (Stiftskirche) (Y) ⊘ – A Gothic hall-church built in the 15C. The rood-screen and the canopied **pulpit★** are in the Flamboyant style. The chancel is in fact the burial place of the Princes of Württemberg. Note the funerary monument of Eberhard the Bearded, original founder of the university, and the Renaissance **tombs★★** of Duke Ludwig and his wife, adorned with fine alabaster relief work. From the top of the church tower, there is an interesting **view★** of the river, the castle promontory and, in the distance, the Swabian Jura.

Castle (YZ) – The present edifice was built on mid-11C foundations during the Renaissance. It now houses several Departments of the university. In the cellars are prison cells and a 1548 vat which held no less than 850hl - 18 700 gallons of wine. From the bastion terraces there are, again, good views of the Neckar and the old town.

Tübingen

Hölderlin Tower (Hölderlinturm) (Z A) – *Bursagasse 6.* Once part of the fortifications, this tower was turned into a dwelling house and inhabited by Hölderlin (1770-1843). Now a museum, it displays many souvenirs of the poet.

Bebenhausen Hospital (Bebenhausener Pfleghof) (Y B) – Once the tithe barn of Bebenhausen Abbey (see below), this building dates from the 15C. Jutting from the tall, steep roof is a three-storey dormer through the windows of which the grain was passed into the lofts.

Fruchtschranne (Y) – Designed as the ducal granary, this wood-walled 15C building has a most unusual roof, since it boasts four storeys, each with mansards.

EXCURSION

★ **Bebenhausen Abbey** – *6km - 3 1/2 miles to the north by the Wilhelmstrasse* (Y).
This ancient Cistercian monastery, founded in 1180 in the solitude of Schönbuch Forest, is an interesting example of Romano-Gothic architecture in Germany. Built to the classic Cistercian plan, but much restored, the abbey church still shows traces of Romanesque design. The **cloister**, in the Flamboyant style, has splendid fan vaulting. Facing the lavabo is the summer refectory; to the west the winter one is now a small museum.

★ **ÜBERLINGEN** Baden-Württemberg   Pop 19 600

Michelin map **413** K 23 - Local map see under Lake CONSTANCE

This ancient Empire outpost on the shores of Lake Constance *(qv)* has become a popular summer resort because of its exceptionally mild climate and the opportunities it affords for water sports. West of the town there is a pleasant **moat walk★** (Stadtbefestigungsanlagen) (A) which leads to the lakeside **Seepromenade** (AB). The town stands on the northern shore of the lake's Überlingersee arm.

ÜBERLINGEN

Christophstraße .... A 3
Franziskanerstraße .... AB 5
Hofstatt .... B
Münsterstraße .... B

Bahnhofstraße.................. A 2
Gradebergstraße............. B 6
Hafenstraße .... B 8
Hizlerstraße .... B 9
Hochbildstraße................ B 10
Jakob-Kessenring-Str. ..... A 12
Klosterstraße................... A 14
Krummebergstraße .... B 15
Landungsplatz .... B 17
Lindenstraße .... B 19
Luziengasse .... B 20
Markstraße....................... AB 22
Obertostraße.................... B 23
Owinger Straße .... B 25
Pfarrhofstraße .... B 26
St-Ulrich-Straße............... B 28
Seestraße.......................... B 29

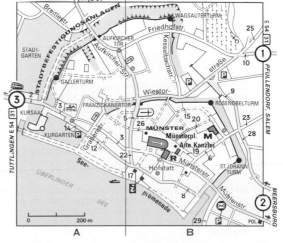

SIGHTS

Münsterplatz (B) – The square lies between the Gothic cathedral, the north façade of the town hall, and the Renaissance municipal chancellery (Alte Kanzlei).

★ **Münster** (B) – The cathedral, or minster, has an enormous central portion with five aisles covered by Gothic fan vaulting. A graceful Swabian work of 1510, the Virgin of the Crescent Moon, stands in the St Elizabeth chapel off the south aisle.

★ **Town Hall** (Rathaus) (B R) – *Enter through the turret on the right and walk up to the first floor.*
The **council chamber**★ (Ratssaal) ⊘ is decorated with great finesse in the Gothic manner: panelled walls embellished with projecting arches; ribbed, and slightly rounded, wooden ceiling; a series of 15C statuettes.

★ **Local Museum** (Städtisches Museum) (B M) – Among the exhibits, housed in a late 15C mansion, is a collection of Krippen (cribs): 18C wood carvings in the folk tradition, representing, scenes from the life of Jesus in miniature.

EXCURSION

★ **Salem Abbey** – *11km - 7 miles to the east. See under Salem Abbey.*

★★ ULM   Baden-Württemberg   Pop 110 000

Michelin map **413** M 21-N 21

The commercial importance of Ulm derives from its situation, at the point where the great Stuttgart-Munich highway, newly descended from the Swabian Jura, crosses a Danube swollen from the inflow of waters from the Iller. If the ancient proverb "the money of Ulm governs the world" no longer applies, local industries, mechanical and electrical, still thrive.
The Nobel Prize physicist Albert Einstein was born in Ulm in 1879.

★★ **General View** – A walk along the **Jahnufer** (the south bank of the Danube) (Z) opens a fine view of gabled houses crowning the ramparts on the far side of the river, of the Metzgerturm (Butchers' Tower) and the cathedral.

★★★ CATHEDRAL (MÜNSTER) (Y)

time: 45 minutes (not counting ascent of the spire)

At a total height of 161m - 528ft, the spire is the tallest in the world. It appears to arrow the entire Gothic building skywards in its slender trajectory. The church's sweeping vertical lines, added to the lightness of the pierced masonry, are wholly admirable. Although the foundation stone was laid in 1377, the two towers and the spire were not erected until 1890.
A beautiful porch with three arcades and a very fine profile precedes the double Renaissance entrance doors (at the pier, an expressive 1429 statue, *Man In Sorrow*, by Hans Multscher).

Interior – The upswept nave, with sharply pointed arches, is emphasized in its soaring flight by the absence of a transept, which also concentrates attention on the chancel.
The pillars of the central nave support a series of graceful early 15C consoles. The pulpit is surmounted by a splendid wooden luffer-board dating from 1510, and above this is what appears to be a second pulpit in the Flamboyant style. This is intended for the Holy Spirit, the invisible preacher. The ciborium, left of the chancel entrance, is in the same style, and so are the four side aisles with fine fan vaulting.

★★★ **Choir Stalls** (Chorgestühl) – A marvellous example of wood carving, executed by Jörg Syrlin the Elder between 1469 and 1474, faces two series of personages, from the Bible and from pagan antiquity, one opposite the other.
Men are grouped on the left, women on the right, the upper gables being devoted to the Church's apostles and martyrs, and the high backs of the stalls to Old Testament figures.
The most expressive sculptures are carved from the sides of the stalls and include sibyls on the right, busts of Greek and Latin philosophers and writers (Pythagoras, Cicero, etc.) on the left. Behind the altar, Syrlin's magnificent triple throne for the priest completes the ensemble. (The sculptor and his wife head the ranks nearest the nave.)

Ascent of the spire – *(768 steps).* From the tower platform or the bulb of the spire, the all-round **panorama**★★ includes the town, the Danube, the plateaux of the Swabian Jura and the Alps.

Ulm Cathedral choir stalls:
a Sibyl

ULM

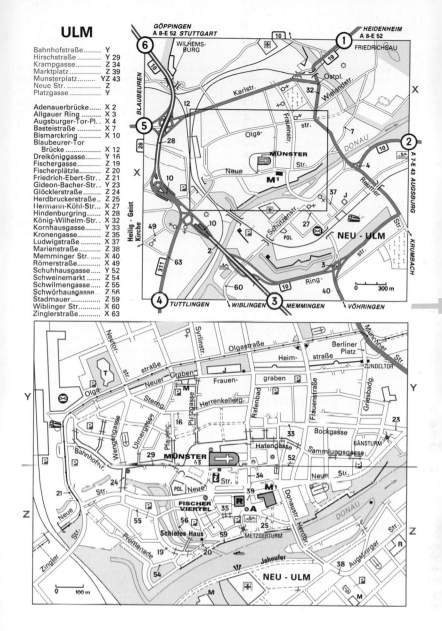

ADDITIONAL SIGHTS

★ **Fishermen's Quarter** (Fischerviertel) (Z). – Start from the Fischerplätzle, a small square shaded in summer by a lime tree. Take an alley on the left that spans a culvert. The picturesque building here, the **Schiefes Haus**, has subsided over a tanners' canal in a curious way.

   Follow the itinerary as far as the Metzgerturm (Butchers' Tower), and then return.

★ **Museum** (Ulmer Museum) (Z M1) ⊙ – The Fine Arts Department of this museum, housed in a mansion that once belonged to a local dignitary, is the most interesting. Among works by the Masters of Ulm, note a reliquary bust by Syrling the Elder, a Virgin and Child by Daniel Mauch, the *Portrait of Eitel Besserer* by Martin Schaffner and Hans Multscher's Bilhafingen Madonna. Picasso, Klee and Kandinsky represent the 20C.

   Town Hall (Z R) – An elegant Gothic and Renaissance building with pierced gables and painted facades, richly decorated in trompe l'oeil. An astronomic clock adorns the fine west façade.
   The **Fischkasten** (Z A) in the nearby Marktplatz is a fountain whose spiral stem was fashioned by Jörg Syrlin the Elder in 1482.

   Church of the Holy Spirit (Heilig-Geist-Kirche) – *To the southwest, via the Römerstrasse* (X). This modern church, distinguished by its bell-tower in the form of a pointing finger, stands on a fine panoramic site above the town.

The letter ß (eszett) which is to be found only in the German alphabet, appears in the text transcribed as "ss".

EXCURSIONS

Wiblingen Abbey – *5km - 3 miles to the south, via the Wiblinger Strasse* (X).
Although its foundation dates back to the 11C, the final touches were not put to
this abbey until the 18C. As at Vierzehnheiligen, more than a third of the abbey
church's floor plan is occupied by the transept, where pilgrims worshipped relics
of the Holy Rood. The flattened domes of this Baroque building could give visitors the impression of being crushed, but this is compensated for by the illusion
of height provided by the painter Januarius Zick in the frescoes which cover them.
The abbey **library★** ⊙, completed in 1760, is one of the finest examples of the
Rococo in Swabia.
The main interest lies in a gallery, supported by 32 columns, which projects into
the centre of the room and at each end. The rhythmically placed columns, painted
alternately pink and blue, combine with the large false relief fresco on the ceiling
to create an ensemble rich in colour and movement.

★ **Blaubeuren** – *18km - 11 miles to the west. Leave by* ⑤ *on the town plan.*
Follow the signposts Blautopf-Hochaltar, in this village of the Swabian Jura
renowned for its fine setting among the rocks, then leave the car near the monumental abbey entrance.

Blautopf – *15 minutes on foot Rtn.* This deep blue pool was formed by a natural
embankment of glacial origin. The shady approaches have been laid out as
walks.

Old Benedictine Abbey – *Time: 1/2 h. Follow the "Hochaltar" signs.*
The premises include a picturesque group of ancient wood-walled buildings. In
the chancel of the old **abbey church** (Benediktinerkloster) ⊙ is the celebrated
Blaubeuren Altarpiece★★ (Hochaltar), a collective work created by the principal studios of Ulm in the 15C.
The themes treated are the Passion, the life of John the Baptist, and the Virgin
among the Saints.

★★ VIERZEHNHEILIGEN CHURCH Bavaria

Michelin map **413** Q 16

This pilgrimage church dedicated to the fourteen Saints of Intercession stands
on an open hillside in the Upper Main Valley, opposite Banz Abbey *(qv)*. The
bold concepts of Balthazar Neumann, master of the Baroque, are evident in the
interior.

The Pilgrimage – In 1445 and 1446, a herdsman on this hillside was blessed
with a number of visions, the last of them identified as the Christ Child among
the "Fourteen Intercessors". The cult of this pious band, actively fostered by
German Dominicans and Cistercians, must be seen in the context of mysticism
prevailing at the beginning of the 15C, when "visions" were frequent (the
"voices" heard by Joan of Arc – born 1412 – were those of St Catherine and
St Margaret, themselves part of this intercessionary group). This devotion to the
holy intercessors remained alive for many years among local people, attracting
crowds of pilgrims to a chapel which was to be superseded, in the 18C, by a
sumptuous Rococo church.

TOUR *about 1/2 hour*

The façade of the church, built between 1743 and 1772 in handsome ochre stone,
is framed by domed towers unusually tall for a Baroque building. The design of
the façade itself is admirably vigorous, with jutting cornices to emphasize the
tiered arrangement of pilasters and columns and the sinous lines of the convex
front. In accordance with the taste of the time – Rococo rather than purely
Baroque – these elements do not simply constitute a covering, as at Ottobeuren
(qv), but form an embellishment in its own right. The four rows of windows, small
at mezzanine or attic level, wide and spacious elsewhere, together with a broken
pediment crowned with statues, are reminiscent of the castles of the period. The
statues, once gilded, represent Jesus Christ between Faith and Charity.

Interior – *Illustration p 25*. The interior arrangement is organized as a succession of three oval bays framed by colonnades and covered by low inner domes.
The true centre of the church is the bay containing the altar to the Saints of
Intercession – to the detriment of the transept crossing, which is invaded by the
bay's colonnade. Circular domes, again, cover the transepts. Such geometric sub-
tleties create an overall perspective concentrating the worshippers' view relentlessly on a central focal point – an ideal haunting 18C architects wearied of the
endless succession of rectangular bays.
Many visitors will be surprised by the restraint and elegance of the church's
Rococo interior decoration. Outstanding are the colour combinations of the painting inside the domes, the lightness of the stuccowork, the richesse of the gold
outlines defining the woodwork of the galleries, and the grace of putti surmounting confessionals and cornice.

★★ **Altar to the Fourteen Saints of Intercession** (Nothelfer-Altar) – A Rococo pyramid with
a pierced baldachin, where every line is nevertheless convex or concave, this
remarkable work was executed by stucco-workers of the Wessobrunn School *(qv)*
in 1764. It stands on the spot where the herdsman's visions are said to have
occurred.

The Altar Statues

Balustrade: 1) St Dionysius - 2) St Blaise - 3) St Erasmus - 4) St Cyriacus (delivery from the Devil at the final hour).

Altar Niches: 5) St Catherine, patron saint of the learned, of students and girls wishing to get married (the model of Christian wisdom). - 6) St Barbara, patron saint of miners, artillerymen and prisoners (the grace of a noble death).

Buttresses: 7) St Achatius (the agonies of death). - 8) St Giles, the only intercessor not to suffer martyrdom (to obtain the grace of a true confession). - 9) St Eustace (converted by the vision of a stag with a Cross between its antlers). - 10) St Christopher, patron saint of travellers.

On top of the baldachin: 11) St Guy (epilipsy). - 12) St Margaret (intercession for the forgiveness of sins). - 13) St George, patron saint of peasants and their possessions - 14) St Pantaleon.

Those who enjoy seeing – or photographing – unusual views should climb the slopes above the church. Before long, Banz Abbey comes into view on the far side of the valley, framed by the Vierzehnheiligen towers, in line with – and apparently resting on – the ridgepole of the church roof.

★ # WALDECK REGION Hessen

Michelin map 412 folds 14 and 15

This small stretch of country on either side of the River Eder lived under the rule of the Waldeck Princes and was half forgotten by the world until 1918. Today its deep forests, the magnificent lake retained by the Eder Dam, and the spa resort of Bad Wildungen make it one of the most popular tourist areas of central Germany.

ROUND TOUR STARTING FROM BAD WILDUNGEN

145km - 90 miles - allow 1 day

Bad Wildungen – The most impressive bathing installations of this spa follow one another on either side of the Brunnenallee, through the Kurpark and as far as the horse-shoe buildings of the George-Viktor spring – the busiest centre of this picturesque region.

In the old town, the **Evangelical Church** (Evangelische Stadtkirche) contains an altarpiece said to be one of the earliest milestones in German painting: the **Wildunger Altar★★**, which dates from 1403.

Embellishing the high altar, these scenes from the life and Passion of Christ are notable for their profundity and for the stylized elongation of the idealized figures.

★ **Waldeck Castle** – Rising above the steep, wooded shores of the artificial lake, the seat of the Waldeck Princes, abandoned in the 17C, is now part hotel, part museum. From the terrace there is a fine view of the lake, curving away out of sight between the wooded heights. The **museum** ⊙ galleries evoke the history of the House of Waldeck. The castle boasts a Witches' Tower (Hexenturm) with three prison cells, one below the other. The Eder Dam, completed in 1914, retains 200 million m³ - 44 000 million gallons of water. In 1943, during the Second World War, a specialized raid by the RAF breached the dam with a single 4-ton bomb, blowing a gap in the stonework 70m - 77 yards wide and 22m - 72ft high, resulting in catastrophic floods.

Drive to Arolsen via Nieder-Werbe, Sachsenhausen, Freienhagen and Landau.

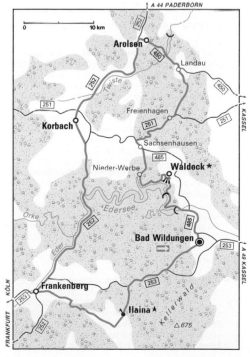

287

Arolsen – Formerly the residence of the Waldeck Princes, this is a small town whose symmetrical plan testifies to its aristocratic origins. The **Palace** ⊙, inspired by Versailles, was built between 1714 and 1728, although the interior decoration was to continue until the beginning of the 19C. The apartments, adorned with stuccowork and painted ceilings (1715-1719), are gained via a vestibule and double staircase. Together with the Baroque Garden Chamber (Gartensaal) and the Great Hall (Grosser Saal), these complete the state rooms.

Korbach – The present town was formed by joining together two fortified settlements: Alstadt (built around the Church of St Kilian – without a tower) and Neustadt (built around the Church of St Nicholas – a tower with a spire). Many old half-timbered houses have been preserved. **St Kilian's** is a Gothic hall-church wider than it is long, a particularity showing Westphalian influence. There is a fine group of statues at the south door: the Virgin stands against the pier, while the Last Judgement is depicted on the tympanum.

Frankenberg an der Eder – The upper town contains impressive wooden houses dating from the 16C, especially around the two central squares, the Obermarkt and Untermarkt. The latter is noteworthy for the **Town Hall★**, bristling with turrets. On the crest behind stands the 13-14 C Church of Our Lady (Liebfrauenkirche), with the **Lady Chapel** (Marienkapelle) abutting on the south transept. The chapel is Gothic, built with an asymmetric polygonal floor plan. It contains a stone altarpiece, now lacking its statues but with a rare decorative perfection.

Haina – The **church** of the former Cistercian abbey, built here in the heart of the woods, is a huge, rather plain Gothic hall. The flat east end, the small columns in the nave broken halfway up by historiated consoles, and the six transept chapels are Romanesque. The cloister, however, shows both Romanesque and Gothic features (note the Romanesque "Lamb of God" entrance).
The road passes through the beechwoods and plantations of oak forming the Kellerwald forest massif before regaining the outskirts of Bad Wildungen.

★ WALDSASSEN Bavaria   Pop 8 000

Michelin map **413** TU 16 and 17

Like its neighbours, Selb and Weiden, Waldsassen owes its prosperity to the glass and ceramics industry. The three towns lie between the Fichtelgebirge and the Oberpfälzer Wald, in a forested region east of Bayreuth that was once a glacial moraine.

★ **Basilica (Stiftsbasilika)** – Completed in 1704, mainly on plans drawn up by Georg Dientzenhofer, this building is distinguished by its unusual length (83m - 272ft) and a chancel occupying more than one third of the floor space – a feature recalling the design of Cistercian churches. The aisles and galleries form two storeys of chapels which communicate vertically by apertures in the vaulting. The decoration is particularly lavish: the stuccowork is by G B Carlone; the **choir stalls★** are by local craftsmen, and so is the red and black marble high altar, with its sculpted reredos (the Annunciation) incorporating a tabernacle in the form of a gilded globe. On the pillars of the transept crossing are imposing statues of the four Fathers of the Church. The whole effects is that of an early example attempting to adapt Italian Baroque to German taste.

★★ **Library** – This is something very special. The visitor is spellbound with admiration before the carved woodwork framing the shelves, decorating the balustrade and, above all, forming the ten life-size statues supporting the gallery. Karl Stilp and Andreas Witt, the local artists who created these masterpieces, brought a profound realism, touched with wry humour, to their task.
The ten figures symbolize, with wit and truth, the different guilds involved in the production of a book.
They include, among others, the rag sorter who provides the raw materials, the shepherd who delivers the animal skins to the bookbinder, the bookseller who distributes the finished work. The stance and characterization of each one is remarkable – and each face, according to the viewpoint of the observer, can show opposing expressions. Thus the oriental bookseller *(2nd statue on the left of the entrance)* presents a noble profile on one side, and features twisted by illness and cunning on the other. The butcher, brandishing a knife, leers maliciously in the direction of his neighbour, the shepherd. The strangest figure is that of the critic *(2nd on the left side of the end door)*: his hands are tied, and a bird of prey, emerging from his head, has seized him by the nose – the inference being that the character has a sharp wit but is nevertheless a prisoner of his pride.
Completed in 1726, this library is one of the finest flowers of lay Baroque art.

EXCURSION

★ **Kappel Church** – *6.5km - 4 miles to the north.*
Isolated in a pastoral **setting★★**, this church dedicated to the Holy Trinity is within sight of the Cheb Basin in Czechoslovakia. It was built in 1689 by Georg Dientzenhofer in the shape of a trefoil rotunda punctuated by three towers. Inside, three apses, each dedicated to one of the three characters forming the Trinity, radiate from a central triangular bay with three columns. Three altar niches have been hollowed out from each apse.

WASSERBURG AM INN Bavaria   Pop 10 500

Michelin map **413** T 22

Wasserburg owes its existence to its site, on a rise encircled by a loop of the River Inn, and its name to a castle built there by the Wittelsbachs. River navigation and the trade in salt contributed to the town's rapid development in the Middle Ages. Coming from the south, the bridge over the river affords an attractive **view**★ of the old town, with the tall facades of the quayside houses reflected in the water. The mixture of flat roofs, stepped gables and ridged roofs behind copings give Wasserburg the half-German, half-Italian look typical of the Inn and Salzach valleys.

SIGHTS

Marienplatz – Bordered by arcaded houses, this main square is closed off by the tall, stepped gable of a **Town Hall** decorated with paintings in which religious subjects alternate with armorial bearings. The façade has Renaissance windows. On the first floor, next to the banqueting hall, there is a **room** with painted panels and walls covered by 16C woodwork beneath carved beams of the same period. On the opposite side of the square, the lovely **Patrizierhaus Kern** displays an outstanding façade with two-storey oriel windows, paintings, and richly ornamented stuccowork by Johann Baptist Zimmermann.

Parish Church (Pfarrkirche St Jakob) – The church is crowned by a tall, square tower. The interior, in the Gothic style, contains a carved wood pulpit dating from 1638.

★ **Local Museum** (Heimatmuseum) ⊙ – The four floors of this huge Gothic building house many different displays. Note Bavaria's oldest postal sleigh *(ground floor)*, exhibitions of furniture *(first and second floors)*, and the craft workshops on the third floor. Examples of religious art from the 15C to the 18C can be seen behind the building in a gallery housed in the former stable block.

EXCURSION

Rott am Inn – *15km - 9 1/2 miles to the south.*
Of the former Benedictine abbey founded in the 11C, only an interesting **church**, to which a number of Baroque features were added in the 18C, remain in Rott today. The remodelling was carried out by Johann Michael Fischer (architect), Franz Xavier Feuchtmayer and Jakob Rauch (stuccowork), Matthäus Günther (frescoes) and Ignaz Günther (sculpture). Together, they achieved a quite remarkable visual harmony.

★★ # WEIMAR Thuringia   Pop 62 000

Michelin map **987** fold 26

To most non-Germans, the name of Weimar recalls the ill-fated republic which existed uneasily between the end of the First World War and the Hitler years. But the town's claim to a place in European history rests shakably on an extraordinary flowering of intellectual talent which has grown steadily over the centuries. Early in its existence it attracted personalities as diverse as Luther, the painter Cranach, Bach, Wieland, Schiller and Liszt. The one genius whose traces it is impossible to escape in Weimar, however, is that greatest of German classicists, Johann Wolfgang von Goethe.

THE "GERMAN ATHENS"

The first historical mention of Weimar occurs in a document dated 975. By 1348 the town had been granted an urban charter, and in 1547 it became the capital of the Duchy of Saxe-Weimar. From this time onwards dates the formidable cultural expansion which made the town the true spiritual capital of Germany.

The Intellectual and Cultural Centre – Weimar's hour of glory coincided with the succession, in 1758, of the Duchess Anna Amalia. It was during her reign that the town's intellectual reputation grew, largely because of **Goethe** (1749-1832). He had first been summoned to the Court at the age of 26 by the Grand Duke Carl August, son of Amalia. In the small provincial capital – at that time numbering no more than 5 000 inhabitants – he was appointed Minister and raised to peerage, and he created the greater part of his work, including Faust. His influence was enormous. For more than 25 years he directed the Weimar Theatre, which soon became accepted as the German National Theatre, renowned for its staging of international classics.

Goethe and Schiller, Weimar

This was the result of a fruitful collaboration with Friedrich von Schiller *(see below)*, who moved permanently to Weimar in 1799. The work produced by these two friends, along with the writings of the theologian **Johann Gottfried Herder** (1776-1803), a disciple of Kant, raised Weimar's literary reputation to the point where the town was considered "the home of German classicism". In the **Goethe-Schiller Archives** *(Jener Strasse)*, which are among the most important literary collections in the country, several posthumous works are conserved, together with letters from almost 1 000 personalities worldwide.

Art and Music in Weimar – It was in Weimar that Lucas Cranach the Elder worked – from 1552 until his death a year later – on his final masterpiece: the altarpiece triptych for the local Church of St Peter and St Paul *(see below)*. Johann Sebastian Bach was organist and choirmaster there from 1708 to 1717. In 1848 Franz Liszt in his turn became choirmaster and surrounded himself with the artistic elite of the period. It was Liszt who was the driving force behind the creation of Weimar's famous school of music, which still bears his name today.

In 1860, an establishment was founded which left an indelible mark on 20C German painting. This was the School of Fine Arts – later to be transformed into the College of Architecture. It was under the influence of such celebrated graduates as Arnold Böcklin (1827-1901) *(qv)* that painters spearheading the contemporary avant-garde movement developed what is known as "the Weimar School".

The Weimar Republic (1919-33) – The constitution of the Weimar Republic was set up by the German National Assembly under Hitler *(see above)*, and it sat at that time in the Weimar National Theatre.

HISTORIC CENTRE

Lucas Cranach House (Lucas-Cranach-Haus) – *Marktplatz*. The famous painter spent the last year of his life in this Renaissance house (1549) with scrolled gables. His studio was on the 3rd floor. The **Town Hall**, opposite, was built *c*1500 but heavily remodelled in the middle of the 19C.

Democracy Square (Platz der Demokratie) – The equestrian statue of the Grand Duke Carl August of Saxe-Weimar-Eisenach (1757-1828), executed by Adolf von Donndorf, stands in this square. On the south side, the former palace (1757-1774) is occupied by the **Franz Liszt Higher School of Music**.

The 16-18C **Green Castle** (Grünes Schloss) today houses the **Central Library of German Classics**. It contains medieval manuscripts, very early printed works, rare documents dating from the 16C and 17C, and above all original, priceless 18C volumes. For many years now, the museum has been collecting manuscripts, publications and translations relating to the "Age of Enlightenment" (Aufklärung) – Kant, Locke, Leibnitz, etc.

Frau von Stein's House (Haus der Frau von Stein) – *Ackerwand 25*. Goethe met Charlotte von Stein, lady-in-waiting to the Duchess Anna Amalia, in November 1775. The first ten years of his stay in Weimar were profoundly influenced by his feeling for her. The house was remodelled in 1776 to his own design.

★★★ **Goethe's House** (Goethehaus) ⊙ – *Frauenplan*. The dramatist-politician lived in this Baroque mansion for more than 20 years, from 1809 until his death in 1832. The interior is for the most part the way he left it. The living-rooms, workroom and library (5 400 volumes) can all be visited. An annexe has been turned into a museum which gives an idea of his personality, his poetical works and his scientific researches.

★★ **Schiller's House** (Schillerhaus) ⊙ – *Schillerstrasse 12*. The writer moved here in 1802 to be nearer to his great friend Goethe. It was here that *William Tell* and *The Bride of Messina* were written. The **Schiller Museum** offers a rundown on his life and his work.

Follow the Schillerstrasse as far as the Theaterplatz.

German National Theatre (Deutsches Nationaltheater) – The present structure, which dates from 1907, was built on the site of a 1779 Baroque building. It was in this old theatre that Schiller's great plays were staged and directed by Goethe; it was here, in 1850, that the first performance of Richard Wagner's Lohengrin was given. And it is in front of the present-day building that the **statues**★★ of Goethe and Schiller, sculpted in 1857 by Ernst Rietschel, are to be found.

Widow's Palace (Wittumspalast) ⊙ – After the death of her husband the Duchess Anna Amalia moved to this 1767 Baroque palace with two wings; it was here that she organized the famous salons of which Goethe, Schiller, Herder and Wieland were so important a part. Today, the **Wieland Museum** illustrates the lifework of "the German Voltaire" – fervent supporter of German classicism, translator and spokesman for the Aufklärung.

Church of St Peter and St Paul (Stadtkirche) – Am Herderplatz. This triple-nave Gothic hall church was built between 1498 and 1500 and much remodelled in the Baroque style between 1735 and 1745. It is also known as the **Herderkirche** *(see "Art and Music", above)*, in memory of the sermons preached there by the philosopher, who is buried in the church. The famous **Cranach Triptych**★★, started by Lucas Cranach the Elder and finished by his son in 1555, represents the Crucifixion on its central panel. This is surrounded by scenes from the Old and New Testanent. On the right, Luther and Cranach the Elder himself appear.

Castle (Stadtschloss) ⊙ – This complex with four separate wings dates from the 15C to the 20C and has frequently been enlarged, most notably by C W Coudray, N Grohmann and N F Thouret. One of the additions to its eastern part is a classical peristyle.

Established in the castle apartments is the **National Research Centre for Classical German Literature**, and with this there is also the **National Art Collection**. This comprises numismatics, prints and – perhaps of wider interest – galleries of paintings. Here, visitors can see: Thuringian altarpieces of the Flamboyant Gothic period; an important **Cranach collection**★★ (*Sybil of Cleves*, *Portrait of Luther*); Flemish and Italian paintings; and work by Hans Baldung Grien, Albrecht Dürer and Bartholomäus Bruyn the Elder. The Weimar School (Von Schwind and Rohlfs) and contemporary German artists (Max Beckmann, Max Liebermann) are also represented.

In the southwestern wing of the complex is the castle tower (1729-1732) with its Baroque cupola, and the 1545 (renovated) keep.

ILM PARK

"Weimar is in fact a park in which they happened to build a town." This approving comment was written by Adolf Stahr in 1851 – and indeed today Weimar is still a city of green spaces, indissolubly linked with its riverside park. From the palace of Tiefurt to the Belvedere, there is a single stretch of greenery centered on the gardens laid out on each side of the Ilm. There was no intention of restraining nature – said Goethe, planning the English-style landscaping – but simply of guiding and at the same time respecting her. The gardens are only a few yards from the city centre.

★★ **Goethe's Pavilion** (Goethes Gartenhaus) – Augustus the Strong made a present of this summer residence to Goethe, and the great man liked it so much that he lived there permanently from 1776 to 1782. It remained his favourite retreat until the end of his life.

Among his works there is even a short poem recording his delight in the place.

> *"It is an unpretentious*
> *Small house beneath a tall roof.*
> *Everyone who came there*
> *Felt light-hearted;*
> *Trees I had planted grew strong and green,*
> *And the spirit as well*
> *Thrived on this blessed ground."*

It was in this house that Goethe wrote *Wilhelm Meister's Theatrical Mission*, important parts of *Iphigenia*, early drafts of *Egmont* and *Torquato Tasso*.

Facing it is the **Borkenhauschen**, Augustus's own favourite retreat. Ten minutes walk away is the **Roman House**, a classical building (1791-1797) conceived by Goethe for the Grand Duke.

Cross the park now in the direction of the Belvederer Allee.

Franz Liszt's House (Franz-Liszt-Haus) ⊘ – *Belvederer Allee*. In this one-time gardeners' lodge at the entrance to the park it is possible to visit the apartments lived in by the composer during his second stay in Weimar, from 1869 to 1886.

The Geschwister-Scholl-Strasse leads to the old cemetery (Alter Friedhof).

Funerary Monument to Goethe and Schiller (Goethe-und Schiller-Gruft) – In the centre of the cemetery, the monument was erected by C W Coudray between 1825 and 1827. The **Russian Orthodox Church** nearby was built between 1859 and 1862 specially for Maria Pavlova, Grand Duchess and daughter-in-law of Augustus.

EXCURSIONS

Tiefurt Palace ⊘ – *2km - 1 mile to the east*. The former summer residence (10C) of the Duchess Amalia is surrounded by English-style gardens. Both palace and gardens were frequently the scene of the literary gatherings she loved. Goethe, the Humboldt brothers and the other members of her cultural coterie were welcome guests. The apartments, in the neo-Classical style, evoke the classical era of Weimar.

Belvedere Castle – *4km - 2 1/2 miles to the southeast*. This is one of the most delightful – and the most artistically successful – stately homes of Thuringia. Comprising a large central block flanked by two low wings, the mansion is completed by four outbuildings and an orangery harbouring a **collection of carriages and barouches**. The grounds, originally formal in the Baroque style, were redesigned and laid out as an English garden between 1814 and 1840.

Buchenwald – *8 km - 5 miles to the west*. Only a few miles from Weimar, cradle of Humanism and first capital (1918) of a democratic Germany, the beechwoods of the Ettersberg hid for eight years one of the largest concentration camps of the Hitler regime.

Between Beeches and Wolves – Established in July 1937 for the internment of Germans who opposed the Nazi ethos, the camp was quick to take the Jews and Gypsies persecuted by the National Socialists – and then, as the invasion of Europe expanded, victims from the occupied countries. A total of almost 300 000 human beings, including innumerable children, took the road that led to Buchenwald; for 65 000 of them, it was a one-way trip.

Despite conditions of unbelievable hardship and a merciless system of surveillance, the camp was liberated, on 11 April 1945, by the inmates themselves. The novel, *Naked Among Wolves*, by Bruno Apitz, remains the most striking testimony to this sinister chapter of German history.

The Concentration Camp (KZ Buchenwald) – Map and descriptive brochure at entrance. The Information Centre shows a film tracing the history of the camp. A tour of the camp starts at the gatehouse, which still retains above the entrance the chilling slogan: **"Jedem das Seine"** ("You get what you deserve").

The position of each hut is marked out on the ground; at the far end, on the right, is the building which was used for storing the inmates' possessions and effects, now transformed into a museum. Outside the camp, a road leads to the quarry where excessively rigorous working conditions resulted in a particularly high death rate among those sent there. Nearly 20 000 Buchenwald prisoners were transferred to a camp named **Dora** *(see local map Harz Mountains)*, for forced labour in an underground factory developing secret weapons. The nature of their work meant that none of them ever saw daylight again.

Memorial (Mahnmal der Gedenkstätte Buchenwald) – *1km - 1/2 mile in the direction of Weimar.* From the entrance, the Steles' Way leads to the Avenue of Nations, which links three mass graves. From the last of these, Liberty Avenue brings you to the memorial bell tower, in front of which is the statuary group of *Eleven Buchenwald Prisoners*, by Fritz Cremer.

★ WERNIGERODE Saxony-Anhalt   Pop 37 000

Michelin map **987** fold 16 - Local map see under HARZ MOUNTAINS

On a marvellous site at the foot of the Harz Mountains, with many of its narrow streets bordered by old, half-timbered houses still intact, Wernigerode is one of the most delightful small towns in this region and an ideal starting point for exploration of the massif.

SIGHTS

★★ **Town Hall** (Rathaus) – *Am Marktplatz.* Considered to be one of the finest half-timbered buildings in Germany, this municipal treasure dates from the first half of the 16C. Its splendid façade includes superimposed oriel windows surmounted by slender spires. Note the double staircase and the carved wood features representing town aldermen.

★★ **Old Houses** (Fachwerkhäuser) – The most picturesque group is on the **Breite Strasse**, as it leaves the Market Place – several rows of town houses built by the rich burghers of Wernigerode in the 16C, 17C and 18C. The wooden sections and joists are often decorated with masks or carved patterns – as for instance on the 1674 house at No 72 known as "The Krummels' House".
An exploration of the lanes between the Breite Strasse and the castle hill to the south is also worthwhile. The houses here are smaller but full of charm. At the highest part of the Kochstrasse (No 43) is the tiniest house of all, which is only 3m - 10ft wide.

St John's Church (Pfarrkirche St Johannis) – Take the Breite Strasse and then, on the left, the Grüne Strasse. This late 15C, triple-aisle Gothic hall church has a four-panel altarpiece in carved wood dating from 1425. It represents the Virgin with angels.

Castle (Schloss) – Extensively remodelled in the late 19C, the castle is in a magnificent position overlooking the town. The main apartments have been organized as a museum, outlining the origins and development of feudalism, with a selection of craftwork and sacred art of the time.

EXCURSION

★★ **Harz Mountains** – *See under Harz Mountains.*

★ WERTHEIM Baden-Württemberg   Pop 21 700

Michelin maps **412** and **413** L 17

Overlooked by the castle ruins, red against the green wooded slopes beyond, Wertheim's overlapping, half-timbered houses are grouped along winding streets where the Main and Tauber rivers meet.

SIGHTS

Market Place – Note the 16C **Zobel-Haus** (bakery) among the half-timbered buildings surrounding this pretty square. Beside the church, the **Angels' Well** (Engelsbrunnen) is a Renaissance monument whose protective coping is surmounted by hooped stone arches adorned with angels.

Church (Stiftskirche) – The chancel is the burial place of the Counts of Wertheim. In the north aisle is the Renaissance **monument★★** to the Count of Isemburg (*c*1590).

Castle – From the ruins, the visitor looks down on the town, the confluence of the rivers and the wooded heights of Spessart (to the north) and the Odenwald (west).

EXCURSIONS

Former Abbey of Bronnbach ⊙ – *10km - 6 miles to the south.*
The late 12C **church★** here has retained its original Romanesque design and, in particular, the groined vaulting above the nave. This was specially conceived to enable tall, deeply pierced windows to be installed, so providing much brighter lighting than was customary in the period. From the Gothic cloister, with its triple-arched windows, there is a good view of the church's south wall, and the tiered roofs above it.

Michelin map ⑬⑬ Q 23 – 10km - 6 miles northwest of Weilheim

This locality in Upper Bavaria is known for the famous **Wessobrunn Prayer** (Wessobrunner Gebet), one of the oldest known documents in the German language. The 9C manuscript, in a Bavarian dialect of Old High German, is kept in the Munich Civic Library.

School of Wessobrunn – In the 17C and 18C, Wessobrunn produced a series of architects and artists of multiple talents who, according to the needs of construction projects or the dictates of their own inspiration, were able at will to exchange the compass for the paintbrush or the tools of the stucco worker. Working in a corporate and family framework known as the Wessobrunn School, these artists of Baroque genius, who were in no way specialists, beautified churches and civic buildings all over Bavaria, Swabia and the Tyrol. The names of the **Feuchtmayer** and **Schmuzer** families stand out brilliantly within the group, though the most celebrated is perhaps **Dominikus Zimmermann**, who was responsible for the Church at Wies (qv).

Former Benedictine Abbey – The history of the abbey goes back to the 8C. After its secularization in 1803, the mother church was destroyed and only the 13C clock tower with its saddleback roof remains today.
On the first floor of the old monastic block is the magnificent **Princes' Gallery**★ (Fürstengang), a 17C masterpiece due to the Wessobrunn School, whose versatility is exemplified in the long hall where painted medallions adorn a vaulted roof covered in stucco-work mingling acanthus leaves, the heads of cherubim and other motifs.

Michelin maps ⑬⑫ and ⑬⑬ I 15
Town plan in the current Michelin Red Guide Deutschland

Until the beginning of the 19C, Wetzlar was a town of lawyers, the seat of one of the law courts of the Holy Roman Empire. Today it is famous for the manufacture of optical and photographic equipment (Leitz). The small format (35mm) film was invented here by the engineer Oscar Barnack in 1924.
The cathedral quarter and three ancient squares, the **Eisenmarkt**, the **Kornmarkt** and the **Schillerplatz**, still bear witness to the town's illustrious past.

SIGHTS

Collegiate Church (Dom) – Of the original 12C Romanesque building, only the north tower of the façade – a sombre construction of dark sandstone and basalt – remains today. Of the subsequent Gothic façade, again, only one Flamboyant 14C tower was completed (in the south). Since this particular stage of the work seems to have been interrupted, the central doorway (whose embellishment, the Coronation of the Virgin, was finished) opens upon nothing.
The sandstone of the south tower is red, in contrast both with the north tower and the light stone in which nave and chancel were eventually finished in 13C Gothic style. Despite its rather bizarre outside appearance, however, the church has two interesting works inside: an ensemble of Gothic frescoes in the south transept; and a fine 14C Pietà in the first chapel off the south aisle.

Local Museum (Stadt-und Industrie Museum) – Closed at present for reorganization.

Lotte's House (Lottehaus) ⊙ – Lotte was Charlotte Buff, the diplomat's fiancée to whom the young Goethe was passionately attracted. The affair – which ended tragically with the suicide of the diplomat – was immortalized by Goethe in The Sufferings of Young Werther, one of the first novels ever to be presented in the form of letters. In this house, which was the young woman's birthplace, glass cases of souvenirs, furniture and other mementoes recall the personality of the heroine.
First editions of Werther, and copies of translations in 30 different languages underline the enormous success of the novel (which Napoleon claimed to have read seven times, one after the other).

Collection of Dr Irmgard von Lemmers-Danforth (Sammlung Dr. Irmgard von Lemmers-Danforth) ⊙ – Kornblumengasse 1. The rooms of a fine 18C house have been transformed into examples of the Renaissance and Baroque styles in Italy, France, Holland and Germany. Paintings, furniture, clocks, jewellery and work by goldsmiths and silversmiths can be admired.

Tribunal Museum (Reichskammergerichtsmuseum) ⊙ – Hofstatt 19. The history of the Holy Roman Empire court in Wetzlar (1693-1806) is evoked by ancient law books, court documents and verdicts, and the portraits of personalities concerned with these trials.

EXCURSIONS

Burg Greifenstein – 17km - 11 miles to the northwest.
This castle was built in the 12C, on a rise overlooking the road from Frankfurt to Cologne – an important trade route in need of protection in the Middle Ages. One of the fortress bastions houses a collection of bells, the oldest of which dates from the 11C.

* **Münzenberg** – *28km - 17 1/2 miles to the southeast.*
Together with those of Gelnhausen and Büdingen *(qv)*, this **feudal stronghold** formed a defensive line destined to protect the Wetterau – an open depression between the Taunus and Vogelsberg massifs. The whole of the depression is visible from the top of the east tower. The ruins are very well preserved, with the outer wall and its bastions emerging from the surrounding greenery. Between the two keeps, fine examples of Romanesque interior decoration can be seen in the living quarters.

* **Arnsburg** – *30km - 18 1/2 miles to the southeast.*
The early Gothic chapter house of this one-time **abbey** is still standing; the abbey **church★**, entirely in ruins, was built to the Cistercian plan, with a flat chevet. The remains of massive columns with Romanesque capitals can be seen in the old transept crossing.

★★ WIES CHURCH (WIESKIRCHE) Bavaria

Michelin map **413** P 23 - Local map see under German ALPINE ROAD

A masterpiece of Bavarian Rococo, Wies Church stands amid the forests, meadows and peat bogs whose gentle undulations characterize the final slopes of the Ammergau Alps between the Lech and the Ammer.

The Architect – It was **Dominikus Zimmermann** (1685-1766), one of the most brilliant members of the **Wessobrunn School** *(qv)*, who was entrusted with the task of building this pilgrimage church "in der Wies" (in the meadow), and dedicated to Jesus Scourged. Aided by his brother Johann Baptist, a painter at the Bavarian court, Zimmermann started the work in 1746, soon after he finished Steinhausen *(qv)* and completed it in 1754. Indeed, much of the church was based on the Steinhausen design: the focal point, as in the earlier edifice, was an oval cupola, which lent itself to painted decorations and emphasized the Rococo approach.

Zimmermann was so pleased with the result, which he considered the most successful of all his works, that he spent the last ten years of his life in a small house near the church.

Church ⊙ – A certain sobriety in the exterior leaves the visitor unprepared for the splendour and magnificence of the oval bay and the long, narrow chancel which prolongs it. Gilded stucco, wood carvings and vividly coloured frescoes stand out from the whitewashed walls, while the richly glowing effect is enhanced by an abundance of light entering through windows whose elaborate design is typical of the architect – an essential feature of the whole, both inside and out.

It is in fact this same finesse in the adaptation of detail to the global effect that strengthens the balance between architecture and ornamentation and achieves that visual harmony for which Wies is renowned. The lower parts of the interior, for example – the walls and paired pillars defining the ambulatory in the usual manner of pilgrimage churches – are deliberately sparsely decorated because they symbolize, in the mind of the designer, the earth. The upper reaches, on the other hand, symbolizing the heavens, vibrate with a profusion of paintings, stucco and gilded work. The immense **cupola fresco** represents the Second Coming, the Gates of Paradise (still closed) and the Court of the Last Judgement with the throne of the Judge himself yet to be occupied.

The decoration of the choir is unparalleled: columns, balustrades, statues, gilded stuccoes and frescoes combine to form a symphony of colour. The wide reredos painting is of Christ Made Man. The richness and delicacy of the lavish ornamentation adorning the organ loft and pulpit mark the high point of the Rococo style in southern Germany.

*The **Michelin Motoring Atlas Great Britain***
provides the motorist in Great Britain
with the best possible information
for route-planning and choosing where to go.

WITTENBERG Saxony-Anhalt   Pop 5 000

Michelin map **987** fold 17

In a pleasant situation between the wooded hills of Fläming and the Elbe, this small town is mainly known because of its connection with Martin Luther.

A Key Town in the Reformation – Summoned by the Elector Friedrich the Wise (1502) to teach philosophy in the university he had just founded, Luther was at the same time appointed the town preacher. After the celebrated public burning of a Papal Bull, Luther was forced to appear before the Imperial Diet at Worms *(qv)*. Then, installed again in Wittenberg in 1522, he was obliged to temper the excesses of his own followers, especially Thomas Müntzer *(qv)*. A year after Luther's death, in 1546 at Eisleben *(qv)*, and eight years before he signed the Peace of Augsburg, allowing freedom of worship to the Lutherans, the Emperor Charles V seized Wittenberg and is said to have meditated over the tomb of the great Reformer.

SIGHTS

★ **Castle Church** (Schlosskirche) – *Am Schlossplatz, in the western part of the town*. The church attached to the royal residence was burned down in 1760 and rebuilt in the Baroque style. It was on the original doors that Luther had pinned up his famous 95 Articles condemning the abuses practised by the Church (1517). The new church contains the text, which was cast in bronze in 1855. Luther's tomb, too, is in this church, and that of Melanchthon *(see below)*, as well as the bronze epitaph to Friedrich the Wise executed in 1527 by Peter Vischer.

★ **Market Place** – In front of the Late Gothic (1440) Town Hall stand statues of Luther (by Schadow, 1821) and his friend and disciple Melanchthon (Drake, 1860). The square is bordered by houses with gables, that in the southwest corner having been the home of the painter Lucas Cranach the Elder from 1505 to 1547, when he was the town's mayor.

Parish Church (Stadtkirche) – *Am Kirchplatz, east of the Market Place*. This triple-aisle Gothic (14C and 15C) church was redecorated in neo-Gothic style in the 18C. The fact that Luther preached here is celebrated in one panel of the 1547 Cranach **Reformation Altarpiece★**. Melanchthon is represented on the left-hand panel.

Melanchthon's House (Gedenkstätte und Museum Melanchthon) ⊙ – *Collegien-strasse 60*. The building in which Luther's companion lived and died is a Renaissance edifice topped by a gable of particularly elegant form. A man of moderate temperament, more tolerant than Luther, the author of the Confession of Augsburg *(qv)* worked for most of his life trying to reconcile the different factions of the Reformation. His study, and many documents relating to his work, can be seen in this house.

★ **Luther's House** (Lutherhaus) ⊙ – *At the far end of the Collegienstrasse*. Occupied by Luther from 1524 onwards, this house faces the courtyard of the Collegium Augusteum, the town's old university. The **Reformation Museum**, housed here since 1883, exhibits collections of antique Bibles, manuscripts, and original editions of Luther's works. One department displays a selection of fine arts from Luther's time: portraits of the Reformer, prints and paintings by Cranach the Elder, canvases by Hans Baldung (Grien), etc.

EXCURSIONS

★★ **Wörlitz Park** (Wörlitzer Park) – *18km - 11 miles to the west*. This huge park in the English style extends over more than 100ha - 250 acres. Landscaped at the end of the 18C, it embraces lakes and several bends of the Elbe. A number of different amenities add to the pleasures of the park. **Wörlitz Castle★** ⊙, for instance, built in the neo-Classical style, houses works by Canaletto, Pesne, Ruysdael and others. The **Gothic House** is a strange building – in fact neo-Gothic – where paintings by Cranach the Elder are on view, along with 15C and 16C stained glass from Switzerland.
A boat trip takes in all these attractions as well as the park itself, with its wealth of statues and wide variety of plants.

★★ WOLFENBÜTTEL Lower Saxony   Pop 50 000

Michelin map 411 O 10

For three centuries, until the Court transferred to Brunswick in 1753, Wolfenbüttel was the seat of the Dukes of Brunswick and Lüneburg. The precise, spacious **plan** of the small town, with die-straight streets linking large squares of symmetrical shape, makes it one of the most successful examples of Renaissance town planning in Germany.

SIGHTS

★★ **Half-timbered Houses** (Fachwerkhäuser) (ABY Z) – Picturesque groups of these houses in different styles reflect the town's social structure under the Dukes. Lining the Kanzleistrasse, the Reichstrasse and the west end of the Harzstrasse, for instance, majestic facades with overhangs on either side of the main entrance distinguish the homes of high Court officials, most of them built c1600. The corbelled upper floors of these houses are supported on brackets. The decoration of smaller houses owned by lesser dignitaries and merchants, oddly enough, is more elaborate. A single gable normally tops their wide, flat facades (Lange Herzogstrasse, Brauergildenstrasse, Holzmarkt, Krambuden). At No 12 Harzstrasse, note the curious grimacing heads above cornices carved with Biblical inscriptions. The simpler, two-storey houses of the less well-to-do (Krumme Strasse, Stobenstrasse) are prettily ornamented with coloured fan designs. The corner houses with oriels which project only slightly are characteristic of Wolfenbüttel. The most harmonious single group of these half-timbered houses is to be found surrounding the main square (Stadtmarkt).

★ **Stadtmarkt** (AZ) – On the north and west side of the square, the Town Hall comprises a number of buildings with splayed beams filled in by brickwork. The Weights and Measures Office has a distinctive arched doorway surmounted by King Solomon's Edict and the Wolfenbüttel coat of arms. Picturesque weather vanes creak in the wind. The philologist **Schottelius**, or Schottel, known as "the father of German grammar", lived in the square in about 1650.

WOLFENBÜTTEL

A statue of Duke Augustus the Young (1635-1666) honours one of the most cultivated princes of the House of Brunswick and Lüneburg.

Castle (Schloss) (AZ) ⊘ – This is reached via an attractive narrow street bordered by arcades known as the Krambuden. Originally a 12C stronghold conquered by Henry the Lion *(qv)*, the building was the subject of many transformations before it evolved into the Baroque residence visible today, complete with several pediments and overlooked by a fine Renaissance **tower★**. In the 16C and 17C, under the rule of several ducal patrons, the castle became a centre of literature and sacred music.

The Ducal Apartments – *Access via a stairway, on the right beneath the porch.* Rare furniture, tapestries, porcelain and valuable paintings recreate the atmosphere of court life, especially during the reigns of Duke Anton-Ulrich and Augustus-Wilhelm (early 18C). Mythological scenes, executed in marquetry with an ivory inlay, adorn the walls of the small study.

Library (Herzog-August Bibliothek) (AYZ) ⊘ – Founded in 1572 by Augustus the Young, and rebuilt at the end of the 19C, this was the largest, most important library in Europe in the 17C. Still an invaluable treasure-house for researchers and scholars, it houses today some 600 000 volumes. Among the priceless manuscripts and illuminated documents from the Middle Ages are *The Story of the Lovely Melusina*, by Jean d'Arras (1478), a rare example of the 14C *Saxon Mirror*, and the first *Helmarshausen Gospel* (12C) said to have belonged to Heinrich the Lion. These are exhibited in the Augusteer Halle and in the room below it. On the left of the latter are two globes, terrestrial and celestial, as well as ancient maps and a portulan (marine chart) which provide interesting information on the state of geographic knowledge and the advances in cartography during the 15C, 16C and 17C. On the right (shown in rotation) are books illustrated by great artists of the present century.

Lessing's House (Lessinghaus) (AZ) ⊘ – Lessing, the great forerunner of German theatre, lived in Wolfenbüttel from 1770 to 1781, working as official ducal librarian and writing, among other works, *Nathan the Wise*. His last home was this mansarded pavilion just before the library on the north side of the esplanade. An evocation of his life and works is on view inside.
On the right of the Lessing house is the **Arsenal** (Zeughaus 1613), a distinctive Renaissance building with projecting gables flanked by obelisks and scrolls. Note the fine rusticated west doorway.

Protestant Church (Hauptkirche) (BZ) – Built on the Kornmarkt in 1608, this Protestant church is laid out in the Gothic manner, with very tall windows and pointed vaulting, but it also has features characteristic of the Late Renaissance.

Note the lateral gables, whose pediments embellished with niches and columns boast a curiously thick decoration of twisted scrollwork. The massive tower with its Baroque roof resembles the castle tower in shape.

Trinity Church (Trinitatiskirche) (BZ) – The church, which closes off the east end of the Holzmarkt, was built in 1719. In its construction, the architects made use of an existing, twin-towered structure which was once a city gate. This explains the strangely flat silhouette of the church. Behind it, a deconsecrated burial ground has been transformed into a romantic **public garden**.

★ **WORMS** Rhineland Palatinate   Pop 76 000

Michelin maps 🔢 and 🔢 I 18 - Local map see under RHINELAND PALATINATE

The city of Worms was, like Speyer and Mainz, an imperial Residence on the banks of the Rhine, a town with a legendary past, a town of history and prestige. Today it extends along the river irrigating the rich soil of the Palatinate Plain vineyards. The **Church of Our Lady** (Liebfrauenkirche – *leave by Remeyerhofstrasse* – B), which stands amidst the vines in the northern suburb, has given its name to the most famous of all Hocks: Liebfrauenmilch (Milk of Our Lady).

Remains (now restored) of the medieval walled town destroyed during the Thirty Years War are visible near the **Torturmplatz (B)** and the **Karolingerstrasse (B 22)**.

Luther before the Diet – Every English schoolboy forced to learn European history has made feeble jokes about "the diet of worms". In fact this particular Diet had perhaps the most far-reaching consequences of any conference before the two world wars (see "The Reformation and the Thirty Years War: Luther"). Summoned before it by the young Charles V in 1521, after a Papal Bull condemning everything he believed in, Luther arrived in Worms "as though going to the torture chamber". He went nevertheless without hesitation, held back by the anxiety of his friends but acclaimed by enthusiastic crowds. Refusing to retract his beliefs, he was banned to the outer parts of the Empire *(see also Wittenberg)*.

★★ **CATHEDRAL (DOM ST PETER) (A)** *time: 30 minutes*

The cathedral is a Romanesque building with two apses quartered in each case by two round towers. From the outside, the **west chancel★★** of this four-towered structure, completed c1230, is one of the finest Romanesque creations in Germany, with its double tier of Rhineland dwarf galleries *(qv)*.

Interior – the best way to go in is through the south (Gothic) doorway. On the tympanum: The Coronation of the Virgin. A splendid Christ in Judgement is on the far side of the door, dating from the 12C. A very old sculpture in the first chapel on the south side represents Daniel in the Lions' Den.

WORMS

The east chancel, with its pointed vaulting, is the oldest: the high altar is the work of Balthazar Neumann *(qv)*. Nine Imperial tombs of relatives of Emperor Konrad II are beneath the choir. The transept crossing, surmounted by a Rhineland cupola on squinches, is admirable.

The Romanesque nave, which has vine bays with diagonally ribbed vaulting, is embellished with blind arcades whose intricate carving typifies the later development of the style. The west chancel, the last to be built, is extremely elegant, with rose windows, a chequered frieze and arches added to its blind arcades.

Five **Gothic sculptures★** in the north aisle (Reliefs aus dem Leben Christi) represent the Annunciation, the Nativity, the Entombment, the Resurrection and the Tree of Jesse.

ADDITIONAL SIGHTS

Luther Monument (Lutherdenkmal) (A) – Unveiled in 1868, the monument commemorates the Reformer's appearance before the Diet. Luther himself, in the centre, is surrounded by the precursors of the Reformation: Pietro Valdo, John Wycliffe, Jan Hus and Savonarola. At the four corners are (back) the Reform theologians Melanchthon and Reuchlin, (front) the Landgrave of Hessen Philip the Magnanimous *(see under Marburg)* and the Elector of Saxony who protected Luther. Seated women symbolize the towns of Speyer, Augsburg and Magdeburg.

★ **Heylshof Museum** (Kunsthaus Heylshof) (A M¹) ⊘ – Installed in the salons of a former town house, this museum displays **paintings★** from the 15C to the 19C. Among them are works by Rubens, Van Loo, Mignard and Knaus. Also on view are ceramics (from Winterthur, Delft and China), glassware and crystal, 300 pieces of Frankenthal porcelain, and examples of 15C and 16C stained glass windows.

★ **Jewish Cemetery** (Judenfriedhof) (A) – Worms was one of the most highly-esteemed centres of Jewish culture in Germany. This ancient burial ground, in use since the 11C, is studded with more than 2 000 steles carved in Hebrew.

Synagogue (B) – Dating also from the 11C (and rebuilt in 1961), this is the oldest synagogue in Germany. Nearby is the Women's Bath-house and the **House of Raschi** (Raschi-haus – B B), an old Jewish school restored to exhibit archives, ceremonial items and other examples of life in the Rhineland Jewish community.

Municipal Museum (Städtisches Museum) (A M²) ⊘ – The historic and prehistoric exhibits are displayed in the Romanesque buildings of a former monastery. Note the collection of helmets in the Roman section. The church contains sacred art, with a lapidary museum in the cloister.

Holy Trinity Church (Dreifaltigkeitskirche) (A D) – Only the tower and façade of the original Baroque (18C) buildings remain. The interior commemorates the Reformation.

St Martin's Church (A E) – The Romanesque west door is flanked by eight columns with crocheted capitals. Note the decorative interlacing of vine stems and leaves on the tympanum.

EXCURSIONS

★ **Rhineland Palatinate** – *See under Rhineland Palatinate.*

★★ WÜRZBURG Bavaria   Pop 124 000

Michelin map **413** M 17

On the far side of the Main and below the episcopal citadel of Marienburg, the original semicircular layout of Würzburg was planned between 1650 and 1750 by three Prince-Bishops of the Schönborn family, who were also responsible for the Baroque churches of the old town and the Residenz palace.

The Master of Würzburg – This was the title bestowed on the great Flamboyant Gothic sculptor **Tilmann Riemenschneider** (1460-1531), who came to live in Würzburg in 1483 and was the town's mayor in 1520 and 1521. Riemenschneider's work was never purely decorative: his whole interest centred on human beings, whose faces, hands – even their clothes – served as vehicles to express emotion and sensitivity. A gravity that is almost melancholy distinguishes his finest work. Among this are the magnificent altarpieces at Creglingen and Rothenburg, the statues in Würzburg's local museum, and the tomb of Heinrich II in Bamberg Cathedral – all priceless treasures of Franconian art.

★★ PALACE (RESIDENZ) (Z) ⊘ *guided tour: 1 hour*

This superb Baroque palace, one of the biggest in Germany, was built between 1720 and 1744 under the direction of that architect of genius, **Balthazar Neumann** *(qv)*, supplanting the old Marienberg stronghold as the bishops' residence.

The monumental **Grand Staircase★** (Treppenhaus), which ends in a double flight and occupies the whole northern part of the vestibule, is one of Neumann's masterpieces. The huge **fresco★★** (600m2 - 6 400sq ft) decorating the vaulted ceiling is by the Venetian, **Tiepolo** (1753). This gigantic work depicts the homage of the four continents then known to the Prince-Bishop Karl-Friedrich von Greiffenklau.

Fresco by Tiepolo in the Imperial Hall of Würzburg Palace

In the Weisser Saal (White Room), between the Grand Staircase and the Imperial Hall, the stuccoes, also Italian, are the work of Antonio Bossi.

The oval **Imperial Hall★★** is splendid. Situated on the first floor, it, too, is adorned with **frescoes by Tiepolo**. Following a fashion current in the Baroque period, the artist makes an impeccable transition, moving imperceptibly from sculpture to false relief painting.

It is also possible to visit the **Imperial Apartments** (Paradezimmer), a luxurious suite of rooms restored in all their splendour with Rococo stucco-work, tapestries and German furniture.

★★ **Church** (Hofkirche) – The architectural fantasy and audacity displayed by Neumann in this building are astonishing. The complex positioning of oval arching, the pink-veined marble columns, the white and gold of false marble highlighting the warm tints of frescoes by the Court painter Rudolf Byss – all of these combine to form a colourful composition rich in contrasts. Two more Tiepolo paintings hang above the side altars: the Assumption and the Fall of the Angels.

★ **Gardens** (Hofgarten) – Astute use of old, stepped bastions has produced a layout of terraced gardens with majestic ramp approaches. From the eastern side, the whole 167m - 545ft of the palace façade, with its elegant central block, is visible. The stucco is the work of Johann Peter Wagner.

★ **Martin von Wagner Museum** – *In the south wing*. On the second floor there is a **painting gallery★** exhibiting German and other European work from the 14C to the 19C. Particularly noteworthy: altar paintings by the Masters of Würzburg (14-16C) and Franconian sculpture, especially that of Riemenschneider. Dutch and Italian painters from the 16C to the 18C are well represented (Tiepolo again).

On the third floor, there is a collection of **antiquities** displaying an interesting series of **painted Greek vases★** (particularly from the 6C to the 4C BC). The department also exhibits Roman pottery, earthenware items, and jewellery from Ancient Egypt. Note the Greek and Roman sculpture and implements made from bronze.

ADDITIONAL SIGHTS ON THE
EAST BANK OF THE MAIN

Cathedral of St Kilian (Dom) (Z) – This basilica with columns and four towers, rebuilt in 1945, preserves its original (11-13C) silhouette, although the interior is marked by many other centuries. The Baroque stucco-work of the chancel contrasts with the high ceiling and simplicity of the Romanesque nave; the **Altar of the Apostles** in the south transept was conceived in 1967 by H Weber as a resting place for three **sandstone sculptures★** by Riemenschneider which were created between 1502 and 1506.

Against the pillars on either of the great nave, **funerary monuments★** to the Prince-Bishops, ranging from the 12C to the 17C, stand in proud array. Those by the 7th and 8th pillar on the north side (Rudolf von Scherenberg and Lorenz von Bibra) are also by Riemenschneider.

The **crypt**, accessible via the north transept, houses a monument (13C) to the founder of the cathedral, Archbishop Bruno. Off the north transept is the **Schönborn Chapel**, built between 1721 and 1736 by Balthazar Neumann and the architect Maximilian von Welsch to take the tombs of the Prince-Bishops of that House. The 15C Gothic **cloister** abuts on the south face of the Cathedral.

Neumünster (YZ B) – The imposing Baroque **west façade** of this church (1710-1716) is attributed to Johann Dientzenhofer. The twin superimposed gables of the central section, sharply curved and richly decorated, lend power to the whole façade.

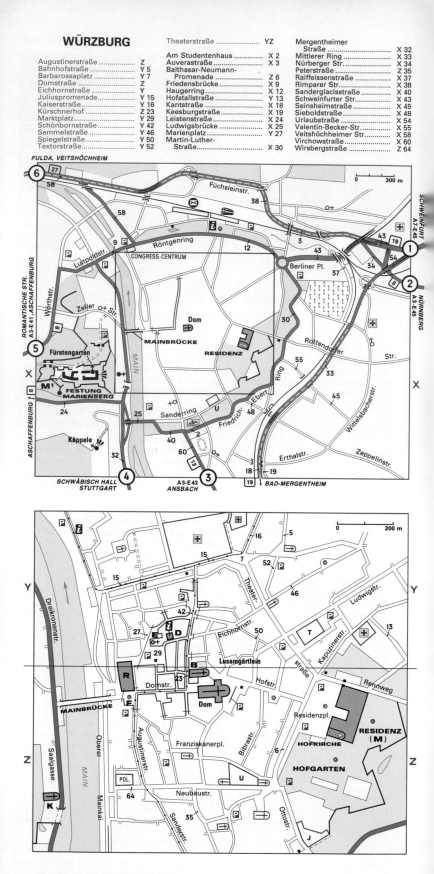

WÜRZBURG

The three-aisle nave inherited from the original Romanesque building was extended at the beginning of the 18C by a huge domed bay at the western end. In niches below this cupola are a Riemenschneider Virgin and Child and a Christ in an unusual pose with arms folded below the chest (14C).

In the west crypt is the **tomb of St Kilian**, apostle, patron of Franconia and missionary, executed in Würzburg in 689.

North of the chancel, on the left, is the entrance to the **Lusamgärtlein**, a small garden laid out on the site of a medieval cloister. It was here, so they say, that the troubadour-poet Walther von der Vogelweide *(qv)*, who died in 1231, is buried.

St Mary's Chapel (Marienkapelle) (Y E) – This fine Gothic hall-church with its lovely upswept lines was built by the town burghers in the 14C and 15C. There is an attractive Annunciation on the tympanum of the north doorway (c1420). Inside the west front is the 1502 tombstone of Konrad von Schaumberg, carved by Riemenschneider and, on the north side, a **Virgin in silver** made by the Master of Augsburg, J Kilian, in 1680.
East of the chapel is the **Falcon House★** (Haus zum Falken) **(D)**, with its graceful 1752 façade decorated in the Rococo style (reconstructed after the war).

★ **Old Bridge (Mainbrücke) (Z)** – Built between 1473 and 1543, the bridge was adorned in the Baroque era with twelve huge sandstone statues of saints.

Town Hall (Rathaus) (YZ R) – A 13C building, once an episcopal residence. The painted façade dates from the 16C. The interior courtyard is charming. The western part, known as the **red building** (Roter Bau), is an example of the Late Renaissance (1659) architectural art. The **fountain (F)** in front of the Town Hall (Vierröhrenbrunnen) dates from 1765.

SIGHTS ON THE WEST BANK OF THE MAIN

★ **Fortress of Marienberg (Festung Marienberg) (X)** ⊘ – From 1253 to 1719, this stronghold was the home of the Prince-Bishops of Würzburg. Built on a commanding height above the west bank of the Main, the original early 13C medieval castle was transformed into a Renaissance palace by Julius Echter c1600. It was under the Schönborn bishops that it became one of the fortresses of the Empire from 1650 onwards.
Marienberg today forms a complex around a rectangular central courtyard in which stand a fine 13C **circular keep**, a circular chapel dedicated to the Virgin (Marienkirche) and a Renaissance covered well that is 104m - 341ft deep. The chapel, crowned by an impressive cupola decorated with Baroque stucco-work, dates back to the early 8C (it was consecrated in 706). It houses many episcopal tombstones.
From the terrace of the **Princes' Garden** (Fürstengarten): a fine **view★** of the town.

★★ **Franconian Museum of the Main (Mainfränkisches Museum) (X M1)** ⊘ – *The entrance is on the right in the fortress's first courtyard.* Among the displays of local art and crafts in this former arsenal (Zeughaus, 1702-1712) is a collection of **Riemenschneider sculptures** (Gallery 3, first floor).
In the splendid vaulted galleries of the **Echterbastei**, religious gold and silver plate, Gothic easel paintings and examples of Franconian folk art can be seen. In the cellars are old wine presses.

St Burkard's Church (Z K) – The chancel of the Romanesque-Gothic (11-15C) riverside church straddles the Uferstrasse (covered passageway). The bust of a Riemenschneider Madonna enlivens the south transept.

Käppele (X) – At the top of a monumental Way of the Cross, this well-situated pilgrim sanctuary comprises a central Baroque chapel with curious bulbous domes and decorations that include Matthäus Günther frescoes and Rococo stucco-work by Johann Michael Feuchtmayer. The finest **view★★** of Würzburg and the river is from the chapel terrace, with the fortress of Marienberg rising from the vineyards in the foreground.

EXCURSIONS

★ **Veitshöchheim Palace** – *7km - 4 miles to the northwest by ⑥ on the town plan.* The castle, built at the end of the 17C and enlarged around 1750 after plans drawn up by Balthazar Neumann, contains splendid Rococo and Empire furniture, including gaming and billiard tables. But it was above all the **park★** that received particular attention from the Prince-Bishops, who improved it so consistently that by the end of the 18C it was an entirely Rococo creation. In the southern part, formalized in the French manner, comical statues people the shaded walks and leafy arbours, brightening avenues bordered by artistically clipped lime trees. In the middle of the great lake stands the superb **Parnassus Group** (Pegasus, the Muses and Apollo), which was carved in 1766.

★ **The Main Valley Vineyards** (Bocksbeutelstrasse) – *Round tour of 87km - 55 miles - allow 1 day. Leave Würzburg via ③ on the town plan.*
It was monks at the beginning of the Middle Ages who introduced viticulture to the Franconian region of the Main – an area with a mild climate and hot, dry summers. The 4 500ha - 11 115 acres under the vine produce mainly white wines from the **Müller-Thurgau** and traditionally fruity Silvaner grape stock. Such wines adapt perfectly to the essentially rich Franconian cooking.

Sommerhausen – A small Franconian walled town. The picturesque gables of the 16C Town Hall and the castle overlook the main street.

Ochsenfurt – Another town still encircled by ancient **ramparts★** punctuated by gates. In the centre, many old half-timbered houses and hotels are adorned with wrought iron statuettes or signs. A clock with mechanical figurines striking the hours is an attraction at the **New Town Hall** (late 15C). At the southwest corner of the building is a graceful 1498 statue of the Virgin. **St Andrew's Church** (Andreaskirche), built between the 13C and the 15C, is noteworthy for its interior decoration.

Frickenhausen – A fortified town dating from late medieval times. There is a beautiful Renaissance gateway with ramshorn scrollwork decorating the pediment. The Town Hall is Late Gothic.

Marktbreit – Here there is a fine **Renaissance ensemble★** formed by the Town Hall, dating from 1579, a bridge (Breitbachbrücke) and the gateway beyond it (Maintor, c1600). Two Baroque houses with corner oriels complete the picture.

Sulzfeld – Another fortified town. The gables of the 17C Town Hall are decorated with projecting scrollwork.

Pass through Kitzingen and Mainstockheim (on the east bank of the Main), and take the road for Dettelbach.

★ **Dettelbach** – This charming fortified market town stands on the northern slopes of the Main valley. See the Late Gothic (c1500) Town Hall and the mid-15C parish church, whose principal tower is linked by a wooden bridge to the smaller staircase tower. Northeast of the upper town is the **Pilgrimage Church "Maria im Sand"** (1608-1613), an interesting example of the transition between Flamboyant Gothic and a Renaissance already tainted by the Baroque. The 1623 **Renaissance doorway★** was made by Michael Kern, who was also responsible for the sandstone and alabaster **pulpit★** (1626).

From Dettelbach to Neuses am Berg, the road crosses an open plateau planted with vines, with good views of the neighbouring slopes. It then drops down again to the valley of the Main and the peaceful village of **Escherndorf**. From Escherndorf, a small ferry crosses the river to Nordheim.

★ **Volkach** – This delightful little wine-growing town lies on the east (outer) side of a wide oxbow curve in the Main. Of the original medieval enclave only two gates remain: the **Gaibacher Tor** and the **Sommeracher Tor**, one at each end of the main street. On one side of the Marktplatz is the **Renaissance Town Hall** (tourist information centre), built – with its double-flight outside stairway and corner turret – in the middle of the 16C. The building known as the **Schelfenhaus**, a civic mansion in the Baroque style dating from c1720, is worth seeing for its interior decorations *(in the Schelfengasse, north of the market place).*

At the northwestern limit of the town *(about 1km - half a mile, in the direction of Fahr)* stands the 15C **Pilgrimage Church "Maria im Weingarten"**, in the middle of vineyards covering the Kirchberg. Inside is the famous **Virgin with Rosary★** (Rosenkranzmadonna), a late work (1512-1524) of Tilmann Riemenschneider, in carved lime wood.

From the Kirchberg there is a superb **panorama** including Volkach, the vineyards and the valley of the Main.

XANTEN Rhineland-Westphalia · Pop 16 000

Michelin map **412** C 12

Xanten, birthplace of Siegfried, hero of the Nibelungen saga *(qv)*, was originally a Roman town and honours St Victor, martyr of the Theban Legion. Traces of the medieval fortifications, such as the 1393 **Cleves Gate** (Klever Tor), can still be found.

★ **St Victor's Cathedral (Dom)** – The south doorway is being restored. One of the finest Gothic buildings in the Lower Rhineland. A Romanesque church was erected here in the 12C on the site of an earlier sanctuary founded by St Helen to house the relics of St Victor. The towers and Westwerk *(qv)* of this, damaged in the Second World War, are nevertheless still standing. The present Gothic structure was begun in 1263, although the five-aisle nave was not completed until the 16C.

The high altar, harbouring the shrine of St Victor, has a handsome reredos by Bartholomäus Bruyn the Elder (1530) which illustrates the lives of St Victor and St Helen. Heinrich Douvermann, the Master Sculptor of Kalkar, created the 1536 Altarpiece of the Virgin, with its intricately worked predella, in the south aisle. The north aisle houses the Altarpiece of St Anthony, which dates from 1500. The outer panels were painted by Derick Baegert. The Gothic **cloister** is 16C.

Cathedral Museum – *Closed for renovation.*

Regional Museum (Regionalmuseum) ⊙ – Roman and Celtic discoveries from archaeological excavations nearby are exhibited on the ground floor. There is a Department of Prehistory. The first floor is reserved for temporary exhibitions.

Archaeological Park (Archäologischer Park) ⊙ – North of the town, near the site of the digs, a Roman town has been reconstituted, complete with perimeter wall, amphitheatre, bath-house, etc.

Each year
the Michelin Red Guide Deutschland
revises its selection of stars for cuisine (good cooking)
mentioning the culinary specialities and local wines;
and proposes a choice of simpler restaurants offering
well prepared meals often regional specialities, at a
moderate price.

★ ZITTAU MOUNTAINS (ZITTAUER GEBIRGE) Saxony

Michelin map 987 fold 18

This range extends for 20km – 12 miles in a southeast-northwest direction, forming an abrupt barrier towering over the Zittau Basin. A favourite region for rock climbers, mountaineers and winter sports enthusiasts, it is also noted for such spas as Lückendorf, Oybin and Jonsdorf, and the trips that can be made from them.
The highest peaks in the range – Lausche (793m - 2 602ft), Hochwald (749m - 2 457ft) and Jonsberg (681m - 2 234ft) – are steep phonolithic (clinkstone) cones extruded among sandstone beds. The juxtaposition of sandstone and limestone heights with the remains of volcanic and igneous eruptions is characteristic of the Zittau Mountains.

ROUND TOUR STARTING FROM ZITTAU

26km - 16 miles - allow about 3 hours

Zittau – The depression in which the town lies is hemmed in by the Zittau Mountains, the Lausitz range and its eastern foothills, and the region drained by the Neisse river. The town's **market place** is dominated by the **Town Hall** (1840-1845), which was built after plans originally drawn up by Karl-Friedrich Schinkel *(qv)* in the Italian Renaissance style.
St John's Church (Johanniskirche, 15-19C) has also been restored on the basis of plans by Schinkel. The **Church of St Peter and St Paul**, once part of a Franciscan monastery, is a Flamboyant Gothic structure (15C) built on Romanesque foundations. The upper part of the tower is Baroque.

Leave Zittau and take the road signposted to Lückendorf.

The road runs through a delightful, hilly landscape punctuated by woods and forests of conifers. The many sandstone outcrops recall the "Swiss Saxony" area *(qv)*.

At Lückendorf, leave the car in the parking place on the right of the road, opposite the Kurhaus "Karl Lucas".

Oybinblick – After ten minutes' walk, there is a fine view of Lückendorf and, on the far side of the frontier, the nearer reaches of Czechoslovakia. Twenty-five yards past the viewpoint, bear left in the direction of Oybinblick, from where there is another splendid view of the Oybin spa and the rock masses of the Grosser Wetterstein and the Kelchstein.

At the exit from Jonsdorf, there is a large car park from which there are opportunities for interesting walks and rambles towards the Steinbruchschmiede, the Waldbühne and the Carola Rock.

West of Jonsdorf rises the bulk of the Lausche, the highest peak in the Zittau range.

Return through Jonsdorf to Zittau.

★★★ THE ZUGSPITZE Bavaria

Michelin map 413 P 24

With a summit at 2 962m - 9 718ft, the Zugspitze is the highest peak on German territory. It is the northwest pillar of the Wetterstein limestone massif, a rocky barrier enclosing the valley of the Loisach.
The matchless panorama it offers, added to extensive ski slopes which can be used up to the beginning of summer in the Schneeferner corrie, have meant that the mountain is particularly well served so far as tourist arrangements are concerned. It can be reached by cable car, either from Schneefernerhaus, terminus of the rack-railway rising from Garmisch, or directly from the Eibsee, or again from the Zugspitzkamm station in Austria, terminus of the cable car from Ehrwald.

THE ASCENT ⊙ *(Be sure to wear warm clothing)*

From Garmisch-Partenkirchen – Departure from the Zugspitzbahn station or the terminus at the Eibsee *(qv)*, accessible by road from Garmisch.
The whole trip lasts 65mn, a 5 000-yd tunnel bored through the mountain ending the rack-railway climb to the Schneefernerhaus. As long as the snow is good (from October to May), the lower part of the corrie known as the Zugspitzplatt offers a skiable area of some 7.5km - almost 3sq miles, equipped with many ski-tow installations reached by leaving the hotel via a short cable-car descent.
To reach the summit **(Gipfelbahn)**, take a lift inside the hotel to the 5th floor, from where the cable-car climb starts.

From the Eibsee – By rack-railway *(see above)*. Cable car direct to the summit.

From the Zugspitzkamm (Austrian Tyrolese side) – *See the current Michelin Green Guide Austria*. The cable car from Ehrwald is linked, at the Zugspitzkamm station (where it is necessary to change cars), to the line reaching the summit. From the Zugspitzkamm, the Schneefernerhaus can be reached on foot via an 800-yd tunnel which is both steep and icy *(20 minutes walk; customs formalities)*.

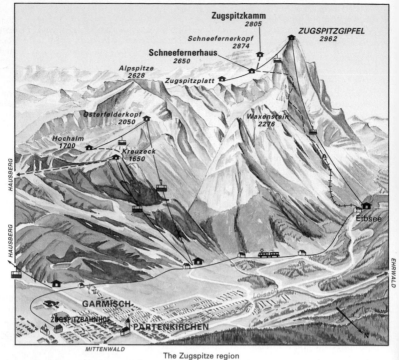

The Zugspitze region

★★ THE SUMMIT (ZUGSPITZGIPFEL)

The upper terminals of the Gipfelbahn and the Eibsee cable car are on the German side, next to the eastern peak of the mountain where a cross has been planted. After that come the "Münchner Haus" refuge and an observatory. The terrace-belvedere by the Gipfelbahn is at an altitude of 2 962m - 9 718ft. On the Austrian side is the upper station of the cable car from the Zugspitzkamm.

The **panorama★★★** to the east reveals the forward bastions of the Kaisergebirge, the Dachstein and the Karwendel, the glacial peaks of the Hohe Tauern (Grossglockner, Gross Venediger), the High Alps of the Tirol (Zillertal, then Stubai and Ötztal to the south) as well as the Ortler and the Bernina.

Nearer, towards the southwest, the mountains of the Arlberg (Silvretta, Rätikon) stand in front of the Säntis in the Appenzell Alps and, further away to the west and northwest, the Allgäu and Ammergau ranges. To the north, the Bavarian lowlands are visible, together with the Ammersee and Starnbergersee lakes.

ZWICKAU Saxony   Pop 116 000

Michelin map 987 fold 27

The geographic site of Zwickau, on the northern edge of the Erzgebirge ("the ore mountains") has played an all-important role in the town's economic development. Since 1316, mines south of the town have been exploited for copper, iron and silver, but it was above all the discovery in 1470 of richer silver-bearing lodes at Schneeberg, a few miles away, which brought prosperity to the city.

On the cultural level, Zwickau is famous as the birthplace of the composer **Robert Schumann** (11810-1856).

SIGHTS

★ **St Mary's Cathedral (Dom St Marien)** – This three-aisle hall-church in the Flamboyant Gothic style was built between 1453 and 1565 on an earlier (13C) construction. Successive stages in the work were directed by the architects N Eichhorn, P Harlass and C Teicher. The Baroque octagonal superstructure crowning the west tower was designed by J Marquardt (1671-1677). The austerity of the cathedral's exterior contrasts vividly with an interior bathed in light, where star-vaulting which appears to leap upwards and outwards from well-spaced slender pillars forms an audacious visual statement.

The jewel of the cathedral's interior decorations is the 1479 **high altar★★** (*sometimes on display in the Municipal Museum, see below*). The six painted panels of the altarpiece, depicting the life of Mary and the Passion of Christ, were executed by Michael Wolgemut of Nuremberg. Also from the School of Nuremberg is the major work of Michael Heuffner, the 1507 **Holy Sepulchre★** (between the two south pillars of the chancel). **The Lamentation of Christ★** (1502), carved in lime wood, is by Peter Breuer, a Master of Zwickau. Paul Speck, a sculptor from Freiberg, executed the **pulpit★** and the **baptismal font** (1538).

The decorations embellishing the various parts of the entrance and the rail leading to the pulpit foreshadow already in their richness the style of the Renaissance (note for instance the terra-cotta medallions with portraits created by J Elsesser in 1560).

Robert Schumann's House ⊘ – *At No 5, Hauptmarkt*. The birthplace of the composer (1810-1856) is arranged to present a retrospective view of his life and works. Schumann passed his childhood in Zwickau but left it at the age of 18 when his education was complete.

Market Place (Marktplatz) – The Marktplatz is surrounded by burghers' houses built at various times between the 15C and the 19C. The **Town Hall** was restored in neo-Gothic style in 1862, although the Council Chamber (formerly St James' Chapel) has preserved its original Gothic lineaments.
The **Gewandhaus**, which has served as a municipal theatre since 1823, unites elements from the Late Gothic and Early Renaissance. It dates from 1525.

Municipal Museum (Städtisches Museum) ⊘ – *At No 1, Lessingstrasse*. Documentation on the history and development of Zwickau, an important collection of minerals and fossils, and sculptures and painting ranging from the 16C to the mid-20C (including, among others, the works of Peter Breuer).

★★ ZWIEFALTEN CHURCH Baden-Württemberg

Michelin map **413** L 22

This village, on the Danubian edge of the Swabian Jura, has a remarkable Baroque church. Like most Baroque edifices in this region, the building contrasts a sober exterior with an interior noteworthy for the sumptuousness of its decoration.

Entering the church, which was built by Johann Michael Fischer between 1739 and 1753, the initial impression is of an extraordinary profusion of luminous colours, a richness and exuberance in the decoration and an extreme virtuosity on the part of the stucco-workers. The eye, intoxicated at first by this deluge of painting, stucco and statues, finally settles on the details: the ceiling paintings devoted to the Virgin, the Feuchtmayer pulpit, the angels and cherubs, in every attitude and from every corner, addressing themselves to the pilgrims.

The choir is separated from the nave by an altar to the Virgin surrounded by superb grilles dating from 1757. The stalls are richly carved and gilded. Before leaving the church, note the most unusual confessionals built to resemble grottoes.

Interior of Zwiefalten Church

EXCURSIONS

★★ The Baroque Churches of Upper Swabia – *Round tour of 84km - 52 miles - allow 4 hours.*
Between Ulm and Lake Constance, the Upper-Swabian Plateau, with its gentle hills and soft light, is scattered with Baroque churches whose fluid, low-key decorations in pastel tints harmonize perfectly with the landscape.

Obermarchtal – The old **abbey church** ⊘ in this small town, dating from 1686, was one of the first to be completed by the Vorarlberg School *(qv)*. The rigidity of the architecture – a Baroque still undeveloped – is accentuated by the heaviness of the furnishings: only the Wessobrunn *(qv)* stucco-work lightens the overall effect.

★ Steinhausen – Designed by Dominikus Zimmermann *(qv)*, master of the Baroque in this part of the country, the abbey church in this hamlet comprises a single nave and a small chancel, both of them oval. A crown of pillars, which supports the inner shell of the vaulting, marks the limit of a gallery circling the nave. The capitals, cornices and window embrasures, carved and coloured, are adorned with birds and insects or flowers with heavy corollas.

Bad Schussenried ☉ – A pleasant small town. The old abbey buildings (now a psychiatric hospital) and the **abbey church** owe their sumptuous Baroque appearance to former Premonstratensian abbots. In the church, the upper panels of the intricately decorated choir stalls (1717) are separated by 28 statuettes representing men and women who founded religious orders. The **library★** has a huge painted ceiling and a sinuous gallery and Rococo balustrade supported by twin columns. The column pedestals are embellished alternately with vivacious cherubim in burlesque costumes and effigies of Fathers of the Church.

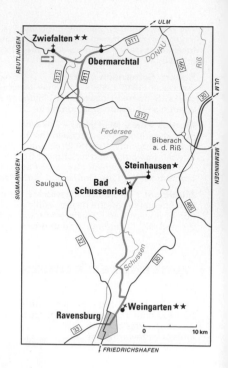

★★ **Weingarten** – A dominant position in this town of 23 000 inhabitants is held by the abbey church, with its fine bare sandstone façade. Consecrated in 1724, the church rivals Ottobeuren as the largest Baroque sanctuary in Germany. It is 102m long and 44m wide at the transepts (335 [88] 144 ft). The west front, framed by two short but elegant towers, is rounded. This, with the construction of a dome on a drum with wide window openings above the transept crossing, betrays an Italian influence transmitted by way of Salzburg.

The interior vistas are amplified by openings pierced through the dividing piers in a manner typical of the Vorarlberg School. The painting and strucco-work, relatively restrained, were entrusted to the masters of the day. Scenes on the vaulting by Comas Damien Asam are full of virtuosity.

Take Route 30 to return to **Ravensburg** *(qv).*

Practical
Information

TRAVELLING TO GERMANY

Formalities – Holders of British, Irish and US passports require no visa to enter Germany, though visas may be necessary for visitors from some Commonwealth countries.

Custom Regulations – Tax-free allowances for various commodities are decided by the EC, but remember that the islands have different regulations.

By air – Various international airline companies operate regular services to one or all of Germany's international airports (Bremen, Cologne/Bonn, Düsseldorf, Dresden, Frankfurt/Mainz, Hamburg, Hanover, Leipzig, Munich, Münster/-Osnabrück, Nürnberg, Stuttgart, Saarbrücken and Berlin).

By rail – The principal travel routes by rail and sea are from:

London, Victoria Station, via Dover and Ostend (sailing: 4 hours; jetfoil: 1 hour 40min) or Sheerness and Vlissingen (sailing: 9 hours);

London, Liverpool Street Station, via Harwich and the Hook of Holland (sailing: 7-9 hours) or Hamburg (sailing: 20 hours);

Hull to Rotterdam (sailing: 13 hours).

By road – When driving to the continent the ideal ports of entry for Germany are **Hamburg** (from Harwich), **Rotterdam** (from Hull), the **Hook of Holland** (from Harwich), **Zeebrugge** (from Hull, Felixstowe and Dover) as well as **Ostend** and **Calais** (both from Dover). From these ports there is a wide choice of routes using motorway or national roads into Germany.
Hamburg to Berlin 289km - 180 miles. Rotterdam to Berlin via Hanover 721km - 448 miles. Vlissingen to Munich via Cologne, Bonn, Mainz, Stuttgart and Augsburg 895km - 556 miles. Ostend to Munich via Regensburg 787km - 489 miles.

TRAVELLING IN GERMANY

By car

Documents – A valid driving licence is required and third-party insurance is compulsory; it is advisable to obtain an International Motor Certificate or a Green Card issued by insurance companies.

Driving Regulations – The **maximum speed** permitted in built-up areas is 50kph - 31mph. On the open road the maximum increases to 100kph - 62mph. There is no official limit on motorways (Autobahnen), but drivers are recommended not to exceed 130kph - 81mph. In Germany careless or reckless driving is considered a serious offence and fines can be stiff.
German motorways are **toll-free** and are well equipped with service areas. These are usually open round the clock and provide the following facilities: petrol, spare parts and accessories, washrooms, toilets, public telephones, refreshments, accommodation and first-aid equipment.
The wearing of **seat belts** is obligatory, in the back as well as in the front of the car. It is necessary to carry the regulation **red triangle**, warning other motorists of a breakdown or enforced roadside halt.
In Germany emergency services are always given priority and drivers should pull to the side of the road.

Breakdown Service – This is taken care of on main roads and motorways by the ADAC (the Auto Club Europa in the eastern part of the country). On-the-spot repairs are free, only the cost of replacement parts being charged.
ADAC Central Breakdown Service, ☎ (01 30) 81 92 11. The Michelin Red Guide Deutschland lists the numbers to use to contact this service in all big towns.

Petrol – The following grades of petrol are available in Germany:
Super Verbleit: Super leaded
Super Plus Bleifrei: Super unleaded (98 octane)
Super Bleifrei: Standard unleaded (95 octane)

Car Hire – Cars may be hired only if the driver is over 23 and has had a driving licence for more than one year.
The major car hire firms (Autohansa, Avis, Europa Service, Hertz, Severin & Co, SU Inter-Rent and Sixt-Budget-Autovermietung) have offices at airports and main stations and in large towns.

Important warning signs:

Anfang/Start	beginning	Rechts einbiegen	turn right
Ausfahrt	exit	Links einbiegen	turn left
Baustelle	road works, site	Rollsplitt	gravel chips
Einbahnstrasse	one-way street	Stau	hold-up, jam
Ende	end	Unfall	accident!
Einfahrt	entrance	Umleitung	deviation
Gefährlich	dangerous	Verengte Spur	road narrows
LKW	heavy lorries, trucks	Vorrang	priority
PKW	private cars	Vorsicht	attention! Look out!

By train

Tickets and fares – Special offer tickets (German National Rail Pass, Two Month Leisure Return, Five Day Return and 10 Day Super Saver) and discount fares (senior citizens and under 26) make good buys. Generally speaking children under 4 travel free and children aged 4-11 years inclusive pay half fare. For further information and reservations apply to:

London – German Rail Sales, c/o DER Travel Service, 18 Conduit Street, London W1R 9TD. ☎ (071) 499 0577;
German Federal Railway, Suite 118, Hudson's Place, Victoria Station, London SW1.

New York – German Rail, 747 Third Avenue, New York NY 10017, ☎ (212) 3 08 31 00.

Los Angeles – German Rail, 11933 Wilshire Bld, Los Angeles, CA 90025. ☎ (213) 4 79 27 72.

Toronto – German Rail, 1290 Bay Street, Toronto, Ontaria M5R 2C3. ☎ (416) 9 68 32 72.

The two railway systems (Deutsche Bundesbahn – DB and the Deutsche Reichsbahn – DR) have a network of some 28 000km and provide a quick and reliable means of transport. Over 50 towns are served by the InterCity and Inter-Regional services. The DB InterCity express operates on certain high-speed routes.

GENERAL INFORMATION

Currency – The unit of currency in Germany is the German Mark (DM), subdivided into 100 Pfennige (Pf).
Although it is unwise to rely entirely on credit cards, they are widely accepted but at times it may be more convenient to make a purchase in cash obtained with a "Eurocard" or "American Express" card.
Banks are open on weekdays from 8.30am to 1pm and 2.30pm to 4pm (5.30pm on Thursdays). They are closed on Saturdays and Sundays.

Post Offices – Post offices are open Mondays to Fridays 8am to 6pm and Saturdays from 8am to 12 noon.
Addresses should always show the international abbreviation W or O in front of the post code of the place concerned.
Post offices with poste restante facilities *(postlagernde Sendungen)* are shown on the town plans in this guide. Poste restante mail is only issued on presentation of a passport or identity card.

Telephone – Off-peak rates apply at weekends. Phonecards for the card-operated call-boxes are available from any post office.
From the UK dial 01049 followed by the local dialling code (omitting the 0) and the subscriber's number.
To telephone the UK from Germany dial 0044 followed by the local code (omitting the 0) and then the subscriber's number.
Ireland: 00353; United States and Canada: 001; Australia: 0061; New Zealand: 0064.

Shops – Normally open between 9am and 6pm Mondays to Fridays; Saturday mornings 9am and 1pm (4-6pm on the first Saturday in the month). Some shops are open until 8.30pm on Thursdays.

Public Holidays – 1 January, Good Friday, Easter Monday, 1 May, Ascension Day, Whit Monday, Corpus Christi (in Catholic regions), 3 October (Day of German Unity), 1 November: All Saints' Day (observed in Baden-Wurttemberg, Bavaria, Rhineland-Palatinate, Rhineland-Westphalia and Saar), Day of Repentance and Prayer (third Wednesday in November) and 25 and 26 December.

ACCOMMODATION

Germany offers a wide range of traditional (Hotel, Gasthof, Gasthaus) accommodation. Lists of local hotels, pensions and boarding houses can be obtained at any tourist information centre.

Hotels – The Michelin Red Guide Deutschland is revised annually and gives a choice of hotels and restaurants based on inspectors' reports. The selection is wide, from the modest inn to the most luxurious grand hotel, from the centrally situated modern establishment catering to the needs of today's businessman to the secluded retreat.
Places listed in the Red Guide are underlined in red on the Michelin map series at a scale of 1:400 000 (maps **411**, **412** and **413**).

German Hotel Reservation Service (ADZ) – Reservations in all hotels, inns and pensions can easily be made through this German reservation centre.
ADZ Allgemeine Deutsche Zimmerreservierung (German Hotel Reservation Service), Corneliusstrasse 34, W-6000 Frankfurt am Main 1. ☎ (069) 74 07 67. Fax (069) 75 10 56. Reservations should be made 4 or 5 weeks in advance. A deposit will be required. English spoken.
Hotel Reservation Service, Drususgasse 7-11, W-5000 Köln 1. ☎ (02 21) 2 07 70. Fax (02 21) 20 77 66 88. Immediate reservation. English spoken.

Bed and Breakfast – The sign *Zimmer Frei* indicates that guest rooms are available. Bookings can be made during office hours, Mondays to Fridays, at the tourist information centres.

Camping and Caravanning – Numerous sites are available to tourists. To obtain a full list and discover the amenities offered by each site, write to:
- ADAC, Am Westpark 8, D-8000 München 70.
- Deutscher Camping-Club (CG), Mandistrasse 28, W-8000 München 40.
- Camping-und-Caravanverband, Postfach 105, W-1080 Berlin.

Youth Hostels (JH) – German youth hostels are open to all young people who are members of the German Youth Hostel Association or of another youth hostel association affiliated to the International Youth Hostel Federation. Priority is given to young people under 26. The stay may not exceed three consecutive nights at any one youth hostel. For lists of all youth hostels apply to the German National Tourist Office. To reserve in advance write to:
Deutsches Jugendherbergswerk, Hauptverband, Bismarckstrasse 8, W-4930 Detmold.
For the Länder of Saxony, Thuringia, Saxony-Anhalt, Mecklenburg-West Pomerania and Brandenburg, write to:
Jugendtourist GmbH, Alexanderplatz 5, O-1026 Berlin. ☎ (0 30) 2 40 62 50.

Holiday villages, flats and bungalows – Details from the German National Tourist Office.

Where to eat – The current Michelin Red Guide Deutschland lists a large selection of restaurants in which tourists can discover for themselves and enjoy the best and most original specialities of each German region (*see the section headed Food and Drink*).
Generally speaking, hotel breakfasts are substantial. But that familiar sinking feeling at midday can easily be assuaged at an "Imbiss". These small fast-food concerns can be found everywhere, in town, on motorways or beside the road. They offer the traditional snack Bratwurst (grilled sausage), sometimes accompanied by a potato salad, and usually washed down with beer (often on draught – Bier vom Fass).
An afternoon break can be taken in a café (tea-room). Such places, which always smell delicious, customarily have a large selection of cakes, notably Schwarzwälder Kirschtorte (Black Forest cherry tart/cake) and Käsekuchen (cheesecake). The coffee served with these pastries is always accompanied by cream (Kaffeesahne).
The Weinstube (wine cellar or wine bar) is an agreeable place, with a pleasant atmosphere, where the best wines can be bought and tasted by the glass.

Spas and Hydrotherapy

Apart from the towns traditionally known for their cures (water or mud), a series of medium-altitude health resorts, and seaside resort thermal establishments, Germany offers a wide choice of spas specializing in what is known as the Kneipp System.

Sebastian Kneipp (1821-1897), curate and then priest at Wörishofen, evolved after an illness, the set of treatments named after him which consists of baths, an alternation of warm and cold showers and a "healthy" life-style. In the Kneipp cure, the latter involves a strictly controlled diet, plenty of walking and medication based on plants.
Among the principal cure towns are: Baden-Baden, Badenweiler, Bad Brückenau, Bad Doberan, Bad Düben, Bad Ems, Bad Homburg, Bad Kissingen, Bad Kreuznach, Bad Langensalza, Bad Orb, Bad Pyrmont, St Peter-Ording, Bad Reichenhall, Bad Stölz, Bad Vilbel, Bad Wiessee and Bad Wildungen.
The best-known climatic health resorts are: Bayrischzell, Bad Bergzabern, Braunlage, Freudenstadt, Garmisch-Partenkirchen, Hahnenklee, Bad Herrenalb, Königstein im Taunus, Isny, Oberstdorf, Rheinsberg, Rottach-Egern, St Blaisen, Schönwald, Bad Suderode and Titisee-Neustadt.
On the North Sea Coast are: Borkum, Helgoland, Juist, Norderney, Wangerooge, Westerland auf Sylt, Wyk auf Föhr;
and on the Baltic coast: Damp, Grömitz, Heiligenhafen, Scharbeutz-Haffkrug, Timmendorfer-Strand and Heiligendamm.
Details of these and other health resorts can be obtained by writing to: Deutsche Bäderverband zur Verfügung, Schumannstrasse 11, W-5300 Bonn 1.

Gourmands or gourmets
Each year the **Michelin Red Guide Deutschland**
gives an up-to-date selection
of establishments renowned for their cuisine.
German gastronomic specialities
are described on page 34.

TOURIST INFORMATION

German National Tourist Offices

London: German National Tourist Office, Nightingale House, 65 Curzon Street, GB W1Y 7PE, ☎ (071) 495 3990;

New York: German National Tourist Office, 747 Third Avenue, 33rd floor, New York, NY 10017, ☎ (212) 308 3300;

Chicago: German National Tourist Office, c/o German American Chamber of Commerce, 104 S Michigan Avenue, Suite 600 Chicago, IL 60603 5978, ☎ (312) 782 8557;

Toronto: German National Tourist Office, 175 Bloor Street East, North Tower, 6th floor, Toronto, Ontario M4W 3R8, ☎ (416) 968 1570;

Sydney: German National Tourist Office, Lufthansa House, 12th floor, 143 Macquarie Street, Sydney 2000, ☎ (02) 367 3890.

Tourist Offices of the German Länder

Schleswig-Holstein – Fremdenverkehrsverband, Schleswig-Holstein e.V, Niemannsweg 31, W-2300 Kiel 1. ☎ (04 31) 5 60 00. Fax: (04 31) 56 98 10.

Hamburg – Tourismus-Zentrale Hamburg GmbH, Buchardstrasse 14, Postfach 102249, W-2000 Hamburg 1. ☎ (0 40) 30 05 10. Fax: (0 40) 30 05 12 53.

North Sea – Lower Saxony – Bremen – Fremdenverkehrsverband Nordsee-Niedersachsen-Bremen, e.V., Bahnhofstrasse 19-20, Postfach 1820, W-2900 Oldenburg. ☎ (04 41) 92 17 10. Fax: (04 41) 9 21 71 90.

Harz – Harzer Verkehrsverband, Marktstrasse 45, W-3380 Goslar. ☎ (0 53 21) 2 00 31. Fax: (0 53 21) 2 33 68.

Westphalia – Landesverkehrsverband Westfalen e.V., Friedensplatz 3, W-4600 Dortmund. ☎ (02 31) 52 75 06/07.

Rhineland – Landesverkehrsverband Rheinland e.V., Rheinallee 69, Postfach 200861, W-5300 Bonn 2. ☎ (02 28) 36 29 21/22. Fax: (02 28) 36 39 29.

Rhineland-Palatinate – Fremdenverkehrs- und Heilbäderverband, Rheinland-Pfalz e.V., Löhrstrasse 103-105, Postfach 1420, W-5400 Koblenz. ☎ (02 61) 3 10 79. Fax: (02 61) 1 83 43.

Saar – Fremdenverkehrsverband Saarland e.V.,Dudweiler Strasse 53, Postfach 242, W-6600 Saarbrücken. ☎ (06 81) 3 53 76 and 3 70 88. Fax: (06 81) 3 58 41.

Hessen – Hessischer Fremdenverkehrsverband e.V., Abraham-Lincoln-Strasse 38-42, W-6200 Wiesbaden. ☎ (06 11) 77 88 00. Fax: (06 11) 77 42 66.

Baden-Württemberg – Landesfremdenverkehrsverband Baden-Württemberg, Esslinger Strasse 8, W-7000 Stuttgart 10. ☎ (07 11) 24 73 64. Fax: (07 11) 24 23 61.

Fremdenverkehrsverband Schwarzwald e.V., Bertoldstrasse 45, Postfach 1660, W-7800 Freiburg. ☎ (07 61) 3 13 17/18. Fax: (07 61) 3 60 21.

Fremdenverkehrsverband Bodensee-Oberschwaben, Schützenstrasse 8, W-7755 Konstanz. ☎ (0 75 31) 2 22 32. Fax: (0 75 31) 1 64 43.

Bavaria – Landesfremdenverkehrsverband Bayern e.V, Prinzregentenstrasse 18, Postfach 221352, W 8000 München 22. ☎ (0 89) 22 94 91/93. Fax: (0 89) 29 35 82.

Mecklemburg-West Pomerania – Landesfremdenverkehrsverband Mecklenburg-Vorpommern e.V., Hauptgeschäftsstelle, Platz der Freundschaft 1, O-2500 Rostock 1.

Saxony-Anhalt – Landesfremdenverkehrsverband Sachsen-Anhalt e.V., Trothaer Strasse 9 h, O-4050 Halle/Saale. ☎ (03 45) 34 00 86. Fax: (03 45) 2 84 73.

Thuringia – Thüringer Landesfremdenverkehrsverband e.V., Staufenberger Allee 18 a, O-5025 Erfurt. ☎ (03 61) 5 15 01.

Saxony – Landesfremdenverkehrsverband Sachsen e.V., Maternistrasse 17, O-8010 Dresden. ☎ (03 51) 4 84 53 75. Fax: (03 51) 4 84 55 61.

Brandenburg – Landesfremdenverkehrsverband Brandenburg e.V., Friedrich-Ebert-Strasse 115, 0-1560 Potsdam. ☎ (03 31) 4 22 21.

Berlin – Verkehrsamt Berlin, Martin-Luther-Strasse 105, O-1000 Berlin 62. ☎ (0 30) 21 23 4. Fax: (0 30) 21 23 25 20.

Informationszentrum, Am Fernsehturn, 1020 Berlin-Mitte. ☎ (00 37) 2/2 12 46 75.

*The current **Michelin Red Guide Deutschland** offers*
a selection of pleasant hotels in convenient locations.
Each entry specifies the facilities available (gardens,
tennis courts, swimming pool, beach facilities)
and the annual opening and closing dates.
There is also a selection of establishments recommended for their
cuisine – well-prepared meals at moderate prices; stars for good cooking.

DISCOVERING GERMANY

If the traditional summer holiday tour allows visitors to discover the richness and beauty of Germany under the best possible conditions (pleasant climate, plenty to see and do), there are many other ways to appreciate the warmth of German hospitality and explore the charms of this great country.

The tourist routes – Very clearly signposted, these "thematic" itineraries provide an original means of crisscrossing the country and getting to know it better. Among the most famous are:

The **German Holiday Route** (Deutsche Ferienstrasse), which links the Baltic Sea (Puttgarden) with the Alps (Berchtesgaden);

The **German Alpine Road** (Deutsche Alpenstrasse), from Lindau to Berchtesgaden;

The **German Wine Road** (Deutsche Weinstrasse), from Heidelberg to Nuremberg;

The **Castles Route** (Burgenstrasse), from Würzburg to Füssen;

The **Upper Swabian Baroque Route** (Oberschwäbische Barockstrasse), from Ulm to Weingarten.

Rambling – Those who long for peaceful holidays will delight in the countrywide network of footpaths and ramblers' routes, all of them clearly signposted. Whether it's a matter of a three-day hike or a simple walk around a chosen area, many maps are available for the preparation of an itinerary. KOMPASS maps and guides cover the most popular tourist regions.

Carnival Time – The three days before Ash Wednesday unite a population traditionally calm and sober in a continuous fête that is both joyful and boisterous. The carnival is at its liveliest in Cologne, Düsseldorf, Mainz, Munich and the towns of the Black Forest.

Cologne Carnival: details from the Verkehrsamt der Stadt Köln, Unter Fettenhennen 19, W-5000 Köln 1. ☎ (02 21) 2 21 33 40.

Munich Carnival: details from Fremdenverkehrsamt München, Postfach, W-8000 München 1. ☎ (0 89) 2 39 11.

In the Rhineland regions, the Thursday of the week preceding Ash Wednesday is known as the "Fetter Donnerstag" or "Schmutziger Donnerstag". This is in fact a "Ladies Choice" day, on which the initiative is taken by the female sex.

The Fools Procession, Rottweil

Cruises

Rhine, Moselle, Main and Elbe – For cruises on the Moselle and Main, and Rhine cruises from Cologne to Mainz as well as those on the Elbe from Hamburg to Dresden, all the relevant details can be obtained by writing to KD, Köln-Düsseldorfer, Frankenwerft 15, W-5000 Köln 1. Information ☎ (02 21) 2 08 80. Reservations ☎ (02 21) 20 88 288, Fax (02 21) 20 88 231 + 229

At Dresden it is possible to prolong the trip as far as Prague. Ask for the dates.

The North Sea – From Cuxhaven or Hamburg to Helgoland, from Travemünde to Rostock, and from Travemünde to Rodbyhavn (Denmark), details can be obtained from: Seetouristik, Eppendorfer Weg 127, D-2000 Hamburg 20. ☎ (0 40) 40 29 29, Fax (0 40) 490 33 88.

Connections between Stralsund, Rügen, the Isle of Usedom and Poland – These are all operated by Die "Weisse Flotte" GmbH, O-2300 Stralsund. ☎ (0 38 31) 69 23 70, Fax (0 38 31) 69 23 67.

Germany seen from the train – This is another, and equally attractive , way of seeing the country. The German National Rail Pass – or German Rail Youth Pass for those under 26 years of age – allows unlimited acces to all scheduled DB and DR trains and buses, and boats on the Rhine and Moselle. A series of Regional Rail Passes also exists (*see p 309*).

Winter Sports – In Germany there is a wide variety of ski stations, all of them well equipped and easy to reach.

RESORTS	Michelin map no and map co-ordinates	Min and max altitude (in metres) of resort	Cable cars and chair lifts	Ski lifts	Extent (in km) of trails for downhill skiing	Extent (in km) of trails for cross-country skiing	Beds available
OBERSTAUFEN	413 N 24	800/1 700	3	34	30	120	7 000
IMMENSTADT	413 N 24	730/1 750	3	12	40	67	3 750
RETTENBERG/KRANZEGG	413 N 24	850/1 700		15	30	30	1 200
HINDELANG/OBERJOCH	413 O 24	850/1 600	1	16	32	45	7 000
FISCHEN im ALLGÄU	413 N 24	760/1 665	5	26	50	100	5 215
OBERSTDORF	413 N 24	843/2 224	7	19	42	80	16 700
FÜSSEN	413 P 24	800/1 800	3	7	15	60	5 500
PFRONTEN	413 O 24	900/1 840	2	14	25	65	5 400
NESSELWANG	413 O 24	860/1 600	2	6	8	40	3 000
GARMISCH-PARTENKIRCHEN	413 Q 24	720/2 720	15	39	73	32	10 050
BAD TÖLZ	413 R 23	700/1 237	1	4	8	75	4 400
MITTENWALD	413 Q 24	920/2 244	1	7	22	40	5 835
BAD WIESSEE							
GMUND							
KREUTH	413 S 23	735/1 700	2	18	15	95	14 000
ROTTACH-EGERN							
TEGERNSEE							
SCHLIERSEE-SPITZING	413 S 23	800/1 700	4	15	30	30	4 000
INZELL	413 V 23	700/900		5	5	40	5 500
REIT IM WINKL	413 U 23	700/1 850	3	20	50	80	4 800
RUHPOLDING	413 U 23	690/1 670	4	16	35	60	6 400
BAD REICHENHALL	413 V 23	470/1 800	4	1	11	18	10 000
BERCHTESGADEN	413 V 24	540/1 800	5	24	40	57	25 200
BISCHOFSMAIS	413 W 20	720/1 100		5	3	60	2 500
BODENMAIS	413 W 19	600/1 456		7	9	65	4 900
GRAFENAU	413 X 20	700		2	1	65	3 000
ZWIESEL	413 W 19	560/1 456		9	10	120	3 000
BAIERSBRONN	413 I 21	560/1 000		9	4	62	12 000
FELDBERG	413 H 23	900/1 493		17	42	45	4 200
FREUDENSTADT	413 I 21	700/1 000		4	2	120	6 596
HINTERZARTEN	413 H 23	900/1 200		3	2	15	3 000
SCHÖNWALD	413 H 22	950/1 150		4	2	42	3 800
St-GEORGEN	413 I 22	800/1 050		5		33	1 500
TITISEE-NEUSTADT	413 H 23	850/1 050		4	2	54	4 685
TODTNAU	413 G 23	660/1 388		21	40	60	4 500
TODTMOOS	413 G 23	800/1 263		4	7	27	4 000
ALTENAU	411 O 11	420/930		5	1	30	6 500
BAD HARZBURG	411 O 11	300/900		3	2	40	4 500
BAD LAUTERBERG	411 O 12	500/700		1		42	4 000
BAD SACHSA	411 O 12	450/700		3	4	48	3 500
BRAUNLAGE	411 O 11	560/980		9	12	46	7 900
HAHNENKLEE	411 O 11	600/730		2	4	21	5 600
St-ANDREASBERG	411 O 11	600/900		9	8	42	2 700

Alps

Bavarian Forest

Black Forest

Harz

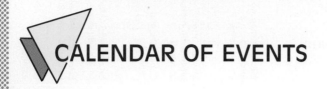

CALENDAR OF EVENTS

1 January
Garmisch-Partenkirchen . . . New Year's Day International Ski Jump

Last 10 days in January
Berlin. . . . . International Green Week

Sunday before Shrove Tuesday
Munich. München Narrisch – Carnival

Shrove Monday
Cologne, Düsseldorf, Mainz Rosenmontagszug – Rose Monday: procession, street carnival

Shrove Monday and Tuesday
Rottweil. Narrensprung Carnival: elaborate traditional costumes and expressive wooden masks – Dance of the Fools

Mid-April to the end of June
Karlsruhe. . . . . European Cultural Festival: theatre, music and exhibitions

30 April
Towns in the Harz region . Walpurgisnacht - Witches Sabbath festivities

Night of 30 April - 1 May
Marburg. . . . . Students Festival

One Sunday per month: Easter to September
**Rothenburg
ob der Tauber** . . . . Schäfertanz - Shepherds Dance

End of April to end of May
Wiesbaden. . . . . May Festival: theatre and music

Mid-May to mid-September: Sundays at noon
Hamelin. Rattenfängerspiel: pageant retracing the legend of the Pied Piper

Friday after Ascension
Weingarten . . . . Blutritt - mounted cavalcade in honour of the Sacred Blood

May to June
Schwetzingen. . . . . Festival of Classical Music

End of May, beginning of June
Dresden. Music Festival

Whit Sunday
Schwäbisch Hall . . . . Küchen- und Brunnenfest : dance of the salt-workers in 16C costume

Whit Monday
Kötzing. Pfingstritt - mounted cavalcade

Tuesday after Whitsun
Deidesheim . . . . Historische Geissbockversteigerung - auction sale of a goat (period costumes, folk dancing and local fair)

Last Saturday in May
Merfelder Bruch . . . . Roundup of wild horses, rodeo

Friday, Saturday and Whit Sunday; 2nd Sunday in July; 1st Sunday in September
**Rothenburg
ob der Tauber** . . . . Meistertrunk - performance of the "Long Drink" legend; evocation of the Thirty Years War by the population in period costume; local festival

Corpus Christi Day

Munich..................... Solemn procession through the decorated town

Cologne.................... Procession of boats on the River Rhine

Hüflingen .... Procession through flower-decked street

14 days after Whitsun, from Friday to Monday

Schwalmstadt .... Salatkirmes (Salad Fair) commemorating the introduction of the potato in Hessen, local costume

Mid-June to mid-August

Schwäbisch Hall .... Open-air theatre performances

First weekend in June and September; second weekend in July

Heidelberg .... Castle illuminations, firework displays

June-August

Chorin...................... Chorin Music Festival

Feuchtwangen............. Cloister Festival (theatre)

Bad Hersfeld .... Festival of Drama and Opera in the abbey ruins

Last week in June

Kiel........................ Kiel Week - International Sailing Regatta

End of June to mid July, every four years (next time: 1993)

Landshut................... Landshuter Hochzeit (the Landshut Marriage) – pageant in period costume

July-August

Different places in Schleswig-Holstein .... Schleswig-Holstein Music Festival

First Sunday of July

Hanover.................... Markmen's Festival - procession of marksmen

Second weekend of July

Speyer .... Brezelfest - Bretzel Festival

Mid-July to mid-August

Pommersfelden............ Collegium Musicum (daily musical performances)

Mid-July, every four years (next time: 1994)

Ulm .... Fischerstechen (Day of the Fisherman)

One week from the Friday preceding the third Monday in July

Dinkelsbühl .... Kinderzeche (commemorating the saving of the town by a deputation of children)

Penultimate Monday in July

Ulm .... Schwörmontag (day of the vows) – procession of boats on the Danube

Third Sunday and Monday of July

Kaufbeuren .... Tänzelfest – great historic cavalcade featuring local schoolchildren

Last Saturday of July to 1st Sunday in August

Hitzacker................... Summer Music Festival

End of July to end of August

Bayreuth .... Richard Wagner Festival

Second Saturday of August

Koblenz .... The Rhine Ablaze – illumination of the river valley from Braubach to Koblenz

Constance.................. Seenachtsfest – night-time festival by the lake

Second week of August

Furth im Wald .... Der Drachenstich (Death of the Dragon) – the legend of St George, enacted as a pageant with a procession in period costumes

Saturday following August 24

Markgröningen .... Schäferlauf – shepherds race

First Sunday of September

Bad Dürkheim .... Wurstmarkt (sausage fair) and important wine fair

Third Saturday of September

St. Goar.................... Illumination of the Rhine and its castles

End of September - beginning of October

Bad Cannstatt .... Cannstatter Volksfest – popular local festival

Munich.................... Oktoberfest – the beer festival

First week of October

**Neustadt
an der Weinstrasse** .... Wine Fair, election of the Queen of Wine

First or second ten days of October

Frankfurt am Main......... Frankfurt Book Fair

Third weekend in October

Donaueschingen........... Donaueschingen Music days (especially
contemporary music)

Last ten days of October

Bremen .... Bremer Freimarkt : the city's free market, the most
popular fair in northern Germany

6 November (St Leonard)

Bad Tölz .... Leonhardifahrt – equestrian procession in honour
of St Leonard

Sunday following the 6 November

Benediktbeuren............ Leonhardifahrt *(see above)*

10 November

Düsseldorf .... Martinmas Festival – procession of children
carrying Chinese lanterns

From the Friday before Advent to the 24 December

Nuremberg................. Christkindlesmarkt – Christmas Market, Christmas
tree decorations and gifts, seasonal performances
by children

24 December

Villingen-Schwenningen... Kuhreihenblasen – concert of Sheperds' Horns

Christmas Eve and New Years' Eve

Berchtesgaden............. Weihnachtsschiessen ; Neujahrsschiessen –
Christmas and New Year shooting matches

*Help us in our constant task of keeping up to date.
Send your comments and suggestions to*

**Michelin Tyre PLC
Tourism Department
Davy House
Lyon Road
HARROW Middlesex HA1 2DQ
Fax: 081 863 0680**

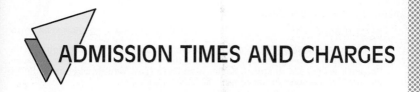

ADMISSION TIMES AND CHARGES

As admission times and charges are subject to modification due to increases in the cost of living, the information printed below is given for guidance only.

The following list details the opening times and charges (if any) and other relevant information concerning all sights in the descriptive part of this Guide accompanied by the symbol ⊙. The entries below are given in the same order as in the alphabetical section of the Guide.

*Normally, especially in the case of large towns, the telephone number and/or address of the local Tourist Information Centre, indicated by the symbol **i**, is given. Generally most efficient, these organizations are able to help passing tourists find accommodation (hotel, pension, camp site, youth hostel...) as well as providing information on exhibitions, performances, guided tours and other items of interest locally.*

The prices quoted apply to individual adults but many places offer reduced rates for children, OAPs and some a discount family ticket.

The times are those of opening and closure but remember that some places do not admit visitors during the last hour or half hour.

A

AACHEN   **i** Friedrich-Wilhem-Platz ☎ (02 41) 1 80 29 60.

Cathedral and Cathedral Treasury Open Mondays from 10am to 2pm; Tuesdays to Saturdays from 10am to 6pm (5pm from October to the end of March); Sundays and public holidays from 10.30am to 5pm. Closed Mondays, Good Friday, 25 December and during the carnival season. Guided tour (1 hour 30min) available. 3DM. ☎ (02 41) 4 77 09 27.

Town Hall – Open daily from 8am (10am Saturdays and Sundays) to 1pm, and from 2pm to 5pm. 1DM. ☎ (02 41) 1 80 29 60.

Couven Museum – Open daily from 10am to 6pm (1pm Sundays). Closed Mondays and public holidays. 2DM. ☎ (02 41) 4 32 44 21.

Suermondt-Ludwig Museum – Same times and charge as for the Couven Museum above. ☎ (02 41) 4 32 44 00.

Ludwig International Art Forum – Open daily from 11am to 7pm (10pm Thursdays). Closed Mondays. 4DM (entrance free the 1st Sunday of each month). ☎ (02 41) 18 07 0.

German ALPINE ROAD

Wendelstein – Funicular Railway : departures hourly from the lower (Brannenburg-Waching) station : May to October 9am to 3pm (last return from the upper station, 5pm); December to the end of April, 9am to 1pm (last return 4pm). Length of journey: 1 hour. 32.50DM Rtn. ☎ (0 80 34) 20 71.

Annaberg-Buchholz

The Frohnau Forge – Guided tours (1 hour) daily from 9am to 11.45am and from 1pm to 4pm. Closed Mondays from October to the end of April, and on 24, 25, 31 December and 1 January. 3DM. ☎ (0 37 33) 20 00.

Ansbach   **i** ☎ (09 81) 5 12 43.

Castle – Guided tours (1 hour): April to September at 9am, 10am, 11am, 2pm, 3pm and 4pm; October to March at 10am, 11am, 2pm and 3pm. Closed Mondays. 3DM (entrance free for children under 16). ☎ (09 81) 31 86.

Aschaffenburg   **i** ☎ (0 60 21) 3 04 26

Castle:

State Gallery – Open: April to September, from 9am to 12 noon and from 1pm to 5pm; October to March, from 10am to 12 noon and from 1pm to 4pm. Closed Mondays, also 1 January, 1 November, 24, 25 and 31 December. 3DM. ☎ (0 60 21) 2 24 17.

Municipal Museum – Open daily from 9am (10am from October to the end of March) to 12 noon and from 1pm to 5pm. Closed Mondays, also 1 November, 24 and 25 December. 3DM. ☎ (0 60 21) 3 04 46.

AUGSBURG
🅹 Bahnhofstrasse 7. ☎ (08 21) 50 20 70.

Municipal Art Gallery – Open daily from 10am to 5pm (4pm from October to the end of April). Closed Mondays, and also the Sunday before Shrove Tuesday, Shrove Tuesday, Good Friday, Easter Monday, 1 May, Whit-Monday and the 24, 25 and 31 December. Entrance free. ☎ (08 21) 3 24 21 75.

Maximilian Museum – Same opening hours as the Municipal Art Gallery. 3DM. ☎ (08 21) 3 24 21 74.

Mozart Family House – Open Mondays, Wednesdays and Thursdays from 10am to 12 noon and from 2pm to 5pm, Fridays until 4 pm only, Saturdays and Sundays from 10am to 12 noon. Closed Tuesdays. 2DM; entrance free Saturdays, Sundays and public holidays. ☎ (08 21) 3 24 21 96.

State Gallery – Open the same hours as the Municipal Art Gallery, except that on Wednesday evening closing time is at 9pm. 3DM; entrance free Saturdays, Sundays and public holidays. ☎ (08 21) 3 24 21 78.

B

BADEN-BADEN
🅹 Augustaplatz 8. ☎ (0 72 21) 27 52 00.

New Castle – Guided tour (3/4hour) from May to the end of September at 3pm. Closed Saturdays, Sundays and holidays. 4DM. ☎ (0 72 21) 2 55 97.

Roman Baths – Open Good Friday to 31 October, daily from 10am to 12 noon and from 1.30pm to 4pm. 2.50DM. ☎ (0 72 21) 2 75 or 9 36.

BADENWEILER Excursions
🅹 ☎ (0 76 32) 7 21 10.

Bürgeln Castle – Guided tours (45min) from February to the end of November at 11am, 2pm, 3pm, 4pm, 5pm. Closed Tuesdays. 4DM. ☎ 0 76 26/227.

BAD HERSFELD
🅹 ☎ (0 66 21) 20 12 74.

Abbey Church Ruins – Open 15 March to 30 April and from 15 September to 31 October, daily except Mondays from 10am to 12.30pm and from 2pm to 5pm. Closed from November to mid-March and during the Festival of Dramatic Art (May to mid-September). 1DM. ☎ (0 66 21) 20 12 95.

BAD KREUZNACH
🅹 ☎ (06 71) 9 23 25.

Römerhalle – Open daily from 10am to 5pm. Closed Mondays. 2DM. ☎ (06 71) 92-2 48.

BAD MERGENTHEIM
🅹 ☎ (0 79 31) 5 71 35.

Castle of the Teutonic Order – Open: Tuesdays to Fridays, daily from 2.30pm to 5.30pm, Saturdays, Sundays and public holidays from 10am to 12 noon and from 2.30pm to 5.30pm (from November to the end of February, Saturdays, Sundays and public holidays only). 3DM. ☎ (0 79 31) 5 71 35.

Excursions

Stuppach Parish Church – Open: March and April daily from 10am to 5pm; May to October daily from 9am to 5.30pm; November to February daily from 11am to 4pm. Closed 25 and 31 December. 1.50DM. ☎ (0 79 31) 26 05.

BAD REICHENHALL
🅹 ☎ (0 86 51) 30 03.

Old Salt Works – Guided tours (45min): April to October, daily from 10am to 11.30am and from 2pm to 4pm; November to March, Tuesdays and Thursdays only, from 2pm to 4pm. 6DM. ☎ (0 86 51) 70 02-0.

BAD TÖLZ Excursions
🅹 ☎ (0 80 41) 7 00 71.

Benediktbeuern Abbey Church – Open 9am (10am Sundays and public holidays) to 6pm. Entrance free.

BAD WIMPFEN
🅹 ☎ (0 70 63) 5 31 51.

Church of St Peter and St Paul: Cloister – Guided tours (1 hour) daily from 9am to 5pm by arrangement only: ☎ 0 70 63/70 75.

Sinsheim Automobile and Technical Museum – Open daily from 9am to 6pm. 13DM. ☎ (0 72 61) 6 11 16.

Gutlenberg Castle – Open from March to end of October, daily from 10.30am to 5pm. 3.50DM. ☎ (0 62 66) 13 73.

Hornberg Castle – Open daily from 8am to 8pm. 3.50DM. ☎ (0 62 61) 50 01.

Neckarsulm German Cycle and Motorcycle Museum – Open daily from 9am to 12 noon and from 1.30pm to 5pm (9am to 5pm uninterrupted on Sundays). 5DM. ☎ (0 71 32) 3 52 71.

BAMBERG
𝒊 Gayersworthstrasse 3. ☎ (09 51) 2 10 40.

Diocesan Museum – Open April to October, daily from 10am to 5pm. Closed Mondays and Good Friday. 2DM. ☎ (09 51) 50 23 29.

New Residence – Guided tours (45min) daily from 9am to 12 noon and from 1.30pm to 5pm (4pm from October to the end of March). Closed 1 January, Shrove Tuesday, 1 November, 24, 25 and 31 December. 3DM. ☎ (09 51) 5 63 51.

Hoffmann's House – Open May to the end of October, 4pm to 6pm Tuesdays to Fridays ; 10am to 12 noon Saturdays, Sundays and public holidays. Closed Mondays. 1DM.

Excursions

Pommersfelden Castle – Guided tours (30min to 1 hour) from April to the end of October, daily from 9am to 12 noon and from 2pm to 5pm. Closed Mondays. 3-6DM. ☎ (0 95 48) 2 03.

BAVARIAN FOREST

Grosser Arber – The chairlift is in service from 8am to 5.45pm in summer, approximately 4.45pm in winter. No service from mid-October to mid-December. 8DM. ☎ (0 99 25) 5 42.

BAUTZEN

Museum of Sorbian History and Culture – Open daily from 10am to 12.30pm and from 1pm to 5pm (4pm from November to the end of March). 2DM. ☎ (0 35 91) 4 24 03.

BAYREUTH
𝒊 Luitpoldplatz 9. ☎ (09 21) 8 85 88.

Margraves' Opera House – Guided tours (15min) April to September, from 9am to 12 noon, and from 1.20pm to 5pm ; October to March, from 10am to 12 noon, and from 1.30pm to 3pm. Closed Mondays and also 1 January, 1 November, 24, 25 and 31 December. 2DM. ☎ (09 21) 6 53 13.

New Castle – Guided tours (30min) April to September from 10am to 12 noon and from 1.20pm to 5pm ; October to March from 10am to 12 noon and from 1.30pm to 3.30pm. Closed Mondays and also 1 January, 1 November, 24, 25 and 31 December. 1.50DM. ☎ (09 21) 6 53 13.

Richard Wagner Museum – Open daily from 9am to 5pm. Closed on 1 January, Easter Sunday, Whit-Sunday, 24 and 25 December. 3DM. ☎ (09 21) 25 404.

Festival Theatre – Guided tours (30min) daily at 10am, 10.45am, 11.30am, 1.30pm, 2.15pm and 3pm. During the Festival (late July to late August), mornings only. Closed Mondays and the month of November. 2DM. ☎ (09 21) 2 02 21.

Hermitage Castle – Guided tours (30min) daily from 9am to 12 noon and from 1pm to 5pm (3pm from October to the end of March). Closed Mondays, Shrove Tuesday and also 1 November, 24, 25 and 31 December. 2DM. ☎ (09 21) 9 25 61.

Excursions

Teufelshöhle Caves – Guided tours (45min) . from Easter to 1 November, daily from 9am to 5pm ; from 2 November to 25 December, Tuesdays and Saturdays only from 10am to 12 noon ; from 26 December to 6 January daily from 1.30pm to 3.30pm ; from 7 January to Easter, Tuesdays and Saturdays only from 10am to 12 noon. 4.50DM. ☎ (0 92 43) 8 33.

Sansparell

Zwernitz Castle – Open mid-April to mid-October, daily from 9am to 12 noon and from 1.20pm to 5pm. Closed Mondays. 1.50DM. Guided tour of the Oriental Building : 1.50DM.

Rock Garden – Entrance free daily the whole year. ☎ (0 92 74) 3 30.

Kulmbach
𝒊 ☎ (0 92 21) 80 22 16.

Plassenburg Castle – Guided tours (45min) daily from 10am to 4.40pm (3.30pm from October to the end of March). Closed Mondays, also 1 January, Shrove Tuesday, 1 November, 24, 25 and 31 December. 2DM. ☎ (0 92 21) 41 16.

BERCHTESGADEN
𝒊 ☎ (0 86 52) 50 11.

Castle – Guided tours (45min) from 10am to 1pm (last tour starts at 12 noon) and from 2pm to 5pm (last tour starts 4pm). Closed Saturdays from Easter to September ; Saturdays and Sundays from October to Easter. 5DM. ☎ (0 86 52) 20 85.

Salt Mines – Guided tours (1 1/2 hours) 1 May to 15 October, daily, from 8.30am to 5pm ; from 16 October to 30 April, daily except Sundays, from 12.30pm to 3.30pm. Closed Good Friday, Whit-Monday and 24 and 31 December. 13.50DM. ☎ (0 86 52) 60 02 0.

Obersalzberg and the Kehlstein – Bus service between Obersalzberg and the Kehlstein from May to the end of October (weather permitting), daily from 8am to 4pm. 17DM for bus and mountain lift. ☎ (0 86 52) 50 11.

Königssee – Boat trips (1 hour 45min). Timetable variable according to season. Approximate sailing times: High Season (end of June to mid-August), daily from 7.15am to 5.30pm, every 10 to 20min; Pre-Season, from 8.15am or 9am to 3.45 or 4pm, every 15 or 30min; Late Season, from 8.15am to 4.45pm every 15 to 30min; Winter, from 9.45am to 3.45pm, every 45min. For further details and exact times enquire at Königssee pier. 16.50DM. ☎ (0 86 52) 40 27.

The Rossfeld Road – This is a toll road: 3DM per person.

THE BERGSTRASSE

Lorsch Torhalle – Open daily from 10am to 4.30pm (3.30pm from November to the end of February). Closed Mondays, also 1 January, 24, 25, 26 and 31 December. 2DM. ☎ (0 62 51) 5 14 46.

Auerbach Castle – Open February to end of December, daily from 10am to 6pm. Closed Mondays. Entrance free. ☎ (0 62 51) 7 29 23.

BERLIN   🛈 Europa-Center, Budapester Strasse. ☎ (0 30) 2 62 60 31.

St Nicholas: March Museum Permanent Exhibition – Open Tuesdays to Fridays from 9am to 5pm; Saturdays from 9am to 6pm; Sundays from 10am to 5pm. Closed Mondays. 2.05DM. ☎ (0 30) 21 71 31 46.

Pergamon Museum – The Middle-East Museum and the Collection of Antiquities are open daily from 10am to 6pm. The Pergamon Museum as a whole is open at the same times from Wednesday to Sunday. Closed 1 January (partially), 24 December, 25 December (partially) and 31 December. 2DM. ☎ (0 30) 20 35 54 44.

National Gallery – Open daily from 10am to 6pm. Closed Mondays, Tuesdays and certain public holidays. 1DM. ☎ (0 30) 20 35 54 44.

Bode Museum – Open daily from 10am to 6pm. Closed Mondays, Tuesdays, and 3 October, 24, 25 and 31 December. 1DM. ☎ (0 30) 20 35 54 44.

Old Museum – Times, charges and telephone number as for National Gallery above.

Victory Column – Open daily from 9am (3pm Mondays) to 6pm. 1.20 DM. ☎ (0 30) 3 91 29 61.

Zoological Gardens – Open April to September, daily, from 9am to 6.30pm; October to March, daily, from 9am to 5 or 6pm. Closed 24 December. 7.50DM. ☎ (0 30) 25 40 10.

Aquarium – Open daily from 9am to 6pm (9pm the last Saturday of the month). 7.50DM. ☎ (0 30) 25 40 10.

Museum of Decorative Arts (Tiergarten Quarter) – Open daily 9am (10am Saturdays and Sundays) to 5pm. Closed Mondays. Entrance free. ☎ (0 30) 2 66 26 02.

New National Gallery – Open daily from 9am (10am Saturdays and Sundays) to 5pm. Closed Mondays. Entrance free. ☎ (0 30) 2 66 26 62.

Philharmonia – Guided tours (30min) available Mondays to Saturdays from 9am to 5pm, provided there are no rehearsals scheduled (find out first). Entrance free. ☎ (0 30) 2 54 88 0.

Musical Instruments Museum – Open from 9am (10am Saturdays, Sundays and public holidays) to 5pm daily. Closed Mondays, and also 1 January, Good Friday, Easter Monday and Whit-Monday, 1 May, Thursday of Ascension, 3 October, Day of Repentance and Prayer (a Wednesday in November), 24, 25 and 26 December. Entrance free. ☎ (0 30) 25 48 11 39.

Charlottenburg – Open daily from 9am (10am Saturdays, Sundays and public holidays) to 5pm. Guided tours to central block every 50min. Closed Mondays, Tuesdays after Easter and Whitsun, and also 1 May, 24, 25 and 31 December. 7DM for the whole castle. ☎ (0 30) 3 20 91-1.

Museum of Antiquities – Open daily from 9am (10am Saturdays, Sundays) to 5pm. Closed Fridays and also 1 January, 1 May, 24, 25 and 31 December. Entrance free. ☎ (0 30) 32 09 12 15.

Egyptian Museum – Hours of opening and closing as for Museum of Antiquities above. Entrance free. ☎ (0 30) 32 09 12 61.

Bröhan museum – Open daily from 10am to 6pm. Closed Mondays and also 24 and 31 December. 4DM ☎ (0 30) 3 21 40 29.

Dahlem Museums – Open daily from 9am (10am Saturdays, Sundays) to 5pm. Closed Mondays and also 1 January, Tuesdays after Easter and Whitsun, 1 May, 24, 25 and 31 December. Entrance free. ☎ (0 30) 83 01-2 16.

Berlin Museum of Post and Telecommunications – Open daily from 9am (10am Saturdays, Sundays) to 5pm. Closed Fridays. Entrance free. ☎ (0 30) 21 28-2 01.

Transport and Technical Museum – Open daily from 9am to 5pm (10am to 6pm Saturdays, Sundays). Closed Mondays. 3.50DM. ☎ (0 30) 2 54 84-1 25.

Kathe-Köllwitz Museum – Open daily from 11am to 6pm. Closed Tuesdays, and also 24 and 31 December. 6DM. ☎ (0 30) 8 82 52 10.

Martin-Gropius Museum – Open daily from 10am to 8pm. Closed Mondays. 6DM. ☎ (0 30) 2 54 86-1 08.

"Topography of Terror" – Open daily from 15 June to 31 December, 10am to 6pm. Closed Mondays. Entrance free. ☎ (0 30) 2 54 86-7 03.

Berlin Museum – Open daily from 10am to 10pm. Closed Mondays. 4DM. ☎ (0 30) 25 86 28 39.

Berlin Wall Museum – Open daily from 9am to 10pm. 7.50 DM. ☎ (0 30) 2 51 10 31.

March Museum – Open daily from 10am to 6pm. Closed Mondays and Tuesdays. 2DM. ☎ (0 30) 2 70 05 14.

Museum of Decorative Arts (Kopenick Castle) – Open from 10am to 6pm, except Mondays and Tuesdays. 1DM. ☎ (0 30) 6 57 15 04.

Botanical Gardens – Open daily from 9am. Gates closed at 8pm from May to the end of August, 7pm in April and September, 5pm in March and October, 4pm from November to the end of February. The glasshouses close earlier. 2.50DM. ☎ (0 30) 83 00 61 19.

Botanical Museum – Open daily from 10am to 5pm. Closed Mondays, Tuesdays after Easter and Whitsun, and on 1 May, 24 and 31 December. Entrance free. ☎ (0 30) 83 00 61 19.

Brücke Museum – Open daily from 11am to 5pm. Closed Tuesdays. 3.50DM ☎ (0 30) 8 31 20 29.

Grunewald Pavilion – Open daily from 10am to 6pm (5pm March and October, 4pm November to February). Closed Mondays, also Tuesdays after Easter and Whitsun, 1 May, 24, 25 and 31 December. 2.50DM. ☎ (0 30) 3 20 91-1.

Peacock Island : Castle – Guided tours (30min) from 10am to 5pm, daily from April to September ; from 10am to 4pm in October. Closed Mondays and from November to March. 3DM. ☎ (0 30) 8 05 3042.

Radio Tower – Open daily from 10am to 11pm. 5DM. ☎ (0 30) 30 38 29 96.

German Radio Museum – Open daily from 10am to 5pm. Closed Tuesdays. 3DM ☎ (0 30) 3 02 81 86.

Bauhaus Museum – Open daily from 11am to 5pm. Closed Tuesdays, and also 24 and 31 December. 3DM. ☎ (0 30) 2 54 00 20.

Memorial of Plötzensee – Open from March to September, daily from 8am to 6pm ; the rest of the year : from 8.30am to 5.30pm in February and October, 4.30pm January and November, 4pm in December. Entrance free. ☎ (0 30) 3 44 32 26.

Tegel Mansion – In the course of restoration. For reopening dates, enquire at the Tourist Information Bureau.

Spandau Citadel – Open daily from 9am (10am Saturdays and Sundays) to 5pm. Closed Mondays. 1.50DM. ☎ (0 30) 33 91-1.

Excursions

Sachsenhausen Concentration Camp – Oranienburg. Open : April to September from 8am to 6pm daily ; October to March from 8.30am to 4.30pm. Closed Mondays and the 24 and 25 December. Entrance free. Film documentary 1DM. ☎ (0 33 01) 35 16.

Chorin Abbey – Open daily from 9am to 6pm (4pm from November to the end of March). 2DM. ☎ (03 33 66) 196-2 06.

BERNKASTEL-KUES   🄸 ☎ (0 65 31) 40 23

St Nicholas' Hospice – Open daily from 8am (10am Saturdays and Sundays) to 12 noon, and from 2pm to 6pm. Entrance free. Guided tour of the Library, 3DM. ☎ (0 65 31) 22 60.

BLACK FOREST

Gutach : Black Forest Open-Air Museum – Open from April to 1 November, daily from 8.30am to 6pm. 5DM. Brochure in English. ☎ (0 78 31) 2 30.

Triberg : Black Forest Museum – Open May to September, daily from 9am to 6pm ; October to April, from 10am to 12 noon and from 2pm to 5pm. Closed for three weeks in November. 4DM. ☎ (0 77 22) 44 34.

Furtwangen : Horological Museum – Open from April to October, daily from 9am to 5pm ; from November to March, by arrangement. 3DM. ☎ (0 77 23) 6 56-1 17.

St Peter : Abbey Library – Guided tours (45min) by arrangement. ☎ (0 76 60) 2 05.

BONN   🄸 Münsterstrasse 20. ☎ (02 28) 77 34 66

Rhineland Museum – Open Tuesdays and Thursdays from 9am to 5pm, Wednesdays from 9am to 8pm, Fridays from 9am to 4pm, Saturdays and Sundays from 10am to 5pm. Closed Mondays, 1 January, Thursday and Sunday before Shrove Tuesday, 1 May and 24, 25, 31 December. 4DM (entrance free the 1st Sunday each month). ☎ (02 28) 7 29 41.

Beethoven's Birthplace – Open from April to September, 10am to 5pm (1pm Saturdays, Sundays and public holidays); October to March, 10am to 4pm (1pm Saturdays, Sundays and public holidays). Closed 1 January, Good Friday, Easter Sunday, 1 May, Whit-Sunday, Corpus Christi Day, 1 November, Day of Repentance and Prayer (a Wednesday in November), and from 24 to 26 December. 5DM. ☎ (02 28) 63 51 88.

Bad Godesberg : Castle Ruins – Access to the keep : Wednesday to Sunday from 10am to 6pm, April to the end of October. 0.50DM. ☎ (02 28) 31 60 71.

Excursions

Drachenfels – The funicular is in service from 1 January to 15 November (from May to the end of September, departures every half hour from 9am to 8pm). 10DM Rtn. ☎ (0 22 23) 2 25 56.

Remagen : Peace Museum – Open March to the end of November, daily from 10am to 5pm. 2DM. ☎ (0 26 42)2 01 12.

BREMEN
🚺 Bahnhofplatz. ☎ (04 21) 30 80 00.

Tour of the Port – Sightseeing trips by boat depart from the landing-stage near St Martin's Church at 10am, 11.30am, 1.30pm, 3.15pm, and 4.40pm, from mid-February to the end of November. Length of trip 1 hour 15min. 10DM. ☎ (04 21) 32 12 29.

Town Hall – Guided tours from March to the end of October at 10am, 11am, noon (11am and noon only on Sundays and public holidays). Entrance free. ☎ (04 21) 3 61 23 91.

Roselius and Paula Modersohn-Becker Houses – Reopening scheduled for 1992. Since the opening times are not known as this Guide goes to press, visitors are advised to apply to the Tourist Information Bureau. 5DM.

St Martin's Church – Open daily from mid-May to mid-September, 10.30am to 12.30pm. Closed Sundays and public holidays. ☎ (04 21) 32 48 35.

Art Gallery – Open daily from 10am to 5pm (9pm Tuesdays). Closed Mondays. Prices vary according to the exhibitions. ☎ (04 21) 32 90 80.

Overseas Museum – Open daily from 10am to 6pm. Closed Mondays. 2DM. ☎ (04 21) 3 97 83 57.

Focke Regional Museum – Open daily from 10am to 6pm. Closed Mondays and certain holidays. 2DM. ☎ (04 21) 4 96 35 75.

BREMERHAVEN
🚺 Columbus-Center, Obere Bürger 13. ☎ (04 71) 4 30 00.

National Maritime Museum – Open daily from 10am to 6 pm. Closed Mondays and also 25 and 31 December. 4DM (combined ticket admitting also to Open Air Museum, see below).

Wilhelm Bauer Submarine Museum – Open daily from April to the end of October, 10am to 6pm. 2.50DM. ☎ (for all three museums) (04 71) 4 82 07-0.

Open Air Museum – Open April to the end of September, from 10am to 6pm. Closed Mondays. 4DM combined ticket, see above.

North Sea Aquarium and Zoo Caves – Open daily from 8am to 7pm (5pm from September to the end of April). 3DM. ☎ (04 71) 5 90 25 16.

Excursions

Cuxhaven : Wreck Museum – Open from mid-March to the end of October, daily from 9am (10am Saturdays and Sundays) to 12 noon and from 3pm to 6pm. Closed Mondays. 3DM. ☎ (0 47 21) 2 33 41.

BRUCHSAL
🚺 ☎ (0 72 51) 7 27 71.

Castle : Central Block – Open daily from 9am to 5pm. Closed Mondays, Shrove Tuesday, and 24, 25 and 31 December. 2DM. ☎ (0 72 51) 74 26 61.

Mechanical Musical Instruments Museum – Guided tours (1 hour) every hour from 9am to 5pm. Closed Mondays, Shrove Tuesday, and 24, 25 and 31 December. 5DM (including visit to the castle). Telephone number as for the Castle, above.

Municipal Museum – Open Tuesdays to Fridays, 2pm to 5pm ; Saturdays and Sundays, 9am to 1pm, and 2pm to 5pm. Closed Mondays, Shrove Tuesday, and 24, 25 and 31 December. Entrance free. ☎ (0 72 51) 79-2 53.

BRUNSWICK
🚺 Hauptbahnhof. ☎ (05 31) 7 92 37.

Duke Anton-Ulrich Museum – Open daily from 10am to 5pm (8pm Wednesdays). Closed Mondays, Easter Sunday and Whit-Sunday, 1 May and 24, 25 and 31 December. Entrance free. ☎ (05 31) 4 84 24 00.

Medieval Art Collection – Open daily from 10am to 5pm. Closed Mondays. Entrance free. Telephone number as for Anton-Ulrich Museum above.

BÜCKEBURG
🚺 ☎ (0 57 22) 2 06 24.

Castle – Conducted tours (45min) daily from 9am to 12 noon, and from 1pm to 6pm. 6DM. ☎ (0 57 22) 50 39.

Helicopter Museum – Open every day from 9am to 5pm. 4DM. ☎ (0 57 22) 55 33.

Excursion

Mining Museum – Guided tours (30min) Tuesdays, Fridays, Saturdays, Sundays and public holidays from mid-April to the end of October, 10am to 4pm. Last tour starts one hour before closing. 10DM. ☎ (05 71) 39 94 38.

BURGHAUSEN

Painting Gallery – Open daily from 9am to 12 noon and from 1pm to 5pm (4pm from October to the end of March). Closed Mondays from October to the end of March, and also on Shrove Tuesday, 1 November, 24, 25 and 31 December. 1.50DM. ☎ (0 86 77) 46 59.

Museum – Same opening times and charges as Painting Gallery above.

C

THE CASTLES OF MÜNSTERLAND

Wasserburgen – Coach excursions leave Münster every Saturday from April to mid-October. For details apply at the Tourist Information Bureau, Berliner Platz 22, 4400 Münster. ☎ (02 51) 51 01 80.

Anholt Castle – Open: 15 March to 15 October, daily from 10am to 6pm (except Sundays); 14 October to 14 March 10am to 6pm Sundays only. Closed 24, 25, 26 and 31 December and 1 January. Castle: 6DM; Gardens: 5DM; Combined Ticket: 8DM. ☎ (0 28 74) 4 53 53.

Gemen Castle – The castle being also a training centre, visits are not always possible. Ask beforehand. ☎ (0 28 61) 50 68.

Hülshoff Manor – Open from mid-March to mid-December, daily from 9.30am to 6pm. 4DM. ☎ (0 25 34) 10 52.

Lembeck Castle – Guided tours (45min) from March to the end of October, daily from 10am to 5pm. 5DM. ☎ (0 23 69) 71 67.

Vischering Castle – Open: April to October, from 9.30am to 12.30pm and from 2pm to 5.30pm; November to March, from 10am to 12.30pm and from 2pm to 4.30pm. Closed Mondays, also 1 January and 25 December. 2DM. ☎ (0 25 91) 36 21).

CELLE ☐ Markt 6. ☎ (0 51 41) 12 12.

Castle – Guided tours (45min) daily at 10am, 11am, 12 noon, 2pm, 3pm and 4pm (2pm, 3pm and 4pm only on public holidays). Closed Good Friday, the Day of Repentance and Prayer (a Wednesday in November), and the 24, 26 and 31 December. 2DM ☎ (0 51 41) 1 23 73.

Bomann Museum – Open: April to October, daily from 10am to 5pm; November to March, Sundays and public holidays only, from 10am to 1pm. 2DM. ☎ (0 51 41) 12-3 72.

Excursions

Wienhausen Convent – Guided tours (1 hour) from April to 1 November: weekdays at 10am, 11am, 2pm, 3pm, 4pm and 5pm; Sundays and public holidays at 11.30am, 1pm, 2pm, 3pm, 4pm and 5pm (from October onwards, last admissions 4pm). 5DM. ☎ (0 51 49) 3 57.

CHEMNITZ ☐ Strasse der Nationen 3. ☎ (03 71) 6 20 51.

Natural History Museum – Open daily from 9am to 6pm. Closed Mondays. 2.50DM. ☎ (03 71) 6 22 45.

Fine Arts Museum – Times and charge as for the Natural History Museum above.

Excursions

Augustusburg Castle:

Museum of Game and Ornithology – Open April to October, daily, from 8.30am to 6pm. November to March from 9am to 5pm. Closed 25 December and 1 January. 3DM. ☎ (03 72 91) 2 67.

Motorcycle Museum – Open April to October, daily, from 8.30am to 6pm, November to March 9am to 5pm. Closed 25 and 31 December. 5DM. ☎ (03 72 91) 2 67 or 3 40.

CHIEMSEE

Prien-Stock Landing-stage – Allow 15min crossing for the Herreninsel, 1/2 hour for the Fraueninsel. Price: 7DM Rtn for the Herreninsel, 8DM for the two islands. ☎ (0 80 51) 60 90.

Herrenchiemsee Castle – On the island of Herreninsel. Guided tours (1/2 hour to 45 min): April to September from 9am to 5pm; October to March from 10am to 3.45pm. Closed 1 January, Shrove Tuesday, 1 November, 24, 25 and 31 December. 5DM. ☎ (0 80 51) 30 69.

COBURG

🖬 ☎ (0 95 61) 7 41 80.

Princes' Palace – Guided tours (1/2 hour): April to October, from 9.30am to 12 noon and from 2pm to 4pm; November to March, from 2pm to 3.30pm. Closed Mondays. 3.50DM. ☎ (0 95 61) 9 20 88.

Art Collections – Open April to October, daily from 9.30am to 1pm, and from 2pm to 5pm; November to March, daily from 2pm to 5pm only. Closed Mondays. 3.50DM. ☎ (0 95 61) 9 50 55.

Ehrenburg Castle – Guided tours (1 hour) at 10am, 11am, 1.30pm, 2.30pm, 3.30pm and 4.30pm daily (from October to the end of March, last tour at 3.30pm). Closed Mondays, also 1 January, Shrove Tuesday, 1 November, 24, 25 and 31 December. 3DM. ☎ (0 95 61) 7 67 67.

Excursions

Banz Abbey – Guided tour (1 hour 15min) available every other Thursday at 2pm. 2DM. Enquire at the Tourist Information Bureau, Staffelstein: ☎ (09 573) 41 92.

COLOGNE

🖬 Am Dom. ☎ (02 21) 2 21 33 40.

Cathedral:

Choir – Open daily from 7am to 7pm. Guided tours (times vary) free of charge.

Treasury – Guided tours (1/2 hour): April to October, Mondays to Saturdays from 9am to 4pm, Sundays from 12.30pm to 4pm; November to March, Mondays to Saturdays from 9am to 4pm, Sundays from 12.30pm to 4pm. Closed 1 January, Monday before Shrove Tuesday, and 25 December. 2DM. ☎ (02 21) 21 75 15.

Germano-Roman Museum – Open daily from 10am to 5pm (8pm Wednesdays and Thursdays). Closed Mondays, 1 January, during the Carnival, and 24, 25 December. 3DM. ☎ (02 21) 2 21 44 38.

Wallraf-Richartz and Ludwig Museums – Open Tuesdays to Thursdays from 10am to 8pm, Fridays to Sundays and public holidays from 10am to 6pm. Closed Mondays, 1 January, and during the Carnival. 3DM (including visit to the **Museum of Photography**). ☎ (02 21) 2 21 23 79.

Museum of Photography – As for Wallraf-Richartz Museums above. ☎ (02 21) 2 21 24 11.

Diocesan Museum – Open daily from 10am to 5pm (1pm Sundays and public holidays). Closed Thursdays. 2DM. ☎ (02 21) 24 45 46.

St Ursula's: Treasury – Open Mondays and Thursdays from 11am to 12 noon, Wednesdays and Fridays from 3pm to 4pm, Saturdays from 4pm to 5pm. Closed Tuesdays, Sundays and public holidays. 1.50DM. ☎ (02 21) 13 34 00.

Schnütgen Museum – Open daily from 10am to 5pm (8pm the 1st Wednesday of the month). Closed Mondays and certain holidays. 2DM. ☎ (02 21) 23 10-36 20.

Museum of East Asian Art – Open daily from 10am to 5pm (8pm the 1st Friday of the month). Closed Mondays and 1 January, 24 and 25 December. 4DM. ☎ (02 21) 40 50 38.

Museum of Applied Arts – Open daily from 10am to 5pm (8pm Tuesdays). Closed Mondays and 1 January, 24 and 25 December. 3DM. ☎ (02 21) 2 21-67 14.

Metropolitan Historical Museum – Open daily from 10am to 5pm (8pm Thursdays). Closed Mondays. 2DM. ☎ (02 21) 2 21 23 98.

Rautenstrauch-Joest Ethnographic Museum – Open daily from 10am to 5pm (8pm the last Wednesday of the month). Closed Mondays. Prices vary according to the temporary exhibitions on display. ☎ (02 21) 31 10 65.

Flora Botanical Park – Open daily from 8am until nightfall. Glasshouses from 10am to 12 noon and from 1pm to 6pm (Sundays from 10am to 6pm continuously). Admission free. ☎ (02 21) 76 43 35.

Excursions

Brühl: Augustusburg Castle – Guided tours (45min) daily from 9am to 12 noon and from 1.30 to 4pm. Closed Mondays and in December and January. 3DM. ☎ (0 22 32) 4 24 71.

CONSTANCE

🖬 Bahnhofplatz 13. ☎ (0 75 31) 28 43 76.

Rosgarten Museum – Open April to October, daily from 10am to 5pm (4pm Saturdays and Sundays); November to March, from 11am to 5pm (4pm Saturdays and Sundays). Closed Mondays and public holidays. Entrance free. ☎ (0 75 31) 28 42 46.

Excursions

Mainau Island – Open to visitors: mid-March to mid-October, daily from 6am to 7pm (12DM); otherwise from 9am to 5pm (5DM). ☎ (0 75 31) 3 03-0.

For a quiet place to stay
consult the annual **Michelin Red Guide Deutschland**
which gives a choice of pleasant hotels.

D

DARMSTADT   🛈 Luisen-Center, Luisenplatz 5. ☎ (0 61 51) 13 27 80.

Hessen Museum – Open Tuesdays, Thursdays, Fridays and Saturdays from 10am to 5pm; Wednesdays from 10am to 1pm and from 2pm to 9pm; Sundays and public holidays from 11am to 5pm. Closed Mondays. Entrance free. ☎ (0 61 51) 12 54 34.

Castle – Guided tours (1 hour): Mondays to Thursdays from 10am to 1pm, and from 2pm to 5pm; Saturdays, Sundays and public holidays, from 10am to 1pm only. Closed Fridays. 2.50DM. ☎ (0 61 51) 2 40 35.

Prince George's Palace – Same times and charge as for the Castle. ☎ (0 61 51) 29 12 16.

Excursions

Kranichstein Pavilion – Closed for restoration. Re-opening date not known at the time of going to press.

DETMOLD   🛈 ☎ (0 52 31) 76 73 28.

Castle – Guided tours (45min) from 9.30am to 1.30pm, and from 2pm to 5pm, daily. Closed 25 December. 4DM. ☎ (0 52 31) 12 25 07.

Westphalian Open-Air Museum – Open daily from 9am to 6pm (last admissions 5pm). Closed Mondays. 3DM. ☎ (0 52 31) 7 06-0.

Arminius Monument – Open in summer from 9am to 6.30pm; in winter from 9.30am to 4.30pm. 1DM. ☎ (0 52 61) 2 50 20.

Excursions

Externsteine – Open April to the end of October from 9am to 7pm; the rest of the year, depending on weather conditions. 1DM. ☎ (0 52 34) 32 00.

DONAUESCHINGEN   🛈 ☎ (07 71) 38 34.

Princely Collections – Open daily from 9am to 12 noon and from 1.30pm to 5pm. Closed Mondays and the month of November. 5DM.

Castle – Guided tours, Easter to the end of October, from 9am to 12 noon and from 1.45pm to 5pm. Closed Tuesdays. 5DM.

DORTMUND   🛈 Hauptbahnhof. ☎ (02 31) 14 03 41.

Westphalia Park – Open daily from 9am until nightfall. 4.50DM. ☎ (02 31) 13 82-0.

Brewery Museum – Open daily from 10am to 6pm. Closed Mondays and 24, 25 December. Entrance free. ☎ (02 31) 15 41 32 89.

Museum of Art and Civilization – Open daily from 10am to 6pm. Closed Mondays. Entrance free. ☎ (02 31) 5 42-2 55 25.

Ostwall Museum – Open daily from 10am to 6pm. Closed Mondays. Entrance free. ☎ (02 31) 5 42-2 32 47.

DRESDEN   🛈 Prager Strasse 10. ☎ (03 51) 4 95 50 25.

Zwinger:

Old Masters Gallery – Open daily from 9am to 5pm (6pm Wednesdays). Closed Mondays, and 24, 25 and 31 December. 5DM (the same ticket admits also to the Gallery of 19C and 20C Painters, below). ☎ (03 51) 4 84 01 19.

Porcelain Collection – Open daily from 9am to 5pm. Closed Fridays, and the 24, 25 and 31 December. 3DM. ☎ (03 51) 4 84 01 19.

Salon of Mathematics and Physics – Open daily from 9.30am to 5pm. Closed Fridays, and 1 January, 3 October, 25 and 31 December. 3DM. ☎ (03 51) 4 95 13 64.

Albertinum:

Gallery of 19C and 20C Painters – Same times, charge, ticket and telephone number as the Old Masters Gallery, above.

Green Vault Collections – Open daily from 9am to 5pm (6pm Wednesdays). Closed Thursdays, and 24, 25 and 31 December. 5DM. ☎ (03 51) 4 84 01 19.

Historical Museum of the City of Dresden – Open daily from 10am to 6pm. Closed Fridays, and 1 January, 24 and 25 December. 2DM. ☎ (03 51) 4 95 23 02.

Museum of Arts and Crafts – Open daily from 10am to 5pm. Closed Mondays, and 24, 25 December. 2DM. ☎ (03 51) 4 84 01 19.

Excursions

Moritzberg Castle – Open April to the end of December from 10am to 5pm (4pm in November and December). Closed Mondays, also 25 and 31 December. 3.50DM. ☎ (03 52 07) 4 39.

Pillnitz Castle – Open May to the end of September, daily from 9.30am to 5.30pm. Weekly closing: Tuesdays for the Wasserpalais, Mondays for the Bergpalais. 3DM. ☎ (03 51) 3 93 25.

DÜSSELDORF
ℹ Konrad-Adenauer-Platz. ☎ (02 11) 35 05 05.

Fine Arts Museum – Open daily from 11am to 6pm. Closed Mondays and Thursdays, also Shrove Tuesday, 1 May and 24, 25 and 31 December. 5DM. ☎ (02 11) 8 99 22 90.

Rhineland-Westphalia Collection – Open daily from 10am to 6pm. Closed Mondays, also the Sunday before Shrove Tuesday, 1 May, and 24, 25 and 31 December. 5 DM. ☎ (02 11) 13 39 61.

Hetjens Museum – Open from 11am to 5pm. Closed Mondays, also 1 January, the Sunday before Shrove Tuesday, Good Friday, Easter Sunday, Whit-Sunday, 1 May, the Thursday before Ascension, 1 November, 24, 25 and 31 December. 3DM. ☎ (02 11) 8 99 42 10.

Land Economics Museum – Open Mondays, Tuesdays, Thursdays, Fridays from 9am to 5pm; Wednesdays from 9am to 8pm; Sundays from 10am to 6pm. Closed Saturdays, also 1 January, the Sunday and Monday before Shrove Tuesday, Easter Sunday, Whit-Sunday, 1 May, 24 and 25 December. 1DM. ☎ (02 11) 4 92 11 08.

Löbbecke Museum and Aquatic Zoo – Open daily from 10am to 6pm. Closed 1 January, Monday before Shrove Tuesday, 1 May, 24, 25 and 31 December. 7DM. ☎ (02 11) 8 99 61 50.

Excursions

Benrath Mansion – Guided tours (1 hour) from 10am to 5pm (last tour starts 4pm). Closed Mondays. 5DM. ☎ (02 11) 8 99 72 71.

Neanderthal Prehistoric Museum – Open daily from 10am to 5pm (from 11am to 6pm Sundays). Closed Mondays, also 1 January, 24 and 25 December. 2DM. ☎ (0 21 04) 3 11 49.

E

EICHSTÄTT
ℹ ☎ (0 84 21) 79 77.

Cathedral : Diocesan Museum – Open from April to the end of October, Mondays to Saturdays from 9.30am to 1pm and from 2pm to 5pm, Sundays and public holidays from 11am to 5pm continuously. Closed Mondays, and Good Friday, Easter Sunday and Whit-Monday. 2.50DM. ☎ (0 84 21) 5 02 48.

Former Episcopal Residence – Guided tours (15min) : April to the end of October, Mondays to Thursdays at 10am, 11am, 2pm and 3pm; Fridays at 10am and 11am; Saturdays, Sundays and public holidays, in the framework of a guided tour of the town only (reservations : ☎ (0 84 21) 79 77). Entrance free. ☎ (0 84 21) 7 02 20.

St Willibad's Castle :

Jura Museum – Open April to September, from 9am to 12 noon and from 1pm to 5pm; October to March, from 10am to 12 noon and from 1pm to 4pm. Closed Mondays, and 1 January, Shrove Tuesday, 1 November, 24, 25 and 31 December. 4DM. ☎ (0 84 21) 29 56.

Historical Museum – Open April to September, from 9am to 12 noon and from 1pm to 5pm; October to March, from 10am to 12 noon and from 1pm to 4pm. Closed Mondays, 1 January, Shrove Tuesday, 1 November, 24 and 25 December. 4DM. ☎ (0 84 21) 60 01 74.

Excursions

Weissenburg
ℹ ☎ (0 91 41) 90 71 24.

Roman Baths – Open from Palm Sunday to 1 November, daily from 10am to 12 noon and from 2pm to 5pm. Closed Mondays. 2DM. ☎ (0 91 41) 9 07-1 24.

Roman Museum – Open from March to the end of December, daily from 10am to 12.30pm and from 2pm to 5pm. Closed Mondays and 24, 25 December. 3DM. ☎ (0 91 41) 9 07-1 24.

EINBECK Excursions

Alfeld Regional Museum – Open daily from 10am to 12 noon and from 3pm to 5pm. Closed Saturday and Sunday afternoons, Mondays and public holidays. Entrance free. ☎ (0 51 81) 70 31 78.

EISENACH
ℹ Bahnhofstrasse 3. ☎ (0 36 91) 48 95.

Castle : Thuringian Museum – Closed for restoration.

Luther's House – Open, May to September, daily from 9am to 1pm and from 2pm to 5pm; October to April, closed public holidays and Sunday mornings. Closed 1 January. 3DM. ☎ (0 36 91) 49 83.

Bach's House – Open Mondays from 1.30pm to 4.30pm, Tuesdays to Saturdays from 9am to 4.30pm, Sundays and public holidays from 9am to 12 noon and from 1.30pm to 4.30pm. 5DM. ☎ (0 36 91) 37 14.

Wartburg Automobile Museum – Open daily from 9am to 5pm. Closed 24 and 31 December. 2.50DM. ☎ (0 36 91) 5 98 09.

Fritz Reuter and Richard Wagner Museum – Open daily from 10am to 5pm. Closed Mondays. 2DM. ☎ (0 36 91) 39 71.

Wartburg Fortress – Guided tours (45min): April to October from 8.30am to 4.30pm, November to March from 9am to 3.30pm. 5DM (access to courtyard only 1DM). ☎ (0 36 91) 30 01 to 30 03.

EMDEN   ✦ ☎ (0 49 21) 2 00 94.

East Frisian Museum – Open: April to September, Mondays to Saturdays from 10am to 1pm and from 2pm to 5pm; Sundays from 11am to 1pm (5pm in June, July and August); October to March, Tuesdays to Saturdays from 10am to 1pm and 3pm to 5pm, Sundays from 11am to 1pm. Closed 1 May, 3 October, 24 and 31 December. 3DM. ☎ (0 49 21) 8 74 78.

ERFURT   ✦ Bahnhofstrasse 37. ☎ (03 61) 2 62 67.

Augustinian Monastery – Guided tours (45min) from 1 April to 10 November, Tuesdays to Saturdays at 10am, 11am, 12 noon, 2pm, 3pm and 4pm; Sundays after Mass. Closed Mondays. 4.50DM. ☎ (03 61) 2 36 03.

Anger Museum – Open 10am to 5pm (8pm Wednesdays). Closed Mondays, also 1 January, Good Friday, Thursday of Ascension, Whit-Sunday, 3 October, Day of Repentance and Prayer (a Wednesday in November) and 25 December, 3DM. ☎ (03 61) 2 33 11.

Franciscan Church – Open daily from May to the end of October, from 10am to 1pm and 2pm to 5pm. Closed Mondays and the same holidays as the Anger Museum above. 2DM. ☎ (03 61) 6 40 10.

Excursions

Arnstadt

Local History Museum – Open daily from 8.30am to 12.30pm and from 1pm to 5pm. Closed Saturday mornings and Sundays. 1.60DM. ☎ (0 36 28) 29 78.

New Palace – Open 1 May to 15 October from 8.30am to 12 noon, and from 1pm to 4.30pm; 16 October to 30 April from 9.30am to 3.30pm. Closed Mondays, at Easter and Whitsun, and on 25 December and 1 January. 2.50DM. ☎ (0 36 28) 29 32.

ESSEN   ✦ Hauptbahnhof. ☎ (02 01) 23 54 27.

Industrial Design Centre – Open from 10am to 6pm (4.30pm Saturdays). Closed Sundays, Mondays and public holidays. Entrance free. ☎ (02 01) 22 79 95.

Folkwang Museum – Open 10am to 6pm (9pm Thursdays). Closed Mondays, also Good Friday, Easter Sunday, Whit-Sunday, 1 May, 24, 25 and 31 December. 5DM. ☎ (02 01) 88 84 12.

Cathedral: Treasury – Open from 10am to 5pm. Closed Mondays, also 1 January, Easter Sunday, Whit-Sunday, 26 and 31 December. 2DM. ☎ (02 01) 2 20 42 06.

Villa Hügel: Krupp Collections – Open daily from 10am to 6pm. Closed Mondays. 1.50DM. ☎ (02 01) 1 88-48 37.

F

FLENSBURG   ✦ Norder Strasse 2. ☎ (04 61) 2 30 90.

Ferries to Denmark – From Flensburg there are continuous daily sea services to Glücksburg and the small neighbouring ports on the Danish coast.

Municipal Museum – Open from 10am to 5pm (1pm Sundays). Closed Mondays, also 1 January, Easter Sunday, Whit-Sunday, 1 May, Thursday of Ascension, 3 October, Day of Repentance and Prayer (a Wednesday in November) and 25 December. 2DM. ☎ (04 61) 85 29 26.

Excursions

Glücksburg Castle – Open May to September daily from 10am to 5pm, in October from 10am to 4.30pm. Guided tours only (1 hour) in November, December, March and April, from 10am to 12 noon and from 2pm to 4pm. Closed Mondays (except from June to the end of August). 6DM. ☎ (0 46 31) 22 43.

FRANKFURT AM MAIN   ✦ Hauptbahnhof. ☎ (0 69) 21 23 88 49.

Henninger Turm – Opening hours not being fixed as the Guide goes to press, visitors are advised to enquire by telephone ☎ (0 69) 6 06 36 00. 3.50DM.

Römer and Römerberg: Imperial Hall – Open from 9am to 6pm (5pm from October to the end of March). Closed 1 January, Saturday and Sunday before Shrove Tuesday, Shrove Tuesday, Whit-Sunday, Corpus Christi Day, Day of Repentance and Prayer (a Wednesday in November), 24, 25 and 31 December. 1DM. ☎ (0 69) 3 58 75.

Cathedral Museum – Open daily from 10am (11am Sundays and public holidays) to 5pm. Closed Mondays and 24, 31 December. 2DM. ☎ (0 69) 28 92 29.

Historical Museum – Open daily from 10am to 5pm (8pm Wednesday). Closed Mondays and certain public holidays. Entrance free. Exhibitions : 3DM. ☎ (0 69) 2 12-3 55 99.

Goethe's House and the Goethe Museum – Open weekdays from 9am to 6pm (4pm from October to the end of March); Sundays and public holidays from 10am to 1pm throughout the year. Closed 1 January, Good Friday and 24, 25 and 31 December. 3DM. ☎ (0 69) 29 18 84.

Modern Art Museum – Open daily from 10am to 5pm (8pm Wednesdays). Closed Mondays and certain public holidays. Entrance free. ☎ (0 69) 2 12-3 88 19.

Jewish Museum – Open daily from 10am to 5pm (8pm Wednesdays). Closed Mondays. Entrance free. ☎ (0 69) 2 12-3 50 00.

Städel Museum and Municipal Gallery – Open daily from 10am to 5pm (8pm Wednesdays). Closed Mondays and certain public holidays. 6DM (admission free Sundays). ☎ (0 69) 60 50 98-0

Museum of Applied Arts – Open daily from 10am to 5pm (8pm Wednesdays). Closed Mondays and certain public holidays. Entrance free. ☎ (0 69) 2 12-3 40 37.

German Cinema Museum – Open daily from 10am to 5pm (8pm Wednesdays). Entrance free. Temporary exhibitions, 10am to 8pm : 2DM. Closed Mondays and 24, 31 December. ☎ (0 69) 21 23 88 30.

Liebig Museum of Sculpture – Open daily from 10am to 5pm (8pm Wednesdays). Closed Mondays and certain public holidays. Entrance free. ☎ (0 69) 2 12-3 86 17.

Postal Museum – Open daily from 10am to 5pm (8pm Wednesdays). Closed Mondays and certain public holidays. Entrance free. ☎ (0 69) 60 60-0.

German Architectural Museum – Open daily from 10am to 5pm. Closed Mondays. 4DM. ☎ (0 69) 2 12-3 88 44.

Museum of Ethnography – Open daily from 10am to 5pm (8pm Wednesdays). Closed Mondays.

Zoo – Open from 8am. Closing times : 7pm from mid-March to the end of September; 6pm from 1 to 15 October and from mid-February to mid-March; 5pm from mid-October to mid-February. 8DM for the zoo ; 4.50DM for the Exotarium ; combined ticket 9.50DM. ☎ (0 69) 21 32 37 15.

Senckenberg Natural History Museum – Open daily from 9am to 5pm, Wednesdays until 8pm, Saturdays, Sundays and public holidays until 6pm. Closed Good Friday and 24 December. 5DM. ☎ (0 69) 75 42-0.

Tropical Gardens – Open from 9am. Closing times: 6pm from April to September ; 5pm March and October ; 4pm January, February, November and December. Closed Shrove Tuesday and 24, 31 December. 5DM. ☎ (0 69) 21 23 39 39.

Excursions

Offenbach Leather Museum – Open from 10am (2pm Saturdays) to 5pm (8pm Wednesdays). Closed 1 January, Shrove Tuesday afternoon, and 24, 25, 31 December. 3.50DM. ☎ (0 69) 81 30 21.

Königstein im Taunus: Feudal Ruin – Open: April to September from 9am to 7pm, October from 9.30am to 4pm, November to February from 9.30am to 3pm (4pm Sundays), March from 9.30am to 4.30pm. 1.50DM. ☎ (0 61 74) 20 22 51.

Grosser Feldberg : Tower Observation-platform – Access (163 steps) from 11am to 9pm in summer, until nightfall in winter. Closed in bad weather. 2DM. ☎ (061 74) 2 22 19.

FREIBURG IM BREISGAU   🖪 Rotteckring 14. ☎ (07 61) 3 68 90 90.

Cathedral :

Chancel – Open mid-June to the end of September, Mondays to Fridays, daily from 10am to 12 noon and from 2.30pm to 5pm. Guided tour (45min) daily at 2pm (Saturday at 11am, Sunday at 2.30pm). 1DM. ☎ (07 61) 3 10 99.

Ascent of the West Tower – From April to September: Mondays to Saturdays, daily from 9.30am to 5.30pm, Sundays 1pm to 5pm ; October to March, Tuesdays to Saturdays, daily from 10am to 4pm, Sundays from 1pm to 4pm. 1.50DM. ☎ (07 61) 3 10 99.

Augustinian Museum – Open daily from 9.30am (10.30 Saturdays and Sundays) to 5pm. Closed Mondays. Entrance free. ☎ (07 61) 2 16 33 00.

Schlossberg : cable-car – Departure from the Stadtgarten. Services : from the beginning of May to the end of September, 10am to 8pm (5pm Tuesdays) ; from the beginning of March to the end of April and from October to January, 11.30am to 6pm (closed Tuesdays). No service in February. 3DM Rtn. ☎ (07 61) 3 17 29.

FRISIAN ISLANDS

Eastern Frisians – For details of embarkation ports, sailing times, prices, etc., consult the current Michelin Red Guide Deutschland, under the names of the individual islands.

FRITZLAR
🚹 ☎ (0 56 22) 8 03 43.

Collegiate Church – Open: in summer, Mondays to Fridays from 9am to 12 noon and from 2pm to 6pm, Saturdays 9am to 12 noon, Sundays 2pm to 5pm; winter, Mondays to Fridays from 10am to 12 noon and from 2pm to 4pm, Saturdays 10am to 12 noon, Sundays 2pm to 4pm. 2.50DM. ☎ (0 56 22) 30 15.

Treasury and Museum – Open: in summer, Mondays to Saturdays from 10am to 12 noon and from 2pm to 5pm; winter, Mondays to Saturdays from 10am to 12 noon and from 2pm to 4pm, Sundays 2pm to 4pm. 2DM. ☎ (0 56 22) 30 15.

FULDA
🚹 Schlossstrasse 1. ☎ (06 61) 10 23 46.

Cathedral Museum – Open Mondays to Fridays, daily from 10am to 5.30pm, Saturdays from 10am to 2pm, Sundays and public holidays from 12.30pm to 5.30pm. Closed in January. ☎ (06 61) 8 72 07.

Excursions

Pheasantry Castle – Guided tours (1 hour) from April to the end of October, daily from 10am to 5pm (last tour starts at 4pm). Closed Mondays. 4DM. ☎ (06 61) 4 19 13.

FÜSSEN
🚹 Ausburger Torplatz 1. ☎ (0 83 62) 70 77.

Former Abbey of St Magnus: Regional Museum – Open daily from 11am (2pm from November to March) to 4pm. Closed Mondays. 3DM. ☎ (0 83 62) 50 53 45.

G

GARMISCH-PARTENKIRCHEN
🚹 Dr-Richard-Strauss-Platz. ☎ (0 88 21) 18 06.

Excursions

Wank Cable-Car – Summer service from 8.30am to 5pm; winter service from 9am to 4.30pm. No service in April or from mid-November to mid-December. 22DM Rtn. ☎ (0 88 21) 7 53-3 33.

Mittenwald: Lutheran Museum – Open daily from 10am to 12 noon and from 2pm to 5pm (Saturdays and Sundays, morning times only). Closed November and part of December. 2DM. ☎ (0 88 23) 25 11

GELNHAUSEN
🚹 ☎ (0 60 51) 82 00 54.

Imperial Palace Ruins – Open daily from 10am to 1pm and from 2pm to 5.30pm (4.30pm from November to the end of February). Closed Mondays, and also 1 January, 24, 25, 26 and 31 December. 1DM. ☎ (0 60 51) 38 05.

Excursions

Büdingen Castle – Guided tours (1 hour), from April to the end of October, at 2pm, 3pm and 4pm daily. Closed Mondays. 3.50DM. ☎ (0 60 42) 66 22.

Steinau Castle: Brothers Grimm Memorial – Open daily from 10am to 12 noon and from 1pm to 5pm (4pm from November to the end of February). Closed Mondays and certain public holidays. 2DM. ☎ (0 66 63) 68 43.

GÖRLITZ

Municipal Museum – Open daily from 10am to 1pm and from 2pm to 4pm (6pm Tuesdays and Wednesdays). Closed Sundays and Mondays. 2DM. ☎ (0 35 81) 6 73 51.

GOSLAR
🚹 Markt 7. ☎ (0 53 21) 28 46.

Animated Chiming Clock – The mechanical figurines work at 9am, 12 noon, 3pm and 6pm.

Town Hall: Chamber of Allegiance – Guided tours (15min) from 10am to 5pm (4pm from November to the end of March). Closed 1 January, Day of Repentance and Prayer (a Wednesday in November), and on 24, 25, 26 and 31 December. 2DM. ☎ (0 53 21) 7 04-2 41.

Siemens House – Open Mondays to Fridays from 9am to 12 noon, by prior arrangement. Entrance free. ☎ (0 53 21) 2 38 37.

Imperial Palace – Open daily from 10am to 5pm (4pm from November to the end of March). Closed 1 January, Good Friday, Day of Repentance and Prayer (a Wednesday in November) and from 24 to 26 December. 2.50DM. ☎ (0 53 21) 7 04-3 58.

Domvorhalle – In the course of restoration. Re-opening scheduled during 1992.

Goslar Museum – Same times and charge as for the Imperial Palace above. ☎ (0 53 21) 7 04-3 59.

GÖTTINGEN

📗 ☎ (05 51) 5 40 00

Municipal Museum – Open daily from 10am to 5pm (1pm Saturdays and Sundays). Closed Mondays, Good Friday, Easter Sunday, Whit-Sunday and the Day of Repentance and Prayer (a Wednesday in November). Entrance free. ☎ (05 51) 4 00 28 43.

H

HAIGERLOCH

📗 ☎ (0 74 74) 6 97 26.

Atom Museum – Open from 10am to 12 noon and from 2pm to 5pm: daily from May to the end of September; Saturdays, Sundays and public holidays only in March, April, October and November. Closed from December to the end of February. 1DM. ☎ (0 74 74) 6 97 26.

HALBERSTADT

St Stephen's Cathedral – Unaccompanied tours possible 10.30am to 11.30am; 12 noon to 2pm; 2.30pm to 3.30pm; and from 4pm to 5pm.

Treasury – Guided tours (1 hour, including tour of the Cathedral): May to October, Mondays to Fridays at 10am, 11.30am, 2pm, 3.30pm, Saturdays at 10am and 2pm, Sundays and public holidays at 11.30am and 2.30pm; November to April, Mondays to Saturdays, at 10am and 2pm, Sundays and public holidays at 11.30am. Donation. ☎ (0 39 41) 2 42 37.

Municipal Museum – Open daily from 9am (10am Saturdays and Sundays) to 5pm. Closed Mondays, and 1 January, 24, 25 and 31 December. 2DM. ☎ (0 39 41) 2 42 16.

HALLE

📗 Roter Turm, Marktplatz. ☎ (03 45) 2 33 40

Handel's House – Open daily from 9.30am to 5.30pm (7pm Thursdays). 2DM. ☎ (03 45) 2 46 06.

Saltworks Museum – Open daily from 10am to 5pm (4pm from October to the end of March). Closed Mondays. 1.50DM. ☎ (03 45) 2 50 34.

Moritzburg National Gallery – Open Tuesdays from 11am to 8.30pm, Wednesdays to Fridays from 10am to 5.30pm, Saturdays and Sundays from 10am to 6pm. Closed Mondays and 24, 31 December. 3DM (5DM during special exhibitions). ☎ (03 45) 3 70 31.

HAMBURG

📗 Burchardstrasse 14. ☎ (0 40) 30 05 10.

Aussenalster – Boat trips from the Alsterschiffahrt: daily from April to the end of October, sailings every half hour from 10am to 6pm (length of trip 50min). 10DM.

St Michael's Church: Tower – Access: May to October from 9am (11.30am Sundays and public holidays) to 5.30pm; November to April from 10am (11.30am Sundays and public holidays) to 4pm. Closed Wednesdays. 1.80DM.

Fine Arts Museum – Open daily from 10am to 6pm. Closed Mondays, and 1 May, 25 and 31 December. 3DM. ☎ (0 40) 24 86 26 12.

Museum of Decorative Arts – Same times and charge as the Fine Arts Museum, above. ☎ (0 40) 24 86 26 30.

Historical Museum – Open daily from 10am to 6pm. Closed Mondays. 3DM. ☎ (0 40) 35 04 23 60.

Boat trip around the port – In the tourist season (April until 22 September), boats leave the HADAG every half hour from 9am (8.30am Sundays) to 6pm. Otherwise, times and frequence vary (enquire on the spot). 12DM.

Postal Museum – Open Tuesdays, Wednesdays and Fridays from 10am to 3pm, Thursdays until 6pm. Closed Mondays, Saturdays, Sundays and certain public holidays. Entrance free. ☎ (0 40) 3 57-24 11.

Television Tower – Access from 10am (9am Sundays and public holidays) to 11pm. Closed 24 December. Lift. 4DM. ☎ (0 40) 43 80 24.

Planten un Blomen Park – Fountains, Son-et-Lumière, every evening at 10pm from May to the end of August (at 9pm in September). Entrance free.

Ethnographic Museum – Open daily from 10am to 6pm. Closed Mondays. 3DM. ☎ (0 40) 44 19 55 24.

Hagenbeck Zoo – Open daily from 8am to 6pm (7pm during summer holidays, 4.30pm in winter). 15DM (adults); 10DM (children). Dolphinarium 6DM and 4DM. ☎ (0 40) 54 00 01 07.

Excursions

Altona and Northern Germany Museum – Open from 10am to 6pm. Closed Mondays and certain public holidays. 3DM. ☎ (0 40) 38 07-5 14.

Villa Jenisch – Open : April to October from 2pm (11am Sundays) to 5pm ; November to March from 1pm (11am Sundays) to 4pm. Closed Mondays, and also 1 January, Good Friday, Easter Sunday, Whit-Sunday, 25 and 31 December. 1.50DM. ☎ (0 40) 82 87 90.

Ernst Barlach House – Open daily from 11am to 5pm. Closed Mondays and 24, 31 December. 3DM. ☎ (0 40) 82 60 85.

Wedel : Ernst-Barlach Museum – Open daily from 10am to 12 noon and from 3pm to 6pm. Closed Mondays, also 1 January, 24, 25 and 31 December. 5DM. ☎ (0 41 03) 1 51 50.

Ahrensburg Castle – Open : April to September, daily from 10am to 12.30pm and from 1pm to 5pm ; November to January, daily from 1pm to 3pm ; Feburary, March and October from 1pm to 4pm. Closed Mondays, Good Friday, the Day of Repentance and Prayer (a Wednesday in November), and from 24 December to 1 January. 4DM. ☎ (0 41 02) 4 25 10.

HAMELIN
🚹 ☎ (0 51 51) 20 26 17.

Hämelschenburg Castle – Guided tours (45min) from April to the end of October : Tuesdays to Saturdays at 10am, 11am, 12 noon, 2pm, 3pm, 4pm and 5pm ; Sundays and public holidays at 10am, 11am, 12 noon, 1.30pm, 2pm, 2.30pm, 3pm, 3.30pm, 4pm, 4.30pm and 5pm. Closed Mondays (except Easter Monday and Whit-Monday). 5DM. ☎ (0 51 55) 85 39.

Fischbeck Abbey – Guided tours (1 hour 30min) from Easter to 15 October, daily except Mondays : Tuesdays and Fridays from 9am to 11am and from 2pm to 4pm ; Wednesdays, Thursdays, Saturdays and Sundays in the afternoon only. 4DM. ☎ (0 51 52) 86 03.

HANOVER
🚹 Ernst-August-Platz 8. ☎ (05 11) 1 68 23 19.

Town Hall – Access to the dome by lift from 10am to 5pm. 2DM. ☎ (05 11) 1 68 23 19.

Wilhelm Busch Museum – Open daily from 10am to 5pm. Closed Mondays, Good Friday and 24 December. 2DM. ☎ (05 11) 71 40 76.

Kestner Museum – Open from 10am to 4pm Tuesdays, Thursdays and Fridays, 6pm Saturdays and Sundays, 8pm Wednesdays. Closed Mondays, and also 1 January, Good Friday, Easter Sunday, Whit-Sunday, 1 May, the Thursday of Ascension, 3 October, 24, 25 and 31 December. Entrance free. ☎ (05 11) 1 68-21 20.

Museum of Lower Saxony – Open daily from 10am to 5pm (7pm Thursdays). Closed Mondays. Entrance free. ☎ (05 11) 88 30 51.

Sprengel Museum – Open daily from 10am to 6pm (10pm Tuesdays). Closed Mondays, and also 1 January, Easter Sunday, 24, 25 and 31 December. Entrance free. ☎ (05 11) 1 68-38 75.

Historical Museum – Open from 10am to 4pm Wednesdays, Thursdays and Fridays, 6pm Saturdays and Sundays, 8pm Tuesdays. Closed Mondays, and also 1 January, Good Friday. Easter Sunday, Whit-Sunday, 1 May, 3 October, 24, 25 and 31 December. Entrance free. ☎ (05 11) 1 68-23 52.

Zoological Garden – Open : April to the end of September from 8am to 5.30pm (6pm Saturdays, Sundays and public holidays) ; March and October from 8am to 5pm ; November to the end of February from 8am to 4.30pm. 7DM. ☎ (05 11) 28 07 40.

HARZ MOUNTAINS

Clausthal-Zellerfeld
🚹 ☎ (0 53 23) 8 10 24.

Upper Harz Mine Museum – Open daily from 9am to 5pm. 4.50DM. ☎ (0 53 23) 8 16 33.

St. Andreasberg
🚹 ☎ (0 55 82) 8 03 36.

Old Silver Mine – Guided tours (1 hour) daily from 8am to 12 noon and from 2pm to 5pm. Closed Sundays and the month of November. 4.50DM. ☎ (0 55 82) 12 49.

Rübeland

Hermann's Grotto – Guided tours (45min) : mid-May to mid-September, daily from 9.45am to 5.15pm ; 2 January to mid-May and from mid-September to the end of December, daily from 9.15am to 4.15pm. Closed 1 January and 24 December. 5DM. ☎ (0 39 54) 91 32.

HEIDELBERG
🚹 Hauptbahnhof. ☎ (0 62 21) 2 13 41.

Castle – Guided tours of the interior (1 hour) daily from 9am to 5pm. 4DM. The Great Vat can be visited separately. ☎ (0 62 21) 2 00 70.

German Pharmaceutical Museum – Open : April to October daily from 10am to 5pm ; November to March Saturdays, Sundays and public holidays only from 11am to 5pm. Closed 25 December. 3DM. ☎ (0 62 21) 2 58 80.

University Library – Open: Easter to 1 November, Mondays to Saturdays from 10am to 7pm; Sundays 11am to 4pm; 2 November to Good Friday, Mondays to Saturdays from 10am to 7pm only. Closed 1 January, Epiphany, the Day of Repentance and Prayer (a Wednesday in November) and 24, 25, 26 December. Entrance free. ☎ (0 62 21) 54 25 39.

Electoral Palatinate Museum – Open daily from 10am to 5pm (9pm Thursdays). Closed Mondays. 3DM. ☎ (0 62 21) 58 34 02.

Students' Gaol – Open daily from 9am to 5pm. Closed Sundays and public holidays. 1DM.

Museum of Sacred and Liturgical Art – Open: July to September from 10am (12.30pm Sundays) to 5pm, closed Mondays; October to June, Saturdays from 10am to 5pm, Sundays from 12.30pm to 5pm. Closed from 20 December to mid-January. 2.50DM. ☎ (0 62 21) 47 56 22.

Excursions

Schwetzingen   🛈 ☎ (0 62 02) 49 33.

Park – Open every day: April to September, from 8am to 8pm; October to March, from 9am to 5pm. 2.50DM. ☎ (0 62 02) 8 14 81.

Castle – Guided tours (1 hours) March to the end of October, daily from 10am to 4pm (9am to 4.30pm Sundays). Closed Mondays. 7DM. ☎ (0 62 02) 8 14 81.

Königstuhl Funicular – From April to the end of October, departures every 10-20min from 9am to 7pm. For winter service, enquire on the spot. Price: 5.50DM Rtn from the Heidelberg-Kornmarkt station, 3.50DM Rtn from Molkenkur. ☎ (0 62 21) 5 13-0.

HELGOLAND   🛈 Landungsbrücke. ☎ (0 47 25) 8 08 50.

Access – There is a regular boat service (passengers only) from Cuxhaven. The "Seetouristik" company runs a transfer service (train, coach, boat) leaving the main railway station (Hauptbahnhof) in Hamburg. Day Excursions allow visitors approximately 4 hours on the island (Departure from Hamburg at 8am, from Cuxhaven at 10.30am; return to Cuxhaven at 6.30pm, Hamburg approximately 9.30pm). Price: 66DM Rtn from Hamburg, 55DM Rtn from Cuxhaven. Services also run from Busum (44DM Rtn), Bremerhaven (55DM) and Wilhelmshaven (54DM).
For the autumn and winter sea service from Cuxhaven, apply for details at the "Cassen Eils" navigation company. ☎ (0 47 21) 3 50 82.

HILDESHEIM   🛈 ☎ (0 51 21) 1 59 95

Cathedral – Open: April to October, Mondays to Saturdays from 9.30am to 5pm, Sundays from 12 noon to 5pm; November to March, Mondays to Saturdays from 10am to 4.30pm, Sundays from 12 noon to 5pm. Closed Good Friday. 0.50DM. ☎ (0 51 21) 3 20 21.

Pelizaeus and Roemer Museums – Open daily from 10am to 4.30pm. Closed Mondays, 1 January and 25 December. 3DM. ☎ (0 51 21) 1 59 79.

THE HOHENLOHE

Schöntal Abbey – Open daily from 9am to 6pm (30min guided tour for the abbey buildings. 2DM). ☎ (0 74 93) 20 83.

Langenburg Castle – Guided tours (45min) from Easter to mid-October, 8.30am to 12 noon and from 1.30pm to 6pm (last admissions 5.15pm). 3.50DM. ☎ (0 79 05) 2 64.

Neuenstein Castle – Guided tours (45min) from mid-March to mid-November, daily from 9am to 12 noon and from 1.30pm to 6pm. Closed Mondays. 5DM. ☎ (0 79 42) 22 09.

HOHENZOLLERN   🛈 ☎ (0 74 71) 18 51 13.

Castle – Guided tours (45min) daily from 9am to 5.30pm (4.30pm from November to the end of March). Closed 24 December. 6DM. ☎ (0 74 71) 24 28.

HUSUM   🛈 ☎ (0 48 41) 6 69 91.

North Frisian Museum – Open: April to October, daily from 10am to 5pm; November to March, Mondays to Fridays from 10am to 12 noon and from 2pm to 4pm, Sundays and public holidays from 10am to 4pm. Closed 1 January, Good Friday, the Day of Repentance and Prayer (a Wednesday in November), and 24, 25, 31 December. 3DM. ☎ (0 48 41) 25 45.

Excursions

Seebüll: Nolde Museum – Open: March to the end of October, daily from 10am to 6pm; in November from 10am to 5pm. Closed from December to the end of February. 4DM. ☎ (0 46 64) 3 64.

I

IDAR-OBERSTEIN 🚇 Nahe-Center, Bahnhofstrasse 13. ☎ (0 67 81) 2 70 25.

German Museum of Precious Stones – Open daily from 9am to 6pm (5pm from October to the end of April). Closed 25 December. 7DM. ☎ (0 67 81) 48 21.

Local Museum – Open daily from 9am to 5.30pm. Closed 25 December. 4DM. ☎ (0 67 81) 2 46 19.

Old Stonecutting Centre – Open from Easter to the end of October: Mondays to Saturdays from 9am to 5pm, Sundays from 10am to 4pm. Entrance free. ☎ (0 67 81) 3 31 65.

INGOLSTADT 🚇 Hallstrasse 5. ☎ (08 41) 30 54 17.

Bavarian Army Museum – Open daily from 8.45am to 4.30pm. Closed Mondays, also Good Friday, 1 November, 24, 25 and 31 December. 3.50DM. ☎ (08 41) 3 50 67.

Excursions

Neuburg an der Donau 🚇 ☎ (0 84 31) 5 52 40.

Castle Museum – Open daily from 10am to 5pm. Closed Mondays, also 1 January, Shrove Tuesday, 1 November, 24, 25 and 31 December. 3DM. ☎ (0 84 31) 88 97.

J

JENA 🚇 Löbderstrasse. ☎ (0 36 41) 2 46 71.

Local Museum – Open daily from 10am to 1pm and from 2pm to 5pm (6pm Wednesdays). Closed Mondays. 2DM. ☎ (0 36 41) 2 39 98.

Goethe Museum – Open from 15 April to 15 October, daily from 9am to 1pm. Closed Mondays. Entrance free. ☎ (0 36 41) 8 22 23 11.

Schiller Museum – Open Tuesdays to Fridays from 10am to 12 noon and from 1pm to 4pm, Saturdays from 11am to 4pm. Closed Sundays and Mondays. 1DM. ☎ (0 36 41) 8 22 23 53.

Planetarium – Astro-shows at 10am, 11am, 3pm and 8pm. Closed Mondays and 31 December. 5DM. ☎ (0 36 41) 2 73 15.

Optical Museum – Open daily from 9am to 5.30pm (4pm Saturdays). Closed Sundays, Mondays and public holidays. 3DM. ☎ (0 36 41) 83 34 04.

K

KARLSRUHE 🚇 Bahnhofplatz 6. ☎ (0 56 72) 10 22.

Fine Arts Museum – Open daily from 10am to 5pm (6pm Sundays). Closed Mondays, also Shrove Tuesday and 24, 31 December. Entrance free. ☎ (07 21) 1 35 33 55.

Baden Regional Museum – Open daily from 10am to 5.30pm (7.30pm Thursdays). Closed Mondays, also Shrove Tuesday and 24, 25, 31 December. Entrance free. ☎ (07 21) 1 35-65 42.

Botanical Gardens – Open daily from 8am until nightfall. Entrance free. Glasshouses (Pflanzenschauhäuser) open Tuesdays to Fridays from 9am to 4pm, Saturdays and Sundays from 9am to 12 noon and 1pm to 5pm (4pm in winter). 1DM.

KASSEL 🚇 Inter-City Bahnhof Wilhelmshöhe. ☎ (05 61) 3 40 54.

Wilhelmshöhe Castle – Open daily from 10am to 5pm. Closed Mondays, also 1 May, 24, 25, 31 December. Entrance free. ☎ (05 61) 3 60 11.

Hessen Museum – Same times as castle above. Entrance free. ☎ (05 61) 78 00 36.

New Gallery – Same times as castle above. Entrance free. ☎ (05 61) 1 52 66.

Brothers Grimm Museum – Open daily from 10am to 5pm. Closed certain public holidays. Entrance free. ☎ (05 61) 10 32 35.

Natural History Museum – Open daily from 10am to 4.30pm (1pm Sundays). Closed Mondays. Entrance free. ☎ (05 61) 7 87-40 14.

Excursions

Wilhelmsthal Castle – Guided tours (45min) daily from 10am to 4pm (3pm from November to the end of February). Closed Mondays, also 1 January, 25 and 26 December. 2DM. ☎ (0 56 74) 68 98.

KIEL

⊞ Sophienblatt 30. **☎** (04 31) 67 91 00.

Town Hall – Guided tours (45min) from May to the end of October, Wednesday and Sundays only from 12.30pm to 1.15pm. 1DM. **☎** (04 31) 6 79 10-0.

Excursions

Schleswig-Holstein Open-Air Museum – Open: April to mid-November, Tuesdays to Saturdays (Mondays also from July to mid-September) from 9am to 5pm, Sundays from 10am to 6pm; mid-November to the end of March, Sundays and public holidays only – providing the weather is fine – from 10am until nightfall. 5DM. **☎** (04 31) 6 55 55.

Laboe: German Naval War Memorial – Open daily from 9am to 4.30pm in March and April, to 5.30pm in May, 6pm from June to August, 5pm in September and October, 4pm from November to February. Closed 24 December. Memorial: 3.50DM; Submarine: 2.50DM. **☎** (0 43 43) 87 55.

KOBLENZ

⊞ ☎ (02 61) 3 13 04.

L

LAHN VALLEY

Schaumburg Castle – Open from Easter to the end of October, daily from 10am to 5pm. Closed Mondays. 5DM. **☎** (0 64 32) 37 84.

Diez: Oranienstein Castle – Closed for restoration until 1994.

Weilburg Castle – Guided tours (45min) daily from 10am to 4pm (3pm from November to the end of February). Closed Mondays, also 1 January, 24, 25, 26 and 31 December. 4DM. **☎** (0 64 71) 22 36.

Museum – Open: April to October, Tuesdays to Sundays from 10am to 12 noon and from 2pm to 5pm; November to March, Mondays to Fridays at the same times. Closed Good Friday and from 23 December to mid-January. 3DM. **☎** (0 64 71) 3 14 59.

LANDSHUT

⊞ ☎ (08 71) 2 30 31.

Palace – Guided tours (45min) daily from 9am to 12 noon and from 1pm to 5pm (4pm from October to the end of March). Closed Mondays, and also 1 January, Shrove Tuesday, 1 November, 24 and 25 December. 2DM. **☎** (08 71) 2 26 38.

Trausnitz Castle – Same times and charges as for the Palace above. **☎** (08 71) 2 26 38.

LEIPZIG

⊞ Sachsenplatz 1. **☎** (03 41) 7 95 90.

Town History Museum – Open daily from 9.30am to 6pm (5pm from November to the end of April) (last admissions 30min before closing time). Closed in January. 2DM. **☎** (03 41) 8 13 92.

Egyptian Museum – Open Tuesdays to Fridays from 2pm to 6pm, Sundays from 10am to 1pm. Closed Mondays and Saturdays. 1DM. **☎** (03 41) 28 21 66.

Grassi Museum – Open from 10am to 6pm Tuesdays and Thursdays, 8pm Wednesdays, 1pm Fridays, 5pm Saturdays and Sundays. Closed Mondays, also 24 and 31 December. 3.50DM. **☎** (03 41) 29 15 43.

Fine Arts Museum – Open daily from 9am to 5pm (from 1pm to 9.30pm Wednesdays). Closed Mondays, also 1 January, 24, 25 and 31 December. 2DM. **☎** (03 41) 31 31 02.

Battle of the Nations Monument – Open: May to September daily from 9.30am to 4.30pm; October to April daily from 9am to 4pm. Closed 1 January, 24, 25 and 31 December. 2DM. **☎** (03 41) 8 04 71.

LEMGO

⊞ ☎ (0 52 61) 21 33 47.

House of the Witches' Burgomaster – Open daily from 10am to 12.30pm and from 1.30pm to 5pm (Saturdays from 10am to 1pm). Closed Mondays, and between Christmas and 1 January. 1.50DM. **☎** (0 52 61) 2 13.

Karl Junker's House – Open from mid-March to mid-November, daily from 10am to 12.30pm and from 2pm to 5pm. Closed Mondays. 1.50DM. **☎** (0 52 61) 2 13-2 76.

LIMBURG AN DER LAHN

⊞ ☎ (0 64 31) 61 66.

Diocesan Museum – Open from 15 March to 15 November, daily from 10am to 1pm and from 2pm to 5pm (Sundays from 11am to 5pm). Closed Mondays. 2DM. **☎** (0 64 31) 29 52 33.

LINDAU

⊞ ☎ (0 83 82) 2 60 00.

Municipal Museum – Open from March to the end of October, daily from 10am to 12 noon and from 2pm to 5pm. Closed Mondays, also 1 May, Whit-Sunday and Corpus Christi (partially). 4DM. **☎** (0 83 82) 27 54 05.

LINDERHOF ☎ (0 88 22) 5 34.

Castle – Guided tours (1 hour 30min) : April to September, daily from 9am to 5.30pm ; October to March, daily from 10am to 4pm. Spectacular fountains play every hour from 9am. Visitors may have to wait in summer. The Grotto of Venus and the Moorish Pavilion are closed in winter. 7DM in summer, 5DM in winter. Admission to the park free. ☎ (0 88 22) 5 12.

LÜBECK 🛈 Markt. ☎ (04 51) 1 22 81 06.

St Anne's Museum – Open daily from 10am to 5pm (4pm from October to the end of March). Closed Mondays, also 24, 25 and 31 December. 3DM. ☎ (04 51) 1 22 41 33.

Behnhaus and Drägerhaus – Same times and charge as museum above. ☎ (04 51) 1 22 41 53.

LUDWIGSBURG 🛈 ☎ (0 71 41) 91 02 52.

Palace – Guided tour of the apartments (1 hour 30min) : mid-March to the end of October from 9am to 12 noon and from 1pm to 5pm ; the rest of the year, Mondays to Fridays at 10.30am and 3pm, Saturdays at 10.30am, 2pm and 3.30pm, Sundays and public holidays at 10.30am and from 1.30pm to 4pm. 4DM. Combined ticket (castle and park) 6DM. ☎ (0 71 41) 18 64 40.

Excursions

Marbach am Neckar 🛈 ☎ (0 71 44) 10 22 45.

Schiller National Museum – Open daily from 9am to 5pm. Closed 24, 25, 26 and 31 December. 2DM. ☎ (0 71 44) 1 57 84.

LÜNEBURG 🛈 Rathaus, Marktplatz. ☎ (0 41 31) 3 22 00.

Town Hall – Guided tours (45min) every hour from 10am to 4pm (3pm from mid-October to the end of March). Closed Mondays. 3.50DM. ☎ (0 41 31) 2 30-3 09.

Excursions

Lauenburg an der Elbe 🛈 ☎ (0 41 53) 59 09 81.

Elbe Navigation Museum – Open : March to October, daily from 10am to 1pm and from 2pm to 5pm (Sundays from 10am to 5pm) ; November to February, Wednesdays, Fridays and Saturdays from 10am to 1pm and from 2pm to 4.30pm, Sundays from 10am to 5pm. Closed 24 and 31 December. 2DM. ☎ (0 41 53) 59 09-84.

Ebstorf Benedictine Abbey – Guided tours (1 hour 15min) : from April to September, Mondays to Saturdays from 10am to 11am and from 2pm to 6pm, Sundays and public holidays at 11.15am and from 2pm to 6pm ; from 1 to 14 October, Mondays to Saturdays from 10am to 11am and from 2pm to 4pm, Sundays and public holidays at 11.15am and from 2pm to 4pm. Closed Good Friday and from mid-October to the end of March. 5DM. ☎ (0 58 22) 23 04.

Suhlendorf Museum – Open daily from 10am to 6pm. Closed Mondays, from 21 to 31 December, and in the month of January. 3DM. ☎ (0 58 20) 3 70.

Walsrode Ornithological Park – Open March to mid-November, daily from 9am to 7pm. 12DM. ☎ (0 51 61) 20 15.

M

MAGDEBURG 🛈 Alter Markt 9. ☎ (03 91) 3 16 67.

Abbey of Our Lady – Open daily from 10am to 6pm. Closed Mondays, also 1 January, 24, 25 and 31 December. 2.05DM. ☎ (03 91) 3 37 41.

MAINZ 🛈 Bahnhofstrasse 15. ☎ (0 61 31) 23 37 41.

Gutenberg Museum – Open daily from 10am to 6pm (1pm Sundays). Closed Mondays and certain public holidays. Entrance free. ☎ (0 61 31) 12 26 40.

Romano-German Museum – Open daily from 10am to 6pm. Closed Mondays, also 25 and 31 December and in January. Entrance free. ☎ (0 61 31) 23 22 31.

Central Rhineland Museum – Open from 10am to 5pm (4pm Fridays). Closed Mondays, also 1 January, during carnival time, and 24, 25, 31 December. Entrance free. ☎ (0 61 31) 23 29 55.

MANNHEIM 🛈 Kaiserring 10. ☎ (06 21) 10 10 11.

Fine Arts Museum – Open daily from 10am to 5pm (from 12 noon to 8pm Thursdays). Closed Mondays. 4DM. ☎ (06 21) 2 93 -64 13.

Reiss Municipal Museum – Open daily from 10am to 5pm (1pm to 8pm Thursdays). Closed Mondays. 4DM. ☎ (06 21) 2 93 22 19.

Museum of Archaeology and Ethnology – Same times, charge and telephone number as the Municipal Museum above.

Palace – Open from 10am to 12 noon and from 3pm to 5pm : April to October, every day except Mondays; from November to March, Sundays only. Closed 1 January, 1 May and 25 December. 2DM. ☎ (06 21) 2 92-28 90.

Boat Museum – Open daily from 10am to 5pm (8pm Wednesdays). Closed Mondays (except at Easter and Whitsun), also Shrove Tuesday, Good Friday and 24, 25, 31 December. Entrance free. ☎ (06 21) 2 92-47 30.

Regional Museum of Industrial Techniques – Open the same days and times as the Boat Museum above. 4DM. ☎ (06 21) 2 92-47 30.

MARBURG
ℹ Neue Kasseler Strasse 1. ☎ (0 64 21) 20 12 49.

St Elizabeth's Church – Open: from Easter Sunday until the end of September, from 9am to 6pm (from 11.15am to 5.30pm Sundays); the rest of the year, from 10am (11.15am Sundays) to 4pm. Closed the 24 December. 2DM. ☎ (0 64 21) 6 55 73.

Castle – Open daily from 11am to 1pm and from 2pm to 5pm. Closed Mondays. Entrance free. ☎ (0 64 21) 28 58 71.

Fine Arts Museum – Open daily from 11am to 1pm and from 2pm to 5pm. Closed Mondays. Entrance free. ☎ (0 64 21) 28 23 55.

MAULBRONN

Abbey – Open: April to the end of October, from 8.30am to 6.30pm; in March and November, from 9am to 5pm; from December to the end of February, from 9.30am to 1pm and from 2pm to 5pm. Closed for certain public holidays. 3DM. ☎ (0 70 43) 74 54.

MEISSEN
ℹ An der Frauenkirch 3. ☎ (0 35 21) 44 70.

National Porcelain Factory – Exhibition: open daily from 8.30am to 4pm. 3DM. Workshops: Guided tours (45min) from 8.30am to 12 noon and from 1pm to 3.45pm. 3DM. Closed Mondays, also 24, 25 and 31 December. ☎ (0 35 21) 5 41-3 91.

Castle – Open daily from 10am to 6pm (last admissions 5pm). Closed Mondays and for the month of January. 3DM. Slides and diorama 4DM. ☎ (0 35 26) 29 20.

MINDEN
ℹ Grosser Domhof 3. ☎ (05 71) 8 93 85.

Cathedral Treasury – Open Tuesdays, Thursdays, Saturdays and Sundays from 10am to 12 noon; Wednesdays and Fridays from 3pm to 5pm. Closed Mondays. Entrance free. ☎ (05 71) 2 30 74.

Local History Museum – Open Tuesdays to Saturdays from 10am to 1pm and from 2.30pm to 5pm, Sundays from 11am to 6pm. Closed Mondays. Entrance free. ☎ (05 71) 8 93 16.

Excursions

Porta Westfalica: Television Tower – Access from Easter to the end of October, daily from 10am to 6pm. 1DM. ☎ (05 71) 79 12 82.

MÖNCHENGLADBACH
ℹ Bismarckstrasse 23-27. ☎ (0 21 61) 2 20 01.

Abteiberg Municipal Museum – Open daily from 10am to 6pm. Closed Mondays, also 1 January, Easter Sunday, Whit-Sunday, 24, 25 and 31 December. 3DM. ☎ (0 21 61) 25 46 14.

Rheydt Castle – Until 1994, part of the castle is being restored. The remainder, notably the department of weaving, is open daily from 10am to 6pm (from 11am to 5pm from November to the end of February). Closed Mondays, also 1 January, 24, 25 and 31 December. 3DM. ☎ (0 21 66) 2 01 01.

Excursions

Dyck Castle – Guided tours (45min) from April to the end of November, every hour from 10am to 5pm. Closed Mondays. 3DM. ☎ (0 21 82) 40 61.

MONSCHAU
ℹ ☎ (0 24 72) 33 00.

Red House – Open from Good Friday to the end of November at 10am, 11am, 2pm, 3pm and 4pm. Closed Mondays. ☎ (0 24 72) 33 00.

Excursions

Nideggen Castle – Open in season daily from 10am to 5pm, in winter according to the weather. Closed Mondays. 2.50DM. ☎ (0 24 27) 63 40.

MOSELLE

River Cruises – From mid-May to mid-October there is a daily service between Koblenz and Cochem (price approximately 45DM Rtn; supplement for the hydrofoil). Two- and three-day cruises between Frankfurt and Trier (via Koblenz), or between Trier and Cologne (via Koblenz), are organized in season. For details, apply at the pier offices or to the secretariat of the Köln-Düsseldorfer company, Frankenwerft 15, W-5000 Köln. ☎ (02 21) 2 08 80.

Beilstein Castle – Open from April to the end of October, daily, from 9am to 6pm. 2DM. ☎ (0 26 73) 14 49.

Cochem Castle – Guided tours (45min) from 15 March to 10 November, daily from 9am to 5pm. 3.50DM. ☎ (0 26 71) 2 55.

Eltz Castle – Guided tours (45min), April to the end of October, daily from 9.30am to 6pm. 6.50DM. ☎ (0 26 72) 13 00.

MUNDEN Excursions

Bad Karlshafen   🄸 ☎ (0 56 72) 10 22.

Huguenot Museum – Open: March to the end of October, Tuesdays to Saturdays from 2pm to 6pm, Sundays from 11am to 6pm ; November and December, Wednesdays and Saturdays only from 2pm to 6pm, Sundays from 11am to 6pm. Closed 25 and 31 December. 2.50DM. ☎ (0 56 72) 14 10.

Fürstenberg   🄸 ☎ (0 52 71) 51 01.

Porcelain Museum – Open from 9am (10am Sundays and public holidays) to 5pm daily. Closed Mondays, also 1 January and 25 December. 3DM. ☎ (0 52 71) 40 11 04.

MUNICH   🄸 Hauptbahnhof. ☎ (0 89) 2 39 12 56.

German Hunting and Fishing Museum – Open daily from 9.30am to 5pm (9pm Mondays and Thursdays). Closed 24 and 31 December. 4DM. ☎ (0 89) 22 05 22.

The Palace :

Treasury – Open from 10am to 4.30pm. Closed Mondays, also 1 January, Shrove Tuesday, Good Friday, Easter Sunday, Whit-Sunday, 1 May, 1 November, 24, 25 and 31 December. 3.50DM. ☎ (0 89) 2 90 67-1.

Palace Museum – Same opening and closing times as the Treasury, above. To make sure of seeing all the exhibits, follow both the morning and afternoon guided tours, 3.50DM each. Same telephone number as the Treasury.

Palace Theatre – Open daily from 2pm (10am Sundays) to 5pm. 2DM. Same telephone number as the Treasury.

Old Pinakothek – Open daily from 9.15am to 4.30pm. Evening opening from 7pm to 9pm Tuesdays and Thursdays. Closed Mondays, also 1 May, Corpus Christi, 1 November, 24 and 25 December. 4DM. ☎ (0 89) 2 38 05-2 15.

New Pinakothek – Same times and charge as Old Pinakothek. Closed Mondays, Good Friday, and 1 May, Corpus Christi, 1 November, 24 and 25 December. ☎ (0 89) 2 38 05-1 95.

Glyptothek – Open daily from 10am to 4.30pm (8.30pm Thursdays). Closed Mondays, also 1 January, Good Friday, 1 May, Whit-Sunday, 3 October, 24 and 25 December. 3.50DM. ☎ (0 89) 5 59 15 51.

Collection of Antiquities – Open daily from 10am to 4.30pm (Wednesdays from 12 noon to 8.30pm). Closed Mondays, also Good Friday, Easter Sunday, and 1 May, Corpus Christi, 1 November, 24 and 25 December. 3.50DM. ☎ (0 89) 5 59 15 51.

Villa Lenbach Collections – Open daily from 10am to 6pm. Closed Mondays, also Shrove Tuesday and 24, 31 December. 5DM (entrance free Sundays and public holidays). ☎ (0 89) 52 82 50.

German Museum – Open daily from 9am to 5pm. Closed 1 January, Shrove Tuesday, Good Friday, Easter Sunday, Whit-Sunday, 1 May, Corpus Christi, 1 November, 24, 25 and 31 December. 8DM. ☎ (0 89) 21 79-1.

Bavarian National Museum – Open daily from 9.30am to 5pm. Closed Mondays and certain public holidays. 3DM. ☎ (0 89) 21 68-0.

State Gallery Modern Art Collection – Open daily from 9.15am to 4.30pm (and again from 7pm to 9pm Thursdays). Closed Mondays, also 1 January, Good Friday, Easter Sunday, Whit-Sunday, 1 May, Corpus Christi, 1 November, 24 and 25 December. 3DM. ☎ (0 89) 29 27 10.

Nymphenburg Palace – Open: April to September, daily from 9am to 12.30pm and from 1.30pm to 5pm ; October to March, daily from 10am to 12.30pm and from 1.30pm to 4pm. Closed Mondays, also 1 January, Shrove Tuesday, 1 November, 24, 25 and 31 December. 2.50DM. ☎ (0 89) 17 90 86 54.

Amalienburg – Same opening and closing times as Nymphenburg Palace above. 2DM. Same telephone number as the Palace.

Carriage Museum and Porcelain Collection – Open: April to September, daily from 9am to 12 noon and from 1pm to 5pm ; October to March, daily from 10am to 12 noon and from 1pm to 4pm. Closed the same days as Nymphenburg Palace above. 2.50DM. ☎ (0 89) 17 90 86 54.

Botanical Gardens – Open daily from 9am to 7pm from May to the end of August, 8pm in April and September, 5pm in February, March and October, 4.30pm in November, December and January. Glasshouses are closed 30min earlier and also between 11.45am and 1pm. Closed 24 and 31 December. 3DM. ☎ (0 89) 1 79 23 10.

Villa Stuck – Open daily from 10am to 5pm. Closed Mondays. 6-8DM according to the special exhibitions.

City Historical Museum – Open daily from 10am to 5pm (8.30pm Wednesdays). Closed Mondays, also the Sunday of carnival week, Shrove Tuesday, Good Friday, Easter Sunday, Whit-Sunday, 1 May, 1 November, 24 and 25 December. 5DM. ☎ (0 89) 23 32 23 70.

Hellabrunn Zoological Gardens – Open April to September, daily from 8am to 6pm; October to March from 9am to 5pm. 6DM. ☎ (0 89) 62 50 80.

Bavaria Film Studios – Guided tours (1 hour 30min) from March to the end of October, daily from 9am to 4pm. 11DM. ☎ (0 89) 64 99 23 04.

Olympiapark – Open from mid-April to mid-October, daily from 8.30am to 6pm, otherwise from 9am to 4pm. 7DM for the whole park; 1DM for the Olympic Stadium; 5DM for the tower (Olympiaturm) lift. ☎ (0 89) 3 06 13-1.

BMW-Museum – Open daily from 9am to 5pm (last admissions 4pm). Closed 24 and 31 December. 4.50DM. ☎ (0 89) 38 95-30 14.

Excursions

Schleissheim Castle – Open daily from 10am to 12.30pm and from 1.30pm to 5pm (4pm from October to the end of March). Closed Mondays, also 1 January, Shrove Tuesday, 1 November, 24, 25 and 31 December. 2DM. ☎ (0 89) 3 15 02 12.

Andechs Benedictine Abbey Church – Visitors are welcome without payment throughout the year. From Mondays to Fridays in July and August, guided tours are available from 2.30pm. 2DM. ☎ (0 81 52) 3 76-0.

Dachau Concentration Camp: Ruins, Commemorative Monuments and Museum – Open daily from 9am to 5pm. Closed Mondays and the 24 and 31 December. Entrance free. ☎ (0 81 31) 17 41.

MÜNSTER   🛈 Berliner Platz 22. ☎ (02 51) 51 01 80.

Cathedral: Treasury – Open daily from 10am to 12 noon and from 2pm to 6pm. Closed Sundays mornings, Mondays, and 1 January, 24, 25, 26 and 31 December. 1DM. ☎ (02 51) 4 26 71.

Fine Arts Museum – Open daily from 10am to 6pm. Closed Mondays. Entrance free. ☎ (02 51) 59 07 01.

Town Hall: Peace Hall – Open Mondays to Fridays from 9am to 5pm, Saturdays from 9am to 4pm, Sundays from 10am to 1pm. Closed 1 January and 25 December. 1.50 DM. ☎ (02 51) 4 92-2745.

Westphalian Museum of Natural Science – Open daily from 9am to 6pm. Closed Mondays, also 24 and 31 December. Entrance free. Planetarium 3DM. ☎ (02 51)5 91 60 98 (Planetarium) (02 51) 8 94 23).

Open-Air Windmill Museum – Open: April to October, daily from 10am to 5pm; November to March, Mondays to Saturdays from 1.30pm to 4.30pm, Sundays from 11am to 4.30pm. 4DM. ☎ (02 51) 8 20 74.

Excursions

Telgte Local Museum – Open daily from 9.30am to 12 noon and from 1.30pm to 5pm. Closed Mondays, 24, 25 and 31 December, and also during preparations for special exhibitions. Ask before going. 2DM. ☎ (0 25 04) 17 36.

N

NENNIG

Roman Villa – Open: April to September, daily from 8.30am to 12 noon and from 1pm to 6pm; October to March, daily from 9am to 12 noon and from 1pm to 4.30pm. Closed Mondays. 1DM. ☎ (0 68 66) 13 29.

NÖRDLINGEN   🛈 ☎ (0 90 81) 43 80.

Municipal Museum – Open from March to the end of November, daily from 10am to 12 noon and from 1.30am to 4.30pm. Closed Mondays, also Good Friday, 1 May and the Day of Repentance and Prayer (a Wednesday in November). 2DM. ☎ (0 90 81) 43 80.

NÜRBURGRING

Motor Racing Museum – Open: March to October, daily from 10am to 6pm; November to February, Tuesdays to Sundays from 10am to 5pm. 8.50DM. ☎ (0 26 91) 30 21 47.

NUREMBERG   🛈 Hauptbahnhof. ☎ (09 11) 23 36 32.

German National Museum – Open daily from 10am to 5pm (9pm Thursdays). Closed Mondays, also 1 January, Shrove Tuesday, Good Friday, 1 May, 3 October, 24, 25 and 31 December. 5DM. ☎ (09 11) 1 33 10.

Dürer's House – Open: March to October, Tuesdays to Sundays from 10am to 5pm (9pm Wednesdays); November to February, Tuesdays to Fridays from 1pm to 5pm (9pm Wednesdays), Saturdays and Sundays from 10am to 5pm. During the period of Advent, the summer timetable applies. Closed Mondays, also 1 January, Shrove Tuesday, Good Friday, 1 May, 24, 25 and 31 December. 3DM. ☎ (09 11) 2 31-22 71.

Castle – Guided tours (30min): April to September, daily from 9am to 12 noon and from 12.45pm to 5pm (last admissions 4.30pm); October to March, daily from 9.30am to 12 noon and from 12.45pm to 4pm (last admissions 3.30pm). Closed 1 January, Shrove Tuesday, 1 November, 24, 25 and 31 December. 3DM. ☎ (09 11) 22 57 26.

Toy Museum – Open daily from 10am to 5pm (9pm Wednesdays). Closed Mondays, also 1 January, Shrove Tuesday, Good Friday, the Tuesdays after Easter and Whitsun, 1 May, 24, 25 and 31 December. 3DM. ☎ (09 11) 2 31-31 64.

Transport Museum – Open daily from 9.30am to 5pm. Closed 1 January, Shrove Tuesday, Good Friday, Easter Sunday, Whit-Sunday, 1 May, 3 October, the Day of Repentance and Prayer (a Wednesday in November), 24 and 31 December. 4DM. ☎ (09 11) 2 19 24 28.

O

OBERSTDORF
🛈 ☎ (0 83 22) 70 00.

Nebelhorn: Cable Car/Chairlift – Services run from 8.15 am to 5pm daily. Inclusive Rtn fare: 25DM. ☎ (0 83 22) 10 95.

Excursions

Breitachklamm – Accessible from 8am to 4pm daily (alteration of times possible in March and April because of melting snows). From May to October, guided tours available. 3DM. ☎ (0 83 22) 48 87.

ODENWALD

Eulbach Park – Open daily from 8.30am to 5pm. ☎ (0 60 62) 37 00.

Michelstadt
🛈 ☎ (0 60 61) 7 41 46.

Odenwald Museum – Open from 10am to 12 noon and from 2pm to 5pm; every day except Mondays from the 2nd Saturday before Easter to 1 November; Thursdays to Sundays only during the weeks of Advent, from the 25 to 31 December, and from 1 to 6 January. 2DM. ☎ (0 60 61) 7 41 46.

Amorbach Abbey Church – Guided tours (30min) every 40min: April to the end of September from 10am (11.20am Sundays) to 6pm; March and October from 10am to 12 noon and from 1.20pm to 4.40pm (Sundays from 11.20am to 4.40pm); November to the end of February from 10am to 11.40am and from 2pm to 3.20pm (afternoons only on Saturdays). 3DM. ☎ (0 93 73) 12 52.

OLDENBURG
🛈 Wallstrasse 14. ☎ (04 41) 1 57 44.

Regional Art and History Museum – Open daily from 9am (10am Saturdays and Sundays) to 5pm. Closed Mondays, also 1 January, Good Friday, Easter Sunday, Whit-Sunday, 1 May, 24, 25, 31 December. Entrance free. ☎ (04 41) 2 20 26 00.

Municipal Museum – Open daily from 9am (10am Saturdays and Sundays) to 5pm (12 noon Saturdays). Closed Mondays, also Easter Saturday and 24, 31 December. Entrance free. ☎ (04 41) 2 35 28 81.

Augusteum – Same times as Regional Museum above; same telephone number; entrance free.

Natural History Museum – Open daily from 9am (10am Saturdays and Sundays) to 5pm (3pm Fridays). Closed Mondays, also 1 January, Easter Sunday, Whit-Sunday, 1 May, 24 and 25 December. Entrance free. ☎ (04 41) 2 65 72.

Excursion

Cloppenburg Museum-Village – Open March to October, daily from 8am (9am Sundays and public holidays) to 6pm; November to February, daily from 9am (10am Sundays and public holidays) to 5pm. Closed 24, 25 and 31 December. 5DM. ☎ (0 44 71) 25 04.

OSNABRÜCK
🛈 Markt 22. ☎ (05 41) 3 23 22 02.

Town Hall – Open Mondays to Fridays from 8.30am to 6pm, Saturdays and Sundays from 10am to 1pm. Closed certain public holidays. Entrance free. Telephone number as above.

OTTOBEUREN
🛈 ☎ (0 83 32) 68 17.

Abbey Church – Open daily from 10am to 12 noon and from 2pm to 5pm (in winter, the church closes at nightfall). ☎ (0 83 32) 7 98-0.

Abbey Buildings – Open March to the end of November, daily from 10am to 12 noon and from 2pm to 5pm. In winter, visits can be arranged on Sundays. 2DM. Telephone number as for the Abbey Church above.

P

PADERBORN
🖸 ☎ (0 52 51) 2 64 61.

Diocesan Museum – Work in progress until the end of 1992.

PASSAU
🖸 ☎ (08 51) 3 34 21.

Glass Museum – Open daily from 10am to 5pm. 3DM. ☎ (08 51) 3 50 71.

POTSDAM
🖸 Friedrich-Ebert-Strasse 5. ☎ (03 31) 2 11 10.

Sans-Souci:

Great Gallery – Open mid-May to mid-October, daily from 9am to 12 noon and from 12.45pm to 5pm. Closed the fourth Wednesday of each month and 24 and 31 December. 3DM. ☎ (03 31) 2 26 55.

Sans-Souci Palace – Guided tours (45min): April to the end of September from 9am to 5pm daily (4pm in February, March and October, 3pm from November to the end of January). Break between 12.30pm and 1pm. Closed the first and third Wednesday of each month, also 24 and 31 December. 6DM. ☎ (03 31) 2 39 31.

New Palace – Unaccompanied tours. Same hours of opening as the Palace, but break from 12 noon to 12.30pm. Closed Fridays, also 24, 31 December. 6DM. ☎ (03 31) 97 31 43.

Hydraulic Waterworks – Guided tours (30min): mid-May to mid-October, Wednesdays to Sundays from 9am to 12 noon and from 1pm to 5pm; mid-October to mid-May, Saturdays and Sundays only from 9am to 4pm. Closed 24 and 31 December. 3DM. ☎ (03 31) 2 41 06.

Cecilienhof – Open daily from 9am to 5pm (4pm from November to mid-May). Closed the second and fourth Monday of each month. 3DM. ☎ (03 31) 2 25 79.

Excursions

Lehnin Abbey – Open from July to the end of September, daily from 10am to 12 noon and from 1pm to 5pm. Closed Sunday mornings and Thursday afternoons. ☎ (0 33 82) 4 31.

Q

QUEDLINBURG
🖸 ☎ (0 39 46) 28 66.

Klopstock Museum – Open: May to September, daily from 10am to 6pm; October to April, daily from 9am to 5pm. Closed Mondays and Tuesdays. Entrance free. ☎ (0 39 46) 26 10.

Feininger Gallery – Open daily from 10am to 12 noon and from 1pm to 6pm (5pm from October to the end of March). Closed Mondays. 3DM. ☎ (0 39 46) 22 38.

Castle Museum – Open: May to September, daily from 10am to 6pm; October to April, daily from 9am to 5pm. Closed Mondays. 2.50DM. ☎ (0 39 46) 27 30.

R

RASTATT
🖸 ☎ (0 72 22) 3 30 53.

Castle – Guided tours (45min) daily from 9.30am to 5.30pm (last admissions 4.15pm). Closed Mondays and certain public holidays. 4DM. ☎ (0 72 22) 38 73 85.

Military Museum – Open daily from 9.30am to 5pm. Closed Mondays, also 1 January, 24, 25 and 31 December. Entrance free. ☎ (0 72 22) 3 42 44.

Excursions

The Favourite's Castle – Guided tours (1 hour): mid-March to the end of September, daily from 9am to 11am and from 2pm to 5pm; October to mid-November, daily from 9am to 11am and from 1pm to 4pm. Closed from mid-November to mid-March. 4DM. ☎ (0 72 22) 4 12 07.

RATZEBURG
🖸 ☎ (0 45 41) 80 00 81.

Barlach Memorial – Open from March to the end of November, daily from 10am to 12 noon and from 3pm to 6pm. Closed Mondays. 2DM. ☎ (0 45 41) 37 89.

RAVENSBRÜCK

National Ravensbrück Memorial – Open daily from 8am to 6pm (5pm from October to the end of March). Last admissions 30min before closing time. Closed Mondays, also 1 January, 24, 25, 26 and 31 December. Entrance free. ☎ (03 30 93) 20 25.

REGENSBURG 🛈 Altes Rathaus. ☎ (09 41) 5 07 21 41.

Cathedral:

Treasury – Open: April to the end of October, daily except Mondays from 10am (11.30am Sundays) to 5pm ; December to the end of March, Fridays and Saturdays from 10am to 4pm, Sundays and public holidays from 11.30am to 4pm. Closed in November. 2DM. ☎ (09 41) 5 76 45.

Cloister – Restoration in progress: re-opening scheduled for 1993.

St-Ulric's Diocesan Museum – Open from April to the end of November, daily from 10am to 5pm. Closed Mondays. 3DM. ☎ (09 41) 5 16 88.

Old Town Hall: Reichstag Museum – Guided tours (45min) daily from 9.30am to 12 noon and from 2pm to 4pm (Sundays from 10am to 12 noon only). 3DM. ☎ (09 41) 5 07 21 41.

Thurn und Taxis Castle and Transport Museum – Guided tours can be arranged. Enquire at the Castle or by telephone: ☎ (09 41) 50 48-1 81.

City Museum – Open daily from 10am to 4pm (1pm Sundays). Closed Mondays, also 1 January, 1 May, 1 November, 24, 25 and 31 December. 2.50DM. Admission free the 1st Sunday of each month. ☎ (09 41) 5 07 34 40.

Excursions

Valhalla – Open: April to the end of September from 9am to 17.45pm; October from 9am to 4.45pm; November to the end of March from 10am to 11.45pm and from 1pm to 3.45pm. Closed Shrove Tuesday and 24, 25, 31 December. 1.50DM. ☎ (0 94 03) 39 09.

Liberation Monument – Open: April to September, daily from 8am to 6pm ; October to March, from 9am to 12 noon and from 1pm to 4pm. Closed Shrove Tuesday, 1 November, 24, 25 and 31 December. 1.50DM. ☎ (0 94 41) 70 12 34.

Wettenburg Abbey – Open daily from 8am to 6pm (except during services). Entrance free. ☎ (0 94 41) 16 62.

RHINELAND PALATINATE

Hambach Castle – Open from March to the end of November, daily from 9am to 6pm. 3DM. ☎ (0 63 22) 7 96-3 28.

Ludwigshöhe Castle – Open daily from 9am to 1pm and from 2pm to 6pm (5pm from October to the end of March). Guided tours (1 hour) of the historic apartments every hour from 10am to 3pm. Closed Mondays and for the month of December. 3DM. ☎ (0 63 23) 31 48.

Trifels Castle – Open: April to the end of September, daily from 9am to 6pm ; March and October from 9am to 5pm ; November, January and February from 9am to 1pm and from 2pm to 5pm (closed Mondays). The castle is closed during the month of December. 3DM. ☎ (0 63 46) 22 00.

RHINE VALLEY

Pfalz Castle – Open daily from 9am to 1pm and from 2pm to 6pm (5pm from October to the end of March). Access by ferry: 2DM. ☎ (0 67 74) 5 70.

Marksburg Castle – Guided tours (45min): Easter to October, from 10am to 5pm ; November to Easter, 11am to 4pm. Closed from 24 to 31 December. 5.50DM. ☎ (0 26 27) 2 06.

Lahneck Fortress – Guided tours (45min) from April to the end of October, daily from 10am to 5.30pm. 4DM. ☎ (0 26 21) 27 89.

Stolzenfels Castle – Guided tours (1 hour) daily from 9am to 1pm and from 2pm to 6pm (5pm from October to the end of March). Last admissions 30min before closing. Closed Mondays and in the month of December. 2DM. ☎ (02 61) 5 16 56.

Gedeonseck – The chair lift is in service from April to the end of October, daily from 10am to 6pm. 7DM. ☎ (0 67 42) 25 10.

Rheinfels Fortress – Open April to the end of October, daily from 9am to 5pm. 3DM. ☎ (0 67 41) 3 83.

Sooneck Fortress – Guided tours (30min) daily from 9am to 1pm and from 2pm to 6pm (5pm from October to the end of March). Last admissions 45min before closing time. Closed Mondays and in the month of December. 3DM. ☎ (0 67 43) 60 64.

Reichenstein Castle – Open mid-March to mid-November, daily from 9am to 6pm. 5DM. ☎ (0 67 21) 61 01.

Rheinstein Castle – Open March to the end of November, daily from 9am to 7pm. 5DM. ☎ (0 67 21) 63 77.

ROMANTIC ROAD

Weikersheim Castle – Guided tours (1 hour): April to October from 9am to 6pm daily ; November to March from 10am to 12 noon and from 1.30pm to 4.30pm daily. Closed 24 and 31 December. ☎ (0 79 34) 83 64.

Harburg Castle – Guided tours (30min) daily from 9am to 11.30am and from 1.30pm to 5.30pm (4.30pm in October). Closed Mondays, and from November to 15 March. Entrance from 3 to 8DM according to the number of people. ☎ (0 90 03) 12 68.

ROSTOCK
🛈 Schnickmannstrasse 13. ☎ (03 81) 2 52 60.

Boat trip around the port – Embarcations from Kabutzenhof Pier (Rostock) or Alter Strom/Neuer Strom Piers (Warnemünde) every hour from 10am. Length of tour: 1 hour to 1 hour 30min. 10DM.

Navigational Museum – Open daily from 9am to 5pm. Closed Fridays, also 24, 25 and 31 December. 2DM. ☎ (03 81) 2 26 98.

Historical Museum – Open dialy from 10am to 6pm. Closed Mondays, also 24 and 31 December. 3DM. ☎ (03 81) 3 47 05.

Excursions

Güstrow : Ernst-Barlach Museum – Open daily from 9am to 12 noon and from 1pm to 5pm. Closed Mondays and 1 January, 24 and 25 December. 3DM. ☎ (0 38 43) 6 22 06.

ROTHENBURG OB DER TAUBER
🛈 Rathaus. ☎ (0 98 61) 4 04 92.

Museum of Medieval Justice – Open daily from 9.30am to 6pm (2pm to 4pm only from November to the end of March). 4DM. ☎ (0 98 61) 53 59.

Museum – Open daily from 10am to 5pm (1pm to 4pm only from November to the end of March). 3DM. ☎ (0 98 61) 4 04-58.

THE ROYAL CASTLES

Hohenschwangau Castle – Guided tours (30min) : April to October, from 8.30am to 5.30pm ; November to March, from 10am to 4pm. Closed 24 December. 8DM. ☎ (0 83 62) 8 11 27.

Neuschwanstein Castle – Guided tours (45min) : April to October, daily from 9.30am to 5.30pm ; November to March, daily from 10am to 4pm. Closed 1 January, Shrove Tuesday, 1 November, 24, 25, 31 December. 8DM. ☎ (0 83 62) 8 10 35.

RÜDESHEIM AM RHEIN Excursions

Eberbach Abbey – Open April to September, daily from 10am to 6pm ; October to March, daily from 11am to 4pm. Closed between Christmas and 1 January. 1.50DM. ☎ (0 67 23) 42 28.

THE RUHR

Bochum
🛈 ☎ (02 34) 1 30 31.

German Mining Museum – Open 8.30am to 5.30pm weekdays, 9am to 1pm Sundays and public holidays. Closed Mondays and certain holidays. 5DM. ☎ (02 34) 58 77-1 26.

Railway Museum – Open Wednesdays and Fridays from 10am to 5pm, Sundays and public holidays from 10am to 12.45pm. Closed from 20 December to 6 January. 4DM. ☎ (02 34) 49 25 16.

Bochum Museum – Open Tuesdays to Fridays from 12 noon to 8pm ; Saturdays, Sundays and public holidays from 10am to 6pm. Closed Mondays. Entrance free. ☎ (02 34) 22 37.

Hagen
🛈 ☎ (0 23 31) 1 35 73.

Open-Air Technical Museum – Open from April to the end of October, daily from 9am to 5.30pm (last admissions 5pm). Closed Mondays. 3DM. ☎ (0 23 31) 78 07-44.

Karl-Ernst Osthaus Museum – Open from 11am to 6pm (10pm Thursdays, 4pm Sundays). Closed Mondays and 1 January, Easter Monday and 25 December. Entrance free. ☎ (0 23 31) 2 07-5 76.

Recklinghausen
🛈 ☎ (0 23 61) 50 28 93.

Icon Museum – Open daily from 10am to 6pm (11am to 5pm Sundays). Closed Mondays, also 1 May, Easter Sunday, Whit-Sunday and 25 December. 2.50DM. ☎ (0 23 61) 50-19 41.

Solingen-Gräfrath
🛈 ☎ (02 12) 2 90 23 33

Blade Museum – Open daily from 10am to 5pm. Closed Mondays. 3DM. ☎ (02 12) 5 98 22.

Wuppertal
🛈 ☎ (02 02) 5 63 21 80.

Early Industrialization Museum – Open daily from 10am to 1pm and from 3pm to 5pm. Closed Mondays, also 1 January, 1 May, Easter Sunday and 24, 25 December. Entrance free. ☎ (02 02) 5 63 64 98.

Van der Heydt Museum – Open daily from 10am to 5pm (9pm Thursdays). Closed Mondays, also Easter Sunday, Whit-Sunday and 25 December. 5DM. ☎ (02 02) 5 63 22 23.

S

SAALE VALLEY

Rudolstadt : Heidecksburg Castle – Guided tours (45min) daily from 9.30am to 5pm. Closed Mondays, also 24 and 31 December. 2.50DM. ☎ (0 36 72) 2 21 45.

Saalfeld : Museum of Thuringia – Open April to the end of December, daily from 8am to 12 noon and from 1pm to 4pm (Sundays from 9.30am to 12 noon and from 1pm to 5pm). Closed Mondays. 1.50DM. ☎ (0 36 71) 3 50 10.

Fairy Grottoes – Guided tours (45min) February to 1 November, daily from 9am to 5pm. 4DM. ☎ (0 36 71) 23 51.

SALEM ⓘ ☎ (0 75 53) 70 11.

Abbey Church and Abbey Buildings – Guided tours (1 hour) April to the end of October, daily from 9am to 12 noon and from 1pm to 5pm (Sundays from 11am to 5pm). Closed Good Friday. 6DM. ☎ (0 75 53) 8 14 37.

THE SAUERLAND

Attendorn : Attahöhle Grotto – Guided tours (45min) daily in summer from 9.30am to 4.30pm, in winter from 10am to 4pm. 5.50DM. ☎ (0 27 22) 30 41.

SCHLESWIG ⓘ ☎ (0 46 21) 81 42 26.

The Nydam Boat – Open : April to October, daily from 9am to 5pm ; November to March, Tuesdays to Sundays from 9.30am to 4pm. Closed 1 January, the Day of Repentance and Prayer (a Wednesday in November), and 24, 25, 31 December. 3DM (ticket also admits to Schleswig-Holstein Regional Museum). ☎ (0 46 21) 8 13-3 00.

Gottorf Castle – Same times and charges as for the Nydam Boat. ☎ (0 46 21) 8 13-2 22.

Haithabu Viking Museum – Open : April to October, daily from 9am to 6pm ; November to March, Tuesdays to Fridays from 9am to 5pm, Saturdays and Sundays from 10am to 6pm. Closed 1 January, 24 and 25 December. ☎ (0 46 21) 8 13-3 00.

SCHWÄBISCH HALL ⓘ ☎ (07 91) 75 12 46.

Regional Museum – Open daily from 10am to 5pm (8pm Wednesdays). Closed Mondays and 24, 25 December. Entrance free ☎ (07 91) 7 51-3 60.

Excursions

Hohenlohe Open-Air Museum – Open : May to September, daily from 9am to 6pm ; April to October, daily from 10am to 5.30pm. Closed Mondays and from November to the end of March. 5DM. ☎ (07 91) 8 40 61.

Gross Comburg Abbey – Open from mid-March to the end of October, daily from 10am to 12 noon and from 1.30pm to 5pm. Closed Mondays, Sunday mornings and Good Friday. 2DM. ☎ (07 91) 75 12 12.

SCHWERIN ⓘ Am Markt 11. ☎ (03 85) 81 23 14.

Castle – Open daily from 10am to 5pm. Closed Mondays and 24, 31 December. 3.05DM. ☎ (03 85) 81 28 65.

National Museum – Open daily from 10am to 5pm. Closed Mondays and certain public holidays. 2.05DM. ☎ (03 85) 5 75 81.

SIGMARINGEN ⓘ ☎ (0 75 71) 10 62 23.

Castle – Guided tours (45min) daily from 8.30am to 12 noon and from 1pm to 5pm (4pm in December and January). Closed Shrove Tuesday and Saturdays and public holidays in January and December. 5DM. ☎ (0 75 71) 7 29-0.

SPEYER ⓘ Maximilianstrasse 11. ☎ (0 62 32) 1 43 95.

Cathedral – Open daily from 9am (2pm Sundays and public holidays) to 6pm. ☎ (0 62 32) 10 22 06.

Crypt – Same times and conditions as for the Cathedral above.

Palatinate Museum – Open daily from 9am to 5pm. Closed 1 January, 24, 25 and 31 December. Charges vary according to exhibitions on display. ☎ (0 62 32) 13 25-10.

THE SPREEWALD

Lübbenau Barge Trip – Services run from mid-April to mid-October, from 9am to 4pm (according to the weather). Length of trip : 2 hours 30min (including stopover at Lehde). 2DM. ☎ (0 35 42) 22 25.

STADE ⓘ ☎ (0 41 41) 40 14 50.

Local Museum – Open daily from 10am to 5pm (6pm Sundays). Closed Mondays. Entrance free. ☎ (0 41 41) 32 32.

🛈 ☎ (0 03 79 21) 21 61 86

Havelberg : St Mary's Cathedral – Open Wednesdays to Sundays from 10am to 12 noon and from 1pm to 6pm (5pm from October to the end of March) ; Mondays and Tuesdays by arrangement only. 3DM. ☎ (03 93 87) 7 02.

STRALSUND 🛈 Alter Markt 15. ☎ (0 38 31) 24 39.

Oceanographic Museum and Aquarium – Open : July and August, daily from 9am to 6pm (5pm Fridays, Saturdays and Sundays) ; May, June, September and October, daily from 10am to 5pm ; November to the end of April, daily from 10am to 5pm (closed Mondays and Tuesdays). 3DM. ☎ (0 38 31) 51 35.

Historical Museum – Open daily from 10am to 5pm. Closed Mondays, 24 and 31 December and certain public holidays. 3DM. ☎ (0 38 31) 21 80.

STRAUBING

Metten Benedictine Abbey – Guided tours of the library (45min) daily – except during Easter week – from 10am to 3pm. 3DM. ☎ (09 91) 9 10 80.

STUTTGART 🛈 Königstrasse 1. ☎ (07 11) 2 22 82 40.

Linden Museum – Open daily from 9am to 5pm (8pm Thursdays). Closed Mondays. Entrance free. Temporary exhibitions : 5DM. ☎ (07 11) 1 23-12 42.

State Gallery – Open daily from 10am to 5pm (8pm Tuesdays and Thursdays). Closed Mondays, Good Friday, 24 and 25 December and certain public holidays. Entrance free. ☎ (07 11) 2 12-50 50.

Old Castle : Württemberg Regional Museum – Open daily from 10am to 5pm (7pm Wednesdays). Closed Mondays. Entrance free. ☎ (07 11) 2 79-34 00.

Stuttgart City Gallery – Open daily from 10am to 6pm (5pm Sundays). Closed Mondays. Entrance free. ☎ (07 11) 2 16 21 88.

National Museum of Natural Sciences – Work in progress. Re-opening scheduled for 1993. Afterwards, same times and conditions as Museum am Löwentor below.

Museum am Löwentor – Open : weekdays, 9am to 5pm Tuesdays, Thursdays and Fridays, 6pm Saturdays, 8pm Wednesdays ; Sundays from 10am to 6pm. Closed Mondays, and 24 December. Entrance free. ☎ (07 11) 89 36-0.

Killesberg Park – Open throughout the year. Entrance charge of 1.50DM from May to the end of September. ☎ (07 11) 25 89-0.

Mercedes-Benz Museum – Open daily from 9am to 5pm. Closed Mondays and certain public holidays. Entrance free. ☎ (07 11) 1 72 32 56.

Excursions

Solitude Castle – Open : April to October, daily from 9am to 12 noon and from 1.30pm to 5pm ; November to March, from 10am to 12 noon and from 1.30pm to 4pm. Closed Mondays. 2.50DM. ☎ (07 11) 69 66 99.

Swabian Brewery Museum – Open daily from 10.30am to 5.30pm. Closed Mondays and public holidays. Entrance free. ☎ (07 11) 73 70-2 01.

Porsche Museum – Open weekdays from 9am to 12 noon and from 1.30pm to 4pm. Closed Saturdays, Sundays and public holidays. Entrance free. ☎ (07 11) 8 27-54 84.

SWABIAN JURA

Holzmaden : Hauff Museum – Open daily from 9am to 12 noon and from 1pm to 5pm. Closed Mondays and 25 December. 4.50DM. ☎ (0 70 23) 28 73.

Lichtenstein Castle – Guided tours (30min) from April to the end of October, daily from 9am to 12 noon and from 1pm to 5.30pm (without interruption on Sundays) ; in November, February and March, Saturdays, Sundays and public holidays only from 9am to 12 noon and from 1pm to 5pm. Closed December and January. 5DM. ☎ (0 71 29) 41 02.

Bärenhöhle Grotto – Guided tours (30min) : April to October, daily from 9am to 5.30pm ; November and March, Sundays and public holidays only from 9am to 5.30pm. Closed December, January and February. 3DM. ☎ (0 71 28) 6 96.

Beuron Abbey – The Abbey Church is open daily from 6am to 8pm. Entrance free. Gregorian Chants : 10am Mass Sundays, 11.15am Mass weekdays. From May to the end of October, Sundays at 1.30pm, slides and diorama illustrating the history of the Abbey. Apply at the gate. ☎ (0 74 66) 17-0.

SWISS SAXONY

Grossedlitz Gardens – Open until nightfall. Guided tours (1 hour) by arrangement. 2DM. ☎ (0 35 29) 7 92 12 or 7 66 60.

SYLT ISLAND

Access by Rail – From **Niebüll**: between 17 and 24 departures daily according to season (no reservations). Price: from 51DM for the car; no charge for passengers (single tickets only). ☎ (0 46 61) 42 33.

Access by Car Ferry – From **Havneby** (Denmark): a dozen departures daily from mid-June to the end of August. Price: from 67 to 77DM Rtn for cars (passengers included) ; 8DM for travellers without a car. Information and reservations : ☎ (00 45) 74 75 53 04 at Havneby (Denmark), ☎ (0 46 52) 4 75 at List (Germany), or at all travel agencies.

T

Forest of THURINGIA

Marienglas Cave – Guided tours (30min) daily from 9am to 5pm (4pm from October to mid-April). 4.05DM. ☎ (0 36 23) 49 53.

TRIER
🖪 An der Porta Nigra. ☎ (06 51) 97 80 80.

Porta Nigra – Open: January, February, March and November, daily from 9am to 1pm and from 2pm to 5pm (closed Mondays) ; April to the end of October, daily from 9am to 6pm ; December, daily from 10am to 4pm. 2DM. ☎ (06 51) 4 80 71.

Municipal Museum – Open Tuesdays to Fridays, daily from 9am to 5pm ; Saturdays and Sundays from 9.30am to 3.30pm. Closed Mondays. 2DM. ☎ (06 51) 7 18 24 40.

Cathedral : Treasury – Open from 10am to 12 noon and from 2pm to 5pm (4pm November to the end of March). Closed Sunday mornings. 1DM. ☎ (06 51) 7 58 01.

Episcopal Museum – Open daily from 9am to 1pm and from 2pm to 5pm (Sundays from 1pm to 5pm). Closed 1 January, also the Monday before Shrove Tuesday and 24, 26 December. 1DM. ☎ (06 51) 71 05-2 55.

Rhineland Museum – Open: Mondays from 10am to 4pm, Tuesdays to Fridays from 9.30am to 4pm, Saturdays from 9.30am to 1pm, Sundays from 9am to 1pm. Closed 1 January, 1 May, 24, 25, 26 and 31 December. Entrance free. ☎ (06 51) 4 35 88.

Imperial Roman Baths – Same times and charge as for Porta Nigra, above. ☎ (06 51) 4 80 71.

Municipal Library Treasury – Open : Easter to the end of October, Mondays to Fridays from 1pm to 5pm, Saturdays from 10am to 1pm ; otherwise on application only. (Closed Sundays and public holidays). Otherwise by arrangement only. 2DM. ☎ (06 51) 7 18 24 35.

Karl Marx House – Open every day : April to October, from 10am to 6pm ; November to March, from 10am to 1pm and from 3pm to 6pm. Closed from 24 December to 2 January. 3DM. ☎ (06 51) 4 30 11.

St Barbara's Baths – Open: January, February, March and November, daily from 9am to 1pm and from 2pm to 5pm (closed Mondays) ; April to the end of October, daily from 9am to 6pm (break between 1pm and 2pm Mondays). Closed in December. 2DM. ☎ (06 51) 4 80 71.

Roman Amphitheatre – Same times and charge as for Porta Nigra and Imperial Baths, above. ☎ (06 51) 4 80 71.

Tübingen
🖪 An der Eberhardsbrücke. ☎ (0 70 71) 3 50 11.

Collegiate Church of St George – Open: April to October, from 10am to 5pm on Fridays, Saturdays, Sundays and public holidays only (daily during Baden-Württemberg school holidays – for dates enquire on the spot). From November to March, the tombs can only be seen by arrangement, after a telephone reservation. Interior: 1DM ; Tower: 1DM. ☎ (0 70 71) 5 25 83.

Hölderlin Tower – Open Tuesdays to Fridays from 10am to 12 noon and from 3pm to 5pm ; Saturdays, Sundays and public holidays from 2pm to 5 pm only. Closed Mondays. ☎ (0 70 71) 2 20 40.

U

ÜBERLINGEN
🖪 ☎ (0 75 51) 40 41.

Town Hall : Council Chamber – Open daily from 9am to 12 noon and from 2.30pm to 5pm. Closed Sundays and public holidays throughout the year, and Saturday afternoons also from mid-October to mid-April. Entrance free. ☎ (0 75 51) 8 72 11.

Local Museum – Open daily from 9am to 12.30pm and from 2pm to 5pm (10am to 3pm on Sundays). Closed Mondays throughout the year and Sundays from November to the end of March. 2DM. ☎ (0 75 51) 8 72 17.

ULM

ℹ Münsterplatz. ☎ (07 31) 6 41 61.

Museum – Open daily from 10am to 5pm (8pm Thursdays). Closed Mondays. Entrance free. ☎ (07 31) 1 61-43 00.

Excursions

Wiblingen Abbey : Library – Guided tours (15min) : April to October, Tuesdays to Sundays from 10am to 12 noon and from 2pm to 5pm ; November to March, Tuesdays to Fridays from 2pm to 4pm, Saturdays, Sundays and public holidays from 10am to 12 noon and from 2pm to 4pm. Closed Mondays and 25 December. 2DM. ☎ (07 31) 6 41 61.

Blaubeuron Abbey Church – Open from Palm Sunday to 1 November, daily from 9am to 6pm. 1.50DM. ☎ (0 73 44) 63 06.

W

WALDECK REGION

Waldeck Castle Museum – Open from mid-March to the end of October, daily from 10am to 5pm. 2.50DM. ☎ (0 56 23) 5 89-0.

Arolsen Palace – Guided tours (45min), May to the end of September from 10am to 4.15pm. 4DM. ☎ (0 56 91) 30 44.

WALDSASSEN

ℹ ☎ (0 96 32) 88 28.

Library – Guided tours (30min) daily from 10am to 11.30am (11am Sundays) and from 2pm to 4.45pm. Closed Easter week and from 1 to 25 December. 3DM. ☎ (0 96 32) 18 31.

WASSERBURG AM INN

ℹ ☎ (0 80 71) 1 05 22

Local Museum – Open : May to September, from 10am to 12 noon and from 1pm to 4pm (Saturdays, Sundays and public holidays from 11am to 3pm continuously) ; October to mid-December and February to April, from 1pm to 4pm (Saturdays, Sundays and public holidays from 10am to 12 noon only). Closed Mondays, and from mid-December to the end of January. 3DM. ☎ (0 80 71) 1 05-42.

WEIMAR

ℹ Marktstrasse 4. ☎ (0 36 43) 53 84.

Goethe's House – Open daily from 9am to 5pm (4pm from November to the end of February). Closed Mondays, also 1 May, 24, 25 and 31 December. 5DM. ☎ (0 36 43) 43 86.

Schiller's House – Open daily from 9am to 5pm (4pm November to the end of February). Closed Tuesdays, also 1 May, 24, 25 and 31 December. 5DM. ☎ (0 36 43) 43 86.

Widow's Palace – Open : April to October, Tuesdays to Sundays from 9am to 12 noon and from 1pm to 5pm ; November to March, Wednesdays to Sundays from 9am to 12 noon and from 1pm to 4pm. Closed 1 May, 24, 25 and 31 December. 3DM. ☎ (0 36 43) 43 86.

Castle – Open daily from 9am to 5pm (6pm in July and August). Closed Mondays, also 1 May, 24, 25 and 31 December. 4DM. ☎ (0 36 43) 6 18 31.

Franz Liszt's House – Open daily from 9am to 1pm and from 2pm to 5pm (4pm November to the end of February). 3DM. ☎ (0 36 43) 43 86.

Excursions

Tiefurt Palace – Open : April to October, Tuesdays to Sundays from 9am to 1pm and from 2pm to 5pm ; November to March, Tuesdays to Sundays from 9am to 1pm and from 2pm to 4pm. Closed 1 May, 24, 25 and 31 December. 3DM. ☎ (0 36 43) 43 86.

Belvedere Castle – Work in progress ; part of the building only can be viewed. Ask for details : ☎ (0 36 43) 6 18 31.

Buchenwald Concentration Camp – Open daily, April to September, from 9.45am to 5.45pm ; October to March from 8.45am to 4.45pm. Closed Mondays, and also 1 January, 1 May and 25 December. Entrance free. ☎ (0 36 43) 6 74 81.

WERNIGERODE

ℹ ☎ (0 39 43) 3 30 35.

Castle Museum – Open daily from 10am to 6pm (last admissions 5.30pm). Closed Mondays, 1 January and 25 December. 3DM. ☎ (0 39 43) 3 20 95.

WERTHEIM Excursions

ℹ ☎ (0 93 42) 10 66.

Bronnbach Abbey – Guided tours, daily from April to the end of November : 9.30am to noon, and 2pm to 5pm. 2DM. ☎ (0 93 42) 3 95 96.

WESSOBRUNN

Former Benedictine Abbey – Guided tours (45min) daily at 10am, 3pm and 6pm (Sundays and public holidays 3pm and 6pm only). Closed Easter Sunday and 25 December. 2DM. ☎ (0 88 09) 2 11.

WETZLAR ☷ ☎ (0 64 41) 40 53 38.

Lotte's House – Open daily from 10am to 1pm and from 2pm to 5pm. Closed Mondays, also Good Friday, the Day of Repentance and Prayer (a Wednesday in November) and 26 December. Entrance free. ☎ (0   64 41) 4 05-2 69.

Collection of Dr Irmgard von Lemmers-Danforth – Guided tours (1 hour) daily from 10am to 1pm and from 2pm to 5pm. Closed Mondays. Entrance free. ☎ (06 44) 4 05-2 69.

Tribunal Museum – Open daily from 10am to 1pm and from 2pm to 5pm. Closed Mondays. Entrance free. ☎ (0 64 41) 4 72 85.

WIES

Church – Open daily from 8am to 7pm (5pm from October to the end of March). ☎ (0 88 62) 5 01.

WITTENBERG ☷ ☎ (0 34 91) 22 39.

Melanchthon's House – Open daily from 9am to 5pm (last admissions 4.30pm). Closed Fridays, also 1 May, 24 and 31 December. 2DM. ☎ (0 34 91) 32 79.

Luther's House – Open daily from 9am to 5pm (last admissions 4pm). Closed Mondays, also 24 and 31 December. 4DM. ☎ (0 34 91) 26 71.

Excursions

Wörlitz Castle – Guided tours (45min for the Castle, 30min for the Gothic House): May to September, daily from 10am (1pm Mondays) to 6pm; April and October from 10am (1pm Mondays) to 5pm. Last admissions: 1 hour before closing time for the Castle, 30min for the Gothic House. Castle: 4DM; Gothic House: 3.50DM; entrance to the park free. ☎ (03 49 05) 3 29.

WOLFENBÜTTEL ☷ ☎ (0 53 81) 8 64 87.

Castle – Open daily from 10am to 1pm (also from 3pm to 5pm Wednesdays, and 3pm to 6pm Fridays and Saturdays). Closed Mondays. Entrance free. ☎ (0 53 31) 57 13.

Library – Open daily from 10am to 5pm. Closed 1 January, Easter Monday, Whit-Monday, 1 May, 3 October and 25 December. 5DM. ☎ (0 53 31) 80 80.

Lessing's House – Same times and charge as for the Library above. ☎ (0 53 31) 80 80.

WORMS ☷ ☎ (0 62 41) 85 35 60.

Heylshof Museum – Open: May to September, Tuesdays to Sundays from 10am to 5pm; the rest of the year, Tuesdays to Saturdays from 2pm to 4pm, Sundays from 10am to 12 noon and from 2pm to 4pm. Closed Mondays, also Good Friday, 24 December, the month of January and part of February. 2DM. ☎ (0 62 41) 85 33 36.

Municipal Museum – Open daily from 10am to 12 noon and from 2pm to 5pm. Closed Mondays, also Good Friday, 1 May, and from 24 December to 1 January. 2DM. ☎ (0 62 41) 85 33 36.

WÜRZBURG ☷ Hauptbahnhof.☎ (09 31) 3 74 36.

Palace – Open daily from 9am to 5pm (10am to 4pm from October to the end of March). Closed Mondays, also 1 January, Shrove Tuesday, 1 November, 24, 25 and 31 December. 4.50DM. ☎ (09 31) 5 27 43.

Fortress of Marienberg – Open: April to September from 9am to 12.30pm and from 1pm to 5pm; October to March from 10am to 12.30pm and from 1pm to 4pm. Closed Mondays, also 1 January, 1 November, 24, 25 and 31 December. 3DM. ☎ (09 31) 4 38 38.

Franconian Museum of the Main – Open daily from 10am to 5pm (4pm from November to the end of March). Closed Mondays and 25 December. 3DM. ☎ (09 31) 4 30 16.

Excursions

Veitshöchheim Castle – Guided tours (30min) from April to the end of September, daily from 9am to 12 noon and from 1pm to 5pm (fountains play in the afternoons). Closed Mondays and from October to the end of March. 2.50DM. ☎ (09 31) 5 27 43.

X

XANTEN ☷ ☎ (0 28 01) 3 72 38

Regional Museum – Open: Tuesdays to Fridays, from 9am (10am from October to the end of April) to 5pm daily; Saturdays, Sundays and public holidays from 11am to 6pm throughout the year. Closed Mondays, also 24, 25 and 31 December. 3DM. ☎ (0 28 01) 33 11.

Archaeological Park – Open: February to the end of October, daily from 9am to 6pm; the rest of the year, open according to the weather. 5DM. ☎ (0 28 01) 29 99.

Z

ZUGSPITZE

Access from Garmisch-Partenkirchen – Funicular as far as the **Schneefernerhaus**: departures hourly from 7.35am and 3.35pm (2.35pm in winter); length of journey, 75min. From Schneefernerhaus to the summit by cable car: departures every 30min; length of journey, 4min. Returning, the funicular leaves every hour between 9am and 5pm (4pm in winter). Price: 55DM Rtn. ☎ (0 88 21) 7 97 9 51.

Access from Eibsee – Cable car departures every 30min between 8am and 5.30pm (4.30pm in winter). Length of journey: 10min. Price: 55DM Rtn. ☎ (0 88 21) 7 97 9 51.

ZWICKAU
🖪 ☎ (03 75) 2 60 07.

Robert Schumann's House – Open daily from 10am to 5pm (12 noon Sundays and public holidays); last admissions 30min before closing time. Closed Mondays, also Good Friday, 24, 25, 26 and 31 December. 3DM. ☎ (03 75) 2 52 69.

Municipal Museum – Open daily from 9am (10am Saturdays and Sundays) to 5pm. Closed Mondays. 2DM (entrance free between 9am and 7pm the first Thursday of each month). ☎ (03 75) 2 37 07.

ZWIEFALTEN CHURCH Excursions

Abbey Church – Work in progress (parts of the complex only). Enquire: ☎ (0 73 75) 4 99.

Bad Schussenried : Abbey Library – Open: April to October, daily from 10am to 12 noon and from 2pm to 5pm; November to March, Mondays to Fridays from 2pm to 4pm, Saturdays, Sundays and public holidays from 10am to 12 noon and from 2pm to 4pm. Closed from mid-December to mid-January. 2DM. ☎ (0 75 83) 33-0.

Lindau

INDEX

Swabian Jura . . . .   Towns, sights and tourist regions followed by the name of the Land. Isolated sights (castles, ruins, lakes, islands...) are listed under their proper name.

Barlach, Ernst . . . .   People, events and artistic styles mentioned in the guide.

Botanical Gardens . . . . . .   Sights of important towns.

This index, like the other alphabetical lists in this guide, follows the normal alphabetical order and differs from the Michelin Red Guide Deutschland, where the vowels ä, ö, ü are classified under ae, oe and ue respectively.

The Spa Establishment, Baden-Baden

ACKNOWLEDGEMENTS – ILLUSTRATIONS

p. 11 Bridgeman/GIRAUDON, Paris
p. 13 Streichan/ZEFA, Paris
p. 19 Lausat/EXPLORER, Paris
p. 22 INTER NATIONES, Bonn
p. 23 JURGENS OST-EUROPA, Cologne
p. 24 After photo HIRMER Fotoarchiv (top of page)
p. 24 CESA, Marburg
p. 26 RÉUNION DES MUSÉES NATIONAUX, Paris
p. 28 Kunsthalle, Karlsruhe
p. 29 Lausat/EXPLORER, Paris
p. 30 Eichhorn/EXPLORER, Paris
p. 31 EXPLORER, Paris
p. 35 FOTOGRAM-STONE, Paris
p. 37 HUBER, Garmisch
p. 41 After photo Erich Müller
p. 42 JURGENS OST-EUROPA, Cologne
p. 52 After photo R. Schuler
p. 61 U. Watzmann/ZEFA, Paris
p. 67 Gregor/EXPLORER, Paris
p. 68 R. Truchot/EXPLORER, Paris
p. 72 K. Kerth/ZEFA, Paris
p. 80 J. Ducange/TOP, Paris
p. 97 Streichan/ZEFA, Paris
p. 108 After photo Lauterwasser
p. 111 Jogschies/EXPLORER, Paris
p. 123 Jogschies/EXPLORER, Paris
p. 124 Jogschies/EXPLORER, Paris
p. 144 R. Elsen/HELGA, Frankfurt
p. 149 INTER NATIONES, Bonn
p. 159 FOTOGRAM-STONE, Paris
p. 181 FOTOGRAM-STONE, Paris
p. 182 W. Kaehler/FOVEA, Paris

p. 188 JURGENS OST-EUROPA, Cologne
p. 190 INTER NATIONES, Bonn
p. 201 W. Germany/EXPLORER, Paris
p. 203 Müller/EXPLORER, Paris
p. 205 Cherville/FOTOGRAM-STONE, Paris
p. 208 P. Tetrel/EXPLORER, Paris
p. 219 H. Champollien/MICHELIN, Paris
p. 228 CESA, Marburg
p. 231 Jogschies/EXPLORER, Paris
p. 235 H. Champollien/MICHELIN, Paris
p. 243 W. Wilke/FOTOGRAM-STONE, Paris
p. 254 JURGENS OST-EUROPA, Cologne
p. 265 CESA, Marburg
p. 271 W.H. Mueller/ZEFA, Paris
p. 273 INTER NATIONES, Bonn
p. 276 Jogschies/EXPLORER, Paris
p. 279 Meier/EXPLORER, Paris
p. 283 H. Champollien/MICHELIN, Paris
p. 284 After photo Langewiesche Bücherei
p. 289 H. Champollien/MICHELIN, Paris
p. 299 H. Veiller/EXPLORER, Paris
p. 304 After drawing by Sepp Reindl, Garmisch
p. 305 CESA, Marburg
p. 307 GIRAUDON, Paris
p. 312 Städt. Verkehrsbüro, Rottweil
p. 348 B. Duke/SUPERBILD, Munich
p. 355 Waldkirch/Bildagentur SCHUSTER Oberursel

MANUFACTURE FRANÇAISE DES PNEUMATIQUES MICHELIN
Société en commandite par actions au capital de 2 000 000 000 de francs
Place des Carmes-Déchaux - 63 Clermont-Ferrand (France)
R.C.S. Clermont-Fd B 855 200 507

Printed in France 3-93-45

Photocomposition : D.S. TYPE, à Bruxelles - Impression : I.M.E., Baume-les-Dames n° 8619
Brochage : AUBIN, Poitiers